1,000,000 Books

are available to read at

Forgotten Books

www.ForgottenBooks.com

Read online
Download PDF
Purchase in print

ISBN 978-1-331-89751-4
PIBN 10251260

This book is a reproduction of an important historical work. Forgotten Books uses state-of-the-art technology to digitally reconstruct the work, preserving the original format whilst repairing imperfections present in the aged copy. In rare cases, an imperfection in the original, such as a blemish or missing page, may be replicated in our edition. We do, however, repair the vast majority of imperfections successfully; any imperfections that remain are intentionally left to preserve the state of such historical works.

Forgotten Books is a registered trademark of FB &c Ltd.
Copyright © 2018 FB &c Ltd.
FB &c Ltd, Dalton House, 60 Windsor Avenue, London, SW19 2RR.
Company number 08720141. Registered in England and Wales.

For support please visit www.forgottenbooks.com

1 MONTH OF FREE READING

at
www.ForgottenBooks.com

By purchasing this book you are eligible for one month membership to ForgottenBooks.com, giving you unlimited access to our entire collection of over 1,000,000 titles via our web site and mobile apps.

To claim your free month visit: www.forgottenbooks.com/free251260

* Offer is valid for 45 days from date of purchase. Terms and conditions apply.

English
Français
Deutsche
Italiano
Español
Português

www.forgottenbooks.com

Mythology Photography **Fiction**
Fishing Christianity **Art** Cooking
Essays Buddhism Freemasonry
Medicine **Biology** Music **Ancient Egypt** Evolution Carpentry Physics
Dance Geology **Mathematics** Fitness
Shakespeare **Folklore** Yoga Marketing
Confidence Immortality Biographies
Poetry **Psychology** Witchcraft
Electronics Chemistry History **Law**
Accounting **Philosophy** Anthropology
Alchemy Drama Quantum Mechanics
Atheism Sexual Health **Ancient History**
Entrepreneurship Languages Sport
Paleontology Needlework Islam
Metaphysics Investment Archaeology
Parenting Statistics Criminology
Motivational

WALKER'S
PATENT SHIP-LOGS

Known throughout the world for their accuracy and durability

Walker's Patent
"CHERUB II" SHIP-LOG.

Also Makers of the
"TRIDENT" SHIP-LOG.
"TRIDENT" ELECTRIC SHIP-LOG.
"ROCKET" SHIP-LOG.
"EXCELSIOR" YACHT LOG.
A1 & A2 HARPOON SHIP-LOGS, Etc.

To be obtained from all Marine Opticians and Ship Chandlers.

THOS. WALKER & SON, LTD.
Makers to the leading Navies and Shipping Companies of the World.
58, OXFORD STREET, BIRMINGHAM, Eng.

SHIPBUILDERS.
ENGINEERS.
DOCK OWNERS.
FORGE MASTERS.
LOCOMOTIVE BUILDERS.
WATER-TUBE BOILER BUILDERS.

BUILDERS OF ALL TYPES OF VESSELS AND MACHINERY.

R. & W. HAWTHORN, LESLIE & Co., Ld.,
NEWCASTLE-ON-TYNE.

Builders of
TORPEDO BOATS and DESTROYERS :—

"SUNFISH."	"RACEHORSE."	"NEMESIS."
"OPOSSUM."	"ROEBUCK."	"NEREIDE."
"RANGER."	"VELOX."	"NYMPHE."
"CHEERFUL."	"DERWENT."	"JACKAL."
"MERMAID."	"EDEN."	"TIGRESS."
"VIPER."	"WAVENEY."	"CHRISTOPHER."
"GREYHOUND."	"BOYNE."	"COCKATRICE."
"DOON."	"GHURKA."	"CONTEST."
"KALE."	4 1st cl. T.B.'s	"MENTOR."
"ZULU."	"SCOURGE."	"MANSFIELD," &c., &c.

RECENT WARSHIPS ENGINED :—

(Battleship)	"TEMERAIRE."	(Battleship)	"COLLINGWOOD."
(Battleship)	"AGAMEMNON."	,,	"MONARCH."
(1st Cl. Cruiser)	"ACHILLES."	(1st Cl. Cruiser)	"HAMPSHIRE."
,,	"DUKE OF EDINBURGH."	,,	"CORNWALL."
(2nd Cl. Cruiser)	"BLANCHE."	,,	"LANCASTER."
(Fleet Scout)	"ADVENTURE."	,,	"KENT."
,,	"ATTENTIVE."	(Battleship)	"BULWARK."
(Battleship)	"CENTURION."	(Cruiser)	"BIRMINGHAM."
	"MARLBOROUGH."		&c., &c.

27th July, 1917.

Dear Sir,

It is with great pleasure that on my appointment as First Lord of the Admiralty, I write to wish your paper "The Fleet" a continuance of the success which it has already achieved. The loyalty, devoted service, and splendid courage of the men of the Royal Navy, are known to the whole world, and need no words of mine to commend them.

Letter from Sir ERIC GEDDES, K.C.B.

THE FLEET ANNUAL — 1917

J. Samuel White & Co., Ltd.

East Cowes, Isle of Wight

Telephone. No. 3 Cowes.   Telegrams "White, East Cowes."

Vedette Boats

Steam & Motor Lifeboats

Steam, Petrol and Paraffin Launches for Police, Customs or Patrol Duties

Torpedo Boats

T.B. Destroyers

Stern-wheel and Screw-in-Tunnel Vessels

Special Service Vessels

London Office.
28, Victoria Street, S.W.
Telephone 4501 Victoria.   Telegrams: Carnage, London.

Ernest B. H. Lander 125

1917 — AND NAVAL YEAR BOOK — vii

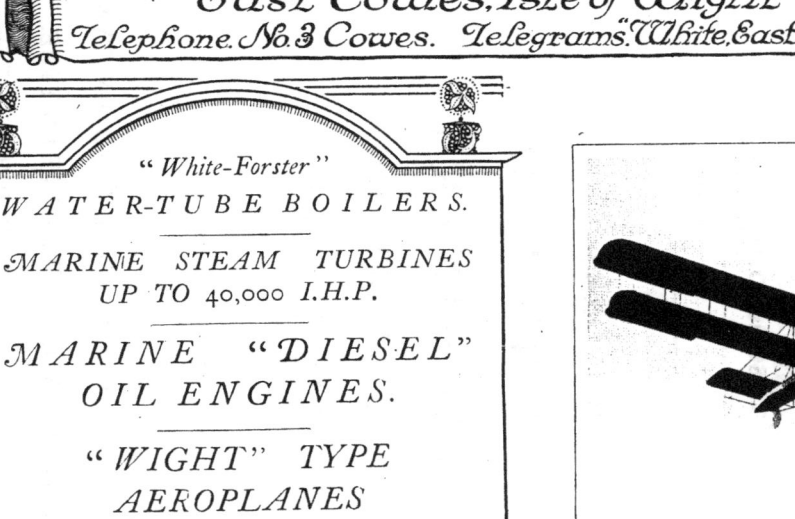

J. Samuel White & Co. Ltd.
East Cowes, Isle of Wight

Telephone. No. 3 Cowes. Telegrams "White, East Cowes."

"White-Forster"
WATER-TUBE BOILERS.

MARINE STEAM TURBINES UP TO 40,000 I.H.P.

MARINE "DIESEL" OIL ENGINES.

"WIGHT" TYPE AEROPLANES & SEAPLANES.

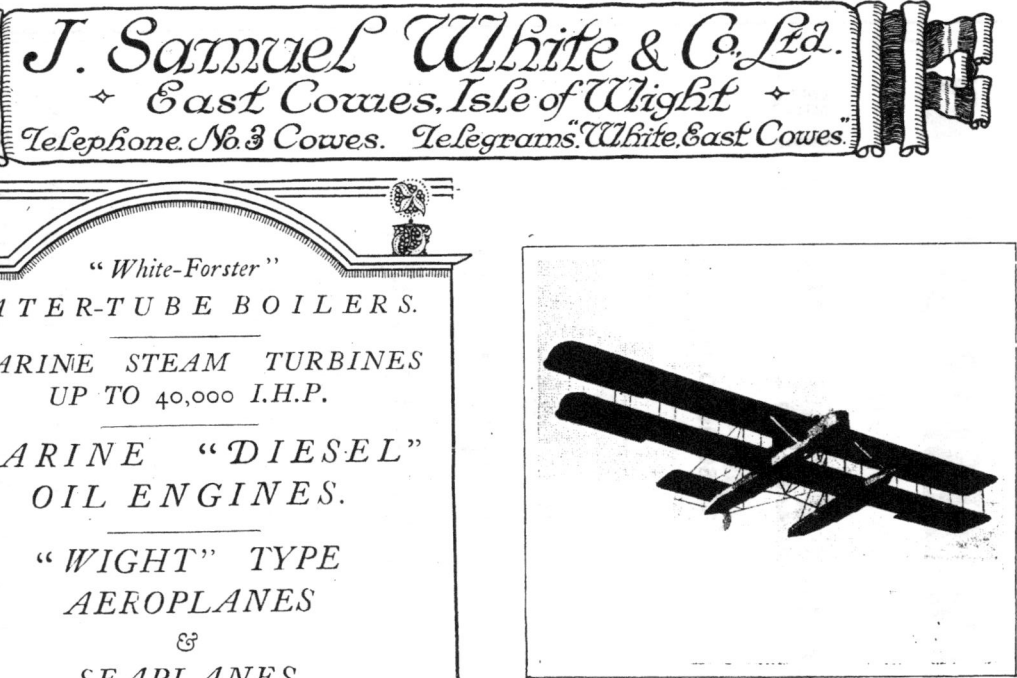

London Office.
28, Victoria Street, S.W.
Telephone. 4507 Victoria. Telegrams. Carnage, London.

x — THE FLEET ANNUAL — 1917.

Vickers' Contribution to the British Naval Fleet up to August, 1914.

At their Naval Construction Works at Barrow-in-Furness, Messrs. Vickers Limited, have built for the British Naval Fleet.

130 Ships of all Classes

Battleships, Battle Cruisers, High Speed Scout Cruisers, Destroyers, Submarines, Airships, and Aeroplanes, the total tonnage being nearly 240,000 tons.

Engines: Steam Turbines, Oil and Steam Reciprocating, have been supplied for 170 ships of all classes, aggregating 900,000 Horse Power.

Armour, guns, ordnance machinery, and electrical gear, have been supplied for these ships, and for many others built in the Royal and other Establishments.

Tubular
Steel Davits, Derricks

TUBULAR PILLARS, MASTS, CRANE
& DERRICK POSTS, STERN TUBES.

Iron & Steel Main Steam Pipes

AS SUPPLIED TO

The Navy & Mercantile Services

Feed Pipes, Water Pipes, Circulating Pipes, Dredger Suction and Delivery Mains.

Steel Castings. BOILER TUBES. *Ship & Boiler Plates.*

Stewarts and Lloyds Ltd.

41 OSWALD STREET   BROAD ST. CHAMBERS   WINCHESTER HOUSE
GLASGOW.   BIRMINGHAM.   LONDON, E.C.

PALMERS
Shipbuilding & Iron Co.
WORKS AT
Ltd.
HEBBURN & JARROW-ON-TYNE

Shipbuilders and Engineers.

Iron and Steel Manufacturers.

Iron and Brass Founders.

Ship Repairers. Forgemasters.

Galvanisers.

Builders of all Classes of War and Mercantile Vessels, with Reciprocating or Turbine Engines, also Floating Docks.

GRAVING DOCKS:
HEBBURN—Length 700 ft. by 90 ft. width entrance.
JARROW—Length 440 ft. by 70 ft. width entrance.

SLIPWAY:
JARROW—Length 600 ft.

Address: Palmers Shipbuilding & Iron Co., Ltd., Hebburn
Telegrams: " Palmers, Hebburn."

'EMPIRE' AUTOMATIC CONTROL

The controllers shewn are a few examples of the work designed and completely built by British Labour in our Glasgow Factory for operating:

FANS, PUMPS, HYDRAULIC ACCUMULATORS, AIR COMPRESSORS, CAPSTANS, HOISTS, LIFTS, CRANES AND EVERY KIND OF MOTOR-DRIVEN PLANT

Supplied to H.M. Government Departments,

British Corporations and Railways, and installed in Mines, Docks, Factories, Engineering Shops, Steel Mills, and Shipyards in Great Britain, all the Colonies, and most Allied Countries.

The controllers shewn are from 10 H.P. to 900 H.P. and 10 amps to 1000 amps.

ELECTRIC **C**ONTROL **L**IMITED

GLASGOW

Telegrams: "Control, Glasgow."

Code: A.B.C. 5th Edition.

WILLIAM BEARDMORE & Co. Ltd.

STEEL MANUFACTURERS, SHIPBUILDERS & ENGINEERS

Glasgow & Dalmuir.

SHIPYARD AND ENGINE WORKS.

Warships of all Types

High Speed Mail, Passenger, and Merchant Ships of all kinds

Engines, Boilers, Turbines, Oil Motors

Fitting Out Shop & Basin

Completion and Repairs of Warships, Passenger, and Merchant Vessels.

Aircraft & Aero Engine Manufacturers.

STEELWORKS, ROLLING MILLS, FORGE, FOUNDRY, &c., &c

Armour Plates for Warships
Naval, Land & Field Guns
Armoured Gun Turrets
Projectiles
Heavy and light forgings
Shaftings of all sizes
Ship and Boiler Plates, Bars
Steel Castings of all dimensions
Marine Boiler Furnaces
Pressed Motor Frames
Railway Wheels, Tyres, and Axles.

BABCOCK & WILCOX MARINE BOILER
(View with Casing Removed, shewing Tubes and Baffles).

Babcock & Wilcox Ltd.

PATENT

WATER-TUBE MARINE BOILERS

Over **3,800,000** h.p. installed in the British, U.S.A. and Foreign Navies, and in the Mercantile Marine.

Large Saving in Space and Weight
Suitable for all Classes of Vessels
Constructed for the Highest Pressures

THE MOST ECONOMICAL STEAM BOILER *in the* WORLD

FIRED WITH WOOD, COAL OR OIL.

OIL FIRING arranged either on the Oil Pressure System or with Compressed Air or Steam as Spraying Agents Under Babcock & Wilcox & J. S. White & Co. Patents

BABCOCK & WILCOX also supply as Joint Manufacturers and General Licensees with J. Samuel White & Co., Lim., the WHITE-FORSTER BOILERS for Destroyers, Torpedo Boats, Pinnaces, etc.

Telegrams: "BABCOCK, LONDON."

Head Offices:

Telephone: No. CITY 6470 (8 lines).

Oriel House, Farringdon St. London E.C.

Works: RENFREW, SCOTLAND.

TURBINE DRIVEN PUMP. 16500 GALS. PER MINUTE.

MARINE CIRCULATING PUMPS
PETER BROTHERHOOD, LTD.
PETERBOROUGH.

RECIPROCATING ENGINES AND PUMPS. EACH 12,000 GALS. PER MINUTE.

1917 AND NAVAL YEAR BOOK xix

Peter Brotherhood, Ltd.
PETERBOROUGH

200 K.W. TURBO-GENERATOR AND CONDENSOR FOR BATTLESHIP.

For forty years it has been our privilege to serve our Navy, and our aim has always been that our machinery supplied to ships may in quality and reliability be worthy of the men that man them. To achieve this is an ideal high indeed.

Diving Apparatus
AND OTHER SUBMARINE APPLIANCES.

Actual Makers of all Patterns in present day use.

Prompt Delivery of complete Apparatus and Accessories of every description.

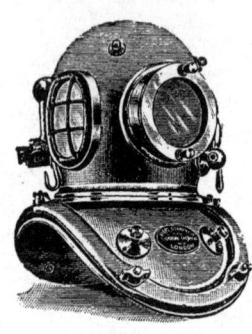

Contractors to British Admiralty, most Foreign Navies, War Office, India Office, Trinity House, Crown Agents for the Colonies and principal Harbour and Dock Work, and Pearl and Sponge Fisheries of the World.

DIVING BELLS EXPLODING MACHINES
ELECTRIC LAMPS
Also
PATENT TELEPHONIC APPARATUS
AIR COMPRESSORS VACUUM PUMPS
CENTRIFUGAL PUMPS

Siebe, Gorman & Co., Ltd.,
"Neptune" Works,
And 187 Westminster Bridge Rd., London, S.E.

Telegrams: "Siebe, Lamb, London."   Telephone No. Hop 3401
Cables: "Siebe, London."   (2 lines).
Codes used :—
A.1., A.B.C. (4th and 5th eds.)
Western Union, Engineering and Private.

International Convention for the Safety of Life at Sea

SMOKE HELMETS

Approved Types as recommended by the above Convention.

Adopted by the Principal Steamship Lines, Oil Tankers, Dock Companies, Oil Companies, Collieries, Fire Brigades, Chemical Works, Etc., Etc.

Light and portable. Extremely simple in use. Nothing to get out of order.

A man requires no training in the use of these appliances, and can be ready to go into noxious atmospheres without delay.

Also Makers of

SELF-CONTAINED OXYGEN BREATHING APPARATUS, of various patterns for use in irrespirable atmospheres.

OXYGEN RESUSCITATING APPARATUS for the apparently drowned or asphyxiated.

RESPIRATORS, RESPIRATOR HOODS, MASKS, GOGGLES, Etc.

Siebe, Gorman & Co., Ltd.,

"Neptune" Works,

And 187 Westminster Bridge Rd., London, S.E.

Telegrams: "Siebe, Lamb, London."
Cables: "Siebe," London."
Telephone No. Hop 3401 (2 lines).

Codes used:—
A.1., A.B.C. (4th and 5th eds.)
Western Union, Engineering and Private.

HADFIELDS LTD.
SHEFFIELD

HADFIELDS' "HECLON" CAPPED ARMOUR-PIERCING PROJECTILES, 13·5-inch, 14-inch, and 15-inch Calibres, after perforating armour plates of the latest type, from 12-inches to 15-inches in thickness.

HADFIELDS' PATENT "ERA" CAST STEEL ARMOUR
Conning Towers, Armoured Tubes, Gun Shields, Roofs and other Shipbuilding Components in use by all the principal Navies of the World.

HADFIELDS LTD.

Workmen employed over 14,000. **Hecla Works, SHEFFIELD** Works area 125 acres.
ENGLAND.

London Office: NORFOLK HOUSE, LAURENCE POUNTNEY HILL, E.C. 4.

Managing Directors:	*Supt. Ordnance Dept.:*
SIR ROBERT HADFIELD, M. Inst. C.E.	MAJOR A. B. H. CLERKE
ALEXANDER M. JACK, M. Inst. C.E.	(late R.A.), Director.

Telegrams: "Hecla, Sheffield," "Requisition, London." | *Telephones:* No. 1050 Sheffield, No. 2 City London

---

FIRST IN ATTACK
Hadfields' Projectiles

PROJECTILES IN FORGED STEEL

CAST STEEL & CAST IRON of all Types and Calibres up to 16-in.
ARMOUR PIERCING, COMMON, SHRAPNEL & HIGH EXPLOSIVE SHELL. Either Empty, or Filled and Fused, together with Gun Charges.

FIRST IN DEFENCE
Hadfields' 'Era' Steel Armour

SOLE MAKERS OF
HADFIELDS' PATENT "ERA" STEEL

Which has been adopted by the British Admiralty and War Office, also by other Powers. The Supreme Material for Ammunition and Communication Tubes, Conning and Director Towers, and all Armoured Parts exposed to Shell Fire; also for Gun Shields for Naval and Land Service.

Contractors to the British Admiralty and War Office, Colonial Offices, The United States, Japanese, and other Foreign Governments.

STEEL CASTINGS & FORGINGS of every description

CHADBURN'S
NEW PATENT HORO-MECHANICAL TURBOMETER MARK I.

An absolute dead reckoning instrument, registering the actual number of revolutions of a shaft per minute, giving corrected readings every 10 seconds.

ADOPTED BY THE BRITISH ADMIRALTY

CHADBURN'S
(Ship) TELEGRAPH Co. Ltd.

Original Inventors
and Patentees of Ships' Telegraphs

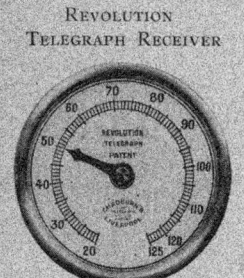

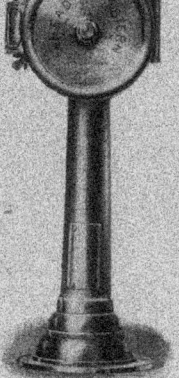

FITTED THROUGHOUT
HIS MAJESTY'S NAVY

Head Office and Works:

CYPRUS ROAD, BOOTLE
LANCASHIRE.

xxvi THE FLEET ANNUAL 1917

Bell's United Asbestos Co. LTD

(OLDEST ASBESTOS MANUFACTURERS IN EUROPE)

SOUTHWARK STREET, LONDON, S.E.

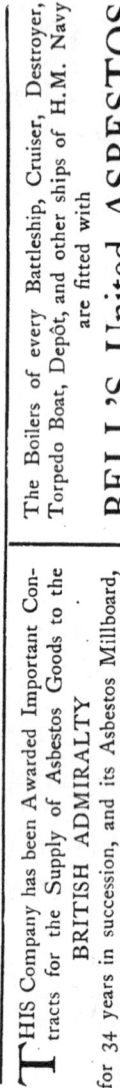

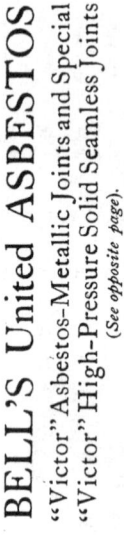

By Special Authority.

THIS Company has been Awarded Important Contracts for the Supply of Asbestos Goods to the BRITISH ADMIRALTY for 34 years in succession, and its Asbestos Millboard, Packing, Fibre, and other Special Asbestos Goods are used throughout H.M. NAVY.

The Boilers of every Battleship, Cruiser, Destroyer, Torpedo Boat, Depôt, and other ships of H.M. Navy are fitted with

BELL'S United ASBESTOS

"Victor" Asbestos-Metallic Joints and Special
"Victor" High-Pressure Solid Seamless Joints
(See opposite page).

BELL'S UNITED ASBESTOS "Salamander" Patent AIR-SPACE MATTRESSES

Results of Tests conducted by The National Physical Laboratory:—

Covered Bare
Surface Surface
Mean Tem. of Surface 370°F.
Ditto over cover 114°F.
Ditto of air 60°F.
Total Loss of Heat } 104 1000
per sq. ft. per hour } B.T.U. B.T.U.
Saving on bare surface loss 89½ per cent. by using these Mattresses.

Price 2/- to 2/6 per sq. ft.

"DECOLITE"

Jointless Fire-Proof Flooring.

FOR DECKS, GANGWAYS, &c., &c.

Bell's Corrugated Asbestos Insulating Slabs.
Bell's Asbestos (*Wadmit*) Protective Mattresses
EXTENSIVELY USED IN THE BRITISH NAVY.

"POILITE" (ASBESTOS-CEMENT) BUILDING SHEETS AND ROOFING TILES.

Over 130,000,000 sq. ft. of "Poilite" have been supplied to the British War Department for Soldiers' Huts, Hospitals, &c., &c.

PRICES & PARTICULARS OF ABOVE ON APPLICATION

1917 AND NAVAL YEAR BOOK xxvii

Bell's United Asbestos
SPECIAL "VICTOR" H.P.
SOLID Seamless JOINTS
For Water-Tube Boilers.

These "VICTOR" Joints are used in every Ship in His Britannic Majesty's Navy, AND HAVE NEVER BEEN KNOWN TO FAIL.

Price 7/6 to 10/6 per lb. according to size and shape.

TYPES of Packing used in His Britannic Majesty's Navy, by several Foreign Navies, and the Principal Steamship Companies throughout the World.

TRADE MARK

BELL'S UNITED ASBESTOS DAGGER PACKING
Millions of feet supplied annually.
N.B.—Every length of Genuine Packing bears the Trade Mark
Price 5/6 per lb.

BELL'S UNITED ASBESTOS 'SYREN' (B) PACKING
Used with great success for many years.
Price 4/6 per lb.

BELL'S UNITED ASBESTOS 'Syren' Automatic Packing
Mark "C" for Steam, Mark "D" for Water.
Price 4/6 per lb.
Described as "Automatic" since the working pressure keeps the gland perfectly tight. In the "D" Packing the Packing acts as a raw feather.

BELL'S UNITED ASBESTOS "VICTOR" Asbestos Metallic PACKING
Price 4/6 per lb.

BELL'S UNITED ASBESTOS "VICTOR" Asbestos-Metallic JOINTS
For MANHOLE DOORS, &c. Exclusively used in every Ship in HM Britannic Majesty's Navy for many years. These Joints have an absolutely clean record for reliability
Price 6/- to 9/- per lb. according to size and shape.

BELL'S UNITED ASBESTOS Co. Ltd.
SOUTHWARK STREET, LONDON, S.E.

xxviii THE FLEET ANNUAL 1917

PETTER
DIRECT REVERSING MARINE CRUDE OIL ENGINES

76 B.H.P. Direct-Reversing Marine Engine.

One, Two & Four Cylinders
10 to 300 B.H.P.

It will pay you to consider the special merits of the Petter Crude Oil Engines, which result in their being simpler, more reliable and more economical than any other oil engine on the market. Consumption of crude oil guaranteed not to exceed half a pint per B.H.P. per hour. No water injection used under any circumstances.

FULL INFORMATION FROM

PETTERS LIMITED,
Marine Department,
73 Queen Victoria St., London, E.C.

Works: YEOVIL, ENGLAND.

1917 AND NAVAL YEAR BOOK xxix

WESTLAND AIRCRAFT WORKS
BRANCH OF
PETTERS LTD
YEOVIL. ENG.

AIRCRAFT CONSTRUCTORS
—TO THE ADMIRALTY.—

ORDERS CAN BE ACCEPTED
FOR COMPLETE MACHINES: PROPELLERS: PARTS:

TELEGRAMS: "AIRCRAFT YEOVIL."
TELEPHONE: YEOVIL 129.

TRADE MARK

Telephone No.1102 Holborn

TAYLOR TUNNICLIFF & Co. LTD
23 HOLBORN VIADUCT LONDON
Estd. 1867

MANUFACTURERS OF
INSULATORS
for
WIRELESS & HIGH-TENSION POWER PURPOSES
TELEGRAPHS & TELEPHONES

Sole Manufacturers of
The patent leading-in insulators
for telephonic purposes adopted by
HIS MAJESTY'S GOVERNMENT
Patent No. 2959/07

HENLEY'S CABLES
for Ships

Photo by]   R.M.S. "AQUITANIA."   *[Frank & Son*

HENLEY'S CABLES SUPPLIED THROUGHOUT.

MANY Ships of War and Ships of Commerce are installed with Henley's Cables. We manufacture Electric Cables of every kind, from the finest dynamo wire to the heaviest armoured cable.

The name of Henley has been associated with the Electrical Industry since 1837

W. T. HENLEY'S TELEGRAPH WORKS CO., LTD.
Blomfield Street,
LONDON
E.C.

Brand: *Park Gate Yorkshire Steel*.

P.G. YORKSHIRE (TRADE MARK)

Works Established 1823.

THE PARK GATE IRON & STEEL CO., Ltd.
ROTHERHAM, ENGLAND.

London Office: 38 Victoria St., Westminster, London, S.W. 1

Manufacturers of HIGH-CLASS STEEL by Siemens' Process only.

STEEL PLATES
FOR MARINE, LANCASHIRE, LOCOMOTIVE, LAND & OTHER BOILERS.

Also BRIDGE AND TANK PLATES, SHEETS, AND CHEQUERED PLATES to Admiralty Pattern.

Steel supplied to the British Admiralty for Marine & other Boilers

ALSO

HIGH TENSILE STEEL
(*in Plates, Sheets and Bars*), FOR
BATTLESHIPS, TORPEDO BOATS, DESTROYERS

STEEL BARS *in rounds, squares, flats, angles, tees and sectional bars of all descriptions.*

WELDING AND CASEHARDENING STEEL.

STEEL SUPPLIED TO BRITISH ADMIRALTY, WAR OFFICE, BOARD OF TRADE, LLOYDS, ENGLISH & FOREIGN RAILWAYS.

John Oakey & Sons, Ltd.

MANUFACTURERS OF GENUINE

EMERY CLOTH & GLASS PAPER

GARNET AND FLINT PAPERS, GLASS CLOTH, EMERY, BLACK LEAD, PUMICE, CROCUS, TRIPOLI, &c.

Oakey's "Flexible Twilled" Emery Cloth

For Engineers, Sewing Machine, Lock and Scale Makers, and all purposes where great Strength, Durability and Perfect Flexibility are required.

OAKEY'S FLEXIBLE GLASS PAPER

Unequalled for Strength & Durability. Each Sheet is Warranted and Stamped "OAKEY'S."

FLINT AND GARNET SAND PAPERS

IN SHEETS AND ROLLS.

EXTRA QUALITY, specially made for Machine use, Covering Drums and Discs, making Belts and Bands, &c., for Boot and Shoe Finishing Machines, Wood Working Machines, &c. Extra Strong Manilla Paper with an Extra Heavy Coating of Flint or Garnet.

In Rolls 50-yds. long, 18-in., 20-in., 24-in., 30-in., 36-in., 40-in., 42-in., and 48-in. wide.

All Papers and Cloths are supplied in Rolls. Sheets, Strips, and Bands can be made to Special Sizes to suit the requirements of Purchasers.

**WELLINGTON EMERY & BLACKLEAD MILLS
LONDON, S.E.**

WRIGHTS'
Highest Quality
STEEL WIRE ROPES

in Flattened Strand, Locked Coil, and other Special Constructions for Mining, Aerial Ropeways, Oil Boring, Logging, and Marine and General Engineering Purposes

WRIGHTS' Special Flattened Strand Ropes for Giant Cranes in Ordnance Works and Shipyards

Launching Ropes, Slipway Ropes

CONTRACTORS TO H.M. ADMIRALTY

JOHN & EDWIN WRIGHT, LTD.

"Universe" Wire Rope Works,
BIRMINGHAM.

Telegrams: "Universe, B'ham."

Telephone: B'ham, 6914 Central (3 lines)

CONTRACTORS TO H.M. GOVERNMENT

"LION" *Patent* PACKINGS

THE KING OF PACKINGS

The only PACKING that combines the Packing Quality of Fibre with the Wearing Quality of Metal.

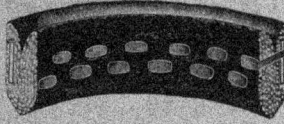

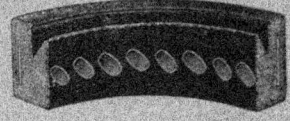

"*Lion*" *Expanding Steam Type*   "*Lion*" *Automatic Water Type*

REFUSE ALL IMITATIONS.

"GOLDEN WALKERITE"
JOINTING

A COMPRESSED ASBESTOS JOINTING THAT IS **ALL BRITISH**

REFUSE ALL IMITATIONS.

For Steam, Water, Ammonia, Petroleum and every description of joint.

WORKING SAMPLE ON APPLICATION

Sole Manufacturers and Patentees:

JAMES WALKER & CO.
LTD.

LION WORKS, GARFORD STREET,
WEST INDIA DOCK ROAD, LONDON, E.

WRITE FOR CATALOGUE "32."

PYROMETERS
FOR
MARINE ENGINEERS.

Portable and Fixed Installations for Flue Gases, Fuel Bed Temperature, Superheated Steam, Compressed Air, &c., &c.

Full Particulars from :—

FOSTER INSTRUMENT Co.

CHAS. E. FOSTER, Sole Proprietor, British,

LETCHWORTH, HERTS, ENGLAND.

Northern Depot—9 Newton Road, POTTERNEWTON, LEEDS.

GUN MOUNTINGS.—STEEL PIVOT PLATE CASTING.

Steel Castings, Tool Steel, Files, Saws, Twist Drills, Ore Crushers, Manganese Steel, Gratings, etc.

Edgar Allen & Co., Ltd. Imperial Steel Works Sheffield.

THE
Excelsior Wire Rope Co., Ltd.
CARDIFF.

Managing Director: D. MORGAN REES.

Manufacturers of
MINING ROPES
(Langs Lay, Ordinary Lay, Flattened Strand, Etc.)

SHIPPING ROPES

CRANE ROPES

And all kinds of Steel and Iron Wire Ropes

MAKERS TO THE ADMIRALTY, WAR OFFICE, INDIA OFFICE, ETC.

Works: MAINDY, CARDIFF.   Docks Depot: LOUDOUN SQUARE
Telegraphic Address: "ROPES, CARDIFF"
Telephone Nos. Head Office: 3093 and 3094.   Docks Depot: 2153
London Office: NORFOLK HOUSE, LAURENCE POUNTNEY HILL

A "Wolseley" Car on War Service.

"WOLSELEY"

EVER since the beginning of the war the Wolseley workshops at Adderley Park have been engaged in supplying the needs of His Majesty's Naval and Military Forces.

Hundreds of Wolseley Engines and Cars are now demonstrating, on active service, the sterling qualities for which they have long been deservedly famous.

"WOLSELEY" AUTOCARS
AVIATION ENGINES
AIRCRAFT
MARINE MOTORS
MOTOR CRAFT
COMMERCIAL VEHICLES

WOLSELEY MOTORS L^{TD.}

Proprietors: VICKERS, LIMITED

ADDERLEY PARK, BIRMINGHAM

LONDON DEPOT:
YORK STREET, WESTMINSTER, S.W.

MARINE DEPT.:
EAST COWES, I.O.W.

York Minster.

AFTERWARDS, when the end for which we are enduring all things, has been secured, the exiles will renew acquaintance with the delightful home roads and quaint old country towns.

Meanwhile the serious business is to "carry-on"; and to aid the successful prosecution of the war, we have ceased

BELSIZE

Wensley Green, Yorks.

temporarily to produce Belsize Cars—our whole energies being devoted to war work.

When we again turn our attention to the building of cars, our pre-war policy of sound workmanship and beauty of design will be pursued ; and the after-war Belsize will reflect all the experience gained during this (the " melting pot ") period.

Earmark Belsize for future reference.

The "after-war" car.

Belsize Motors Ltd.—Clayton, Manchester.

Austin

COMMERCIAL & PRIVATE
MOTOR CARS

AIRCRAFT & AIRCRAFT ENGINES. PORTABLE POWER UNITS for ELECTRIC LIGHTING AND OTHER PURPOSES

CULTI-TRACTORS FOR FARM WORK

Contractors to the Admiralty, the War Office, the Russian Government, the Crown Agents for the Colonies, etc.

A COMMANDER AND HIS AUSTIN.

THE AUSTIN MOTOR Co. L^D

Head Office and Works:
NORTHFIELD BIRMINGHAM ENGLAND.
LONDON.   PARIS.   MANCHESTER.   NORWICH.

Rudge Multi

Shore Leave

Means a lot more to the Naval man who owns a Rudge-Multi. He can get about quickly, saving heaps of time in travelling and enjoying every mile of his journey.

The Rudge is always in perfect running order because every one of its parts is thoroughly proved and tested before the final assembly.

It is absolutely the ideal Mount for the man with no time to spare for "breakdowns" and no desire to waste money on high running costs.

Get the Rudge Motor Bicycle Catalogue —post free—for full particulars. It includes a lot of useful information on motor cycling.

Rudge-Whitworth, Ltd., (Dept. 236) COVENTRY

London Depôts: 230 Tottenham Court Road (Oxford Street end), W. 1.
23 Holborn Viaduct, E.C. 1.

By Appointment Cycle Makers to H.M. King George

Correct Lubrication

SCIENCE *versus* GUESSWORK

Friction in any power plant—whether steam engine or automobile—is the worst enemy of economy and efficiency. The necessity of reducing friction brought about the first use of lubricants.

The rapid development of machinery in every branch of industry demonstrated that *any* lubricant would not do.

The lubricating problems thus set up demanded scientific solution.

The Vacuum Oil Company were pioneers in the field of scientific lubrication, and were the first manufacturers of petroleum residual lubricants which possess marked advantage over others.

Gargoyle lubricants properly selected and carefully applied ensure better lubrication and a saving in running costs.

GARGOYLE Lubricants

USED BY THE ALLIED NAVIES
A grade for every purpose

VACUUM OIL CO. Ltd.
CAXTON HOUSE,
WESTMINSTER, S.W. 1.

Telegrams: "Vacuum, Vic., London."   *Telephone:* Victoria 6620

B.S.A

The Birmingham Small Arms Company Limited,

Contractors to His Majesty's Government, the War Office, the Admiralty, the India Office, the Post Office, and Colonial and Foreign Governments.

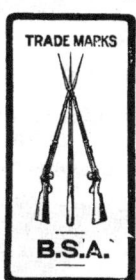

Manufacturers of

- MOTOR CARS.
- MOTOR BICYCLES,
- BICYCLES,
- BICYCLE FITTINGS,
- and SPECIALITIES.
- MACHINE GUNS.
- MILITARY MAGAZINE RIFLES.
- MATCH RIFLES.
- REPEATING SPORTING RIFLES, For BIG and SMALL GAME.
- MINIATURE RIFLES (SINGLE SHOT and MAGAZINE).
- AIR RIFLES.
- PATENT RIFLE SIGHTS, &c.
- HIGH-SPEED STEEL TWIST DRILLS,
- MILLING CUTTERS, REAMERS, &c.

ENQUIRIES INVITED.

The Birmingham Small Arms Company Limited,

Registered Offices - - - - - Small Heath, Birmingham.
Works - - - Small Heath, Sparkbrook, Redditch and Coventry.
Telegrams: "Smallarms, Birmingham." Telephone: 6440 Central (9 Lines).
Codes: A.B.C. 4th and 5th Editions, Lieber's, Western Union.

IMPORTANT.—All communications should be addressed to the Head Offices, SMALL HEATH, BIRMINGHAM.

Webley & Scott Ltd.

Manufacturers of Revolvers, Automatic Pistols, and all kinds of High-class Sporting Guns and Rifles.
Contractors to His Majesty's Army, Navy, Indian and Colonial Forces.

SINGLE SEMI-HAMMERLESS EJECTOR GUN.

Interchangeable Single Ejector Gun made entirely throughout in our factories.

AUTOMATIC PISTOLS

·455 AUTOMATIC PISTOL,
As adopted by the British Government.

HAMMERLESS AUTOMATIC PISTOL
·25 or 6·35 Calibre.

ADVANTAGES OF WEBLEY AUTOMATIC.

No Tools required for dismounting.

Can be used as a Single Loader, Magazine being reserved for emergency.

Double Security Lock.

Greater Smashing and Stopping Power than any other Automatic on the Market.

Great Accuracy at Long Ranges. Solidity, Accuracy, Durability. Reliability, Simplicity and Efficiency.

The Smallest and Lightest Automatic Pistol made.

COMBINED PISTOL AND RIFLE, ·22 R.F.

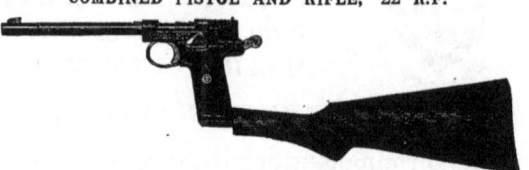

An ideal Combination Arm. Can be used either as a pistol, for Target work, or as a Short Rifle, making an extremely close diagram at 150 yards.

To be obtained from all Gun Dealers, and Wholesale at—

Weaman St., Birmingham & 78 Shaftesbury Avenue, London W.

Webley & Scott Ltd.

Contractors to His Majesty's Navy, Army, Indian & Colonial Forces

REVOLVER & AUTO-PISTOL WORKS.

Webley & Scott Revolvers and Automatic Pistols have a World-wide reputation. The Company has supplied to the British Government upwards of 150,000 of their celebrated **Service Model** Revolvers.

British Officers going on foreign service now arm themselves with the **Webley-Fosbery** Automatic Revolver, which is the only automatic weapon taking the present Service cartridge.

Elaborate trials and experiments have been conducted by the Admiralty with the .455 Automatic Pistol, which is a high velocity weapon of great smashing power and extreme accuracy.

The Webley & Scott .32 **"M.P."** (Metropolitan Police) model Automatic Pistol has been adopted by the following Police Forces:

    London Metropolitan   **Adelaide (Australia)**
           " City   **Switzerland**
     Dublin Metropolitan   **Manchester**
                   Isle of Man,

and many of the principal Town and County Forces in the United Kingdom.

The Webley & Scott Automatic Pistol requires no tools for stripping, and the high velocity weapons have a positive security bolt, and are lighter, stronger, simpler and more efficient than any other Automatic at present on the Market.

Webley & Scott are the largest manufacturers of high-class Sporting Guns and Rifles in the United Kingdom

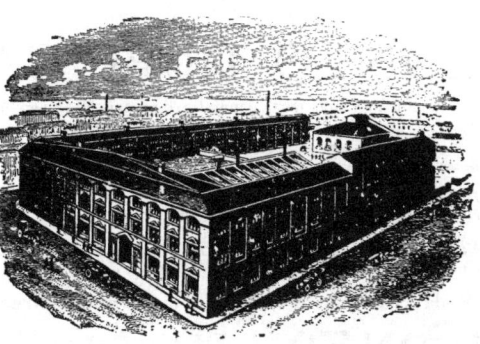

GUN WORKS.

Used by the Navy, the Army and all Government Departments

THERE are many Ships in the Grand Fleet and many Orderly Rooms in the Field that are using the Roneo Duplicator. It is speedy, cleanly and efficient. It **produces forms, reports, etc., in record time** — each copy being perfect, whilst charts, diagrams, drawings or plans reproduced by means of the Roneo Duplicator are as clear and distinct as the originals.

THE RONEO DUPLICATOR No. 10

is the machine most generally used for Navy and Army work. It is used by :—

Argyle & Sutherland Highlanders
Black Watch (Royal Highlanders)
Duke of Cornwall's L.I.
King's Own (Royal Lancaster Regt.)
King's Own (Yorkshire L.I.)
King's Royal Rifles
King's Own Scottish Borderers
King's Liverpool Regiment
London Regiment
H.M.S. "Erin"
H.M.S. "Royalist"
H.M.S. "Excellent"
H.M.S. "Vernon"
Loyal North Lancs. Regt.
Manchester Regiment
Middlesex Regiment
Northumberland Fusiliers
Rifle Brigade
Royal Fusiliers
Royal Welsh Fusiliers
Somerset Light Infantry
West Yorkshire Regiment
Welsh Regiment
York and Lancaster Regiment
ETC., ETC., ETC.

Would you like to know more about it. Write for free Illustrated Catalogue to-day.

RONEO LTD., 5/11 Holborn, London, E.C.

SHIPS FANS — ELECTRIC HEATERS — SHIPS FITTINGS

EDISWAN
Everything Electrical

All Ediswan Electrical Manufactures for ships' use have found exceptional favour afloat on account of their efficiency. Ediswan Fans, Heaters, Fittings, Engine-room Switchboards, Royal Ediswan Lamps, etc., have a reputation amongst shipping circles second to none. May we have the pleasure of knowing your requirements which will have every attention.

Tele.: 520 Enfield.　　　　Telegrams: Ediswan, Enfield

THE EDISON SWAN ELECTRIC CO., LTD.
PONDERS END WORKS, MIDDLESEX

LIVERPOOL. 48 Duke Street
NEWCASTLE. 34 Grainger Street West
SOUTHAMPTON. 123 High Street
HULL. 54 King Edward Street
GLASGOW. 153 West George St.
BRISTOL. 71 Victoria Street
CARDIFF. Westgate Street
DUNDEE. 13 Castle St.
and other Provincial Towns

THE MONOTYPE

*The name of a typesetting machine
that is a guarantee of good printing*

Type is the first consideration in all printing. It is the medium that is to convey the message to the person whose attention you wish to attract. That is why discriminating purchasers of printing specify

Monotype Composition

The "Monotype" way is the most efficient method of setting type, and will produce the kind of printing that the buyer has the right to expect.

There are no limits to the capacity of the "Monotype" to handle your work.

Its popularity with buyers of printing has been built upon Quality, the only foundation upon which to construct a business.

Further particulars may be obtained of

The Lanston Monotype Corporation Limited

43 & 43a, FETTER LANE, LONDON, E.C. 4.

Prudential Assurance Company, Limited

Chief Office—HOLBORN BARS, LONDON.

Funds exceed £99,000,000.

Summary of the Report presented at the Sixty-Eighth Annual Meeting, held on March 1st, 1917.

ORDINARY BRANCH.—The number of policies issued during the year was 48,258, assuring the sum of £5,080,989, and producing a new annual premium income of £373,309. The premiums received during the year were £5,230,170, being an increase of £72,654 over the year 1915.

The claims of the year amounted to £4,573,917, of which £249,689 was in respect of War Claims. The number of deaths was 12,407. The number of endowment assurances matured was 27,065, the annual premium income of which £146,894.

The number of policies including annuities in force at the end of the year was 932,539.

INDUSTRIAL BRANCH.—The premiums received during the year were £8,897,723, being an increase of £391,660.

The claims of the year amounted to £4,005,251, of which £827,879 was in respect of 49,625 War Claims. The bonus additions included in the claims amounted to £112,565. The total number of claims and surrenders, including 16,741 endowment assurances matured, was 398,917.

The number of free policies granted during the year to those policyholders of five years' standing and upwards who desired to discontinue their payments, was 69,775, the number in force being 2,004,282. The number of free policies which became claims during the year was 50,016.

The total number of policies in force in this Branch at the end of the year was 21,305,330; their average duration exceeds thirteen and a quarter years.

The War Claims paid during the year, in both Branches, number 52,433 and amount to £1,077,568. The total paid up to the present on this account since the outbreak of War exceeds £1,860,000 in respect of over 88,000 claims.

GENERAL BRANCH.—Under the Sickness Insurance Tables the Premiums received during the year were £7,780, and £3,974 was paid in Sickness claims. Under the new Memorandum of Association thirteen sinking fund policies were issued during the year, assuring a capital sum of £131,300, and producing an annual income of £2,531. The whole of the Fund of £23,399 is reserved for future liabilities.

The assets of the Company, in all branches, as shown in the balance sheet are £99,123,746, being an increase of £4,328,948 over those of 1915.

In the Ordinary Branch the surplus shown is £1,418,240, including the sum of £219,331 brought forward from last year. Out of this surplus the Directors have added £400,000 to the Investments Reserve Fund, which stands as at 31st December, 1916, at £2,000,000. In addition, £800,000 has been added to the Special Contingency Fund, which stands at £1,500,000, and £218,240 has been carried forward. The Directors have decided to continue the payment of a bonus on all participating policies of this Branch which become claims either by death or maturity during the financial year. They much regret, however, that the present circumstances do not justify them in making a general distribution of bonus, and the shareholders will again receive no part of the profits of this Branch. The Directors have every confidence, however, that the interests of the participating policy holders are fully secured by the Special Contingency Fund referred to above.

In the Industrial Branch the surplus shown is £1,000,892, including the sum of £249,282 brought forward from last year. Out of this surplus the Directors have added £415,082 to the Investments Reserve Fund, which, after deducting £15,082, representing realised loss on Securities, stands as at 31st December, 1916, at £1,400,000.

The provisions relating to Industrial Assurance contained in the Courts (Emergency Powers) Act, 1914, have again resulted in a severe strain upon the Company's resources, which has reduced the surplus shown on the operations of the year, and whilst these provisions remain in force the strain must continue. In these circumstances the Directors have not felt justified in drawing upon the £350,000 set aside last year to meet contingent liabilities created by the Act, but have met the loss out of revenue. The Courts (Emergency Powers) Act Reserve therefore stands, as at 31st December, 1916, at £350,000.

The profit sharing scheme in the Industrial Branch provides that after payment of a fixed dividend to the shareholders, any surplus profit shall be divided into six parts, one part being retained by the shareholders, one distributed among the outdoor staff of the Company, the remaining four parts being allotted by way of bonus to the policy-holders of the Industrial Branch.

The sum which has already been paid or allotted under this scheme, by way of bonus to the Industrial Branch policyholders and outdoor staff, amounts to £2,825,000. The Directors regret that the amount of surplus shown this year does not permit of any increase being made to this sum: there is, however, still a balance remaining, from which bonus additions will be made to the sums assured on all policies in the Industrial Branch on which at least thirty years' premiums have been paid, and which become claims either by death or maturity of endowment from the 2nd of March, 1917, to the 7th of March, 1918, both dates inclusive.

In addition to the reserves held against the liabilities shown by the valuation, the total amount reserved for contingencies, including amounts carried forward, exceeds £5,650,000.

The Balance Sheet includes amounts totalling over £17,750,000 in British Government Securities; this represents an increase, compared with last year, of about £4,500,000.

During the year the Company has lent or sold to the Treasury under the various mobilisation schemes securities of the nominal value of £6,955,159.

The Prudential Approved Societies formed under the National Insurance Act, 1911, continue to make satisfactory progress, and the valuable services rendered to the members by the Agency Staff are highly appreciated. The amount distributed in benefits to the members at their homes during the year amounted to £1,320,397, making a total exceeding £5,700,000 since the Act came into operation. An arrangement has been made and approved by the Insurance Commissioners whereby the Prudential Approved Society for Miners is absorbed into the Prudential Approved Society for Men, and the Society for Laundresses is absorbed into the Society for Women as from the 31st December, 1916, thus reducing the number of Prudential Approved Societies to four.

During the year the Government has continuously availed itself of the services of the Company and its officials. It has been a matter for congratulation that the services so rendered have met with the greatest appreciation.

The indoor and outdoor Staffs have been further depleted during the year by naval and military demands, and the Company is now supplying more than ten thousand men to the fighting strength of the nation.

Messrs. Deloitte, Plender, Griffiths & Co. have examined the securities, and their certificate is appended to the balance sheets.

THOMAS C. DEWEY, *Chairman.*

W. J. LANCASTER. } *Directors.*
D. WINTRINGHAM STABLE.

J. BURN, *Actuary.*   A. C. THOMPSON.

G. E. MAY, *Secretary.*   *General Manager.*

The full Report and Balance Sheet can be obtained upon application.

THE UNION JACK CLUB

This picture shows the Union Jack Club as it will appear when the much needed Extension is added.

Facts about the Union Jack Club
The Club with 5,000,000 Members

It is the Greatest National and Personal Memorial to our Sailors and Soldiers

I. The Union Jack Club is the Club of the W.O.'s, P.O.'s, N.C.O.'s, and Men of the Royal Navy, Army, and Marines, and is in Waterloo Road, London, S.E. 1.
II. It was opened by H.M. King Edward VII in 1907 as a memorial to the men who lost their lives in the South African War.
III. It is open to every man in both Services.
IV. It is entirely self-supporting, and now asks for money from the public for extension purposes only.
V. It has 355 bedrooms, besides dining-rooms, billiard-rooms, reading-rooms, bath-rooms, etc.
VI. A bedroom costs 1s. a night, and meals are charged for on the same modest scale.
VII. It has a hostel for married men and their wives.
VIII. Men from the fleet and front invariably use it when passing through London.
IX. 241,056 men slept at the Club during 1916. Thousands were turned away for want of accommodation.

Subscriptions should be sent to the Hon. Treasurer, G. J. Marjoribanks, Esq., The Union Jack Club, 91a Waterloo Road, London, S.E.

Hon. Organiser Extension Fund : Sir Herbert Morgan.

BURBERRY NAVAL KIT

AND NAVAL YEAR BOOK

BURBERRYS are expert in all branches of Naval Outfitting, and, as skilled craftsmen, supply correct and well-tailored Uniforms, as well as every detail of equipment.

SERVICE KIT, made in Burberrys' exclusive Weave-Proof materials, ensures better protection against rain or storm, more warmth in cold weather, and greater comfort at all times, besides withstanding hard wear longer than any other kit available.

Every Burberry Garment is labelled "Burberrys"

Naval Uniforms
Burberry materials surpass all others for proofness, durability and fine appearance.

The Burberry
unlike oilskins and rubberproofs, provides an efficient safeguard against wet, yet is healthful to wear.

Illustrated Naval Catalogue Post Free on Request

The Burfron
Winds round the figure without leaving openings anywhere to admit rain or wind, and is held together securely by a button at the neck. A belt gives it a smart Service appearance.

Husky Suit
Made in thick, fleecy cloth, and worn under a weatherproof, provides a plentiful supply of warmth in very cold weather.

The Tielocken
Ensures that, from chin to knees, every vulnerable part of the body is doubly covered. Another advantage is its quick adjustment. A belt holds it securely—no buttons to fasten.

Officers' Complete Kits in 2 to 4 Days or Ready for Use

Burberry Husky Suit

SUNLIGHT SOAP

IN HOME WATERS.

WORDS could not express more perfectly all that is told in this picture. Neither can words fully convey the nation's gratitude to our gallant navy. Therefore, we leave our illustration to express all we would say of Jack, of his good wife, bonny son and happy home. Likewise we think that the Quality and Efficiency of SUNLIGHT SOAP with the satisfaction and leisure they bring are also best expressed in this illustration of

SUNLIGHT IN HOME WATERS.

£1,000 GUARANTEE OF PURITY ON EVERY BAR

The name Lever on Soap is a Guarantee of Purity and Excellence.
LEVER BROTHERS LIMITED, PORT SUNLIGHT.

SPRATT'S DOG CAKES AND PUPPY BISCUITS

"INDISPENSABLE"

Fry's PURE BREAKFAST Cocoa

MAKERS TO H.M. THE KING.

CONTRACTORS TO THE ALLIED FORCES.

SMOKE
"CAPSTAN"
NAVY CUT
TOBACCO
AND
CIGARETTES

W. D. & H. O. WILLS
BRISTOL AND LONDON

Branch of the Imperial Tobacco Company (of Great Britain & Ireland), Ltd.

Hall's Barton Ropery Co., Ltd., Hull

MANILA ROPE

STEEL WIRE ROPE

HEMP ROPE

COIR ROPE

COTTON ROPE

TRAWL NETS & TRAWL TWINES

CANVAS

HALL'S BARTON ROPERY Co. Ltd.
83 HIGH STREET, HULL

London Office : (John Munro, 83 Gracechurch Street)

Works : Barton-on-Humber

LLOYDS BANK LIMITED.

HEAD OFFICE: 71, LOMBARD ST., LONDON, E.C.

CAPITAL.
Subscribed:
£31,304,200
Paid-up:
£5,008,672
Reserve Fund:
£3,600,000

Savings Bank Department.

The services of the Bank, with its widespread system of Branches, are at the disposal of the public for the deposit of savings, however small.

Wherever a Branch of Lloyds Bank is established, such deposits can be made, and interest will be allowed thereon, on terms as to rate, withdrawal, &c., which can be obtained on application.

THIS BANK HAS NEARLY 900 OFFICES IN ENGLAND AND WALES.

French Auxiliary: **LLOYDS BANK (FRANCE) LIMITED.**
Offices at PARIS, BORDEAUX, BIARRITZ, HAVRE and NICE.

STOCK LINE:—WATER-TIGHT, GUN METAL

CABLE JOINT BOXES

For EMERGENCY REPAIRS.

A. REYROLLE & CO. Ltd.
HEBBURN-ON-TYNE.

Makers of Armoured Switch-gear for Shipyards, Factories and Mines, W.T. Plugs and Sockets for Dockyards.

CONTENTS

PART I

	PAGE
Letter from Sir Eric Geddes, K.C.B.	v
Foreword	5
A Brief History of the War	7
Submarine Warfare à Outrance	57
British Losses by Enemy Submarines	60
Navy Separation Allowances	63
Naval Prize Money	71
NAVAL DESPATCHES—	
The Dover Patrol	72
Evacuation of Gallipoli	73
Operations of H.M. Ships against German East Africa	81
For Distinguished Service	89

PART II

The British Navy	3
The French Navy	13
The Russian Navy	18
The Japanese Navy	21
The Italian Navy	25
The Brazilian Navy	27
The U.S.A. Navy	28
The Greek Navy	32
The Chilian Navy	33
The Spanish Navy	33
The German Navy	34
The Austro-Hungarian Navy	40
Uniforms of the World's Navies	43
Distinguishing Badges	46

PART III

The Navy's Immortal Names

MILKMAID Café au Lait
(KAFFAY-O-LAY)

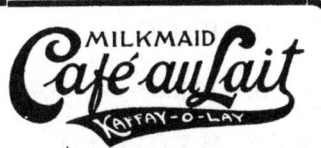

Coffee, Milk, and Sugar, read for use. Only boiling water required. Keeps any length of time. No waste. Just the thing for camp use, refreshing, portable, handy, and easy to make.

Leaves no 'grounds' for complaint.

Sold by all Grocers, Canteen Dealers and Stores, in tins and half-tins.

MILKMAID MILK-COCOA
The Cocoa with the Milk-Chocolate flavour

There is nothing more warming and comforting than a cup of Cocoa.

It is the very thing for Sailors and Soldiers or anyone who desires to make a delicious cup of Cocoa hastily

MILKMAID MILK - COCOA is Cocoa, Milk, and Sugar, ready for use. Only boiling water is required to mix it.

Ask your grocer for it.

MILKMAID CREAM

is delicious with tinned, dried or stewed fruits, and is excellent with porridge and other cereals.

Put up in sterilized cans of various sizes.

Sold by all Grocers and Stores.

Never go to sea without IDEAL MILK
The Everyday Milk

IDEAL MILK is fresh milk concentrated to the consistency of cream. No sugar added. Undiluted in place of cream. Diluted with two or three parts water it replaces fresh milk.

AS SUPPLIED TO THE ARMY AND NAVY.

Sold by all Grocers and Stores.

LIST OF ILLUSTRATIONS

Part I

	PAGE
"Anyway, I never Paid my Mess Bill!"	Frontispiece
Sir Eric Geddes, K.C.B., P.C.	2
Admiral Sir David Beatty, K.C.B., M.V.O., D.S.O.	6
Sir Reginald Tyrwhitt, K.C.B.	9
Captain Evans, C.B., D.S.O.	13
Lieut.-Com. R. R. Turner	21
Petty Officer Whales	25
Captain E. Unwin, V.C.	31
Commander A. L. Snagge	35
Captain A. P. Addison	39
Commander H. C. Woolcombe-Boyce	41
Commander F. H. H. Goodhart, D.S.O.	47
Engineer-Commander James Hughes	53
Naval Cadets in the Workshops at Osborne	87
Commander Gordon Campbell, V.C., D.S.O.	88

Part II

Uniforms of the World's Navies	43
Distinguishing Badges	46

CATALOGUES

Will be in great request after the War. Nearly all Catalogues are now out of date. Revised ones will be wanted for old customers and large supplies wanted for new customers. The most important thing in preparing an Illustrated Catalogue is to get good

BLOCKS

See that you have the very best.

ANDRÉ, SLEIGH & ANGLO, Ltd.

ENGRAVERS BY EVERY KNOWN PROCESS

Head Office: Milford House, Milford Lane, Strand

A SPECIMEN COPY OF OUR MAGAZINE "ILLUSTRATION" SENT ON REQUEST

By Special Appointment to
HIS MAJESTY THE KING

CROSSE & BLACKWELL
Soho Square, London, W.

The C. & B. Products are renowned the World over for their Quality and Excellence. They are absolutely pure and wholesome, being manufactured from the finest ingredients and under ideal conditions.

CROSSE & BLACKWELL

Jams, Jellies, Marmalade, Sauces, Soups, Pure Pickles & Potted Meats. Preserved Fish & Provisions, Sausages in Tins, Salad Oil, Pure Malt Vinegar.

OF ALL GROCERS & STOREKEEPERS THROUGHOUT THE WORLD

Save Your Life

As so many Naval men have already done by wearing a

"GIEVE" LIFE-SAVING WAISTCOAT

An officer of a big ship, recently torpedoed, remarks: "I should not be here with you to-day, but for my 'Gieve' Waistcoat."

Worn as an ordinary waistcoat under uniform, fitted with a brandy flask, inflates easily in few seconds.

Price: **50/- net.**

Angle of 65 degrees, face uppermost, head and shoulders well clear of water

Lives saved from the following ships:

H.M.S.
FORMIDABLE
GOLIATH
INDIA
TRIUMPH
MAJESTIC
IRRESISTIBLE
LYNX
ROYAL EDWARD

S.S. FALABA
MONGONA
BAYANO
LUSITANIA
ARABIC
HESPERIAN
PERSIAN
MALOJA

PATROL BOATS

MINE SWEEPERS

And numerous others.

Sold everywhere, or direct from the following addresses:

PORTSMOUTH: The Hard.
LONDON: 65 South Molton St. W.
DEVONPORT: 44 Fore Street.
CHATHAM: Railway Street.
WEYMOUTH: 1 & 2 Grosvenor Place.
SHEERNESS: 72 High St., Blue Town.
EDINBURGH: 30 George Street.
HARWICH: Kingsway, Dovercourt.

Made by the well-known Royal Naval Outfitters—

GIEVE'S LIMITED

Humour in the Navy

"Anyway, I never paid my mess bill!"

Drawn by Bram. Scholey, R.N.

Sir Eric Geddes, K.C.B., P.C.
First Lord of the Admiralty
Photograph : Elliott & Fry

The Third Great War Number of

THE FLEET ANNUAL

AND NAVAL YEAR BOOK
1917

COMPILED BY
LIONEL YEXLEY

TWELFTH YEAR

PUBLISHED FOR "THE FLEET" BY
CHAPMAN & HALL LIMITED
11 HENRIETTA STREET, COVENT GARDEN, W.C.
1917

THE WESTMINSTER PRESS
411A HARROW ROAD
LONDON W

Foreword.

THIS is the Third War Edition of THE FLEET ANNUAL, and judging from the success of the other two, and the numerous letters of enquiry as to when this one would be ready, its success is already assured. A tragic incident has somewhat delayed its issue, as when it was almost ready, news came of the destruction of H.M.S. "Vanguard," and although THE ANNUAL only deals with events up to June 30th, 1917, it was felt that in face of the magnitude of the disaster mentioned, the officers and men who went down should be included in the Navy's Immortal Names at once, instead of waiting till 1918. Hence a slight delay in publication.

In Part II, instead of eliminating the losses from ships' lists and showing them separately, ships lost are retained in the lists but printed in italics, also the method of destruction and date, a method appreciated by the readers of THE ANNUAL. It has not been possible to show the whole of the British losses in this way, owing to the decision of the Admiralty, in the early part of the year, not to publish the names of vessels lost, especially torpedo and small craft.

Last year, owing to the impossibility of printing a Second Edition, several hundred applicants for copies had to be refused: "Sold out." This year we have based the supply on last year's demand, and hope there will be sufficient to go round.

One fact I should like to make clear—the War Edition of THE FLEET ANNUAL does not profess to pass any expression of opinion on events; it is compiled exclusively from official documents and records, and therefore may be looked on as absolutely authentic.

Lionel Yexley

Admiral Sir David Beatty, K.C.B., M.V.O., D.S.O.
Commander-in-Chief of the Grand Fleet.
Photo: Central News.

THE FLEET ANNUAL AND NAVAL YEAR BOOK, 1917.

A BRIEF HISTORY OF THE WAR FROM THE NAVAL POINT OF VIEW:

PART III.—June 30th, 1916—June 30th, 1917.

PART I.—June 29th, 1914—March 1st, 1915 (FLEET ANNUAL, 1915).
PART II.—March 1st, 1915—June 30th, 1916 (FLEET ANNUAL, 1916).

CONTINUING our Brief History of the War, a matter of interest was dealt with on Monday, July 3rd, 1916, when, in the Prize Court, Sir Samuel Evans granted £3,580 as prize money to the Commander, officers and crew of H.M.S. "Highflyer" for their services in sinking the German auxiliary cruiser "Kaiser Wilhelm der Grosse" in the Atlantic in August, 1914. The bounty is at the rate of £5 per head of the crew.

Commander Maxwell Anderson presented the case for the applicants, and called Captain Henry Tritton Buller, M.V.O., R.N., who stated that he chased the "Kaiser Wilhelm der Grosse" at full speed, and called on her to surrender. She signalled that she would not do so, and he fired a shot to the right of her. She at once opened fire in return, and the action became general. After firing for about an hour, the "Kaiser Wilhelm der Grosse" was sunk. The action ended near the shore, and all the crew of the enemy warship got to land in boats, so that Captain Buller was not able to say what exactly had been the complement of the German vessel. However, from his knowledge of ships of this class, he was able to say it was approximately 500.

An affidavit was put in made by Sir Graham Greene, Secretary of the Admiralty, who reported that the official casualty list of the "Kronprinz Wilhelm," a sister ship to the "Kaiser Wilhelm der Grosse," was 516.

On the same day there appeared a detailed report from the German Admiralty of the Battle of Jutland. It said :

> The High Sea Fleet, consisting of three battleship squadrons, five battle-cruisers, a large number of small cruisers, and several destroyer flotillas, was cruising in the Skager Rak on May 31st for the purpose, as on earlier occasions, of offering battle to the British Fleet. The vanguard of small cruisers, at 4.30 p.m., suddenly encountered, 90 miles west of the Hanstholm, a group of eight of the newest cruisers of the "Calliope" class and from 15 to 20 of the most modern destroyers. While the German light forces and the First

Cruiser Squadron, under Admiral von Hipper, were following the British, who were retiring to the north-west, the German battle-cruisers sighted to the westward Admiral Beatty's Battle-cruiser Squadron of six ships, including four of the "Lion" type and two of the "Indefatigable" class, which formed into battle line on a south-easterly course. Admiral Hipper formed line ahead on the same general course, and approached for a running fight and opened fire at 5.49 p.m. with his heavy guns at a range of 13,000 metres against a superior enemy. The weather was clear, with a light sea and a light north-west wind. After about a quarter of an hour a violent explosion occurred in the last cruiser, the "Indefatigable," caused by a heavy shell, which destroyed the ship. About 6.20 p.m. five ships of the "Queen Elizabeth" class, coming from the west, joined the British battle-cruiser line, powerfully reinforcing it with 15 in. guns.

DESTROYERS' DUEL.

To equalise this superiority Admiral Hipper ordered destroyers to attack the enemy. British destroyers and small cruisers interposed, and a bitter close-range engagement ensued, in which the light cruisers participated. The Germans lost two torpedo-boats, the crews of which were rescued by sister ships under a heavy fire. Two British destroyers were sunk by artillery, and two others, the "Nestor" and the "Nomad," were crippled, and were later destroyed by the main fleet, after the German torpedo-boats had rescued all the survivors. A mighty explosion, caused by a big shell, destroyed the "Queen Mary," and a third ship in the line at 6.30. Soon afterwards the German main battleship fleet was sighted southwards, steering north. The hostile fast squadrons thereupon turned northward, closing the first phase of the fight, which lasted about an hour. The British retired at high speed before the German Fleet, which was following hotly. The German battle-cruisers continued the artillery combat with increasing intensity, particularly with the division of the "Queen Elizabeths," in which the leading German battleship division intermittently participated. The hostile ships showed a desire to run in a flat curve ahead of the point of our line and across it. At 7.45 p.m. British small cruisers and destroyers launched an attack against our battle-cruisers, which avoided the torpedoes by manœuvring ; while the British battle-cruisers retired from the engagement, in which they did not participate later, as far as can be established. Shortly after the German reconnoitring group, which was carrying out a destroyer attack, received a heavy fire from the north-east, in which the cruiser "Wiesbaden" was soon put out of action. Parts of the German torpedo flotillas, which immediately attacked the heavy ships that were appearing shadow-like from the bank of haze to the north-east, made out a long line of at least 25 battleships, which, first on a north-west to westerly course, sought a junction with the British battle-cruisers and the "Queen Elizabeths," and then turned to an east-south-east course.

Sir Reginald Tyrwhitt, K.C.B.

Photograph : Russell & Son

Third Phase of the Battle.

With the advent of the British main fleet, whose centre consisted of three squadrons of eight battleships with fast divisions of three "Invincibles" on the northern wing, and three of the newest "Royal Sovereigns," armed with 15 in. guns, at the southern end, began about eight in the evening the third phase of the engagement, embracing the combat of the main fleets. Vice-Admiral von Scheer determined to attack the British main fleet, which, as is now recognised, was completely assembled and about doubly superior. The German battleship squadrons, headed by the battle-cruisers, steamed first towards the extensive bank of haze to the north-east, from which the crippled "Wiesbaden" was still receiving a heavy fire. Around the "Wiesbaden" stubborn individual fights in quickly-changing conditions now occurred. Enemy light forces, supported by the armoured cruiser squadron and five ships of the "Minotaur," "Achilles," and "Duke of Edinburgh" classes, coming from the north-east, encountered (apparently surprised by the decreasing visibility) our battle-cruisers and leading battleship divisions. They thereby came under a violent fire, whereby a small cruiser and the "Defence" and the "Black Prince" were sunk. The "Warrior" regained her own line as a wreck and sank. Later a small cruiser was severely damaged. Two destroyers had already fallen victims to an attack by German torpedo-boats against the leading British battleships, and a small cruiser and two destroyers were damaged. In the haze shortly after 8 p.m. the enemy Battle Squadron turned north, and finally east. The Germans observed amidst the artillery combat signs of the effect of their good shooting. Several officers of the German ships observed that a battleship of the "Queen Elizabeth" class blew up under conditions similar to the "Queen Mary." The "Invincible" sank, severely hit.

Steaming in a Circle.

A ship of the "Iron Duke" class had earlier received a torpedo hit, and one ship of the "Queen Elizabeth" class was observed steaming in a circle, apparently hit in the steering gear. The "Lützow" was hit by at least fifteen heavy shells, and was unable to maintain her place in the line. Admiral Hipper therefore transferred his flag by torpedo-boat, under heavy fire, to the "Moltke." The "Derfflinger" meantime temporarily took the lead. Parts of the German torpedo flotillas which attacked the enemy main fleet heard detonations. The Germans lost a torpedo-boat by a heavy hit. An enemy destroyer was seen hit by a torpedo and in a sinking condition. After this first violent onslaught against the mass of the superior enemy force the opponents lost sight of one another in the smoke and powder clouds. After a short cessation of the artillery combat, Admiral Scheer ordered a new attack by all the available forces of the German battle-cruisers, which, with several light cruisers and torpedo-boats, again headed the line, and encountered soon after nine o'clock a renewed heavy fire from

… A Brief History of the War   11

the mist, which was answered by them and then by the leading division of the main fleet. The armoured cruisers now flung themselves in a reckless onset at extreme speed against the enemy line in order to cover an attack by torpedo-boats, and approached the line under heavy fire to within 6,000 metres. Several German torpedo flotillas then dashed forward to the attack, fired their torpedoes, and returned, losing only one boat, despite the heaviest counter-fire. A bitter artillery fight was again interrupted by smoke from the guns and funnels, and several torpedo flotillas, which were ordered to attack somewhat later, found, after penetrating into the smoke-cloud, that the enemy fleet was no longer before them. Nor when the Fleet Commander again brought the German squadrons upon a southerly and south-westerly course could the enemy be found.

Detached Fighting.

Only once more, shortly before 10.30 p.m., did the battle flare up for a short while in the twilight, when the German battle-cruisers sighted to the northward four enemy capital ships, and opened fire immediately. As the two German battleship squadrons attacked the enemy turned and vanished in the darkness. The older German light cruisers of the fourth reconnaissance group were also engaged with the older enemy armoured cruisers in a short fight. This ended the day of battle. The divisions, which after losing sight of the enemy took a night course in a southerly direction, were attacked until dawn by enemy light forces in rapid succession. The attacks were favoured by the general strategic situation, and particularly by the dark night. The cruiser " Frauenlob " was severely damaged during the engagement between the fourth reconnaissance group and a superior cruiser force, and was lost from sight. Then one armoured cruiser of the " Cressy " class suddenly appeared close to the German battleships, and was shot into, and sank in four minutes. Five destroyers were sunk by ours, some in a few seconds. One destroyer was cut in two by the ram of a German battleship. Seven destroyers were hit and severely damaged, these including the " Tipperary " and the " Turbulent," which, after the saving of the survivors, were left behind in a sinking condition and drifted past our lines. The wakes of countless torpedoes were sighted by German ships, but only the " Pommern " fell an immediate victim. The torpedo-cruiser " Rostock " was hit, but remained afloat. The " Elbing " was damaged by a German battleship in an unavoidable accident. After vain endeavours to keep the ship afloat, the " Elbing " was blown up, but only after the crew had embarked on torpedo-boats. A German torpedo-boat struck a mine laid by the enemy.

A supplement to The *London Gazette* issued on Saturday, July 8th, contained the Order in Council withdrawing all orders made under the Declaration of London issued since the commencement of the war.

His Majesty declares by the advice of his Privy Council that it is, and always has been, his intention, as it is and has been that of his Allies, to exercise their belligerent rights at sea in strict accordance with the law of nations. On account of the changed conditions of commerce and the diversity of practice, doubts might arise in certain matters as to the rules which the Allies might regard as being in conformity with the law of nations, and it is expedient to deal with such matters specifically. It is ordered that the following provisions shall be observed :—

(*a*) The hostile destination required for the condemnation of contraband articles shall be presumed to exist until the contrary is shown, if the goods are consigned to or for an enemy authority or an agent of the enemy State, or to or for a person in territory belonging to or occupied by the enemy, or to or for a person who during the present hostilities has forwarded contraband goods to an enemy authority or an agent of the enemy State, or to or for a person in territory belonging to or occupied by the enemy, or if the goods are consigned "to order," or the ship's papers do not show who is the real consignee of the goods.

(*b*) The principle of continuous voyage or ultimate destination shall be applicable both in cases of contraband and of blockade.

(*c*) A neutral vessel carrying contraband with papers indicating a neutral destination, which, notwithstanding the destination shown on the papers, proceeds to an enemy port, shall be liable to capture and condemnation if she is encountered before the end of her next voyage.

(*d*) A vessel carrying contraband shall be liable to capture and condemnation if the contraband, reckoned either by value, weight, volume or freight forms more than half the cargo.

It is further ordered : Nothing herein shall be deemed to affect the Order in Council of March 11th, 1915, for restricting further the commerce of the enemy, or any of His Majesty's Proclamations declaring articles to be contraband of war during the present hostilities. Nothing herein shall affect the validity of anything done under the Orders in Council hereby withdrawn. Any cause or proceeding commenced in any Prize Court before the making of this Order may, if the Court thinks just, be heard and decided under the provisions of the Orders hereby withdrawn, so far as they were in force at the date when such cause or proceeding was commenced, or would have been applicable in such cause or proceeding if this Order had not been made. This Order may be cited as " The Maritime Rights Order in Council, 1916."

On July 9th a U.S.A. report stated :

A German submarine named the "Deutschland" arrived here this morning. She left some German port on June 23rd, Captain König commanding, and carries a crew of 29 men, a cargo of 1,000 tons, a quantity of mails, and a message to President Wilson from the Kaiser. The vessel is more than 300 feet long, with a beam of 30 ft. She draws 17 ft. when travelling on the surface, and has twin

Captain Evans, C.B., D.S.O.
H.M.S. "Broke."

screws, driven by two engines of 2,600 h.p., with a speed of 14 knots.

On July 10th, Sir Samuel Evans awarded Commander Horton, the officers and crew of the E 9 prize bounty at the rate of £5 per head of the crew on board the German vessels—in the case of the cruiser "Hela" £1,050, and in the case of the destroyer £350.

On July 10th a Turkish official report stated :—

Black Sea.—The "Yavas Selim" and the "Midilli" attacked a couple of hostile transports off the coast of the Caucasus, sank four steamers and several sailing ships, and bombarded new harbour works south-east of Novo Rossisk, causing a conflagration in a large petroleum depôt and setting fire to war material.

Mediterranean.—An enemy monitor from a distance fired some shells, without success, at the island of Makronisi, and then retired. A hostile torpedo-boat which approached Fotcha was driven off by our artillery fire. Last Friday a British aeroplane parent ship and a French torpedo-boat arrived off Beirut. An aeroplane ascended from the ship and dropped bombs in the vicinity of the port, wounding three civilians.

On Wednesday, July 12th, the Field-Marshal Commanding-in-Chief, Home forces, reported :—

At 10.30 last night a German submarine appeared off the small undefended port of Seaham Harbour. She approached within a few yards of the town, and then opened fire. Some thirty rounds of shrapnel were fired from a 3-inch gun. Twenty rounds fell in the direction of Dalton-le-Dale, and a dozen rounds fell in and about Seaham Colliery. A woman who was walking through the colliery yard was seriously injured, and died this morning. One house was struck by a shell. No other casualties or damage occurred.

Seaham Harbour, which has a population of about 12,000, is in Durham, seven miles south of Sunderland and ten miles north of the Hartlepools. Coal export is the main industry.

On Wednesday, July 12th, the Admiralty announced :—

Information has been received from the British Admiral in the Adriatic that on July 9th the Austrian cruiser "Novara" came upon a group of H.M. drifters on patrol duty. The "Astrum Spei" and the "Clavis" were sunk, and the "Frigate Bird" and "Ben Bui" were damaged, but were able to return to their port. The crew of the "Astrum Spei" were taken prisoners, and among the remainder of the boats there were ten killed and eight wounded.

This incident is grossly exaggerated in the following German wireless message :—Our cruiser "Novara" met in the Otranto Straits a group of four (or, according to statements made unanimously by prisoners who were taken, five) armed English patrol ships, and destroyed them all with cannon fire. All the steamers sank in flames, and three of them after an explosion of the boilers. The "Novara" was only able to save nine men of their crews.

On July 12th the German Admiralty reported :—

On July 11th one of our submarines in the North Sea sank a British auxiliary cruiser of about 7,000 tons. On the same day, off the English East Coast, three armed English patrol boats were sunk by submarine attacks. The crews of these patrol boats were taken prisoners. One gun was captured.

This was followed by an Admiralty announcement to the following effect :—

With reference to the Berlin communique issued by the Naval General Staff, announced in the Wireless of the 15th inst, reporting the sinking of an English auxiliary cruiser in the North Sea on July 11th and " three armed English guardships," there is no truth in the report of the sinking of an auxiliary cruiser, and the " guardships " were armed trawlers.

A German official report, dated July 15th, said :—

On July 11th one of our submarines shelled ironworks at Seaham, on the English East Coast.

During the period July 10th-14th our submarines on the East Coast sank seven British steam trawlers and two fishing boats. It should be added that British fishermen are keeping watch and doing intelligence work for the British Navy, whether chartered by the Admiralty or not.

The following official report was also issued in Berlin on the same day :—

On the night of July 22nd, German torpedo-boats from Flanders undertook a raid, which brought them close to the mouth of the Thames, without sighting hostile naval forces there.

On the return journey on the morning of July 23rd, our torpedo-boats encountered several small British cruisers of the "Aurora" class, with destroyers. A short artillery engagement followed, in which we obtained some lucky hits. Our torpedo-boats have returned to their bases undamaged.

On Monday, July 24th, a Turkish official report stated :

On Saturday the cruiser " Midilli " (formerly the " Breslau ") encountered strong enemy naval forces south of Sebastopol. As the latter tried to intercept the "Midilli," the cruiser was compelled to accept battle with a new Russian warship of the " Imperatritza Maria " type and four new destroyers. The engagement lasted four hours, but in spite of all their attacks and the fact that the enemy continually summoned reinforcements, the "Midilli" broke through the hostile envelopment and return undamaged.

On Monday, July 24th, the Admiralty announced:—

About midnight on July 22nd, near the North Hinder light vessel, some of our light forces sighted three enemy destroyers, which retired before damage could be inflicted on them.

Subsequently, off the Schouwen Bank, six of the enemy destroyers were engaged, and a running fight ensued, during which the enemy were repeatedly hit, but escaped on reaching the Belgian coast. One of our vessels was hit once, and one officer and one man were slightly wounded. There were no other damage or casualties.

In the Prize Court, on Monday, July 24th, Sir Samuel Evans was asked to award prize bounty to Lieutenant Norman Holbrook, V.C., commander of the British submarine B 11, and her ship's company, for sinking the Turkish battleship "Mesudieh" off Chanak, in the Dardanelles, on December 13th, 1914, after the submarine had dived under five lines of enemy mines. The "Mesudieh" normally carried a complement of 600, but it was contended she had many more on board at the time. She was torpedoed because of German ratings and troops.

His Lordship: I don't think this is a case where I ought to encourage any splitting of straws. I declare the officers and crew of submarine B 11 are entitled to prize bounty as being the only vessel present that brought about the destruction of the Turkish battleship "Mesudieh," and I think I am justified in adding a percentage to the complement ordinarily carried by that battleship. I declare the number on board to be 700. Nobody can say I am wrong, and I hope I am right. The prize bounty awarded will be £3,500.

An official announcement, issued in Berlin on July 26th, stated:

On July 20th, off the British naval base at Scapa Flow, Orkneys, one of our submarines attacked a large British line-of-battle ship, and obtained two hits.

The British Admiralty denied this, and stated that the actual facts are that a small auxiliary off the North of Scotland was attacked by an enemy submarine on the date mentioned. She was not hit.

In the Prize Court on Friday, July 28th, Commander Nasmith, V.C., of E 11 and his crew were awarded £4,330 for exploits in the Sea of Marmora.

Lieut.-Commander Kenneth James Duff-Dunbar's affidavit told how E 16 got home with a torpedo which sank a large armed fleet auxiliary in the Bight of Heligoland in spite of her large escorting flotilla of enemy ships.

Sir Samuel Evans said he would declare that prize bounty to the extent of £625 should be paid, and he would declare the people entitled to the distribution on Monday, when an affidavit could be produced showing that nobody else was present at the sinking.

Commander C. S. Baring, of E 5, in an affidavit, said he fell in with a large German armed auxiliary cruiser of about 4,000 tons, about the size of the "Moewe," and sank her on Christmas-day, 1915, off Borkhum. Prize bounty of £1,000 was awarded.

On August 5th the Admiralty announced:

The "Clacton," an auxiliary mine-sweeping vessel, was torpedoed and sunk in the Levant on August 3rd.

August 5th.—An Italian official statement was issued to the effect that:

On Wednesday morning one of our submarines torpedoed an Austrian destroyer in the Upper Adriatic.

On Monday, August 14th, the Secretary of the Admiralty announced:

H.M.S. "Lassoo" (destroyer) was sunk on the 13th inst. off the Dutch coast, after being torpedoed or mined.

An official statement issued in Berlin on the same day said:

One of our submarines yesterday morning torpedoed in the English Channel the British destroyer "Lassoo."

Another submarine torpedoed in the Channel between August 2nd and 10th seven British and three French sailing vessels and three British and two French steamers.

[It is to be noticed that the "Lassoo" was sunk a few miles off the coast of Holland, and not in the English Channel as the German Admiralty pretends.]

Monday, August 21st.—The Secretary of the Admiralty makes the following announcement:

Reports from our look-out squadrons and other units showed that there was considerable activity on the part of the enemy in the North Sea on Saturday. The German High Sea fleet came out, but learning from the scouts that the British forces were in considerable strength, the enemy avoided engaging and returned to port. In searching for the enemy we lost two light cruisers by submarine attack—H.M.S. "Nottingham" (Capt. C. B. Miller, R.N.) and H.M.S. "Falmouth" (Capt. J. D. Edwards, R.N.). All the officers of the former were saved, but there are 38 men of the crew missing. All officers and men of the "Falmouth" were saved, but one leading stoker (Norman Fry) died of injuries.

One enemy submarine has been destroyed; another has been rammed and possibly sunk. There is no truth in the German statement that a British destroyer was sunk and a British battleship damaged.

The enemy claim was as follows:

Our submarines, in the waters of the English East coast on August 19th, sank one hostile small cruiser and one destroyer.

Another small cruiser and one battleship were badly damaged by torpedoes.

On Tuesday, August 22nd, the Secretary of the Admiralty announced :

Submarine E 23 (Lieut.-Commander Robert R. Turner, R.N.), which has returned to-day from the North Sea, reports that on the morning of Saturday last (August 19th) she made a successful torpedo attack upon a German battleship of the "Nassau" class.

The commanding officer reports that while the ship was being escorted by five destroyers back to harbour in a damaged condition he attacked again and struck her with a second torpedo, and he believes that she was sunk.

In the Prize Court on August 22nd, application was made by Admiral Sturdee for prize bounty for the sinking of German warships by six of His Majesty's vessels.

The German ships were the "Scharnhorst," having on board a complement of 872, "Gneisenau" with 835, "Leipzig" with 341, and "Nurnberg" with 384. The total of the enemy crews on which prize bounty was asked for at the rate of £5 per head was 2,432, making a total bounty of £12,160. The "Dresden," it will be remembered, escaped in the battle. The officers of Admiral Sturdee's squadron desired to claim for a common action. Sir Samuel Evans awarded them prize bounty £12,160.

A claim for the sinking of the German raider "Emden" subsequently came before the Prize Court. Capt. John Collings Taswell Glossop, C.B., and the ship's company of H.M. Australian ship "Sydney" claimed nearly £2,000 prize bounty.

His Lordship, delivering judgment, said a point was raised as to the complement of the "Emden." It was given at 397, but 68 men had left, some to destroy a wireless apparatus on British territory, and others to direct a British vessel which the "Emden" had captured. The Act said prize bounty should be reckoned at £5 per head on the number on board. The lower figure would yield £1,645 prize bounty, the larger £1,985. He preferred to award the larger sum. The 397 total was the complement of the ship; and those who were absent were engaged on the same kind of business.

August 25th.—The Secretary of the Admiralty announced :

His Majesty's armoured yacht "Zaida," which was on detached service in the Gulf of Alexandretta, where she had been destroying petrol stores, etc., has been reported as being considerably overdue.

A recent German official report stated that a patrol boat had been sunk in those waters. There is no doubt that this information referred to the "Zaida," as news has now been received through Turkish sources that four officers and 19 men of her crew have been taken prisoners; but there is no information as to the fate of the remainder of the crew—two officers and eight men—and it must be assumed that they are lost.

August 26th.—The Secretary of the Admiralty announced :

H.M. armed boarding steamer "Duke of Albany" (Commander

George N. Ramage, R.N.R.) was torpedoed and sunk in North Sea on 24th instant by enemy submarine.

On Wednesday, August 28th, a German official notice admitted that the battleship "Westfalen" was hit and slightly damaged by a British torpedo on August 19th. The notice asserted that the ship was able to proceed under her own steam, and would shortly be repaired. The second English torpedo, it is said, missed its aim.

On Friday, September 1st, thirty British and French warships arrived off the Piræus.

Official details regarding a fire and subsequent explosion on board the Italian Dreadnought "Leonardo da Vinci," which resulted in the sinking of the vessel on August 2nd, were published for the first time on September 11th, as follows:

> The warship was moored in a position sheltering her from any possibility of hostile attack. Fire broke out near the aft magazine. The prompt action, which was worthy of all praise, of the officer on duty secured the immediate flooding of the magazine and prevented the complete destruction of the ship. As a result, however, of a subsequent explosion the hull sustained damage, and there was an inrush of water. The ship settled on the bottom at a depth of 11½ metres. Effective measures for the rescue of the crew succeeded in saving many of those on board. Out of the 34 officers and 1,156 men composing the crew, 21 officers and 227 men fell victims to their duty.

A Berlin official report, dated September 19th, said:

> Our aeroplanes again attacked with good success off the coast of Flanders an enemy naval force of two monitors, 16 destroyers, and 1 aeroplane mother-ship. A hit was observed on the mother-ship. Again, an aeroplane of an enemy squadron which came into action against our machines was obliged to land on Dutch territory.

With reference to the above, the Secretary to the Admiralty stated that none of H.M. ships was hit or damaged in any way.

A report issued by the German Admiralty Staff on October 11th said:

> In the Mediterranean one of our submarines, on October 2nd, sank the small French cruiser "Rigel," built as a submarine-destroyer, sending her to the bottom with two torpedo shots.

On October 4th the French auxiliary cruiser "Gallia" was sunk by one torpedo. Of the Serbian and French troops on board the "Gallia," which was on the way to Salonika, about a thousand perished. The ship sank within fifteen minutes.

On Saturday, October 21st, the Secretary of the Admiralty announced:

> One of our submarines, which has just returned from duty in the North Sea, has reported that she attacked and hit with a torpedo a

German light cruiser of the "Kolberg" class early on the morning of Thursday last. When last seen the cruiser was steaming slowly, in evident difficulties, towards her home waters.

A Berlin official statement, issued October 23rd, referring to the British Admiralty statement regarding the torpedoing by a British submarine, on the 19th Oct., of a German cruiser of the "Kolberg" class, says that this was the small cruiser "Munchen," which was slightly damaged, but returned to harbour.

Monday, October 23rd.—The Secretary of the Admiralty announced that there was no truth in the statement contained in a Berlin official telegram, dated October 21st, that a British destroyer operating off the coast of Flanders was hit by a bomb dropped from a German seaplane squadron.

On October 27th, the Secretary of the Admiralty made the following announcement:

One of our mine-sweeping vessels, H.M. ship "Genista" (Lieutenant-Commander John White, R.N.) was torpedoed by an enemy submarine on 23rd instant and sunk; all her officers and seventy-three men were lost, and twelve men were saved. When last seen the ship was sinking, but was still engaged with the enemy submarine.

Friday, October 28th.—The Secretary of the Admiralty issued the following announcement for publication:

During last night the enemy attempted a raid with ten destroyers on our cross-Channel transport service. The attempt failed. One empty transport, the "Queen," was sunk. The whole of her crew were saved. Two of the enemy destroyers were sunk and the rest driven off.

H.M. torpedo-boat destroyer "Flirt" (Lieut. Richard P. Kellett, R.N.) is missing, and it is feared she may be lost, but nine of the crew have been saved. H.M. torpedo-boat destroyer "Nubian" (Commander Montague Bernard, R.N.) was disabled by a torpedo and taken in tow, but owing to the bad weather the tow parted, and she has grounded.

An official statement issued in Berlin the same day said:

On Thursday night portions of our torpedo-boat forces moved from German Bay (Deutsche Bucht) through the Straits of Dover and Calais to a line from Folkestone to Boulogne, into the English Channel. According to the report of Commander Michelsen, at least eleven patrol steamers and two or three destroyers or torpedo-boats were sunk quite near hostile ports. Some members of the crews were saved and captured. Several other guard vessels and at least two destroyers were heavily damaged by torpedoes and artillery fire. Further, the British Mail steamer "Queen" was sunk south of Folkestone. The crew had time to leave the ship. In the Channel, near

Lieut.-Com. R. R. Turner, H. M. Submarine E23, which torpedoed the German Battleship "Westfalen."

Photo : Russell.

the Varne Lightship, there was remarkable activity on the part of hospital ships. Our torpedo-boats returned safely to German waters without having suffered any loss.

On November 6th, the Secretary of the Admiralty announced:

One of our submarines operating in the North Sea reports that she fired torpedoes at a German battleship of the "Dreadnought" type near the Danish coast yesterday. The vessel was hit, but the extent of the damage is not known.

On the same day the Secretary of the Admiralty announced:

The German Press are trying to make capital out of what they describe as a second "Baralong" case. One object may be conjectured to be the incitement of American opinion against Britain; another, the provision of arguments in favour of an "unrestrained" submarine campaign. The facts are perfectly simple. On the morning of September 24th, 1915, in the Western Channel, the U 41 was engaged in sinking a merchant steamer. Whilst she was so engaged a converted merchant vessel, commissioned as one of H.M. auxiliary ships, approached the submarine and the sinking vessel.

Its character was not at once recognized, and in order that the submarine might not submerge before it was within range she hoisted neutral colours, a perfectly legitimate *ruse de guerre*. When within range she hoisted the White Ensign, as all British ships of war are required to do, fired on and sank the submarine. The immediate preoccupation of her commander was to rescue the crew of the British vessel sunk by the submarine, who had been compelled to take to their boats 50 miles from the nearest port.

When this had been done H.M. ship closed with one of the boats of the sunken steamer which had broken adrift, into which two survivors of the submarine's crew had climbed. These were rescued in the same way as the British seamen, but after their victims.

The use of a neutral flag in order to approach within range of an enemy is a recognised practice of naval warfare, and has been repeatedly adopted by the Germans themselves in this war. The "Möwe," for instance, secured most of her victims by this method. It is difficult to believe that anybody except a German would base on these facts an accusation of "brutality" on the ground that it was the English and not the German survivors who were saved first by a matter of a few minutes. The whole allegation affords a very fine example of the typical German mentality. It is the first obligation of the non-German to save German life; no reciprocal obligation rests on the German. Any surprise or *ruse de guerre* by the Germans is legitimate; all become illegitimate when practised against the Germans.

The statement that the Admiralty had ever issued orders that survivors of German submarines need not be rescued is an absolute lie, and was explicitly denied in the Note of H.M. Government on the "Baralong" case, dated February 25th, 1916.

On November 7th the Secretary of the Admiralty announced :

With reference to yesterday's communique, a further report has now been received from the Commanding Officer of the submarine. He now claims to have hit two "Dreadnought" battleships of the "Kaiser" class.

Sir Samuel Evans, in the Prize Court on Monday, November 13th, heard an application for prize bounty for the destruction of the German ship "Meteor" on August 9th, 1915. The Commodore related how the squadron, while cruising in the North Sea, spread for search and came upon the German mine-layer "Meteor," abandoned and in a sinking condition. She was eventually seen to founder. From a neutral vessel the "Arethusa" rescued the crew of the British vessel "Ramsey," and then learned that the "Meteor" had sunk the "Ramsey" and was on her way back to Germany when she was informed by airships of the approach of the British squadron. The British squadron had been kept under observation by enemy airships, but on account of the disposal of H.M. ships it was impossible for the "Meteor" to escape. She was therefore scuttled and blown up by her crew, who went on board a Swedish vessel which was not far away. The squadron took no prisoners, and it was only at a later date that the Commodore received information which convinced him that the crew of the minelayer numbered 131.—His lordship awarded £655 prize bounty.

On Tuesday, November 14th, the Secretary to the Admiralty announced :

The Admiralty on November 6th issued a statement as to the circumstances of the destruction of the German submarine U 41 on September 24th, 1915. This was a plain account of the facts intentionally as brief as possible, as it was not supposed that any reasonable person would pay attention to the obviously absurd embellishments of the story as published in the German Press. The result has, however, been that the German Government have issued a further statement, in which it is alleged that " the Admiralty, by its eloquent silence, indirectly admits that the rest of the German report is true on all points." In order to make it absolutely clear that the embellishments referred to are pure fiction the commanding officer of H.M. ship which sank the U 41 has been called on for a report on the German allegations, and his statement is appended. It is also necessary to advert to the extraordinary statement that the Admiralty have " morally corroborated " the German allegation " that there exists an order of the British Admiralty according to which it is not necessary to rescue survivors of the crews of German submarines.". The first denial of this allegation was contained in the British Note of February 5th, 1916, on the "Baralong," and was to the following effect : " The German Government are in error. . . . . It is not true that the British Admiralty have ever desired to retaliate by refusing mercy to an enemy who has been put out of action . . . nor do they now propose to vary their methods of warfare."

This was apparently not explicit enough for the German Government, and accordingly the British communique of November 6th contains the following : " The statement that the Admiralty had ever issued orders that survivors of German submarines need not be rescued is an absolute lie."

As this seems to be still lacking in lucidity or definiteness for German comprehension the Admiralty affirm that it is directly, explicitly, and completely untrue to allege that there exists, or ever has existed, an Admiralty order that it is not necessary to rescue survivors of the crews of German submarines.

The statement of the commanding officer of H.M. ship which sank U 41 on September 24th, 1915, is as follows :—

" H.M. ship under my command was now headed towards the boat in which were the two survivors. On approaching this boat, finding that the ship had too much way on, I reversed engines, at the same time putting the helm hard a-port. The boat was not struck by the ship, and came past along the port side. The prisoners, however, when the boat in which they were was some 20 yards from my bows, both dived overboard. The boat was in no way damaged ; in fact, I towed her astern some 120 miles to port, where she arrived safely, although on account of the weather another of the ship's lifeboats, which was also towing astern, was lost. The two prisoners again climbed into the boat, which by this time was about 30 yards from my port quarter, and I endeavoured to come astern in order to pick them up out of the boat. On account of the direction of sea and wind, and also the fact that my ship was single-screwed, I could not prevent the stern flying up into the wind, and had in consequence to back right away and come ahead again to pick them up, which was successfully done about ten minutes later. No surgeon was borne, and the wounded prisoner was treated with as great care as possible, and his wounds were washed and bandaged to the best of the ability and appliances available. The prisoners were not confined in any close space, but were kept in the poop, where comfortable beds, with mattresses, pillows, and blankets were laid down for them in two large open-fronted lockers. The dimensions of these would be, roughly, 12 feet long by 5 feet broad and 5 feet high, closed in at the ends, top and one side, with the other side open. The weather was fine and mild. The open side had a canvas cover, which could be brought down if required. The prisoners, however, as far as I could make out from them, were perfectly comfortable and satisfied with their accommodation. They were both in a state in which their chief requirement was to be left alone in bed and not disturbed, for which

Petty Officer Whales, Quartermaster, H.M.S. "Castor."
Photo : Cribb.

purpose the places described were eminently suitable and 'airy' without being in any way cold or unprotected.

"Medical aid was given to the wounded prisoner on arrival in port (about 1 a.m. on the following day, September 25th) by a doctor, who came on board with the senior naval officer immediately we anchored. The prisoners were kept on board for two days until the completion of arrangements for their disposal. During this period the unwounded prisoner was kept in an empty storeroom under the poop 15ft. by 20ft. by 10ft, which had a scuttle, bedding and a seat. The man apparently had no complaint with this accommodation. The officer, being confined to bed, still remained, as described, in the poop. The fleet surgeon in charge of him medically considered it quite suitable and comfortable. The prisoners were supplied with dry clothing immediately they got on board, and were given from the ship's stores flannels, socks, drawers and boots. The boots supplied, which were the largest size procurable—the largest size in the service— in the case of the seaman (?) were too small, and hurt him. I believe he preferred most of the time to go without them. There could be no cause for complaint on the above head, the paymaster having my full permission to supply all they asked for, which he did. The petty officer was evidently pleased with his treatment, as he always smiled when spoken to, and said in broken English, 'No more fighting.' The officer was surly, but this was probably due to the seriousness of his wounds. Both the prisoners when originally rescued were in a highly nervous and excited state, and were not in a position to judge what was being done for them. Two days after being rescued the officer told me, before one of my ship's officers, that he had no recollection how he got out of the submarine or what he did subsequently."

A Russian official report dated November 17th said :

Baltic Sea.—On the night of November 10th a flotilla of enemy destroyers of modern type, with a speed of 36 knots, penetrated the Gulf of Finland, and thick fog prevented their approach being discovered. Consequently, for some minutes the enemy had time to fire on Port Baltic nearly a hundred shells, mostly shrapnel. Seven people were killed, of whom five were children, and two soldiers. A woman and four soldiers were wounded. Some buildings were damaged, and twelve horses were killed. As they beat a hasty retreat we sank the majority of the destroyers. Pursuit of the remainder of the flotilla was hindered by the timely discovery of enemy mines, and was stopped. We had no losses.

A Berlin official telegram of the same date stated :

On Friday a German torpedo flotilla on a reconnoitring expedition advanced into the Gulf of Finland as far as Port Baltic, and effectively shelled the harbour buildings of this Russian naval base at short range.

Tuesday, November 20th.—The Secretary of the Admiralty, on the authority of the French Ministry of Marine, announced:

No French war vessel, destroyer or otherwise, was sunk on the 14th instant in the English Channel, as is claimed in the official German report received from Amsterdam on the 21st instant.

The German official report was as follows:—"On the 14th instant, in the English Channel, sank a French guard vessel, apparently a destroyer of the "Arc" or "Contelas" class, besides six enemy merchantmen."

Wednesday, November 22nd.—The Secretary of the Admiralty made the following announcement:

The British hospital-ship "Britannic" was sunk by mine or torpedo yesterday morning (November 21st) in the Zea Channel of the Ægean Sea. There are about 1,100 survivors, 28 of whom are injured, and it is estimated that about 50 persons are lost.

The "Britannic," reputed to have a tonnage of more than 48,000, was, so far as is known, the world's largest steamship. Built at Belfast for the White Star Line, she was completed some months ago, and taken over by the Government as a hospital ship. The "Britannic" was larger than the "Olympic," which has a tonnage of 45,324.

The same day an official German announcement said:

Portions of our naval forces during the night of November 23rd—24th advanced against the mouth of the Thames and towards the northern outlet of the Downs. With the exception of a patrol vessel, which was sunk by gunfire, no enemy forces whatever were encountered. The fortified place of Ramsgate was subjected to artillery fire. When, after this, nothing was seen of the British fleet, our forces withdrew, and returned safely to their home base.

The Petrograd Naval Staff issued the following on November 23rd:

At 6 a.m. on October 20th a fire broke out in the forward magazine of the "Imperatritsa Maria." An internal explosion followed at once, and the fire spread rapidly, and reached the petrol tanks. The officers and crew strove with the utmost bravery to localize the effect of the explosion and to flood the magazine. The Commander-in-Chief, Vice-Admiral Koischak, went on board and took personal control of the operations. Shortly after 7 a.m., however, the vessel sank. The greater part of the crew have been saved. An officer, two first-class petty officers, and 140 sailors are missing, and 64 of the crew have since succumbed to the effects of burns. The position of the ship, which lies in shallow water, gives cause for hope that she may be refloated and completely repaired in a few months. Her bridge at present is only a yard below water.

The "Imperatritsa Maria" was a battleship of 22,500 tons displacement, operating in the Black Sea. She was only completed last year at Nikolaieff.

Saturday, November 25th.—The Secretary of the Admiralty announced:

During the night of November 23rd-24th six German destroyers attempted to approach the north end of the Downs, and were seen by a patrol vessel. The enemy fired about twelve rounds quickly and steamed off at once. One shell hit a drifter without injuring any of the crew, and only damaging her upper works. No shell fell anywhere near the open town of Ramsgate.

Monday, November 27th.—The Secretary of the Admiralty announced:

A recent incident is of interest as showing what occurs when the commanding officer of a German submarine departs from his ordinary practice of sinking all the ships he meets, and follows in a particular instance the procedure of civilized cruiser warfare.

On November 13th the Norwegian steamship "Older," on a passage from Newport to Gibraltar, was captured by a German submarine, which placed a prize crew on board. For a time, it appears, the submarine remained in company, committing the usual acts of piracy on other ships which were met with. Eventually, however, the "Older" separated from the submarine, apparently with the intention of making for a German port, but was intercepted by one of H.M. ships, recaptured in spite of an attempt to blow her up, and brought to an English port. The prize crew are now prisoners of war in this country.

The following Berlin official communique was issued on Tuesday, November 28th.

The Admiralty staff announces that a portion of our naval forces again executed a raid until close to the British coast, not far from Lowestoft. An enemy watching vessel was sunk, and the crew captured. Some neutral steamers were also stopped and searched, but while transported no contraband was released (?). Our naval forces returned without finding touch with the enemy.

In this connection the Secretary of the Admiralty made the following announcement:

A report has been received that the armed trawler "Narval" was on duty off the East Coast on the night of the 26th, and is missing. This is presumably the vessel referred to.

December 3rd.—The Secretary of the Admiralty made the following announcement:

With reference to the statement in the German war list issued to-day, that the British cruiser "Newcastle" struck a mine on November 15th, and sank at the entrance to the Firth of Forth, and that 27 of her crew are dead and 45 wounded, none of His Majesty's ships were sunk or mined during the week, the 12th November to the 18th, in the North Sea. The whole story, with its circumstantial details, is a fabrication.

The *London Gazette* announced that the King has appointed Mr. Balfour, Admiral Sir John Jellicoe, Admiral Sir Cecil Burney, Rear-Admiral F. C. Tudor-Tudor, Captain Lionel Halsey, The Earl of Lytton, and Sir Francis Hopwood to be Commissioners for executing the office of Lord High Admiral of the United Kingdom. The new members are Admiral Jellicoe, Admiral Burney, and Captain Halsey, who take the places of Admiral Sir Henry Jackson (First Sea Lord), Vice-Admiral Sir Somerset Gough-Calthorpe (Second Sea Lord), and Commodore Cecil Foley Lambert (Fourth Sea Lord).

December 8th.—The Secretary of the Admiralty announced :—

A report has been received that a German armed and disguised vessel of the mercantile type was sighted in the North Atlantic on December 4th. There is no further information as to her proceedings.

Friday, December 10th.—The French Ministry of Marine announced :

The battleship "Suffren," which left on November 24th for Lorient, has not arrived, and is believed to be a total wreck. The crew comprised 18 officers and 700 men.

In the Prize Court on Monday, December 11th, Commander Graham Richard Leicester Edwards, of H.M. torpedo-boat destroyer "Laforey," with the officers and ships' companies of three other torpedo-boat destroyers, claimed prize bounty for the sinking of two German torpedo-boats in the North Sea on May 1st, 1915.

Commander Edwards, of the "Laforey," who was senior officer of a division of torpedo-boat destroyers, consisting of these four vessels, had made an affidavit, in which he stated that while cruising in the North Sea he received information from British trawlers on patrol duty that they had been attacked by German torpedo-boats, which had steamed by and gone out of sight. The Commander gave orders for chase, and spread his division on an arc of search. The enemy vessels were overtaken, and the division closing in, brought them to action off the Noord Hinder light vessel. Both German craft were sunk by the destroyers' gunfire. From survivors and other sources it had been ascertained that there were at least 32 persons on each of the enemy vessels. Sir Samuel Evans made an award of £320, to be divided between the four vessels.

In the Prize Court on Monday, December 18th, the commander, officers and crew of H.M.S. "Canopus" applied for an order that they were entitled to share in a prize bounty awarded in respect of the battle of Falkland Islands and declared due under decree made last August.

Counsel for the "Canopus" said that vessel was sent from the Falkland Islands to the Mediterranean, and Rear-Admiral Grant and his officers knew nothing of the bounty proceedings until they saw the report in the newspapers. They then got the consent of the Admiralty to lay their claim before the Court. Counsel read a letter from Admiral Sturdee in which he said : "Our second anniversary is approaching. All congratulations." Judgment was reserved.

Sir Samuel Evans, the President, gave judgment in the Prize Court on Thursday, December 21st, with reference to the application of Rear-Admiral H. S. Grant and officers and crew of H.M. ship "Canopus" for a declaration that they were entitled to share in the prize bounty which his lordship awarded on August 22nd last to the officers and crews of the British squadron in respect of the destruction of German warships in the Falkland Islands battle. The total bounty amounted to £12,160, being £5 per head of persons on board the enemy vessels.

The President said the "Canopus" did not and could not join in the chase. Her speed was much less than that of the slowest of the British squadron. The naval action was at its height over a hundred miles away, and the first German armoured cruiser was being destroyed while the "Canopus" remained at her post of duty at Port Stanley. Therefore they were not entitled to share in the bounty allowed. The application was accordingly dismissed.

The following details show the more important of the cases in respect of which bounty awards have been made during 1916 :

	£
Four German warships sunk in Falkland Islands battle by British warships	12,160
Three Turkish war vessels in Sea of Marmora and Dardanelles by E 11	4,330
Turkish battleship in Dardanelles by B 11	3,500
German cruiser "Prinz Adalbert," sunk in Baltic by E 8	3,000
German auxiliary cruiser "Kaiser Wilhelm der Grosse," sunk by H.M.S. "Highflyer," in the Atlantic	2,580
German armed cruiser "Cap Trafalgar," sunk off East Coast of America by British auxiliary ship "Carmania"	2,115
German cruiser "Emden" sunk by H.M.A.S. cruiser "Sydney" on North Keeling Island	1,985
German armed vessel "Greif" sunk by H.M. ships "Alcantara" and "Andes" in North Sea	1,605
German cruiser "Undine" sunk in Baltic by E 19	1,410
Four German torpedo-boats sunk by British torpedo-boats "Lance" "Legion" "Loyal" and "Lennox" and cruiser "Undaunted" in North Sea	1,400
German cruiser "Hela" sunk in North Sea by E 9	1,050
German fleet auxiliary ship, in North Sea by E 5	1,000
H.M.S. "Yarmouth" for rescue of Greek steamer "Pontoporos" from German cruiser "Emden" (salvage award)	7,335

December 20th.—The German Admiralty Staff issued the following :

One of our submarines torpedoed and sank on November 20th an enemy ship of the line, about 50 miles north-west of Lisbon. This vessel was the French battleship "Suffren," which was reported by the French Admiralty on December 8th as having been lost with the entire crew.

On December 21st the Berlin *Lokal Anzeiger* reported that :

The German submarine officer, Lieut. Cromton, has been sent to Germany as a prisoner to be exchanged. Lieut. Cromton and

Captain E. Unwin, V.C.
Who won the Cross for most distinguished service at the Gallipoli landing.
Photo: Cribb.

Seaman Godan were the sole survivors of U 41, which was sunk by the treacherous attack made upon her by a British merchantman whilst flying the American flag. After vain effort to get rid of the two witnesses by ill-treating them, the British authorities detained Cromton in spite of the fact that the first and second Swiss Medical Commission recommended him for exchange. Only after publication of the facts regarding the treatment meted out to them was the fate of the prisoners ameliorated.

To which the Secretary of the Admiralty replied that, in spite of complete denial and disproof of the German allegations regarding the sinking of the U 41 by a British armed auxiliary, and the subsequent rescue of survivors, the message quoted above contains a reiteration of unfounded charges in connection with the alleged ill-treatment of Cromton.

The injury which this officer sustained while engaged in the piratical occupation of sinking, contrary to international law, unarmed merchantmen, was the loss of one eye, and he suffered no other permanent disability. At the time of his examination by the first Swiss medical commission such disability did not constitute a ground for transfer to Switzerland. A revised schedule was, however, subsequently agreed upon between the belligerent Powers, whereupon Cromton, as soon as the next visiting commission had certified his disability, was immediately sent to Switzerland.

Monday, December 25th.—The Secretary of the Admiralty made the following announcement :

Two of H.M. torpedo-boat destroyers were sunk in collision in the North Sea on December 21st during very bad weather, resulting in the loss of six officers and 49 men, the relatives of whom have all been notified.

The names of the destroyers were not disclosed.

A bulletin issued by the Ministry of Marine at Rome on December 25th, said:

On the night of December 23rd several enemy vessels began an attack on some small guardships in the Straits of Otranto, but were immediately perceived by French destroyers. After a very lively and violent fire on both sides, the enemy, pursued also by Italian and other Allied units which had been sent to assist, succeeded in the darkness of night in escaping. It is not known how much damage the enemy suffered. One French destroyer and one guardship in the Straits sustained insignificant material damage.

The Austrian fleet Command reported the next day as follows :

During the night of December 23rd four of our destroyers, in an advance into the Straits of Otranto, sank two armed guard vessels in an artillery battle. On their return journey their way was barred by

Ostend after a Naval Bombardment

Key to lettering on photograph :—A Shell-hole. B Shell damaging entrance gates to basin ; the gates on the right-hand side can be seen shored up. C Destroyer damaged on her side. D Pier damaged. G Corner of shop demolished. H Skylight of shop blown out by explosion inside. Q Destroyer with side damaged. W Wreckage. Y Top of submarine shelter depressed. Z Damage to a jetty.

six enemy destroyers of a powerful and speedy type. As our destroyers broke through a violent engagement ensued, during which an enemy destroyer was set on fire. At least three others were hit many times at close range, and were put to flight. Amongst these was a destroyer of a yet more powerful and unknown type. Of our destroyers one received two hits in the funnel; the second one was hit in the superstructure; one man was killed. There were no wounded.

The following was issued by the Minister of Marine in Paris on December 30th:

The battleship "Gaulois" was torpedoed in the Mediterranean on December 27th, and sank in half an hour. Thanks to the discipline which prevailed on board to the last minute, the coolness of the crew, and the rapid arrival of patrol boats to the scene of the attack, only four sailors lost their lives.

Wednesday, January 3rd, 1917.—The Ministry of Marine issued the following communique:

A German wireless message to-day states that the French battleship "Verité" was torpedoed by a German submarine in the neighbourhood of Malta, was seriously damaged, and was laid up in port. The statement is absolutely false. The "Verité," which forms part of the squadron detached in Greek waters, is at present at one of our naval bases. No accident of any kind has happened to her. Since the torpedoing of the "Gaulois" which occured on December 27th, at nine o'clock in the morning, no French or Allied warship has been torpedoed in the Mediterranean.

January 3rd.—The Secretary of the Admiralty stated that "efforts are being made in the German wireless press messages to cast doubt upon the strictly defensive character of the armament carried by British merchant ships, and that, in support of this contention, use is being made by the Germans of unofficial and unauthorised comments that appear from time to time in British newspapers. In this connection the policy of His Majesty's Government is quite clear, and is defined in the following authoritative statement, which was made by the First Lord of the Admiralty in the House of Commons on December 21st last":

His Majesty's Government cannot admit any distinction between the rights of unarmed merchant ships and those armed for defensive purposes. It is no doubt the aim of the German Government to confuse defensive and offensive action, with the object of inducing neutrals to treat defensively-armed vessels as if they were men-of-war. Our position is perfectly clear: that a merchant seaman enjoys the immemorial right of defending his vessel against attack or visit or search by the enemy by any means in his power, but that he must not seek out an enemy in order to attack him, that being a function reserved to commissioned men-of-war. So far as I am aware, all neutral Powers, without exception, take the same view, which is clearly indicated in the Prize Regulations of the Germans themselves.

January 4th.—The Secretary of the Admiralty announced:

The outrage perpetrated by a German submarine in torpedoing the Furness-Withy liner "Rappahannock" without taking measures to ensure the safety of the crew, all of whom were presumably drowned, was announced by the Secretary of the Admiralty on Nov. 24th last. The vindictive shelling of the survivors of the steamship "Westminster" by another German submarine on December 14th has already been exposed in the statement published in the press on December 30th. A further case of this callous disregard for the lives of non-combatant seamen has now come to light. The British steamship "North Wales," proceeding in ballast from Hull to Canada, was reported by the German Wireless Press on November 9th as having been torpedoed. Beyond the pieces of varnished wood marked "North Wales" found in Sennen Cove, and bodies washed ashore on the Cornish coast, nothing further has been heard of her, and it is presumed that the crew took to their boats in the gale raging at the time, and were drowned.

January 5th.—A Berlin official report stated that the German submarine U 46, which was reported by the French to have been sunk off St. Nazaire, had safely returned to her home port; also, it is added, another German submarine was not destroyed as reported.

Thursday, January 11th.—The Secretary of the Admiralty announced:

H.M.S. "Cornwallis" (Captain A. P. Davidson, D.S.O.) was sunk by enemy submarine on January 9th in the Mediterranean. The captain and all the officers are saved, but there are 13 men missing. It is feared that they were killed by the explosion.

Friday, January 12th.—The Ministry of Marine, Rome, announced:

On the night of December 11th the battleship "Regina Margherita" struck two mines and sank with almost the whole of her crew. Out of a total complement of 945 men, 270 were saved. The commander and fourteen officers were drowned. The battleship disappeared in a few minutes.

Saturday, January 13th.—The Ministry of Marine, Rome, announced:

The enemy submarine U C 12 which the German Navy had ceded to Austria-Hungary, has fallen into our hands, and has become a unit in our torpedo-boat flotillas. Another enemy submarine, the U 12, belonging to the Austro-Hungarian Navy, is also in our possession.

Monday, January 15th.—An explosion occurred in the magazine of the Japanese battle-cruiser "Tsukuba," anchored in the harbour of

Commander A. L. Snagge.
Mentioned in Sir Archibald Murray's Despatch.

Yokosuka, setting fire to the ship. The first report estimated the casualties at 400.

The story of the Battle of the Dogger Bank on January 24th, 1915, was told in the Prize Court on Monday, January 15th, in affidavits of Admiral Sir David Beatty and Commodore Tyrwhitt. A group of British warships applied for prize bounty for their part in the sinking of the German battleship "Blücher" which at the time had a complement of 1,050, a displacement of 15,000 tons, and carried a mixed armament. Commander Maxwell Anderson, R.N., as counsel, conducted the case for 37 claimants, who asked for prize bounty of £5,250. Admiral Beatty, in his affidavit, stated that the squadron of H.M. ships under his command patrolling the North Sea included the battle-cruisers "Lion," "Princess Royal," "Tiger," "New Zealand," and "Indomitable," and the light cruisers "Southampton," "Nottingham," "Birmingham," and "Lowestoft." The light cruisers and torpedo-boat flotillas were under the command of Commodore Reginald York Tyrwhitt. Sir Samuel Evans, awarding £5,250 prize bounty, said it was clear that the claimants in this case had taken the right line. They were all entitled to participate. The prize bounty would be distributed among the claimants. These included, in addition to the vessels whose names have already been given, the "Arethusa," "Aurora," "Undaunted," "Meteor," "Miranda," "Mentor," "Mastiff," "Attack," "Minos," "Morris," "Legion," "Lark," "Lawford," "Laforey," "Lydiard," "Louis," "Lysandor," "Landrail," "Hornet," "Sand-fly," "Hydra," "Jackal," "Acheron," "Ariel," "Lapwing," "Tigress," "Defender" "Druid," "Ferret," "Forester," "Look-Out," "Goshawk," "Phœnix," "Milne," "Lucifer," "Laurel," "Liberty," and "Laertes."

January 17th.—The Secretary of the Admiralty announced:

For some time past it has been assumed that the following British and French merchant vessels, which have been long overdue, have been sunk by a German raider :—

British—"Dramatist," "Radnorshire," "Minich" (?) "Netherby Hall," "Mount Temple," "King George," "Georgette," "Voltaire."

French—"Nantes," "Asnières."

Definite information has now been received from Pernambuco concerning this assumption. On the afternoon of January 15th the Japanese steamship "Hudson Maru" arrived at Pernambuco, having on board the masters and 237 men of the crews of some of the lost vessels, which were sunk on various dates between December 12th and January 12th. In addition, the steamship "St. Theodore" was captured, and a prize crew put on board, and the steamship "Yarrowdale" was captured and sent away with about 400 men of the crews of the other sunk vessels, who were to be landed. No further news has yet been received of their whereabouts.

The presence of an armed and disguised German raider on the high seas was first reported by the Admiralty on December 8th, the vessel having been sighted in the North Atlantic four days earlier.

Friday, January 19th.—A Berlin official report said :

One of our submarines, commanded by Captain Hartwig, on the 9th instant, 60 sea miles south-east of Malta, torpedoed and sank the British battleship "Cornwallis," which was covered by light craft.

January 23rd.—The Secretary of the Admiralty issued the following announcement :

Last night, whilst our light forces were patrolling in the North Sea, not far from the Dutch coast, they met a division of enemy torpedo-boat destroyers. A short engagement took place, during which one of the enemy torpedo-boat destroyers was sunk. The rest scattered, having suffered considerable punishment. Darkness prevented the full results of the action from being observed. During this night there was also a short and sharp engagement between enemy torpedo-boat destroyers and our own destroyers in the vicinity of the Schouwen Bank. During this engagement one of our torpedo-boat destroyers was struck by a torpedo, the explosion killing three officers and 44 men of the crew. She was subsequently sunk by our own ships. The relatives have been informed. Our ships suffered no other casualties.

January 24th.—An official return issued at Berlin said :

In the course of an enterprise by portions of our destroyer forces, an engagement took place in the early morning off Hossten with the British light naval forces, in the course of which an enemy destroyer was sunk and a second destroyer was observed by one of our aeroplanes to be in a sinking condition. One of our torpedo-boats, which was in distress owing to damage sustained, has, according to reports, run into the Dutch harbour of Ymuiden. All of our boats have returned, with slight losses.

January 25th.—The Secretary of the Admiralty announced :

In view of the repeated allegations in the German official communiques, it is necessary to state again quite clearly that no British vessel engaged in the fight on the morning of January 23rd was rammed by an enemy ship, or in any way damaged, other than the torpedo-boat destroyer reported sunk after being torpedoed.

January 28th.—The Secretary of the Admiralty announced :

H.M. auxiliary cruiser "Laurentic" (Captain R. A. Norton, R.N.) was sunk off the Irish coast by a German submarine or mine late on January 25th. Twelve officers and 109 men have been saved.

The "Laurentic" was the well known White Star liner which was built at Belfast in 1908, and displaced nearly 15,000 tons. She had a length of 550 feet, a breadth of 67 feet, and her hold depth was 41 ft.

A claim by Commander Edward Courtney Boyle, V.C., on behalf

of himself and the officers and ship's company of H.M. submarine E 14, for prize bounty in connection with two Turkish vessels destroyed in the Sea of Marmora in May, 1915, came before the Prize Court on Monday, January 29th. Mr. Roche, for claimants, said one of the two ships' was a Turkish gunboat, name unknown, and the number of persons on board was 75 ; the other was a Turkish transport, and in addition to the crew of 200 there were 6,000 troops on board. Known as the "Gul Gamal," she was a permanent constituent of the Turkish Navy. Commander Boyle, in his affidavit, stated that the gunboat broke in half and sank in about a minute after the torpedo struck her. No survivors were rescued nor prisoners taken, but it was estimated that her crew consisted of not less than 75 persons. In regard to the transport "Gul Gamal," late "Ottawa," late "Germania," having discharged a torpedo at her, he saw her settle down by the stern, but owing to the darkness and the activities of the convoying warship her actual sinking could not be observed. From a report made by Lieut. Slade he believed that the transport sank. From the same report it appeared that she carried 6,000 troops, and it was believed a crew of 200. The President reserved judgment, remarking that the question to be determined was whether the claim came within the terms of the Act, and affected not only these officers and men and their comrades, but the public generally.

The following official notice was issued at Berlin on January 31st :

During last December 152 enemy merchant steamers, with an aggregate tonnage of 329,000, including British vessels totalling 240,000 tons, were sunk as the result of the war measures of the Central Powers. Besides these, 64 neutral merchant vessels, aggregating 86,500 tons, were sunk, owing to their having on board contraband for the belligerents. The grand total of tonnage sunk during December was thus 415,500.

Since the outbreak of war, up to December 31st, 1916, the total tonnage of the enemy merchant vessels sunk as a result of the war measures of the Central Powers was 4,021,500, including British vessels aggregating 3,069,000 tons, being 15 per cent of the total British tonnage before the outbreak of war. Besides the foregoing, 401 neutral vessels, of a total tonnage of 537,000, have been accounted for owing to transport of contraband, or have been condemned as prizes. It is stated on good authority that at the outbreak of war there were in the ports of the Central Powers 99 enemy vessels, aggregating 189,000 tons, including 75 British, of 173,500 tons. They were all seized.

Friday, February 9th.—The Secretary of the Admiralty made the following announcement :

One of his Majesty's torpedo-boat destroyers of an older type, employed on patrol duty in the Channel, struck a mine last night and

Captain A. P. Addison, H.M.S. "Dartmouth."
In the Scrap in the Adriatic.

sank. All the officers were lost. There are five survivors among the crew. All the relatives have been informed.

(The name of the vessel was not disclosed.)

The First Lord of the Admiralty (Sir Edward Carson) stated in the House of Commons on Monday, February 26th, that one of our destroyers on patrol duty in the Channel encountered a force of several enemy destroyers between 11 p.m. and midnight on Sunday night, and that a short engagement ensued. Our destroyer was not damaged, although under heavy fire. The effect of her fire on the enemy could not be ascertained. The enemy vessels were followed, but lost sight of in the darkness.

About the same time another force of enemy destroyers bombarded for about a quarter of an hour the undefended towns of Broadstairs and Margate. The enemy withdrew before the arrival of our vessels, and in the darkness could not be located. The casualties, so far as could be ascertained, were one woman and one child killed and two children injured. He believed that two houses were damaged.

The claim to prize bounty of the submarine E14 for sinking the Turkish transport "Gul Gamal" with 6,000 troops on board and a crew of 200, came before Sir Samuel Evans in the Prize Court on Wednesday, February 21st.

His Lordship, in giving judgment, said he awarded £375 to Commander Boyle and the ship's company of E14 for sinking a Turkish gunboat with 75 men on board. The claim to prize bounty concerned only this gunboat and the troopship "Gul Gamal." As to the latter, the question arose: (1) Was she an enemy armed ship? (2) If she was, should bounty be estimated according to the crew of 200 on board, when the amount would be £1,000? and (3) Should bounty be reckoned according to the total number on board, when it would be £31,000?

On March 4th the Secretary of the Admiralty announced:

One of His Majesty's destroyers was sunk with all hands in the North Sea on March 1st, as the result, it is thought, of striking a mine. All the next-of-kin have been informed.

(The name of vessel was not disclosed.)

On Wednesday, March 7th, the French Ministry of Marine announced:

The destroyer "Cassini," on patrol service in the Mediterranean, was torpedoed by an enemy submarine at 1 a.m. on February 28th. The magazine blew up, and the vessel sank in less than two minutes. The Commander, six officers, and 100 petty officers and men perished. Two officers and 32 petty officers and men were saved.

From the narratives of the survivors it appears that while they were struggling in the water in the darkness, endeavouring to reach the floating rafts, they heard voices shouting in French: "This way, comrades." They discerned the dark mass of a submarine, which

Commander H. C. Woolcombe-Boyce.
Drowned.
Photo: Russell.

opened fire on them from a machine gun or rifles, while one shell was also fired. The latter just grazed a life-raft.

The "Cassini" was built in 1894, and had a displacement of 1,050 tons. She was a mine-layer converted from a torpedo-gunboat. A sister-ship, the "Casabianca," was sunk in June, 1915.

Friday, March 16th.—The Secretary of the Admiralty announced:

One of H.M. torpedo-boat destroyers, of an old type, struck a mine in the Channel yesterday (March 15th) and sank. All the officers were saved, but one man was killed, and 28 are missing and are presumed drowned. All the next-of-kin have been informed.

(The name of the vessel was not disclosed.)

On Monday, March 19th, the Secretary of the Admiralty announced:

Enemy destroyers shelled the undefended watering-place of Ramsgate for a few minutes on the night of the 17th-18th. They retired hurriedly before our local forces, and escaped in the darkness. It was not possible to ascertain the damage inflicted on them.

At almost the same time enemy destroyers engaged one of our destroyers on patrol to the eastward of the Straits of Dover, sinking her with a torpedo. She returned the fire, using torpedoes and guns. The result is not known. There were eight survivors from the crew, but all the officers were drowned.

A second British destroyer was torpedoed, but not seriously damaged.

Whilst picking up the survivors of the first destroyer, a British merchant vessel from the northern part of the Downs was sunk by a torpedo during the night of the 17th-18th. The next-of-kin have been informed.

The German official report is as follows:

One of our naval aeroplanes on Saturday afternoon dropped bombs on the gasworks at Dover. On Saturday night portions of our naval forces again penetrated the Straits of Dover and the mouth of the Thames. The southern attacking group sank a hostile destroyer of the Channel patrol in a fight at close quarters, and a second destroyer was seriously damaged. The northern attacking group torpedoed a merchant vessel of about 1,500 tons near the North Foreland, and sank (?) two outpost vessels by artillery fire. Subsequently this group effectively shelled the fortified port of Margate at close range. Enemy land batteries replied unsuccessfully, and our naval forces returned absolutely free from damage or casualties.

In the Prize Court on Monday, March 19th, Sir Samuel Evans was asked to grant prize bounty to the crew of the submarine E 2, for sinking three Turkish naval vessels in August, 1915. Com. Maxwell Anderson, counsel for the claimants, read an affidavit of Commander D. de Beauvoir Stocks, who stated that on August 14th, 1915, he was in the Sea of Marmora, on Oraburnu Lighthouse, when he saw an enemy naval vessel 250 feet long, which he took to be a Turkish mine-layer. He sank her with his first torpedo, and when she came to the surface only the tops of her masts were visible. He was fired at twice by the enemy ship, which he believed, carried two guns. He saw some of her crew being rescued in dhows, and estimated their number at 80. On August 17th, off Kalolinmo, he observed another enemy ship of about the same size carrying three or four guns, and three days later this craft fired on him at the entrance to Artaki Gulf. The submarine dived, and the vessel ran into Artaki Bay, where he torpedoed her. She sank broken in halves. From the speed and rapidity of her fire and other factors, it was estimated that she carried a crew of 120. Two days later, off Mudania, E 2 sank a rather larger Turkish vessel, estimated to have a crew of fifty on board. His Lordship awarded £1,250 prize bounty for the sinking of these three ships. Prize bounty was also applied for by Commander Geoffrey Basil Spicer Simson, D.S.O., who was in command of the British Naval Expeditionary Force which went out against the Germans on Lake Tanganyika about Christmas, 1915. Commander Simson, in his evidence, said he was in command originally of two motor launches—" Mimi " and " Toutou "—which he had brought from England. Each was armed with a gun. In addition, he had a small motor boat, obtained on the lake, as supply ship, laden with petrol. On Boxing-day he encountered and brought to action off Ngubw, the enemy armed vessel " Kingani," armed with one gun, and manned by a crew of six Europeans and 11 native ratings. In the engagement three of the Europeans and three of the native crew were killed. The " Kingani " surrendered, then went down, and was afterwards salved and repaired by the British force. On February 9th, 1916, when 12 miles east of Mtoa, with the " Fifi," " Mimi," and the small supply boat, he brought to action the German armed vessel " Hedwig von Wissmann." She was armed with three guns, and was manned by 14 Europeans and 12 native ratings. After an hour's fighting, the " Hedwig von Wissmann " was sunk, and 21 of her crew, including the commanding officer, were taken prisoners. Sir Samuel Evans awarded £215 prize bounty.

Wednesday, March 21st.—The Secretary of the Admiralty announced :

Two of H.M. mine-sweeping vessels have struck mines and sunk. In one case there were no casualties, and in the second case there were 14 missing, presumed drowned.

On March 25th the French Ministry of Marine announced that the French battleship " Danton " was torpedoed by a hostile submarine on Monday last in the Mediterranean :

The vessel was struck by two torpedoes and sank in 30 minutes. 806 men were saved by the escorting destroyer " Massue," and patrol vessels arrived on the scene at the distress signal. The number of lost is 296. The submarine, whose periscope was seen some minutes after the torpedoing, was attacked with bombs from the "Massue" but immediately disappeared and was not seen again.

Tuesday, March 27th.—The Secretary of the Admiralty announced:

One of H.M. destroyers has recently struck a mine in the Channel and sunk. Four officers and 17 men were saved. Another of these vessels was sunk to-day, after being in collision with a steamer. One man lost his life in the collision: there were no other casualties. All the next-of-kin have been informed.

(The name of the vessel was not disclosed.)

March 28th.—The Secretary of the War Office issued the following:

The Admiralty transport "Tyndareus," having on board a battalion of the Middlesex Regiment, struck a mine at eight p.m. on February 9th, 1917, off Cape Agulhas. A strong south-easterly gale was blowing, and immediately after the explosion the ship began to settle by the head, with her propellers well out of water. The "Assembly" was at once sounded, and the men put on their lifebelts, and paraded in perfect order. Roll was called, and upon the order "Stand easy" being given the whole battalion began to sing. Two steamers were at once despatched to the rescue, and arrived upon the scene half an hour later. During this trying time, although faced by the probability of imminent death, the troops maintained the same steadfast courage and discipline. It was noteworthy that the incident took place not far from the spot where the "Birkenhead" was lost: and never was a tradition of the British Army more worthily upheld than on this occasion. Thanks to the devotion and perseverance of the captain, ship's officers, and engine-room staff, the ship was saved. The troops were transferred to the two steamers, and taken to Simonstown, where the Tyndareus subsequently returned, under her own steam, with two holds flooded and another leaking. His Majesty the King was graciously pleased to express his deep admiration of the conduct of all ranks in upholding the cherished tradition of the "Birkenhead."

The Tyndareus is a steamer of 11,000 tons gross, built at Greenock in 1915, and owned by the Ocean Steamship Company (Limited) (A. Holt and Co., managers), her port of registry being Liverpool.

Wednesday, March 28th.—The following was issued by the French naval authorities:

During the night March 25th—26th, about 2 a.m., German torpedo boat destroyers opened fire on the town of Dunkirk, firing some 60 projectiles. The bombardment lasted three minutes, and there were two victims. The destroyers immediately retired at full speed.

On March 30th, the Secretary of the Admiralty announced:

During the night of March 28th—29th some firing was observed some miles off the shore from Lowestoft. Our patrols were sent to the scene at the utmost speed, but nothing was seen of the enemy, who had made off.

On April 4th, the Secretary of the Admiralty announced :

One of our mine-sweeping vessels of an old type struck a mine and sank on the 3rd instant. Twenty-four of the crew are missing. All the next-of-kin have been informed.

(The name of the vessel was not disclosed.)

Sunday, April 8th.—The Secretary of the Admiralty announced that the Vice-Admiral, Dover, had reported :

Attacks were carried out on Zeebrugge Mole by seaplanes of the R.N.A.S. on the night of the 7th—8th, and many bombs were dropped. Attacks were also made, in co-operation with the military, on ammunition dumps in Ghent and Bruges. All machines returned safely. Other operations were carried out off Zeebrugge during the same night, as the result of which two enemy destroyers were torpedoed. One of these was seen to sink. The fate of the second is not certain, but she was very severely damaged. We sustained no casualties.

Thursday, April 12th.—The Secretary of the Admiralty announced :

One of H.M. patrol vessels struck a mine and sank in the Channel on April 10th. Two officers and 14 men are missing.

(Name of vessel not given.)

April 21st.—The Secretary of the Admiralty announced :

The Vice-Admiral at Dover reports as follows :—On the night of April 20-21 five German destroyers attempted a raid on Dover. The The raid resulted in their firing a number of rounds into a ploughed field a few miles distant from Dover. The enemy appears then to have steered in the direction of some of our shipping, possibly with the intention of attacking, but was met by two vessels of the Dover patrol. In five minutes these two vessels [H.M.S. "Broke" and "Swift"] engaged and sank at least two, and possibly three, of the five enemy boats, the remainder making off at high speed during the short engagement, and escaping in the darkness.

Our vessels suffered no material damage, and our casualties were exceedingly slight in comparison with the results obtained. Our patrol vessels were handled with remarkable gallantry and dash, and the tactics pursued were a very fine example of destroyer work. We were fortunate in being able to save the lives of 10 German officers and 108 men from the vessels which were sunk.

The official German report was as follows :

During the night of April 20-21 light German naval forces pushed forward into the eastern Channel and against the mouth of the Thames. The fortresses of Dover and Calais were effectively shelled at close range with a total of 650 shots. Calais was unguarded. An outpost vessel encountered before Dover was destroyed. As no further opponent was sighted on the return journey, the German naval forces, under the leadership of Corvette-Captain Gautier, again directed their course towards the Channel exit. They then encountered east of Dover a great number of English destroyers and "leader" ships, whereupon sharp engagements ensued at close quarters.

An enemy "leader" ship was sunk by a torpedo. Several others were heavily damaged by artillery hits. One of the latter was probably sunk in the same manner. Of the German torpedo-boats, G 85 and G 42 did not return from these encounters, and must be regarded as lost. All the other boats have returned without damage or losses. A portion of the German forces which pushed forward south of the mouth of the Thames encountered no enemy war vessels, and was only able to bring in prisoners from a merchant vessel.

Monday, April 23rd.—The Secretary of the Admiralty announced :

One of H.M. airships left on patrol from an East Coast air station on the morning of April 21st, and has not returned. Reports received state that an airship was seen to descend in flames in the Straits of Dover about noon of the same day. An aeroplane, or seaplane was seen in the vicinity shortly before the occurrence, and it is believed that the missing British airship has been destroyed by hostile aircraft. The position given is a considerable distance from the area in which the airship should have been working, and it is probable that her engine power had failed, and that she had drifted a long distance with the wind. Extensive search has been made where she fell, but no trace of the crew nor any portion of the ship has been found, and it must be assumed that all the crew are lost. The relatives have been informed.

Sunday's German official report contained the following :

Naval aviators off Nieuport brought down an enemy airship, which fell into the sea in flames.

In the Prize Court on Monday, April 23rd, Captain Maurice S. Fitzmaurice, C.M.G., and Commander Wellwood G. C. Maxwell claimed £6,000 head money for bringing about the surrender of the port of Tsingtau. They found in the harbour after their bombardment seven German warships sunk, whose complement would be a total of 1,200.

Counsel said there was a problem in this case which was last before the Court a hundred years ago. It was a question as to what constituted a conjoint expedition, and whether the operation of military forces with the naval forces destroyed the claim of the Navy to bounty. The case a hundred years ago was that of "La Bellone," one of the several ships captured at the taking of Mauritius. That case did appear to support the argument that the co-operation of soldiery with the naval

Commander F. H. H. Goodhart, D.S.O.
Of "E 8" submarine fame. Drowned.

forces destroyed the title of the Navy to bounty ; but the times had changed.

Commander Anderson argued that without the work of the Navy these ships, having steam, could have proceeded to sea whenever they liked. This was the great difference made by modern conditions. Judgment was reserved.

Tuesday, April 24th.—The Secretary of the Admiralty announced :

The Vice-Admiral at Dover states that he has received a report from Dunkirk to the effect that on the afternoon of April 23rd reconnaissance machines reported the presence of hostile destroyers, and three British naval machines were despatched to attack them. Five enemy destroyers were seen at 4.10 p.m., steaming between Blankenberge and Zeebrugge in a north-easterly direction, five miles off the coast. The leading machine attacked, dropping 16 bombs, one of which was seen to obtain a direct hit. The remaining four destroyers scattered, and were attacked by the two remaining machines, 32 bombs being dropped. The leading destroyer was observed to take a list to port and remain stationary after all bombs had been dropped. The four destroyers closed on the disabled craft.

A hostile seaplane attacked our machines, but was easily driven off.

At 6.10 p.m. four destroyers were reported by reconnaissance machines entering Zeebrugge Harbour. It is considered most probable that one destroyer was sunk.

April 27th.—The Secretary of the Admiralty announced :

On the night of April 26th-27th several enemy destroyers opened fire in the direction of Ramsgate. The fire was immediately returned, and the enemy were driven off after they had fired a large number of rounds.

In connection with the above, Field-Marshal Lord French reported :

The damage and casualties occasioned by the enemy during his bombardment of the East Kentish coast are as follows :—Killed : One man, one woman. Injured : One man, two women. Damage : Twenty-one dwelling-houses, two stables (one horse killed). The larger number of projectiles fell in the open country.

The Admiralty reported that the following telegram was sent on Friday, April 27th, to the Vice-Admiral, Dover :

His Majesty the King commands that you should convey to the commanders, officers and men of "Swift" and "Broke" his hearty congratulations on the skill, dash, and bravery displayed on the night of April 20th-21st off Dover, which resulted in the sinking of two enemy destroyers.

On Wednesday, May 2nd, the Secretary of the Admiralty announced:

The British steamer "Gena" was sunk yesterday (May 1st) by a torpedo discharged from a German seaplane off Aldeburgh. All

Supplement to The Fleet Annual, 1917

H.M. THE KING'S
VISIT TO THE
GRAND FLEET
1917

Men of H.M. Ships marching past the King.

The King and Admiral Beatty.

Supplement to *The Fleet Annual*, 1917

Petty Officer W. E. Wheele who was decorated by the King with the D.S.M.

Admiral Sturdee receives the King on board his Flagship.

A Brief History of the War 49

hands were saved. Another seaplane concerned in this attack was brought down by gunfire from the steamship "Gena," and the crew were made prisoners.

In connection with the above, the Admiralty states that this method of attack was first practised successfully by R.N.A.S. pilots in August, 1915, when they sank several ships in the Dardanelles by torpedoes from seaplanes.

On Friday, May 4th, the Admiralty announced:

One of H.M. destroyers of an older type struck a mine on the 2nd instant in the Channel and sank. One officer and 61 men are missing, and presumed drowned. All the next-of-kin have been informed.

(The name of ship was not divulged.)

On May 10th, the Secretary of the Admiralty made the following announcement:

A scouting force, consisting of light cruisers and destroyers from Harwich, under Commodore Tyrwhitt, while cruising between the Dutch and English coasts this morning, sighted a force of eleven German destroyers at about four o'clock Greenwich mean time, on a parallel course, and to the southward. Our forces immediately closed, and on our opening fire the enemy at once made off at full speed to the southward, under cover of a dense smoke screen. Chase was continued for one hour and twenty minutes, and the enemy was engaged at long range, but our force was unable to overtake them. Four British destroyers chased the eleven German destroyers to within range of the guns of the batteries of Zeebrugge. Our casualties were one man slightly wounded. Enemy's destroyers were seen to be hit by our fire.

May 12th.—Berlin issued the following official report of the North Sea engagement on the 10th:

During an advance of German light naval forces in the Hoofden on May 10th, enemy forces were sighted at 5.40 a.m. to the east of the North Hinder Lightship, which as they came nearer were recognised as three small modern English cruisers and four destroyers. A firing engagement at once developed in the direction of the Flemish coast, and continued until as far as Thornton Bank. There the enemy cruisers fell back. Our forces reduced speed, so as to allow the enemy to come within closer range.

During the latter part of the engagement an explosion occurred on a destroyer in the enemy line as the result of our artillery fire—apparently a boiler explosion. The damaged destroyer, with a list to starboard, sank shortly afterwards, as was reliably observed.

Our forces then advanced upon the enemy destroyers, which had turned away at full speed to join the now distant cruisers, and finally ceased fire as the enemy disappeared from view to the north. Neither damage nor losses occurred on our side.

May 13th.—The Secretary of the Admiralty made the following announcement:

A very heavy bombardment of an important area at Zeebrugge was successfully carried out on the morning of 12th instant by a portion of the forces under the orders of the Vice-Admiral, Dover. The Royal Naval Air Service rendered valuable co-operation, and over fifteen aerial combats took place, in which four enemy machines were destroyed and five others driven down out of control. Two of our machines failed to return, one of which came down in Dutch territory and has been interned.

News from Berlin sent through the wireless stations of the German Government on May 13th said:

The English cruiser "Cordelia" ran on a mine in the Northern Channel, betwen Ireland and Scotland, and, according to the *Neue Zuricher Nachrichten*, was heavily damaged and towed to Barrow.

In giving the above statement, as a specimen of German official veracity, or of the value of the enemy's Intelligence Department, we are authorised to state that neither His Majesty's ship "Cordelia" nor any ship of her class ran on a mine between Ireland and Scotland, nor has any of His Majesty's ships been heavily damaged and towed to Barrow.

May 14th.—The Secretary of the Admiralty issued the following announcement:

Our naval forces destroyed Zeppelin L 22 in the North Sea this morning.

An unofficial telegram said that news was received early on the morning of the 14th that Zeppelin L 22 was approaching the coast. A squadron of naval aircraft went off in pursuit, and the invader was attacked by a battleplane, by which it was overhauled as it attempted to escape. L 22 was seen to burst into flame. Two of the crew jumped into the sea, but the rest disappeared with the burning mass. The scene of the encounter was fifty miles from the Dutch coast and about 200 miles from the British.

Far-reaching and important changes at the Admiralty were announced by the First Lord in the House of Commons on May 14th, in reply to a question of which private notice had been given. Sir Edward Carson said the King has been pleased to approve the following appointments:

Admiral Sir John R. Jellicoe, G.C.B., O.M., G.C.V.O., the present First Sea Lord, to have the additional title of Chief of the Naval Staff.

Vice-Admiral Sir Henry F. Oliver, K.C.B., M.V.O., the present Chief of the Staff, to become an additional member of the Board of Admiralty, with the title of Deputy Chief of the Naval Staff.

Rear-Admiral Alexander L. Duff, C.B., at present in charge of the Anti-submarine Division of the War Staff, to become an additional member of the Board of Admiralty, with the title of Assistant Chief of the Naval Staff.

Rear-Admiral Lionel Halsey, C.B., C.M.G., the present Fourth Sea Lord, to become Third Sea Lord, in succession to Rear-Admiral Frederick C. T. Tudor, C.B., who will be appointed Commander-in-Chief of the China Station in due course.

Sir Eric Geddes to become an additional member of the Board of Admiralty, with the title of Controller, and with the honorary and temporary rank of Vice-Admiral.

Rear-Admiral Hugh H. D. Tothill, C.B., to become Fourth Sea Lord, in succession to Rear-Admiral Halsey.

On Friday, May 18th, the Admiralty announced :

From reports received from the Rear-Admiral Commanding the British Adriatic Squadron, supplemented by an Italian communique issued to the Press, it appears that early on the morning of the 15th inst. an Austrian force, consisting of light cruisers, which were subsequently reinforced by destroyers, raided the Allied drifter line in the Adriatic, and succeeded in sinking 14 British drifters :—2284 "Admirable," 2114 "Avondale," 2112 "Coral Haven," 2271 "Craignoon," 1399 "Felicitas," 1869 "Girl Gracie," 2714 "Girl Rose," 2274 "Helenora," 2414 "Quarry Knowe," 2711 "Selby," 2186 "Serene," 2155 "Taits," 2434 "Transit," 1916 "Young Linnet." From which (according to an Austrian communiqué) 72 prisoners were taken.

H.M.S. "Dartmouth" (Capt. A. P. Addison, R.N.) with the Italian rear-admiral on board, and H.M.S. "Bristol," immediately chased the enemy off, assisted by French and Italian torpedo-boat destroyers. The chase was continued with the enemy, under heavy and continuous fire, until near Cattaro, when, some enemy battleships coming out in support of their cruisers, our vessels drew off.

Italian airmen, after a battle in the air, attacked the Austrian warships outside Cattaro, and they confidently assert that one of the enemy cruisers was heavily on fire and was being taken in tow off Cattaro in a sinking condition. One other enemy cruiser is reported by the British Admiral as being "badly damaged."

During her passage back H.M.S. "Dartmouth" was struck by a torpedo from an enemy submarine, but returned into port with three men killed and one officer and four men missing (believed dead) and seven wounded. There were no other casualties to our ships.

May 19th.—The French Minister of Marine announced the following :

The French destroyer "Bountefeu" has been sunk after striking a mine. The officers and almost the whole of the crew have been saved.

May 20th.—The Minister of Marine stated that during the night of May 19—20 a patrol of four French torpedo-boats met off Dunkirk a flotilla of German destroyers making for that port. After a short engagement the enemy flotilla withdrew at full speed. Our four torpedo-boats returned to Dunkirk, one of them slightly damaged.

An official telegram from Berlin referring to the above engagement says the French vessels were repeatedly hit by artillery, and the German vessels returned without damage.

May 22nd.—The Secretary of the Admiralty announced:

A flotilla of United States destroyers has recently arrived in this country to co-operate with our naval forces in the prosecution of the war. Rear-Admiral Sims, U.S.N., is in general command of all United States naval forces that are sent to European waters, and he is in daily touch with the Chief of the Naval Staff. The services which the United States vessels are rendering to the Allied cause are of the greatest value, and are deeply appreciated.

To celebrate this historic happening, Sir David Beatty wired as follows to Admiral Mayo, United States Atlantic Fleet:

The Grand Fleet rejoices that the Atlantic Fleet will now share the task of preserving the liberties of the world and maintaining the chivalry of the sea.

Admiral Mayo replied as follows:

The United States Atlantic Fleet appreciates the message from the British Fleet, and welcomes the opportunities for work with the British Fleet for the freedom of the seas.

Tuesday, May 29th.—The Secretary of the Admiralty made the following announcement:

His Majesty's hospital ship "Dover Castle" was torpedoed without warning at 6 p.m. on the 26th instant in the Mediterranean. At 8.30 p.m. she was again torpedoed and subsequently sunk. The whole of the hospital patients and hospital staff were safely transferred to other ships, and the crew were also saved with the exception of six men missing and feared killed by the explosions.

His Majesty's armed mercantile cruiser "Hilary" (Act. Capt. F. W. Dean, R.N.) has been torpedoed and sunk in the North Sea. There were four men killed by the explosion.

One of His Majesty's torpedo-boat destroyers has been in collision and sunk. There were no casualties.

Tuesday, June 5th.—The Secretary of the Admiralty made the following announcement:

The Vice-Admiral at Dover reports that the enemy's naval base and workshops at Ostend were heavily bombarded in the early hours of this morning, and a large number of rounds were fired with good

Engineer-Commander James Hughes.
Promoted for services in Channel fight.
Photo: Russell.

results. The enemy's shore batteries returned our fire, but our bombarding forces suffered no damage.

Commodore Tyrwhitt also reports that early this morning a force of light cruisers and destroyers under his command sighted six German destroyers and engaged them at long range. In a running fight one of the enemy's destroyers, S 20, was sunk by our gunfire and another was severely damaged. Seven survivors from S 20 have been picked up and made prisoners. There were no casualties on our side.

Wednesday, June 6th.—The Secretary of the Admiralty issued the following :

During the night of the 4th—5th June a successful bombing raid was carried out on hostile shipping in the harbour of Bruges. A big explosion was observed and many smaller ones. This was followed by another raid on the same objective at daybreak. In all many tons of bombs were dropped. A hostile kite balloon was shot down by one of our machines. In every case all our machines returned safely.

A photographic reconnaissance over Ostend shows that as a result of yesterday's bombardment from the sea the majority of the workshops in the Dockyard were either seriously damaged or totally destroyed. The entrance gate to the Dockyard basin, the wharf, the submarine shelter, and a destroyer under repair were badly damaged. It appears also that several vessels were sunk.

June 7th.—The Secretary of the Admiralty made the following announcement:

An attack was carried out yesterday by a squadron of naval aeroplanes on the enemy's aerodrome at Nieumunster, about fifteen miles south-south-west of Blankenberghe. A number of bombs were dropped, one big shed being hit, and several bombs fell close to two machines on the aerodrome. On the return journey the bombing machines were attacked by four hostile aircraft, which were driven off. All our machines returned safely.

June 10th.—The Secretary of the Admiralty announced :

The Vice-Admiral, Dover, reports that the latest reconnaissance of Ostend shows that all large shipping has been removed from that harbour. The two destroyers lately reported as being towed to Zeebrugge are probably those damaged during the bombardment, which have been removed from the basin. The harbour presents a deserted appearance.

On Monday, June 11th, the Admiralty issued the following report by the Vice-Admiral at Dover :

About 5 a.m. to-day one of H.M. drifters, "I. F. S." (Lieut. H. B. Bell-Irving, R.N.V.R., in command), whilst on patrol duty, encountered a group of five enemy seaplanes and engaged them.

One machine was destroyed, the pilot being rescued by another enemy machine. This machine was in turn attacked by the drifter, and both pilots were taken prisoners, the machine being so badly damaged that it sank while being towed into harbour. The remaining three enemy seaplanes made good their escape.

June 14th.—The Secretary of the Admiralty issued the following:

The Commander-in-Chief, East Indies, reports that on the morning of the 12th instant H.M. ships under his command captured the fort at Saliff, after a resistance of three hours. The fort is situated on the eastern shore of the Red Sea, in Kamaran anchorage, 180 miles north of Perim, between Loheiya and Hodeida. Ninety-four prisoners were taken, three machine and two mountain guns, military stores, camels, and harbour plant were captured. We had one man killed.

Zeppelin L 43 was destroyed this morning by our naval forces in the North Sea. Soon after being attacked she burst into flames fore and aft, broke in two, and fell into the sea. No survivors were seen.

June 15th.—The Secretary of the Admiralty issued the following statement:

The German wireless news of June 12th contains very grave accusations of inhumanity against the British destroyers which engaged German torpedo craft off the Belgian coast on the morning of June 5th, sinking the German destroyer S 20, and seriously damaging three other destroyers, which were in company with her. The German story is that the rescuing boat picked up only seven of the survivors of S 20, and that twenty or twenty-five other Germans were left in the water. The further statement is made that the sea was perfectly smooth, and that the boat could without danger have embarked at least another twenty men.

The facts are as follows:

The commanding officer of the rescuing torpedo-boat destroyer found on approaching S 20 that those of her crew who remained on deck trained one of the starboard torpedo-tubes on him after his boat had been lowered, and was actually picking up survivors who had jumped overboard. He nevertheless continued his efforts to pick up survivors by means of life-lines, life-belts, etc. The Germans in the water, however, mostly tried to swim away from the torpedo-boat destroyer, evidently having received orders to avoid capture. The commanding officer then recalled his boat and hoisted her in, as three enemy seaplanes were overhead, apparently about to drop bombs (as was done in similar circumstances when the survivors of the "Blücher" were being rescued), and he himself was under fire from the shore batteries, his boats and upper works being repeatedly hit. Seven men had been picked up by the whaler, and she was, in fact, in danger of capsizing when she was recalled and hoisted. Nothing more could possibly be done, and grave risks had already been incurred for the sake of humanity.

H.M. armed merchant cruiser "Avenger" (Captain Arthur L. Ashby, R.N.) was torpedoed in the North Sea during the night of 13th—14th, and subsequently sank. All the ship's company and officers were saved, with the exception of one man killed by the explosion.

June 17th.—The Secretary of the Admiralty made the following announcement :—

There is no truth in the report contained in a German wireless message of the 17th instant, that a German submarine has sunk an English destroyer of the "L" class, of about 1,000 tons, in the Mediterranean, on June 11th.

On the same date the Japanese Naval Attaché communicated the following :

On June 11th one of the Japanese destroyer flotillas attacked enemy submarines in the Mediterranean ; the result is not known. On that occasion "Sákiki" received some damage by enemy torpedo, with loss of 55 lives. She was, however, towed safely into port.

The Secretary of the Admiralty added the subjoined note :

This is one of the destroyers which so gallantly aided in rescuing troops and crew from the torpedoed transport "Transylvania," at imminent risk of being herself torpedoed. Her handling on that occasion by her commanding officer, who placed her and kept her in the most advantageous position for carrying on the rescue work in very bad weather, won the admiration of everybody, and especially of the captain and ship's company of the "Transylvania."

June 18th.—The Secretary of the Admiralty issued the following :

The Japanese Naval Attaché communicates the following :—One of the Japanese flotillas in the Mediterranean on the evening of June 12th encountered an enemy submarine and immediately attacked, with, it is believed, good success, and in all probability sank it.

June 27th.—An official statement issued by the Navy Department, U.S.A., stated that the second-class cruiser "Olympia," which was Admiral Dewey's flagship at the battle of Manila, went ashore on Block Island on Monday evening, and now lies in 4½ fathoms of water on the edge of the Cerberus Shoals. The crew were taken off on Tuesday. One life was lost.

June 29th.—The French Ministry of Marine stated that the French cruiser "Kléber," from Dakar for Brest, struck a mine on the morning of the 27th instant off Cape St. Mathieu and sank. Thirty-eight of the crew, including three officers, are missing.

SUBMARINE WARFARE À OUTRANCE.

The following is the text of the German Note presented to the American Ambassador at Berlin on Thursday, February 1st, 1917 :

"Your Excellency was good enough to communicate to me on January 22nd the Message which the President of the United States on the same day delivered to the American Senate. The Imperial Government has taken cognizance of the contents of the Message with the serious attention due to the President's utterances, which are inspired by a high sense of responsibility. It affords it great satisfaction to declare that the guiding lines of this important declaration agree to a wide extent with the principles and wishes which Germany professes. Hereto belongs, in the first place, the right of all nations to self-government and equal rights.

"In acknowledging this principle Germany would sincerely rejoice if peoples like those of Ireland and India, who do not enjoy the blessings of political independence, now obtained their freedom.

"Sublime Aims."

"Alliances which drive peoples to competition in power and entangle them in the net of selfish intrigues are rejected also by the German people. Its joyful collaboration is assured to all efforts which aim at the prevention of future wars. Freedom of the seas, as the pre-requisite of the free existence of, and peaceful intercourse between, the peoples, and the opening of the door for trade by all nations, have always belonged to the leading principles of German policy. The Imperial Government regrets all the more deeply that the attitude of its enemies, being hostile to peace, renders it impossible for the world to begin with the realization of these sublime aims at once. Germany and her allies were ready to enter forthwith into peace negotiations, and had declared as their basis the security, existence, honour, and freedom of development of their peoples. Their plans, as they expressly emphasized in the Note of December 12th, 1916, were not aimed at the destruction or crushing of their enemies, and were, according to their conviction, quite compatible with the rights of other nations.

No Annexation of Belgium.

"Especially as regards Belgium, which is the object of the warm sympathy of the United States, the Imperial Chancellor a few weeks ago declared that the annexation of Belgium was never intended by Germany. In the peace to be concluded with Belgium, Germany solely wanted to take the precaution that this country, with which the Imperial Government desires to live in good neighbourly relations, should not be used by the enemy for the promotion of hostile designs. Such a precaution is the more urgent because the enemy statesmen, in repeated speeches, especially in the resolutions of the Paris Economic Conference, undisguisedly pronounce their intention not to recognize Germany as possessing equal rights even after the re-establishment of peace, but to continue to fight systematically. The peace efforts of the four allies failed owing to the lust of conquest of their opponents, who desire to dictate peace. On the pretext of the principle of nationalities they disclosed their war aim to disintegrate and dishonour Germany, Austria-Hungary, Turkey, and Bulgaria.

New Decisions.

"They desire to fight to the utmost. Thus a new situation has arisen, which forces Germany also to new decisions.

"For 2½ years Britain misused her naval power in the wicked attempt to force Germany into submission by hunger. Brutally ignoring international law, the group of Powers led by Britain prevented not only the legitimate commerce of their opponents, but by ruthless pressure they force neutral States also to abandon commercial intercourse which is not agreeable to the Entente, or to restrict their commerce according to the Entente's arbitrary regulations. The American people knows the efforts which were undertaken to induce Britain and her Allies to return to international law and to respect the law of freedom of the seas. The British Government persists in the starvation war, which in truth does not hit the fighting forces of its opponent, but compels women, children, the sick, and the old to suffer for the Fatherland's sake grievous privations, which are endangering the people's strength. Thus the British lust of power cold-bloodedly increases the sufferings of the world without regard to any law of humanity, without regard to the protests of severely-prejudiced neutrals ; and to the desire for reconciliation they oppose the will to destruction, even without regard to the silent desire for peace among the peoples of her own Allies.

FIGHT FOR EXISTENCE.

" Every day by which the terrible struggle is prolonged brings new devastations, new distress, new death ; every day by which the war is shortened preserves on both sides the lives of thousands of brave fighters, and is a blessing to tortured mankind. The Imperial Government would not be able to answer before its own conscience, before the German people, and before history if it left any means whatever untried to hasten the end of the war. With the President of the United States it had hoped to attain this aim by negotiations.

" After the attempt to reach an understanding was answered by the enemy with the announcement of intensified war, the Imperial Government, if it desires in the higher sense to serve humanity and not to do wrong against its own countries, must continue the battle for existence, which is forced on it anew, with all its weapons.

" It must, therefore, abandon the limitations which it has hitherto imposed on itself in the employment of its fighting weapons at sea.

" Trusting that the American people and its Government will not close their eyes to the reasons for this resolution and its necessity, the Imperial Government hopes that the United States will appreciate the new state of affairs from a high standpoint of impartiality, and will also on their part help to prevent further misery and sacrifice of human lives which might be avoided.

" While I venture, as regards the details of the projected war measures to send the attached Memorandum, I wish at the same time to express the expectation that the American Government will warn American ships against entering the blockaded zones described in the Memorandum and its subjects against entrusting passengers or goods to vessels trading with harbours in the blockaded zones."

The Memorandum annexed to the German Note to neutral nations is as follows :

From February 1st, 1917, within the barred zones around Great Britain, France, Italy, and in the Eastern Mediterranean, all sea traffic will forthwith

Submarine Warfare

be opposed by all means. Neutral ships plying within the barred zones do so at their own risk. Although precautions are taken that neutral ships which were on February 1st on their way to ports in the barred zones shall be spared for appropriate time, yet it is urgently advised that they be warned and directed to other routes by all means at their disposal. Neutral ships lying in the ports of the barred zones can with the same safety abandon the barred zones if they sail before February 5th, and take the shortest route into the open zone.

Traffic of regular American passenger steamers may go on unmolested if:

(a) Falmouth is taken as the port of destination.

(b) On the first and return journey to the Scillies, as well as a point 50 deg. N. 20 deg. W. are steered. On this route no German mines will be laid.

(c) Steamers bear the following special signs, allowed only to them in American ports: Coat of paint on the ship's hull and on the superstructure three metres broad, vertical stripes, alternating white and red. On every mast a large flag chequered white and red; on the stern the American national flag. During darkness the national flag and coat of paint to be as easily recognizable as possible from far away, and ships must be completely illuminated brightly.

(d) One steamer runs in each direction every week, arriving at Falmouth on Sundays, and leaving Falmouth on Wednesdays.

(e) Guarantees are given by the American Government that these steamers carry no "contraband" according to the German list of contraband.

Maps in which the barred zones are outlined are added in two copies. It is further stated that Germany is prepared, in view of the need for Continental passenger traffic, that every week day a Dutch paddle steamer shall receive free and unobstructive right of passage in each direction between Flushing and Southwold, on condition that said paddle steamers only pass through the barred zones by daylight, and that they steer by the North Hinder lightship on both the outward and homeward voyage. On this route no German mines will be laid. The marks on the ships making these voyages to be the same as those given regarding American passenger steamers.

On Tuesday, February 13th, a Berlin official statement said:

"The period of grace, which until now has not been made public, for neutral steamers which the announcement of the blockade zone could not reach in time, elapsed on the night of the 12th inst. as regards the blockaded zone in the Atlantic and the English Channel. For the North Sea the period of grace expired on the night of the 6th, and for the Mediterranean on the night of the 10th.

"From now, in the blockaded zones generally, the warning which has been issued is in force, according to which shipping can no longer expect individual warning. Vessels which, in spite of this, enter the blockaded zones do so with the full knowledge of the danger threatening them and their crews.

"It is expressly stated that all news spread from the enemy side regarding the torpedoing without warning of neutral ships before the dates mentioned for the various blockaded zones is incorrect.

"The periods of grace mentioned were also in force for enemy passenger vessels, because it was possible that on them were neutral passengers who were perhaps without knowledge of the sea blockade."

BRITISH LOSSES BY ENEMY SUBMARINES.

IN the last issue of THE FLEET ANNUAL we dealt at some length with the future of the submarine. Since that article was written[*] submarine activities have moved apace, so that there is no necessity for dealing at any length with the subject here. The following table shows British shipping losses since the week ending February 25th, 1917—the time when Germany started her unrestricted submarine policy:

Week ending	Arrivals of Ships at U.K. Ports.	Sailings of Ships from U.K. Ports.	BRITISH VESSELS SUNK.			British Vessels unsuccessfully attacked by Submarines.
			Ships of 1,600 tons and over.	Ships of under 1,600 tons.	Fishing Vessels.	
Feb. 25	2,280	2,261	15	6	4	12
Mar. 4	2,528	2,477	14	9	3	12
Mar. 11	1,985	1,959	13	4	3	16
Mar. 18	2,528	2,554	16	8	21	19
Mar. 25	2,314	2,433	18	7	10	13
April 1	2,281	2,399	18	13	6	17
April 8	2,406	2,367	17	2	6	14
April 15	2,379	2,331	19	9	12	15
April 22	2,585	2,621	40	15	9	27
April 29	2,716	2,690	38	13	8	24
May 6	2,374	2,499	24	22	16	34
May 13	2,568	2,552	18	5	3	19
May 20	2,664	2,759	18	9	3	9
May 27	2,719	2,768	18	1	2	17
June 3	2,693	2,642	15	3	5	17
June 10	2,767	2,822	22	10	6	23
June 17	2,897	2,993	27	5	—	31
June 24	2,876	2,923	21	7	—	22
July 1	2,745	2,846	15	5	11	16

[*] Cf. "A Retrospect and Forecast," p. 68 FLEET ANNUAL, 1916.

British Losses by Enemy Submarines

Statement by Sir Edward Carson, First Lord of the Admiralty, in the House of Commons, February 21, 1917 :

SHIPS LOST.

I must now state our losses. Their real significance can be only realized by comparing them with the volume of our shipping. I propose to compare first the total of British, Allied, and neutrals. Taking the first 18 days of December, January, and February, I am going to give you the figures of merchant vessels of over 100 tons net lost through submarines and mines, excluding fishing vessels, which I exclude because they are not brought within the comparison with ships that enter and clear our ports every day.

Steamers of over 1,000 tons each lost in the first 18 days of the following three months :—

BRITISH, ALLIED, AND NEUTRAL.

December.		January.		February.	
No.	Tonnage	No.	Tonnage.	No.	Tonnage.
69	201,934	65	183,533	89	268,671

BRITISH ONLY.

| 24 | 92,573 | 23 | 82,153 | 47 | 169,927 |

STEAMERS UNDER 1,000 TONS: BRITISH, ALLIED, AND NEUTRAL.

| 10 | 6,292 | 7 | 4,379 | 14 | 6,957 |

BRITISH ONLY.

| — | — | 1 | 466 | 8 | 3,468 |

SAILING VESSELS: BRITISH, ALLIED, AND NEUTRAL.

| 39 | 151,509 | 19 | 10,231 | 31 | 28,968 |

BRITISH ONLY.

| 6 | 2,531 | 2 | 2,193 | 7 | 8,334 |

TOTAL VESSELS LOST.

| 118 | 223,122 | 91 | 191,233 | 134 | 304,596 |

GERMAN BOASTS AND THE FACTS.

Let us now see what those losses were in comparison with the volume of trade. Of vessels of over 100 tons arriving at United Kingdom ports, exclusive of fishing craft and of coastwise sailing vessels and estuarial traffic, for the first 18 days of February we had 6,076 ships, and we had clearances for the same 18 days of 5,873 ships. That shows the enormous amount of shipping which goes on, notwithstanding the German blockade.

Statement of Lord Curzon in the House of Lords :

SHIPS OF 100 TONS AND UPWARDS.

BRITISH MERCANTILE MARINE:

	June, 1914.	Dec., 1916.
Ships	10,124	9,757
Tonnage	20,523,706	19,765,516

ALL OTHER COUNTRIES:

Ships	14,320	13,749
Tonnage	24,880,171	24,293,000

In other words, the British mercantile marine comprised 45.3 of the total mercantile tonnage of the world before the war, and 45.2 last December. Even more important, however, were the figures dealing only with the larger vessels :

SHIPS OF 1,600 TONS AND UPWARDS.

BRITISH MERCANTILE MARINE :

	June, 1914.	Mar. 31, 1917.
Ships	3,900	3,500
Tonnage	16,900,000	16,000,000

In ships of this tonnage the British share was about 50 per cent. of the whole. It should also be observed that the latter set of figures comes down to March 31 of this year, and therefore includes the results of two months of unrestricted submarine warfare.

NAVY SEPARATION ALLOWANCES
(*Extracts from Admiralty Orders*).
January, 1917.

MEN.
A.—WIVES AND CHILDREN.

1. For the period of the present war, separation allowance is being paid to the wives and families of Naval ratings, Marines and Reservists borne on the books of H.M. Ships, *provided that in each instance the man voluntarily declares an allotment of at least 5s. a week in favour of his wife.* The allowance is in no circumstances issuable in connection with compulsory allotments obtained under the Naval Discipline (No. 2) Act, 1915.

2. The weekly rates of allowance for wives and children are as follows:

SCALE A.

Ratings.	Wife, per week	Children, per week.
SAILOR. Class I :— Ordinary Seaman Able Seaman Leading Seaman 2nd Class P.O. and equivalent ratings	6s.*	1st child, 4s. 2nd child, 3s. 3rd child, 2s. 4th and subsequent children, 1s. each.
Class II :— Petty Officer P.O. 1st Class and equivalent ratings	7s.*	Ditto.
Class III :— C.P.O. and equivalent ratings	8s.*	Ditto.
Motherless children, 5s. a week each, irrespective of the father's rating.		
MARINE ON SHIP'S BOOKS. Class I :— Private Corporal Sergeant and equivalent ranks	6s.*	1st child, 4s. 2nd child, 3s. 3rd child, 2s. 4th and subsequent children, 1s. each.
Class II :— Colour-Sergt. and equivalent ranks	7s.*	Ditto.
Class III :— Warrant Officer (Class II), Quartermaster-Sergt. and Staff-Sergt.	8s.*	Ditto.
Class IV :— Warrant Officer, Royal Marines (except Royal Marine Gunners)	9s.*	Ditto.

Motherless children, 5s. a week each, irrespective of the father's rank.

* These rates are increased by 3s. 6d. a week in the case of women eligible for London allowance.

In cases where there are children under 14, allowances in addition to those shown in the foregoing scale may be paid for periods not earlier than the 18th January, 1917, the scale of the extra payment being as follows :

SCALE B.

No. of Children under 14.	Class I.	Class II.	Class III.	Class IV.
1	2s.	1s.	—	—
2	3s. 6d.	2s. 6d.	1s. 6d.	6d.
3	5s.	4s.	3s.	2s.
4	6s.	5s.	4s.	3s.
5	7s.	6s.	5s.	4s.
6	8s.	7s.	6s.	5s.
7	9s.	8s.	7s.	6s.
8	10s.	9s.	8s.	7s.

Motherless children, 2s. a week for the first child and 1s. a week for each other child under 14, irrespective of the father's rating or rank.

On a child attaining the age of 14 the extra allowance ceases, but the normal rates continue until the age of 16 is reached.

3. The payment in respect of children is made ordinarily for those under 16 years of age, but may be granted beyond that age on the recommendation of the Local Education Authority in the cases (1) of apprentices receiving not more than nominal wages, and (2) of children being educated at secondary schools, technical schools or universities. It may also be continued to the age of 21 in the case of children unable to support themselves owing to mental or physical infirmity. Allowances under Scale B. (par. 2) are not payable for these children in any circumstances.

4. Allowance is made for children adopted prior to the war, subject to the production—
   (i) of the deed of adoption, or
   (ii) of a statutory declaration to the effect that the child was and is permanently maintained as a member of the man's family.

5. In certain circumstances the Admiralty has power under the Naval Discipline Act to enforce an allotment not in excess of 7s. a week in the case of Petty Officer ratings, or of 3s. 6d. a week in that of lower ratings. Such allotments do not carry separation allowance.

6. Separation allowance is not issuable for—
   (i) inmates of Asylums, Workhouses or kindred institutions, or for
   (ii) wives living apart from their husbands,
except that in the case of a Reservist who, prior to his mobilisation, was contributing for such a person's maintenance a sum larger than his Naval pay now admits of his paying, the question of the issue of some allowance could be considered, provided the man voluntarily allotted as much as his pay would allow. Women under (ii) have no claim to payment for children living in their care any more than for themselves.

Navy Separation Allowances

Procedure.

7. As soon as information is received that a man has declared an allotment of at least 5s. a week in favour of his wife, a form of application to enable her to apply for a Navy separation allowance is issued to her direct from the Admiralty (or in the case of a Marine from the Marine Division to which he is attached). Until she receives this form it is consequently unnecessary for her to take any action in the matter beyond desiring her husband to declare the requisite allotment.

8. Separation allowance for wives is issuable from the Thursday following the date of entry if the qualifying allotment is declared within a month of entry; otherwise from the Thursday on which the qualifying allotment becomes operative, the allowance and the allotment being made payable in one combined sum at whatever Post Office is named by the payee (*see* par. 33). In the case of a wife resident outside the United Kingdom payment is effected by Foreign Money Order or other suitable means.

B.—Motherless Children.

9. The condition as to an allotment of at least 5s. a week will not be insisted upon in the case of motherless children, but men are expected to allot to the guardians of their children. If the children are not all in the care of one guardian, two or more allotments may be declared in favour of the two or more guardians.

Application for an allowance for a motherless child should be made by forwarding a statement giving the child's name, sex, date of birth, and address, and also its guardian's full name. The man should arrange with the child's guardian to produce its birth or baptismal certificate when called upon to do so.

Children by a former wife cannot be regarded as motherless while their stepmother is alive and in receipt of an allowance.

C.—Dependants, other than Wives and Children.

10. Subject to proof of actual dependence prior to the war or prior to the man's entry, if later, separation allowance is also issuable to dependants *provided the man himself makes an allotment to his dependant.* As from 1st February 1915 the term "dependant" has been extended to include any person who is found as a fact to have been dependent on the man before the war (or his entry, if later). The necessary investigations are made by the Local Old Age Pension Authorities of the district in which the dependant resides, and the rate of allowance in each case is assessed after consideration of the reports of those Authorities.

Scale of Allowance.

11. Separation allowance to a dependant naturally cannot exceed the scale for a wife, *i.e.,* the allowance for a wife, including London allowance where it would be applicable (*see* pars. 2 and 16 [*c*]) is a maximum which cannot in any circumstances be exceeded for one dependant. (For cases in

which there are more dependants than one, (*see* footnote*.) *Within* that maximum the allowance to be awarded *is governed strictly by the extent to which dependence existed* prior to the war or prior to the man's entry into His Majesty's Service, if later, and cannot exceed half the amount of such dependence. (As regards subsequent changes which have taken place in a dependant's circumstances, (*see* par. 24.) When the sum paid by the man to his dependant covered the cost of his own keep, a suitable deduction is made on that account in computing the amount of the benefit derived from his payment.

12. Within the maximum of the rate payable to a wife the allowance to the dependant of an active service rating will equal half the amount of the dependence, as defined above, provided he continues to allot a sum equal to the amount of such dependence. If he allots a smaller sum the allowance will be proportionately reduced, but if he is able to allot more, the allowance will remain unaltered. Thus in the case of an active service rating the allowance granted will not exceed half the amount of the dependence or half the amount of the current allotment, *whichever is the less*.

13. In the case of a reservist, if he allots half the amount of the dependence, *i.e.* half the amount which he was in the habit of paying in civil life (less the cost of his keep where that was included), the Admiralty will pay the other half as separation allowance. In this case also if he allots a smaller sum the allowance will be proportionately reduced, but if he is able to allot more, the allowance will remain unaltered. Consequently, in the case of a reservist the allowance granted will not exceed half the amount of the dependence or the amount of the current allotment, *whichever is the less*.

14. Men who have entered "for hostilities" are regarded as reservists, that being to the advantage of their dependants.

15. Although the claim of an unmarried wife to an allowance for herself (and her children, if any) has to be investigated by the Local Old Age Pension Authorities, especially as regards pre-war (or if later pre-entry) dependance, the allowance is awarded upon the scale for a wife and under the Regulations governing allowances for wives and children (*e.g.*, the minimum qualifying allotment of 5s. a week is applicable).

16. Examples of the method of assessment of allowances for dependants:

Active Service Ratings:—

    (a) A stoker, 1st class, allowed his mother 7s. a week before the war. The maximum allowance issuable to her is half the degree of the pre-war dependence, namely, 3s. 6d. a week, and

---

* If there are several persons dependent on *one* seaman, the maximum is increased to the scale for a wife and a number of children corresponding to the number of additional dependants, provided the total amount of dependence and the rate of the current allotment admit of such increase. If, however, there are two seamen and three dependants, for instance, two of the dependants are earmarked to the two men and only the third is regarded for allowance purposes as a child. In the case of one person being dependent on two or more men holding different ratings, the maximum allowance to be awarded, provided the degree of dependence before the war and the rate of the current allotment admit, is that payable for the wife of the man holding the rating carrying the highest allowance. *See* examples (par. 16).

When under this footnote increases become possible for additional dependants within the scale for children, the maximum is that provided by Scale A., not by Scale B., in par. 2.

an allowance of that amount would be awarded if his current allotment were one of 7s. a week; if he decided to raise his allotment the amount of the separation allowance would not be affected, but if he lowered the allotment, say, to 4s., separation allowance of 2s. per week only would be payable. (Wife's scale maximum, 6s.)

(b) A Petty Officer Telegraphist (N.S.) used to contribute 21s. a week to the support of his two sisters. The maximum separation allowance issuable to them is 10s. 6d. a week; and an allowance for that amount would be granted provided the man's current allotment were not less than 21s. a week (wife's scale maximum 11s. being as for a wife (7s.) and one child (4s.)

(c) A Chief Petty Officer used to allow his mother and sister 27s. a week. The maximum separation allowance issuable to them would be half the degree of the pre-war dependence, supposing the scale for a Chief Petty Officer's wife and one child would admit of it; that scale, however, limits the allowance to 12s. a week (8s. + 4s.), except in a case in which if the allowance had been for a wife, London allowance would have been payable. In that event an allowance of 13s. 6d. would be issued, provided the man allotted not less than 27s. a week to his dependants.

It is to be observed from this example that London allowance is not added *in its entirety* to the amount of dependant's separation allowance, but serves *to raise* what would otherwise have been the limiting maximum given by the wife's scale, *i.e.*, in the case of a dependant the London allowance of 3s. 6d. a week is not paid in addition to the ordinary separation allowance, but enables a higher allowance to be awarded in cases in which the degree of the pre-war dependence and the rate of the current allotment would justify such higher allowance.

Reservists :—

(d) A reservist of Chief Petty Officer rating used to allow his widowed sister for herself and her two children 24s. a week before the war. The maximum separation allowance issuable is half the pre-war dependence, namely 12s. a week, and an allowance of that amount would be granted if the reservist's current allotment were not less than 12s. a week. It will be observed that this allowance of 12s. a week happens to correspond with the allowance for a Chief Petty Officer's wife and one child only, but seeing that the contribution made before the war is the measure of the dependence, this is the full allowance that can be paid, even though there is a second child (*see* footnote to par. 11).

(e) A reservist of Petty Officer rating allowed his mother 11s. a week before the war. She would be entitled to a separation allowance of 5s. 6d. a week, namely, half the pre-war dependence, provided that her son allotted her at least 5s. 6d. a week (wife's scale maximum 7s).

Procedure.

17. A man wishing a person who was in fact dependent upon him prior to the war or his entry into His Majesty's Service, if later, to receive a separation allowance should make a declaration on A.G. Form No. 11 in addition to declaring an allotment in favour of his dependant.

18. Provided a new entry declares an allotment *and* completes A.G. Form No. 11 within one month after entry, the allowance will be payable from the Thursday following his entry; otherwise it will only be payable from the Thursday following the date on which he completes the necessary action. *Every facility is therefore to be given for men on entry to declare an allotment and to complete A.G. Form No. 11* (par. 33). These forms are to be in the custody of the Accountant Officer, and in every case in which a new entry declares an allotment in favour of a dependant, other than a wife, he should be asked whether he wishes to apply for separation allowance on behalf of his dependant, and supplied with a copy of the form if he does wish to apply for the allowance.

19. Before the form is issued the man's name, rating and official number are to be inserted upon it and the date of his entry given, but as the declarations on these forms must be regarded as strictly private the Accountant Officer is only required to see that no form is issued without those details. Where therefore a man prefers to fill up the form and to despatch it himself he is to be allowed to do so, but Accountant Officers are relied upon to afford any assistance that is required.

The completed form should be sent to the Admiralty, or, in the case of a Marine, to the Marine Division to which he belongs. It will then be forwarded to the Old Age Pension Authorities for investigation, and on the receipt of their report, the rate of allowance will be determined.

20. If the dependant is dissatisfied with the Pension Authorities' assessment of his or her dependence, it is open to him or to her to lodge an appeal by completing an A.G. Form No. 15, which is obtainable at any Post Office.

D.—REGULATIONS AFFECTING SPECIFIC CASES.

21. Where an allowance is being paid for a wife and children, an allowance to a dependant cannot also be granted in respect of the same seaman or marine. Similarly, if an allowance is payable for a motherless child or children, this precludes the issue of an allowance for a dependant.

22. If both a father and a son are serving, the wife may be granted a dependant allowance in respect of her son in lieu of a child's allowance in respect of her husband, if to her advantage. A wife without a child or children in her care is ineligible for a Navy dependant allowance in respect of her serving son in addition to a wife's allowance in respect of her husband, whether he be in the Navy, Marines or Army.

23. *Allowances for Children all of whom are not living in the care of the Man's Wife.*—When some of the children are in the care of the wife and others in that of some other person, the total allowance payable in respect of them is the same as if they all lived together, the allowance being divided between the wife and the guardian according to the ages of the children, *i.e.*, the highest rate is paid for the eldest child; but if any of the children are maintained in a charitable institution they are regarded as junior to those remaining in the mother's care.

24. *Changes which have taken place in a dependant's circumstances since the outbreak of war* or since the man's entry, if later, cannot be taken into account in assessing separation allowance, that allowance being awarded solely by reference to pre-war or pre-entry conditions. These and other isolated cases in which the Regulations would be productive of hardship have, however, been provided for by the establishment of the War Pensions (Statutory) Committee, 22, Abingdon Street, Westminster, and dependants of men may apply for supplementary or special separation allowances to the Local Committee appointed for the district in which they reside. The address of such Committee will be obtainable on inquiry at the Town Hall or of any representative of the Soldiers' and Sailors' Families Association,

25. *Boys who have had less than three months' service, and who under the Training Service Regulations consequently cannot allot to their dependants.*— Subject to the usual proof of dependence, separation allowance is issued in these cases in anticipation of the boy declaring an allotment in his dependant's favour as soon as the Regulations will admit of his so doing.

26 Only in exceptional circumstances will an allowance be paid to a dependant resident outside the United Kingdom.

27. *Men undergoing Detention; in a state of Desertion; or in Debt.*— Separation allowance is naturally not issuable for any period during which a man is in a state of desertion, but is continuable for periods of detention, irrespective of allotment, and in the case of men in debt, provided that the allotment is re-declared at the earliest date practicable.

E.—WIDOWS, CHILDREN AND OTHER DEPENDANTS.

28. In those cases in which separation allowance is in force at the date of the death of a Warrant Officer, Seaman or Marine, it is continuable, together with whatever allotment was then operative, for a period of twenty-six weeks following that date.

In cases, however, in which an allotment only was in force, and separation allowance had not been applied for and refused, the allotment will be continued for a period of four weeks from the date of the official announcement of the casualty.

Any pension or other allowance that may be awarded is then issued.

Warrant Officers, R.N., and R.M. Gunners.

29. For the duration of hostilities separation allowance is also granted in respect of Warrant Officers (but *not* Commissioned Warrant Officers) of the Royal Navy and Reserve Forces and Royal Marine Gunners.

30. Generally the issue of the allowance is governed by the Regulations applicable to separation allowance in the case of men. Thus the allowance is only payable in respect of Warrant Officers who are borne on the books of one of H.M. Ships, and in no circumstances is it issuable in respect of Officers paid at a Mercantile rate of pay. A minimum allotment of 20s. a week is required to qualify a wife for consideration for an allowance.

31. The scale of payment is 8s. a week for the wife, 4s. for the first child, 3s. for the second, 2s. for the third, and 1s. for each other child. Additional allowances of the type specified in par. 2, Scale B., are payable when there are children under 14; namely, 1s. 6d. a week where there are two children under that age, 3s. when there are three, and an additional 1s. a week for each such child beyond that number. The allowance for motherless children is 5s. a week each with additions under Scale B. for children under 14 years of age. Allowances for dependants are granted by reference to the three limiting factors specified in pars. 11 to 13, viz. :—

(1) The degree of the pre-war or pre-entry dependence;
(2) The amount of the current allotment; and
(3) The scale allowance for a wife (and children if there are more dependants than one).

32. An allowance for a dependant should be applied for on an A.G. Form No. 11, which should be adapted as necessary. In issuing such a form to a Warrant Officer the Accountant Officer should see that the Officer's name and rank have been correctly inserted on the form.

The regulations contain the following injunctions to Commanding Officers, viz. :—

33. All men are, immediately on entry, to be questioned as to whether they desire to allot, and, except in the case of men who allot to their wives, as to whether they wish to complete an A.G. Form No. 11.

It cannot be too clearly realised how essential it is that every facility should be afforded to new entries to declare allotments at the earliest possible opportunity after entry. Not only does delay in the matter keep the man's wife or other dependant without the support which he or she needs and has been accustomed to receive from him, but it involves delay in the grant of any separation allowance that may be payable—and, in fact, if the allotment is not declared within a month of the man's entry, arrears of separation allowance are forfeited (*see* pars. 7, 8 and 18).

34. All ratings must clearly understand that these allowances are intended not as a means of relieving them of any part of their obligations to their wives and children or other dependants, but as an additional provision which should free men from anxiety on their relatives' behalf during the period of the war. In this connection it is especially desirable that Commanding Officers should see that allotments are not reduced without sufficient reason.

NAVAL PRIZE MONEY.

REGULATIONS FOR DISTRIBUTION.

An Order in Council, dated February 9th, 1917, repealed an Order in Council dated December 5th, 1865, in respect to the distribution of naval prize money, and substituted a new scheme to come into operation forthwith. The new regulations are as follows :

All money distributable among the officers and crew of any of His Majesty's ships of war shall be forthwith paid to the account of His Majesty's Paymaster-General at the Bank of England on account of naval prize, or to the Accountant-General of the Navy, in order that it may be transferred to the said account.

Before any money distributable is actually distributed, notification shall be given in the " London Gazette."

No assignment of prize money may be made by any officer or man in respect of any advance or consideration, but any assignment made by an officer before the date of this Order shall be discharged as heretofore.

Any amounts due in respect of deceased officers and men shall be paid in the manner prescribed for the disposal of residues of naval assets generally.

Shares due to persons of unsound mind shall be dealt with in all respects as are balances of pay and allowances payable to such persons.

Payment shall be made in such manner as the Admiralty may from time to time direct.

Prize money which is unclaimed, or to which a claim has not been proved to the satisfaction of the Admiralty, shall be deemed to be forfeited after the expiration of six years from the 1st day of April following the date when it first became distributable; but when the relative accounts have not been finally closed the Admiralty may, if good cause is shown, remit such forfeiture and pay the amount out of the naval prize cash balance.

All accounts relative to any prize money shall be finally closed at the expiration of forty years from the date of distribution.

The net amounts brought to account in any year in respect of percentage reductions and of forfeitures under the Naval Discipline Act shall be regarded as finally transferred to the Exchequer Consolidated Fund at the expiration of the sixth year after that in which they were brought to account.

An account showing all the receipts and expenditure on account of prize money made up to March 31st in each year, and signed by the Accountant-General of the Navy, shall be laid annually before the House of Commons.

NAVAL DESPATCHES.
The Dover Patrol.

A supplement to the *London Gazette*, issued July 25th, 1916, contained the following despatch, dated May 29th, from Vice-Admiral Sir Reginald H. S. Bacon, K.C.B., C.V.O., D.S.O., commanding the Dover Patrol, reporting the operations of the Dover Patrol since December 3rd last :

Since my last despatch to their lordships on December 3rd, 1915, the varied duties of this patrol have been carried out with unremitting energy on the part of the officers and men under my command.

During the winter months offensive operations on the Belgian coast were much impeded by the shortness of the daylight hours and by gales of wind and bad weather. These same factors that impeded offensive action facilitated the work of the enemy in laying mines and in attacking our commerce in these narrow waters, since it assisted them to elude our patrols of protective vessels.

The services of the Dover Patrol can be best appreciated from the following facts :

Over 21,000 merchant ships, apart from men-of-war and auxiliaries, have passed through this patrol in the last six months. Of these 21 have been lost or have been seriously damaged by the enemy. The losses in merchant vessels, therefore, have been less than one per thousand. On the other hand, to effect this very considerable security to our merchant shipping I regret that over 4 per cent. of our patrol vessels have been sunk and the lives of 77 officers and men lost to the nation. No figures could emphasize more thoroughly the sacrifice made by the personnel of the patrol and the relative immunity ensured to the commerce of their country.

Besides the foregoing, the patrol assists in the protection of the flank of all the sea transport to and from our army in France. The number of vessels that have passed, and also of the troops that have been carried, are known to their lordships, but it is well to call attention to the fact that this vast transport of troops has been so thoroughly safeguarded that not one single life has been lost during the sea passage.

ATTACKS ON ENEMY POSITIONS.

The work of the destroyer flotilla throughout the winter has been incessant and arduous, and thoroughly well carried out.

Certain opportunities have arisen of bombarding the enemy's positions in Belgium. On these occasions the necessary minor operations have been carried out.

NAVAL AIRMEN'S SERVICES.

In addition to the daily reconnaissance and protective work performed by the Royal Naval Air Service on the coast, 11 organized attacks against the enemy's aerodromes and 13 attacks on enemy vessels have been carried out. Nine enemy machines and one submarine have been destroyed by air attacks and appreciable damage has been inflicted on military adjuncts.

The services rendered by the naval airmen in Flanders, under Acting Capt. Lambe, have been most valuable. It is equally advantageous to maintain the offensive in the air as it is to do so on land or at sea. It is with considerable satisfaction, therefore, that I am able to report that, with only one exception, all the aeroplanes destroyed were fought over the enemy's territory and that all the seaplanes were brought down into waters off the enemy's coast.

ENEMY'S SUBMARINE ATTACKS.

The advent of spring weather has lately enabled me to take measures to limit the extent to which the submarine and other vessels of the enemy had free access to the waters off the Belgian coast. The success achieved has so far been considerable, and the activities of submarines operating from the Belgian coast have been much reduced. We have destroyed several of the enemy's submarines and some of his surface vessels. Our losses, I regret to say, were four officers killed, one wounded ; men, 22 killed, two wounded.

It is to the energy and endurance of the officers and men of the vessels that have been employed, and who are now daily on patrol, that the success of these operations has been due. Whether of our Royal Navy, of the French Navy, of our mercantile marine, or our fishermen, all have exhibited those qualities most valued at sea in time of war.

My cordial thanks are due to Rear-Admiral de Marliave for the hearty co-operation he has afforded me during the whole of the foregoing period.

During these operations I was afforded much assistance by Commodore R. Tyrwhitt, C.B., Commodore C. D. Johnson, M.V.O., D.S.O., and Capt. F. S. Litchfield-Speer, as well as Commandant Excelman, of the French Navy.

Capt. H. W. Dowring, D.S.O., acted most ably as chief of my staff throughout the operations.

Evacuation of Gallipoli.

A supplement to the *London Gazette*, issued on Wednesady, April 11th, 1917, contains the following despatches to the Admiralty from Vice-Admiral Sir John M. de Robeck, K.C.B., late Vice-Admiral Commanding the Eastern Mediterranean Squadron, and Vice-Admiral Sir Rosslyn E. Wemyss, K.C.B., K.C.M.G., M.V.O., late Senior Naval Officer, Mudros, describing the naval operations in connection with the withdrawal of the Army from the Gallipoli Peninsula :

ADMIRAL WEMYSS
" Lord Nelson," at Mudros, *22nd December*, 1915.

Sir,—Be pleased to lay before the Lords Commissioners of the Admiralty the following report on the operations connected with the evacuation of the position at Suvla and Anzac.

The evacuation was carried out in three stages, as follows :

(*a*) A Preliminary Stage.

During this stage all personnel, animals, and vehicles not necessary for a winter campaign were removed. This necessitated no special arrangement, and was completed by the date on which definite orders to evacuate Suvla and Anzac were received.

(*b*) An Intermediate Stage.

During this stage all personnel, guns, and animals which were not absolutely necessary for the defence of the positions in the event of an enemy attack at the last moment were removed. This also was carried out without special arrangements beyond the withdrawal of increased amounts of material each night.

(c) Final Stage.

Special and detailed orders were necessary for the operations of this stage, which had to be completed in thirty-six hours, and which included the embarkation of all personnel remaining, and of all guns and animals not previously withdrawn.

The principle decided upon for all three stages was secrecy and the attempt to take the enemy entirely by surprise. It was hoped that he would ascribe any unusual activity, if observed, to the preparation for an attack. Every effort was therefore made during the whole of the operations to maintain the beaches, offing, etc. in their usual appearance, and all embarkations were carried out during the dark hours. The increase in the number of motor lighters, boats, etc., in use at the beaches were hidden as far as possible during the daytime.

The preliminary stage was completed satisfactorily by 10th December, when the definite orders to evacuate were received.

It had been computed that ten nights would be required for the intermediate stage, on each of which 3,000 personnel and a proportion of guns and animals would be embarked from each beach. This estimate was eventually reduced, special efforts being made in order to take advantage of the fine weather, the duration of which could not be relied on at this season.

The intermediate stage was completed on the night of the 17th-18th December and, from the absence of any unusual shelling of the beaches during these nights, it was apparent that the enemy had no idea of the movement in progress.

Some 44,000 personnel, nearly 200 guns, numerous wagons, and 3,000 animals, were evacuated during this period, together with a large amount of stores and ammunition.

The final stage commenced on the night of the 18th-19th December, and was completed on the night of the 19th-20th December. The fixing of the date for this stage had been a question of some discussion. On the one hand, it was deemed most advisable that the operation should be carried on with the utmost despatch and without loss of time for fear of the weather breaking; on the other hand, the moon on the 18th was very near its full. It was considered, however, that this fact might not altogether be a disadvantage, as the benefit accruing to us would probably counteract any advantage gained by the enemy. The weather conditions, however, proved to be ideal. An absolutely smooth sea, no wind, and a cloudy sky caused grey nights, which were of the utmost benefit to the work on the beaches, and were apparently not sufficiently light to enable the enemy to get an idea of what was taking place.

On each of the two nights of the final stage it was necessary to evacuate rather more than 10,000 personnel from each beach, and for this special arrangements were necessary. The chief possible difficulties to contend with were two: Firstly, the bad weather to be expected at this season; secondly, interference by the enemy.

After some heavy winds, fine weather set in with December, and, except for a strong north-easterly wind on the 15th, continued until 24 hours after the completion of the evacuation. This prolonged period of fine weather alone made possible the success which attended the operation. It enabled light piers, and improvements of a temporary nature to existing piers, to be carried out. A southerly wind of even moderate force at any time during this period must have

Evacuation of Gallipoli 75

wrecked piers, and have caused very considerable losses among the small craft assembled for the operations, and would have necessitated the embarkation being carried out from the open beaches. Such loss of small craft would have made anything in the nature of rapid evacuation an impossibility, and would have enormously increased the difficulties. To cope with such an eventuality a reserve of small craft up to 50 per cent. would not have been too great ; actually the reserve maintained had to be very much smaller.

Interference by the enemy would have been most serious, as the beaches were fully exposed to shell fire, and the damage inflicted to personnel, small craft, piers, etc., might have been most serious, as he would have had no inducement to husband his ammunition.

Under such conditions it was most improbable that anything beyond personnel could have been evacuated. Casualties would also have been heavy, and removal of wounded out of the question. To meet the latter possibility arrangements were made to leave the hospital clearing stations intact, with a proportion of medical staff in attendance, and thus ensure that our wounded would not suffer from want of attention, which the enemy, with all the good will in the world, might have been unable to supply. It was also arranged that in such circumstances an attempt would have been made to negotiate an armistice on the morning after the evacuation to collect and, if possible, bring off our wounded. Fortunately, neither of these two dangers matured, but the probability of either or both doing so made this stage of the operations most anxious for all concerned.

The final concentration of the ships and craft required at Kephalo was completed on the 17th December, and in order to prevent enemy's aircraft observing the unusual quantity of shipping, a constant air patrol was maintained to keep these at a distance.

Reports of the presence of enemy submarines were also received during these two days ; patrols were strengthened, but no attacks by these craft were made.

The evacuation was carried out in accordance with orders. No delays occurred, and there were no accidents to ships or boats.

On the night of the 18th-19th December, when I embarked in H.M.S. " Arno," accompanied by General Sir William Birdwood, the embarkation was finished at Suvla by 3 a.m., and at Anzac by 5.30 a.m., and by daylight the beaches and anchorages at these places had resumed their normal aspect.

The second night's operations, as far as the Navy was concerned, differed in no wise from the first, precisely the same routine being adhered to. The weather conditions were similar, and could not have suited our purpose better. On this night I hoisted my flag in H.M.S. " Chatham," and was accompanied by General Sir William Birdwood and members of our two staffs.

The last troops left the front trenches at 1.30 a.m., and I received the signal that the evacuation was complete at 4.15 a.m. at Anzac and 5.39 a.m. at Suvla.

A large mine was exploded at about 3.15 a.m. by the Australians, and at Suvla all perishable stores which had not been taken off, and which were heaped up in large mounds with petrol poured over them, were fired at 4 a.m., making a vast bonfire which lighted everything around for a very long distance.

In spite of all this, the enemy seemed perfectly unaware of what had taken place. As day dawned, soon after 6.30, the anchorages of both places were clear of all craft, except the covering squadrons, which had been ordered up during the night, and when the sun had sufficiently risen for objects to be made out, the bombardment of the beaches commenced, with the object of destroying everything that remained. At Suvla this consisted only of some water tanks and four motor lighters, which, I regret to say, had been washed ashore in the gale of 28th of November, and which had never been recovered, owing principally to lack of time. At Anzac it had been deemed inadvisable to set a light to the stores which had been found impossible to embark, so that here the bombardment was more severe and large fires were started by the bursting shells.

A curious spectacle now presented itself, certain areas absolutely clear of troops being subjected to a heavy shell fire from our own and the enemy's guns.

It seems incredible that all this work had taken place without the enemy becoming aware of our object, for although the utmost care was taken to preserve the beaches and offing as near as possible normal, yet it proved quite impracticable to get up boats and troop carriers in sufficient time to carry out the night's work and yet for them not to have been visible from some parts of the Peninsula.

The morning bombardment lasted but a very short time, for I felt that the use of much ammunition would merely be a waste; moreover, the risk of submarines appearing on the scene of action had never been absent from my mind at any time during the whole operation. Consequently at 7.25 a.m. I ordered the squadron to return to Kephalo, leaving two specially protected cruisers to watch the area. These subsequently reported that they had caused a good deal of damage amongst the enemy when they eventually swarmed down to take possession of the loot, the realization of which, I trust, was a great disappointment to them.

All the arrangements were most admirably carried out, and the time-table previously laid down was adhered to exactly.

Before closing this despatch I would like to emphasize the fact that what made this operation so successful, apart from the kindness of the weather and of the enemy, was the hearty co-operation of both Services. The evacuation forms an excellent example of the cordial manner in which the Navy and Army have worked together during these last eight months.

For the Army the evacuation was an operation of great probable danger, shared by the naval beach personnel; it was also, specially for the former, one of considerable sadness. Throughout the whole proceedings nothing could have exceeded the courtesy of Generals Sir William Birdwood, Sir Julian Byng, and Sir Alexander Godley and their respective staffs, and this attitude was typical of the whole Army.

The traditions of the Navy were fully maintained, the seamanship and resources displayed reaching a very high standard. From the commanding officers of men-of-war, transports, and large supply ships, to the midshipmen in charge of steamboats and pulling boats off the beaches, all did well.—I am, sir, your obedient servant,

R. E. WEMYSS.

Evacuation of Gallipoli

ADMIRAL DE ROEBECK.

"Lord Nelson," *26th January*, 1916.

Sir,—I have the honour to forward the following despatch dealing with the withdrawal of the Army from the Gallipoli Peninsula.

In considering the evacuation of the Helles position, it was laid down by Sir Charles Monro, for the guidance of the Army, that :

(*a*) The withdrawal should be conducted with the utmost rapidity, the final stage being limited to one night.

(*b*) Every effort should be made to improve embarkation facilities at as many points on the coast as could be used, other than W and V beaches.

(*c*) Every endeavour should be made to evacuate as many as possible of the following :

British : 18pdr. guns, 4.5-inch howitzers, 60pdr. guns, 6-inch guns.
French : 75mm. guns, heavy guns.

Also artillery ammunition and such small-arm ammunition as could safely be withdrawn before the final stage.

(*d*) The period of time which must elapse before the final stage could be undertaken would be determined by the time required to collect necessary shipping and to make essential preparations ashore (work on beaches, pathways, etc.), taken in conjunction with the necessity for evacuating the superfluous personnel and as much as possible of the material mentioned in (*c*).

(*e*) During the "intermediate stage," the duration of which would be determined by the foregoing considerations, such other animals, material, stores, and supplies as could be embarked without prolonging this period would also be evacuated.

Forty-eight hours before the evacuation was completed, the number of men remaining on the peninsula was to be cut down to 22,000.

Of these, 7,000 were to embark on the last night but one, leaving 15,000 for the final night ; at the request of the military the latter number was increased to 17,000.

As few guns as possible were to be left to the final night, and arrangements were made to destroy any of these which it might be found impossible to remove or which, by reason of their condition, were considered not worth removing.

The original intention was to use Gully, " X," " W," and " V " beaches for the embarkation of troops on the final night ; this was deemed advisable in consequence of the very accurate and heavy fire which the enemy could bring to bear on " W " and " V " beaches, on to both of which their guns were carefully registered.

The decision not to use " X " beach and to use Gully beach only to embark the last 700 men was arrived at on the 6th January.

This alteration of plan was recommended by General Sir Francis Davies, commanding the 8th Corps ; he based his objections to the use of " X " and Gully beaches to :

(*a*) The probability of bad weather. Embarkation from these beaches, even in a moderately strong northerly blow, was impossible.

(*b*) " X " and Gully beaches had not been used for a considerable time as landing-places, and should the movements of ships and boats off the beaches be observed by the enemy, it might awaken their suspicions as to what was taking place.

The essence of the operations being secrecy, the second of these reasons decided me to concur in this change of plan almost at the eleventh hour.

The preliminary stage commenced on the night of the 30th-31st December, and terminated on the night of the 7th-8th January.

During this stage all personnel except 17,000 were removed, as well as the majority of the guns and a great quantity of animals, stores, etc.

The amount of stores remaining on shore after the preliminary stage was greater than was anticipated or intended; this was almost entirely due to the unfavourable weather conditions and, as men were evacuated, to a shortage in working parties.

On 1st January the weather showed signs of breaking; on the 2nd and 3rd strong north-easterly winds blew all day; the morning of the 4th was calm, but the weather broke at 7 p.m., and by 11 p.m. it was blowing a gale from the N.E., which, however, moderated on the evening of the 5th; on the 6th and 7th the weather conditions were favourable.

Fortunately the wind remained in the north to north-east, which permitted work to continue on " V " and " W " beaches. The transfer of guns, animals and stores, etc., from motor lighters to transports and supply ships lying off the beaches was a matter of great difficulty under such conditions of weather.

During the whole of this period " V " and " W " beaches were subjected to a heavy and accurate shell fire from the enemy's batteries mounted on the Asiatic shore, and also from guns firing from positions to north of Achi Baba.

All these guns were accurately registered on to the beaches, and the shelling continued day and night at frequent and uncertain intervals; that the actual loss of life from this fire was very small borders on the miraculous; the beach parties were completely exposed, and piers and foreshore constantly hit by shells while officers and men were working on them; even when resting in the dug-outs security from enemy's fire could not be assured, and several casualties occurred under these conditions.

The work on the beaches was practically continuous; during the daytime motor lighters, etc., were loaded up with stores, etc., to be transferred to store ships at night; by night the work was most strenuous.

During the whole time there remained the paramount necessity of preventing the enemy gaining intelligence of what was in progress; this added greatly to the difficulties of work during daylight. Enemy aircraft paid frequent visits to the peninsula; on these occasions, whilst the " Taube " was in evidence, animals and transports approaching the beaches were turned and marched in the opposite direction, and stores and horses already in lighters were even unloaded on to the beaches to give the appearance of a disembarkation.

On the afternoon of the 7th the enemy delivered a very heavy artillery attack against certain portions of our advanced position, probably the most intense bombardment our trenches in the Helles area have ever been subjected to.

Attempts were made by the enemy to follow up this bombardment by an infantry attack, but the few Turks who could be persuaded to quit their trenches were instantly shot down, and the infantry advance was a complete failure.

This bombardment and attack most fortunately took place at a time when our forward position was fully manned and when there were still about sixty guns in position on the peninsula, with a very large supply of ammunition.

The ships supporting the left flank opened a heavy fire on the Turkish position. H.M.S. " Grafton " (Capt. Henry E. Grace), H.M.S. " Raglan " (Capt. Cecil D. S. Raikes) and H.M. destroyer " Wolverine " (Lt.-Com. Adrian St. V. Keyes) were on duty in position to support the Army, which they did most ably, undoubtedly inflicting heavy loss on the enemy. They were reinforced by H.M.S. " Russell," H.M.S. " Havelock," and H.M. destroyer " Scorpion."

Arrangements were also made to reinforce Helles with one brigade of infantry from Imbros, should such a step become necessary.

The principal reasons the enemy did not discover that the evacuation was taking place were, I consider :

(a) The excellent arrangements made by the military and the beach parties to prevent the enemy noticing any change in the landscape or any undue activity on the beaches.

(b) The probable unexpected force encountered in their attack on the 7th. It appears reasonable to suppose that the enemy, having thus convinced himself that the peninsula was still held in force by us, was satisfied that no evacuation would take place for some days.

(c) The fact that on the 8th the wind was in the south and blowing on to " W" and " V " beaches, and that by 9 p.m. it had freshened so considerably as to render any evacuation a most difficult and hazardous proceeding.

The enemy was certainly deceived as to the date of our final departure from his shores, and his artillery fire on the final night of the evacuation was negligible.

The decision arrived at on the 6th to evacuate practically all the personnel of the final night from " W " and " V " beaches necessitated some rearrangement of plans, as some 5,000 additional troops had to be embarked from these beaches.

To use motor lighters from the already crowded piers would have lengthened the operation very considerably, and it was therefore decided to employ destroyers to embark 5,200 men from the blockships, which were fitted with stagings and connected with the shore ; thus existing arrangements would be interfered with as little as possible. The result was excellent. The destroyers which were laid alongside the blockships, in spite of a nasty sea, being handled with great skill by their commanding officers, once more showing their powers of adaptability.

The necessary amendments to orders were issued on the morning of the 7th, and, in spite of the short notice given, the naval operations on the night of the 8th-9th were carried out without confusion or delay, a fact which reflects great credit on all concerned, especially on the beach personnel, who were chiefly affected by the change of plan.

On January 8th the weather was favourable, except that the wind was from the south ; this showed no signs of freshening at 5 p.m., and orders were given to carry out the final stage.

The actual embarkation of the 8th commenced at 8 p.m., and the last section were to commence embarking at 6.30 a.m.

By 9 p.m. the wind had freshened considerably, still blowing from the south ; a slight sea got up, and caused much inconvenience on the beaches.

A floating bridge at "W" beach commenced to break up, necessitating arrangements being made to ferry the last section of the personnel to the waiting destroyers.

At Gully beach matters were worse, and, after a portion of the 700 troops had been embarked in motor lighters and sent off to H.M.S. "Talbot," it was found impossible to continue using this beach (one motor lighter was already badly on shore—she was subsequently destroyed by gunfire), and orders were given for the remainder of the Gully beach party to embark from "W" beach; this was done without confusion, special steps having been taken by the beachmaster to cope with such an eventuality.

After a temporary lull the wind again increased, and by 3 a.m. a very nasty sea was running into "W" beach.

It was only by the great skill and determination displayed by the beach personnel that the embarkation was brought to a successful conclusion, and all the small craft except one steamboat damaged in collision) got away in safety.

The last troops were leaving at 3.45 a.m., after which the beach personnel embarked.

Great difficulty was experienced in getting the last motor lighters away, owing to the heavy seas running into the harbour.

This was unfortunate, as the piles of stores which it had been found impossible to take off, and which were prepared for burning, were lit perhaps rather sooner than was necessary, as were also the fuses leading to the magazine.

The latter blew up before all the boats were clear, and, I regret to report caused the death of one of the crew of the barge, which was amongst the last boats to leave.

It was fortunate that more casualties were not caused by the explosion, debris from which fell over and around a great many boats.

The success of the operations was due principally to:

(a) Excellent staff work.

(b) The untiring energy and skill displayed by officers and men, both Army and Navy, comprising the beach parties.

(c) The good seamanship and zeal of the officers and crews of the various craft employed in the evacuation of the troops.

(d) The excellent punctuality of the Army in the arrival of the troops for embarkation at the different beaches.

The Navy has especially to thank Generals Sir William Birdwood and Sir Francis Davies for their forethought and hearty co-operation in all matters.

The staff work was above reproach, and I hope I may be permitted to mention some of those military officers who rendered special assistance to the Navy. They are:

      Maj.-Gen. the Hon. H. A. Lawrence,
      Brig.-Gen. H. E. Street, and
      Col. A. B. Carey, R.E.,

the latter of whom performed work of inestimable value in the last few days by improving piers and preparing means of rapid embarkation from the blockships.

The programme and plans as regards the Naval portion of the operations were due to the work of my chief of staff, Commodore Roger J. B. Keyes, to whom too great credit cannot be given; to Capt. Francis H. Mitchell, R.N., attd. to General Headquarters; Maj. William W. Godfrey, R.M.L.I., of my staff; Capt. Cecil M. Staveley (principal beachmaster at Cape Helles); Capt. Henry F. G. Talbot, in charge of the vessels taking part; and Act.-Com. George F. A. Mulock (chief assistant to Capt. Staveley).

The organization of the communications, on which so much depended, was very ably carried out by my fleet wireless officer (Com. James F. Somerville) and my signal officer (Lieut. Hugh S. Bowlby). The arrangement by which H.M.S. " Triad " (on board of which was the general officer commanding Helles Army) was anchored close in under Cape Tekeh, and connected with the shore telephone system by two cables, thus leaving her wireless installation free for communicating with the ships of covering squadron, etc., was especially good.

The naval covering squadron was under the command of Rear-Admiral Sydney R. Fremantle in H.M.S. " Hibernia," who had a most able colleague in Capt. Douglas L. Dent, of H.M.S. " Edgar," whose ability had done so much to improve the naval gun support to the Helles Army.

The work of this squadron was conducted with great energy, and was in every way satisfactory. It controlled to a great extent the enemy's guns firing on to the beaches.

Whenever the enemy opened fire, whether by day or night, there were always ships in position to reply, a result which reflects much credit on the officers named.

The Army Headquarters gave us again the invaluable assistance and experience of Lt.-Col. C. F. Aspinall in arranging details, and I cannot help laying special stress on this officer's excellent co-operation with my staff on all occasions.

I now have the pleasure of bringing to your notice the loyal support and assistance we received now, as always, from our French friends.

Contre Adml. de Bon was responsible for the French naval programme of evacuation, and on its completion he rendered us every assistance with his beach parties, who were under the immediate command of a most able and gallant officer—Capitaine Frégate Bréart de Boisanger—an officer whom I have already brought to your lordships' notice in a previous despatch.

There are many officers and men who have performed meritorious service in connection with this evacuation; their names will be forwarded in due course in a separate letter.—I have the honour to be, sir, your obedient servant,

J. M. DE ROEBECK, *Vice-Admiral.*

German East Africa.

ADMIRALTY, 15*th June*, 1917.

The following despatch has been received from the Commander-in-Chief, Cape of Good Hope Station, describing the later coastal operations by H.M. ships against German East Africa:

H.M.S. " Hyacinth," 28*th January*, 1917.

SIR,—Be pleased to lay before their Lordships the following report of the later coastal operations against German East Africa by H.M. ships under my orders.

These operations may be said to have commenced with the occupation, on the 1st August, 1916, of the town of Saadani by naval forces, assisted by a detachment of the Zanzibar African Rifles. The capture of this coast town was undertaken at the request of General Smuts, and was well and effectively carried out under the immediate supervision of Captain A. H. Williamson, M.V.O., of " Vengeance " (flying my flag) for the outer squadron, and of Captain E. J. A. Fullerton, D.S.O., of " Severn " for the inshore squadron ; Commander R. J. N. Watson of " Vengeance " being in command of the landing party.

The force was landed in boats from " Vengeance," " Talbot " (Captain R. C. Kemble Lambert, D.S.O.), " Severn," and " Mersey " (Commander R. A. Wilson, D.S.O.) about one mile to the north of the town at 6 a.m., " Severn " and " Mersey " covering the landing with their guns. But slight opposition was experienced, only three casualties being sustained. The fort was enclosed in a " boma," which had been constructed originally to keep out leopards and savages, and was surrounded by the native village and dense bush, which had to be cleared.

During the period of naval occupation a few encounters took place between our advanced patrols and those of the enemy, but no attack in force was made and our energies were confined to consolidating the position.

On the 5th August the whole of the naval forces, except the Marines and a few special details, re-embarked on military forces being landed to relieve them.

On the 13th August I received a wireless message from the military officer in command at Saadani, giving the enemy force at Bagamoyo at about ten whites and forty Askaris, and asking if the Navy would take the town, as its earliest occupation was essential. I replied that this would be done, and issued orders accordingly.

Although the information given me indicated that the enemy force was small, I knew that it would be strongly entrenched and would have Maxims, and I therefore decided to land what force I could raise from the ships immediately available, together with all machine guns, and to have a strong covering force of light-draught ships inshore with heavy-draught ships outside.

As it turned out the intelligence was very much at fault, the enemy having one 4.1-in. gun, one five-barrelled pom-pom, and two Maxims, their total force being more numerous than the landing party.

At 5 p.m. on the 14th August, " Vengeance " (Flag), with " Challenger " (Captain A. C. Sykes) and " Manica " (Commander W. E. Whittingham, R.N.R.) in company, left Zanzibar, anchoring at 3.24 a.m. on the 15th off Bagamoyo, the landing party leaving " Vengeance " at 4.40 a.m., under the command of Commander R. J. N. Watson.

There was a slight swell, little wind, and a bright moon, so that a complete surprise was not to be expected ; but the landing turned out to be as near a surprise as was possible in the circumstances, and it is believed that the boats were not seen until they had left the monitors at 5.30 a.m.

Owing to the skill with which the advance was conducted by Commander Watson and Commander (acting) W. B. Wilkinson, and an alteration of course when some little way from the shore, the enemy were completely deceived as to the point of landing, and found themselves under a heavy fire from the monitors and motor boats, which effectually prevented them from firing on the landing party.

The latter proceeded and landed close under the 4.1-in. gun position to the left of the town, at a point where the gun, owing to its position some 30 feet back from the ridge on which it was sited, could not be sufficiently depressed to bear on them.

On the other hand this gun came under the enfilading fire of the 3-pounders, one each in my steam barge "Vengeance's" picket boat, and the tug "Helmuth." This fire, at from 800 to 500 yards, so seriously discomposed the enemy that they abandoned the gun as soon as attacked by the shore party. This gun had come from Tanga in tow of 500 coolies, and had arrived at the position in which it was taken on the 9th August. Its capture was, in my opinion, a most remarkable piece of work, reflecting the greatest credit on the boats and the attacking section.

Meanwhile the "Manica" had got up her kite balloon and was spotting, but her seaplane had engine trouble and was forced to come down in the breakers at the mouth of the Kingani River, returning undamaged. I accordingly called on "Himalaya" (Captain Colin Mackenzie, D.S.O.), which was just leaving Zanzibar, and at 6 a.m. her seaplane flew across from Zanzibar, and at once dropped bombs on the enemy in trenches, afterwards spotting. "Himalaya" herself followed and took a useful part in the subsequent bombardment.

At 6.30 a.m. it was reported from three sources—kite balloon, portable W.-T. set ashore, and W.-T. from seaplane—that the enemy were retiring between the French Mission and the sea, and were around the Mission.

The cause of this retreat was the endeavour of Captain von Bok to rush his troops round to the opposite side of the town to oppose our landing. About this time the pom-pom gun was hit by a 6-in shell from "Severn" (Commander (acting) W. B. C. Jones) and nearly pulverised, Captain von Boedecke being killed. Shortly after Captain von Bok was also killed, and with both leaders gone all initiative on the part of the enemy was lost, and our men were able to firmly establish themselves in a small but important quarter of the town, from which they subsequently spread and gathered in all the Arabs, Indians, and natives. Beyond slight damage from shell fire and a fire in the native village—where an occasional fire is beneficial—the town is intact.

The importance of the capture of this town on the native mind was very great, as it is the old capital of the slave trade and the starting place of the great caravan routes into the interior.

The result from a military point of view was immediately apparent in the demoralisation of the enemy forces, particularly the native portion, and in the evacuation of the Mtoni Ferry, a strategic and strongly-defended position about six miles above the town over the Kingani River, thereby giving our troops moving south from Saadani and Mandera an open road.

It is with deep regret that I record the death of Captain Francis H. Thomas, D.S.C., Royal Marine Light Infantry, whilst gallantly leading his men. He had taken part in all recent operations, and was a most promising officer. Our other casualties were two seamen and two marines wounded, while the Zanzibar African Rifles had one sergeant and one Askari killed and one Askari wounded. Two native porters were also wounded.

The enemy casualties were estimated at two officers, one white soldier, and eight Askaris killed, three white and eight Askaris wounded, and four white and fifteen Askaris taken prisoner.

On the 20th August the naval forces were relieved by the military and re-embarked in their ships.

On the 21st August, in continuance of the policy of harassing Dar-es-Salaam "Vengeance" and "Challenger" bombarded various gun positions; and during that night "Challenger" carried out a further bombardment, firing 50 rounds of 6-in. over the town into the railway station. On the 23rd, 26th, 28th, 30th and 31st August, and on the 1st September, other limited bombardments took place, and on the 3rd September the whalers " Pickle " (Lieutenant H. C. Davis, D.S.C., R.D., R.N.R.), " Fly " (Lieutenant D. H. H. Whitburn, R.N.R.) " Childers " (Lieutenant V. C. Large, R.N.R.), and " Echo " (Lieutenant C. J. Charlewood, D.S.C., R.N.R.), under Flag Commander the Hon. R. O. B. Bridgeman, D.S.O., simulated a landing at Upanga and attacked the front at short range from West Ferry Point to Ras Upanga. They were received with shrapnel fire from a field battery, but escaped injury.

Meanwhile preparations for the advance on Dar-es-Salaam were in full swing, and on the 31st August the military advance started from Bagamoyo, the main body marching south and being strongly reinforced at Konduchi on the 2nd September, for which landing they themselves formed the covering party. The plan succeeded admirably, the enemy retiring and making little attempt to oppose the advance, so that in the end the final reinforcements actually landed in face of the very formidable entrenchments at Mssassani Bay.

With the military column went six naval maxims, six Lewis guns, one 3-pounder Hotchkiss on field mounting, and a medical section, the party being under the command of Commander H. D. Bridges, D.S.O., of " Hyacinth."

Communication between the main column and the small craft inshore was maintained by a naval wireless party.

The march of 36 miles proved exceedingly arduous, the road turning into little better than a sandy track through a waterless district. Porters were short and speedily dropped behind with provisions, to add to which the first regiment of African descent which arrived at Mssassani consumed the 12,000 gallons of water and three days' provisions for the force.

On the 3rd September, following on the simulated landing from the whalers, a brisk bombardment of gun positions to the northward of the town, and in advance of our troops, was carried out for half an hour until 7 a.m., when firing ceased and our troops continued their advance to the outskirts of the town.

As matters now appeared ripe to demand the surrender of the town, on the morning of the 4th September, " Challenger," flying a white flag, proceeded to Makatumbe with a written demand, signed by me and by the Officer commanding troops. This was transferred to the " Echo," which took it as far as the boom and then sent it ashore in her boat.

About 8 a.m., the deputy burgomaster, the bank manager, and an interpreter came off in the " Echo " and agreed to the conditions of the demand, giving all the required guarantees. Our troops were at once told by wireless to advance into the town. All ships entered Dar-es-Salaam Bay, and during the afternoon the monitors entered the harbour after destroying the hawsers of the boom across the entrance.

I landed with my staff at 2.30 p.m., and at 3 o'clock the Union Jack was hoisted over the Magistracy with full honours.

Following on the occupation of Dar-es-Salaam it became necessary to seize other coast towns further south, and thus prevent the enemy from retreating by the coast to Lindi and the southern ports.

In consequence, on the 7th September, a simultaneous attack was made on the two Kilwas (Kivinje and Kisiwani), with the object of getting possession of these towns and holding the two hills, Singino Hill and Mpara Hill, which command Kilwa Kivinje and Port Beaver respectively. After four 12-in. shrapnel had been placed on the top of Singino Hill by " Vengeance," a white man was seen endeavouring to haul down the German colours at Kivinje and to hoist his boy's white " kanzu " in their place. This was observed just in time to prevent fire being opened from " Vengeance " with 6-in. guns on the trenches along the beach. A flag of truce was sent in, the town surrendered unconditionally, and a force was landed and occupied the town and the hill. Meanwhile, Kilwa Kisiwani had surrendered unconditionally to " Talbot," who landed a party and occupied Mpara Hill.

Operations against the three Southern Ports of Mikindani, Sudi and Lindi commenced on the 13th September, when 200 Marines, 700 Indian troops, 200 Zanzibar and Mafia African Rifles, 12 naval machine guns, 2 Hotchkiss guns and 950 porters were landed at Mikindani in boats from " Vengeance," " Tal-' bot," " Himalaya," and " Princess " (Captain C. La P. Lewin), assisted by the gunboats " Thistle " (Commander Hector Boyes) and " Rinaldo " (Lieutenant-Commander H. M. Garrett), and the kite balloon ship " Manica," and the transport " Barjora." There was no opposition, and the town was occupied by 9 a.m.

On the 14th September our troops commenced their advance towards Sudi, while " Vengeance," " Hyacinth," " Talbot," and " Himalaya," with " Barjora," proceeded round to the anchorage outside there. Whalers entered the inner harbour at daylight on the 16th, experiencing no resistance.

The whole force, having left a garrison of 100 men at Mikindani, marched to Sudi, arriving there at noon, when the marines, naval guns and African Rifles were embarked, the intention being to land these as a covering party outside Lindi under the guns of the squadron, while the main force marched from Sudi to Lindi, where, if any resistance was put up, they would have held a commanding position on the south side of the river.

Early on the 16th the ships proceeded to Lindi Bay and the Naval Brigade was landed after a short bombardment of the selected beach with 6-in. guns. An attempt to send in a flag of truce was made, but no answer could be obtained, and from seaplane observations the town appeared to be deserted. Supported by " Thistle," the force advanced along the beach and occupied the town.

The troops—who were thus saved a long and arduous march from Sudi to Lindi—were re-embarked at Sudi on the evening of the 16th, leaving a garrison of 100 men there. They arrived at Lindi on the 17th, and relieved the Naval Brigade and African Rifles, who we re-embarked.

The same evening " Talbot," " Thistle," and " Barjora," with a detachment of Indian troops on board, left Lindi, and by 8 a.m. on the 18th Kiswere was occupied without any opposition, the troops remaining as a garrison.

.. This was the last town of any importance on the coast of German East Africa, and the whole coast line is now occupied with the exception of the Rufiji Delta.

In connection with the operations covered by this despatch I append a list of officers and men whom I specially desire to bring to the notice of their Lordships for meritorious services :

I have the honour to be, Sir, your obedient servant,
(Signed) E. CHARLTON, *Rear-Admiral, Commander-in-Chief*.

The Fleet Annual

Officers.

Capt. A. H. Williamson, M.V.O., H.M.S. "Vengeance."
Capt. A. C. Sykes, H.M.S. "Challenger."
Comdr. R. J. N. Watson, H.M.S. "Vengeance."
Comdr. Philip H. Trimmer, H.M.S. "Talbot."
Lieut. E. S. Brooksmith, H.M.S. "Vengeance."
Flag Lt.-Com. Cyril Goolden, H.M.S. "Hyacinth."
Flgt.-Lt. E. R. Moon, R.N.A.S.
Flgt.-Lt. J. E. B. Maclean, R.N.A.S.
Engr.-Com. F. J. Roskruge, H.M.S. "Hyacinth."
Flt.-Paymr. W. F. Cullinan, H.M.S. "Hyacinth."
Paymr. (Actg.) H. G. Badger, H.M.S. "Challenger."
Actg.-Paymr. (Emergency) Charles H. Griffith, H.M.S. "Hyacinth."
Asst.-Paymr. A. B. Johnston, H.M.S. "Hyacinth."
Mr. John Mackay, C.-Gnr., H.M.S. "Hyacinth."
Mr. Frank Goldsmith, Gnr. (T.), H.M.S. "Talbot."
Sub-Lt. F. G. J. Manning, R.N.R., H.M.S. "Talbot."

Petty Officers and Men.

C.P.O. (C.) James Noonan, R.N.A.S.
C.P.O. Francis Ernest Strong, H.M.S. "Talbot."
P.O. William James Grills, H.M.S. "Vengeance."
P.O. John James Mitchell Lawes, H.M.S. "Talbot."
P.O. Charles Ernest Pease, H.M.S. "Vengeance."
P.O. Arthur John Pidgeon, H.M.S. "Talbot."
P.O. Frank Reynolds, H.M.S. "Echo."
P.O. William Henry James Vennal, H.M.S. "Mersey."
P.O. William Young, H.M.S. "Vengeance."
L.S. George Brunker, H.M.S. "Hyacinth."
L.S. Cecil William Saunders, H.M.S. "Challenger."
A.B., R.F.R., Vincent Burrage, H.M.S. "Talbot."
A.B., R.F.R., Samuel Charles Cubitt, H.M.S. "Severn."
A.B. Michael Fitzgerald, H.M.S. "Echo."
A.B., R.F.R., Edward White Rose, H.M.S. "Vengeance."
Yeo. of Sigs. Ernest James Templeman, H.M.S. "Vengeance."
Sigmn. John Joseph Collins, H.M.S. "Vengeance."
P.O. Teleg. Albert French, H.M.S. "Hyacinth."
P.O. Teleg. Percival Charles King, H.M.S. "Hyacinth."
Ldg. Teleg. George Ambler, H.M.S. "Pickle."
Teleg. William Gilbert Gardiner, H.M.S. "Challenger."
Eng.-Rm.-Art., R.N.R., William Gordon, H.M.S. "Mersey."
Eng.-Rm.-Art., 2nd Cl., Harry Hopkins, H.M.S. "Hyacinth."
L.Sto., R.F.R., Bernard Sinden, H.M.S. "Severn."
Sto. P.O. Charles Arthur Cronshaw, H.M.S. "Pickle."
C. Writer Ernest Hambly, H.M.S. "Challenger."
Ship's Stewd. Albert Edward Tull, H.M.S. "Hyacinth."
Sick-Berth Stewd. Sampson Woodcock, H.M.S. "Challenger."
Co. Ser-Major Percy Evan Smith, R.M.L.I., H.M.S. "Hyacinth."
Colr.-Sergt., R.M.L.I., Walter James Fouracre, H.M.S. "Challenger."
Sergt., R.M.L.I., Harry Carter, H.M.S. "Hyacinth."
Corpl. Ernest Victor Dean, R.M.L.I., H.M.S. "Talbot."
Lce.-Corpl. William Bradley, R.M.L.I., H.M.S. "Talbot."
Pte. William Dennis, R.M.L.I., H.M.S. "Talbot."
Air Mechanic, 1st Grade, Frederick Wilmshurst, R.N.A.S.

Naval Cadets in the Workshops at Osborne.
Photo: Cribb.

Commander Gordon Campbell, V.C., D.S.O.
Photo: Russell.

FOR DISTINGUISHED SERVICE.

EVACUATION OF GALLIPOLI.

In addition to the honours notified in the supplements to the *London Gazette* dated 14th March, 15th May, and 31st May, 1916:

D.S.O.

Capt. Alexander V. Campbell, M.V.O., R.N.
 Performed meritorious service whilst in command of H.M.S. "Prince George," which took part in the actions of February 25th and March 18, 1915. "Prince George" supported the Army from inside the Straits between April 25th and May 10th, 1915, and also at Suvla for several weeks continuously under fire. Capt. Campbell also did good service during the evacuation.

D.S.C.

Lieut. Kenneth Edwards, R.N.
 Performed good service at the landing and at the evacuation of Helles. Set a fine example to his men whilst assisting at salvage operations on Monitor M.30 under fire from enemy's guns.

Lieut. Charles Leonard Fawell, R.N.V.R.
 For consistent good service, often under heavy fire, whilst in command of motor gunboat in the Smyrna inner patrol.

D.S.M.

C.P.O. Arthur James.
P.O. Walter Alger.
L.S. Harry T. Coleman.
C.E.R.A. Samuel Fletcher.
Armr's. Mate Chas. H. Hazel.
First Writer Walter J. V. Keeble.
Ship's Stewd. Wm. H. Bromidge.
C. Motor Mech. T. Thurburn.
Sgt. Albert V. Proctor.

MENTIONED IN DESPATCHES.

Capt. Michael H. Hodges, M.V.O., R.N.
Capt. Francis Clifton Brown, R.N.
Capt. Edmund C. Carver, R.N.
Com. Morton Smart, R.N.V.R.
Lt.-Com. (now Com.) Basil H. Piercy, R.N.
Lt.-Com. Claude P. Champion de Crespigny, R.N.
Lt.-Com. Henry C. Summers, R.N.V.R.
Gnr., R.N., Hugh F. Bevan.
Gnr. (now Mate), R.N., Charles E. A. W. Cox.
Gnr., R.N., Leonard W. Brock.
Signal Boatswain Philip J. Jones.
P.O. Thomas Hoban.
P.O. James Mather.
P.O. Lawrence V. Parsons.
L.S. Thomas G. Maylor.
Yeo. of Sig. Samuel R. J. Hillier.
C.E.R.A., 2nd Cl., David Thompson.
C. Sto. James W. French.
C. Writer H. J. W. Gains.
Pte. John Gollop, R.M.L.I.

A supplement to the *London Gazette*, issued on Friday, July 14th, 1916, says:

The Lords Commissioners of the Admiralty have received with much satisfaction from the officers in charge of the Auxiliary Patrol areas at home and abroad reports on the services performed by the officers and men serving under their orders during the period January 1st, 1915, to January 1st, 1916. These reports show that the officers and men serving in armed yachts, trawlers, and drifters of the Auxiliary Patrol during the period in question have carried out their duties under extremely arduous and hazardous conditions of weather and exposure to enemy attack and mines with marked zeal, gallantry, and success.

The King has been graciously pleased to give orders for the following appointments in recognition of the services referred to above:

D.S.O.

Capt. William Vansittart Howard, R.N.
Comdr. Sutton Smith, R.N.
Comdr. Evelyn Leonard Berridge Boothby, R.N.
Comdr. William Marshall, R.D., R.N.R.
Comdr. Alfred Spencer Gibb, R.D., R.N.R.
Lt.-Com. Hugh Edward M. Archer, R.N.R.
Lt.-Com. (Act.-Com.) G. W. Cavendish Venn, R.N.R.

Distinguished Service Cross.

Lieut. George Metcalf Mercer, R.N.R.
Lieut. Albert James Coles, R.N.R.
Lieut. Horace Bowyer Smith, R.N.R.
Lieut. V. Lamonnarie Delves Broughton, R.N.R.
Lieut. George Worley, R.N.R.
Lieut. Henry James Bray, R.N.R.
Lieut. Hugh Holmes, R.N.R.
Lieut. Frederick Henry Peterson, R.N.R.
Lieut. William Rodger Mackintosh, R.N.R.
Lieut. Albert Charles Allman, R.N.R.
Lieut. Allan Lansley, R.N.R.
Sub-Lt. (now Act. Lt.-Com.) W. Olphert, R.N.R.
Act.-Lt. Walter George Morgan, R.N.R.
Act.-Lt. Robert Linaker, R.N.R.
Sub-Lt. Thomas Francis Lanktree, R.N.R.
C. Gnr. (now Lieut.) Michael Carey, R.N.
Skipper Jabez George King, R.N R.
Skipper Alexander Watt, R.N.R.
Skipper Albert Wators, R.N.R.
Skipper William Bruce, R.N.R.
Skipper Andrew Noble Duthie, R.N.R.
Skipper Leonard Morley, R.N.R.
Skipper Alfred Alexander, R.N.R.
Skipper James Edwin Mitchell Duncan, R.N.R.

Distinguished Service Medal.

P.O., 1st Cl., Charles Reid, R.F.R.
L.S. James Bright, R.F.R.

The following officers are mentioned for their services in vessels of the Auxiliary Patrol:

Comdr. Odiarne Unett Coates, R.N.
Comdr. Ronald Scott Jervoise Wigram, R.N.
Comdr. Samuel Robson Crabtree, R.N.
Lt.-Com. John Walter Pugh, R.N.
Lieut. Charles Wood, R.N.R.
Lieut. Charles Claude Humphreys, R.N.R.
Act.-Lt. Joseph Cowie Gibson, R.N.R.
Act.-Lt. Henry Brodie Conby, R.N.R.
Eng. Sub-Lt. E. S. Manning, R.N.R. (since died).
Skipper Thomas May, R.N.R.
Skipper William Parker, R.N.R.
Skipper Herbert Knights, R.N.R.
Skipper James Sidney Harris, R.N.R.

Skipper George Daniel Thacker, R.N.R.
Skipper William Alfred Capps, R.N.R.

The Retreat from Serbia.

The King has also been pleased to give orders for the following appointments and awards in recognition of their services in connection with the evacuation of the Serbian Army and Italian troops from Durazzo in December, 1915, and January and February, 1916:

D.S.O.

Capt. Denis Burke Crampton, M.V.O., R.N.
Comdr. James Olden Hatcher, R.N.
Lt.-Com. Morris Edward Cochrane, R.N.

Distinguished Service Cross.

Act.-Lt. Arnaud Adams, R.N.R.
Act.-Lt. Edward Maitland Rae, R.N.R.
Act.-Lt. Harry Cuthbertson Campbell Fry, R.N.R.
Skipper Robert Aaron George, R.N.R.
Skipper John Hughes, R.N.R.
Skipper Frederick James Andrews, R.N.R.
Skipper William James Dow, R.N.R.
Skipper William Cowie, R.N.R.
Skipper Walter Charles Alfred Scrivener, R.N.R.
Skipper Hugh Mortimer Nesling, R.N.R.

The following officer is mentioned:
Sub-Lt. Harold Barnett Deakin, R.N.R. (killed in action).

OTHER SERVICES,

D.S.O.

Comdr. the Hon. R. O. B. Bridgeman, R.N.
Comdr. Bridgeman displayed great courage and coolness on the 19th August, 1915, in command of two whalers which proceeded into Tanga Harbour. The manner in which the whalers endeavoured, though subjected to a heavy and accurate fire, to carry out their orders and board the s.s. "Markgraf" was worthy of the best traditions of the Royal Navy.

Comdr. Henry Dalrymple Bridges, R.N.
Comdr. Bridges proceeded into Sudi Harbour with two whalers on the 11th April, 1916, and remained under fire with his vessels in a very hot corner, spotting the fall of shot from H.M.S. "Hyacinth" to enable her to destroy a storeship which was in the harbour. In order to reach the requisite position the whalers were obliged to run up a narrow harbour, where they were confronted with a heavy fire from 4in. guns at close range.

Distinguished Service Cross.

Lieut. Howard Canute Davis, R.D., R.N.R.
Lieut. Davis was in command of the whaler which led the way into Tanga Harbour on the 19th August, 1915.

Lieut. Herbert Keer Case, R.N.R.
Lieut. Case was in command of one of the whalers which proceeded into Sudi Harbour on the 11th April, 1916, and handled his vessel under fire in the confined waters of the harbour with great skill and gallantry. His quiet and calm behaviour set a perfect example to those under him.

Boatswain John Park Mortimore, R.N.
Mr. Mortimore was in one of the whalers which entered Sudi Harbour on the 11th April, 1916, and gave every assistance to his captain, encouraging the guns' crews, making good spotting corrections, and rendering first-aid readily and efficiently to the wounded.

CONSPICUOUS GALLANTRY MEDAL.

A.B. Lawrence J. Walsh, R.N.R.
In recognition of his services in one of the whalers which entered Sudi Harbour on the 11th April, 1916. He continued to steer the whaler after bring seriously wounded, his leg being badly shattered, until out of range of gun fire, when it was possible to remove the conning tower plates and relieve him.

DISTINGUISHED SERVICE MEDAL.

P.O., 1st Cl., G. E. Hayman, R.F.R.
L.-Sig. T. Down, R.F.R.

The following officers are mentioned for their services in the action between H.M.S. "Alcantara" and S.M.S. "Greif" on February 29th, 1916:

Lieut. Ernest Alva Hernandez, R.N.R.
Surg. John Parton Berry, R.N.
Act.-Lt. George Henry Walker Williamson, R.N.R.
Sub-Lt. Alfred Wallace Kay, R.N.R.
Eng. Sub-Lt. Reginald J. Mackintosh, R.N.R.

PROMOTIONS.

Royal Naval Reserve.—Temp. Eng.-Sub-Lts. to be Temp. Eng. Lts.:—Alfred King, Alexander Stevenson, Hugh Marr, Bert John Parker, David Robbie, William Henry Johns, Francis John Bradshaw, William Youngman Streader, Jim Horace Osborn, James Reston Campbell, Aaron Dann, Thompson Reid, Edward Jones, William Curtis Martin, John Mariott Clinch, to date July 14th, 1916.

A special supplement to the *London Gazette*, issued September 6th, 1916, contained the following awards:

ORDER OF ST. MICHAEL AND ST. GEORGE.

The King has been graciously pleased to give directions for the following appointments to the Most Distinguished Order of St. Michael and St. George, in recognition of services with the Royal Naval Division in the Gallipoli Peninsula:

THIRD CLASS, OR COMPANIONS.

Lt.-Col. (now 2nd Comdt.) E. J. Stroud, R.M.L.I.
Lt.-Col. A. R. H. Hutchison, R.M.L.I.
Temp. Lt.-Col. L. O. Wilson, D.S.O., M.P. (Res. of Off., R.M.).
Fleet-Surg. E. J. Finch, R.N.

D.S.O.

The King has been graciously pleased to give orders for the appointment of the undermentioned officers to be Companions of the Distinguished Service Order:

Lt.-Com. T. S. L. Dorman, R.N.
For his gallant conduct at Reshire on September 9th, 1915, when he volunteered and endeavoured to bring a machine-gun into action, exposed to a heavy fire from the enemy, at about 300 yards' range. A Yeoman of Signals, who accompanied Lt.-Com. Dorman, was mortally wounded.

Eng. Lt.-Com. W. H. Clarke, R.N.
After his ship had been holed below the water-line in action off the Belgian coast, he kept the engines running under most difficult conditions.

Lt.-Com. W. M. Egerton, R.N.V.R.
St.-Surg. A. F. Fleming, R.N.
Capt. (temp. Maj.) R. D. H. Lough, R.M.L.I.
In recognition of their services with the Royal Naval Division in the Gallipoli Peninsula.

D.S.C.

The King has further been graciously pleased to give orders for the award of

For Distinguished Service

the Distinguished Service Cross to the undermentioned officers :

Lieut. F. S. Kelly, R.N.V.R.
Capt. B. G. Weller, R.M.L.I.
Temp. Lieut. T. N. Riley, R.M.
In recognition of their services with the Royal Naval Division in the Gallipoli Peninsula.

Flight Sub.-Lt. R. S. Dallas, R.N.A.S.
Flight Sub-Lt. Dallas, in addition to performing consistently good work in reconnaissances and fighting patrols since December, 1915, has been brought to notice by the V.-A., Dover Patrol, for the specially gallant manner in which he has carried out his duties. Amongst other exploits is the following : On May 21st, 1916, he sighted at least 12 hostile machines which had been bombing Dunkerque. He attacked one at 7,000 feet, and then attacked a second machine close to him. After reloading, he climbed to 10,000 feet, and attacked a large hostile two-seater machine off Westende. The machine took fire and nose-dived seawards. Another enemy machine then appeared, which he engaged and chased to the shore, but had to abandon owing to having used all his ammunition.

Sub.-Lt. (now Act. Lt.) C. B. Oxley R.N.
Sub-Lt. Oxley was acting as observer with Flight-Lt. Edward H. Dunning, D.S.C., as pilot, on escort and reconnaissance patrol for a flight of bombing machines on the Bulgarian coast, on June 20th, 1916. Two enemy machines were engaged at close range and forced to retire, and as our machine withdrew Flight-Lt. Dunning was hit in the left leg and the machine itself was badly damaged. Sub.-Lt. Oxley, having first improvised a tourniquet, which he gave to Flight Lt. Dunning, took control of the machine, whilst the latter put on the tourniquet. The pilot was obliged to keep his thumb over a hole in the lower part of the petrol tank in order to keep enough fuel to return to the aerodrome, where he made an exceedingly good landing.

Flight Sub-Lt. D. E. Harkness, R.N.A.S.

Flight Sub-Lt. R. H. Collett, R.N.A.S.
In recognition of their services on the morning of August 9th, 1916, when they dropped bombs on the airship sheds at Evere and Berchem St. Agathe. Flight Sub-Lt. Collett dropped all his bombs on the shed at Evere from a height of between 300 and 500 feet, under very heavy rifle, machine-gun, and shrapnel fire from all directions. Flight Sub-Lt. Harkness could not descend so low owing to the very heavy anti-aircraft fire which had by this time opened on the machines, but he dropped some of his bombs on the shed, and then proceeded to Berchem St. Agathe, which he also bombed.

Act.-Lt. F. S. Lofthouse, R.N.R.
Lieut. Lofthouse showed admirable presence of mind on the occasion of the attack by an Austrian cruiser on a group of drifters in the Adriatic on July 9th, 1916. When the cruiser opened fire on his drifter at point-blank range, this officer ordered the crew to put on lifebelts, and immediately went to the wireless apparatus himself and twice sent out a message as to the presence of the cruiser. Whilst he was sending this message three shots hit the ship. He then came on deck, and, finding his ship was sinking, he got his crew overboard, and by his example and

behaviour kept them together until they were picked up six hours later.

Skipper H. J. Goldspink, R.N.R.

Skipper J. Ritchie, R.N.R.
Skipper Ritchie behaved in an admirable manner, and displayed great coolness under fire on the occasion of the attack by an Austrian cruiser on a group of drifters in the Adriatic on July 9th, 1916. He was instrumental in saving many lives by taking his drifter alongside damaged drifters and by picking up men who were in the water.

Skipper F. G. Harris, R.N.R.
Skipper Harris showed most seamanlike qualities on the occasion of the attack by an Austrian cruiser on a group of drifters in the Adriatic. He went to the assistance of the damaged drifters, took them in tow, and brought them safely into harbour.

C.G.M. AND D.S.M.

The following awards have also been approved:

Conspicuous Gallantry Medal.

Pte. T. H. Hoskins, R.M.L.I.
For conspicuous gallantry at Gaba Tepe, on April 30th, 1915, when, after volunteering for the duty, he moved across the open under very heavy and very close range fire to another sector of the outpost line with an urgent message for ammunition and water. Having delivered the message, he courageously attempted to return to his unit, and in doing so was twice wounded.

Distinguished Service Medal.

L.S. F. W. Andrews.
L.S. C. J. Colbran.
Act. L. Sto. H. Heath.
Qrmr. J. Drinkall; Mercantile Rating.
Pte. G. Yates, R.M.L.I.

Royal Naval Division:
Corpl. J. McDowell. R.M.L.I.
Corpl. A. R. Grainger, R.M.L.I
Pte. C. R. Bell, R.M.L.I.
Sergt. J. C. Dunn, R.M.L.I.
Sergt. M. W. Minter, R.M.L.I.
A.B. G. Ramsey, R.N.V.R.
Lce.-Corpl. D. G. Denyer, R.M.L.I.
Pte. H. Mills, R.M.L.I.
Pte. A. Dunkley, R.M., Medical Unit.
Pte. P. Berry, R.M.L.I.
Sto. T. Bell, R.N.V.R.
Lce.-Sergt. P. Wolstenholme, R.M.L.I.
Sto. T. Arnold.
Sapper W. Bottomley, R.M.
Sergt. A. H. Hunting, R.M.L.I.
A.B. G. W. James, R.N.V.R.
A.B. D. Bullen, R.N.V.R.
Pte. F. Hunt, R.M.L.I.

Nigerian Marine (Natives): Isaac, Deckhand; Yesufu, Boatswain. Angus, Chief Engineer; Sam Druder, Boatswain; William M'Beh, Quartermaster.

Bar to D.S.M.

The undermentioned rating has been awarded a Bar to his Distinguished Service Medal for a subsequent act of gallantry:

L. Sig. I. Overton.
The award of the Distinguished Service Medal was notified in the *Gazette* dated August 16th, 1915, page 8,135.

Promotions.

The following promotions have been made for distinguished service with the Royal Naval Division, with effect from May 1st, 1911, inclusive:

To be Brevet Lieutenant-Colonels

Major (temp. Lt.-Col.) J. A. Tupman (Reserve of Officers, R.M.).
Major J. A. M. A. Clark, R.M.L.I.
Major (temp. Lt.-Col.) N. O. Burge, R.M.L.I.

For Distinguished Service

To be Brevet Major.

Capt. (temp. Major) M. C. Festing, R.M.L.I.

Mentioned in Despatches.

The following have been mentioned in despatches for good services in action:

Lt.-Com. A. J. L. Murray, R.N.
Yeo. Sigs. F. S. Wood (killed in action).
Nigerian Marine (Natives): Joshua Cockburn, Master of the Flotilla Storeship "Trojan."
Nigerian Marine (Natives): Isiah Briggs, Quartermaster; Pom Pom: Deckhand; Micassa Dumba (locally entered); Ndgea Noah (locally entered)

Corrections.

The name of Deckhand Roger Brown Martin, R.N., Trawler Reserve, O.N. 1377 D.A., which appeared in the list of men awarded the Distinguished Service Medal on page 87 of the *Gazette* of January 1st, 1916, should read: Trimmer Robert Martin, R.N.R. (Trawler Section), O.N. 654 T.S.

The name of C.P.O. Harry Nelson, R.N.A.S., O.N. F.8945, which appeared in the list of men mentioned in despatches on page 4,833 of the *Gazette* of May 15th, 1916, should read: C.P.O. Mechanic Hugh Nelson, R.N.A.S. O.N. 272016.

DOVER PATROL.

List of Recommendations.

The following is the list of officers and men recommended by R.-A. Sir R. Bacon in his despatch dealing with the operations of the Dover Naval Patrol:

Capt. F. S. Litchfield-Speer, D.S.O.
Carried out several important operations under difficult circumstances off the enemy's coast.

Comdr. George Louis Downall Gibbs.
Commanded a division of destroyers with marked ability and dash in action against the enemy.
Comdr. Henry Gerard Laurence Oliphant, M.V.O.
Commanded a division of destroyers in action and on patrol duties off the enemy's coast.
Comdr. Reginald Lionel Hancock.
Carried out surveying operations of considerable importance under heavy gun fire off the enemy's coast.
Lieut. Henry Forrester.
Carried out dangerous patrol duties with marked ability.
Lieut. Rudolf Henry Fane De Salis.
Commanded a detached division on several occasions in close proximity to the enemy's coast.
Act.-Lt. James Towrie Muir, R.N.R.
In command of a division of drifters during several operations off the enemy's coast.
Skipper Robert George Hurren, R.N.R.
Distinguished conduct which led to the destruction of an enemy submarine boat.
C.Art. Eng. Thomas Robson Hall, R.N.
Exceptional services during war operations.
Comdr. Edward Ratcliffe Garth Russell Evans, C.B., R.N.
Lt.-Com. John Stewart Gordon Fraser, R.N.
Lt.-Com. Montague Robert Bernard, R.N.
Lieut. John Cracroft-Amcotts, R.N.
Lieut. James Douglas Godfrey, D.S.C., R.N.
Sub.-Lt. Robert Don. Oliver, R.N.
Skipper Isaac Lilly Manthorpe, R.N.R.
C.-Gunr. John Steel, R.N.
Art.-Eng. William George Jackson, R.N.

Men Recommended.

Yeo. of Sigs. A. W. Harding.
C. Sto. J. Brown.

L. Sig. J. Wise.
P.O. 1st Class, C. W. Moore.
C. E.R. Art. R. Sheppard.
C.P.O. H. Barber.
C.E.R. Art. Robert Shires.
E.R. Art. 1st Class, H. H. Robertson.
C.E.R. Art. 1st. Cl., G. F. Cockrell.
Act. C.P.O. Wm. Ewles.
Sto. P.O. A. A. Bradley.
Stoker Edward Madden.
C.P.O. Charles Darton.
Ch. Armourer J. T. Lewis.
Ch. Armourer H. Goodwin.
P.O. J. Hailstone.
Elec.-Art., 2nd Cl., H. A. Hughes.
L.S. C. H. Holmes.
C.P.O. T. A. W. Collard.
Sig. J. C. Duley.
C.P.O. Jas. Southwood.
2nd Hand J. Gardiner, R.N.R.
2nd Hand W. J. Sutton.
2nd Hand F. W. Saunders, R.N.R.
Ch. Motor Boatman G. Culverwell.
C.E.R. Art. G. Barrowman.
L.Sig. G. V. McKenzie.
L.Sig. C. W. Lumley.
L.Sig. R. Giddings.
C.E.R. Art. A. Matthews.
C.E.R. Art. J. E. Pether.
L.Sig. T. Young.
E.R. Art. L. C. Boggust.
P.O. Charles Nason.
L.S. Albert Mercer.
P.O. William Foley.
Act. C.P.O. W. J. Brown.
A.S. William Austin.
P.O. W. A. Osborne.
L.S. E. Savage.
Yeo. of Sig. W. C. Chapman.
A.B. William Austin.
A.B. O. J. Broers.
P.O., 1st Cl., G. Arlingham.
P.O. G. J. L. Staff.
P.O. J. Penman.
Engineman J. Berry, R.N.R.
Stoker (Act. Engineman) D. B. Knowles, R.N.R.
A.B. W. J. Hunt, R.N.R.
Deck Hand James Latta, R.N.R.

L. Deck Hand William Wigg.
Deck Hand Francis William Beamish, R.N.R.

The Admiralty further announces that the King has been graciously pleased to give orders for the following appointments to the Distinguished Service Order and for the award of the Distinguished Service Cross to the undermentioned officers in recognition of their services as mentioned in the foregoing despatch:

TO BE COMPANIONS OF THE DISTINGUISHED SERVICE ORDER.

Comdr. George Louis Downall Gibbs, R.N.
Comdr. Reginald Lionel Hancock, R.N.
Comdr. Henry Gerard Laurence Oliphant, M.V.O., R.N.

TO RECEIVE THE DISTINGUISHED SERVICE CROSS.

Lieut. Henry Forrester, R.N.
Act. Lt. James Towrie Muir, R.N.R.
Skipper Robert George Hurren, R.N.R.
C.Art. Eng. Thomas Robson Hall, R.N.

TO RECEIVE THE DISTINGUISHED SERVICE MEDAL.

C.P.O. Harry Barber.
C.P.O. Thomas Arthur William Collard.
C.P.O. Charles Darton.
C.P.O. James Samuel Southwood.
Act. C.P.O. William Ewles.
P.O. Jesse Hailstone.
P.O., 1st Cl., Charles William Moore.
L.S. Charles Henry Holmes.
Yeo. of Sig. Alfred William Harding.
L.Sig. Joseph Wise.
Signalman Joseph Charles Duley.
C.E.R. Art., 1st Cl., George Frederick Cockrell.
C.E.R. Art., 2nd Cl., Richard Sheppard.

For Distinguished Service

C.E.R. Art., 2nd Cl., John Robert Shires.
E.R. Art., 1st Cl., Harry Robertson.
Elec. Art., 2nd Cl., Harold Archibald Hughes.
C.Sto. James Brown.
Sto. P.O. Arthur Alfred Bradley.
Stoker, 1st. Cl., Edward Madden.
Ch. Armourer Harry Goodwin.
Ch. Armourer Jams Thomas Lewis.
Ch. Motor Boatman W. G. Culverwell.
Second Hand John Gardiner, R.N.R.
Second Hand Florence Westgate Saunders, R.N.R.
Second Hand Walter James Sutton, R.N.R.
Deck Hand Francis William Beamish, R.N.R.

The following officers and men are commended for service in action :

Capt. Frederick Shirley Litchfield-Speer, D.S.O., R.N.
Comdr. Edward Ratcliffe Garth Russell Evans, C.B., R.N.
Lieut. Rudolf Henry Fane De Salis, R.N.
Lt.-Com. John Stewart Gordon, R.N.
Lt.-Com. Montague Robert Bernard, R.N.
Lieut. John Cracroft-Amcotts, R.N.
Lieut. James Douglas Godfrey, D.S.C., R.N.
Sub-Lt. Robert Don Oliver, R.N.
Skipper Isaac Lilly Manthorpe, R.N.R.
Ch. Gunner John Steel, R.N.
Art. Eng. William George Jackson, R.N.
Act. C.P.O. William Joseph Brown.
P.O., 1st Cl., George Allingham.
P.O. William Foley.
P.O. Charles Nason.
P.O. William Arthur Osborn.
P.O. James Penman.
P.O. George John Louis Staff.
L.S. Ernest Savage.
L.S. Albert Mercer.
A.B. William Charles Austen.
A.B. Oliver Joseph Broers.
A.B. William Joseph Hunt.
Yeo. of Sig. Wilfred Cubit Chapman.
L.Sig. Robert Giddings.
L.Sig. Charles William Lumley.
L.Sig. George Victor Mackenzie.
L.Sig. Thomas Young.
C.E.R. Art., 2nd Cl., George Dunsmuir Barrowman.
C.E.R. Art., 2nd Cl., Arthur Matthews,
C.E.R. Art., 2nd Cl., John Ernest Pether.
E.R. Art. 2nd Cl., Limbrough Charles Boggust.
Deck Hand James Latta, R.N.R. (Special service).
L. Deck Hand William Wigg, R.N.R. (Special service).
Engineman John Berry, R.N.R.
Stoker David Bannerman (Act. Eng.),
Stoker (Act. Engineman) David Bannerman Knowles, R.N.R.

Admiralty, S.W., 15th Sept., 1916.

The following despatch has been received from Admiral Sir John R. Jellicoe, G.C.B., G.C.V.O., Commander in-Chief, Grand Fleet :

" Iron Duke," Aug. 23rd, 1916.

SIR,—With reference to my despatch of 24th June, 1916, I have the honour to bring to the notice of the Lords Commissioners of the Admiralty the names of the following officers who are recommended for honours and special commendation.

Where all carried out their duties so well it is somewhat invidious and difficult to select officers for special recognition. As regards the Flag Officers, I would again draw the attention of their Lordships to the remarks made in that despatch on the subject of their services, and I would recommend for honours :

Adml. Sir Cecil Burney, K.C.B., K.C.M.G.

D

V.A. Sir Thomas Henry Martyn Jerram, K.C.B.
V.A. Sir Frederick Charles Doveton Sturdee, Bart., K.C.B., C.V.O., C.M.G.
V.A. Sir David Beatty, K.C.B., K.C.V.O., D.S.O. (Commanding the Battle Cruiser Squadron).
R.A. Hugh Evan-Thomas, C.B.,M.V.O.
R.A. Alexander Ludovic Duff, C.B., (Civil).
R.A. William Christopher Pakenham, C.B., M.V.O.
R.A. Arthur Cavenagh Leveson, C.B., (Civil).
R.A. Ernest Frederic Augustus Gaunt, C.M.G.
R.A. Osmond De Beauvoir Brock, C.B.

Although R.A. Evan-Thomas has but recently received the C.B., I would draw attention to the fact that he commands a Battle Squadron which was closely engaged, and that he is, with the exception of R.A. Heath, the senior R.A. in the Grand Fleet.

R.A. Herbert Leopold Heath, C.B., M.V.O.,
would have been recommended for an honour had he not so recently received the C.B.
Commodore Charles Edward Le Mesurier,
whose squadron was handled with great ability.
R.A. Trevylan Dacres Willes Napier, C.B., M.V.O.
would have been recommended for an honour had he not so recently recently received the C.B.
R.A. William Edmund Goodenough, C.B., M.V.O.,
who with great tenacity kept touch with the enemy's battle fleet during the afternoon of 31st May, and
Commodore Edwyn Sinclair Alexander-Sinclair, C.B., M.V.O., A.D.C.,
who first gained touch with the enemy forces. would have been recommended for an honour had they not so recently received the C.B.

2. The remarks of the Flag or Commanding Officers of the Squadrons concerned, in which I concur, have been inserted after the names of the officers recommended in the following list:

LIST OF OFFICERS RECOMMENDED FOR HONOURS FOR SERVICE IN THE BATTLE OF JUTLAND.

Capt. Frederic Charles Dreyer, C.B., (Civil), R.N.
Commanded and handled the Fleet Flagship most ably during the action. The rapidity with which hitting was established on ships of the enemy's fleet was the result of long and careful organisation and training of the personnel.

Comdr. Geoffrey Blake, R.N.
Gunnery and principal control officer of H.M.S. "Iron Duke," whose zeal, knowledge, and devotion to duty throughout the war and coolness and skill in action resulted in severe damage being inflicted by "Iron Duke's" 13.5inch guns on a German battleship of the "Koenig" class in the action off the coast of Jutland on May 31st.

Remarks of Admiral Sir Cecil Burney.

Capt. Edmund Percy Fenwick George Grant, R.N. (Commodore 2nd Cl.).
My Chief of Staff, who afforded me very valauble assistance during the action.

Capt. George Parish Ross, R.N.
My Flag Captain, who helped me greatly during the action. He fought his ship well, and subsequently, after she was torpedoed, successfully

For Distinguished Service

took "Marlborough" back to harbour, avoiding attack by two submarines on the way.

Capt. Lewis Clinton-Baker, R.N.
The Senior Captain in the First Battle Squadron at the time of the action. His valuable services are worthy of recognition.

Comdr. Hugh Schomberg Currey, R.N.
Executive officer of "Marlborough," whose untiring energy and skilful work greatly assisted in saving the ship after she was torpedoed.

Engineer Comdr. Reginald William Skelton, R.N.
A valuable officer whose department during the action reflected credit on his organisation.

Fleet Surgeon Henry William Finlayson, M.B., R.N.
A zealous and hardworking officer, who organised his department in an efficient manner for the action.

Staff Paymaster Herbert Patrick William George Murray, R.N. (Secretary to Second in Command).
My Secretary, whose services were most valuable to me during the action.

Lt.-Com. James Buller Kitson, R.N.
My Flag Lieutenant-Commander, who was of very great assistance to me during the action.

Remarks of Vice-Admiral Sir Martyn Jerram.

Capt. Michael Culme-Seymour, M.V.O., R.N., (now Rear-Admiral).
Sub-Divisional Leader, An officer of great experience, who handled his sub-division with excellent judgment throughout the action.

Capt. Hugh Henry Darby Tothill, A.D.C., R.N.
Sub-Divisional Leader. Handled his sub-division most skilfully throughout the action, and amply justified the high opinion I have always held of him.

Capt. Frederick Laurence Field, R.N.
Handled " King George V." as leader of the line of battle with great skill under very difficult conditions. His previous good services in the Signal School and Vernon are well known.

Deputy Inspector - General Robert Forbes Bowie, R.N.
Displayed a high degree of ability during the action in the working of the medical department.

Eng.-Comdr. William Cory Sanders, R.N.
A very capable and zealous officer, who showed great ability throughout the action in the working of the engine-room department.

Comdr. Richard Horne, R.N.
An officer of great ability, who conned "Orion" throughout the action with ability and skill.

Comdr. John Walsh Carrington, R.N.
An officer of great ability, who conned " King George V." throughout the action with good judgment and prompt decision. He was navigating officer of H.M.S. " Inflexible " in the action off the Falkland Islands and in the Dardanelles.

Remarks of V.A. Sir Doveton Sturdee.

Capt. William Coldingham Masters Nicholson, R.N. (now R.A.).
Took his ship into action in a fine manner, and by the effective gunfire of his command materially assisted in forcing the enemy to retire.

Eng.-Capt. John Richardson, R.N.
Was personally responsible for the excellent organisation of the engine

room and stokehold departments in every ship of the squadron. The maximum speeds were obtained in all cases without mishap, though in the older ships the authorised horse-power was exceeded.

Lt.-Col. Charles Edwin Collard, R.M.L.I.
Very materially assisted in controlling the gunfire of H.M.S. "Benbow" from an exposed position. This officer has seen much war service previously in East and South Africa.

Fleet Surgeon Joseph Agnew Moon, R.N.
Was responsible for the excellent medical arrangements for dealing with the wounded in H.M.S. "Benbow" which were very efficient.

Capt. Henry Wise Parker, R.N.
Was of great assistance to me as my Flag Captain. He showed great coolness and judgment in his handling of the ship and its fighting power. Captain Parker was Commander of the "Lion" in the Heligoland action of 28th August, 1914.

Paymaster Cyril Sheldon Johnson, R.N.
Rendered valuable services as my Secretary in keeping records and generally assisting me during the action. His name was mentioned in despatches after the Falkland Islands action.

Eng.-Comdr. Robert Spence, R.N.
By his general management of the machinery and stokers under his orders in H.M.S. "Vanguard" enabled the ship to be taken into and maintained in action in a most effective manner.

Remarks of R.A. Evan-Thomas.

Capt. Edward Montgomery Phillpotts, R.N.
At a critical time, when the Fifth Battle Squadron was turning to form astern of the battle fleet, under a heavy fire, "Warspite," owing to a breakdown in her steering gear, turned towards the enemy and got into a very dangerous position. She was splendidly handled, however, and got away to the northward clear of the enemy's fire. Also when nearing the Firth of Forth, much damaged, she was attacked by three submarines and was handled in such a manner as to get her safely into port. Captain Phillpotts is the senior Captain in the ships of the Fifth Battle Squadron which were engaged, and I strongly recommend him for an honour worthy of his great services.

Capt. Maurice Woollcombe, R.N.

Capt. Arthur William Craig, R.N.
The Rear-Admiral Commanding reports that the ships under his orders were handled and fought by their Captains in the manner one would expect from those officers and in accordance with the best traditions of the British Navy.

Comdr. Humphrey Thomas Walwyn, R.N.
Commander Walwyn, from the moment the first shell struck the ship, managed to be everywhere where attention was necessary in putting out fires, plugging holes, shoring, etc., with the fire brigade and repair parties. Considering the size of the ship and the damage sustained, and also the fact that he was keeping the Captain fully informed of her condition, the work effected by Commander Walwyn in the short space of time was marvellous, and the Captain considers it greatly due to his prompt action that much water was prevented from access into the port wing and main engine rooms.

For Distinguished Service

Rev. Anthony Pollen (Roman Catholic Chaplain).

The Reverend Anthony Pollen carried men injured by severe burns from the battery deck to the distributing station, he himself being severely burned at the time. Aged 56.

Lieut. John Gordon Cliff-McCulloch. R.N.R.

Lieut. Cliff-McCulloch was in charge of the port battery, and immediately went across and in a short space of time the fire had been got under and the situation was in hand, and Nos. 1 and 6 6-inch starboard were ready to open fire in ten minutes from the explosion. This is due to the prompt action taken by Lieut. McCulloch, and his example had undoubtedly a good effect on a large number of very young men stationed there.

Comdr. Henry John Studholme Brownrigg, R.N.

Comdr. Brownrigg took charge of and conducted the operations in connection with dealing with fires and repairs to damage by shell. He was continually in positions of greatest danger and where the conditions were most trying to the nerves. His example inspired all those under him, and he was largely instrumental in keeping the ship in effective fighting condition to the end of the action, notwithstanding the severe damage from shell fire.

Remarks of R.A. Herbert L. Meath.

Capt. Eustace La Trobe Leatham, R.N.

For the very able and efficient manner in which he handled his ship throughout the action.

Capt. John Summarez Dumaresq, M.V.O., R.N.

For the very able and efficient manner in which he handled his ship throughout the action.

Capt. Arthur Cloudesley Shovel Hughes D'Aeth, R.N.

For the untiring zeal and energy displayed throughout the action, and during the events preceding and subsequent thereto, when he handled my flagship with marked ability and was of the greatest assistance to me.

Eng.-Capt. Arthur Frederick Kingsnorth, R.N.

Engineer-Captain of the First Cruiser Squadron recommended by the R.A. Commanding Second Cruiser Squadron.

Comdr. James Geoffrey Penrose Ingham, R.N.

Eng.-Comdr. Henry Walton Kitching, R.N.

Remarks of Commodore Charles E. Le Mesurier.

Staff - Surgeon Bertram Raleigh Bickford, R.N.

For great gallantry and devotion to duty in action. This officer, though severely wounded by a shell splinter, persisted in attending to the wounded, only yielding to a direct order from myself to place himself on the sick list.

Remarks of V.A. Sir David Beatty

Capt. Rudolf Walter Bentinck, R.N. (Chief of Staff to Vice-Admiral Commanding Battle Cruiser Fleet).
For very valuable services in the action and throughout the war.

Act. Paymaster Frank Todd Spickernell, R.N. (Secretary to the V.A. Commanding Battle Cruiser Fleet).
For very valuable services in the action and throughout the war.

Lt.-Com. Ralph Frederick Seymour, R.N. (Flag Lt.-Com. to V.A. Commanding Battle Cruiser Fleet)
For very valuable services in the action and throughout the war.

Capt. Alfred Ernle Montacute Chatfield, C.V.O., C.B., R.N. (Flag Capt. to V.A. Commanding Battle Cruiser Fleet).
Commanded and fought my Flagship with great skill and gallantry.

Lt.-Com. Gerald Fortescue Longhurst, R.N. (now Comdr.).
Gunnery Officer of my Flagship. Controlled the fire of "Lion" with greatest coolness, courage, and skill, and inflicted immense damage on the enemy. This is the third time he has controlled the fire of the "Lion" in action.

Fleet-Surgeon Alexander Maclean, M.B., R.N.
Performed his exhausting duties with the greatest zeal and courage. The medical staff was seriously depleted by casualties; the wounded and dying had to be dressed under very difficult conditions on the mess deck, which was flooded with a foot of water from damaged fire mains. Fleet-Surgeon Maclean has suffered considerably since the action from his devotion to duty.

Lieut. (E.) Stewart Magee Walker, R.N.
The command of the mess deck devolved on Lieut. Walker in the absence on duty of the commander of the ship. He grappled successfully with very difficult and trying situations, putting out extensive fires in a blinding and suffocating atmosphere, saving life from asphyxiation, clearing compartments of water, and flooding magazines.

Capt. Walter Henry Cowan, M.V.O., D.S.O., R.N.
Commanded and fought the "Princess Royal" with great skill and gallantry.

Eng. Lt.-Com. Albert Arthur Green Martell, R.N.
In charge of all fire and salvage parties, and directed and led them with complete success, setting an example of coolness and vigour of action which unquestionably prevented far more serious damage.

Art.-Eng. Joseph House, R.N.
When the ship was hit and badly damaged, effected repairs to pipes under very difficult circumstances of smoke and darkness, whereby fires were got under which otherwise must have been a very grave danger.

Capt. Henry Bertram Pelly, M.V.O., R.N.
Commanded and fought "Tiger" with great skill and gallantry.

Lieut. Percy Harrison, R.N.V.R.
His work with the fire brigade was beyond praise. He was gassed badly, but continued work until noon the next day, clearing debris, etc., and only gave up when his lungs would stand no more, and he was placed on the sick list.

Carpenter-Lt. John Norman Matheson, R.N.
Did splendid work below. Although taken to the dressing-station twice, once gassed, and once nearly drowned he insisted on going back to his work, and only rested when ordered by the Commander to do so on the following morning.

Capt. John Frederick Ernest Green, R.N.
Commanded and fought "New Zealand" with great skill and gallantry.

Capt. Francis William Kennedy, R.N. (now R.A.).
Commanded the Third Battle Cruiser Squadron after the loss of R. A. Hood

and fought his ship with great skill and gallantry.

Capt. Edward Henry Fitzhardinge Heaton-Ellis, M.V.O., R.N.
Commanded and fought "Inflexible" with great skill and gallantry.

Comdr. Hubert Edward Dannreuther, R.N.
The senior of the two surviving officers of the "Invincible.' Up to the moment when the ship blew up Comdr. Dannreuther controlled the fire of "Invincible" in a manner which produced visible and overwhelming results on the enemy.

Capt. Bertram Sackville Thesiger, C.M.G., R.N.
Assumed command of a Light Cruiser Squadron when "Galatea" was temporarily disabled by shell fire, and fought his ship with great skill and gallantry.

Capt. Charles Blois Miller, R.N.
Commanded and fought "Nottingham" with great skill and gallantry.

Lieut. Arthur Malcolm Peters, R.N.
His coolness and clearness on this occasion, and his constant care and attention in regard to the signals and communications of the squadron during the past three years, enabled the fullest advantage to be taken when reporting the enemy's battle fleet.

Comdr. Malcolm Henry Somerled Macdonald, R.N.
For his coolness in the night action, when he extinguished the fires on the mess deck, and his prompt action in preventing the fore magazine from being flooded.

Capt. John Douglas Edwards, R.N.
Commanded and fought the "Falmouth" with great skill and gallantry.

Capt. Edward Bamford, R.M.L.I.
In after control when it was blown to pieces by a shell burst. Slightly burnt in face and slightly wounded in leg. Then assisted to work one gun with a much reduced crew, and controlled another gun. Assisted in extinguishing a fire, and in general showed great coolness, power of command, judgment, and courage, when exposed to a very heavy fire.

Lieut. Frederick Joseph Rutland, R.N. (Flight-Lt., R.N.A.S.).
For his gallantry and persistence in flying within close range of four enemy light cruisers, in order to enable accurate information to be obtained and transmitted concerning them. Conditions at the time made low flying necessary.

Lt.-Com. Laurence Reynolds Palmer, R.N.
For his gallantry, when his destroyer was disabled, in proceeding to the assistance of "Onslow" and taking her in tow under heavy shell fire. He succeeded in towing her in a heavy sea until relieved by tugs when in sight of land.

Lieut. Jack Ernest Albert Mocatta, R.N.
Supported Commander Bingham, "Nestor," in his gallant action against destroyers, battle cruisers, and battleships, in the most courageous and effective manner.

Lt.-Com. Roger Vincent Alison, R.N.
For promptness and gallantry in taking advantage of the opportunity of attacking the enemy's vessels with the torpedo on two occasions, as described in my original despatch.

Lt.-Com. Montague George Bentinck Legge, R.N.
Having defeated the enemy destroyers, gallantly pressed home attack with torpedoes on the enemy battle cruisers.

Lt.-Com. Cuthbert Patrick Blake, R.N
Having defeated the enemy destroyers, gallantly pressed home attack with torpedoes on the enemy battle cruisers.

RECOMMENDED FOR VICTORIA CROSS·

Comdr. the Hon. Edward Barry Stewart Bingham, R.N. (prisoner of war).

For the extremely gallant way in which he led his division in their atttack first on enemy destroyers and then on their battle cruisers.

He finally sighted the enemy battle fleet, and followed by the one remaining destroyer of his division (" Nicator "), with dauntless courage he closed to within 3,000 yards of the enemy in order to attain a favourable position for firing the torpedoes. While making this attack, " Nestor " and " Nicator " were under concentrated fire of the secondary batteries of the High Sea Fleet. " Nestor " was subsequently sunk.

Major Francis John William Harvey, R.M.L.I.

Recommended for Posthumous Victoria Cross.

Whilst mortally wounded and almost the only survivor after the explosion of an enemy shell in " Q " gunhouse, with great presence of mind and devotion to duty ordered the magazine to be flooded, thereby saving the ship. He died shortly afterwards.

Remarks of Capt. Percy M. R. Royds.

Lt.-Com. Cecil Charles Brittain Vacher, R.N.

For controlling the fire from the ship in the coolest manner from a very exposed position under extremely heavy fire.

Lieut. Cuthbert Coppinger, R.N.

For navigating the ship in the coolest manner from a very exposed position under extremely heavy fire.

Remarks of Capt. Walter L. Allen.

Lt.-Com. Gordon Alston Coles, R.N.

The commander of his division speaks highly of the way he conned his ship. Ambuscade fired three torpedoes, and the rapid reloading under fire reflects credit on all concerned, and proves the ship is in a high state of efficiency.

Comdr. Loftus William Jones, R.N.

Recommended the posthumous honour For fighting his ship until she sank, after having been seriously wounded.

Act. Sub.-Lt. Newton James Wallop William-Powlett, R.N. (now Sub-Lt.).

Very strongly recommended. This officer showed wonderful coolness under most trying circumstances, and his pluck and cheerfulness after the ship sank were certainly the means of saving the lives of several who would otherwise have given in and succumbed. I cannot speak too highly of this young officer's conduct throughout.

Surgeon Probationer Douglas George Patrick Bell, R.N.V.R.

Devoted great attention to the wounded, and amputated a limb single-handed in the dark.

Ch. Art. Eng. Alexander Noble, R.N.

Went twice into the after stokehold, but was driven out by steam. Succeeded at the third attempt and shut off auxiliary feed pump and auxiliary stop valve.

Remarks of Commodore James R. P. Hawkesley.

Staff-Surgeon James McAlister Holmes M.B., R.N.

For the very efficient manner in

which the wounded were attended to whilst under fire and subsequently.

Lt.-Com. Henry Ruthven Moore, R.N.
For the assistance he gave the Commodore (F), both during the day and night action, and the manner in which he carried out his duties.

Comdr. Harold Ernest Sulivan, R.N.
As second in command of the flotilla he manœuvred his half very ably during the daytime, and at night, when " Castor" could make no signals owing to damage by gunfire, he very ably turned his half-flotilla and kept clear of the first half-flotilla manœuvring.

Remarks of Capt. (D) Anselan J. B. Stirling.

Comdr. John Pelham Champion, R.N.
Handled his division with great ability whilst in action, and led his division to attack an enemy battle squadron with great gallantry.

Lieut. John Hinton Carrow, R.N.
Was on the bridge the whole time during the action, and carried out the duties of navigating officer in a most exemplary manner, and was of the greatest assistance to me in keeping me informed of the range and bearing of the enemy, especially during the night attack.

Eng.-Lt.-Com. John Kirk Corsar, R.N.
Kept his department in good order and kept the boiler water going in spite of evaporator being semi-disabled most of the time and out of action entirely for some period.

Remarks of Capt. Berwick Curtis.

Eng.-Lt.-Com. Harold Bertram Tostevin, R.N.
This officer's organisation of the engine-room department and general energy at all times, keeping the machinery of the ship in a thoroughly efficient state, contributed largely to the success of " Abdiel's " operations on the night of 31st May observing that the ship proceeded at full speed for over six hours.

Staff of the Commander-in-Chief (with remarks of Admiral Sir John Jellicoe).
V.A. Sir Charles Edward Madden, K.C.B., C.V.O., (Chief of the Staff).

Commodore Lionel Halsey, C.B., C.M.G., A.D.C. (Capt. of the Fleet).
The very valuable services of these officers are mentioned in my despatch of the 24th June, 1916. Commodore Halsey would have been recommended for an honour had he not so recently received the C.B.

Comdr. the Hon. Matthew Robert Best, M.V.O., R.N.
Has performed valuable staff work during the war and services during the action.

Comdr. Charles Morton Forbes, R.N.
My Flag Comdr., who has always afforded me great assistance. This officer was Executive Officer of H.M.S. " Queen Elizabeth " during the whole period that ship was employed at the Dardanelles.

Comdr. Alexander Riall Wadham Woods, R.N.
Controlled the visual signal work with great coolness and accuracy.

Comdr. Richard Lindsay Nicholson, R.N.
Controlled the wireless telegraph work with great coolness and most marked efficiency, and reaped the reward of the excellent organisation for which he is responsible.

Fleet- Paymaster Hamnet Holditch Share, C.B., R.N. (Secretary).
I should have recommended my Secretary, Fleet-Paymaster Share,

for an honour for his invaluable work during the war and assistance during the action had he not recently been awarded a C.B.

Fleet - Paymaster Victor Herbert Thomas Weekes, R.N. (Additional Secretary).
Has been of great assistance to me during the war and took valuable records throughout the action.

Admiralty, Sept., 15th, 1916.

The King has been graciously pleased to approve of the grant of the Victoria Cross to the following officers in recognition of their bravery and devotion to duty as described in the foregoing despatch :

Comdr. the Hon. Edward Barry Stewart Bingham, R.N. (prisoner of war in Germany).

Major Francis John William Harvey, R.M.L.I. (killed in action).

OTHER HONOURS.

Order of Merit.

The King has been graciously pleased to make the following appointment to the Order of Merit, to date from the 31st May, 1916 :

Adml. Sir John Rushworth Jellicoe, G.C.B., G.C.V.O., Commander-in-Chief, Grand Fleet.

Order of the Bath.

The King has been graciously pleased to give orders to the following promotions in, and appointments to, the Most Honourable Order of the Bath, in recognition of the services mentioned in the foregoing despatch. The promotions and appointments to date from May 31st, 1916 :

G.C.B. (Military Division) Additional Member.

V.A. Sir David Beatty, K.C.B., K.C.V.O., D.S.O.

K.C.B. (Military Division) Additional Members.

R.A. Hugh Evan-Thomas, C.B. M.V.O.

R.A. William Christopher Pakenham, C.B., M.V.O.

Posthumous K.C.B's.

The King has been graciously pleased to approve of the posthumous honour of Knights Commanderships of the Most Honourable Order of the Bath being conferred on the late R.A. Sir Robert Keith Arbuthnot, Bart., C.B., M.V.O., and the late R.A. the Hon. Horace Lambert Hood. C.B., M.V.O., D.S.O., who were killed in action on May 31st, 1916, in recognition of their services mentioned in the foregoing despatch.

C.B. (Military Division). Additional Members.

R.A. Alexander Ludovic Duff, C.B. (civil).

R.A. Arthur Cavenagh Leveson, C.B. (civil).

R.A. Ernest Frederic Augustus Gaunt, C.M.G.

R.A. Francis William Kennedy.

R.A. Michael Culme-Seymour, M.V.O.

R.A. William Coldingham Masters Nicholson.

Capt. Hugh Henry Darby Tothill A.D.C., R.N.

Capt. Henry Bertram Pelly, M.V.O., R.N. (Commdore, 2nd Cl.).

Capt. Lewis Clinton-Baker, R.N.

Capt. John Frederick Ernest Green, R.N.

Capt. Edward Montgomery Phillpotts, R.N.

For Distinguished Service

Capt. Walter Henry Cowan, M.V.O., D.S.O., R.N.
Capt. Maurice Woollcombe, R.N.
Capt. Rudolf Walter Bentinck, R.N.
Capt. Edmund Percy Fenwick George Grant, R.N. (Commodore, 2nd Cl.).
Capt. Frederick Laurence Field, R.N.
Capt. Charles Edward Le Mesurier, R.N. (Commodore, 2nd Cl.).
Capt. Edward Henry Fitzhardinge Heaton-Ellis, M.V.O., R.N.
Capt. Arthur William Craig, R.N.
Capt. Charles Blois Miller, R.N.
Capt. Eustace La Trobe Leatham, R.N.
Capt. John Douglas Edwards, R.N.
Capt. John Saumarez Damaresq, M.V.O., R.N.
Capt. Bertram Sackville Thesiger, C.M.G., R.N.
Capt. Frederic Charles Dreyer, C.B. (civil), R.N.
Capt. Arthur Cloudesley Shovel Hughes D'Aeth, R.N.
Capt. George Parish Ross, R.N.
Capt. Henry Wise Parker, R.N.
Eng.-Capt. John Richardson, R.N.
Eng.-Capt. Arthur Frederick Kingsnorth, R.N.
Dep.-Insp.-General of Hospitals and Fleets, Robert Forbes Bowie.
Major (temporary Lieut.-Col.) Charles Edwin Collard, R.M.L.I.
Fl.-Pm. Victor Herbert Thomas Weekes, R.N.

ORDER OF ST. MICHAEL AND ST. GEORGE.

The King has been graciously pleased to give directions for the following promotions in, and appointments to, the Most Distinguished Order of Saint Michael and Saint George, in recognition of the services mentioned in the foregoing despatch, the appointments to date from May 31st, 1916:

Adml. Sir Cecil Burney, K.C.B., K.C.M.G.
V.A. Sir Thomas Henry Martyn Jerram, K.C.B.
V.A. Sir Frederick Charles Doveton Sturdee, Bart., K.C.B., C.V.O., C.M.G.
V.A. Sir Charles Edward Madden, K.C.B., C.V.O.
R.A. Osmond De Beauvoir Brock, C.B.
Capt. Alfred Ernie Montacute Chatfield, C.V.O., C.B.

The King has been graciously pleased to give orders for the following appointments to the Distinguished Service Order and for the award of the Distinguished Service Cross to the following Officers in recognition of their services as mentioned in the foregoing despatch:

DISTINGUISHED SERVICE ORDER.

Comdr. Harold Ernest Sulivan, R.N.
Comdr. Hugh Schomberg Currey, R.N.
Comdr. Richard Horne, R.N.
Comdr. the Hon. Matthew Robert Best, M.V.S.O, R.N.
Comdr. Humphrey Thomas Walwyn, R.N.
Comdr. Alexander Riall Wadham Woods, R.N.
Comdr. John Walsh Carrington, R.N.
Comdr. Charles Morton Forbes, R.N.
Comdr. Henry John Studholme Brownrigg, R.N.
Comdr. Malcolmn Henry Somerled Macdonald, R.N.
Comdr. James Geoffrey Penrose Ingham, R.N.
Comdr. Geoffrey Blake, R.N.
Comdr. Hubert Edward Dannreuther, R.N.
Comdr. John Pelham Champion, R.N.
Comdr. Richard Lindsay Nicholson, R.N.
Comdr. Gerald Fortescue Longhurst, R.N.
Lt.-Com. Gordon Alston Coles, R.N.

108   The Fleet Annual

Lt.-Com. James Buller Kitson, R.N.
Lt.-Com. Montague George Bentinck Legge, R.N.
Lt.-Com. Roger Vincent Alison, R.N.
Lt.-Com. Ralph Frederick Seymour, R.N.
Lt.-Com. Cuthbert Patrick Blake, R.N.
Lt.-Com. Laurence Reynolds Palmer, R.N.
Lt.-Com. Henry Ruthven Moore, R.N.
Lt.-Com. Cecil Charles Brittain Vacher R.N.
Lieut. Jack Ernest Albert Mocatta, R.N.
Eng.-Comdr. William Cory Sanders. R.N.
Eng.-Comdr. Robert Spence, R.N.
Eng.-Comdr. Reginald William Skelton R.N.
Eng.-Comdr. Henry Walton Kitching, R.N.
Eng.-Lt.Com. Harold Bertram Tostevin, R.N.
Eng. Lt.-Com. John Kirk Corsar, R.N.
Eng. Lt.-Com. Albert Arthur Green Martell, R.N.
Fl.-Surg. Joseph Agnew Moon, R.N.
Fl.-Surg. Alexander Maclean, M.B., R.N.
Fl.-Surg. Henry William Finlayson, M.B., R.N.
Staff-Surg. Bertram Raleigh Bickford, R.N.
Staff-Surg. James McAlister Holmes, M.B., R.N.
Staff-Payr. Herbert Patrick William George Murray, R.N.
Payr. Cyril Sheldon Johnson, R.N.
Asst.-Payr. (Act-Payr.) Frank Todd Spickernell, R.N.
Capt. Edward Bamford, R.M.L.I.

DISTINGUISHED SERVICE CROSS.

Lieut. Arthur Malcolm Peters, R.N.
Lieut. Cuthbert Coppinger, R.N.
Lieut. John Hinton Carrow, R.N.
Lieut. Stewart Magee Walker, R.N.
Flight-Lieut. Frederick Joseph Rutland, R.N. (Lieut., R.N.).

Lieut. John Gordon Cliff-McCulloch, R.N.R.
Lieut. Percy Harrison, R.N.V.R.
Carpenter Lieut. John Norman Matheson, R.N.
The Rev. Anthony Pollen (Roman Catholic Chaplain).
Sub-Lieut. Newton James Wallop William Powlett, R.N.
Surg. Probationer Douglas George Patrick Bell, R.N.V.R.
Ch.-Art.-Eng. Alexander Noble, R.N.
Art.-Eng. Joseph House, R.N.

———

Admiralty, Sept. 15th, 1916.

The following despatch has also been received from Admiral Sir John R. Jellicoe, G.C.B., G.C.V.O., Commander-in-Chief, Grand Fleet:

"Iron Duke," July 15th, 1916.

Sir,—With reference to my despatch of 24th June, 1916, after full and careful consideration of the recommendations for promotion received from Flag Officers commanding Squadrons and Officers in command of Flotillas, the following lists are submitted for the favourable consideration of the Lords Commissioners of the Admiralty.

I am, Sir, your obedient servant,

J. R. JELLICOE,
Admiral.

The Secretary of the Admiralty.

OFFICERS RECOMMENDED FOR PROMOTION.

Commanders to Captain.

Walter Lingen Allen.
 H.M.S. "Broke" was very badly damaged and casualties very great, but the morale seems to have been unshaken and the ship was successfully steamed back to port.

For Distinguished Service

Hon. Arthur Lionel Ochoncar Forbes-Sempill.
A very able executive officer, who had the arrangements for fire, repair and other parties extremely well organised, and who was of great help throughout the action.

Joseph Charles Walrond Henley.
Admiral Sir Cecil Burney reports: Commander Henley rendered me very valuable assistance as my Flag-Commander during the action, and has done very valuable work in the gunnery training of the squadron. He is a most excellent and capable officer. He has served as my Flag-Commander and Second in Command of my Flagship during the past five years, and was of the greatest assistance to me in the occupation and administration of Scutari in 1913. He has been previously recommended for promotion by me.

Edward Astley Rushton.
Displayed great promptitude and powers of leadership, especially during and after the night action of 31st May, in which Southampton suffered considerably in casualties and damages. Was skilful and resourceful in effecting temporary repairs in a rising sea. Strongly recommended.

Berwick Curtis.
Carried out an operation on the night of 31st May-1st June with conspicuous skill, gallantry, and success.

George William McOran Campbell.
Throughout the various actions handled his division with great ability, sinking an enemy destroyer with his division. Attacked enemy battle squadron in company with flotilla, and undoubtedly assisted in blowing up one enemy battleship.

Arthur Goodenough Craufurd.
The Captain of the "Tiger" reports that he cannot speak too highly of the valuable and untiring work of this officer between decks under the most painful and trying conditions.

The Hon. Reginald Almer Ranfurley Plunkett.
Vice-Admiral Sir David Beatty reports: "Was most valuable in observing the effect of our fire, thereby enabling me to take advantage of the enemy's discomfiture."

Francis Arthur Marten.
Vice-Admiral Sir David Beatty reports: "Was of great assistance to the Commodore throughout the action. The work of the light cruisers was very much to be commended."

Lieut.-Comdrs. to Commander.

Guy Charles Cecil Royle.
Admiral Sir Cecil Burney reports: "It was entirely owing to his organisation and work that the ship fired so extremely well, quickly and accurately, during the action, especially so after she had been struck by a torpedo and took up a considerable list. He is a very efficient and capable officer.

Geoffrey Charles Candy.
Strongly recommended by Vice-Admiral Sir Martyn Jerram for his work in connection with the wireless telegraph of the squadron.

Henry Purdon Boyd.
Recommended by Vice-Admiral Sir Doveton Sturdee for valuable work.

Richard Wyville Bromley.
Remained exposed outside the conning tower, and, inspite of being wounded in leg, arm, and neck, took his captain personal reports of the various damages suffered and got the ship in tow afterwards.

Paul Whitfield (now prisoner of war in Germany).
In command of "Nomad," made a most gallant attack on the enemy

battle-cruisers, after having assisted to drive off an enemy flotilla which was endeavouring to attack our battle-cruisers. "Nomad" was disabled by shell fire from the enemy battle-cruisers and subsequently sank.

Gerald Fortescue Longhurst.
Gunnery officer of "Lion." This officer controlled the fire of "Lion" with the greatest coolness, courage, and skill, and inflicted immense damage on the enemy.

Cecil Burnaby Prickett.
Gunnery officer of "Princess Royal." Controlled the fire of "Princess Royal" under very difficult conditions with conspicuous success. This is the third time he has controlled the fire of a battle cruiser in action. A most efficient and resourceful officer. Strongly recommended.

Lachlan Donald Ian Mackinnon.
First Lieutenant and Gunnery officer. By his zeal and skill obtained excellent results. Under his control the firing of the ship was accurate and rapid.

Charles Gwillim Robinson.
In command of "Engadine." Was prompt in sending up a seaplane to scout. Handled his ship in a skilful and seamanlike manner. and towed "Warrior" for 75 miles, subsequently succeeding in taking off her crew, thus saving their lives.

Geoffrey Corlett.
Led his division into action in a most gallant manner and fought a successful action with enemy destroyers, in which they were forced to retire.

John Cronyn Tovey.
For the persistent and determined manner in which he attacked enemy ships as occasion offered, even though his destroyer was disabled by shell fire and unable to proceed at more than 10 knots.

Robert Stedman Macfarlan.
This officer's coolness, ability, and resource, especially after he had had a miraculous escape in the torpedo control tower, was most praiseworthy, and the fact that very few communications and lighting failed is entirely due to this officer's work both before and during the action.

Stephen Dowell Tillard.
Recommended for good service in action.

Errol Manners.
Executive officer of "Comus" and gunnery officer of the Squadron. An excellent officer, already strongly recommended for promotion, who has contributed very materially to the good gunnery work of the Squadron.

Reginald Stannus Goff.
This officer reported immediately presence of enemy. Subsequently he exhibited initiative with success, and eventually escorted "Porpoise" back to harbour and berthed her alongside in a most seamanlike manner.

Clarence Walter Eyre Trelawny.
This officer, by skilful handling of his ship, managed to ram an enemy cruiser instead of being rammed by her, thereby saving his ship. He showed great coolness and afterwards successfully returned to harbour with his ship in a very damaged condition.

John Ouchterlony Barron.
This officer stood by the "Shark" under a very heavy fire, and although engine-room was wrecked and steering gear broken down and the ship a practical wreck, he successfully, by the aid of "Nonsuch," returned into harbour.

Gerald Charles Wynter.
Seeing "Castor" being engaged with

For Distinguished Service

two enemy ships, closed them and fired a torpedo at the second enemy ship. This was followed by an explosion. It may be taken for certain that it was "Magic's" torpedo that struck the second ship in the enemy's line.

Eric Quintin Carter.
Handled his ship with skill and judgment, as is usual with this officer.

Edwin Anderson Homan.
This officer handled his ship with great skill throughout the action under difficult circumstances.

OFFICERS RECOMMENDED TO BE NOTED FOR EARLY PROMOTION.

Lieutenant-Commanders.

Ralph Frederick Seymour (Flag-Lieut-Comdr.).
Sir David Beatty reports: "Carried out his duties with great coolness on the manœuvring platform, and maintained efficient communications under the most difficult cirumstances despite the fact that signalling appliances were continually shot away.

Stephen St. Leger Moore.
Commodore Le Mesurier reports: "This very promising officer has served as 1st and (G) of "Calliope" since the ship commissioned, and has been of the very greatest assistance to me in every way, while a large portion of the credit due for the gunnery efficiency of the ship is his.

OFFICERS RECOMMENDED FOR PROMOTION.

Sub-Lieutenants to Lieutenant.

Charles Saumarez Daniel.
Performed very good service as officer in charge of a turret.

John Catterall Leach.
Performed very good service as officer in charge of a turret.

Douglas Stanley Swanston.
Controlled the 6-inch guns with marked ability, hitting the enemy destroyers, and is believed to have sunk one.

Harry William Algernon Kemmis.
For taking command and bringing the ship back to harbour after the commanding officer and first lieutenant had been killed.

Eric Vernon Lees.
Rendered invaluable service in attending the wounded for five hours after a shell had struck the ship and killed two officers (one of whom was the surgeon) and five men, and wounded seven.

Leicester Charles Assheton St. John Curzon-Howe.
In charge of fore transmitting station and carried out his duties in a manner specially to be commended. Was mentioned in despatches after the action of the Falkland Islands.

Roderick Larken Moore.
Is reported by his commanding officer to have been of invaluable assistance, taking charge of the torpedo armament with excellent results.

Roger Prideaux Selby.
In charge of the transmitting room, the working of which was in every way admirable. Showed coolness in dangerous situations.

Robert Reginald Gibbons.
For good service in action. He has only recently recovered from wounds received in action of 24th January, 1915.

Francis Adrian Blaydes Haworth-Booth.
Recommended for good service in action.

Herbert Annesley Packer.
Was in charge of "A" turret during

the action, and is an extremely able officer.

Eric Sydney Brand.
He was of the very greatest assistance to the gunnery officer throughout the action.

OFFICERS RECOMMENDED TO BE NOTED FOR EARLY PROMOTION

Sub-Lieutenants.

John Gerald Yerburgh Loveband.
Performed very good service as control officer of secondary armament.

George Sidney Godolphin Cavendish.
Performed very good service as control officer of secondary armament.

Humphery Ranulph Brand.
Strongly recommended for excellent service.

Newton James Wallop William-Powlett.
Very strongly recommended. This officer showed wonderful coolness under most trying circumstances, and his pluck and cheerfulness after the ship sank was certainly the means of saving the lives of several who would otherwise have given in and succumbed. Captain (D), 4th Flotilla, reports: " I cannot speak too highly of this young officer's conduct throughout."

Herbert Claude Millett.
Strongly recommended for good service in action.

George Evelyn Paget How.
Recommended for good service in action.

Cecil Spurstow Miller.
In command of the 4-inch guns' crews, most of whom were killed or wounded. Sub-Lieutenant Miller, himself very badly injured and burnt by shell-fire, stuck to his work, reorganised what was eft, and set a fine example.

Mates.

Alfred Bowman.
Second officer of " Y " turret. Highly commended by his officer of the turret for good work during the action.

Matthew McClure.
In charge of forecastle group of 4-inch guns. Wounded by a shell splinter, but continued to carry on.

OFFICERS RECOMMENDED FOR PROMOTION.

Engineer Lieutenant-Commander to Engineer Commander.

Arthur Lee Picton.
Recommended for good service in action.

Engineer Lieutenant to Engineer Lieutenant-Commander.

Geoffrey Morgan.
Captain Molteno, late of " Warrior," reports: " Utmost gallantry and conspicuous devotion to duty in remaining in the engine-room after the explosion and endeavouring to take action for the safety of the ship, by which delay he was imprisoned under the grating for over two hours, and very narrowly escaped losing his life by drowning scalding, and suffocation. Was almost, overcome when rescued. He afterwards took part with energy and coolness in the work of salving the ship. This officer, under the able supervision of Engineer Commander Kitching, has run the engine-room department extremely well, and greatly increased " Warrior's " steaming efficiency."

OFFICERS RECOMMENDED TO BE NOTED FOR EARLY PROMOTION

Engineer Commanders.

William Toop.
Rendered most valuable services

For Distinguished Service

after the ship was struck by a torpedo, and his excellent work in keeping the water under in the flooded compartments was largely instrumental in the saving of the ship. He is a most capable engineer officer.

Herbert Brooks Moorshead.
His zeal and ability and care of the main and auxiliary engines and boilers throughout the war, and coolness in action, contributed largely to the efficient working of the engine-room department in the action on 31st May.

John Downie Wilson.
For the great efficiency of the engine-room department and the example he set to his officers and men during a period of considerable stress, steaming at between 18 and 20 knots for four consecutive days.

Charles Frederick Dun.
Senior Engineer Commander in the 5th Battle Squadron. The Captain of "Warspite" reports: "I consider that this officer is worthy of reward, as the efficiency of his department has proved to be excellent, and no further remarks are necessary beyond the fact that I was able to obtain full speed whenever I deemed it safe, considering the damage the ship had sustained from shell fire."

John Benjamin Hewitt.
Recommended for service in action.

Engineer Lieutenant-Commanders.

Bertram Harvey.
The Senior Engineer Lieutenant-Commander in the 2nd Battle Squadron. Very highly recommended by his captain.

Harold Benjamin Main.
Was appointed to "Canada" whilst completing, and has carried out the duties of Senior Engineer since the ship joined the Squadron in a most satisfactory manner. The Engineer Captain speaks very highly of him.

Harold Edwin Brook.
For services as Senior Engineer of "Valiant," and largely responsible for the high speed maintained.

Albert Knothe.
The Captain of "Indomitable" reports that it is principally due to this officer that the ship steamed during the action faster than ever before. A most efficient officer, strongly recommended for promotion. Was mentioned in Vice-Admiral Beatty's despatch after the action of 24th January, 1915.

Arthur Ellis Lester, D.S.O.
Recommended for good service in action.

Engineer Lieutenant.

William David Smith.
Senior Engineer of "Calliope." Responsible under the Engineer Commander, for the excellent steaming of the ship and behaviour of the engine-room department during the action.

Temporary Engineer Sub-Lieuts.

Harry Hunter.
Was in charge of "A" boiler-room, and kept steam regulated under very trying conditions, with the boiler-room full of smoke and fumes. He afterwards went to the hydraulic engine-rooms and endeavoured to cope with the damage to S.F. Hydraulic E.R., and afterwards made temporary repairs to the port telemotor pipes.

Mackenzie Dallas.
By promptness and at great danger personally assisted in directing and heading the hoses and arresting the spread of igniting cordite.

The Fleet Annual

OFFICERS RECOMMENDED TO BE NOTED FOR BREVETS OR EARLY PROMOTION.

Major Arthur George Troup, R.M.A.
Recommended for service in action.

Capt. Robert Edgar Kilvert, R.M.A.
Was in command of "X" turret during the action, and as commanding officer of the Marine detachment, is recommended as having specially contributed to the general efficiency of the ship.

Capt. Richmond Campbell Shakespear Waller, R.M.L.I.
Vice-Admiral Sir Doveton Sturdee reports: "This officer has served continuously in the Home and Grand Fleets from April, 1913, and has been in charge of the wireless organisation of a Battle Squadron since the commencement of hostilities. The squadron was composed of new ships of various types which had been hurriedly completed and the work entailed in bringing the wireless installations of ships designed for foreign Powers into effective working order was carried out entirely satisfactorily. Is unceasing in his endeavours to improve the wireless of the squadron, and has been of valuable assistance since I have been in command; an excellent Marine officer."

Lieut. Harold Marsland Franks, R.M.A.
Vice-Admiral Sir David Beatty reports: "W.T. Officer on my Staff. Showed great skill and resource in maintaining the vitally important wireless communications throughout the action, despite the fact that aerials were shot away and required constant repair. An officer of high technical skill."

Lieut. Henry Loftus Mitchell McCausland, R.M.L.I.
The senior Marine subaltern in the squadron. Very highly recommended by his captain.

OFFICERS RECOMMENDED TO BE NOTED FOR EARLY PROMOTION.

Fleet Surgeons

Robert Hill, C.V.O.
The principal Medical Officer of the Fleet Flagship and on my staff. His excellent organisation and services before and after the action were of great assistance, and contributed much to the well-being of the wounded.

Arthur Reginald Bankart, C.V.O., M.B., K.H.P,
Has organised his department for action in a most efficient manner.

Alexander Maclean, M.B.
Performed his exhausting duties with the greatest zeal and courage. The medical staff was seriously depleted by casualties. The wounded and dying had to be dressed under very difficult conditions on the mess deck, which was flooded with a foot of water from damaged fire mains. Fleet Surgeon Maclean has suffered considerably since the action from his devotion to duty.

Ernest Alfred Penfold, M.B.
Was in the fore medical distributing station when a heavy shell burst just outside, killing and wounding many. Fleet Surgeon Penfold was himself knocked down and bruised and shaken, but personally assisted in the removal of wounded and afterwards tended the wounded with unremitting skill and devotion for forty hours without rest. His example was invaluable in keeping up the moral of the wounded and of the medical party under very trying conditions.

Christopher Louis White Bunton, M.B.
Did good work, being hard pressed

For Distinguished Service

with many sudden casualties of a serious nature.

Staff Surgeon.

Arthur Reginald Schofield, M.B.
For skilful and untiring attention to the wounded.

Temporary Surgeon.

Richard Stocker Carey.
For skilful and untiring attention to the wounded.

Fleet Paymasters.

Charles Henry Rowe.
Has voluntarily undertaken the duties of Rate-keeper in the foretop, which he has with great zeal inspired himself to perform with great efficiency. During the action he was of great assistance to the Fire Control, being cool and accurate in his work.

Harold Boxer Pearson.
Recommended for good service.

Staff Paymaster.

Herbert Patrick William George Murray (Secretary).
Admiral Sir Cecil Burney reports: "Rendered me very valuable personal services as my secretary both during and before the action. His valuable services as my secretary have now extended over a period of ten years.

Paymasters.

James Meade Loughnan Cusack.
Recommended for good service in action.

Harry Sampson Orchard.
Recommended for good service in action.

Assistant Paymasters.

Clarence Teasdale-Buckell (Acting Paymaster).
Recommended for good service in action.

Geoffrey Thomas Smyth (Secretary) (Acting Paymaster).
Commodore Le Mesurier reports: "In charge of coding staff during the action, and has been of great assistance to me in every way as my secretary.

Harry Ewart Flint (Acting Assistant Paymaster).
Recommended for good service in action.

Officers Recommended for Promotion.

Chief Gunner to Lieutenant.

Alexander Grant.
With the greatest zeal and coolness went from magazine to magazine to encourage the crews in maintaining a rapid supply of ammunition; also in taking charge of fire parties under Lieut. Walker and extinguishing several extensive fires.

Carpenters to Chief Carpenters.

John William Sparks.
The Captain of "Princess Royal" reports that the indefatigable resource of this officer in dealing with fires and damage throughout the action was in the highest degree admirable and a splendid example to all who saw it.

Henry Ham.
Rendered invaluable service with repair parties, and was conspicuous in directing men until wounded.

Officers Recommended to be Noted for Early Promotion.

Chief Gunners.

Edwin Stanley Norman.
Recommended for good service in action.

John Dick Jamieson.
A most reliable and trustworthy officer of exceptional ability.

Edward Fox.
Recommended for good service in action.

William James Cann.
This Commissioned Warrant Officer was appointed to H.M.S. "Canada" whilst completing, and has carried out his duties in a most able manner. There have been very few of the difficulties usually experienced in ships designed for foreign Powers, and this fact is largely attributable to him.

Charles Richard Ponton.
Recommended for good service in action.

Harry Hoggett.
Recommended for good service in action.

Joshua Ernest George Chubb.
Recommended for good service in action.

Gunners.

William James Newton.
Recommended for good service in action.

John Williams.
Recommended for good service in action.

Herbert Daniel Jehan.
Is stationed in "Iron Duke's" lower top as principal control officer of the 6-inch guns. These guns were employed during the action in repelling two attacks of German t.b.d.'s on our battle fleet, and were controlled with coolness and good judgment, as a result of which one German t.b.d. was seen to sink.

George Ernest Freeme.
Recommended for good service in action.

William Johnston.
The rapid rate of fire maintained by "Marlborough" was largely due to this officer's able performance of his duties as director layer.

Chief Boatswain.

George Enock Turner.
The senior Chief Boatswain in the 2nd Battle Squadron and 3rd on list of Chief Boatswains. A very conscientious and capable officer.

Boatswain.

William Henry Fenn.
Specially recommended. Was in charge of the after repair party and worked in fumes until he was overcome and removed. He returned again to the same work as soon as he had regained consciousness, and rendered invaluable services. Mr. Fenn had only returned from hospital the day before the action, and was on light duty.

Signal Boatswains.

Ernest Albert Dunk Collins.
Admiral Sir Cecil Burney reports: "Rendered excellent service during the action in charge of the signal staff, and also, after the transfer of my flag, re-organised the signal staff very quickly into one suitable for a flagship.

John Joseph Gowen.
Recommended for good service in action.

Harry Albert Pitt.
Mr. Pitt was on deck throughout the action and did excellent work.

Chief Carpenters.

George Campbell Grant.
The Captain of "Superb" speaks most highly of this officer's suitability for Carpenter-Lieutenant. He has served in "Superb" for the whole war.

Albert Edward Scarlett.
The senior Chief Carpenter in 2nd Cruiser Squadron. Recommended for good service in action.

For Distinguished Service

Albert Edward Lamb.
  The senior Chief Carpenter in 2nd Battle Squadron. A very capable and thoroughly efficient officer.

Carpenters.

William Ernest Mutton.
  Recommended for good service in action.

Charles Alfred Morley Brown.
  Recommended for good service in action.

George Emmerson.
  Recommended for good service in action.

William Morrissey.
  Rendered excellent services after the ship was torpedoed and on passage to port.

Chief Artificer Engineer.

James Henry Fenton.
  Performed good services in stopping gaps caused by carrying away of foremost funnel and damage to second funnel, thus preserving considerably the steaming capabilities of the ship.

Commissioned Mechanician.

Clayton Hartnup.
  Recommended for good service in action,

Artificer Engineers.

Joseph Fegan.
  Rendered valuable service during the action and after the ship had been struck by a torpedo.

William Perry Hill.
  For efficient work and good leadership in repairing damage to the ship.

Frederick Samuel Heath.
  A very capable officer.

Gilbert Mager McWhirter.
  Recommended for good service in action.

Thomas John Gard.
  Recommended for good service in action.

Charles Keeling.
  Displayed conspicuous resource and initiative at a critical period.

Francis William John Patterson.
  For exceptionally good work in charge of the stokeholds.

Royal Marine Gunners.

George Allan.
  Vice-Admiral Sir Doveton Sturdee reports: "This officer has served afloat for the whole of the war, and is the Senior Warrant Officer, R.M., in the Squadron. He was recommended for commissioned rank by the Squadron selection committee on 14th Januray, 1916. Is fully worthy of promotion."

John Edward Flower.
  Recommended for good service in action.

Warrant Telegraphist.

Samuel Lewington.
  Was in charge of the auxiliary W.T. cabinet during the whole operations, and carried out his work with conspicuous coolness and ability.

OFFICER RECOMMENDED FOR PROMOTION.

Lieutenant R.N.R., to Commander, R.N.R.

Robert Milne Porter.
  After having been severely burned in the cordite explosion at No. 2 starboard 6-inch gun, Lieutenant Porter personally superintended the extinction of the fire and removal of wounded, and remained at his post for two hours after, when swelling from burns had closed his eyes and rendered his hands useless. His condition when he reached the medical party was critical.

OFFICERS RECOMMENDED TO BE NOTED FOR EARLY PROMOTION.

Lieutenants R.N.R.

Robert Beaufin Irving.
Recommended for good service in action.

Reginald Slaughter Triggs.
Vice-Admiral Sir Doveton Sturdee reports: "Is the Senior R.N.R. Lieutenant in the Squadron. He has served in H.M.S. "Canada" since commissioned in June, 1915, and prior to that, whilst serving in H.M.S. "Chatham" was wounded in action at the Ruffegi River, where he lost the use of his right arm."

Bertram Elliott.
Recommended for good service in action.

Reginald John Finlow.
Recommended for good service in action.

Charles Leonard Dettmar.
Ably carried out his duties as a turret officer during the action. He is an exceptionally able officer, strongly recommended for promotion by his Commanding Officer.

John Alexander Macdonald (Acting).
Recommended for good service in action.

Wilfred Charters (Acting).
Ably performed his duty in charge of 6-inch guns during the action.

William Groggan Lalor (Acting).
Ably performed his duties as a turret officer during the action.

Sub-Lieutenant R.N.R.

Jeremiah Aylmer Bunting.
This officer carried out his duties as officer of quarters in the 6-inch battery in a most praiseworthy manner while the ship was under heavy fire.

Temporary Midshipman, R.N.R.
Charles Gordon Denning.
For the cool and skilful way in which he, as officer of the quarters, while continuously under heavy fire controlled the foremost 4-inch gun, the primary control having broken down.

Assistant Paymaster, R.N.R.
Thomas Emrys Daniel.
Recommended for good service in action.

Warrant Engineers, R.N.R.
Stanley Perigrine Oxnard.
For efficient work and good leadership in repairing damage to the ship.
John Cameron Allen.
For exceptionally good work in charge of the stokeholds.

Lieutenants, R.N.V.R.

Leonard Bampfylde Cogan.
Recommended by Commodore commanding for good service during the action.

Alexander Percy McMullen.
Ably carried out his duties in charge of 12-in. transmitting station.

William Cleveland Stevens.
For good organisation of W.T. department.

Surgeon, R.N.V.R.

William James Aitken Quine, M.B.
For his assiduous care of, and attention to, the wounded, of whom he was in sole charge for over 40 hours, the Staff Surgeon having been severely wounded.

PROMOTIONS.

Admiralty, Sept. 15th, 1916.

The following promotions, etc., have been made in recognition of the ser-

For Distinguished Service

vices mentioned in the foregoing despatch:

Commanders already promoted to Captain to date June 30th.

Walter Lingen Allen, the Hon. Arthur Lionel Ochoncar Forbes-Semphill, Joseph Charles Walrond Henley, Edward Astley Rushton, Berwick Curtis, Francis Arthur Marten, George William McOran Campbell, Arthur Goodenough Cranford, the Hon. Reginald Aylmer Ranfurly Plunkett.

Lt.-Coms. already promoted to Comdrs., June 30th: Paul Whitefield, Richard Wyville Bromley, Clarence Walter Eyre Trelawny, Henry Purdon Boyd, Chales Gwillim Robinson, Reginald Strannus Goff, Robert Stedman Macfarlan, Geoffrey Corlett, John Ouchterlony Barron, Gerald Charles Wynter, Lachlan Donald Ian Mackinnon, Edwin Anderson Homan, Stephen Dowell Tillard, Gerald Fortescue Longhurst, Cecil Burnaby Prickett, Geoffrey Charles Candy, Errol Manners, Eric Quintin Carter, Guy Charles Cecil Royle, John Cronyn Tovey.

Eng.-Comdr. William Toop to be Engr.-Capt.

Eng.-Lt. Comdrs. Arthur Lee Picton and Bertram Harvey to be Engr.-Comdrs.

Eng.-Lieut. Geoffrey Morgan to be Eng. Lt.-Com.

Major Arthur George Troup, R.M.A., to be Bt. Lieut.-Col.

Capt. Robert Edgar Kilvert, R.M.A., to be Major.

Capt. Richmond Campbell Shakespear Waller, R.M.L.I., to be Brevet-Major.

Lieut. Harold Marsland Franks, R.M.A. to be Capt. and Brevet-Major.

Flt.-Surg. Robert Hill, C.V.O., to be Deputy Surg.-General.

Paymaster James Meade Loughnan Cusack to be Staff Paymaster.

Sub.-Lts. (Actg. Lts.) Duglas Stanley Swanston and Robert Reginald Gibbons to be Lieuts.

All the above to date June 30th, 1916.

The Seniority as Actg.-Lieut. of the following to be ante-dated to June 30th, 1916: Charles Saumarez Daniel,* John Catterall Leach.*

The following Sub.-Lts. to be promoted to Actg.-Lieut., to date June 30th, 1916: Leicester Charles Assheton St. John Curzon-Howe,* Francis Adrian Blaydes Haworth-Booth,* Herbert Annesley Packer,* Eric Vernon Lees,* Roger Prideaux Selby,* Harry William Algernon Kemmis,* Roderick Larken Moore.*

* All these Officers to be confirmed in their Acting Seniority subject to completion of their courses; any time gained for meritorious examinations to be in addition subject to a minimum of six months' service as Sub.-Lt.

The following temporary Engr.-Sub.-Lts. to be Engr.-Lieuts., to date, June 30th, 1916, and to be noted for early promotion to Engr.-Lt.-Com. should they be transferred to the Permanent List: Harry Hunter, Mackenzie Dallas, Asst.-Payr. (Actg.-Payr.) Clarence Teasdale-Buckell to be Payr.

Chief Gnr. Alexander Grant to be Lieut., under the provisions of Art. 299, Clause 4, of the King's Regulations and Admiralty Instructions.

Chief Art.-Engr. James Henry Fenton to be Engr.-Lieut.

Carp. John William Sparks to be Chief Carp.

Carp. Henry Ham to be Chief Carp.

R.M. Gnr. George Allan to be Lieut., R.M.

R.M. Gnr. John Edward Flower to be Lieut., R.M.

All the above to date June 30th, 1916.

The following officers have been noted for early promotion :

Comdr. the Hon. Arthur Charles Strutt
Lt.-Coms. Stephen St. Leger Moore and Ralph Frederick Seymour.
Engr.-Coms. Herbert Brooks Moorshead, Charles Frederick Dunn, and John Downie Wilson.
Engr. Lt.-Coms. Arthur Ellis Lester, D.S.O., Harold Edwin Brook, Harold Benjamin Main, and Albert Knothe.
Engr.-Lt. William David Smith.
Flt.-Surg. Alexander Maclean, M.B., Ernest Alfred Penfold, M.B., Arthur Reginald Bankart, C.V.O., M.B., K.H.P., and Christopher Louis White Bunton.
Staff-Surg. Arthur Reginald Schofield, M.B.
Temp.-Surg. Richard Stocker Carey should he be transferred to the permanent list.
Flt.-Payr. Charles Henry Rowe.
Staff-Payr. (Secretary) Herbert Patrick William George Murray.
Payr. Harry Sampson Orchard.
Sub.-Lts. George Evelyn Paget-How, John Gerald Yerburgh Loveband, Humphrey Ranulph Brand, Cecil Spurstow Miller, Eric Sydney Brand, George Sidney Godolphin Cavendish.
Actg. Sub.-Lt. (now (Sub.-Lt.) Newton James Wallop William-Powlett.
Actg. Sub.-Lt. Herbert Claude Millett.
Mates Matthew McClure and Alfred Bowman.
Asst. Payr. (Actg. Payr. and Sec. Geoffrey Thomas Smyth.
Chief. Gnrs. Edwin Stanley Norman, John Dick Jamieson, Edward Fox, (previously noted for early promotion), William James Cann, Charles Richard Ponton, Harry Hoggett, and Joshua Ernest George Chubb.

Commissioned Mechanician Clayton Hartnup.
Chief Carps. George Campbell Grant, Albert Edward Scarlett, and Alfred Edward Lamb.
Gnrs. William James Newton, John Williams, Herbert Daniel Jehan, George Ernest Freeme, and William Johnston.
Boatswain William Henry Fenn.
Sig. Boatswains Harry Albert Pitt, Ernest Albert Dunk Ollins, and John Joseph Gowen.
Warrant Teleg. Samuel Lewington.
Art.-Engrs. Joseph Fegan, William Perry Hill, Frederick Hamel Heath, Gilbert Mager McWhirter, Thomas John Gard, and Charles Keeling.
Actg. Art.-Eng. Francis William John Patterson.
Carps. William Ernest Mutton, Charles Alfred Morley Brown, George Emmerson, and William Morrissey.

In accordance with the foregoing, Eng.-Lt. Com. Arthur Ellis Lester, D.S.O., has been promoted to the rank of Eng.-Com. in H.M. Fleet, to date, July 25th, 1916.

The following officer is noted for Brevet Major on attaining the rank of Capt. Royal Marines : Lieut. Henry Loftus Michell McCausland, R.M.L.I.

The services of the following Officers have been specially noted :

Eng.-Com. John Benjamin Hewitt.
Flt. Payr. Harold Boxer Pearson.
Actg. Asst.-Payr. Harry Ewart Flint.
Chief Boatswain George Knock Turner, Royal Naval Reserve.
Lieut. Robert Milne Porter to be Comdr.
Sub.-Lt. (Act. Lt.) John Alexander Macdonald to be Lieut.
Temp. Sub.-Lt. (Act. Lt.) Wilfrid Charters to be Lieut. on the permanent list of the R.N.R.

For Distinguished Service

Sub.-Lt. (Act.-Lt.) William Goggan Lalor to be Lieut.

Temp. Sub.-Lt. (Act.-Lt.) Jeremiah Aylmer Bunting to be Lieut. on the permanent list of the R.N.R.

Midshipman Charles Gordon Denning to be transferred to the Royal Navy as Act.-Sub.-Lt.

All the above to date, June 30th, 1916.

The following Officers have been noted for early promotion.

Lieuts. Robert Beaufin Irving, Reginald Slaughter Triggs, Bertram Elliott, Reginald John Finlow, and Charles Leonard Dettmar.

Warrant Engrs. Stanley Perigrine Oxnard and John Cameron Allen.

The services of the following officer have been specially noted:

Asst. Payr. Thomas Emrys Daniel.

Royal Naval Volunteer Reserve.

Noted for early promotion:

Surg. William James Aitken Quine, M.B.

The services of the following officers have been specially noted:

Lieut. Leonard Bampfylde Cogan, Temp. Lieuts. Alexander Percy McMullen and William Cleveland Stevens.

With reference to the dispatch of Admiral Sir John Jellicoe, G.C.B., G.C.V.O., Commander-in-Chief, Grand Fleet, published in the *London Gazette* of Thursday, July 6th, 1916, the following awards have been approved in connection with the recomemendations of the Commander-in-Chief for services rendered by Petty Officers and men of the Grand Fleet in the action in the North Sea on May 31st-June 1st, 1916:

The King has been graciously pleased to approve the grant of the Victoria Cross to

Boy, 1st Cl., John Travers Cornwell, (died 2nd June, 1916), for the conspicuous act of bravery specified below.

Mortally wounded early in the action, First Class, John Travers Cornwell remained standing alone at a most exposed post, quietly awaiting orders, until the end of the action, with the gun's crew dead and wounded all round him. His age was under sixteen and a half years.

The following awards have also been made:

CONSPICUOUS GALLANTRY MEDAL.

Sto. P.O. William Ackerman.

Sto. P.O. William Ackerman evidenced considerable aptitude and bravery in clearing a suction box in a damaged compartment and freeing the rods in use to keep it clear. It was necessary at one time for him to descend in a diving suit for the purpose.

C. E.R.A., 2nd Cl. Frederick Tinsley Birchall.

C. E.R.A., 2nd Cl., Birchall showed great coolness and resource in removing portions of shafting from forward to enable the after steering position to be successfully operated. His work was carried out under a heavy fire, and he displayed a dexterity and calmness which did him the highest credit.

P.O. Frederick Adolphus Day (alias Parsons).

L.S. James Simpson Watson.

When a shell exploded in the starboard battery of the ship in which P.O. Day and L.S. Watson were serving a considerable blast of flame and smoke caused a quantity of smouldering debris to fall among a hoist of cartridges in bags. P.O. Day showed great coolness and presence of mind in immediately jumping amongst the cartridges, removing the debris. In doing this he was assisted by L.S. Watson, these two dealing with this dangerous situation promptly.

Sto. P.O. Patrick James Hogan.
Sto. P.O Hogan remained for over eighteen hours continuously at his station, where during the action the fans were broken down and the temperature became almost un-bearable; in order to stop leaks in cover joints he had to take off his clothes. He showed great judgment in hurrying on salt water supply at a critical time.

Shipwt. 1st Cl., William Holigan.
Shipwt., 1st. Cl., Holigan acted with great courage when a shell burst in the canteen flat of the ship in which he was serving, killing and wounding about twenty men. He was knocked down and scorched about the head, but immediately plugged leaking pipes which had been shot away.

Sto., 1st. Cl., Joseph Henry Hughes.
Sto., 1st Cl., Hughes was one of the ratings on duty in a compartment immediately above that struck by a torpedo. The deck of this compartment was distorted, and all the lights save one were extinguished, and water was coming into it. Sto. Hughes at once closed a valve, and the last light going out, he proceeded on deck to obtain another, with which he returned closing steam and exhaust valves, although there was then 5 feet of water in the compartment. The action taken by this stoker, who remained alone at his place of duty in spite of the shock and noise of the explosion, and took effective steps to ensure the continued operation of the machinery in it, exhibited great presence of mind and bravery.

Sick Bth.Stwd. Alfred Edward Jones.
Sick Berth Steward Jones showed conspicuous gallantry in bringing hoses to bear on a cordite fire in the vicinity of the midship ammunition lobby, when the supply parties had been driven away by the fumes. He performed his duties in an exemplary manner in very trying circumstances.

C.P.O. Telegraphist Patrick McEvoy.
C.P.O. Telegraphist McEvoy was working on deck almost continuously throughout the action. Four times he repaired or cleared the Main Aerial under fire in a cool and efficient manner. The smoke on the Mess Deck was so intense that he had to feel his way up on deck.

C. Sto. William George Pring.
Although severely wounded early in the action, C. Sto. Pring continued to carry out important duties with repair parties until the action was finished.

P.O. George Arthur Sayer.
P.O. Sayer's leg was shot away when the turret in which he was stationed was disabled, and he thereafter set a fine example by remaining at his post and trying to get his gun into action again.

Act. Sto. P.O. Frederick John Henry Wherry.
Act. Sto. P.O. Wherry, at great risk, flooded the 6-inch magazine of the ship in which he was serving, and then, until gassed, assisted to extinguish a fire in close proximity to the magazine. Subsequently, whilst still suffering from the effect of the fumes, he left the dressing station to unlock the secondary position for 13.5-inch flooding valves, showing great devotion to duty.

For Distinguished Service

P.O. William John Adlam Willis.
P.O. Willis, brought his gun into action after he himself and the whole of his gun's crew had been wounded.

Distinguished Service Medal.

C. E.R.A., 1st Cl., J. G. Ashton.
Sto., 1st Cl., E. R. Allcock.
Sto., 1st Cl., C. O. Anderson.
C. Sto. O. W. Barrett.
Mech. W. Beecroft.
P.O. J. C. Bragg.
A.B. A. Bright.
C. Sto. R. F. Burley.
C.P.O. F. W. Bird.
Shipwright, 1st Cl., Martin Bray.
A.B. H. J. Boutell.
L. Sto. C. E. Blagdon.
A.B. G. C. Bowers.
E.R.A., 1st Cl., J. R. Barss.
L.S. W. J. Barrow.
C. Yeo. of Sig. S. C. Burgess.
C. Sto. J. Brudnell.
C. E.R.A., 1st Cl., J. Bentley.
C. E.R.A., 1st Cl., A. L. Burgess.
Sto. P.O. W. H. Carne.
C.P.O. J. Coughlan.
C. E.R.A., 1st Cl., N. Cawrse.
Ch. Arm. T. Chivers.
L.S. M. J. Cooper.
L. Sig. F. G. Chesters.
Officer's Cook, 1st Cl., H. F. Carter.
C.P.O. A. E. Cleife.
Sto. P.O. T. Crowley.
L.S. M. H. Cox.
L.S. P. Curtis.
Yeo. of Sig. A. J. Colyer.
Sto. P.O. M. Connell.
Shipwright, 1st Cl., E. J. Dunn.
P.O. R. G. Dycer.
C.P.O. W. Demellweek.
C. Yeo. of Sig. T. J. Dalton.
P.O., 1st Cl., H. W. Dudman.
Sto., 1st Cl., A. T. Dunn.
A.B., R.N.V.R., E. W. Dicker.
C. Sto. P. W. Dennis.
P.O. A. M. Eagland.
C. E.R.A., 1st Cl., E. F. Edge.
Wireman, 2nd Cl., G. J. Ellisdon.
Sto. W. F. Elvins.
Sto., 1st Cl., J. Flynn.
Sgt. W. H. Fairs.
C. E.R.A., 1st Cl, F. T. Farmer.
Yeo. of Sig. F. W. Foster (now Actg. Sig. Botsn.)
Sto., 1st Cl., A. J. Fane.
C.P.O. E. Fitzgerald.
P.O. M. Fitzpatrick.
A.B. G. F. French.
Yeo. of Sig. H. J. Fisher.
C.P.O. H. E. Fox.
C.P.O. E. G. Fry.
C.P.O. H. L. Greenhill.
C. E Art 2nd Cl. F. E. Grace.
C. Sick Berth Steward A. E. Gregson.
P.O. B. W. R. Gardiner.
C.P.O. J. J. Greenland.
P.O. M. D. Godin.
P.O. W. H. Graves.
C.P.O. G. Gates.
P.O. W. C. R. Griffin.
L.S. J. Hiram.
C. Yeo. of Sig. A. W. Hogger.
C.P.O. W. W. Higman.
Mech. J. G. Hicks.
C.P.O. W. Harris.
C.P.O. J. D. Hatherley.
C. Sto. A. Harbour.
C. E.R.A., 1st Cl., A. F. W. Hughes.
A.B. J. E. Hines.
L. Sto. E. J. Hignett.
L. Sig. C. Headley.
Sto. P.O. T. Heard.
Sto. P.O. C. G. Hawkins.
P.O. J. W. Harvey.
A.B. G. Hanson.
P.O. W. Halliwell.
P.O., 1st Cl., W. Hooper.
P.O. E. Irving.
C. Sto. W. Johns.
Sto., 1st Cl., S. Jackson.
E.R.A., 2nd Cl., R. G. Jefferson.
P.O. A. E. James.
Boy, 1st Cl., S. J. Keen.
A.B. P. F. Knapman.
C.P.O. W. E. Kent.
P.O. E. Kerry
C. E.R.A. 1st Cl., H. H Lake.

C.P. O.C. Lovell.
P.O., 1st Cl., E. Luckman.
Sto. P.O. W. Long.
C Sto. J. Lyons.
A.B. J. C. Leathers.
C.P.O. J. Matthews.
C. Armr. W. H. Martin.
Sto. P.O. G. H. Manning.
P.O. S. C. A. Medway.
Actg. Bombdr. J. Mulraney.
Armr. I. Mitchell.
C.P.O H. Minns.
Yeo. of Sig. H. R. Mason (now Actg. Sig. Botsn.)
E.R.A., 3rd Cl., R. Monro.
Sto., R.N.R., Y. McConnell.
Sto. P.O. J. McCoy.
E.R.A., 1st Cl, J. S. Marr.
E.R.A., 3rd Cl., M. Macleod.
A.B. C. Mitchell.
C. E.R.A., 2nd Cl., F. Moore.
C.P.O. H. G. Newman.
Sto. P.O. W. Norman.
C. E.R.A., 2nd Cl., C H. Nicholls.
C. E.R.A., 2nd Cl., W. M. Oldrieve.
Sto., R.N.R., J. Orton.
L. Teleg. P. J. Olding.
Sec. Sick Berth Steward H. C. Pridmore.
C.P.O. C. Pengelly.
C.P.O. T. Prebble.
C. Yeo. of Sig. G. H. Pink.
C. P.R.A., 1st Cl., J. L. C. Payne.
C.E.O. C. P. Peckham.
P.O., 1st Cl., G. J. Plummer.
A.B. W. Perrow.
Sig. Boy J. Postles.
C. Shpwrt. J. Pascoe.
Shipwrt., R.N.V.R., H. Peel.
Sick Berth Steward C. Purchase.
C. Armr. H. P. Pike.
C.P.O. J E. Profitt.
P.O. A. H. Potterill.
Yeo. of Sig. W. H. Parker.
C. E.R.A., 1st Cl., F. Rendall.
C.P.O. J. H. Reeves.
C. Armr. H. K. Rounthwaite.
P.O. W. Rennie.

Sergt. H. Ross, R.M.L.I.
Mech. M. Stuart.
C. Yeo of Sig. J. Simmons.
P.O. C. E. Siffleet.
P.O. J. Saddler.
L. Sig. T. Shannon.
P.O. D. Sheppard.
Sto., 1st Cl., R. A. Smith.
C. E.R.A., 1st Cl., J. Searle.
Sto. P.O W R. Seaborne.
Sto., 1st Cl., W. J. Sibley.
C.P.O. R. C. Smith.
P.O. M. Sliney.
P.O. G. E. Smith.
C. Sto. F. C. Smith.
P.O. H. Swales.
C. P.O. T. Sargent.
P.O. Teleg. H..F. Thomas.
C.P.O. E. G. Temlett.
C. Sto. R. Turner.
Ord. Sig. T. S. Tempest.
C. E.R.A., 2nd Cl., S. S. Tozer.
C Sto. A. E. Thurston.
A.B. J. J. Thompson.
C. Sto. F. A. Truscott.
Shipwrt., 2nd Cl., W. S. Walters.
C.P.O. Teleg. G. J. Ward.
Sgt. E. W. Weston.
C.P.O. T. E. Ward.
E.R.A, 3rd Cl., E. Williams.
Boy, 1st Cl., J. E. W. Worn.
Shipwrt., 2nd Cl., H. E. Webley.
Teleg. D. Wyllie.
Actg. C.P.O. J. Webster.
P.O. H. E. Winchester.
Sto., 1st Cl., T. A. Woolley.
Yeo. of Sig. J. V. Wagstaff.
L.-Sgt. A. H. Waterloo, R.M.L.I.
L. Cook's Mate H. G. Walters.
P.O. J. Westlake.

Awarded a Bar to his Distinguished Service Medal for an act of gallantry performed subsequent to that for which the Medal was awarded:

C. Writer S. G. White (award of Medal notified in *Gazette* dated March 3rd, 1915).

For Distinguished Service

COMMENDED FOR GOOD SERVICES.

The following Petty Officers and men are commended for good services in action on the occasion above referred to:

Sto. P.O. H. Allen.
P.O. Teleg. D. Allen.
C. Sto. F. Aldred.
Sick Berth Steward C. R. Allwright.
C.P.O. W. A. Attwood.
P.O. Teleg. E. Ashdown.
Sgt. A. W. Balcombe, R.M.L.I. (killed in action, May 31st, 1916).
Cpl. W. Broadbridge, R.M.A.
Shipwt. 1st Cl. G. H. Brown.
C. Elec. Art. 2nd Cl., S. H. Burchell.
C.P.O. C. F. S. Billing.
C. Sto. A. L. Bond.
Sto. P.O. C. Broadbridge.
Sto. P.O. F. W. Baglin.
C. Yeo. of Sig. S. A. Brooks.
C. Sto. J. D. Brunsdon.
P.O. G. Brummage.
C. E.R.A., 1st Cl., T. A. Bacon.
A.B. F. Barnett.
Boy Teleg. W. Barrett.
Act. C. E.R.A., 2nd Cl., S. Bentley.
P.O., 1st Cl., A. R. Brotherton.
L. Sto. T. Blythin.
Act. L. Sto. A. Bignell.
Sto., 1st Cl., J. H. Bignell.
A.B. H. S. Bevis.
A.B. A. G. Butt.
E.R.A., 2nd Cl., H. Bickerton.
Sgt. H. C. Barlow., R.M.A.
P.O. F. Barber.
A.B. C. B. Brown.
Ord. Smn. F. Baker.
C.P.O. H. Bolton.
L.S. P. T. Belsey.
Act. C.P.O. S. L. Baily.
C. Sto. J. Breen.
Sgt. J. Clerk, R.M.L.I.
Mech. J. Cutlan.
C. Elec. Art., 2nd Cl., A. C. Cornhill.
C. Yeo. of Sig. E. Crompton.
Ship's Cpl., 1st Cl., G. M. Cunningham.
Yeo. of Sig. W. H. J. Campin.
P.O., 1st Cl., A. E. Coulson.
C.P.O. A. G. Clarke.
E.R.A., 3rd Cl., G. W. Coy.
C. Sick Berth Steward, A. G. Camm.
Gnr. E. A. Crawley, R.M.A.
C. Sto. J. D. Cousins.
P.O. Teleg. E. H. Cox.
A.B. A. A. Campbell.
Sgt. F. Cox, R.M.A.
L. Sig. W. Cassin.
L. Teleg. F. Castell.
Act. C.P.O. R. G. Carson.
Sto., 1st Cl., W. C. Cox.
Ship's Steward A. E. Dannan.
C. E.R.A., 1st Cl., F. Dymond.
Sto., 1st Cl., E. Dolphin.
C. E.R.A., 1st Cl., W. A. Dobbie.
Carpenter's Crew E. Dexter.
P.O. J. Deacon.
L. Sto. W. Dane.
C.P.O. J. E. Dudley.
C.P.O. A. G. Dixey.
A.B. P. Driscoll.
A.B. S. T. Ellis (died June 3rd, 1916).
C. Yeo. of Sig. S. F. England.
Act. C. E.R.A., 2nd Cl., E. C. Evans.
C. Stoker W. J. Emery.
Ord. Teleg. A. H. Gordon English.
C.P.O. W. Ewart.
C.P.O. G. W. Epsly.
Musician A. G. S. Flippence, R.M.B.
Mech. D. Finney.
Officers' Steward, 1st Cl., H. Foley.
L. Teleg. E. V. Fossick.
Sto. P.O. E. J. Farley.
Act. C. Ship's Ck. S. G. Frampton.
A.B. R. Fitzgerald.
Sto., 2nd Cl., J. Flynn.
Clr.-Sgt. W. W. Finnigan, R.M.L.I.
Officers' Steward, 1st Cl., C. A. Gravatt.
P.O. G. Grace.
C. Yeo. of Sig. W. H. Gorman.
Mech. W. H. Getheridge.
P.O., 1st Cl., M. Gardiner.
A.B. A. Garden.
Sick Berth Steward W. Gardner.
Ch. Shipwt. F. E. Glew.
Pte. G. W. Green, R.M.L.I.

Sec. Sick Berth Steward H. Gerbert.
Sto. P.O. E. J. Gardner.
C. Yeo. of Sig. W. Gregg.
L. Smn. J. J. Hunt.
L. Smn. A. L. Hill.
E.R.A., 1st Cl., B. W. Hooper.
C. Sto. R. Howard.
P.O. C. R. Hoskin.
P.O. W. H. Hoyle.
C. Sto. F. J. Hooker.
Mech. E. G. Hayter.
P.O. D. Harrington.
C.P.O. A. E. Harry.
C. E.R.A., 1st Cl., G. H. Heal.
C. Elect Art., 2nd Cl., J. Haigh.
Sto. P.O. E. T. Hinds.
Armr. G. W. Heywood.
C. Sto. W. T. Hooker.
Sec. Sick Berth Steward P. C. Harvey.
Shipwt., 1st Cl., J. T. T. Honey.
Sick Berth Steward T. S. Howarth.
C. E.R.A., 1st Cl., G. G. Hill.
Sgt. W. T. Hunt, R.M.L.I.
Pte. W. A. Hamilton, R.M.L.I.
Sto. P.O. F. F. Hills.
C. E.R.A., 2nd Cl., T. W. Hole.
Ship's Cpl., 1st Cl., E. J. Highams.
P.O. C. W. Ives.
C.P.O. H. Jones.
C.P.O. H. T. Jones.
L. Sto. L. J. Jordan.
C. Ship's Ck. T. Jupp.
Shipwrt., 1st Cl., W. G. Jeanes.
Pte. A. J. Jenner, R.M.L.I.
P.O. J. Keane.
C.P.O. R. Kelly.
L.-Sgt. T. Keirby, R.M.L.I.
Sto. P.O. R. Kennedy.
L. Smn. D. J. Keogh (alias Kough).
E.R.A., 3rd Cl., T. C. Kingswell.
C. E.R.A., 2nd Cl., E. Kerkin.
Ship's Steward G. Kingsford.
L.-Sgt. J. R. King, R.M.L.I.
C.P.O. T. Knight.
Act. E.R.A., 4th Cl., R. J. Keating.
C. Writer E. A. Lillicrap.
Bndmr. H. Lodge.
C. Sto. J. W. Lockhart.
Sgt. F. Lefevre, R.M.L.I.

C. Yeo. of Sig. A. Large.
Ship's Steward A. J. Litton.
C. E.R.A., 2nd Cl., R. C. Lee.
Sgt. H. R. Lucas, R.M.A.
C. Arm. W. J. Lewis.
L. Smn. I. Lovell.
Shipwrt., 1st Cl., B. Lucas.
A.B. P. Lawless.
C. E.R.A., 1st Cl., T. H. Love.
L. Sto. M. Lawson.
P.O. H. J. J. Elliot Maxey.
C.P.O. F. L. Marshall.
C. Armr. D. Mansell.
P.O. T. Matthews.
L. Smn. R. V. R. Morris.
Cpl. J. Mulligan, R.M.L.I.
L. Sto. T. McGovern.
Sick Berth Attdt. S. R. Mortimore.
Clr.-Sgt. R. Magson, R.M.A.
Officers' Steward, 1st Cl., J. Miles.
C. E.R.A., 1st Cl., A. McDowall.
P.O. J. Murray.
A.B. A. Oglesby Mudd.
Sgt. A. E. Murrell, R.M.L.I.
L. Smn. L. Martin.
Sgt. E. J. Nichol, R.M.A.
C. Sick Berth Steward J. A. Neal.
C.P.O. R. Oliver.
C. Armr. T. V. Orden.
Shipwrt., 1st Cl., C. A. Osborne.
A.B. E. B. Olivant.
A.B. J. E. Potts.
Boy, 1st Cl., P. P.
C.P.O. W. H. Palmer.
C. Sto. W. Parkinson.
Sto. P.O. G. Parmenter.
Clr.-Sgt. W. H. Potter, R.M.A.
Sec. Sick Berth Steward W. H. Peard.
C.P.O. F. W. Pilcher.
L. Smn. J. H. Pedrick.
Sto., 1st Cl., R. Prout.
Officer's Steward, 1st Cl., A. R. Poor.
Officer's Steward, 1st Cl., R. Picani.
L. Smn. R. W. Pearce.
P.O. A. F. Painter.
L.S. S. J. Pooley.
Pte. W. J. Patterson, R.M.L.I.
    (killed in action, 31st May, 1916).
Officers' Steward, 2nd Cl., F. Pook.

For Distinguished Service

P.O. H. F. Pearce.
Sto. P.O. G. H. Pragnell.
A.B. A. E. Pethybridge.
C.P.O. J. Rye.
A.B. W. Reid.
Clr.-Sgt. L. D. Roberts, R.M.L.I.
P.O. Teleg. R. E. Rendle.
Sgt. J. Reid, R.M.L.I.
C.P.O. W. Reed.
Shipwrt., 1st Cl., A. V. Revans.
C. Armr. E. T. Reeve.
E.R.A., 3rd Cl., E. F. Roser.
Act. E.R.A., 4th Cl., A. D. Reid.
Act. Yeo. of Sig. P. F. Redfern.
Sto., 1st Cl., W. Roberts.
C.P.O. J. H. L. Rundle.
Master-at-Arms W. H. Scott.
P.O. Teleg. M. Skinner.
C. Shipwrt. R. J. Seymour.
Sgt. A. E. Stevens, R.M.A.
C. Writer W. H. Sleep.
Ship's Steward A. J. Sutton.
P.O. L. Silvers.
C. E.R.A., 2nd Cl., P. S. Smith.
Sgt. W. E. Shaw, R.M.A.
Clr.-Sgt. A. Spooner, R.M.A.
C. E.R.A., 1st Cl., C. J. Stobart.
A.B. C. J. Skelsey.
Sto. P.O. C. Sadgrove.
P.O. J. L. Strevens.
C.P.O. C. Smith.
Boy, 1st Cl., H. S. Sears.
L. Sig. D. Smith.
Pte. W. Smith, R.M.L.I.
(killed in action 31st May, 1916).
C.P.O. A. E. Smith.
E.R.A., 3rd Cl., J. V. Shaw.
C. Sto. A. J. Smith.
C.P.O. W. J. Stacey.
C. Sto. W. Tink.
C. Sto. W. H. Trowell.
Act. E.R.A., 4th Cl., R. Thornton.
C. E.R.A., 1st Cl., E. A. Turner.
Sgt. H. L. Vale, R.M.A.
C. Yeo. of Sig. G. Whitby.
P.O. Teleg. J. R. Wolley.
C. Yeo. of Sig. T. White.
C. Writer L. J. Watkins.
L. Teleg. E. J. Weller.

Sto. P.O. R. Whiting.
Sto., 1st Cl., P. Walsh.
C.P.O. W. Williams.
Master-at-Arms E. Warnes.
P.O. J. Weddick.
Yeo. of Sig. H. S. Wilmot.
Pte. H. Willows, R.M.L.I.
Ord. Smn. R. A. Wise.
Pte. A. V. Whatley, R.M.L.I.
Sto., 1st Cl., J. White.
Master-at-Arms A. T. Woodcock.
C. Elect. Art., 2nd Cl., G. Walmsley.
Mech. H. A. Woodman.
C. Sto. S. T. Wade.
L.S. W. Walmsley.
C. Yeo. of Sig. H. Wood.
Ship's Steward Asst. W. Wallace.
L.-Sgt. G. R. Westlake, R.M.L.I.
A.B. C. J. Woodhouse.
E.R.A., 1st Cl., S. A. Webber.
Sto. P.O. J. Watson.
C. E.R.A., 2nd Cl., J. B. Yarrell.
Canteen Assts. F. Percival and W. Rutt.

———

A supplement to the *London Gazette*, issued on Thursday, October 19th, 1916, contained the following list of mentioned for honours conferred by the King for services in connection with the operations in Mesopotamia:

Lt.-Com. J. E. P. Bickford.
Staff-Surg. E. Cameron, M.B.
Mr. H. P. Chapman.
Lt.-Com. C. J. F. Eddis.
Lieut. H. O. B. Firman (killed).
Surg. E. G. Hitch, M.B.
Capt. W. Nunn, C.M.G., D.S.O.
Lieut. G. W. T. Robertson.
Comdr. E. Mc. Rutherfoord.
Com. D. St. A. Wake.
Comdr. C. R. Wason.
Lieut. R. P. D. Webster.
R.A. (Act. V.A.) Sir R. E. Wemyss, K.C.B., C.M.G., M.V.O.
Paymr. S. J. Wright.
Gnr. J. B. Ham.
P.O. J. Robertson.

Gnr. J. B. Spanner.
P.O. W. H. Wakeling.

The King has awarded the following decorations to Naval Officers, February 16th, 1917:

D.S.O.

Flt.-Lt. Stanley James Goble, D.S.C., R.N.A.S.
For conspicuous bravery and skill in attacking hostile aircraft on numerous occasions. On November 7th, 1916, he attacked an enemy scout, and chased it down to 1,500 feet, when it was seen to land, crash into a fence, and turn over in a field. On November 27th, 1916, he attacked four hostile scouts, one of which he brought down in flames. On December 4th, 1916, on six different occasions during the same flight he attacked and drove off hostile aircraft which threatened the bombing machines which he was escorting, one of the hostile machines going down completely out of control.

Capt. Harry Hesketh Smyth, R.N.

Lt.-Com. Malcolm Raphael Joseph Maxwell Scott, R.N.

Lieut. Matthew Armstrong, R.N.R.

Distinguished Service Cross.

Flt..-Com. Williams Geoffrey Moore, R.N.A.S.
In recognition of excellent work which he has done in East Africa, and especially on January 10th, 1917, when he flew a distance of 300 miles from Ubena to Mahenje. He obtained important results in bombing flights.

Flgt.-Lt. Limnel Conrad Shoppee, R.N.A.S.
For conspicuous gallantry and enterprise during a bomb attack by aircraft on an important enemy railway bridge. Subsequent reconnaissance showed that the whole of the centre section of the bridge had collapsed into the river, thereby interrupting important enemy railway communications.

Flgt.-Lt. Edward Rockfort Grange, R.N.A.S.
For conspicuous gallantry and skill on several occasions in successfully attacking and bringing down hostile machines, particularly on January 4th, 1917, when during one flight he had three separate engagements with hostile machines, all of which were driven down out of control. On January 5th, 1917, he attacked three hostile machines, one of which was driven down in a nose dive. On January 7th, 1917, after having driven down one hostile machine, he observed two other enemy aircraft attacking one of our scouts. He was on the way to its assistance, when he was attacked by a third hostile scout. He was hit in the shoulder by a bullet from this machine, but landed his aeroplane safely in the aerodrome on our side of the lines.

Flgt.-Sub-Lt. Robert Alexander Little, R.N.A.S.
For conspicuous bravery in successfully attacking and bringing down hostile machines on several occasions. On November 19th, 1916, he attacked and brought down a hostile machine in flames. On December 12th he attacked a German machine at a range of 50 yards. This machine was brought down in a nose dive. On December 20th he dived at a hostile machine, and opened fire at 25 yards range. The observer was seen to fall down inside the machine, which went down in a spinning nose dive. On January 1st, 1917, he attacked an enemy scout, which turned over on its back and came down completely out of control.

Lieut. John Lawrie, R.N.R.
Lieut. Cedric Naylor, R.N.R.
Act.-Lieut. Philip James Hogg, R.N.R.
C. Gnr. (T.) Richard Hawker, R.N.

BAR TO HIS DISTINGUISHED SERVICE CROSS.

Flgt.-Lieut. Daniel Murray Boyne Galbraith, D.S.C., R.N.A.S.
For conspicuous gallantry. On November 23rd, 1916, he attacked single-handed a formation of six hostile aircraft, no other Allies' machines being in the vicinity. One hostile machine was shot down, a second was driven down not under control, and the remaining four machines then gave up the fight and landed. In several other combats in the air Flgt.-Lt. Galbraith has displayed exceptional gallantry, particularly on November 10th and 16th, 1916, on each of which days he successfully engaged and shot down an enemy machine.

A supplement to the *London Gazette*, issued on Wednesday, October 25th, 1916, contained the following list of appointments and honours bestowed by the King for services during the war:

C.B.

Capt. E. L. Booty, M.V.O., R.N. (Commodore, 2nd Cl.).
Capt. Arthur Kipling Waistell, R.N.

C.M.G.

Capt. Cathcart Romer Wason, R.N.

D.S.O.

Comdr. Ernest William Leir, R.N.
Comdr. Charles Stuart Benning, R.N.
Lt.-Com. Robert Ross Turner, R.N.
Lt.-Com. Robert Henry Taunton Raikes, R.N.

Lieut. George Elliott Harden, R.N.
Lieut. Humphrey Maurice Robson, R.N.
Flt.-Lt. Colin Roy Mackenzie, R.N.A.S.

DISTINGUISHED SERVICE CROSS.

Lieut. Stephen Clive Lyttelton, R.N.
Lieut. Rodolph Henry Fane De Salis, R.N.
Lieut. Anthony Bevis Lockhart, R.N.
Lieut. George Samuel Brown, R.N.
Lieut. James Lawrence Boyd, R.N.
Lieut. Douglas Carteret Sealy, R.N.
Lieut. Adrian Henry James Stokes, R.N.
Flgt.-Com. Tom Harry England, R.N.A.S.
Flgt.-Lt. Charles Teverill Freeman, R.N.A.S.
Flgt.-Sub-Lt. Stanley James Goble, R.N.A.S.
Flgt.-Sub.Lt. Ronald Grahame, R.N.A.S.
Flgt.-Sub-Lt. Daniel M. B. Galbraith, R.N.A.S.
Sub-Lt. (now Act.-Lt.) J. G. Wood, R.N.R.
Lieut. Benjamin Rowley George Kent, R.N.R.
Act.-Lt. Hugh Donald Wynne, R.N.R.
Sub-Lt. Frederick Henry Good, R.N.R.
C. Gnr. Robert John Thomas, R.N.
Act.-Lt. Denis A. Casey, R.N.R.
Act.-Lt. Arthur George Madan, R.N.R.
Gnr. (T.) Reuben James McVittie, R.N.
Skipper Charles Angus, R.N.R.

The King has further been pleased to approve of the award of a Bar to the Distinguished Service Cross of the undermentioned warrant officer for a subsequent act of gallantry:

Skipper Alfred Robert Thompson, D.S.C., R.N.R.

(The award of the Distinguished Service Cross was notified in *Gazette* dated 31st May, 1916).

E

Distinguished Service Medal.

M.A.A. A. Foxwell, R.F.R.
C. Armr. Robert Cook.
C. Shpwrt. Geo. Henry Mears.
P.O. Alfred Charles Barrett.
P.O. Frank Thomas Mill.
Yeo. of Sig. William Hough.
L.S. J. McKinlay, R.F.R.
A.B. F. T. Meade, R.F.R.
A.B. William Charles Austen.
Yeo. of Sig. Wilfred Chapman.
P.O. William Arthur Osborn.
A.B. Charles Donald Jones.
P.O. Teleg. Lewis J. Isaac.
Colr.-Sgt. Geo Burley, R.M.L.I.
P.O. William Henry Murdoch.
P.O. Thomas Powell Sproat.
L.S. James Boland.
Sto. P.O. George Henry Newland.
P.O. Cecil Ernest Edgar Miles.
Sto., 1st Cl., William Goulding.
C.P.O. Sidney Allen Watkins.
L.S. George Cameron.
Engr.-Driver, 1st Cl., Saidu Hoosbein.
P.O., 1st Cl., Henry John Wheeler.
Interpreter, 3rd Cl., Mohammed Nagaf.
Act. L. Sto. John Duncan.
Lce.-Cpl. Robert Emmett, R.M.L.I.
C.E.R.A, 2nd Cl., George Perry.
Act. C. Sto. William Henry Gitsham.
L.S. Norman Harry, R.N.R.
Seaman Albert Edward Bush, R.N.R.
Seaman M. Pottle, R.N.R. (Newfoundland).
C. Fireman William G. Benton, M.R.
Donkeyman Daniel Gartlan, M.R.
Greaser John Longman, M.R.
Greaser Duncan McKenzie, M.R.
Fireman Thomas Harris, M.R.
Engine-room Rating H. W. Longley, M.R.
Sec. Hnd. John Ritchie, R.N.R.
Sec. Hnd. G. E. Smith, R.N.R.

Mentioned in Despatches.

Act. Eng.-Com. James Richard Clay, R.D., R.N.R.
Lt.-Com. William Charles Tarrant, R.N.R.
Act. Lt. Herbert Percival, R.N.R.
Act. Sub.-Lt. (Act.) R. D. Cruickshank, R.N.R.
Temp. Asst.-Payr. R. P. Henery, R.N.R. (now Temp. Lt., R.N.V.R.)
Sub-Lt. A. G. Cameron, R.N.R.-(since killed).
Capt. Harry Hesketh Smyth, R.N.
Lt.-Com. (Act. Com.) John May, R.N.
Com. Anthony Hamilton, S.D.O., R.I.M.
Staff Surg. Ewen Cameron, M.B., R.N.,
Surg. Frederick George Hitch, M.B. R.N.
Shpwt., 2nd Cl., G. L. Thomas.
C.P.O. George Baker.
C.P.O. Edmund Phillippo.
M.A.A. Samuel Rundle.
Ch. Yeo. of Sig. Charles Chapman.
C. Arm. W. E. Butchers.
Elec. Art., 4th Cl., W. J. Hayward.
P.O., 1st Cl., Arthur Banfield James.
Act. Arm. Norvel Birkett Forster.
L.S. W. A. Groves, R.N.V.R.
Sig. Leonard Prosser, R.N.V.R., Wales.
Sgt. Wm. Perkins, R.M.A.
Pte. Joseph Henry Westall, R.M.L.I.
Pte. Ernest Throssell, R.M.L.I.
Seaman John Pritchard, R.N.R.
Seaman William James Findlay, R.N.R.
Trimmer Robert Brown M.R.
P.O. William J. Day.
Yeo. of Sig. John Thirsk.
P.O. Charles Henry Parker.
C. Arm. Alfred Hutchings.
Yeo. of Sig. Walter Seager Briden.
Greaser William Dawkins, (1) M.R.
Fireman Barclay McCann, M.R.

Promotions.

The undermentioned Petty Officers have been promoted to warrant rank in recognition of their services in the battle of Jutland :

Act. C.P.O. John Webster, to be acting boatswain, dated 30th June, 1916.
Shpwrt., 1st Cl., Martin Bray, to be act. carpenter, dated 30th June, 1916.

For Distinguished Service

C.E.R.A., 1st Cl., Ernest Francis Edge, to be act. art.-engr., dated 30th June, 1916.

C.S.B.S. John George Beal, to be Warrant Warmaster, dated 25th September, 1916.

COMMENDED.

The following Petty Officers and men of the Grand Fleet are commended for service in action in the battle of Jutland:

L.S. Samuel Alexander.
L.S. Walter Bamsey.
C. S.B.S. John George Beal.
Armr. Joseph Bellamy.
Shpwt., 1st Cl., Harold P. Bennett.
I.S. Frederick Butterfield.
Ship's Steward Asst. Jeremiah Connor.
L.S. John William Dunn.
Yeo. of Sig. Arthur Friche.
L.S. Walter Henry Fryer.
P.O. Teleg. Montague John Gates.
Ship's Steward Walter John Gunn.
L. Teleg. Stanley Hodkinson.
L.S. George Jennings Hulin.
L.S. Alfred Edward Jordan.
Sec. Sick Berth Steward Vincent Lloyd.
Sec. Sick Berth Steward G. W. Light.
L. Teleg. H. E. G. Newman.
P.O. Thomas Henry Olding.
P.O. William George Pearce.
Sto., 1st Cl., R. H. Regan.
Yeo. of Sig. Frank Rockett.
A.B. Arthur James Rudge.
P.O. William John Albert Shaw.
L. Sig. William Stewart.
P.O. W. A. Wakeling (now acting Gnr.).
Boy, 1st Cl., Robert Walker.
A.B. Frank Robert Watts.
Sto. P.O. Alfred James Webb.
Sto., P.O. George David Wyeth.
Sto., 1st Cl., William Yeo.

A supplement to the *London Gazette*, issued on Monday, January 1st, 1917, contained a long list of honours awarded by the King in connection with naval and military operations. Those bestowed on officers and men of the Navy are as follow:

ORDER OF THE BATH.
K.C.B.
V.A. Willian Lowther Grant.

C.B.
V.A. Richard Bowles Farquhar.
R.A. Godfrey Harry Brydges Mundy.
R.A. Henry Hervey Campbell.
R.A. Edmund Radcliffe Pears.
R.A. Charles Lionel Vaughan-Lee.
Capt. Brian Herbert Fairbairn Barttelot R.N.
Col. (Temp. Brig.-Gen.) Herbert Southey Neville White, R.M.L.I.
Eng.-R.A. William John Anstey.
Insp.-Gen. John Cassitis Birkmyre MacLean, M.B., R.N.
Paymaster-in-Chief William Le Geyt Pullen, R.N.

ADDITIONAL AWARDS FOR THE BATTLE OF JUTLAND.

ORDER OF THE BATH.
C.B.
Capt. Anselan John B. Stirling, R.N., D.SO.
Flt.-Surg. Ernest Alfred Penfold, M.B. R.N.
Comdr. John Coombe Hodgson, R.N.
Lt.-Com. Evelyn Claude O. Thomson, R.N.
Capt. Harold Blount, R.M.A.

DISTINGUISHED SERVICE CROSS.
Mr. Francis William Potter, gunner, R.N.
Mr. Thomas Bazley, Gunner, (T) R.N.

CONSPICUOUS GALLANTRY MEDAL.
Colr.Sgt. Abraham Spooner, R.M.A.
L. Sto. Thomas McGovern (Dev.)

Distinguished Service Medal.

C.E.R.A., 1st Cl., Frank Dymond.
C.E.R.A., 1st Cl., Herbert Neal.
C.E.R.A., 2nd Cl., William Ford.
C.E.R.A., 2nd Cl., Robert Charles Lees.
C.P.O. William Henry Palmer.
C. Sto. Frederick Aldred.
Ship's Steward Arthur James Litton.
Colr.Sgt. Leonard Daw Roberts R.M.L.I.
Sgt. Harry Richard Lucas, R.M.A.
C. Yeo. of Sig. George Whitby.
P.O. William Henry Hoyle.
P.O. Tomson Matthews.
P.O., 1st Cl., Edward Charles Street.
Sto. P.O. George Parmenter.
S.B.S. Charles Robert Allwright.
E.R.A., 3rd Cl., Edward Frank Roser.
Sto., 1st Cl., Patrick Walsh.
A.B. Hubert Samuel Bevis.
Officers' Steward, 2nd Cl., Frank Pook.
Musician Arthur George Sylvester Flippence, R.M.

Sto. P.O. George French.
P.O. Teleg. Neil MacLeod.
E.R.A., 2nd Cl., John Friend Kellaway
E.R.A., 2nd Cl., George Henry Langmead.
E.R.A., 3rd Cl., Henry Cameron Booth
Ship's Cpl., 1st Cl., Samuel Edwin Wills.
S.B.S. Lyonel Ivo Percy Sabin.
Signalman Montague Charles Chandor.
Corpl. Alfred Phipps, R.M.L.I.
L. Ck's. Mate George Edwin Sparks.
Gnr. Charles Beard, R.M.A.
Officers' Steward, 1st Cl., John Spiteri.
Officers' Steward, 3rd Cl., Albert Batty.

Correction.

The name of L. Sto. Ellis James Hignett, which appeared in the list of men awarded the Distinguished Service Medal for services in the battle of Jutland in the *London Gazette* of September 15th, 1916, should read: Sto. Thomas Henry Hignett, R.N.R.

Commended.

Engr. Capt. Archie Russell Emdin, R.N.
Comdr. Guy Plantagenet Brigg-Withers, R.N.
Comdr. Wilfred Frankland French, R.N.
Flt. Payr. Harold Rodham, R.N.
Flt. Lt. Comdr. Sydney Hopkins, R.N.
Paymr. John Duncan Macaulay Cavanagh, R.N.
Lieut. the Hon. Charles A. Colville, R.N.
Asst.-Paymr. Harold Charles F. Foot, R.N.
C.P.O. John Coleman.
C. Shipwt. Arthur Edward Foster.
C. Yeo of Sig. Oscar Charlton Cox.
Flt. C.E.R.A., 1st Cl., Frederick C. Selway.
Act. C.E.R.A., 2nd Cl., Archibald F. Tammadge.
P.O. Ernest Southcott.
P.O. William Henry Winsor.
Sto. P.O. Henry Ernest Woodland.

Mine-Sweeping Operations.

D.S.O.

Comdr. Hugh Seymour, R.N.
Lt.-Com. (Act. Comdr.) Leslie D. Fisher, R.N.
Lt.-Com. Daniel McDowell, R.N.

Distinguished Service Cross.

Lieut. Peter Alexander C. Sturrock, R.N.
Lieut. Arthur Edgar Buckland, R.N.
Tempy. Lieut. J. C. Bird (Lieut., R.I.M., retd.).
Lieut. William G. Wood, R.N.R.
Lieut. Geoffrey Unsworth, R.N.R.
Lieut. Rudolph Lancelot Wikner, R.N.R.
Lieut. William St. Clair Fleming, R.N.R.
Lieut. John Percival Tugwood, R.N.R.
Act. Lieut. William George Duggan, R.N.R.

For Distinguished Service

Skipper Frederick Alfred Sibley, R.N.R.
Skipper Benjamin Robert Joyce, R.N.R.
Skipper George Ferguson, R.N.R.
Skipper Alexander McLeod, R.N.R.
Skipper Alexander McKay, R.N.R.
Skipper Donald McMillan, R.N.R.
Skipper Samson Herbert Hayes, R.N.R.

DISTINGUISHED SERVICE MEDAL.

C.P.O. Thomas Robert Cozens. R.F.R.
C.P.O. James Henry Lancey.
C.P.O. John Edward Perritt, R.F.R.
P.O., 1st Cl., George Charles Day, R.F.R.
A.B. William Robert Bull.
P.O. William Herbert Winton.
P.O., 1st Cl., William A. Adams, R.F.R.
A.B. William Thomas Elliot.
Seaman William Spry, R.N.R.
Boy Teleg. Ernest Kelly.
E.R.A., 1st Cl., Albert George Pearson.
Sto. P.O. William Driver.
Engmn. William Betmead.
Engmn. Fred William Briggs, R.N.R.
Engmn. Harold Cooke, R.N.R.
Engmn. Charles Edward East. R.N.R.
Engmn. William Fleming, R.N.R.
Engmn. James Reid, R.N.R.
Engmn. Charles Edward Vittery, R.N.R.
Engmn. Fred Percy Wilson, R.N.R.
Trimmer Richard Morrison, R.N.R.
Sec. Hnd Richard Combe, R.N.R.
Sec. Hnd. John Noble Stephen, R.N.R.
Sec. Hnd. Francis John Williams, R.N.R.
Dk. Hnd. Alexander Davidson, R.N.R.
Dk. Hnd. Bert Huntingdon, R.N.R.
Dk. Hnd. Daniel Nithsdale, R.N.R.
Dk. Hnd. David William Leon Simpson R.N.R.
Dk. Hnd. Charles Shell, R.N.R.

COMMENDED.

Capt. Hubert Henry Holland, R.N.
Capt. Francis Evelyn Massy-Dawson, R.N.

Comdr. Robert William Dalgety, R.N.
Lieut. Claude Preston Hermon-Hodge, R.N.
Lieut. Howard McGloshan, R.N.R.
Lieut. John Wales, R.N.R.
Lieut. Wilfrid Walter Storey, R.N.R.
Skipper Henry Lead, R.N.R.
Skipper William Parker, R.N.R.
Skipper George Dow Summers, R.N.R.
C.P.O. Robert Ross Howitt.
C.P.O. Thomas Scamaton, R.N.R.
P.O., 1st Cl., Aaron Barker, R.F.R.
P.O., 1st Cl., Henry John Dormer
P.O., 1st Cl., Horace Charles Pallant, R.F.R.
P.O., 1st Cl., John H. Thompson R.F.R.
P.O. Edward Alfred Hatt.
Act. P.O. William George Brown, R.N.R.
L.S. Donald MacDonald, R.N.R.
L.S. George McKay, R.N.R.
C. Yeo. of Sig. Frederick Neal.
L. Sig. John W. Dudley, R.N.V.R.
Sig. William F. Batty, R.N.V.R.
E.R.A., 3rd C.l, George Robert J. Lighton.
L. Sto. George T. McCarthy.
Engmn. Fred Drayton, R.N.R.
Engmn. Charles Thomas, R.N.R.
L. Trimmer George Wouldhave, R.N.R.
Trimmer William Brown, R.N.R.
Trimmer Stephen Balls, R.N.R.
Dk. Hnd. Albert Edward Bull, R.N.R.
Dk. Hand Charles Broughton, R.N.R.
Dk. Hnd. James Roland Brown, R.N.R.
Dk. Hnd. Clifford Andrew Jackson, R.N.R.
Dk. Hnd. Herbert Mayes, R.N.R.
L.S. Walter Carter (mercantile rating).
Sec. Hnd. Ernest Robert Gooder Ham, R.N.R.

SUBMARINE SERVICE.

DISTINGUISHED SERVICE MEDAL.

L.S. Albert William Broadway.
Act. L. Sto. Lionel Elsom Corker.
L. Sig. Frederick Thomas Davis.

E.R.A., 3rd Cl., Sidney Lewis D Frampton.
P.O. William Edmund Goddard.
P.O. William Harry Gunton.
P.O. Richard Charles Hammett.
P.O. Edwin Walter Harrison.
P.O. Edward Haydon.
A.B. George William Hodder.
Act. L. Sto. Walter Humphries.
P.O. John Ilott.
Act. L. Sto. Charles Kessell.
L.S. Benjamin Charles Litchfield.
L.S. Patrick Andrew McEvoy.
C. Sto. George Plain.
P.O. Alfred Albert Ernest Phillips.
Sto., 1st Cl., Percy Sidney Saville.
L. Teleg. Albert Thomas Sibthorpe.
P.O. Roland Thomas Stripp.
L.S. Albert Owen Tilbury.
E.R.A., 3rd Cl., Alfred Alexander Truscott.
Act. C.E.R.A., 2nd Cl., Alexander Weir.
A.B. Harry Winter.

Mentioned in Despatches.

L.S. John Rodway Adams.
L. Sto. Harry James Bentley (since dead).
P.O. Bertram Wabon Brett.
Sto. P.O. John George Bowers.
P.O. Robert John Brown.
Sto. P.O. William Brown.
L. Sto. Albert Edward Byles.
L.S. Robert Diamond.
Act. L. Sto. Sidney Doble.
Act. L. Sto. James William Alfred Formoy.
P.O. Percival George Fry.
C.P.O. Joseph Henry Johnson.
A.B. Joseph Golden Langridge (since dead).
P.O. William Arthur McGill.
P.O. John Neal.
E.R.A., 2nd Cl., Gilbert Oxley (since dead).
A.B. James Patrick O'Regan.
P.O. Ernest Gordon Powell.
A.B. George Thomas Purkiss.
Act. L. Sto. Frank Benjamin Stallard.
P.O. Ernest James Rodgers.
E.R.A., 2nd Cl., Edward Frederick Cowley Sutton.
L.Sto. Frederick Trudgeon.
E.R.A., 3rd Cl., Robert Alfred Wilson.

Miscellaneous Services.

D.S.O.

Comdr. Frederick Edward Ketelbey Strong, R.N.
Comdr. Francis Henry Grenfell, R.N.
Comdr. H. C. V. B. Cheetham, R.D., R.N.R.
Lt.-Com. Arthur Alured Mellin, R.N.
Lt.-Com. John de Burgh Jessop, R.N
Lt.-Com. Henry George Gardiner Westmore, R.D., R.N.R.
Lt.-Com. John Percival, R.N.R.
(The appointment to the Distinguished Service Order was announced in the *London Gazette*, February 24th 1916.)

Distinguished Service Cross.

Flt.-Lieut. Ernest William Norton R.N.A.S.
Surg. Hother McCormack Hanschell R.N.
Lieut. Arthur Darville Dudley, R.N.V.R.
Sub.-Lt. Guy Trevarton Sholl, R.N.V.R.
Gnr. (T.) James Albert Graham, R.N.
Capt. John Couch, master of the transport "Trevorian."

Distinguished Service Medal.

C. Eng. F. L. Angus, Nigeria Marine Contingent.
C.E.R.A., 1st Cl., Albert Charles Burton.
Mechn. Harry Clifford Curtis.
P.O. Herbert Henry Bond Whitty.
Elect. Art., 2nd Cl., Henry Frederick Williams.
A.B. Albert Edward John Stevens.
Pte. William F. Hammond, R.M.L.I.
Corpl. Frederick W. Hemmings, R.M.L.I.

For Distinguished Service

Lce.-Corpl. Albert C. Rutland, R.M.L.I.
P.O. John Butters, R.F.R.
Dk. Hnd. Leonard Findlay, R.N.R.
P.O. Albert Edward Gregory.
P.O. Frederick Dart.
P.O. Joseph Richard Ashfield.
E.R.A., 3rd Cl., Frank William Crabbe
P.O., 1st Cl., William John Adams.
L.S. Daniel Joseph Donovan.
P.O. Thomas Heffernan.
Act. C.-Armr. Albert Henry Hinks.
Armourer's Crew Ernest Charles King
L.S. James Robert Sole.
A.B. Charles George Bremer Barham.
Sgt. Walter Henry France, R.M.A.
Gnr. Adam Fenton, R.M.A.
P.O. William Ernest Sims.
P.O. Mechanic Charles Ernest Cobb, R.N.A.S.
P.O. Mech. Donald McLean Graham, R.N.A.S.
A.B. Herbert William Marsh.
Seaman George Behenna, R.N.R.
Sigmn. George Sydney Tosker, R.N.V.R.

Mentioned in Despatches.

Comdr. Walton Cornelius Grinnell Ruxton, R.N.
Fleet-Surg. Alfred James Hewitt, R.N.
Lt.-Com. Patrick Stewart E. Maxwell, R.N.
Lt.-Com. Andrew Purdon, R.N.R.
Lieut. Roland Arbuthnot Clark. R.N.
C. Writer Frederick Thomas Abbot.
L.S. William John Bryant.
Yeo. of Sig. John Burke.
P.O. George Gill.
A.B. Archibald McLeod Pratt (since dead).
P.O. Teleg. Archibald Williams.
L.-Fireman Michael Keelan (M.R.)
Asst.-Paymr. W. Eastwood, R.N.V.R.
Warrant Officer, 2nd Grade, R. H. Mullin, R.N.A.S.
C.P.O. William Waterhouse.
P.O. Daniel Joseph Murphy.
E.R.A. Hubert Berry, R.N.R.
A.B. William Tanner.

Seaman Jeremiah Brien, R.N.R.
Sto. John Wood, R.N.R.

Promoted for War Service.

Sub.-Lt. Charles Tyrer, R.N.V.R., to to be Lieut., November 28th, 1916.

Noted for Accelerated Promotion

Flt.-Surg. Alfred James Hewitt, R.N. has been noted for accelerated promotion in recognition of the conspicuous gallantry and very exceptional professional ability which he displayed as medical officer of H.M.S. " Pegasus " when that ship was sunk by the " Konigsberg " in September, 1914.

DECORATIONS BY KING OF THE BELGIANS

Ordre de Leopold.
Commandeur.

Capt. Charles Duncan Johnson, M.V.O. D.S.O., R.N. (Commodore 2nd Cl.).

Officier.

Capt. Humphrey W. Bowring, D.S.O., R.N.
Capt. Bernard St. George Collard, R.N.
Comdr. Edward Ratcliffe G. R. Evans, C.B., R.N.
Comdr. Gerald Louis Saurin, R.N.
Comdr. Henry Crosby Halahan D.S.O., R.N.
Capt. Stanley Ray Miller, R.N.

Chevalier.

Lieut. Richard Prescott Kelgwin, R.N.V.R.
Lieut. Arthur William L. Brewill, D.S.C., R.N.
Lieut. Guy Langton Warren, R.N.

Ordre de la Couronne.
Chevalier.

Mr. George Frederick Wheeler, boatswain, R.N.

ORDRE DE LEOPOLD II.
CHEVALIER.

Act. C.P.O. Albert Edward Cocks.
C.P.O. George Hubbard.
C.-Shipwrt. Dennis McCartney.
E.R.A. Robert Alwyn Wainwright, R.N.R.
C.P.O. Harry Barnley.
C.E.R.A., 2nd Cl., Samuel Abbott Earle.
C.P.O. Charles Rose.
Officers' Steward, 1st Cl., Albert Philbrick.
P.O. Hayward George Piper.
Yeo. of Sig. Stanley Wallace Muirhead.

Act. Arm. Edgar Matthews Brown Adcock.
P.O. Herbert Moore.
1st Writer Walter Henry Sheather.
C.P.O. Percy Lionel Crowther.

DECORATION MILITAIRE.
L.S. Bernard Cyril Watson.
Sto., 1st Cl., George Edward Herring.
Sto., 1st Cl., William Driver.
A.B. Edward Charles Woods.
L.-Sig. William Noon.
Sto., 1st Cl., William John Vivian.
A.B. John Mitchell Stewart.
A.B. Charles Ernest Ellwood.

COMMANDER OF H.M.S. "SHARK."
(GOVERNMENT PRESS BUREAU, MARCH 5TH, 1917.)

The King has been graciously pleased to approve of the posthumous grant of the Victoria Cross to the undermentioned officer in recognition of his most conspicuous bravery and devotion to duty in the course of the battle of Jutland. The full facts have only now been ascertained :

Com. Loftus Wm. Jones, R.N. (killed in action)

On the afternoon of May 31st, 1916, during the action, Com. Jones, in H.M.S. "Shark," torpedo-boat destroyer, led a division of destroyers to attack the enemy Battle-Cruiser Squadron. In the course of this attack a shell hit the "Shark's" bridge, putting the steering gear out of order, and very shortly afterwards another shell disabled the main engines, leaving the vessel helpless. The Commanding Officer of another destroyer, seeing the "Shark's" plight, came between her and the enemy and offered assistance, but was warned by Com. Jones not to run the risk of being almost certainly sunk in trying to help him. Com. Jones, though wounded in the leg, went aft to help connect and man the after wheel. Meanwhile the forecastle gun with its crew had been blown away, and the same fate soon afterwards befel the after gun and crew. Com. Jones then went to the midship and only remaining gun, and personally assisted in keeping it in action. All this time the "Shark" was subjected to very heavy fire from enemy light cruisers and destroyers at short range. The gun's crew of the midship gun was reduced to three, of whom an able seaman was soon badly wounded in the leg. A few minutes later Com. Jones was hit by a shell, which took off his leg above the knee, but he continued to give orders to his gun's crew, while a chief stoker improvised a tourniquet round his thigh. Noticing that the Ensign was not properly hoisted, he gave orders for another to be hoisted. Soon afterwards, seeing that the ship could not survive much longer, and as a German destroyer was closing, he gave orders for the surviving members of the crew to put on lifebelts. Almost immediately after this order had been given the "Shark" was

For Distinguished Service

struck by a torpedo and sunk. Com. Jones was unfortunately not amongst the few survivors from the " Shark," who were picked up by a neutral vessel in the night.

The following awards have also been made to the survivors of H.M.S. " Shark " for their services during the action :

DISTINGUISHED SERVICE MEDAL.

Sto. P. O. Charles Filloul.
A.B. Charles Cleeberg Hope.
A.B. Charles Herbert Smith.

A.B. Joseph Owen Glendower Howell.
Sto., 1st Cl., Thomas Wilton Swan.
P.O. William Charles Richard Griffin.

A supplement to the *London Gazette*, of March 12th, 1917, contained a list of honours awarded by the King to officers and men of the " Broke " and " Swift " for their services in the recent action with six German destroyers in the Channel, in which two enemy vessels were sunk. The Secretary of the Admiralty reports that his Majesty signified his approval of the awards in the following words :

I have much pleasure in approving these awards in recognition of the splendid action of the " Swift " and " Broke " with German destroyers. Officers and men in their conduct did more than uphold the grand traditions of the British Navy.

(Signed) GEORGE, R.I.

Below is the text of the document, which adds some interesting details of individual acts of gallantry in what was one of the striking Naval successes of the war :

D.S.O.

The King has been graciously pleased to give orders for the appointment of the undermentioned officers to be Companions of the Distinguished Service Order, in recognition of their services in command of his Majesty's ship " Swift " and his Majesty's ship " Broke " respectively, on the night of April 20th-21st, 1917, when they successfully engaged a flotilla of five or six German destroyers, of which two were sunk :

Cdr. (now Capt.) Ambrose M. Peck, R.N.

Cdr. (now Capt.) Edward R. G. R. Evans, C.B., R.N.

D.S.C.

The King has further been graciously pleased to give orders for the award of the Distinguished Service Cross to the undermentioned officers for their services during this action :

Lieut. Geoffrey V. Hickman, R.N. Navigator and second in command of H.M.S. " Broke." He assisted with great coolness in handling the ship in action. His proper appreciation of the situation when one enemy destroyer was torpedoed, which his commanding officer had made ready to ram, enabled course to be altered in time to ram the next astern.

Lieut. Robert D. King-Harman, R.N. Navigating Officer of H.M.S." Swift."

He was of the utmost assistance to his commanding officer throughout.

Lieut. Maximilian C. Despard, R N.
First and Gunnery Lieut. of H.M.S "Broke." He controlled gun fire and gave the orders which resulted in an enemy destroyer being torpedoed.

Lieut. Henry A. Simpson, R.N.
Executive Officer and Gunnery Lieut. of H.M.S. "Swift." He displayed great coolness and method in the control of fire which he had very ably organised and zealously drilled, and greatly assisted his commanding officer throughout the action.

Surg. Prob. Christopher T. Helsham, R.N.V.R. ("Broke").

Surg. Prob. John S. Westwater, R.N.V.R. ("Swift").
Worked with great energy and ability in attending to the wounded.

Gnr. (T.) Henry Turner, R.N. ("Swift").
Obtained a hit with a torpedo on one of the enemy destroyers.

Gnr. (T.) Frederick Grinney, R.N. ("Broke").
Gave orders for the firing of the torpedo which struck one of the enemy destroyers.

Midi. Donald A. Gyles, R.N.R.
He took charge on the forecastle, and, although wounded on the eye, organised a gun's crew from the survivors of the crews which had suffered heavy casualties and kept the guns on the forecastle going. He repelled the German sailors who swarmed on board from the destroyer which was rammed, and remained at his post until after the action was finished.

The following awards have also been approved.

CONSPICUOUS GALLANTRY MEDAL.

A.B. William G. Rawles.
Although he had four bad wounds in his legs, in addition to other injuries, he continued to steer H.M.S. "Broke" in action until the enemy destroyer had been rammed.

DISTINGUISHED SERVICE MEDAL.

Yeo. of Sig. William Smith.
O.S. Herbert Thomas Huntley Fowle.
Sto. Charles Williams, R.N.R.
Sto., 1st Cl., John Clasper, R.F.R.
C. Sto. William Shearn.
P.O. Tel. Harry Sedgley.
P.O. William Edward Strevens.
P.O. George Henry Froud.
P.O. Albert Last.
A.B. Sidney Clarke.
A.B. Charles Reginald Norton.
A.B. Ernest Ramdsen Ingleson.
A.B. Walter Frederick Mair.
C.P.O. John Crother Ashton.
P.O. Sidney Albert Simmonds.
P.O. Charles Henry Daish.
C. E.R.A. William Culverwell.
P.O. Frederick Percy Mursell.
C. Sto. Henry Simmons.
Sto. P.O. William Edward Hedseman.
Yeo. of Sig. Albert Ebenezer James.
Sto. P.O. James Bryant.
Sto. Edward Gilfillan, R.N.R.
Sto. Sidney Frederick Brooks.

MENTIONED IN DESPATCHES.

The following officers and men have been mentioned in despatches:

Engr. Lt.-Comdr. (now Engr.-Comdr.) James Hughes, R.N.
Engr. Lt.-Comdr. (now Engr.-Comdr.) Thomas George Coomber, R.N.
Lt.-Com. Arthur Jermyn Landon, R.N.
Sub-Lt. Whitworth Brady Nicholson, R.N.
Act. Sub-Lt. Lionel Hill Peppé, R.N.
Wt. Mech. James Coughlan, R.N.
Act. Art.-Engr. Charlie Rodgers Barter, R.N.
Midi. Maurice Theobald Maud, R.N.R.
P.O. Charles Christmas Brown,
L.-Sig. William Page.

For Distinguished Service

L.-Sto. Frank William King.
L.-Sto. Eli Daniels.
E.R.A., 2nd Cl., Walter Blanchard Wellman.
A.B. William George Cleeter.
O.S. Sidney John Thomas Taylor.
Sto., 2nd Cl., Frederick Arthur Hickman.
Sto., 1st Cl., George Henry Doe.
A.B. John Henton.
Sto., 1st Cl., Albert Edward Glover.
A.B. Henry Alfred Hitchin.
L.-Sig. Charles Claude Higgins.
S.B.A. James Gradwell.
Sto., 1st Cl., Ernest Muff.
Sig. Sidney Charles Helps, R.N.V.R.
C. E.R.A. Ralph Victor Nelson.
E.R.A. Henry Albert Riley.
Sto. P.O. Matthew Lawson., R.F.R.
L.-Sto. Frederick Thomas Yapp.
Sto., 1st Cl., John Kempton Falconer.
Sto., 1st Cl., Charles Herbert Harvey.
Sto. P.O. Thomas Davies.
L.-Sto. Charles Edward Walls.
Sto. Albert Boyland, R.N.R.
Sto., 1st Cl., Charles Edward Miller, R.F.R.

Promotions.

The following promotions have been made for service in this action:

COMMANDERS TO BE CAPTAINS.

Comdr. Ambrose Maynard Peck.
Comdr. Edward Ratcliffe Garth Russell Evans, C.B.

ENGR. LT.-COMDRS. TO BE COMMANDERS.

Engr. Lt.-Comdr. James Hughes.
Engr. Lt.-Comdr. Thomas George Coomber.

All to date April 21st, 1917.

The following officers have been noted for early promotion:
Sub-Lt. Whitworth Brady Nicholson, R.N.
Act. Sub-Lt. Lionel Hill Peppé, R.N.
Wt. Mech. James Coughlan, R.N.
Midi. Maurice Theobald Maud, R.N.R.

The following honours (among others) have been awarded to members of the Royal Naval Air Service, May, 1917:

DISTINGUISHED SERVICE ORDER.

Capt. Charles Laverock Lambe, R.N.
Sq.-Com. Geoffrey Rhodes Bromet, R.N.
Sq.-Com. Edward Thomas Newton-Clare, R.N.A.S.

DISTINGUISHED SERVICE CROSS.

Flt.-Com. Bertram Lawrence Huskisson, R.N.A.S.
Flt.-Lt. (now Flt.-Com.) Arthur D. W. Allen, R.N.A.S.
Flt.-Lt. (now Flt.-Com.) B. C. Bell, D.S.O., R.N.A.S.
Flt.-Lt. (now Act. Flt.-Com.) F. Fowler, R.N.A.S.
Flt.-Lt. Frank Thomas Digby, R.N.AS.
Flt.-Lt. Herbert George Brackley, R.N.A.S.
Flt.-Lt. Noel Keeble, R.N.A.S.
Flt.-Lt. Thomas Frederick Le Mesurier, R.N.A.S.
Flt.-Lt. Robert John Orton Compston, R.N.A.S.
Flt.-Lt. William Edward Gardner, R.N.A.S.
Lieut. Russell William Gow, R.N.V.R.
Flt. Sub-Lt. Philip Sidney Fisher, R.N.A.S.
Flt. Sub-Lt. D. A. H. Nelles, R.N.A.S.
Flt. Sub-Lt. Ernest John Cuckney, R.N.A.S.
Flt. Sub-Lt. Walter Ernest Flett, R.N.A.S.

BAR TO DISTINGUISHED SERVICE CROSS.

Flt.-Lt. Ronald Grahame, D.S.C., R.N.A.S.

FOR OTHER SERVICES.

DISTINGUISHED SERVICE ORDER.

Lt.-Com. William W. Hallwright, R.N. (since killed).

Lt.-Com. Charles George Matheson, R.N.R.
Lieut. George Fagan Bradshaw, R.N.
Act.-Lt. Francis Charles Harrison, R.N.
Lieut. Gerald Norman Jones, R.N.R.
Lieut. Frank Watkin Charles, R.N.R.
Lieut. Archibald Dayrell Reed, R.N.R.

DISTINGUISHED SERVICE CROSS.
Lieut. Walter Napier Thomason Beckett, R.N.
Engr.-Lt. Alexander Hargreaves Boyle. R.N.
Lieut. Frank Tomkinson Brade, R.N.R.
Lieut. Alfred Swann, R.N.V.R.
Act.-Lt. James Alexander Pollard Blackburn, R.N.R.
Act.-Lt. William Murdoch McLeod, R.N.R.
Act.-Lt. Arnold George Morgan, R.N.R.
Act.-Lt. Harold William Green, R.N.R.
Asst.-Paymr. John Weston Sells, R.N.R.
Sub-Lt. Harold Drew, R.N.
Act. Sub-Lt. (Act.) Edmund George Smithard, R.N.R.
C.A.E. Edward Ethelbert Rose, R.N.
Gnr. Percy John Joseph Cullum, R.N.
Skipper Joseph Powley, R.N.R.
Skipper William Wood, R.N.R.
Skipper James Thompson.

BAR TO DISTINGUISHED SERVICE CROSS.
Lieut. Walter L. Scott, D.S.C., R.N.R. (since drowned).

CONSPICUOUS GALLANTRY MEDAL.
Sto., 1st Cl., James Davies.

DISTINGUISHED SERVICE MEDAL.
L.-S. George Alfred Smedley.
A.B. James Hartley.
C.E.R.A., 2nd Cl., John Buchanan.
A.B. William Francis Burrows Biss.
Sto. P.O. Lewis David Snell.

A Supplement to the *London Gazette* of March 26th, 1917, announces the following Naval honours :

D.S.O.
Capt. John Locke Marx, M.V.O., R.N.R.
Maj. Charles D'Oyly Harmar, R.M.L.I.
Lt.-Com. Philip Wilfred Sidney King, R.N.
Act. Lt.-Com. W. Olphert, D.S.O., R.N.R.
Lt.-Com. John Whittow Williams, R.N.R.
Lieut. Ernest Mortimer Hawkins, R.N.
Lieut. Edward Vaughan Davies, R.N.R.
Lieut. Ronald Neil Stuart, R.N.R.
Eng.-Lt. Leonard S. Loveless, D.S.C., R.N.

BAR TO D.S.O.
Com. Francis Henry Grenfell, D.S.O., R.N.
Com. Edmund L. B. Lockyer, D.S.O., R.N.
Lt.-Com. Arthur A. Mellin, D.S.O., R.N.

D.S.C.
Capt. John Maurice Palmer, R.M.L.I.
Lieut. Edward Overend Priestley, R.N.
Lieut. Arthur Francis Eric Palliser, R.N.
Lieut. Leon Stopford Acheson, R.N.R.
Lieut. William Arthur Hanna, R.N.R.
Act.-Lt. Francis Cecil Pretty, R.N.R.
Act.-Lt. James Sinclair Campbell, R.N.R.
Act.-Lt. Edgar William Bowack, R.N.R.
Act.-Lt. Stephen P. R. White, R.N.R.
Act.-Lt. Magnus Leo Musson, R.N.R,
Act.-Lt. Francis Robert Hereford. R.N.R.
Asst.-Paymr. William Richard Ashton, R.N.R.

For Distinguished Service

Sub-Lt. Leonard Clifton Warder, R.N.R.
Sub-Lt. Richard Percy Nisbet, R.N.R.
Asst.-Paymr. Reginald Arthur Nunn, R.N.R.
Gnr. (T.) Harry Morgan, R.N.
Gnr. Morris Roseman Cole, R.N.
Skipper George A. Novo, R.N.R.
Skipper David Wallace, R.N.R.
Skipper Philip W. Page, R.N.R.
Skipper Thomas Crisp, R.N.R.

BAR TO D.S.C.

Skipper Walter S. Wharton, D.S.C., R.N.R.

D.S.M.

P.O. Henry Granville.
A.B. S. Proudlove, R.F.R.
P.O. Albert E. Holding.
L.S. A. Wilson, R.F.R.
Pte. James A. Short, R.M.L.I.
Cpl. Thomas H. Wedge, R.M.L.I.
P.O. Francis J. Horwill.
Sto. P.O. S. J. Pollard, R.F.R.
P.O. John Henry Philp.
E.R.A., 2nd Cl., J. H. Green.
Act. E.R.A., 4th Cl., E. Lancaster.

BAR TO D.S.M.

P.O., 1st Cl., William J. Adams.
L.S. Daniel J. Donovan.
C.P.O. G. H. Truscott, R.F.R.

MENTIONED IN DESPATCHES.

Surg. John Desmond Milligan, M.B., R.N.
Lieut. Frank Lionel Tongue, R.N.R.
Act.-Lt. Frederick George Russell, R.N.R.
C.Art.-Eng. Alfred Edward Thomas, R.N.
Act.-Sub-Lt. Dudley Thomas Cary Field, R.N.
Act.-Sub-Lt. Arthur Hubert Stanley, R.N.
Act.-Sub-Lt. Archibald Guthrie Elliot, R.N.
Act.-Sub-Lt. Thomas Norman Becket Cree, R.N.
Wt. Teleg. Allan Andrews, R.N.R.
A.B. E. A. Veale, R.F.R.
A.B. B. R. C. Harris.
A.B. Noble Britton, R.F.R.
S.B.A. George J. Grieve.
Pte. F. T. Gorman, R.M.L.I.
Pte. A. Whittle, R.M.L.I.

BY THE FRENCH PRESIDENT.

LEGION OF HONOUR.

COMMANDER.

V.A. Sir Rosslyn E. Wemyss, K.C.B., C.M.G., M.V.O.
R.A. Cresswell J. Eyres.
Capt. Cyril T. M. Fuller, C.M.G., D.S.O., R.N.

OFFICER.

Capt. Francis H. Mitchell, D.S.O., R.N.
Comdr. Walton C. G. Ruxton, R.N.
Comdr. Robert C. Davenport, R.N.

CHEVALIER.

Maj. and Bt.-Lt.-Col. Lewis C. Lampen, R.M.L.I.
Eng.-Com. (Act.-Eng.-Capt.) Charlie Broadbent, R.N.
Com. George T. C. P. Swabey, D.S.O., R.N.
Lt.-Com. (Act. Com.) Theodore J. Hardinge, R.N.
Maj. Walter L. Huntingford, R.M.A.
Capt. and Bt.-Maj. Stephen C. Wace, R.M.A.
Lt.-Com. Patrick S. E. Maxwell, R.N.
Lieut. Ronald Langton-Jones, D.S.O., R.N.
Lieut. Alick Purdon, R.N.R.

CROIX DE GUERRE AVEC PALME.

Maj. Charles D. O'Harmar, R.M.L.I.
Lieut. Edward O. Priestley, R.N.
Lieut. Arthur F. E. Palliser, R.N.
Capt. John M. Palmer, R.M.L.I.

Lieut. Frank L. Tongue, R.N.R.
Surg. John D. Milligan, M.B., R.N.
Act. Sub-Lt. Dudley F. C. Field, R.N.
Act. Sub-Lt. Arthur H. Stanley, R.N.
Act. Sub-Lt. Thomas N. B. Cree, R.N.
Act. Sub-Lt. Archibald G. Elliott, R.N.
P.O. Henry Granville.
Cpl. Thomas H. Wedge, R.M.L.I.
Pte. James A. Short, R.M.L.I.
Pte. James Cook, R.M.L.I.
Pte. Frank T. Gorman, R.M.L.I.
Pte. Arthur Whittle, R.M.L.I.
Pte. George T. James, R.M.L.I.
S.B.A. George J. Grieve.
Cpl. Christopher J. Conway.
C.P.O. William H. Pysden.
Col.-Sgt. Percy J. Strachan, R.M.L.I.
L.S. Thomas W. Liddiard.

CROIX DE GUERRE.
Com. Henry C. Halahan, D.S.O., R.N.
Wing-Com. Richard B. Davies, V.C., D.S.O., R.N.
Sqn.-Com. Francis K. Huskins, D.S.C., R.N.
Lieut. Denvis C. G. Shoppee, D.S.C., R.N.
Lieut. Viscount Maidstone, R.N.V.R.

BY THE KING OF ITALY.
ORDER OF ST. MAURICE AND ST. LAZARUS.
Grand Officer: R.A. Mark E. F. Korr, C.B., M.V.O.
ORDER OF THE CROWN OF ITALY.
Commander: Capt. John G. Armstrong, R.N.

BY THE KING OF THE BELGIANS.
ORDER OF LEOPOLD.
Chevalier: Act. Flt-Com. Charles C. R. Edwards, R.N.A.S.

A supplement to the *London Gazette*, issued on Saturday, April 20th, 1917, contained the following, among other Naval honours:

VICTORIA CROSS.
Com. Gordon Campbell, D.S., R.N.
In recognition of his conspicuous gallantry, consummate coolness, and skill in command of one of H.M. ships in action.

SERVICE IN PATROL CRUISERS.
In recognition of services in the patrol cruisers, under the command of V.A. Reginald G. O. Tupper, C.B., C.V.O., during the period July 1st-December 31st, 1916:
D.S.O.
Capt. Humphrey Hugh Smith, R.N.
Eng.-Com. Walter Jordan, R.N.R.
DISTINGUISHED SERVICE CROSS.
Asst.-Paymr. (now Paymr.) F. L. Horsey, R.N.
Lieut. Howard Uncles, R.N.R.
Midi. Thomas Edwin Hunter Grove, R.N.R.
DISTINGUISHED SERVICE MEDAL.
C.P.O. W. J. C. Poole (*alias* W. J. Curley), R.F.R.
P.O.1 A. B. James, R.F.R.
L.-Sig. W. T. Isaac, R.F.R.
L.-Sig. Edgar C. Saunders.
MENTIONED IN DESPATCHES.
Eng.-Com. George Thompson Greig, R.N.R.
Asst.-Paymr. Jack Barton, R.N.R.
Sub-Lt. C. J. Leonard Hayward, R.N.R.
Sub-Lt. Arthur Mallorie Coleman, R.N.R.
Sub-Lt. William Mill Ruxton, R.N.R.
A.B. John F. Gainsford, R.F.R.

ROYAL NAVAL AIR SERVICE.
D.S.O.
Flt.-Lt. (Act. Flt.-Com.) B. C. Bell.
DISTINGUISHED SERVICE CROSS.
Flt.-Lt. (now Act. Flt.-Com.) C. C. R. Edwards.
Sub-Lt. Charles Keith Chase, R.N.V.R.
Flt.-Com. A. W. Clemson, R.N.A.S.
Lieut. (now Lt.-Com.) Erskine Childers, R.N.V.R.

For Distinguished Service

Flt.-Sub-Lt. H. E. P. Wigglesworth.
Sub-Lt. (now Lieut.) E. B. C. Betts, R.N.V.R.

Mentioned in Despatches.
Flt.-Lt. Henry Guy Holden, R.N.A.S.

MISCELLANEOUS SERVICES.

D.S.O.
Com. Francis William Hanan, R.N.
Lt.-Com. James Sandbach Parker, R.N.
Lieut. (now Act.-Lt.-Com.) F. A. Frank, R.N.R.

Distinguished Service Cross.
Act.-Lt. John Herman R. Elfert, R.N.R.
Eng.-Sub.-Lt. John Smith, R.N.R.
Gnr. William John Hubbard, R.N.
Act.-Eng. Ernest Thaxter, R.N.

Conspicuous Gallantry Medal.
C. Yeo. of Sig. Albert Arthur Bishop.

Distinguished Service Medal.
Pte. Thomas Mitchell Symons, R.M.L.I.

Mentioned in Despatches.
Capt. Henry Faulconer Aplin, R.N.
Maj. and Bt. Lt.-Col. J. A. M. A. Clark, R.M.L.I.
Com. (now Capt.) G. F. Hyde, R.A.N.
Lt.-Com. William Wybrow Hallwright, R.N.
Lt.-Com. John Henry Webb, R.N.R.
Lieut. Martin Arthur Frankland Hood, R.N.
Lieut. Humphrey Edward Archer, R.N.
Lieut. Philip John Mack, R.N.
Eng.-Lt. William Begg McDonald, R.N.R.
Lieut. Alfred Sand Holmes, R.N.R.
Lieut. William Henry Askew Bee, R.N.R.
Lieut. W. Macpherson McRitchie, R.N.R.
Sub-Lt. Keith Morris, R.N.R.
Asst.-Paymr. Leonard Warren, R.N.R.
Mate (E.) George Edward Harman, R.N.
Gnr. Henry Frank Edwards, R.N.
Carpenter Francis Fernley Smith, R.N.
Skipper Samuel Reid, R.N.R.

BY THE FRENCH PRESIDENT.

Legion of Honour.

Commander.
V.A. Bernard Currey.
Com. Lionel Halsey, R.N.

Officer.
Capt. William L. Elder, R.N. (Wing-Capt., R.N.A.S.)
Maj. and Bt. Lt.-Col. Charles J. Thornton (Temp. Lt.-Col.), R.M.L.I.
Com. William F. Sells, C.M.G., R.N.

Chevalier.
Wing-Com. Richard B. Davies, V.C., D.S.O., R.N.
Capt. Edward M. Compton Mackenzie, R.M.
Lieut. John Couch, R.N.R.

Croix de Guerre.
Flt. Sub-Lt. Horace E. P. Wigglesworth, R.N.A.S.
Flt. Sub-Lt. Fred C. Armstrong, R.N.A.S.
Flt. Sub-Lt. Ronald F. Redpath, R.N.A.S.
Flt. Sub-Lt. Percy G. McNeil, R.N.A.S.
Flt. Sub-Lt. Raymond Collishaw, R.N.A.S.
Air Mech., 1st Cl., Sydney Herbert Pinchen.
Pte. John Jones, R.M.L.I.

BY THE KING OF ITALY.

Order of the Crown of Italy.

Officer.
Maj. Stephen C. Wace, R.M.A.

BY THE KING OF THE BELGIANS.

Order of Leopold Grand Cordon.
Adml. Sir John R. Jellicoe, G.C.B.

Chevalier.
Lieut. Denys C. G. Shoppee, D.S.C., R.N.

Croix de Guerre.
Adml. Sir John R. Jellicoe.
V.A. Sir Reginald H. S. Bacon, K.C.B., K.C.V.O., D.S.O.

WORK ON THE "ZULU."

The King conferred (May 3rd, 1917) the Albert Medal (Second Class) on : Eng.-Room Art., 3rd Cl. (now Act. C. Eng.-Room-Art., 2nd Cl.), Michael Joyce Sto. P.O. (now C. Sto.) Walter Kimber.

H.M.S. "Zulu" was mined on November 8th, 1916. As a result of the explosion the bottom of the after part of the engine-room was blown out and the whole compartment reduced to a mass of debris and broken steam and water pipes. Immediately after the explosion, Joyce and Kimber proceeded to the engine-room, the former having just come off watch. The latter had just left the boiler-room after he had seen that the oil burners were shut off and everything was in order, and had sent his hands on deck.

Hearing the sound of moans coming from inside the engine-room, they both attempted to enter it by the foremost hatch and ladder. As the heat in the engine-room was intense, and volumes of steam were coming up forward, they then lifted one of the square ventilating hatches further aft on the top of the engine-room casing (port side), and climbed into the rapidly-flooding compartment over the steam pipes, which were extremely hot. Scrambling over the debris, they discovered well over on the starboard side Sto. P.O. Smith with his head just out of the water. A rope was lowered from the upper deck, and with great difficulty Smith, who was entangled in fractured pipes and other wreckage, was hauled up alive. At the same time Sto. P.O. Powell was found floating in the water on the port side of the engine-room. The rope was lowered again and passed around Powell, who, however, was found to be dead on reaching the deck. The water was so high that further efforts to discover the remaining artificer left in the engine-room would have been useless, and the attempt had to be abandoned.

A supplement to the *London Gazette* of Saturday, May 12th, 1917, contains a list of honours awarded by His Majesty in the Royal Naval Air Service.

The King has been graciously pleased to give orders for the appointment of the undermentioned officers :

D.S.O.

Capt. C. L. Lambe, R.N.
For his valuable services in command of the R.N.A.S. units on the Belgian Coast; he is very largely responsible for the good service in the varied duties carried out by them against the enemy.

Sqn.-Cdr. G. R. Bromet, R.N.
This officer commanded a squadron of the R.N.A.S., attached to the Flying Corps, with conspicuous ability and success. Under his command the squadron developed into a most efficient and formidable fighting force, which has brought great credit to the Royal Naval Air Service.

Sqn.-Cdr. E. T. Newton-Clare, R.N.A.S.
During the past year he has led his squadron with conspicuous success in numerous bomb attacks, and on many occasions has engaged and driven down hostile machines.

D.S.C.

Flt. Sub.-Lt. W. E. Flett, R.N.A.S.
For conspicuous gallantry during an air raid. Shortly after leaving the objective he was engaged with

three enemy machines—two single-seater and one two-seater. His gunlayer, Air-Mechanic, 1st Grade, R. G. Kimberley, was slightly wounded in the wrist, which numbed his hand. Notwithstanding this he succeeded in bringing down two of the enemy machines, being again wounded by an explosive bullet in the ankle. The machine was riddled with bullets and owing to the damage navigation was most difficult, and the return journey was very slow. Consequently he was again attacked, but although the gunlayer was twice wounded, the enemy machine was driven off.

Flt.-Com. B. L. Huskisson, R.N.A.S.
Flt.-Lt. (now Flt.-Com.) A. D. W. Allen, R.N.A.S.
Flt.-Lt. (now Flt.-Com.) B. C. Bell, D.S.O., R.N.A.S.
Flt.-Lt. (now act. Flt.-Com.) F. Fowler, R.N.A.S.
Flt.-Lt. F. T. Digby, R.N.A.S.
Flt.-Lt. H. G. Brackley, R.N.A.S.
Flt.-Lt. N. Keeble, R.N.A.S.
Flt.-Lt. T. F. Le Mesurier, R.N.A.S.
Flt.-Lt. L. N. C. Clarke, R.N.A.S.
Flt.-Lt. R. J. O. Compston, R.N.A.S.
Flt.-Lt. W. E. Gardner, R.N.A.S.
Lieut. R. W. Gow, R.N.V.R.
Flt. Sub.-Lt. P. S. Fisher, R.N.A.S.
Flt. Sub.-Lt. D. A. H. Nelles, R.N.A.S.
Flt. Sub.-Lt. E. J. Cuckney, R.N.A.S.
Flt. Sub.-Lt. J. E. Sharman, R.N.A.S.

Bar to D.S.C.
Flt.-Lt. R. Grahame, D.S.C., R.N.A.S.

Mentioned in Despatches.
Wing-Com. C. L. Courtney, R.N.
Flt.-Payr. F. R. Waymouth, R.N.
Act. Wing-Com. A. Ogilvie, R.N.A.S.
Sqn.-Com. F. E. T. Hewlett, R.N.
Flt.-Com. W. L. Welsh, R.N.A.S.
Act. Flt.-Com. R. G. Mack, R.N.A.S.
Act. Flt.-Com. B. C. Clayton, R.N.A.S.

Flt.-Lt. G. A. Gooderham, R.N.A.S.
Flt.-Lt. C. D. Booker, R.N.A.S.
Lieut. L. E. Innes-Baillie, R.M.A.
Lieut. O. G. G. Villiers, R.N.V.R.
Lieut. R. G. St. John, R.N.V.R.
Flt. Sub.-Lt. J. de Francis, R.N.A.S.
Flt. Sub.-Lt. F. D. Casey, R.N.A.S.

Miscellaneous Services.
D.S.O.
Lt.-Com. W. W. Hallwright, R.N. (since killed).
Lt.-Com. C. G. Matheson, R.N.R.
Lieut. G. F. Bradshaw, R.N.
Act. Lieut. F. C. Harrison, R.N.
Lieut. G. N. Jones, R.N.R.
Lieut. F. W. Charles, R.N.R.
Lieut. A. D. Reed, R.N.R.

D.S.C.
Lieut. W. N. T. Beckett, R.N.
Engr. Lt. A. H. Boyle, R.N.
Lieut. F. T. Brade, R.N.R.
Lieut. A. Swann, R.N.V.R.
Act. Lieut. J. A. P. Blackburn, R.N.R.
Act. Lieut. W. M. McLeod, R.N.R.
Act. Lieut. A. G. Morgan, R.N.R.
Act. Lieut. H. W. Green, R.N.R.
Asst. Payr. J. W. Sells, R.N.R.
Sub.-Lt. H. Drew, R.N.
Act. Sub.-Lt. (actg.) E. G. Smithard, R.N.R.
Ch. Art. Eng. E. E. Rose, R.N.
Gnr. P. J. J. Cullum, R.N.
Skipper J. Powley, R.N.R.
Skipper W. Wood, R.N.R.
Skipper J. Thompson.

Bar to D.S.C.
Lieut. W. L. Scott, D.S.C., R.N.R. (since drowned).

Mentioned in Despatches.
Lieut. A. F. Sellers, R.N.R.
Eng. Lieut. D. Lyons, R.N.R.
Act. Lieut. J. Jackell, R.N.R.
Act. Lieut. C. H. C. Brown, R.N.R.

A special supplement to the *London Gazette*, issued May 13th, contains the first section of a long list, dated April 9th, of officers, ladies, non-commissioned officers, and men serving, or who have served, in France, whose " distinguished and gallant services and devotion to duty " Sir Douglas Haig considers deserving of special mention. Below is the first part of the section, which covers the Royal Navy.

ROYAL NAVY.

Comdr. G. S. Hewett.
Comdr. W. G. A. Ramsay-Fairfax.
Temp. Surg. H. B. Padwick, D.S.O., B.A.
Act. Comdr. C. R. Rowsell,

Royal Naval Air Service.

Lieut. (Act. Sqn. Com.) G. R. Bromet.
Flt.-Com: B. L. Huskisson.
Temp. Flt.-Lt. (temp. Flt.-Com.) C. R. Mackenzie, D.S.O.
Temp. Flt.-Lt. S. J. Goble, D.S.C.
Temp. Flt.-Lt. B. C. Bell.

Royal Naval Reserve.

Asst. Paymr. R. H. S. Gobbitt.

Royal Marine Artillery.

Maj. A. P. Liston-Foulis.
Capt. (temp. Maj.) W. H. I. Tripp.
Lemp. Capt. (Act. Maj.) C. Micklem.
Tieut. (temp. Capt.) R. C. S. Morrison-Scott.
Lieut. (temp. Capt.) H. Boffey.
Temp. Lieut. L. S. Charleton.
Hon. Lieut. W. T. Webley.

Royal Marines.

Capt. (temp. Lt.-Col.) A. S. Tetley.
Temp. Capt. the Hon. L. Montagu.
Temp. Capt. A. A. Walker.
Temp. Lieut. R. H. Marsland.
Qmr. and Hon. Lieut. S. Geary.
Maj. (temp. Lt.-Col.) F. J. W. Cartwright, D.S.O.
Maj. H. Ozanne.
Temp. Lieut. A. G. Kyle.
Temp. 2nd Lieut. F. W. Goldie.
Temp. 2nd Lieut. J. W. Middleton.
Temp. Surg. J. N. M. Ross, M.B., R.N.
Lt.-Col. A. R. H. Hutchison, C.M.G., D.S.O.
Temp. 2nd Lieut. B. G. Andrews.
Temp. Lieut. W. M. Curtis.

Royal Marine Light Infantry.

Maj. L. W. Miller.
Lieut. (temp. Capt.) G. E. Outcher.

Royal Naval Volunteer Reserve.

Temp. Sub.-Lt. J. M. Wylie.
Temp. Lieut. N. R. Mollor.

Royal Naval Division.

Temp. Sub.-Lt. W. Sterndale-Bennett, D.S.O.
Temp. Sub.-Lt. P. R. H. Fox.
Temp. Sub.-Lt. G. W. Whittaker, D.S.O.
Temp. Lt.-Com. R. H. Shelton.
Temp. Lieut. O. J. Wainwright, (Asst. Paymr., R.N.).
Temp. Lt.-Com. A. M. Asquith.
Temp. Sub.-Lt. (temp. Lieut.) T. B. Green.
Temp. Lieut. J. W. Morrison.
Temp. Lt.-Com. C. S. West.
Temp. Lt.-Com. B. H. Ellis, D.S.O.
Temp. Lt.-Com. H. E. Funnell.
Temp. Lieut. J. Coote.
Temp. Sub.-Lt. T. V. Williams.

Naval Transport Staff.

Paymr.-in-Chief C. E. Byron, R.N.
Fleet Paymr. W. E. R. Martin, R.N.
Comdr. (act. Capt.) A. E. H. Marescaux, R.N.
Comdr. D. M. Hamilton, R.N.
Lt.-Com. W. E. Moses, R.N.R.

Naval Chaplains Department.

Act. Chapalin C. W. G. Moore, M.A.
Rev. S. A. L. Thornton, D.S.O.

The *London Gazette* of Wednesday, May 23rd, contained lists of honours conferred by the King on officers and men of the Royal Navy for services in the war. One list is headed:

MISCELLANEOUS SERVICES.

D.S.O.

Capt. Berwick Curtis, R.N.
Lt.-Com. Basil John Douglas Guy, V.C., R.N.
Lieut. Arthur Walter Forbes, R.N.
Lt.-Com. Thomas Charles Carpenter Bolster, R.N.

In recognition of conspicuously gallant conduct on April 15th, 1917, when he took his destroyer into a mined area to rescue survivors from a hospital ship, which had been sunk by a mine, and from a patrol boat, which had struck a mine in proceeding to the assistance of the hospital ship. His handling of his destroyer in heavy weather and taking her alongside the wreck of the patrol boat was a splendid piece of seamanship.

DISTINGUISHED SERVICE CROSS.

Lieut. Francis William Crowther, R.N.
Lieut. William Strickland Harrison, R.N.R.
Act.-Lt. Charles Bruce Long Filmer, R.N.R.
Sub-Lt. Charles O'Callaghan, R.N.R.
Sub-Lt. Laurence James Meade, R.N.

BAR TO DISTINGUISHED SERVICE CROSS.

Lieut. Cedric Naylor, D.S.C., R.N.R.
Act.-Lt. S. P. Robey White, D.S.C., R.N.R.
Asst.-Paymr. William R. Ashton, D.S.C., R.N.R.

BAR TO DISTINGUISHED SERVICE MEDAL.

A.B. F. E. Pym, R.F.R.

MENTIONED IN DESPATCHES.

Lt.-Com. George Osborne Hewett, R.N.
Lt.-Com. Graham Cunningham Glen, R.N.
Act.-Lt. Francis Allsopp Innes, R.N.R.
Act.-Lt. Robert Roberts, R.N.R.
Sub-Lt. Percy Arthur Morgan, R.N.R.
Sub-Lt. Samuel Robinson, R.N.R.
Act. Sub-Lt. (Act.) S. R. Sunnucks, R.N.R.
Act. Sub-Lt. (Act.) William John Young, R.N.R.
Gnr. (T.) Alexander George Stock, R.N.
Wt. Teleg. Harold Waddington, R.N.R.
Off. Std., 2nd Cl., John C. Bird.

ROYAL NAVAL AIR SERVICE.

D.S.O.

Flt.-Sub-Lt. John Joseph Malone, R.N.A.S.

For successfully attacking and bringing down hostile aircraft on numerous occasions. At about 6.30 a.m. on April 23rd, 1917, while on patrol, he attacked a hostile scout and drove it down under control. He then attacked a second scout, which, after the pilot had been hit, turned over on its back and went down through the clouds. A third scout, attacked by him from a distance of about twenty yards, descended completely out of control. While engaging a fourth machine he ran out of ammunition, so returned to the advanced landing ground, replenished his supply, and at once returned and attacked another hostile formation, one of which he forced down out of control. On the afternoon of April 24th, 1917, he engaged a hostile two-seater machine, and, after badly wounding the observer, forced it to land on our side of the lines.

Distinguished Service Cross.

Flt.-Lt. Lloyd Samuel Breadner. R.N.A.S.
For conspicuous gallantry and skill in leading his patrol against hostile formations. He has himself brought down three hostile machines and forced several others to land. On April 6th, 1917, he drove down a hostile machine which was wrecked while attempting to land in a ploughed field. On the morning of April 11th, 1917, he destroyed a hostile machine, which fell in flames, brought down another in a spinning nose dive with one wing folded up, and forced a third to land.

Flt. Sub-Lt. Joseph Stewart Fall, R.N.A.S.
For conspicuous bravery and skill in attacking hostile aircraft. On the morning of April 11th, 1917, while escorting our bombing machines, he brought down three hostile aircraft. The first he attacked and brought down completely out of control. He was then attacked by three hostile scouts, who forced him down to within about 200 feet of the ground. By skilful piloting he manœuvred his machine close behind one of them, which was driven down and wrecked. Shortly afterwards this officer was again attacked by a hostile scout, which he eventually brought down a short time before recrossing the lines. He then landed at one of the aerodromes, his machine having been riddled with bullets from the hostile machines, and also by rifle fire from the ground.

DESTROYER PATROL FLOTILLAS

The following appointments and awards have been made in recognition of services in the destroyer patrol flotillas, armed boarding steamers, etc., during the period which ended September 30th, 1916:

D.S.O.

Capt. Alan Cameron Bruce, R.N.
Capt. Edwin Harold Edwards, R.N.
Com. Alan Montague Yeats-Brown, R.N.
Act.-Capt. W. B. Compton, M.V.O., R.N.
Com. Arthur Kemmis Betty, R.N.
Com. Lionel John Garfit Anderson, R.N.
Com. Hubert Seeds Monroe, R.N.
Com. Francis Alexander Clutterbuck, R.N.
Com. Aubrey William Peebles, M.V.O., R.N.
Com. Wilfrid Ward Hunt, R.N.
Com. William Herbert Coates, R.D., R.N.R.
Com. John McInnes Borland, R.D., R.N.R.
Lt.-Com. Francis G. C. Coates, R.N.
Lt.-Com. Ernest Cyril Brent, R.N.
Lt.-Com. Astley D. C. Cooper-Key, R.N.
Lt.-Com. John Kelty McLeod, R.N.
Lt.-Com. Frederick Archibald Warner, R.N.
Lt.-Com. Hugh Joseph Woodward, R.N.
Lt.-Com. Herbert Gerald Briggs, R.N.

Distinguished Service Cross.

Lt.-Com. Henry Radcliffe James, R.N.
Lieut. Cecil R. E. W. Perryman, R.N.
Lieut. Keith Richard Farquharson, R.N.
Lieut. Herbert Owen R N.
Lieut. Ernest Kirkbank Irving, R.N.R.
Lieut. William Murray, R.N.R.
Act.-Lt. T. H. Coughtrey, R.N.R.
Act.-Lt. A. E. Trivett Morris, R.N.R.
Asst.-Paymr. Hugh James Leleu, R.N.R.
C. Gnr. Reginald Cardwell Ide, R.N.
C. Art.-Eng. Herbert Edward Pope, R.N.
C. Art.-Eng. John William Farrow, R.N.
Gnr. Thomas Henry Xeyes, R.N.
Art.-Eng. William Thomas Hall, R.N.

For Distinguished Service

BAR TO DISTINGUISHED SERVICE CROSS.

Lieut. Henry Antony Simpson, D.S.C., R.N.

MENTIONED IN DESPATCHES.

Capt. George Napier Tomlin, M.V.O., R.N.
Capt. Ambrose Maynard Peck, D.S.O., R.N.
Com. Robert Arthur Hornell, R.N.
Com. Edward Bathurst Compton, R.N.
Act.-Com. Ernest Kennaway Arbuthnot, R.N.
Com. Arthur Edward Dunn, R.D., R.N.R.
Com. Cecil Wills Burleigh, R.D., R.N.R.
Com. Selwyn Mitchell Day, R.D., R.N.R.
Eng.-Com. William Burgoyne Lakeman, R.N.
Lt.-Com. Charles Wilbraham John Howard, R.N.
Lt.-Com. Arthur Felton Crutchley, R.N.
Lt.-Com. Godfrey Herbert, D.S.O., R.N.
Lt.-Com. Bertram Gregory Drake, R.N.R.
Lieut. Godfrey Ratcliffe Chambers, R.N.
Lieut. George Hector Creswell, R.N.
Lieut. Ernest Edward Lowe, D.S.C., R.N.
Lieut. Arthur Hugh Lloyd Terry, R.N.
Lieut. Robert Johnston Dailey, R.N.
Lieut. Ralph Clement Smith, R.N.
Lieut. Brian Cameron Gourley, R.N.
Lieut. Arthur Cocks, R.N.R.
Lieut. John Ibbotson Harrison, R.N.R.
Act.-Lt. George Wishart Leith, R.N.R.
Eng.-Lt. John Brasano Hyde, R.N.
Eng.-Lt. John Thomas Barrett, R.N.
Asst.-Paymr. Herbert Percy Hunter, R.N.
Asst.-Paymr. S. T. Morris, R.N.R. (Temp. Lt., R.N.V.R.).

Sub-Lt. Alan David James Robertson-Macdonald, R.N.
C. Gnr. Norman Gee Parker, R.N.
C. Gnr. Charles Sanderson, R.N.
C. Art.-Eng. Frederick Smith, R.N.
Gnr. Daniel Patrick Joseph Enright, R.N.
Gnr. Harry Pegg, R.N.
Art. Eng. Andrew Moules, R.N.

SERVICES OF DOVER PATROL.

D.S.O.

Capt. William Douglas Paton, M.V.O., R.N.
Com. George Ronald Beddard Blount, R.N.
Eng.-Lt.-Com. John Blackler Pulliblank, R.N.

DISTINGUISHED SERVICE CROSS.

Lieut. John Brooke, R.N.
Lieut. Sir John Meynell Alleyne, Bart., R.N.
Lieut. Wyndham Charles Johnson, R.N.
Lieut. Charles Herbert Lightoller, R.N.R.
Sub.-Lt. John Douglas Gibbon Chater, R.N.R.
C. Art.-Eng. Henry Taylor, R.N.
Gnr. George Gates, R.N.

MENTIONED IN DESPATCHES.

Com. Kerrison Kiddle, R.N.
Com. Harold Owen Reinold, R.N.
Com. Wion de Malpas Egerton, R.N.
Com. Maurice Baldwin Raymond Blackwood, R.N.
Lt.-Com. Percy Ralph Passawer Percival, R.N.
Lieut. Lionel Moore Bridge, R.N.
Lieut. Mark Peregrine Charles Kerr, R.N.
Lieut. Edmund Hugh Hopkinson, R.N.
Act.-Lt. Stanley Napier Blackburn R.N.
Asst.-Paymr. Charles Bernard Jarrett, R.N.R.

Shpwt., 1st Cl., J. Pile.
P.O. S. R. Sandy.
A.B. G. Ambler.

Chancery of the Order of St. Michael and St. George.

Downing Street,
15th June, 1917.

The King has been graciously pleased to give directions for the following appointments to the Most Distinguished Order of Saint Michael and Saint George in recognition of the services mentioned in the Commander-in-Chief's despatch :

To be additional Members of the Third Class or Companions of the said Most Distinguished Order :

Capt. Adolphus Huddlestone Williamson, M.V.O., R.N.
Was in command of H.M.S. " Vengeance " and in charge of organisation of landing parties in the coastal operations. The shooting of " Vengeance " was remarkably accurate, and contributed largely to the success of the operations.

Capt. Alfred Charles Sykes, R.N.
In command of H.M.S. " Challenger," and frequently carried out duties of Senior Naval Officer. The shooting of " Challenger " during the night bombardment of Dar-es-Salaam on 21st August assisted largely in bringing about the surrender.

Admiralty, *15th June*, 1917.

The King has been graciously pleased to give orders for the following appointments to the Distinguished Service Order and for the award of the Distinguished Service Cross to the undermentioned Officers in recognition of their services in the operations described in the Commander-in-Chief's despatch :

To be Companions of the Distinguished Service Order.

Comdr. Reginald James Newall Watson, R.N.
Was in charge of landing party at Bagamoyo on 15th August, 1916, and displayed great dash and energy in the face of unexpectedly superior forces.

Eng.-Com. Francis John Roskruge, R.N.
Kept the squadron and H.M S. " Hyacinth " in a state of continuous efficiency for over two years with the smallest possible allowance for necessary repairs.

Flgt.-Lieut. Edwin Rowland Moon, R.N.A.S. (now prisoner of war).
Since April, 1916, has carried out constant flights over the enemy's coast, including reconnaissances, bomb-dropping and spotting for gun fire in all weathers. Has shown great coolness and resource on all occasions.

To Receive the Distinguished Service Cross.

Lieut. Eldred Stuart Brooksmith, R.N.
Was in sole command of the defences of the southern part of the defence lines at Bagamoyo, when he showed conspicuous ability ; also contributed largely to the successful firing by the monitors.

Flgt.-Lieut. James Edward Baker Maclean, R.N.A.S.
Since April, 1916, has carried out constant flights over the enemy's coast, including reconnaissances, bomb-dropping and spotting ; was wounded when flying over Bagamoyo.

For Distinguished Service

Mr. John Mackay, C. Gnr., R.N.
Was in command of whaler "Salamander," and did excellent work under fire; organised mine-sweeping with great efficiency.

The following awards have also been made:

TO RECEIVE THE CONSPICUOUS GALLANTRY MEDAL.

Corpl. Ernest Victor Dean, R.M.L.I.
Showed great initiative at Bagamoyo. After Capt. Thomas, R.M.L.I., had been killed he immediately informed the Commanding Officer of the situation, and then taking cover behind a tree shot one German and one Askari, and wounded a second Askari.

TO RECEIVE THE DISTINGUISHED SERVICE MEDAL.

C.P.O. (C.) James Noonan, R.N.A.S.
C.P.O. Francis Ernest Strong.
P.O. William James Grills.
P.O. John James Mitchell Lawes.
P.O. William Young.
L.S. George Brunker.
A.B., R.F.R., Vincent Burrage.
A.B., R.F.R., Samuel Charles Cubitt.
A.B. Michael Fitzgerald. R,F.R.
Pte. William Dennis, R.M.L.I.
P.O. Teleg. Albert French.
Ship's Stewd. Albert Edward Tull.
Sick-Berth Stewd. Sampson Woodcock.
Co. Sergt.-Major Percy Evan Smith, R.M.L.I.
Lce.-Corpl. William Bradley, R.M.L.I.
P.O. Teleg. Percival Charles King.
Air Mechanic, 1st Grade, Frederick Wilmshurst, R.N.A.S.

The King has further approved of the following appointments to the Distinguished Service Order and of the award of the Distinguished Service Cross to the undermentioned Officers in recognition of their services with the East African Military Forces:

TO BE A COMPANION OF THE DISTINGUISHED SERVICE ORDER.

Comdr. George Stanley Thornley, R.N., Senior Naval Officer, Lake Victoria Nyanza.
Rendered most efficient assistance to the Military throughout the campaign.

TO RECEIVE THE DISTINGUISHED SERVICE CROSS.

Sqdn.-Com. Eric Roper Curson Nanson, R.N.A.S.
Organised his unit with great efficiency and zeal, and carried out reconnaissance work under great climatic difficulties.

Lieut. Vincent Holland Pryor Molteno, R.N.
Organised the naval gun detachment which he commanded during part of the Kibata operations.

Flgt. Sub. Lt. Leslie O. Brown.
For bravery, zeal and ability shown in many long flights over enemy territory on reconnaissance work and bomb-dropping expeditions; was repeatedly under fire.

Flgt. Lieut. Norman Gordon Stewart-Dawson.
Carried out reconnaissance over difficult country on 30th May, 1916, when he was obliged to land in the bush.

Lieut. William John King, R.N.V.R.
For continuous good service in the operations of the Umba Valley Field Force; also served as Assistant Transport Officer and as Port Captain, Tanga.

Capt. Ernest William O'Connor, Master of Transport "Barjora."
Showed exceptional ability in the

coast operations, the success of the landings being largely due to his professional capacity and zeal.

The following officers and men have been mentioned in despatches :

Flgt. Lieut. John Robinson, R.N.A.S.
Lieut. Ivor Mackenzie Bellairs, R.N.V.R.
C.P.O. Mechanic, 2nd Grade, Arthur Henry Simmonds.
C.P.O. Mechanic, 3rd Grade, Herbert Russell.
L. Mechanic Savile Aubrey Brooke.
C.P.O., 3rd Grade, William Alfred Chapple.
C.P.O., 3rd Grade, Edward Mathias.
L. Mechanic Alfred Frederick Wardle.
Air Mechanic, 2nd Grade, John Harry Seager.
Actg. Air Mechanic, 1st Grade, Albert Edward Liles.

HONOURS FOR SERVICE IN MINE-SWEEPING OPERATIONS.

The following appointments have been made to the Distinguished Service Order and for the award of the Distinguished Service Cross to the undermentioned officers in recognition of their services in Mine-sweeping operations between the 1st July, 1916, and the 31st March, 1917 :

TO BE COMPANIONS OF THE DISTINGUISHED SERVICE ORDER.

Capt. Francis Evelyn Massy Dawson, R.N.
Capt. William Rawdon Napier, R.N.
Comdr. Robert William Dalgety, R.N.
Comdr. Ronald Scott Jervoise Wigram, R.N.
Comdr. Eric Walter Harbord, R.N.
Comdr. Basil Richard Brooke, R.N.
Lieut.-Com. Cyril Prescott Franklin, R.N.
Lt.-Com. Graham Cunningham Glen, R.N.

TO RECEIVE THE DISTINGUISHED SERVICE CROSS.

Lieut. William Victor Rice, D.S.O., R.N.
Lieut. Claude Preston Hermon-Hodge, R.N.
Lieut. Arthur Perfect Meredith Lewes, R.N.
Lieut. William Dene Keith Dowding, R.N.
Lieut. Archibald Henry L. S. Ruddell, R.N.
Lieut. Ebenezer Gordon, R.N.R.
Lieut. Edward L. Dobson, R.N.R.
Lieut. John H. Pitts, R.N.R.
Lieut. Alfred Havercroft Chafer, R.N.R.
Lieut. Howard McGlashan, R.N.R.
Lieut. Percy Noble Taylor, R.N.R.
Lieut. George B. Musson, R.N.R.
Lieut. Eric Rees, R.N.R.
Lieut. Charles Sidney Mence, R.N.R.
Lieut. Arthur Sandison, R.N.R.
Lieut. Wilfrid Walter Storey, R.N.R.
Lieut. Benjamin Swinhoe Stothard, R.N.R.
Lieut. Fred Collins, R.N.R.
Lieut. Thomas Elliott Hodge, R.N.R.
Lieut. Francis Joseph Woods, R.N.R.
Lieut. Roxburghe Tulloch, R.N.R.
Lieut. Alexander Duff Thomson, R.N.R.
Lieut. Ian Mackenzie Adie, R.N.R.
Eng. Lieut. Joseph Hall, R.N.R.
Actg. Lieut. John Williams Powell, R.N.R.
Actg. Lieut. Alexander Finlayson, R.N.R.
Act. Lieut. Charles Frederick Le Patourel, R.N.R.
Actg. Lieut. Bernard Lawson Parker, R.N.R.
Actg. Lieut. Percy Ridley, R.N.R.
Skipper Alexander McLeod, R.N.R.
Skipper George Mair, R.N.R.
Skipper Francis Thompson, R.N.R.
Skipper John Jolland, R.N.R.
Skipper Horace Edward Nutten, R.N.R.
Skipper Thomas Reid, R.N.R.
Skipper James Edward Calvert, R.N.R.

For Distinguished Service 153

Skipper Robert Barker, R.N.R.
Skipper Samuel Beach Ward, R.N.R.
Skipper George Gill, R.N.R.

The following awards have also been approved :

TO RECEIVE THE DISTINGUISHED SERVICE MEDAL.

Engmn. David Hillock Aitken, R.N.R.
2nd Hnd. Thomas Eynon Bailey, R.N.R.
C.P.O. Alfred Baker.
C.E.R.A., 2nd Cl., William James Bartlett.
Deck Hnd. Thomas Henry Searby Bates, R.N.R.
Sig. William Frederick Batty, R.N.V.R.
Deck Hnd. James Roland Brown, R.N.R.
Deck Hnd. William George Bruce, R.N.R.
Deck Hnd. Albert Edward Bull, R.N.R.
2nd Hnd. Arthur John Bull, R.N.R.
Deck Hnd. Benjamin Bunn, R.N.R.
2nd Hnd. John Clay, R.N.R.
P.O. Ernest William John Claydon.
C.P.O. John Thomas Collier.
W.T. Op., 2nd Cl., Arthur John Collins, R.N.R.
L.S. Reeves Conroy, R.F.R.
Actg. C.P.O. John Cope, R.F.R.
Engmn. Fred Cowen, R.N.R.
2nd Hnd. Amos Craven, R.N.R.
2nd Hnd. George Samuel Crinks, R.N.R.
L.S. Charles Culmer.
2nd Hnd. John Davis, R.N.R.
Deck Hnd. Robert Dixon, R.N.R.
Sig. George Dodds, R.N.V.R.
2nd Hnd. John Draper, R.N.R.
C.P.O. Walter William Easter.
P.O. John Alfred Ellis, R.F.R.
1st Engmn. Thomas Evans, R.N.R.
Engmn. James Everett, R.N.R.
Engmn. Manning Faiers, R.N.R.
C. Writer Leonard Henry Harcourt Finlay.
Deck Hnd. Christopher Gaunt, R.N.R.
L.S. Charles Edward Gill. R.F.R.
Sto. Edward Gillan, R.N.R.
C.P.O. George David Glover, R.F.R.
C. Writer J Evans Hamilton.

Ldg. Trmr. Charles Bertram Hebdon, R.N.R.
Yeo. of Sigs. Robert Hooper.
Deck Hnd. Benjamin Jackson, R.N.R.
Deck Hnd. Charles Richard Johnson, R.N.R.
Sto., 1st Cl., Herbert Jones.
Engmn. Richard Jones, R.N.R.
C.P.O. Thomas Kearns.
L.S. David James Kyle.
Engmn. Edward Lee, R.N.R.
Ord. Teleg. John James Letham Logan, R.N.V.R.
2nd Hnd. George McDonald, R.N.R.
2nd Hnd. William McIlroy, R.N.R.
L.S. Colin McKay, R.N.R.
C.P.O. Lott McKay, R.F.R.
2nd Hnd. Thomas Buchanan Mackenzie, R.N.R.
L.S. William John Mail, R.N.R.
2nd Hnd. John Robert Markham, R.N.R.
2nd Hnd. Robert Marr, R.N.R.
C.P.O. Henry George Marshall, R.F.R.
C.P.O. George Lacey Mottrum, R.F.R.
Sig. Sidney Nobbs, R.N.V.R.
P.O. Frederick Ernest Nottage.
C.P.O. William Thomas Noyes.
Ldg. Trmr. Patrick Joseph O'Toole, R.N.R.
C.P.O. John William Phillips, R.F.R.
Sto. P.O. Arthur Pavey.
P.O. James Porter, R.F.R.
Sto. P.O. James Potter.
P.O. William Power.
Sig. Archibald John Preece, R.N.V.R.
P.O. Charles Henry Price.
C.P.O. John Henry Price.
Trmr. Ernest Redding, R.N.R.
Sig. Fred. Reed, R.N.V.R.
2nd Hnd. George Harry Reed, R.N.R.
L.S. Thomas Reynolds, R.N.R.
C. Sto. James Robertson.
C.P.O. Charles John Rowsell.
2nd Hnd. Frederick Charles Sayer, R.N.R.
2nd Hnd. William Liddle Seaton, R.N.R.
C.P.O. Frederick John Shannon.
C.P.O. William Shepherd, R.F.R.

154   The Fleet Annual

C.P.O. Cecil Taylor.
Trmr. Leonard Thomas, R.N.R.
2nd Hnd. Alfred Albert John Thompson, R.N.R.
P.O. John Walter Turner, R.N.V.R.
Engmn. Joseph Holman Walton, R.N.R.
P.O. Samuel Warren, R.N.R.
2nd Hnd. Joseph Watkinson, R.N.R.
Trmr. William Thomas Weedon, R.N.R.
C.P.O. Henry Albert Wilson.
2nd Hnd. Richard Wilson, R.N.R.
2nd Engmn. Thomas Wouldhave, R.N.R.

The following officers and men have been mentioned in despatches :

Comdr. Francis Hungerford Pollen, R.N.
Comdr. Frederick Richard Harrold, R.N.
Comdr. Harry Francis Cayley, D.S.O., R.N.
Actg. Comdr. Gervase William Heaton Heaton, D.S.O., R.N.
Actg. Comdr. Charles Edward Aglionby, R.N.
Actg. Comdr. Ronald Clinton Mayne, R.N.
Actg. Comdr. Ralph Tindal, R.N.
Comdr. Wilfrid Montague Bruce, R.N.R.
Lt.-Comi. John Edwards, R.N.
Lieut. Stafford Harry Dillon, R.N.
Lieut. Archibald Gordon Cranmer, R.N.R.
Lieut. Frederick William Gray, R.N.R.
Lieut. William George Wood, D.S.C., R.N.R.
Lieut. John Joseph Fulton, D.S.C., R.N.R.
Lieut. Robert Davies, R.N.R.
Lieut. Walter Sumner, R.N.R.
Lieut. Nelson Cooper, D.S.C., R.N.R.
Lieut. Leslie Oswald Hatherley, R.N.R.
Lieut. Charles Kemp Paris, R.N.R.
Lieut. Norman Minshull, R.N.R.
Lieut. Charles Alfred Todd, R.N.R.
Lieut. George Syms, R.N.R.
Lieut. William George Brown, R.N.R.
Lieut. Bertie Warwick, R.N.R.

Lieut. Thomas Rayne Kirby, R.N.R.
Actg. Lieut. William Wilson, R.N.R.
Actg. Lieut. Oswald Frank Pennington, R.N.R.
Actg. Lieut. George Andrew Drummond R.N.R.
Eng.-Lieut. James Jack Andrews, R.N.R.
Eng.-Lieut. Joseph Percy Watts, R.N.R.
Sub-Lt. Frederick Wilson, R.N.V.R.
C. Gnr. William Henry Wilkie, R.N.
C. Bosn. Ernest Robert Parrott, R.N.
C. Warr. Eng. Stanley Peregrine Oxnard, R.N.R.
Skipper Alexander Youngson, R.N.R.
Skipper Edward Warwick, R.N.R.
Skipper John William Eden, R.N.R.
Skipper John William Blyth, R.N.R.
Skipper George John Bird, R.N.R.
Skipper Joseph Renton, R.N.R.
Skipper William Joseph Smith, R.N.
Skipper James Austin, R.N.R.
2nd Hnd. Noah Ayers, R.N.R.
C.P.O. Arthur Samuel Bailey.
P.O. John Beaton, R.N.R.
Deck Hnd. William Walter Berryman, R.N.R.
P.O. Stanley James Bloss.
Trmr. John Bradley, R.N.R.
Cook Eli Braham (Mercantile Marine).
L. Deck Hnd. Frederick William Brown.
Engmn. James William Bryan. R.N.R.
A.B. Frank Ruffin Buckett.
C.P.O. Benjamin Bussey, R.F.R.
Trmr. William Butler, R.N.R.
Engmn. Robert Cameron, R.N.R.
L.S. George William Cardno, R.N.R.
C.P.O. James Carter.
A.B. George Sydney Chisman (Mercantile Marine).
Trmr. Allan Cook, R.N.R.
Trmr. George Cox, R.N.R.
Deck Hnd. George Cutting, R.N.R.
Sig. William Arthur Dearman, R.N.V.R.
Yeo. of Sigs. Charles Harold Dedman.
P.O. John Denby, R.F.R.
Deck Hnd. Alexander Donnison, R.N.R.
L.S. Michael Donovan.

For Distinguished Service

L.S. Percival George Downs, R.F.R.
2nd Hnd. (now Skipper) Alfred Daniel Ellis, R.N.R.
L. Tmr. Tobias Fitzpatrick, R.N.R.
2ne Hnd. William Flett, R.N.R.
Seaman David Frederick, R.N.R.
P.O. Charles Edward Frost, R.F.R.
Engmn. William James Reynolds Gastineau, R.N.R.
Deck Hnd. Charles Francis Godel, R.N.R.
Engmn. Edward Augustus Hackett, R.N.R.
Sig. Percy Thomas Halfhead, R.N.V.R.
Sto., 1st Cl., Robert Harris.
2nd Hnd. Daniel James Harrison, R.N.R.
Shipwt., 1st Cl., Thomas Henry Hill.
Deck Hnd. Robert Hislop, R.N.R.
L.S. Frederick Hosking, R.N.R.
Trmr. William Hyndman, R.N.R.
Deck Hnd. Clifford Andrew Jackson, R.N.R.
Deck Hnd. James Jenkins, R.N.R.
L. Deck Hnd. Mark Hodson Knights, R.N.R.
C.E.R.A. Henry Edward Korn, R.N.R.
P.O. James Croxford Liley, R.F.R.
L.S. Malcolm McIntyre, R.N.R.
Deck Hnd. Thomas Magee, R.N.R.
P.O. William Marlow, R.F.R.
Sig. Davie Midwinter, R.N.V.R.
Trmr. Albert Hindle Miller, R.N.R.
Engmn. Burton George Henry M R.N.R.
Deck Hnd. William John Newman, R.N.R.
2nd Hnd. Harold George Nicholson R.N.R.
Engmn. Charles Niven, R.N.R.
Sto. P.O. Robert Henry Osgood.
2nd Hnd. Thomas Ovenstone, R.N.R.
C.P.O. George Edward Over.
2nd Hnd. (now Skipper) Charles William Penrose, R.N.R.
L. Sig. George Popple.
Engmn. William Rogerson Porter.
L.S. John William Presswell, R.F.R.
Seaman James pugh, R.N.R.

C.P.O. John Rafferty, R.F.R.
L.S. Frederick Reed, R.N.R.
L.S. William Reed.
Deck Hnd. Joseph Anthony Reid, R.N.R.
Deck Hnd. James Ritchie, R.N.
2nd Hnd. Cecil Percy Rogers,
Trmr. William Rollo, R.N.R.
2nd Hnd. Robert Rutter, R.N.R.
Engmn. Harry Smith, R.N.R.
Trmr. Leonard Sparkes, R.N.R.
Engmn. James Stables, R.N.R.
Engmn. James Stirton, R.N.R.
Deck Hnd. William Walker, R.N.R.
C.P.O. William Henry Tapsell.
P.O. Sidney Frederick Waller.
A.B. Frederick Joseph Welch, R.F.R.
C. Sto. Albert Edward White.
2nd Hnd. Morris Wisher, R.N.R.
Seaman Alexander Wood, R.N.R.
2nd Hnd. Robert Wright, R.N.R.

Addendum to List of Officers Appointed Companions of the Distinguished Service Order, which appeared on page 5462 of the "London Gazette," dated 4th June, 1917.

The King has been graciously pleased to give orders for the appointment of the undermentioned Officer to be a Companion of the Distinguished Service Order, in recognition of his services in the prosecution of the war:

Adm. Robert Stevenson Dalton Cuming (temp. Capt., R.N.R.).

A special supplement to the *London Gazette* of June 22nd, 1917, contained the following list of awards to officers, petty officers, and men of the Royal Navy, Royal Naval Volunteer Reserve, Royal Naval Air Service, and Royal Marines for war services:

VICTORIA CROSS.

Act.-Lt. (now Lt.-Com.) William Edward Sanders, R.N.R.
In recognition of his conspicuous

gallantry, consummate coolness, and skill in command of one of his Majesty ships in action.

Lce.-Corpl. Walter Richard Parker, R.M.L.I., R.N. Division.

In recognition of his most conspicuous bravery and devotion to duty in the course of the Dardanelles operations. On the night of April 30th-May 1st, 1915, a message asking for ammunition, water, and medical stores was received from an isolated fire trench at Gaba Tepe. A party of non-commissioned officers and men were detailed to carry water and ammunition, and, in response to a call for a volunteer from among the stretcher-bearers, Parker at once came forward; he had during the previous three days displayed conspicuous bravery and energy under fire whilst in charge of the battalion stretcher-bearers. Several men had already been killed in a previous attempt to bring assistance to the men holding the fire trench. To reach this trench it was necessary to traverse an area at least 400 yards wide, which was completely exposed and swept by rifle fire. It was already daylight when the party emerged from shelter and at once one of the men was wounded. Parker organised a stretcher party, and then going on alone succeeded in reaching the fire trench, all the water and ammunition carriers being either killed or wounded. After his arrival he rendered assistance to the wounded in the trench, displaying extreme courage and remaining cool and collected in very trying circumstances. The trench had finally to be evacuated, and Parker helped to remove and attend the wounded, although he himself was seriously wounded during this operation.

DISTINGUISHED SERVICE ORDER.

Capt. Francis Martin Leake, R.N.
Comdr. (now Capt.) Selwyn Mitchell Day, R.D., R.N.R.
Lt.-Com. Charles Harold Jones, R.N.
Lt.-Com. Kenneth Faviell Sworder, R.N.
Lt.-Com. Geoffrey Warburton, R.N.
Lt.-Com. Geoffrey Robert Sladen Watkins, R.N.
Lieut. Thomas Edward Price, D.S.C., R.N.R.
Lieut. Frederick Henry Peterson, D.S.C., R.N.R.
Lieut. William Donald Beaton, R.N.

BAR TO D.S.O.

Comdr. Victor Lindsay Arbuthnot Campbell, D.S.O., R.N.
Lt.-Com. Robert Henry Taunton Raikes, D.S.O., R.N.

DISTINGUISHED SERVICE CROSS.

Lieut. Hugh Evelyn Raymond, R.N.
Lieut. Reginald Nash, R.N.
Lieut. Edward Arthur Aylmer, R.N.
Lieut. Colin John Lawrence Bittleston, R.N.
Lieut. Leonard Ernest Pearson, R.N.
Act.-Lt. Edward Lyon Berthon, R.N.
Lieut. William Stanley Nelson, R.N.R.
Lieut. Hugh Ross Mackay, R.N.R.
Lieut. John Joseph Fulton, R.N.R.
Lieut. Nelson Cooper, R.N.R.
Lieut. Richard James Turnbull, R.N.R.
Eng.-Lt. Alexander Kenny, R.N.R.
Lieut. Robert Alexander Paterson, R.N.V.R.
Sub.-Lt. James Henry Arnold, R.N.R.
Sub-Lt. Clarence Aubrey King, R.N.V.R.
Skipper Thomas Edward Cain, R.N.R.
Skipper William Henry Brewer, R.N.R.
Skipper William Arthur Mead, R.N.R.
Skipper Adam Forbes, R.N.R.

For Distinguished Service

BAR TO D.S.C.
Lieut. Frederick Henry Peterson, D.S.C., R.N.R.

DISTINGUISHED SERVICE MEDAL.
L.S. J. Whitley, R.N.R.
Engmn. T. Toms, R.N.R.
P.O. J. Campbell.
P.O. F. G. Marchant.
E.R.A., 2nd Cl., A. M. Langley.
C.P.O. W. H. Isted.
E.R.A., 3rd Cl., H. Lang.
Col.-Sgt. N. Sears, R.M.L.I.
Lce.-Corpl. G. Short.
L.-Sig. A. E. Martin.
L.S J. L. Arthurson, R.N.R.
P.O., 1st Cl., W. Lee, R.F.R.
P.O. J. J. B. Norris.
E.R.A., 3rd Cl., J. Smith.
L.S. D. Dorrian.
Ord. Sea. G. M. Burns.
L.S. G. E. Palmer.
E.R.A., 4th Cl., G. Chinchen.
A.B. W. Biggs.
E.R.A. G. N. S. Cromarty, R.N.R.
A.B. G. E. Beresford.
P.O. F. Hobbs.
E.R.A., 1st Cl., J. K. Lawrie.
P.O. R. J. Brown.
P.O. E. J. Rodgers.
Engmn. S. Holman, R.N.R.
P.O. F. Robinson.
C.E.R.A., 2nd Cl., E. Pike.
E.R.A., 1st Cl., J. G. Reason.
L.-Sig. W. Smith.
Sec. Hnd. J. R. Evans, R.N.R.
Engmn. N. Denoon, R.N.R.
L.S. R. Hay, R.N.R.
Sea. A. J. Aldridge, R.N.R.
Donkeyman J. R. H. Page, M.R.
L.S. R. W. O. Dall, R.F.R.
Sea M. Nicholson, R.N.R.
P.O. E. Morrsion, R.N.R.
P.O. F. C. Rockett.
P.O. G. J. Jarrett.
P.O. J. M. Wall.
A.B. C. Holland.
Sto. P.O. G. R. Norman.
Sto., 1st Cl., J. Kennedy.
Shpwt., 1st Cl., W. G. Thomas.
Ck's Mate A. Matthews.
O.S., 2nd Cl., J. C. Chudley.
Ord. Teleg. T. Caldwell, R.N.V.R.
Ord. Teleg. J. Thomas, R.N.V.R.
Dck. Hnd. H. P. Knevitt, R.N.R.
Dck. Hnd. W. Vickers, R.N.R.
Dck. Hnd. R. Crossland, R.N.R.
Dck. Hnd. W. Foley, R.N.R.
Dck. Hnd. J. McCalland, R.N.R.
Dck. Hnd. D. C. McKinnon, R.N.R.
Dck. Hnd. R. Dougherty, R.N.R.
Dck. Hnd. J. H. Knowles, R.N.R.
Dck. Hnd. E. Bastian, R.N.R.
Dck. Hnd. J. McLean, R.N.R.
Dck. Hnd. L. Leathley, R.N.R.
Dck. Hnd. J. Porteous, R.N.R.
Sea. J. A. Townsend, R.N.R.
C.P.O. J. T. Worn, R.F.R.
L.S. W. G. Johnson, R.N.R.
Sea. J. McKillep, R.N.R.
Air Mech., 2nd Cl., W. P. Caston.
Air Mech., 1st Cl., A. E. Shorter.
P.O. G. H. Carlton.
Sto. P.O. A. E. Wilton.

MENTIONED IN DESPATCHES.
Comdr. W. A. Thompson, R.N.
Comdr. J. C. Hodgson, D.S.O., R.N.
Comdr. G. L. D. Gibbs, D.S.O., R.N.
Comdr. G. W. Taylor, R.N.
Comdr. H. H. de Burgh, R.N.
Comdr. A. F. W. Howard, R.N.
Comdr. J. V. Creagh, R.N.
Comdr. H. T. Dorling, R.N.
Lt.-Com. (act.-Comdr.) J. H. Neild, R.N.
Lt.-Com. A. J. Robertson, R.N.
Lt.-Com. E. H. B. Williams, R.N.
Lt.-Com. G. S. F. Nash, R.N.
Lt.-Com. E. R. D. Long, R.N.
Lt.-Com. P. B. Crohan, R.N.
Lt.-Com. A. A. Scott, R.N.
Lt.-Com. R. M. Mack, R.N.
Lt.-Com. E. K. Boddam-Whetham, R.N.
Lt.-Com. H. R. Troup, R.N.
Lt.-Com. W. E. B. Magee, R.N.
Act.-Paymr. K. E. Badcock, R.N.

Act. Eng.-Lt. S. R. Baker, R.N.
Act. Lt. F. H. Lawson, R.N.R. (killed in action).
Sub-Lt. J. W. Cookson, R.N.
Sub-Lt. K. Morris, R.N.R.
Gnr. H. C. Webber, R.N.
Act. Gnr. F. C. Dike, R.N.
Skipper A. Forbes, D.S.C., R.N.R.
C.P.O. H. P. Parfitt.
Yeo. of Sig. A. H. Tompson.
Cr. Arm. H. W. Gobie.
Mech. F. A. Neal.
C. Std. L. Taylor.
Sto. P.O. R. Lambert.
A. B. J. McC. Cullen, R.N.V.R.
A.B. W. Hughes, R.N.V.R.
A.B. W. R. Eames, R.N.V.R.
A.B F. C. Craig, R.N.V.R.
A. B. H. B. Winrow, R.N.V.R.
Sea. J. G. Anderson, R.N.R.
Act. L.-Sto. J. W. Frost.
Sto., 1st Cl., P. Lindsay.
Ord. Teleg. R. Spink.
Dk. Hnd. C. Flane, R.N.R.
Sea. W. Munro, R.N.R.
Sgt. H. J. Jordan, R.M.A.
L.S. J. T. Annis.
E.R.A., 4th Cl., R. Honeywell.
L.Sig. C. H. C. Hodges.

ROYAL NAVAL AIR SERVICE.

DISTINGUISHED SERVICE ORDER.

Flt.-Lieut. Christopher John Galpin, R.N.A.S.

Flt.-Lieut. Herbert George Brackley D.S.C., R.N.A.S.
In recognition of his services on the morning of April 14th, 1917, when he carried out a raid on Bruges Harbour, with good results, in spite of difficult conditions. Great credit is due to him for his persistence and determination. He also dropped bombs on Ostend seaplane base on the night of May 3rd-4th, 1917, making two trips.

DISTINGUISHED SERVICE CROSS.

Flt.-Com. Philip Leslie Holmes, R.N.A.S.

Flt. Sub-Lt. (now Act. Flt.-Com.) Herbert Gardner Travers, R.N.A.S.
In recognition of his services with the Army in France. This officer has himself brought down three hostile aeroplanes completely out of control, and has taken part in two other combats in which enemy machines were forced to land in our lines. He has always shown the greatest determination in leading his flight on offensive patrols, and has on many occasions driven down superior numbers of hostile machines.

Flt.-Lieut. Edward J. Cooper, R.N.A.S.

Flt. Sub-Lt. Charles Reginald Morrish, R.N.A.S.

Flt. Sub-Lt. Henry George Boswell, R.N.A.S.

Flt.-Lt. Charles Langston Scott, R.N.A.S.

Flt.-Lt. Walters Travers Swire Williams, R.N.A.S.

Flt.-Lt. Thomas Grey Culling, R.N.A.S.
In recognition of his services on April 23rd, 1917, when, with two other machines, he engaged a formation of nine hostile scouts and two-seater machines. Two two-seater machines were shot down, one of them by Flt.-Lieut. Culling unassisted.

Flt.-Lt. Francis Dominic Casey, R.N.A.S.
For conspicuous bravery and skill in attacking hostile aircraft on numerous occasions. on April 21st, 1917, he attacked a hostile two-seater machine at a range varying from forty to 100 yards, and brought it down completely out of control. On April 23rd, 1917, on four different occasions during one flight, he attacked hostile machines, one of which was driven down in a spinning nose dive, and another, turning over

For Distinguished Service

on its side, went down completely out of control. This officer has driven down four machines completely out of control, and forced many others down.

Flt.-Lt. Charles Adrian Maitland Heriot, R.N.A.S.
Flt.-Sub-Lt. John Roland Secretan Devlin, R.N.A.S.
Sub-Lt. Rupert Forbes-Bentley, R.N.V.R.

In recognition of their services in a bombing attack on the Kuleli Burgas Bridge on January 4th, 1917, when several direct hits were scored and considerable damage done. The machines were exposed to anti-aircraft, rifle, and machine-gun fire during the attack, and also on the return journey.

Flt. Sub-Lt. Leo Philip Paine, R.N.A.S.
Flt. Sub-Lt. Robert Leckie, R.N.A.S.
Flt. Sub-Lt. Basil Deacon Hobbs, R.N.A.S.
Flt. Sub-Lt. Charles McNicoll, R.N.A.S.
Flt. Sub-Lt. Valentine Edgar Sieveking, R.N.A.S.

In recognition of his services on the night of May 3rd-4th, 1917, when he dropped bombs on Ostend seaplane base with good results, making two trips.

Flt. Sub-Lt. Harold Thomas Mellings, R.N.A.S.

In recognition of his services on March 19th, 1917, when he attacked a hostile aeroplane with great gallantry at heights varying from 12,000 ft. to 20,000 ft.

Flt. Sub-Lt. Frederick Earle Fraser, R.N.A.S.
Flt.-Lieut. (Act. Flt.-Com.) Charles Dawson Booker.

For special gallantry in the field on numerous occasions, especially the following: On April 26th, 1917, he went to the assistance of some of our photographic machines, which were about to be attacked by twelve Albatross scouts. One of these he fired on at close range, and brought it down out of control. On May 24th, 1917, whilst on patrol, he went to the assistance of a formation of our machines, which was being attacked by nine hostile scouts. He attacked one of the latter, which was driven down in flames and crushed. Later in the same day he attacked and drove down out of control another hostile machine. On numerous other occasions he was attacked enemy machines and driven them down out of control.

Flt.-Lt. George Goodman Simpson.

For gallantry and able leadership in aerial fighting, notably on the following occasions: On May 3rd, 1917, he drove down a hostile aeroplane out of control. On May 11th, 1917, while an offensive patrol with five other machines, he attacked six hostile aircraft. One of these he brought down out of control, and a few minutes later he attacked another at close range and brought it down in flames. On May 23rd, 1917, he led a formation of five machines to attack at least twice that number of hostile aeroplanes. Both formations became split up, and a general fight ensued. Five times during the combat he drove off hostile aeroplanes from another of our machines, and one of those which he attacked was seen to go down in a spin.

Bar to D.S.C.

Flt.-Com. Theodore Douglas Hallam, D.S.C., R.N.A.S.
Flt.-Com. Roderic Stanley Dallas, D.S.C., R.N.A.S.

In recognition of his services on April 23rd, 1917, when with two other machines he engaged a formation of nine hostile scouts and two-seater machines. Two two-seater machines were shot down, one of them by Flt.-Com. Dallas, unassisted.

Flt.-Lt. Charles Langston Scott, D.S.C., R.N.A.S.

Flt.-Lt. Robert Alexander Little, D.S.C., R.N.A.S.

For exceptional daring and skill in aerial fighting on many occasions, of which the following are examples: On April 28th, 1917, he destroyed an Aviatik; on April 29th he shot down a hostile scout, which crashed. On April 30th, with three other machines, he went up after hostile machines, and saw a big fight going on between fighter escorts and hostile aircraft. Flt.-Lt. Little attacked one at fifty yards' range, and brought it down out of control. A few minutes later he attacked a red scout with a larger machine than the rest. This machine was handled with great skill, but by clever manœuvring Flt.-Lt. Little got into a good position and shot it down out of control.

DISTINGUISHED SERVICE MEDAL.

Act. Air Mech., 1st Cl., F. Bate.
Air Mech., 2nd Cl., A. G. Flowers.
P.O. Mech., 3rd Cl., J. W. Rose.
Air Mech., 1st Cl., G. B. Clements.
Air Mech., 2nd Cl., S. R. Laycock.
C.P.O., 3rd Cl., V. F. Whatling.
Air Mech., 1st Cl., D. G. Rennett.
Air Mech., 2nd Cl., C. S. Laycock.

MENTIONED IN DESPATCHES.

Sqdrn.-Com. J. R. Wadham Smyth-Pigott, D.S.O. R.N.
Flt.-Com. T. D. Hallam, D.S.C., R.N.A.S.
Flt. Sub-Lt. J. R. Ross, R.N.A.S.
Midi. E. R. Snow, R.N. (since killed).
Air Mech., 1st Cl., W T. Hollidge, (since died of injuries).

PROMOTION FOR SERVICE IN ACTION.
ROYAL NAVAL RESERVE.

Comdr. S. M. Day, R.D., to be Capt.; dated March 16th, 1917.

PART II

SEND TO THE

POLISH VICTIMS RELIEF FUND

for a booklet recording its work

in collaboration with the Poles themselves

and keep the stream of

British Generosity to Poland

flowing, if only by a few pence

The Poles and the Poles only

will benefit by what you give

EXECUTIVE COMMITTEE

Chairman - - - I. J. PADEREWSKI

Major-General Lord Treowen, C.B., C.M.G.
Lieut-Col. Sir Francis Younghusband, K.C.I.E., K.C.S.I.

Father Bernard Vaughan, S.J.
Lieut.-Colonel John Buchan
H. E. Morgan

Hon. Treasurer - - Lord Stuart of Wortley

Hon. Secretary—MISS LAURENCE ALMA TADEMA,
11 Haymarket, London, S.W. 1
Telephone—Gerrard 4130

THE BRITISH NAVY.
BATTLESHIPS
(Pre-War details only.)

Name.	Lgth (feet)	B'am (feet)	Tonnage.	Horse Power.	Spd. (kts.)	Coal (Max.)	Com'ment	Where Built.	Boilers	Completed	Armour.	Armament.
Royal Sovereign Class.												
Ramillies	610	90	25,750	31,000	22	All oil	1000	Dalmuir	Bc. & Y.	1915	Belt: 13½ in.; P.D. 3in.; Guns 13½in.; C.T. 13½in.	15in., eight; 6in., sixteen; 3in., four; torpedo tubes, five.
Resolution								Jarrow	,,	,,		
Revenge						4,000		Barrow	,,	,,		
Royal Oak								Devonport	,,	,,		
Royal Sovereign								Portsmouth	,,	,,		
Canada*	625	92	28,000	37,000	23	4,000	1000	Elswick	Yarrow	1915	Belt: 9 in.; P.D. 3 in.; Turrets 10 in.	14 in., ten; 6 in., sixteen; torpedo tubes, four.
Queen Elizabeth Class.												
Barham	650	92	27,500	58,000	25	All oil.	1000	Glasgow	Bc. & Y.	1915	Belt: 13½in.; P.D. 2¾in.; Guns 13½in.; C.T. 13½in.	15 in., eight; 6in., sixteen; 3in., four; torpedo tubes, five.
Malaya								Newcastle	,,	,,		
Queen Elizabeth						4,000		Portsmouth	,,	1914		
Warspite								Devonport	,,	1915		
Valiant								Govan	,,	,,		
Erin‡	525	91	23,000	31,000	21	3,500	870	Barrow	B'cock	1914	Belt: 12·6 P.D., 3in.	13·5, ten; 6in. sixteen.
Iron Duke Class.												
Benbow	580	90	25,000	29,000	22.5	4,000	900	Glasgow	Bc. & Y.	1914	Belt: 12 in.; P.D. 2¾in.; Guns 12in.; C.T. 12in.	13·5 in., ten; 6in., twelve; 3pr. six; torpedo tubes, five.
Emperor of India								Barrow	,,	,,		
Marlborough								Devonport	,,	,,		
Iron Duke								Portsmouth	,,	,,		
King George V. Class.												
Ajax	555	89	23,600	31,000	21	3,700	900	Greenock	Bc. & Y.	1913	Belt: 12 in.; P.D. 2¾in.; Guns 12in.; C.T. 12in.	13·5in., ten; 4in., sixteen; 3pr., four; torpedo tubes, five.
Centurion								Devonport	,,	,,		
King George V.								Portsmouth	,,	,,		
Agincourt †	632	89	27,500	45,000	22	3,000	1000	Elswick	B'cock	1914	Belt: am, 9in.; P.D. 2¾in.; turrets, 9in.	12in., fourteen; 6in. twenty; 3in. ten.
Orion Class.												
Conqueror	545	88½	22,500	27,000	21	3,500	800	Dalmuir	Bc.&Y.	1912	Belt: 12 in.; P.D. 2¾in.; B'bette 6in.	13·5in., ten; 3pr., four; 4 in., sixteen; torpedo tubes, three.
Monarch								Elswick	,,	,,		
Thunderer								Thames	,,	,,		
Orion								Portsmouth	,,	1911		

NOTE TO ARMOUR.—am.=amidships; f.= forward; a.=aft; P.D.=protective deck. C.T.=Conning tower.

* Ex-Almirante Latorre (Chile); ‡ late Reshadieh (Turkey); † late Rio de Janeiro (Brazil), late Sultan Osman I (Turkey).

THE BRITISH NAVY—continued.

Name.	Lgth (feet)	B'am (feet)	Tonnage.	Horse Power.	Spd. (kts).	Coal Max.	Com' pmt.	Where Built.	Boilers.	Completed	Armour.	Armament.
Colossus Class.												
Colossus	510	86	20,000	25,000	21	2,800	800	Greenock	Bc. & Y.	1911	Belt: am. 10in.; f. 8in.; a. 7in.; P.D. 2¾in.; B'bette and C.T. 11in.	12in., ten; 3pr., four; 4in., sixteen; torpedo tubes, three.
Hèrs			19,900					Jarrow	,,	,,		
Neptune								Portsmouth	,,	,,		
St. Vincent Class.												
Collingwood	500	84	19,250	24,500	21	2,700	724	Devonport	Yarrow	1910	Belt: am. 9¾in.; f. 6½in.; a. 6½in.; P.D. 2¾in.; B'bette 11in.	12in., ten; 3pr., four; 4in., eighteen; machine, six; torpedo tubes, three.
Vanguard			Blown up July 9, '17					Barrow	Babco'k	,,		
St. Vincent								Portsmouth	,,	1909		
Bellerophon Class.												
Bellerophon	490	82	18,600	23,000	21	2,700	870	Portsmouth	Bc. & Y.	1909	Belt: am. 11in.; f. 6in.; a. 4in.; P.D. 2¾in.; B'bette 12in.	12in., ten; 3 pr., four; 4in., sixteen; torpedo tubes, three.
Téméraire								Devonport	,,	,,		
Superb	490	82	17,900	23,000	21	2,700	800	Elswick	Babco'k	1906	,, ,,	12in., ten; 12pr., twenty-four; torpedo tbs, five.
Dreadnought								Portsmouth				
Lord Nelson Class.												
Agamemnon	420	79	16,500	2 090	18	2,500	747	Glasgow	Babco'k	1 97	(Krupp) Belt: am. 12 in.; f. 4in.; a. 4in.; P.D. 2in.; B'bette 12in.; C.T. 12in.	12in., four; 9'2, ten; 3in., i 8pn.; 3pr., lite; machine, ten; torpedo t Us, five.
Lord Nelson								Jarrow	Yarrow	,		
King Edward VII. Class												
Africa	453	78	16,350	18,000	18	2,000	780	Chatham	Babco'k	1906	(Krupp) Belt: am.9in.; f. 6in.; a. 2in.; P.D. 2in.; B'bette 12in.; C.T. 12in.	12in., four; 9'2, four; 6in., ten; 12pr., fourteen; 3pr., fourteen; Maxims, two; tplo tubes, five.
Britannia								Portsmouth	,,	,,		
Cmwealth								Fairfield	,,	1905		
Dominion								Barrow	,,	,,		
i ilia								Devonport	,,	1906		
Hindustan								Clydebank	,,	1905		
King Edward VII.			Mined Jan. 9, '16					Devonport	,,	1904		
Zealandia								Portsmouth	Nicla'se	1905		
Swiftsure Class.												
Swiftsure	450	71	11,800	12,500	20	2,000	700	Elswick	Yarrow	1904	(Krupp) Belt: am.7in.; f. 3in.; a 2in.; P.D. 3in.; B'bettte 10in.; C.T. 10in.;Cas.7in.	10in., four; 7'5, fourteen; 14pr., fourteen; 12pr., two; 6pr., four; Maxims, four; torpedo tubes, two.
Triumph			Torpedoed May 25, '15					Barrow	,,	,,		

NOTE TO ARMOUR.—am.=amidships; f.=forward; a.=aft; P.D.=protective deck   C.T.=conning tower.

THE BRITISH NAVY—continued.

Name.	Lgth (feet)	B'am (feet)	Tonnage.	Horse Power.	Spd. (kts.)	Coal (Max.)	Com' pmt.	Where Built.	Boilers.	Completed	Armour.	Armament.
Formidable Class.											(Krupp) Belt: am.9in.; f. 6in.; P.D. 3in.; B'bette 13in.; C.T. 12in, Casemates 6in.	12in., four; 6in., twelve; 12pr., eighteen; 3pr., six; Maxims, two; torpedo tubes, four.
Bulwark			*Blown up*	*Nov. 26, '14*				Devonport	Belle'le	192		
Formidable			*Torpedoed*	*Jan. 1, '15*				Portsmouth	,,	1901		
Implacable								Devonport	,,	,,		
Irresistible			*Mined*	*Mar. 18, '15*				Chatham	,,	1902		
Queen	420	75	15,000	15,000	18	2,200	760	Portsmouth	,,	194		
Prince of Wales								Devonport	Babco'k	,,		
London								Chatham	Belle'le	192		
Venerable												
Duncan Class.											(Krupp) Belt: a.m. 7in.; f. 5in.; a. 1¾in.; P.D. 2½in.; B'bette 11in.; C.T. 11in. Casemates 6in.	12in., four; 6in., twelve; 12pr., twelve; 3pr., six; Maxims, two; torpedo tubes, four.
Albemarle								Chatham	Belle'le	1903		
Cornwallis			*Torpedoed*	*Jan. 9, '17*				Thames	,,	1904		
Duncan	25	75	14,000	18,000	19	2,000	750	,,	,,	1903		
Exmouth								Birkenhead	,,	,,		
Russell			*Mined*	*A/t. 28, '16*				Jarrow	,,	,,		
Canopus Class.											(Harvey Nic.) Belt: am. 6-in.; f. 2in., a. 1½in.; P.D. 2¾in.; B'bette 12in.; C.T. 12in. Casemates 5in.	12in., four; 6in., twelve; 12pr., twelve; 3pr., six; Maxims, two; torpedo tubes, four.
Aion								Thames	Belle'le	1901		
Canopus								Portsmouth	,,	1899		
Glory	20	74	12,950	13,500	18	2,300	700	Birkenhead	,,	1900		
Goliath			*Torpedoed*	*May 13, '15*				Chatham	,,	,,		
Ocean			*Mined*	*Mar. 18, '15*				Devonport	,,	,,		
Vengeance								Barrow	,,	1902		
Majestic Class.											(Harvey) Belt: am. 9in.; P.D. 4in.; B'bette 14in.; C.T. 14in. Casemates 6in.	12in., four; 6in., twelve; 12 pr., sixteen; 3 pr., twelve; Maxims, two; torpedo tubes, four.
Cæsar								Portsmouth	Cylindcl	1898		
Hannibal								Pembroke	,,	,,		
Illustrious								Chatham	,,	,,		
Jupiter								Clydebank	,,	1897		
Magnificent	412	75	14,900	12,000	17	2,000	750	Chatham	,,	1895		
Majestic			*Torpedoed*	*May 27, '15*				Portsmouth	,,	,,		
Mars								Birkenhead	,,	1897		
Prince G'ge								Portsmouth	,,	1896		
Vict ɔɔis								Chatham	,,	1897		

NOTE TO ARMOUR.—am.=amidships; f.=forward; a.=aft; P.D.=protective deck; C.T.=conning tower.

BATTLE CRUISERS

Name.	Lgth (feet)	B'am (feet)	Tonnage.	Horse Power.	Spd. (kts.)	Coal (Max.)	Com' pmt.	Where Built.	Boilers.	Completed	Armour.	Armament.
Queen Mary Class.												
Queen Mary	670	88	*Gunfire* 28,000	*May 31,'16* 87,500	31	3,800	1000	Jarrow Glasgow	Babco'k ,,	1914 ,,	Belt: 9¾in.; P.D. 3in.; Turrets 10in.	13'5, eight; 4in., sixteen. (Tiger, 6in., twelve).
Tiger												
Lion Class.												
Princess Royal	660	88	26,350	70,000	31	3,500	980	Barrow Devonport	Babco'k	1912 ,,	Belt: 9¾in.; Turrets 10in.; P.D. 3in.	13'5, eight; anti-torpedo, 4in., sixteen.
Lion												
Australian Class.												
Australia	567	82	19,220 18,800	44,000	26	2,500	780	Govan Clydebank	Babco'k	1912 ,,	Belt: 8in.; P.D. 3in.; Turrets 10in.	12in, eight; 4in., sixteen.
New Zealand												
Indefatigable Class.												
Indefatigable	555	80	*Gunfire* 18,750	*May 31,'16* 45,000	26	2,500	800	Devonport Elswick	Babco'k ,,	1911 1908	(Krupp) Belt: am. 7in.; f. 6in.; a. 4-in.; Turrets 10in.; P.D. 2½in.	12-in., eight; anti-torpedo guns, 4in. (1907 model) sixteen; (Indefatigable 20 4in.); t'pedo tubes, three.
Invincible	530	78⅙	*Gunfire* 17,250	*May 31,'16* 41,000	25	2,500	750	Clydebank Gcvan	,, ,,	,, ,,		
Inflexible												
Inomitable												

CRUISERS.

Minotaur Class.												
Defence	520	72	*Gunfire* 14,600	*May 31,'16* 27,000	23	2,000	755	Pembroke Chatham Devon	Yarrow ,, Babco'k	1908 ,, ,,	(Krupp) Belt: am. 6in.; f. 4in.; a. 3in.; P.D. 1¾in.; B'bette 7in.	9'2, four; 7'5, ten; torpedo tubes, three (submerged).
Shannon												
Minotaur												
Dk. of Edinburgh Class												
Achilles	480	73½	*Blown up* *Gunfire* 13,550	*Dec. 30,'15* *May 31,'16* 23,500	23	2,000	720	Elswick Govan Barrow Pembroke ,, Thames	Yarrow & Cylin'l B.Y.B.& W. Babco'k	1907 ,, ,, 1906 1905 1906	(Krupp) Belt: am. 6in.; f. 4in.; a. 3in.; P.D. ¾in.; B'bette 7in.	9'2, six; 7'5, four; twenty-four. 3pr.,
Cochrane												
Natal												
Warrior												
Duke of Edinburgh												
Black Prince												9'2, six; 6in., ten; 3pr., twenty; torpedo tubes, three (submerged).

NOTE TO ARMOUR.—am.=amidships; f.=forward; a.=aft; P.D.=protective deck; C.T.=conning tower.

THE BRITISH NAVY—continued.
CRUISERS

Name.	Lgth (feet)	B'am (feet)	Tonnage.	Horse Power.	Spd. (kts.)	Coal (Max.)	Com'ment	Where Built.	Boilers	Completed	Armour.	Armament.
Ðe Class.												
Antrim	460	68½	*Wrecked* Oct. 16, '15	21,000	22½	1,800	650	Clydebank	Yarrow	1905	(Krupp) Belt: am. 6-in.; f. 2in.; P.D. 2-in.; B'bette 6in.; Casemates 6in.	7·5, four; 6in., six; 12pr., two; 3-pounders, twenty; Maxims, two; torpedo tubes, two (submerged).
Argyll			11,000					Greenock	Babco'k	,,		
Carnarvon								Beardmore	Nicla'se	,,		
Devonshire								Chatham	,,	,,		
Hampshire			*Mined* June 5, '16					Elswick	Yarrow	,,		
R ¹ ₁ᵈrgh								Glasgow	Durr	,,		
Monmouth Class.												
Berwick	450	66	9,800	22,000	23	1,600	537	Beardmore	Nicla'se	1903	(Krupp) Belt: am. 4-in.; f. 2in.; P.D. 2-in.; B'bette 5in.; Casemates, 4in.	6in., fourteen; 12pr, ten; pompoms, ten; 3 pr, three; torpedo tubes, two (submerged).
₁ll								Pembroke	Babco'k	1904		
₁land								Glasgow	Belle'le	,,		
Donegal								Fairfield	,,	1903		
Essex								Pembroke	,,	,,		
Kent								Portsmouth	,,	1904		
₁ ster			*Gun-fire* Nov. 1, '14					Elswick	,,	1903		
Monmouth								Glasgow	,,	1904		
Suffolk								Portsmouth	Nicla'se			
Drake Class.												
Drake	520	71	*Gun-fire* Nov. 1, '14	30,000	23	2,500	900	Pembroke	Belle'le	1902	(Krupp) Belt: am. 6-in.; f. 2in.; P.D. 2-in.; B'bette 6in.; Casemates 6in.	9·2, two; 6in., sixteen; 12pr., fourteen; 3pr., two; machine, six; torpedo tubes, two (submerged).
Good Hope								Fairfield	,,	,,		
King Alfred			14,100					Clydebank	,,	1903		
Leviathan								Barrow	,,	,,		
Cressy Class.												
Aboukir	470	69½	*Torpedoed* Sept. 22, '14	21,000	21	1,600	750	Fairfield	Belle'le	1902	(Krupp) Belt: am. 6-in.; f. 2in.; P.D. 3-in.; B'bette 6in.; Casemates 5in.	9·2, two; 6in., twelve; 12pr., fourteen; 3pr., three; machine, four; torpedo tubes, two (submerged).
Cressy			*Torpedoed* Sept. 22, '14					,,	,,	1901		
Bacchante				12,000				Clydebank	,,	192		
Euryalus								Barrow	,,	1904		
Hogue			*Torpedoed* Sept. 22, '14					,,	,,	1902		
Sutlej								Clydebank	,,	··		

NOTE TO ARMOUR.—am.=amidships; f.=forward; a.=aft; P.D.=protective deck; C.T.=conning tower.

THE BRITISH NAVY—continued.

PROTECTED CRUISERS

Name.	Lgth (feet)	B'am (feet)	Tonnage	Horse Power	Spd. (kts).	Coal (Max.)	Com' pmt.	Where Built.	Boilers.	Completed	Armour.	Armament.
Powerful Class.												
Terrible	520	71	14,400	25,000	22	3,000	840	Clydebank	Belle'le	1898	(H.) P.D. 6in.; B'bette 6in.; Casemates 6in.	9'2, two; 6in., sixteen; 12pr., eighteen; machine, six; torpedo tubes, four (submerged).
Diadem Class.												
Amphitrite	460	69	11,000	10,000	21	2,000	680	Barrow	,,	190	(H.) P.D. 4in.; Casemates 4in.	6in., sixteen; 12pr., fourteen; 3pr., six; Maxims, two; torpedo tubes, three (two submerged).
Andromeda								Pembroke	,,	,,		
Argonaut								Fairfield	,,	,,		
Ariadne								Clydebank	,,	1899		
Diadem								Fairfield	,,	,,		
Europa								Clydebank	,,	,,		
Spartiate								Pembroke	,,	1902		
Edgar Class.												
Crescent	360	60	7,350	12,000	19	1,250	550	Portsmouth	Cylindcl	1893	P.D. 3in.; Casemates 6in.	9'2, two; 6in., ten; 6pr., twelve; 3pr., five; Max., two; torpedo tubes, two (submerged).
Edgar				Torpedoed Oct. 15, '14				Devonport	,,	1893		
Endymion								Hull	,,	1894		
Gibraltar								Glasgow	,,	,,		
Grafton								Blackwall	,,	,,		
Hawke								Chatham	,,	1893		
Royal Arthur								Portsmouth	,,	,,		
St. George								Hull	,,	1894		
Theseus								Blackwall	,,	,,		
Challenger Class.												
Challenger	355	56	5,800	12,500	21	1,225	475	Chatham	Babco'k	1904		6in., eleven; 12pr., nine; 3pr., six; Maxims, two; torpedo tubes, two (submerged).

NOTE TO ARMOUR.— am.=amidships; f.=forward; a.=aft; P.D.=protective deck; C.T.=conning tower.

THE BRITISH NAVY—*continued*.

CRUISERS

Name.	Length (feet).	Beam (feet).	Tonnage.	Horse Power.	Speed (Knots).	Coal (Max.)	Complement.	Where Built.	Boilers.	Completed	Armament.
Highflyer Class.											
Hermes	Torpedoed Oct. 31, '14		5,600	10,000	20	1,100	430	Fairfield	Babcock	1889	6in., eleven; 12pr., nine; 3pr., six; Maxims, two; torpedo tubes, two (sub'd)
Highflyer	350	54						,,	Belleville	,,	
Hyacinth								Glasgow	,,	1900	
Arrogant Class.											
Furious	320	58	5,750	10,000	19	1,180	420	Devonport	Belleville	1896	6in., ten; 12pr., nine; 3pr., three; Maxims, two; torpedo tubes, three (two submerged).
Vindictive								Chatham	,,	1899	
Talbot Class.											
Diana	370	54	5,600	9,600	19.5	1,076	440	Fairfield	Cylindrical	1899	6in., eleven; 12pr., nine; 3pr., seven; Maxims, two; torpedo tubes, three (two submerged).
Dido								Glasgow	,,	1897	
Doris								Barrow	,,	,,	
Eclipse								Portsmouth	,,	,,	
Isis								Glasgow	,,	1898	
Juno								Barrow	,,	,,	
Minerva								Chatham	,,	1896	
Talbot								Devonport	,,	,,	
Venus								Fairfield	,,	1897	
Astræa Class.											
Astræa	320	49½	4,360	9,000	19.5	1,000	320	Devonport	Cylindrical	1894	6in., two; 4.7, eight; 6pr., eight; 3pr., one; torpedo tubes, four (above water).
Bonaventure								Pembroke	,,	,,	
Cambrian								Sheerness	,,	1895	
Flora								Pembroke	,,	,,	
Forte								Chatham	,,	,,	
Fox								Portsmouth	,,	,,	
Hermione								Devonport	,,	,,	

THE BRITISH NAVY—continued.

Name.	Length (feet).	Beam (feet).	Tonnage.	Horse Power.	Speed (Knots).	Coal (Max)	Complement.	Where Built.	Boilers.	Completed	Armament.
Apollo Class.											
Æolus								Devonport	Cylindrical	1893	6in., two; 4"7, six; 6pr., eight; 3pr., one; machine, four; torpedo tubes, four (above water).
Brilliant	300	44	3,500	9,000	20	550	275	Sheerness	,,	,,	
Iris								Glasgow	,,	1892	
Sappho								Barrow	,,	1893	
Scylla								Poplar	,,	,,	
Sirius								Elswick	,,	1892	
Terpsichore								Glasgow	,,	,,	
Adventure Class.											
Adventure	370	38	2,700	16,500	25	450	268	Elswick	Yarrow	1905	12pr., ten; 3prs., eight; torpedo tubes, two.
Attentive								,,	,,	,,	
Foresight								Govan	Thornycroft	,,	
Forward								,,	,,	,,	
Patrol								Laird	Laird	,,	
Pathfinder *Torpedoed Sept. 5, '14*								,,	,,	,,	
Sentinel								Barrow	Normand	,,	
Skirmisher								,,	,,	,,	
Boadicea Class.											
Diamo	360	40	3,000	9,800	23	500	300	Elswick	Yarrow (T.)	1904	4in., twelve; pr., eight; Maxims, two; torpedo tubes, two.
Sapphire								Laird	Reed	1905	
Topaze								Jarrow	,,	,,	
								Laird	Laird	1904	
Arethusa Class.											
Calliope								Chatham		1915	6in., two; 4in., six.
,,								Newcastle		,,	
Chatham	3,740			40,000	30	750 (oil)		Devonport		,,	
Champion								Newcastle		,,	
Carysfort								Pembroke		,,	
Caroline								Birkenhead		,,	
Cordelea								Pembroke		,,	
Royalist								,,		,,	
Phaeton	410	39	3,600	30,000	30	750 (oil)	280	Glasgow		1914	6in., two; 4in., six.
Penelope								Barrow		,,	
Undaunted								Glasgow		,,	
Arethusa *Mined Feb. 14, '16*								Govan		,,	
Aurora								Chatham		,,	
								Devonport		,,	

THE BRITISH NAVY—continued.

Name.	Length (feet).	Beam (feet).	Tonnage.	Horse Power.	Speed (Knots).	Coal (Max.)	Complement.	Where Built	Boilers.	Completed	Armament.
Chatham Class.											
Birmingham	430	48¼	5,400	26,500	25	1000	380	Newcastle	Yarrow	1914	6in., eight; 3pr., four.
Chatham								Chatham	,,	1912	6in., eight ; nine Q.F. and machine.
Dublin								Dalmuir	,,	1913	
Lowestoft								Chatham	,,	1914	
Nottingham	*Torpedoed* Aug. 19, '16							Pembroke	,,	1914	
Southampton								Clydebank	,,	1913	
Bristol Class.											
Bristol								Clydebank	,,	1910	6in., two; 4in., ten; machine, eight.
Glasgow								Fairfield	,,	,,	
Gloucester	430	47	4,800	24,500	27	800	375	Dalmuir	,,	,,	
Liverpool								Barrow	,,	,,	
Newcastle								Elswick	,,	,,	
Weymouth Class.											
Dartmouth								Glasgow	Yarrow	1911	6in., eight ; Q.F. and machine, nine.
Falmouth	*Torpedoed* Aug. 19, '16							Clydebank	,,	,,	
Weymouth	430	48½	5,250	23,500	25	1000	380	Elswick	,,	,,	
Yarmouth								Govan	,,	,,	
Colonial.											
Brisbane								New S.W.	Yarrow	1913	6in., eight ; Q.F. and machine, nine.
Melbourne	460	48½	5,400	25,000	25.5	1000	350	Birkenhead	,,	1912	
Sydney								Glasgow	,,	,,	
Boadicea Class.											
Active								Pembroke	Yarrow	1911	4in., ten ; 3pr., four.
Amphion	*Mined* Aug. 6, '14							,,	,,	1912	
Bellona*								,,	,,	1910	
Blanche	385	41	3,440	20,000	26	600	320	,,	,,	,,	
Blonde								,,	,,	1911	
Boadicea*								,,	,,	1909	
Fearless								,,	,,	1913	

* The Bellona and Boadicea carry only six 6in. guns.

The Monitors : Severn, Humber, Mersey, late Javary, Medeira, Solimoes (Brazil), 1,250 tons, carry two 6 in. and 2 4.7 in. howitzers.

SUBMARINES (pre-war details only).

Class.	No. in Class.	Date of Building.	Speed in Knots.	Displacement.	Horse Power.	Tubes.	Guns.
A	9	1904-06	9-12	200 Tons	150-500	2	
B	10	1904-06	9-13	314 ,,	189-600	2	
C	37	1906-09	10-14	320 ,,	300-600	2	
D	8	1908-11	10-16	580 ,,	550-1,200	3	Two 3in.
E	16	1911-13	10-16	800 ,,	1,950	4	Two 3in.
F	6	1913-14	12-20	1,000 ,,	5,000	6	

TORPEDO CRAFT.

"M" Class (1 g-14) (Displacement, 1,200-1,350 tons; H.P., 27,000; 34 knots; armament, four 4·1; four tin. tubes):—Mary, Meteor, Miff, Milne, Mor, Murray, Myngs, Mystic.

"L" Class (g) (Displacement 980-1,100 tons; H.P., 25,000; ds; armament, three 4·1; four 21in. tubes):—Laforey, Lance, Lan... Lark, Lassoo (Torpedoed August 13, 1916), Laverock, Laertes, Legion, Leonidas, Liberty, Lily, bit, Llewellyn, Louis (Wrecked Nov. a, 1915), Loyal, Lucifer, Lydiard, Lysander.

"K" Class (g-8) Displacement 928-1,100 tons; H.P., 28,000; 30-32 knots; armament, three 4in.; four 2in. tubes):— Ace (Gunfire, May 31, 1916), Midge, Ol... Ophelia, Paragon, Parthian, Pelican, Pellew, Penn, Peregrine, Phoenix, Pigeon, Plover, Portia, Pylades, Lynx (Mined, Aug. 9, 1915), Shark (Gunfire, May 3, 1916), Sparrowhawk (Gunfire, May 31, 1916), Spitfire, Unity, Victor.

"J" Class (1911) (Displ... ton... ts; H.P. ... ts; armament, ... 4in. ... tubes):—Ariel, Attack, Badger, Beaver, ... Druid, Ferret, Fortune (Gunfire, May 31, 1916), Goshawk, Hind, Hornet, Hydra, Jackal, Lapwing, Ll..., Lookout, Lurcher, Lyra.

"H" Class (1910) (Displacement, 9-30 tons; H.P., 13, or 27 l armament, two 4-in.; two tin. tubes):—Basilisk, Beagle, Cameleon, Ca... Ery, Garth, Hope, Ive, Lyra, Mc..., Mill s, Nereide, Nymphe, Redpole, Rifleman, Ruby, Sel... Salmon, Scourge, Veteran.

"G" Class (99) ... 900-1,000 tons; H.P., 2,1 or 27 knots; armament, oe ... dr.; two in. tubes):—Basilisk, Beagle, Bulldog, ... field, Grasshopper, Hy..., Mo..., Mill s, Racoon, Rat..., Renard, Savage, Scorpion, Scourge, Wel...

"F" Class (1907-9) (Displacement, 865-1,050 tons; H.P., ... five ... 33 knots; armament, five ... 2 18in. ... Oer G, 196), Saracen, ...Afridi, ...ian, Viking, ...

"E" Class (g-08) (Displacement, 530-650 tons; H.P., 7,500; 25 knots; armament, four 12pdrs.; two ... :—Arun, Boyne, Ga... rar, Cherwell, Co..., Dee, Derwent, Doon, Eden (Collision, June 6, 19..), Erne (Wrecked, Feb. 6, 1915), Etrick, Exe, Foyle, Garry, It..., J..., d, Kale, Lif..., Liffey, My, N..., Ne..., Ouse, Ribble, Rother, Stour, Swale, Test, Tey, Ure, Usk, Waveney, W..., Well sad.

"D" Class (1895-01) l armament, on ... dr; two ... dr. ... 30 ... ts; armament, oe pdr.; the 6- pds.; two 8in. tubes):—

Angler, A... ger (Mined, March 9, 1916), Cygnet, Cynthia, Desperate, Fame, Mallard, Stag.

"C" Class (1895-01) Displacement, 2-90 tons; H.P., 6,000; 30 knots; armament, oe pdr., five ... five pdrs.; two 18in. tubes):— Albatross, Avon, Bat, Ba... Brazen, Br... By..., Gi..., Gypsy, Greyhound, Kestrel, Le..., Leven, Vixen, Vulture, Hn, Fawn, Flirt (Sunk ... Or 6, 19..) Flying Fish, Racehorse, Recruit (Torpedoed, May 1, 195), Roebuck.

"B" Class (1895-01) Displacement, 9-90 tons; H.P., 6,000; 30 knots; armament, oe ... dr.; five pdrs.; two 18in. to ... tubes):—Albacore, Arab, Bonetta, Ernest, Express, Griffon, Kangaroo, July, M..., Myrmidon, Orwell, Kel, Quail, Seal, Spiteful, Sprightly, Success, Syren, E... Wolf.

"A" Class (1894-95) Displacement, 3- 30 ... tons; H.P., 4,500; 27 l armament, one ... dr.; five pdrs.; two 18in. t tubes):—Conflict, Fervent, Lightning, ... (1907) ... Crane, ... 2,170 tons; I.H.P., 30,000; 35.2 knots; armament, 6r 4in., two 18in. Botha (ex Gil), Broke (ex Riveros), Faul... her (ex Rebol... do), Tipperary (ex Simpson) (Gunfire, May 31, 1916) (1912-13).

Displacement, 80 tons; I.H.P., 27,000; 3¹ knots; armament, six ... is... two ... the 4in., Lightfoot, Ma..., Nimrod, Turbulent (Gunfire, May 31, 1916), (1915-16), Displacement, 1, 90 ... I.H.P., 29,000; 32 l knots; six 4in., five 21 in.

BRITISH NAVY (over l oses).

T.B. No. a, Torpedoed, June a, 1915. T.B. No. 12, Torpedoed, June a, 195. T.B. No. 96. T.B. No. 11, Mined, Meh a, 1916. Nomad and Nestor (Gunfire, May 31, 196).

SUBMARINES—E3, Sunk, Ot. 18, 1914. E7, Sunk, Sept. 8, 1915. E10, Sunk, Aug.—Nov. 1915. E13, Interned, Aug. 8, 1915. E5, Destroyed April 18, 195. E17, Sunk, Jan. 6, 1916. E20, Captured, Nov. 5, 1915. D2, Sunk, Aug.—Nov. 1915. D5, Sunk, Nov. 3, 1914. AE1, Sunk, Sept. 14, 1914. AE2, Sunk, April 31, 1915.

(*Other destroyers have been sunk, but names not disclosed by Admiralty.*)

THE FRENCH NAVY.
BATTLESHIPS

Name.	Lgth (feet)	B'am (feet)	Tonnage.	Horse Power.	Spd. (kts.)	Coal (Max.)	Com'l mnt.	Where Built.	Boilers.	Completed	Armour.	Armament.
BATTLESHIPS.												
Bearne	574	92	25,387	33,000	21	3,000	1100	La Seyne, Brest, Lorient, La Seyne, St. Nazaire	Nicla'se, Guyot, ,, Belle'ile, ,,	1916, 1916, 1916, 1916, 1916	Belt: 12·6 in.; ends 7in.; P.D., 2¾in.; gun positions, 17·2.	13·4in., twelve; 5·5in., twenty-four; torpedo tubes, six.
Bretagne, Provence	546	88½	23,600	29,500	20	3,000		Brest, Bordeaux, L'Orient	Belle'ile, Guyot, Nicla'se	1915, ,, ,,	Belt; am., 11⅜in.; P.D. 2¾in.; Turret 10⅜in.	13·4in., ten; 5·5in., twenty-two; torpedo tubes, four.
	541	88	23,100	29,000	20	2,800	1000	L'Orient, Brest, St. Nazaire, La Seyne	Belle'ile	1913, 1913, 1914, 1914	Belt: am. 10⅜in.: f. 7in., a. 7in.; P.D. 3⅜in.	12in., twelve; 5·5in., twenty-two; eight smaller; torpedo tubes, three.
Danton, Vergniaud	476	84	18,400 *Torpedoed Mar.19,'17*	22,500	19	2,000	680	St. Nazaire, Brest, L'Orient, ,, Bordeaux, La Seyne	Belle'ile & Nicla'se	1 91, ,, ,, ,, ,,	Belt: am. 10in.: f. 6in., a. 6in.; P.D. 3in., B'bette 12in.; C.T. 12in.	12in., four; 9·4in., twelve; 3in., sixteen; torpedo tubes, two.
	439	79½	14,870	18,000	18	1,90	800	Brest, La Seyne, Bordeaux	Belle'ile, Nicla'se, ,,	1907, ,, 1908	Belt: 11in.; 2¼in.: Turret 12in.	12in., four; 7·6, ten: 4in., eight; smaller, twenty-six; torpedo tubes, five (two submerged).
	450	79½	14,865	7,500	18	1,900	800	La Seyne, Brest	,, ,,	1906, ,,	Belt: 11in.; 3in.; Turret 14¼in.	12in., four; 6·4, eighteen; smaller, twenty-five; torpedoed tubes, five (two submerged).
Suffren	420	70	12,730 *Torpedoed Nov.26,'1*	16,300	18	1,200	750	,,	,,	1903	Belt; 12in.; 3in.; Turret 12in.	12in., for; 6·4, ten; 4in., eight; smaller, twenty-four; torpedo tubes, four (two submerged)

NOTE TO ARMOUR.—am.=amidships; f.=forward; a.=aft; P.D.=prot ive deck; C.T.=conning t

13

BATTLESHIPS AND ARMOURED CRUISERS

Name.	Lgth (feet)	B'am (feet)	Tonnage.	Horse Power.	Spd. (kts)	Coal (Max.)	Com' mnt.	Where Built.	Boilers.	Completed	Armour.	Armament.
Charlemagne *Gaulois* ... St. Louis ...	387	67½	11,000 *Torpedoed*	14,500 *Dec. 27,'16*	18	1,100	630	Brest ,, L'Orient	Belle'ile ,, ,,	1899 ,, 1900	(H.) Belt: am. 12¾-in.; f. 10in., a. 10-in.; P.D. 2¾in.; B'bette 15¾in.	12in., four; 5·5, ten; 4in., eight; smaller, 29; torpedo tubes, 4 (submerged)
Henri IV	350	73	8,948	11,500	17·5	1,100	460	Cherbourg	Nicla'se	1899	(H.N.) Belt: 11in., ends 8in; P. D. 5in.-3in.	10.8, two; 5·5, seven; torpedo tubes, 2 (submerg'd)
Bouvet	400	70	12,000 *Mined*	14,000 *Mar. 18,'15*	17½	900	650	L'Orient	Belle'ile	1898	(H.) Belt: am. 15¾-in.; f. 12in.; a. 10in.; P.D. 3½in.	12in., two; 10·8, two; 5·5, eight; 4in., eight; smaller, thirty; torpedo tubes, four
Masséna	370	66	11,700	13,500	18	800	620	St. Nazaire	D'Albert	,,	(H.) Belt: am. 17¾in.; f. 10in.; a. 10in.; P.D. 3½in.	12in., two; 10·8, two; 5·5, eight; 4in., eight; torpedo tubes, four.
Charles Martel ...	400	70	11,880	14,500	18	1,000	650	Brest	,,	1896	(C.) Belt: am. 17¾in.; f. 13½in.; a. 11in.; P.D. 2¾in.	12in., two; 10·8, two; 5·5, eight; torpedo tubes, six.
Carnot	390	70	12,000	15,000	18	700	650	Toulon	,,	1896	(C.) Belt: am. 17¾in.; f. 10in.; a 10in.; P.D. 2¾in.	12in., two; 10·8, two; 5·5, eight, smaller, twenty-four; torpedo tubes, four
Jauréguiberry ...	370	72	11,650	15,000	18	1,100	600	La Seyne	,,	,,	(C.) Belt: am. 17¾in.; f. 9in.; a. 9in., P.D. 2¾in.	12in., two; 10·8, two, 5·5, eight; smaller, twenty; torpedo tubes, six.
ARMD. CRUISERS												
Edgard Quinet Waldeck Rosseau	515	70	13,780	36,000	25	2,300	750	Brest L'Orient	Guyot Belle'ile	1910 1911	(Krupp) Belt: am. 5½in.; f. 3in.; a. 3; P.D. 2¼in.; B'bette 6in.; cas. 6in.	7·6, fourteen; smaller, 30; torpedo tubes, five.
Ernest Renan Jules Michelet	515	70	13,427 12,370	36,000	23½	2,300	674	St. Nazaire L'Orient	Nicla'se Guyot	1909 1908	,,	7·6, four; 6·4, fourteen; smaller, thirty; torpedo tubes, 5 (two submerged).

NOTE TO ARMOUR.—am.=amidships; f.=forward; a.=aft; P.D.=protective deck; C.T.=conning tower.

ARMOURED CRUISERS

Name.	Lgth (feet)	B'am (feet)	Tonnage.	Horse Power.	Spd. (kts.)	Coal (Max.)	Com' mnt.	Where Built.	Boilers.	Completed	Armour.	Armament
Leon Gambetta Jules Ferry ... Victor Hugo...	476	71	*Torpedoed* 12,350	*Apr.* 26,'15 27,000	22	2,100	750	Brest Cherbourg ,,	Nicla'se Belle'ile ,,	1904 1906 ,,	(Krupp) Belt: am. 6¾in.; f. 3in, a 3in.; P.D. 2½in.; B'bette 6in.; casemates 4 in.; .Œin.	7·6, four; 6·4, sixteen; smaller, twenty-four; torpedo tubes, five (two submerged).
Amiral Aube ... Conde ... ... Gloire ... ... Marseilla s10..	460	64	10,000	20,000	21	1,600	600	St. Nazaire L'Orient ,, Brest	,, Nicla'se ,, Belle'ile	1904 ,, 1902 1903	(Krupp) Belt: am. 6¾in.; f. 4in.; a. 4in.; P.D. 2½in.; Turret, 8in; cas., 4in.; C.T. 9in.	7·6, two; 6·4, eight; 4in., six; smaller, twenty; torpedo tubes, five.
Dupetit Thouars Amiral Gueydon Mm ...	452	63	9,519	19,600	21	1,600	580	Toulon L'Orient La Seyne	,, Norm'nd Nicla'se	,, 1902 ,,	(H. N.) Belt; am. 6¾in.; f. 4in.; a. 4in.; C.T. 4in.	7·6, ten; 6·4, eight; 4in., four; smaller, 22.
Jeanne d'Arc ...	480	64	11,270	28,500	22	2,100	620	Toulon	Temple	1903	(H.) Belt: am. 6in.; f. 5in.; a. 3in.; P.D. 2½in.; Turret 7½in.; cas. 5in.; C.T. 6in.	7·6, two; 5·5, fourteen; smaller, twenty; torpedo tubes, two (submerged).
Desaix . Dupleix . Kleber .	430	59	7,700	17,000	21	1,200	500	St. Nazaire Rochefort Bordeaux	Belle'ile ,, Nicla'se	1904 1903 1904	(Krupp) Belt: am. 4in.; f. 3in.; a. 3in.; P.D. 2¾in.; Turret 4in.; C.T. 6in.	6·4, eight; 4in., four; smaller, sixteen; torpedo tubes, two (above water).
Pothuau	370	50	5,360	10,000	19	650	450	Granville	Belle'ile	1896	(Steel) Belt: am. 3 in. f. 1½in., a. 1½in., P.D. 3½in., Turret 9in., casemates 2in., C.T. 9½in.	7·6, two; 5·5, ten; smaller, twenty; torpedo tubes, four (above water)
Bruix ... ... Latouche Treville	360	46	4,750	8,500	19	420	370	Rochefort Havre	, ,	,, 1894	(Ste l)&Belt: am. 3½in., f. 2½in, a. 2½in., P.D. 3in., Turret 3in., C.T. 4in.	7·6, two; 5·5, six; smaller, ten; torpedo tubes, four (above water).

NOTE TO ARMOUR.—am.=amidships; f.=forward; a.=aft; P.D.=protective de k; C.T.=conning tower.

THE FRENCH NAVY—continued
PROTECTED CRUISERS

Name.	Lgth (feet)	B'am (feet)	Tonnage	Horse Power.	Spd. (kts.)	Coal (Max.)	Com' mnt.	Where Built.	Boilers.	Completed	Armour.	Armament.
PTD. CRUISERS.												
Lamotte-Picquet No. 2 No. 3	452	45	4,500	42,000	32	Oil	400	Toulon	Temple-Guyot	—	(Krupp) Belt, 2in.; C.T., 6in.; gun shields, 6in.	5'5, eight; torpedo tubes, 4 (submerged).
Guichen	440	55	8,200	24,000	23	1,800	600	St. Nazaire	D'Allest	1901	(H.) P.D. 2½in.; casemates 1½in.; C.T. 6in.	9'4, two; 5'5, six; smaller, sixteen; torpedo tubes, two (above water).
D'Entrecasteaux	380	58	8,000	13,500	19	1,000	520	La Seyne	Cylindcl	1898	(H.) P.D. 3¼in.; cas. 3in.; Turret 8 in., C.T. 10in.	9'4, two; 5'5, twelve; smaller, sixteen; torpedo tubes, six (two subm'ged).
Jurien de la Gravière	440	49	5,680	17,000	23	1,000	500	L'Orient	Guyot	1901	P.D. 3in.; C.T. 6½in.	6'4, eight; smaller, sixteen; torpedo tubes, two (above water).
Du Chayla Friant	330	45	4,000	10,000	19	650	350	Cherbourg Brest	D'Allest Niclasse	1897 1894		6'4, six; 4in. fır; smaller, sixteen; torpedo tubes, two ; the tar).
D'Estrées	311	49	2,500	990	21	500	250	Rochefort	D'Allest	1900		5'5, two; 4in., 4; smaller, t kre; torpedo tubes, two (the water).
Lavoisier	330	35	2,350	7,000	20	350	250	Rochefort	Belle'ile	1899		5'5, four; 4in., wo; smaller, ke; torpedo tubes, two (above water).

NOTE TO ARMOUR.—am.=amidships; f.=forward; a.=aft; P.D.=protective deck; C.T.=conning tower.

FRENCH DESTROYERS.

New destroyers of not os displacement have been laid 'iee wr started, no details are available.

32-Knot ... (1914). Six originally laid in the ing of 1914 for Turkish Navy :—4in., five; r o tbs, 2in., five; displace-
ths, o tons; all oil.

31-Knot I nt, s (1911):—Aventurier, Intrépide, Opiniâtre, e.: dt, 1,100 ts ; h.p. 19,5 ; , 31 knots ; 4in., four ;
tbs, i, four. t for Argentina as M, Rioja, Salta, and San Juan.) (9-11):—4in., t 9-pdr., four ; tbs,
ue, t 700 e, Bouclier, Boutefeu (mined May 19, 1917), (e Mhl, t ls,
t Riviere, G, Cimeterre, Dague (mined February 24, 1915), Faulx, Fourche, Francis t Bory, Ensigne e,
Lestin, Magon, i, Protet; Renaudin, Roux.

28-Knot s :—9-pdr., is, tbs, three ; ds :
Aspirante-Herbert,) r. Cavalier, Gr, Ensei ne g ly, Fantassin, ld, J ire, Lansquenet, Mmeluke, S hi, Tirailleur,
Voltigeur.

28-Knot s (1905-8): , α 3 dr., is; t ts, n ; t, 330 ds :
Ms (Mined, November, 1915), s, e, Cognée, S t, d, re, Fanion, Fl uret, n, ive, Mortier
Gr, i e, r, Poignard, Sabretache, Sape, fin, it.

28-Knot s (1899-04):—9-pdr., e ; 3-pdr., ix; o ts, two ; t, 300 ds :
Arbalète, , Belier, Bombarde, ulte, Durandal, Epée, , et , e, Pique, Pistolet, Sabre, Sagaie,
Fronde, Hallebarde, Harpon, Javelin, Mousquet (Sunk, r 28, 1914), Mou eton, et t,
Sarbacane, Yatagan.

FRENCH SUBMARINES.

1901.—Displacement, 150 ds :— n, Follet, Francais, n, Sil , Sirene, Triton.

1903-05.—Displacement, 67 ds; 8 l ts :—Aigrette, Alose, Angville, Argonaute, Bonite, Gr, Cigogne (160-280 tons), Dauphin, Esturgeon,
Grondin, Loutre, d, Lynx, Meduse, Naiade, Otarie, , B, Protee, S uffleur Thore, Truite.

1906-08.—Displacement, 380-450 ns; 12 l ts :— , o, Ci e, e, e, Rubis, Saphir (Sunk, January 17, 1915), Topaze, Turquoise
(Destroyed, y, 1915).

1907-12.—Displacement, 400 t 12 ts :—Ampere, Arago, Berthelot, Bernoulli, Brumaire, Calypso (Sunk, July 7, 1914), Circe, Clorinde, Cornelie,
mb, Cugnot, Curie (d, December, 1914), Euler, Faraday, l, Foucalt, Franklin, Fresnal (Gunfire, December 6, 1915), Frimaire,
Fructidor, y, t, Germinal, Giffard, Joule, Le Verrier, Messidor, Monge, Montgolfier, i, n, Papin, Pluviose, Prairial,
Soule, Thermidor, a, Vendemaire, Volta, W.

1909-10.—Di nt, 1,050 t os ; 15 l ts :—Archimede, Bourgeois, Charles , Mariotte (Sunk, July 26, 1915).

1912.—Displ t, 1,050 t os ; d surface, 20 knots ; submerged, 12 :—Gustave Zédé, e.

1913.— e elie. o to 60 tons. Speed: submerged, 10 ots ; surface, 15 ts.

1914-15.—Displacement, 830-100 ns ; I.H.P., 4,000 ; d, 19 l ts su e, 11 l ts, submerged ; 8 torpedo tubes: - Dupuy-de-Lôme, Fulton,
Joule (Sunk, May 1, 1915), Lagrouge, le, Regnault, Sane.

1914-15.—Dis t, 520- 90 t os ; I.H.P., 2 oo ; , 17 nots ; surface, 8 ts submerged ; 8 torpedo tubes:—Amoronte, Amphitrite, Andro-
me, huse, Arione, e, Aal i, Bell e, Daphne, e, Gorgene, Hermoine.

FRENCH NAVY (other losses)

T.B. 219, Sunk, January, 1915. T.B. 347 and 338, Sunk in collision, October 9, 1914. Casabianca, Mine-layer, Mined, June 3, 1915. Zela (T.G.
Gunfire, September 22, 1914. Cassini, destroyer, torpedoed Feb. 28, 1917. This vessel was one of France's latest destroyers, carrying a crew
of 9 officers and 132 men.

THE RUSSIAN NAVY.
BATTLESHIPS AND BATTLE CRUISERS

Name.	Lgth (feet)	B'am (feet)	Tonnage.	Horse Power.	Spd (kts.)	Coal (Max.)	Com mnt.	Where Built.	Boilers.	Completed	Armour.	Armament.
BATTLESHIPS. Borodino Izmail Kinburn Navarin			25,000	15,000	26½			Petrograd	Yarrow	1916 ,, ,, ,,	Belt, 9in.	14in., nine; 5'1. twenty.
Imperatritsa Maria	551	89	22,500 *Sunk*	25,000 *Oct. 20, 16*	21	3½0	900	Nikolaieff	Yarrow	1916 1916 1913	Belt: 12in.; P.D., 3in.; turrets 12in.	12in., twelve; 5'1in., twenty; torpedo tubes, four.
†Ekaterina II Gangoot Petropavlovsk Poltava Sevastopol	590	87	23,000	42,000	23	3½0	900	Petrograd	,,	,, ,, ,, ,,	Belt: 11in.; P.D., 3in.; turrets, 11in.	12in., twelve; 4'7in.. sixteen; torpedo tubes, four.
A. Pervosvanni Imperator Pavel	435	80	17,400	17,600	18	3½0	900	,,	,,	1911 ,,	(Krupp) Belt: am. 8½in.; f. 5, a. 4in.; P.D., 3in., B'bette 12, By 5, C.T. 8in.	12in., four; 8in., four; 4'7, twenty; torpedo tubes, five.
Slava	376	79	13,500	16,500	18	1,300	700	,,	Belleville	1905	(Kr.) Belt: am. 9in.; f. 4, a. 4, P.D. 4in.; Bte 10, T 6, CT 10.	12in., 4; 6in., 12; smaller, 25; tor do tbs, four (two submerged).
Cesarevitch	400	75	12,912	16,500	18	1,400	750	La Seyne	,,	1903	(Kr.) Belt: am. 10, f. 4, a. 4, P.D. 4in.; B'bette 11in.; Turret 6in.; C.T. 10in.	12in., four; 6in., six; 12pr., twenty; smaller thirty; tor do tbs, the (two submerged).
†Panteleimon †Ivan Zlatoust	380	72	12,733	10,500	16	90	700	Nicolaieff Sevastopol	,,	1911 1910	(Kr.) Belt: am. 9, f. 2, a. 2, P.D. 2½in.; Bte 12, By 5 CT a.	12in., f ur; 6in., 16; 12pr., 14; smaller, 16; torpedo tbs, 5 (2 submerged).
†Evstafi	380	72	12,500	10,500	17	1,000	700	Nicolaieff	Cylindcl	1911	(H.) Belt: am. 16in.; P.D. 3in.; B'bette 16in.; Battery 5in.; C.T. 12in.	12in., four; 8in., four; 6in., t lve; smaller, 22.
†Rostislav	350	69	9,000	9,000	16½	900	600	,,	C. & B.	,,	(H.) Belt: 15, P.D. 3in., B'bette 15in.; Batty. 6, C.T. 10in.	10in., four; 6in., eight; smaller, thirty; torpedo tubes four (above water)
†G. Pobiedonosetz	320	68	11,200	13,000	16	90	550	Sevastopol	,,	1895	(G.) it a.m. 18in.:f. 10in.;a. 10in! B'bette 12in.; C.T. 16in.	12in., six; 6in., seven; smaller, twenty; torpedo tubes, six (under water).

NOTE TO ARMOUR.—am.=amidships; f.=forward; a.=aft; P.D.=protective decks; C.T.=conning tower.
† These Ships belong to the Black Sea Fleet.

THE RUSSIAN NAVY—continued.
ARMOURED CRUISERS AND CRUISERS

Name.	Lgth (feet)	B'am (feet)	Tonnage.	Horse Power.	Spd. (kts.)	Coal (Max.)	Com' mnt.	Where Built.	Boilers.	Completed	Armour.	Armament.
AD. CRUISERS												
Rurik	490	75	15,000	20,000	22	2,000	800	Barrow	Bellev'le	1907	(Krupp) Belt: am. 6, f. 4 a. 3, P.D. 1½in. Bte 8, By 3, CT 8. (t.) &t: am. 8in.	in., four; 8·8, eight; 1 light 4·7, 2 rpdo tbs, two submerged).
Admiral Makaroff	443	67	*Torpedoed* Oct. 1, '14 7,900	16,500	21	2,500	570	S. Petersb'g	,,	1908	f. 4. a. 3, P.D. 2in. Bte 7, By 3, CT 6¼	8in., two, 6in., eight; 12pr., twenty; 4 rpdo tbs, two (submerged).
Pallada												
Bayan	470	68	12,400	18,000	20	2,500	800	S. Petersb'g	,,	1910	(H.). Belt 6in.; P.D. 2in.; C.T. 10in.	8in., four; 6in., ether; 12pr., twenty; rpdo tbs, two.
Gromoboi										1910		
								,,	,,	1900		
Rossia	480	68	12,130	18,000	20	2,500	750	,,	,,	1898	(H.) Belt: am. 10in. f. 5, a. 4, P.D. 2½in.; Bulkheads 6, Casemates 2, C.T. 8in.	24; 6in., four; 6in., twelve; rpdo tbes, six (above water).
CRUISERS.												
*Prut	331	47	7,800	12,000	22	600		Putilov	Nicla'se	1904	Belt: 4½in.	6in., two; 4·7in., eight.
Butakoff								Reval	,,	1915		
Grieg	525	50	7,500	35,200	30			Putilov	,,	,,	Belt 3in.	6 in., sixteen.
Sviatlanoff								Reval	,,	,,		
Svietlana									,,	,,		
†Muraviev-Mursky	495	46	4,300	23,000	27			Danzig	,,	,,		
Bogatyr								Stettin	Norman	1902	(Krupp) P.D. 3in.; Casemates 3in.; C.T. in.	6in., twelve; 12pr., twelve; smaller, ten; torpedo tubes, four (two submerged).
Oleg			6,750	20,000	23	1,500	570	S. Petersb'g	,,	1904		
‡Kagul	445	54						Sevastopol	Bellev'le	1905		
‡Pamyat Mra									,,	1906		
Askold	430	49	6,500	20,000	23	1,100	580	Kiel	Th'nycft	1901	(Krupp) P.D. 3in; C.T. 6in.	6in., twelve; 12pr., twelve; smaller, ten; torpedo tubes, six (two submerged).
Diana	420	55	6,600	11,800	20	1,500	500	S. Petersb'g	Bellev'le	1902		6in., eight; 12pr., 22; smaller, 10; torpedo tubes, 4 (above water).
Aurora								,,	,,	,,		
Jemtchug	350	40	3,000 *Torpedoed* Oct. 28, '14	19,000	24	600	350	,,	Yarrow	1904		4·7, eight; 3pr. six; torpedo tubes, four (above water).

NOTE TO ARMOUR.—am.=amidships; f.=forward; a.=aft; P.D.=protective decks; C.T.=conning tower.

* This vessel was the Turkish Medjidieh, mined in Black Sea, April 4, 1915, and salved shortly after.
† These vessels were building by Schicau, Danzig, and were seized by Germany. The light cruiser Elbing, sunk at Jutland, is believed to be one of these.
‡ These ships belong to the Black Sea Fleet.

The Fleet Annual

RUSSIAN TORPEDO CRAFT.

35-Knot Destroyers (1914-15):—I.H.P. 25,000. Speed, 35-knots. Armament, four 4in., four machine; four 18in. tubes. Avtroil, Axard, Brietschislaw, Chios, Desua, Gavril, Gogland, Grom, Grongamn, Kern, Kinsbergen, Koolur, Konstantin Lieut. Belle, Krown, Lictorn, Lieut. Doobassor, Lieut. Illin, Lieut. Lombardo, Michael, Novik, Orphery, Patrass, Poblikitel, Priamshaw, Kouon-Zotof, Rymnick, Samson, Smolensk, Sokol, Stivsooden, Stratilat, Temdos, Theodor, Tsylmettiev, Vladimir Zabeaka.

34-Knot Destroyers (1912-13):—1,050 tons, H.P. 22,500, speed 34 knots. Armament, 34in. Bespokoiny, Bystry, Dersky, Gnievry, Gromky, Pospiechny, Pulky, Pronsiteiny, Stchrastiry.

25-Knot Destroyers (1907):—610 tons, H.P. 6,500. Armament, 6 12-pounders, 3 tubes. Baranoff, Shestakov, Saken, Zatzarenni.

25-Knot Destroyers (1905):—570 tons, H.P. 7,000. Armament, 2 4.7, 6 6-pounders, 2 machine guns, 3 tubes. Amuretz, Bukharski, Dobrovoletz, Finn, Gaidamak, Kondrachenko, Moskritzanin, Okhotink, Pogranechnik, Siberski-Stryelok, Ussurietz, Vsadnik.

26-Knot Destroyers (1904-6):—500 tons, H.P. 6,200. Armament, 2 12-pounders, 4 6-pounders, 2 tubes. Donskoi-Kazak, Kazanetz, Steegushchi, Strashmi, Truskhmenetz, Ukraina, Voiskovoi, Zabaikaletz.

27-Knot Destroyers (1905):—350 tons, H.P. 5,000. Armament, 2 12-pounders, 6 machine guns, 2 tubes. Iskusni, Ispolnitelni, Kryepki, Legki, Letuchi, Lieut.-Burakov, Likhoi, Lovki, Molodetzki, Moshchni, Myetki.

27-Knot Destroyers (1905-6):—300 tons, H.P. 6,000. Armament, 2 12-pounders, 5 3-pounders, 2 tubes. Bditelni, Boevoi, Burni, Dmitriev, Sergyeev, Vnimatelni, Vninoslivi, Vnushitelni, Zuyerev, Yurasovski.

27-Knot Destroyers (1899-07):—350 tons, H.P. 5,500. Armament, 1 12-pounder, 5 3-pounders, 2 tubes. Bezstrashni, Bezshumni, Bezposhchadni, Bodri, Boiki, Bravi, Dostoini, Dyelni, Dyeyatdni, Gromyaschi, Grozni, Grozovoi, Pushchin, Rastoropni, Rozyaschi, Silni, Storozhevoi, Stroini, Vidni, Vlastni, Zavidni, Zavyetni, Zharki, Zhivoi, Zhivuchi, Zhutki, Zorki, Zvonki.

27-Knot Destroyers (1895-05):—24 tons, H.P. 3,800. Armament, 1 12-pounder, 3 3-pounders, 2 tubes. Anastosov, Malyeev, Podvizhni Porazhayuschi, Poslushni, Prochni, Prozorlivi, Pruitki, Retivi, Ryani, Ryezvi, Serditi, Smyeli, Smyetlivi, Statni, Stremiletni, Strogi, Sviryepi, Tochni, Trevozhni, Tverdi.

Russia has also 55 Submarines—37 complete and 29 torpedo-boats of doubtful value.

RUSSIAN NAVY (other losses)

Donitz and Kudonitz (Gunboats), Torpedoed, October 29, 1914. Siroutch (Gunboat), Gunfire, August 19, 1915. Prut (Minelayer), Scuttled, October 29, 1914. Yenessi (Minelayer), Torpedoed, June 6, 1915.

RUSSIAN NAVAL GUNS

Calibre in Inches.	Weight in Tons.	Length in Calibre.	Projectile in lbs.	Muzzle Velocity (F.S.)	Muzzle Energy (F.T.)
14	63	45	1,400	2,600	45,000
12	59	40	725	2,600	22,000
10	32	45	490	2,600	18,800
9	25	45	400	2,500	17,000
8	14	35	190	2,000	11,000
6	7	45	89	2,900	2,800
4.7	2.5	45	46	2,700	2,300

THE JAPANESE NAVY.
BATTLESHIPS

Name.	Lgth (feet)	B'am (feet)	Tonnage.	Horse Power.	Spd. (kts.)	Coal (max.)	Com mnt.	Where Built.	Boilers.	Completed.	Armour.	Armament.
Nagato			32,000		24			Kure	Miyab'a	1915		16in., 12; 6in., 16.
Fu-So	} 630	94	31,000	43,000	22·5	3,000	1030	Kure	,,	1917	Belt: am 12in.; P.D. 2½in.	14in., 12; 6in., 16
Hiuga								Nagasaki	,,	,,		
Ise								Yokosuka	,,	,,		
								Kure				
Kawachi	} 500	84	20,800	26,500	20·5	2,500	960	Kure	,,	1912	(Krupp) Belt: am. 9 in.; f. 5in.; a. 4in.; gun positions, 11in.	12in., 12: 6in., 10; 4'7in., 10.; two tubes, 5 (submerged)
Settsu								Yokosuka	,,	,,		
Aki	} 480	83	19,800	25,000	20½	2,300	980	Kure	,,	1911	(Krupp) Belt: am. 9 in.; f. 6in.; a. 4in. P.D. 3in B'bte 8in.	12in., 4; 10in., 12; 6in., 8; two tubes, 5 (submerged)
Satsuma	480	83	19,350	18,500	20	2,200	980	Yokosuka	,,	,,		
Katori	} 420	78	16,400	17,000	18	2,000	800	Elswick	Nicla'se	1906	(Kr.) Belt: am. 9in.; f. 6½, a. 6¾in.; P.D. 3in., B'bette 9in.; Bty. 6in.; C.T. 9in.	12in., 4; 6in., 4; 6in., 12; 12pr., 12; smaller, 10; torpedo tubes, 5 (submerged)
	420		15,950					Barrow	,,	,,		
Mikasa	430	75½	15,200	15,000	18	1,700	750	,,	Bellev'le	1902	(Kr.) Blt; am. 9in.; f., 4; a. 4in.; P.D. 7in.; B'bette 14in. By, 16; C.T. 12in.	12in.,4;10in.,4;6in.,10;12pr., 14; smaller, 22; torpedo tubes, 4 (submerged)
Shikishima	} 425	76	15,000	14,500	18	1,500	740	Thames	,,	1900	(H.N.) Blt: am.9; f. 4in; a. 4in.; P.D. 3in.; B'bette 14in.; cas. 6in.; C.T. 14in.	12in., 4; 6in., 14; 12pr., 20; smaller, 20; torpedo tubes, 5 (submerged)
Asahi								Clydebank	,,	,,		
Iwami	400	76	13,500	16,500	18	1,250	750	S. Petersbg.	,,	1904	(Krupp) Belt: am. 7¾in.; f. 4in.; a. 4in., P.D. 3in.; Turret 10in., C.T. 10in.	12in., 4; 8in., 6; 12pr., 20; smaller, 20; torpedo tubes, 4 (2 submerged)
Hizen	376	72	12,700	16,000	18	2,000	700	Philadelphia	Nicla'se	1902	(Kr.) Belt: m. 9in.; f. 4in.; a. 3in.; P.D. 3in., Turret 10in.: a. 5in. C.T. 9in.	12in., 4; 8in., 6; smaller, 40; torpedo tubes 4 (2 submerged)

NOTE TO ARMOUR.—am.=amidships; f.=forward; a.=aft; P.D.=protective decks; C.T.=conning tower.

21

THE JAPANESE NAVY—continued.
BATTLESHIPS, BATTLE AND ARMOURED CRUISERS.

Name.	Lgth (feet)	B'am (feet)	Tonnage.	Horse Power.	Spd. (kts.)	Coal (max.)	Com'mnt.	Where Built.	Boilers.	Completed.	Armour.	Armament.
Sagami } Suo }	400	71¼	12,670	14,500	19	2,058	740	S. Petersbg.	Bellev'le	1901	(H.) Belt: am. 9in; f. 4in.; a. 4in.; P.D.; 2¾in.; Turret 10in.; s. 5in. C.T. 10in.	10in., 4; 6in., 10; 12pr, 20; machine guns, 20; torpedo tubes 6 (2 submerged)
Fuji	374	73	12,320	14,000	19	1,200	600	Thames	"	1897	(H.)lt: am. 18in.; f. 4in.; a. 4in.; turret, 14in.; P.D. 3in.	12in., 4; 6in., 10; 3pr., 20; torpedo tubes, 5
Tango	36½	67	11,000	10,000	12	1,000	700	S. Petersbg.	Cylindcl	1898	(C.) Belt: m. 15in.; P.D. 3½in.: T. 10in. s. 5in.; C.T. 12in.	12in., 4; 6in., 12; smaller, 30; torpedo tubes, 4
BAT'L. CRUISERS												
Hiei Kirishima Kongo }	704	92	27,500	70,000	28	3,000	1000	Kobe Yokosuka Nagasaki Barrow	Miyab'a " " "	1915 1914 1915 1913	(Krupp) Belt: am. 9in; 4in.; a. 3in.; P.D. 2¼in.; B'bette 10in.	14in., 8; 6in., 16; smaller, 16
ARM'D. CRUISERS												
Kurama Ibuki }	440	75	14,600	25,000	2·5	2,000	800	Yokosuka Kure	" "	1908 1909	(Krupp) Belt: am. 7in.; f. 4; a. 4in.; P.D. 2in.; B'bette 7in.; Bty. 5in.; C.T. 7in.	12in., 4; 8in., 8; 4·7, 14; torpedo tubes 5 (one above water)
Tsukuba Ikoma }	440	75	13,750	Blown up Jan. 15, '17 20,500	20	2,000	800	" "	" "	1907 "	(K.) Belt: am. 7in.; f. 4in.; a. 4i.; P.D. 2in.; B'bette 7in.; s. 5in.; C.T. 8in.	12in., 4; 6in., 12; 4·7in., 12; torpedo tubes, 5 (oneabove water)
Yakumo	420	65½	9,850	15,000	20	1,300	500	Stettin	Bellev'le	1901	(Kr.) Belt: am. 7in; f. 7½; a. 4½in.; P.D. 2½in.; Tu et 6i.; cas.6in.; C.T 10in.	8in., 4; 6in., 12; 12pr, 12; 3pr., 10; torpedo tubes 5 (4 submerged)
Idzumo Iwate }	400	68½	9,800	14,500	21	1,400	480	Elswick "	" "	" "	(Kr.) Belt: m. 7i.; f. 3½ a. 3½in.; P.D. 2½in.: Turret 5in.; cas.6in.; C.T. ¼in.	8in., 4; 6in., 14; 12pr, 12; machine guns, 12; torpedo tubes 4 (submerged)

NOTE TO ARMOUR.—am.=amidships; f.=forward; a.=alt; P.D.=protective decks; C.T.=conning tower.

THE JAPANESE NAVY—continued.

ARMOURED CRUISERS AND CRUISERS.

Name.	Lgth (feet)	B'am (feet)	Tonnage.	Horse Power.	Spd. (kts.)	Coal (max.)	Com'mnt.	Where Built.	Boilers.	Completed.	Armour.	Armament.
Asama Tokiwa	428	67	9,750	18,000	22	1,300	500	Elswick	Cylindcl "	1900 "	(Kr.) Belt: am. 7in.; f. 3½, a. 3½in.; P.D. 2½in.; Turret 5in.; cas. 6in.; C.T. 14in.	8in., 4; 6in., 14; 12pr., 12; 3pr., 3; torpedo tubes 5 (4 submerged)
Azuma	420	59	9,450	17,000	21	1,300	500	St. Nazaire	Bellev'le	1901	(Kr.) Belt: am. 7in.; f. 3½, a. 3½in.; P.D. 2½in.; Turret 5in.; cas. 6in.; C.T. 10in.	8in., 4; 6in., 12; 12pr., 12; smaller, 10; torpedo tubes 5 (4 submerged)
Aso	443	55	7,800	17,000	20	1,109	400	La Seyne		1900	(Kr.) Belt: am. 8in., f. 4in.; a. 4in.; Turret 7in.; C.T. 6½in.	8in., 2; 6in., 8; 12pr., 20; torpedo tubes, 2 (submerged)
Kasuga Nisshin	370	61¼	7,500	13,500	20	1,100	500	St. Ponente "	Cylindcl "	1904 "	(H.N.) Belt: am. 6in., f. 4½in, a. 4½in., P.D. 1½in.; Turret 6½in.; C.T. 5in.	10in., 1; 6in., 14; 12pr., 12; 8in., 2; Maxims, 2; torpedo tubes, 4 8in., 4; (above water)

CRUISERS.

Name	Lgth	B'am	Tonnage	Horse Power	Spd.	Coal	Com'mnt	Where Built	Boilers	Completed	Armour	Armament
Tsugaru	410	55	6,630	11,500	20	1,500	570	Philadelphia	Nicl'sse	1901	C.T. 4in.; P.D. 3in.	6in., 8; smaller, 28; torpedo tubes, 3
Chikuma Hirado Yahagi	430	43	5,000	22,500	26	1,000	392	Sasebo Kobe Nagasaki	Miyab'a " "	1912 " "	C.T. 4in.; P.D. 3½in.	6in., 6; 12pr., 4; torpedo tubes, 3

NOTE TO ARMOUR.—am. = amidships; f. = forward; a. = aft.; P.D. = protective decks; C.T. = conning tower.

THE JAPANESE NAVY—continued.
CRUISERS

Name.	Length (feet).	Beam (feet).	Tonnage.	Horse Power.	Speed (Knots).	Coal (Max.)	Complement.	Where Built.	Boilers.	Completed	Armament.
Kasagi ...	400	48	4,500	15,000	22	1,000	400	U.S.A.	Cylindrical	1900	8in, 2; 4.7in., 6; 12pr, 12; 3pr., 10; rifle tubes, 4 (above wtr)
Chitose ...	"	"	"	"	"	"	"	"	"	"	6in., 2; 4.7in., 12; torpedo tbs, 3
Tone ...	404	49	4,100	15,000	23	1,000	350	Kobe	Miyabara	1909	6in., 2; 4.7in., 6; 12pr., 4; to tbs 2
Otowa ...	330	41	3,000	10,000	21	900	300	Yokosuka	Niclausse	1905	6in., 6; 12pr., 4; 3pr., 4
Tsushima	350	44	3,400	9,500	20	600	300	"	"	1904	
Niitaka	"	"	"	"	"	"	"	"	"	"	
Soya ...	416	52	6,500	20,000	23	1,250	570	America	" Schulz	1900	6in. 12; 3in. 12; smaller, 6
Satsuya ...	347	39½	3,000	17,000	25	650	40	Germany		1892	4.7, 2; smaller, 8
Suma ...	305	41	2,700	8,500	20	600	270	"	Cylindrical	1898	6in., 2; 4.7in., 6; 3pr., 12; torpedo tubes 2
Akashi ...	"	"	"	"	"	"	"	"	"	"	
Akitsushima	310	46	3,150	8,400	19	500	300	Yokosuka	"	1893	6in., 4; 4.7in., 6; 3pr., 10; torpedo tubes 4 (above water)
Mogami ...	300	32	1,230	8,000	23	800	300	Sasebo	Miyabara	1908	4.7in., 2; 12pr., 4
Yodogava ...	"	"	"	"	"	"	"	"	"	"	
Takachio ...	300 Mined Oct. 17, '14	46	3,700	7,000	18.5	800	350	Elswick	Cylindrical	1885	6in., 8; 6pr., 2; torpedo tubes, 4.

JAPANESE TORPEDO CRAFT.

Building at Kure.—Kaba, Kashima, Kaede, Kiri, Kusu, Matsu, Sakai, Sugi, Take (no tits available), *Building at Kure.*—Amatsukaze, Hamahaze, Isokaze, Hiushi, Kashi, M, Yanagi; 830 ds; 16, 00 h.p.

33-Knot Destroyers (1912). 605 tons; 18,600 I.H.P.—Sakura, Tachibana: 4in., two; 14-prs., four. (1913-14) Kawakaze, Urakaze: 4in., two; 2- prs., 5; tub, two; 3-inch, five; ono tbs, three :— Ume, Yamakaze.

32-Knot Destroyers (1910). 1,150 ds; 90 I.H.P.;; tbs, 3 (?); displ ment, 840 tons; 20,000 h.p.

29-Knot Destroyers (1904-08). Displ mnt, 374 or 6,000 I.H.P.; six 12- prs.; two tbs.:—Arare, Ariake, Asakae, Asatsuyu, Fubuki, Harukaze, Hatsushimo, Hayakaze, Hibiki, Isonami, Kamakaze, Kiki, Kisaragi, Minazuki, Mikazuki, Nagatsuki, Nenohi, Nowaki, Oikase, Oite, Shi uri, g Oto, Shirayuki

Five Wrecked, (Apr 4, 1914), Ushio, Utsuki, Uzanami, Wakaba, Yayoi, Yunami, Yuguri, Yunagi.

33-Knot Destroyers (1901-02). 370 tons; 6,5 od H.P.; one 12-pr.; 5 6- prs., 2 tubes:—Asagiri, Asashio, Kasumi, Me, Shio.

27-Knot Destroyers (1901-02). 240 tons; 3,800 I.H.P.:—Fumitsuki, No.

31-Knot Destroyers (1899-1900). 280 tons; 6,000 I.H.P.; oe 12-pr.; five 6-prs.; two tbs: Oboro, Usugumo.

31-Knot Destroyers (1898-9). 300 ds; 6,000 I.H P.: - Kagero, Murasame, Sazanami, Shiraui, Yugiri.

Japan has also some fifty torpedo boats building and projected, together with fifty thr boats of various ages. Submarines, fifteen, and two building.

THE ITALIAN NAVY.

BATTLESHIPS.

Name.	Lgth (feet)	B'am (feet)	Tonnage.	Horse Power.	Spd. (kts.)	Coal (Max.)	Com mnt.	Where Built.	Boilers.	Completed	Armour.	Armament.
C Conte di Cavour M Giulio Cesare F Leonardo da Vinci	620	92	30,000	49,000	25	Oil	1000	Spezia S. Ponente Genoa Leghorn		1916 1917 1917 1916	Belt: 11in.; P.D. 2¾in.; turrets 11in.	15in., eight; 6in., twenty; 14pdr. twenty-four.
Doria Duilio	570	91	23,025	24,000	23	3,000	1000	Spezia Cast'llamare	Bchy'd'n	1915 1915	Belt: 10½in.; P.D. 1¾in.; turrets 1 d.	12in., thirteen; 6in., sixteen; 12pdr., fourteen; torpedo tubes, three.
Leonardo da Vinci Giulio Cesare	557	92	22,340 *Blown up Aug. 2,'16*	24,000	23	2,500	1000	Spezia Genoa Leghorn	" "	1914 1914 1914	Belt: am. 9¾in.; P.D. 1¾in.; turrets 9¾in.	12in., thirteen; 4·7in., eighteen; 12pdr., fourteen; torpedo tubes, three.
Dante Alighieri	505	85	18,300	26,000	22	2,500	900	Cast'llamare	"	1913	Belt: 9½in.; P.D. 1½in.; turrets 10in.	12in., twelve; 5·5in., twenty; 12pdr., thirteen; tubes, three.
Napoli Regina Elena Roma Vitt. Emanuele	435	73	12,600	20,000	22	2,800	700	Spezia Cast'llamare	Babcock Bellev'le " "	1908 1907 1909 1908	Belt: 10in.; turrets 8in. P.D. 4in.	12in., two; 8in., twelve; smaller, twenty-four; torpedo tubes, four.
Benedetto Brin Regina Margherita	427	78	*Blown up Sept.29,'15* 13,400 *Mined Dec. 11-12, 1916.*	19,000	20	2,000	720	Spezia	Nicla'se	1904 "	Belt: 6in.; P.D. 3in.; turrets 8in.	12in., four; 8in., four; 6in., twelve; smaller, twenty-six; torpedo tubes, four.
A. di St. Bon. Emanuele Filiberto	345	70	9,645	13,500	18	1,000	550	Venice Cast'llamare	Cylindel "	1901 "	Belt: 9¾in.; P.D. 3in.; turrets 9¾in.	10in., four; 6in., eight; 4·7; eight; smaller, twenty; torpedo tubes, four (submerged).

ARM. CRUISERS

San Georgio San Marco	430	69	9,832	18,000	23	1,500	650	Cast'llamare	Nicla'se	1910 1910	Belt: 8in.; P.D. 2in.; turrets 6½in.	10in., four; 8in., eight; smaller, sixteen; torpedo tubes, three.
Amalfi Pisa	430	67	*Torpedoed July 7,'15* 9,956	20,800	23	1,600	687	Genoa Leghorn	Bellev'le	1909 1909	do. do.	do. do.

NOTE TO ARMOUR.—am.=amidships; f.=forward; a.=aft; P.D.=protective decks; C.T.=conning tower; T=Terni steel.

THE ITALIAN NAVY—continued.
ARMOURED AND OTHER CRUISERS.

Name.	L'g'h (feet)	B'am (feet)	Tonnage.	Horse Power.	Sp'd (kts.)	Coal (Max.)	Com'mnt.	Where Built.	Boilers.	Completed	Armour.	Armament.
Franc'sco Ferrucio Giuseppe Garibaldi Varese	346	59	7,400 Torpedoed July 19, 15	13,500	20	1,200	480	Venice Se'-Ponenet Leghorn	Nicla'se ,, 'Believ'le	1903 1901 ,,	Belt: 6in.; P.D. 1½in.; turrets, 6in.	10in., one; 8in., two; 6in., fourteen; smaller, twenty; torpedo tubes, four (sub.)
Go Al bto Vettor Pisani	325	59	6,400	13,000	19	1,000	480	Spezia Cast'llamare	Cylindcl ,,	1898 1897	Belt: a.m. 6in., f. 4in.; a. 4in.; P.D. 1½in.; Gun Shields 4½in.; CT. 6in.	6in., twelve; 4'7, six; smaller, twenty; torpedo tubes, four.
Mo Polo	327	47	4,500	10,500	19	700	350	,,	,,	1895	Belt: 4in.; P.D. 1in.; Gun Shields 4in.; C.T. 6i.	6in., six; 4'7, ten; smaller, twenty, torpedo tubes, five.
CRUISERS.												6in., six; 12pr., six.
Basilicata Ga	249	42	2,560	7,000	18	500	240	,, ,,	Nicla'se ,,	1914 1914		6in., ten; 4'7, eight; smaller, twelve.
Libia	341	47	3,690	12,500	22	600	300	Genoa	,,	1913		4'7, six; 12pr., six.
Go Ma Nino iBo	460	42	3,400	22,500	29	800	197	Venice Cast'llamare ,,	,, ,, ,,	1912 1913 1913		6in., four; 4'7, six; smaller, vary; rdo tbs, two (above water).
Etruria Gl ba Puglia tha	270 290	41 43	2,500 3,500	7,500 7,700	19 17	500 600	230 300	Leghorn Spezia Taranto Cast'llamare	Cylindcl ,, ,, ,,	1893 1895 1900 1887		6in., six; smaller, torpedo tb, four (submerged).

35-Knot Destroyers (1915-16).—Di pit, 450 tos; I.H.P., 40,000; pd, 35 kts; nat, he 4'7in. O.F.; seven dr.; five tb. Originally built for ta as Vi, Vifor, Viyelie, Viscol.
35-Knot Destroyers go).—Di pit, 1,540 t os; I.H.P., 37,000; pd 35 kts (tied for me laying). Carlo Mirabell Grlo Alberta Racchia, Augusto dy.
32-Knot ps (g-14). — 60-1, 00 tos, 50 I.H.P.; 47, oe; 2 dr., 6r; 2 th, Mo Paerio, Mo, Cesare Rassoval, So Rollo, Gto Corini, Englialmo B, Ge A, Ge Siri, I pto Niero, Rdi Im, Rosolino Pino, the Schuassino.
30-Knot Destroyers (1912), 613 ds; 1 50 I.H.P. Mo, Ardente, Adito, Ale, tho, Indomito, I do, Intrepido (Mined, Mr, 1915), Lo.
9— kt Destroyers (1906-10).—376 .16 ds; 6, 00 I.H.P. Mo, Artigliere, Rersagliere, Ge, Corazzi e, Fucili e, Mini, Ge, Go ad Be.
30-Knot Destroyers (1899-1904).—325 t os; 6,000 I.H.P. Auil e, Borea, Dardo, Espero, Euro, Lampo, No, Ostro, St d, Zeffiro, Turbine (Gunfire, May 24, 1915), Zeffiro.
Kn mis.—Argo, Atropo, En (1894), Salea, Is, Fal e, Galileo, Giacinto Ad by Austrians, August, 1 9), Glauco, Medusa (Torpedoed, June 15, 1915), Narvolo, Nautilus, Nereide (Sunk, August, 1915), Ga, Pullino, Salpa, Santina, Squalo, Po (1905-09), Valella, Zoea 9). Building, particulars at available og type); No, Pellegrino, gi, Angelo Eo, No Nn, Lio Mocenigo, bo Mello, Pietro M, Torricelli. Building (Coastal type): Agostino Barbarigo, Ma Provana, Go Ni, So Bo.

ITALIAN NAVAL GUNS

Calibre in Inches.	Weight in Tons.	Length in Calibre.	Projectile in lbs.	Muzzle Velocity (F.S.)	Muzzle Energy (F.T.)
15	102	45	1,650	2,500	70,000
13.5	66	45	1,300	2,600	65,000
12	57	50	850	3,030	55,000
12	52	45	850	2,900	50,000
10.8	41	50	600	3,000	40,800
10.8	34.5	45	600	2,600	27,500
9.45	28	50	400	3,000	27,800
8.2	18.6	50	275	3,000	18,500
7.9	16	50	231	3,000	15,600
6	6.8	50	100	3,000	6,700
4	2.2	55	72	2,500	1,300

THE BRAZILIAN NAVY.

Name.	Lgth (feet)	B'am (feet)	Tonnage.	Horse Power.	Spd. kts.	Coal (Max.)	Com' mnt.	Where Built.	Boilers.	Completed.	Armour.	Armament.
Riachueto	620	95	30,500	45,000	21			Elswick		Building	Belt: am. 13¾in.; also barbettes & conning tower.	15in., eight; 6in., fourteen; 4in., ten; torpedo tubes. two.
Minas Geraes Sao Paulo	500	87	19,281	24,500	21.5	2,400	900	" Barrow	B'bcock "	1910 1910	Belt: am. 9in.; f. 6in.; a. 4in.; turrets, 12'8in.	12in., twelve; 4'7in., twenty-two; 3pr., eight; torpedo tubes, four.
Deodora Floriano	267	48	3,112	3,400	15	236	200	La Seyne "	Lagvald "		Belt: 13⅜ am.; f. 4in.; a. 4in.; turrets, 8in.	9'2in., two; 4'7in., four; 12pr., 2; torpedo tubes, two.
Bahia Rio Grande de Sul	380	39	3,100	17,500	27	650	260	Elswick "	Turbine "	1910 1910		4'7in., ten; torpedo tubes, two.

27-Knot Destroyers (1908-9).—Alajoas, Amazono, Matto Grosso, Para, Parahyba, Piouhy, Rio Grande der Norte, Santa Catharina. 4in., two; 3-pdrs., four; tubes, two; displacement, 550 tons: 8,000 h.p.

Brazil has also a few old cruisers, while three submarines of the Laureaté type are building at Spezia, Italy.

THE U.S.A. NAVY.
BATTLESHIPS.

Name.	Lgth (feet)	B'am (feet)	Tonnage.	Horse Power.	Spd. (kts.)	Coal (Max.)	Com'mnt.	Where Built.	Boilers.	Completed	Armour	Armament.
California / she	600	97	32,000		21	Oil	1080	New York	Babc'ck	1917	Belt: 14in., e ads 8: P.D. 3in.; Turret, 18in.; C.T. 16in.	14in., twelve; 5in., 22; torpedo-tubes (21in.) four.
Ido								"	"	"	P.D. 3in.; Turret, 18in.; C.T. 6in.	14in., twelve; 5in., twenty-two; torpedo tubes (21in.), four.
Mississippi / New Mexico (ex-California) / Arizona	600	97	32,000	32,000	21	Oil	1080	Newport, N. New York	"	"		
Pennsylvania	600	97	31,400	31,500	21	3,500		Newport, N.	"	1916	Belt: 13½in.; P.D. 3in.; Turret, 16in.	14in., twelve; 5in., twenty-; do tbs, four.
Nevada	575	95	27,500	35,000	21	Oil	1014	Quincy, Ms. New York	"	1915	Belt: 13in.; P.D. 3in.; Turret. 13in.	14in., en; 5in. twenty-two; smaller, six; t. tubes, four.
New dik	573	95	27,000	39,000	21	3,500		"	"	1915	Belt: 11in.; P.D 3in.; Turret, 14·8in.	14 in, en; 5in., twenty; smaller, six; t. tubes, four.
Texas			28,367				1100	Newport	"	1914		
Arkansas	554	93	26,000	28,000	21	3,000		in N.J.	"	1913	Belt: 1in.; P.D. 3in.; turets, 11in.	12in., twelve; 5in., twenty-oe; torpedo tubes, two.
Wyoming								Philadelphia	"	1912		
Utah	510	85	27,825	28,000	22	2,500	1100	iden N.J.	"	1911	(Krupp) Belt): 11in.; (Krupp) 11in.: C.T. 12in.	12in., en; 5in., sixteen; smaller, six; torpedo tbs, va.
Del we								Newport		1910	(Krupp) Belt: 11in.: P.D. 3in.; Turret 11in.: C.T. 12in.	12in., ten; 5in. ist en; smaller, six; dr pdo tbs, .
Nth Dakota	510	85	29,000	29,000	21	2,500	950	Quincy,Mas.	"	"		
Michigan	450	80	16,000	16,500	20	2,200	800	rdGen N.J Philadelphia	"	1909	(Krupp) Belt: m. 12in., f. 13½in.; a. 1½in.; P.D. 5in.; C.T. ia	ia., eight; 3-in., twenty-two; maller, 14; torpedo t bs, two.
South Colina									"	"	12in.; C.T. ia	
Kansas Classs.												
ss								en	"	1907	Belt: am.9in.; f. 4in.; a. 4in.; P.D. 3 n.; B'bette 1 io; C.T. 9in.; Battery 7in.	12in., four; 8in., eight; 7in., twelve; smaller, forty; torpedo tubes, four.
New Me	460	77	16,000	16,000	18	2,400	800	Camden N.J.	"	1906		
Vermont								Quincy, Mas.	"	1907		
Connecticut								en N.J.	"	1908		
sa								Nt	"	1906		
New Jersey Cls.												
Georgia								Bath	"	1906	(H.N.) Belt: am. 11-in.; f. 4in.; a. 4in.; P.D. 3in.; B'bette io.; Battery 6in.; C.T. 9in.	12in., four; 8in., eight; 6in., twelve; smaller, thirty; torpedo tubes, four.
Ma	443	78	15,000	19,000	19	2,000	750	Seattle	"	"		
New Jersey								Quincy, Mas.	"	"		
Rhode Isl nd								Nt	"	"		
Virginia									"	"		

NOTE TO ARMOUR.—am.=amidships; f.=forward; a.=aft; P.D.=protective dk; C.T.=conning tower.

THE U.S.A. NAVY—continued.
BATTLESHIPS AND ARMOURED CRUISERS.

Name.	Lgth (feet)	B'am (feet)	Tonnage.	Horse Power.	Spd. (kts.)	Coal (Max.)	Com' mnt.	Where Built.	Boilers.	Completed	Armour.	Armament.
Me Class.												
Me	388	73	13,000	16,000	18	2,000	650	Philadelphia	Babc'ck	1902	(Krupp)Belt: am.11in.; f. 4in.; a. 5in.; P.D. 3in.; be 12in.; a. 6in.; C.T. 12.	12in., four; 6in., ten; smaller, thirty; torpedo tubes, two (submerged).
Missouri								Newport	Thnycft.	1903		
Ohio								S. Francisco	"	"		
Alabama Class.												
Alabama	370	72	11,565	10,000	16	1,500	550	Philadelphia	Cylindcl	1900	(H.N.) Blt: m. 16½ in.; f. 4in.; a. 4in.; D. 4in.; B'bette 14in.	13in., four; 6in., fourteen; smaller, twenty-four; torpedo tubes, four (above water).
Illinois								Newport	"	1901		
Wisconsin								S. Francisco	"	"		
Kearsage Class.												
Kearsage	370	72	11,500	10,500	16	1,400	550	Newport	"	1900	(Do.) Blt: m. 16½ in.; f. 4in.; a. 4in.; P.D. 4in.; Turret 17in.; Battery 5½in.	13in., four; 8in., four; 5in., fourteen; smaller, twenty-six; rdo tubes, four (above wr.).
Kentucky								"	"	"		
Iowa	360	72	11,340	11,000	16½	1,800	470	Philadelphia	"	1897	(H.) Belt: m. 14in.; P.D. 3in.; Turret 14in.; C.T. 10in.	13in., four; 8in., eight; 4in., six; smaller, thirty; torpedo tubes, four (above wr.).
Indiana Class.												
Indiana	350	70	10,300	9,500	15	1,600	470	"	Babc'ck	1895	(H.) Belt: am. 18in.; P.D. 3in.; Turret 17in.; C.T. 10in.	13in., four; 8in., eight; 6in., four; smaller, thirty; torpedo tubes, two (above water).
Massachusetts								"	Cylindcl	"		
Oregon								S. Francisco	"	1896		
ARMD. CRUISERS.												
Washington Class.												
North Carolina	500	73	14,500	25,000	22	2,000	850	Newport	Nicla'se	1908	(Krupp)Belt:am.5in.; f.3in.; a. 3in.; P.D. 3in.; B'bette 7in.; Battery 5in.; C.T. 9in.	10in., four; 6in.. sixteen; 3 in., twenty - two; smaller, twenty; torpedo tubes, four (submerged).
Montana								Philadelphia	"	"		
*Tennessee								"	"	1906		
Washington								Camden, N.J.	Babcock	"		

NOTE TO ARMOUR.—am.=amidships f.=forward; a.=aft; P.D.=protective deck; C.T.=conning tower.
* "Memphis" (four "Tennessees"), wrecked in San Domingo Bay, August 29th, 1916.

THE U.S.A. NAVY—continued.

ARMOURED CRUISERS, SMALLER CRUISERS AND SCOUTS.

Name.	Lgth (feet)	B'am (feet)	Tonnage.	Horse Power.	Spd. (kts.)	Coal (Max.)	Com'mnt.	Where Built.	Boilers.	Completed	Armour.	Armament.
California Cls.												
San Diego	500	70	13,500	23,000	22	2,000	820	S. Francisco	Babcock	1907	(Krupp) Belt: am. 6 in.; f. 3½in.; a., 3½ in.; P.D. 4in.; B'te 6in.; casemates 6 in.; C.T. 9in.	8in., four; 6in., fourteen; 14pr., eighteen; smaller, twenty-eight; torpedo tubes, two (submerged).
Colorado								Philadelphia	Nicla'se	1905		
Pittsburg Md								Newport	Babcock	,,		
South Dakota								Philadelphia	Nicla'se	1908		
West Vir inia g								S. Francisco	Babcock	1905		
								Newport	,,			
St. Louis Class,												
Charleston	424	65	9,700	21,000	22	1,500	550	S. Francisco	Babcock	1906	(Krupp)Belt: am.4in.; P.D. 3in.;casemates 4in.; Battery 3in.; (H.) Belt: 3in.; P.D. 6in.; ends 3in.; B'te 8in.; C.T. 7½in.	6in., fourteen; 14pr., eighteen; smaller, thirty-six; torpedo tubes, four.
St. Louis	400	65	9,215	16,000	21	1,500	500	Philadelphia	,,	1906		8in., eight; 5in., twelve; smaller, twenty-four; torpedo tubes, four.
Brool lyn								,,	Cylindcl	1896		
Saratoga	380	64	8,200	16,500	21	1,200	450	,,	,,	1893	(H.) Belt: 4in.; P.D. 5in.; ends 3in.; B'te 10in.; C.T. 7in.	8in., four; 5in., ten; smaller, sixteen; torpedo tubes,three (above water).
Birmingham	420	45½	3,750	16,000	24	1,200	384	Quincy, Ms.	Belleville	1908		5in., two; 3in., six; torpedo tubes, two (submerged)
C lr								Bath, Me.	,,	1908		
Salem								Quincy, Ms.	,,	,,		
Albany cls	350	44	3,500	7,500	20	700	300	Elswick	Scotch	90		6in., six; 4.7, four; smaller, eighteen; torpedo tubes, two (above water).
New										1898		
Minneapolis	412	58	7,350	20,000	23	1,400	500	Philadelphia	Cylindcl	1894		8in., one; 6in., two; 4in., eight; smaller, twenty; torpedo tubes, four (above water).
								,,	,,	,,		
Cll nd Cls.												
Chattanooga	292	44	3,100	4,500	16.5	700	290	PortElizab'h	Babcock	194		5in., ten; twelve smaller guns.
Clevel nd								Bath	,,	193		
Denver								Philadelphia	,,	1904		
Des Moines								Quincy	,,	,,		
Tacom on								Richmond	,,	,,		
								S.Francisco	,,	,,		

NOTE TO ARMOUR.—am.=amidships; f.=forward; a.=aft; P.D.=protective deck; C.T.=conning tower.

The U.S.A. has a number of old cruisers of little, if any, fighting value.

THE U.S.A. NAVY—continued.
SUBMARINES.

Class.	No. in Class.	Tons.	Date.	Speed.	Horse Power.	Armament.
A	6	125	1901-03	7-8	160	One torpedo tube
B	3	200	1905-06	9-10	250	,, ,, ,,
C	5	270	1907	10-12	500	Two torpedo tubes
D	3	340	1909-10	10-12	600	Four ,, ,,
E	2	400	1911-12	10-14	780	,, ,, ,,
F	3	430	1911-12	10-14	780	,, ,, ,,
G	4	400-500	1912	10-16	1,200	,, ,, ,,
H	3	450	1912-13	11-14	1,200	,, ,, ,,
K	8	500	1912-13	14-20	—	Six ,, ,,
L	11	390—525	1914-15	—	1,000	,, ,, ,,
M	1	706-1200	1915	20-12	5,000	Ten ,, ,,
N	7	—	—	—	—	—

About thirty others provided for. No official data of U.S. Submarines published.

DESTROYERS.

29·5-knot Destroyers (1915-1916).—Allen, Davis, Rowan, Sampson, Shaw, Wilkes: Displacement, 1,125 tons; I.H.P., 18,000 = 29.5 knots. Armament, 4.4in. Q.F.: 12 21in. torpedo-tubes.

29·5-knot Destroyers (1914-1915)—Conynham, Jacob Jones, Porter, Tucker, Wadsworth, Wainwright: Displacement, 1,100 tons; I.H.P., 17,000 = 29·5 knots. Armament, four 4in. Q.F.; eight 21in. torpedo tubes.

29-knot Destroyers (1913).—Displacement, 1,100 tons; I.H.P., 16,000; armament, four 4in.; eight 21in. tubes. Cushing, Ericson, McDougal, Nicholson, O'Brien Winslow.

29-knot Destroyers (1912-13).—Displacement, 1,000 tons; I.H.P., 16,000 = 29 knots; eight 21in. tubes. Aylwyn, Balch, Benham, Cassin, Cummings, Downes, Duncan, Parker.

31-knot Destroyers (1910).—Ammen, Beale, Burrows, Drayton, Fanning, Henley, Jarvis, Jenkins, Jouett, Mayrant, McCall, Monaghan, Patterson, Paulding, Perkins, Roe, Sterrett, Terry, Trippe, Walke, Warrington. Displacement 850 tons, I.H.P. 12,000, speed 31 knots, armament five 3in., six 18in. torpedo tubes.

29-knot Destroyers (1909).—Flusser, Lamson, Preston, Reid, Smith. Displacement, 700 tons; I.H.P., 10,000; speed, 29 knots; armament, four 3in.; six 18in. torpedo tubes

Together with a number of older destroyers.

U.S.A. NAVAL GUNS

Calibre in Inches.	Weight in Tons.	Length in Calibre.	Projectile in lbs.	Muzzle Velocity (F.S.)	Muzzle Energy (F.T.)
14	63	45	1,400	2,600	63,000
12	66	50	870	3,000	54,000
12	53	45	870	2,800	46,000
12	52	40	870	2,600	40,000
10	35	45	500	2,700	27,000
10	33	40	500	2,300	18,000
8	18	45	250	2,000	13,000
8	15	40	250	2,100	8,200
6	8.4	50	105	2,900	6,100
6	7	45	105	2,600	5,000
5	4.6	50	60	2,700	3,000
4	2.6	50	33	2,500	1,400

THE GREEK NAVY.

Name.	Lgth (feet)	B'am (feet)	Tonnage.	Horse Power.	Spd. (kts.)	Coal (Max.)	Com'ment	Where Built.	Boilers.	Completed	Armour.	
Wasilefs Giorgios* (ex Sal amis)	570	82	19,200	40,000	23	2,500	720	Stettin		1908	Belt, 10 in.; P.D. 2½ in.	14 in., eight; 6 in., twelve; 3 in., late; torpedo tubes, five.
Kilkis‡ { {	375	77	13,000	14,000	17	1,700	800	Philadelphia	Bab'ck	1908	Belt: m. 9 in.; 'a. ds, P.D. 3 in.; turrets, 12 & 8 in.	12 in., four; 8 in., eight; 7 in., twelve; 3 in., twenty.
Hydra Psara Spetzia	331	52	5,000	6,700	17	400	440	St. Nazaire Havre Havre	Cylindcl ,, ,,	1891 1892 1891	Belt: 12 in.; ds 4½ in.; P.D. 2½ in.; Gs 13¾ & 12 in.	10.8 in. tk. 6 in., five; several maller.
CRUISERS												
Lambros Kal t roff	450 460	47 69	5,500 10,000	26,000 19,000	26 22.5	700	550	England Leghorn	Bellev'le	1915 ,, 1911	Belt: 3 in.; P.D. 1 in. Belt: 8 in.; ends 3½ in.; turrets 6½ in.	6 in., eight, torpedo tubes (21 in.), eight. 9.2 in., four; 7.5 in., eight; 3 in., sixteen.

Also Acheloos (420 tons), Alphios (420 tons), Eurotas (420 tons), Saktirea (1,000 tons), Helli ex Fie Hung (2,650 tons).

NOTE TO ARMOUR.—am.=amidships; f.=forward; a.=aft; P.D.=protective deck; C.T.=conning tower.

* This vessel was launched from the Vulkan Yard, Stettin, Nov. 11, 1914, and is now a unit in the German Navy.
‡ ex U.S.A. Idaho, purchased 1914.
† ex U.S.A. Mississippi.

DESTROYERS.

32-Knot Destroyers (1912):—980 tons; 19,750 I.H.P.; 32 knots speed; four 4 in.; four 21 in. tubes: Actos, Jerex, Leon, Panthier. *Purchased from Argentine Government.*

32½-Knot Destroyers (1912):—640 tons; 23,500 I.H.P.; 32.5 knots speed; 23-pdr., 2; four 19.5 in. tubes: Keravnos, Neagenea. *Purchased from Vulkan Yard, Stettin.*

30-Knot Destroyers: 400 tons; 6,000 I.H.P.; 30 knots speed: 12-pdr., ten; 6-pdr., four; two 18-in. tubes: Aspis, Doxa, Lonchi, Naphkratoussa, Niki, Sfendoni, Thyella.

THE CHILIAN NAVY.

Name.	Lgth (feet)	B'am (feet)	Tonnage.	Horse Power.	Spd. (kts.)	Coal (Max.)	Com¹ mnt.	Where Built.	Boilers.	Completed	Armour.	Armament.
Almirante Cochrane / *Almirante Latorre	625	93	28,000	37,000	23	4,000	— / 1075	Elswick / ,,	Yarrow / ,,	1915 / 1914	Belt: 9in.; P.D. 3in.; turrets 11in.	14in., ten; 6in., sixteen; torpedo tubes, four.
Esmerelda	436	53	7,020	16,000	22	1,350	500	,,	Cylindcl	1897	Belt: 6in.; P.D. 2in.; Bulkheads 6in.; Guns 4½in.	8in., two; 6in., sixteen; smaller, twenty-two.
O'Higgins	411	62	8,500	16,000	22	1,250	500	,,	,,	1898		

31 Knot Destroyers (1912-14), displacement 1,850 tons, 31 knots, 7,000 h.p.; armament, 4in. six, two machine, three 18in. tubes. Almirante Condell, Almirante Goni, Almirante Lynch, Almirante Riveros, Almirante Robelledo, Almirante Simpson.
30 Knot Destroyers (1896-01), displacement 300-350 tons; 30 knots, 6,000 H.P.; armament, 3in., one, 6pr., five, two 18in. tubes. Capitan Munoz Gamero, Capitan Orella, Capitan O'Brien, Capitan Merino Tarpa, Teniente Serrano, Guardia Marina Riquelme.

*Taken over by British Admiralty. Now H.M.S. Canada.

THE SPANISH NAVY.

Alfonso XIII								Ferrol	Yarrow	1914	Belt, 8in.; ds, 3in.;	12in., eight; 4in., twenty;
Espana	439	79	15,700	15,300	19.5	1,900	700	Ferrol		1913	P.D. 2in.; Turrets,	torpedo tubes, three.
Jaime I								Ferrol		1915	6in. ad 8in.	
Pelayo	330	66	9,950	8,000	16	700	60	La Seyne	Nicla'se	1890	Belt, 16in.; d, 12in. P.D. 3½in.; Guns, 16in.	12.6in., two; 11in., two; 5.5in., nine.
CRUISERS.												
Rña	748	60	7,000	10,000	18	1,200	500	Cartagena	Cyli del	90	Belt, 12in.; 6in. ends;	9.4in., two; 5.5in., eight.
Pdr Asturias								Carraca		1896	P.D. 2¾in.; Gs, 12in. ad 8in.	
V. Eugenia										97		
B.	440	50	5,600	25,500	26			Ferrol	Yarrow	1918	Belt: m, 3in.; P.D., 3in.	6in., nine; 3-pdrs., three; torpedo tubes, two.
C.										1918		
D.										1918		

NOTE TO ARMOUR.—am.=amidships; f.=forward; a.=aft; P.D.=protective deck; C.T.=conning tower.

30-Knot Destroyers.—Proserpine, Az, G. Turor: 14-pds, 2; 6-pdrs., 2; torpedo tubes, 2; 7,500 h.p.; displacement, 460 tons.
28-Knot Destroyers.—Bustamuti, Cardorsss, Villamil; 6-pdrs, 5; torpedo tbes, 2; 6,250 h.p.; displacement, 360 tons.
The latest building programme ples for 28 submarines, to be built in five successive groups.

THE GERMAN NAVY.

BATTLESHIPS

Name.	Lgth (feet)	B'am (feet)	Tonnage.	Horse Power.	Spd. (kts).	Coal (Max.)	Com'mnt.	Where Built.	Boilers.	Completed.	Armour.	Armament.
*E.K. Friedrich III	626	100	Gunfire May 31 '16 28,000	40,000	23	4,800		Kiel Dantzig Kiel	Schulz ,, ,,	1916 1915 1915		15in., eight; 6in., sixteen.
†Baden												
†Bayern												
Markgraf	580	98	27,000 Gunfire	35,000 May 31, '16	23	3,600	1150	Bremen Hamburg Wilh'mshav. Kiel	,, ,, ,, ,,	1914 ,, ,, 1915	Belt: 13in.; P.D. 3in.; Turrets 11in.; C.T., 12in.	12in., ten; 5'9in., fourteen; 3'4in., twelve; torpedo tubes, five.
Grosser Kurfurst												
Konig												
Kronprinz												
Konig Albert	560	98	24,312 Gunfire	28,000 May 31, '16	21	3,600	1000	Dantzig Kiel Hamburg Kiel	,, ,, ,, ,,	1913 ,, ,, ,,	Belt: 13in.; P.D. 3in.; Turrets 11in.; C.T. 12in.	12in., ten; 5'9in., twelve; 3'4in., fourteen; torpedo tubes, six.
Kaiserin												
F. der Grosse												
Kaiser												
P. Regent Luitpold												
Helgoland	546	93	22,435	28,000	20.5	2,700	1000	Kiel Dantzig Wilh'mshav. Bremen	,, ,, ,, ,,	1911 1912 1911 ,,	Belt: 11in.; P.D. 3in.; Turrets 11in.; C.T. 12in.	12in., twelve; 5'9in., fourteen; 3'4in., fourteen; torpedo tubes, six.
Oldenburg												
Ostfriesland												
Thuringen												
Nassau	451	88	18,200	20,000	19	2,700	900	Wilh'mshav Kiel Stettin Bremen	,, ,, ,, ,,	1909 1910 ,, 1909	(Krupp) Belt: am. 11in.; f. 6in.; a. 4 in.; P.D. 4in.; Barbtte, 12in.; C.T.12in.	11in., twelve; 5'9in., twelve; 3.4in., sixteen; torpedo tubes, six.
Posen												
Rheinland												
‡Westfalen												

NOTE TO ARMOUR.—am.=amidships; f.=forward; a.=aft; P.D.=protective decks; C.T.=conning tower.

* Believed to have been the "Pommern," sunk at Battle of Jutland.   † Also reported to be named "Wilhelm II" and "Gannenberg."
‡ Claimed to have been sunk by Submarine E 23 on August 19, 1916.

THE GERMAN NAVY—continued.

Name.	Lgth (feet)	B'am (feet)	Tonnage.	Horse Power	Spd (kts.)	Coal (Max.)	Com'mnt.	Where Built.	Boilers.	Completed	Armour.	Armament.
Deutschland	430	72½	13,200	*Torpedoed July, 1915* 16,000	18	2,000	700	Kiel	Schulz	1906	(Krupp) Belt; am. 9¾in.; f. 4in.; a. 4in.; P.D. 3in.; Barbette 11in.; casemates 6⅜in.; C.T. 12in.	11in., four ; 6·7, fourteen ; 3·4, twenty-two ; smaller, eight ; P.D. torpedo tubes, six (submerged).
Hannover								Stettin	,,	1907		
Pommern								Wilh'mshav.	,,	,,		
Schlesien								Schichau	,,	1908		
Schleswig Holstein								Kiel	,,	,,		
Braunschweig	430	72½	13,200	16,000	18	1,600	700	Kiel	,,	1904	(Kr.) Belt: am. 6in.; f. 4in.; a. 4in.; P.D. 3in.; B'bette 11in.; casemates 6in.; C.T. 12in.	11in., four; 6·7, fourteen; 3·4, twelve ; smaller, twenty; torpedo tubes, six (five submerged).
Elsass								Schichau	,,	,,		
Lothringen								Kiel	,,	1906		
Hessen								,,	,,	1905		
Preussen								Stettin	,,	,,		
Mecklenburg	416	68	11,800	15,000	18	1,400	660	Stettin	,,	1903	(Kr.) Belt: am. 9in.; f. 4in.; a. 4in.; P.D. 3in.; B'bette 10in.; casem'ts. 6in.; C.T. 10in.	9·4, four ; 6in., eighteen ; 15pr., twelve ; smaller, twenty ; torpedo tubes, six (five submerged).
Wettin								Schiehau	,,	1902		
Wittelsbach								Wilh'mshav.	,,	,,		
Schwaben								,,	,,	,,		
Zähringen								Germania	,,	,,		
K. Barbarossa	400	66	10,700	13,000	18	1,100	650	Danzig	Mixed	1901	(Kr.) Belt: am. 12in.; f. 4in.; a. 4in.; P.D. 3in.; B'bette 10in.; casemates 6in.; C.T. 10in.	9·4, four ; 5·9in., fourteen ; 3·4, twelve ; smaller, twenty ; torpedo tubes, six (five submerged).
K. Friedrich III.								Wilh'mshav.	,,	1898		
K. Karl der Grosse								Hamburg	,,	1901		
K. Wilhelm II.								Wilh'mshav.	,,	1899		
K. Wil. der Grosse								Kiel	,,	1901		

NOTE TO ARMOUR.—am.=amidships; f.=forward; a.=aft; P.D. protective decks; C.T. conning tower.

35

THE GERMAN NAVY—continued.
BATTLE AND ARMOURED CRUISERS

Name.	Lgth (feet)	B'am (feet)	Tonnage.	Horse Power.	Spd. (kts.)	Coal (Max)	Com' mnt.	Where Built.	Boilers.	Completed	Armour.	Armament.
B'TL CRUISERS.												
Bismarck	610	96	*Gunfire* 28,000	May 31, '16 100,000	28	3,600	1125	Hamburg	Schulz	1914	Belt, 7in.; P.D. 2½in.	12in., eight; 5'9, twelve.
Lutzow								Danzig	,,	1915		
Hindenberg								Wilh'mshav.	,,	1916		
Derfflinger	610	96	26,600 24,000 *Gunfire*	50,000 May 31, '16	27	3,000	1100	Hamburg ,,	,, ,,	1913	Belt, 8in.; P.D. 2½in.	11in., ten; 5'9, twelve; 3'4, twelve.
Seydlitz												11in., ten; 5'9, twelve; 3'4, twelve.
Moltke	610	96	22,640	70,000	28	3,000	900	,,	,,	1911	Belt, 8in.; P.D. 2½in.	14in., eight; 6in., twelve; 12pr., twelve.
*Goeben	571	82	19,200	40,000	23	2,500	900	Stettin	,,	1915	Belt, 10in.; P.D. 2½in.; C.T. 10in.	
Von der Tanne	561	87	19,000 *Lost* Dec. 1914	44,000	25	2,800	850	Hamburg	,,	1910	Belt, 6in.; P.D. 2½in.	11in., eight; 5'9, ten; 3'4, twelve.
ARM'D CRUISERS.												
Blücher	499	80	15,500 *Gunfire*	40,000 Jan. 24, '15	25½	2,000	760	Kiel	,,	1909	(Krupp); am., 6in.; f. 4in.; a. 4in.; P.D. 2½in.	8in., twelve; 5'9, eight; 3'4, sixteen.
Gneisenau	449	71	*Gunfire* 11,500 *Gunfire*	Dec. 8, '14 26,000 Dec. 8, '14	22½	2,000	650	Bremen Hamburg	,, ,,	1908 1907	(Krupp) Belt: am. 6, f. 3, a. 5, P.D. 2, Bte 6, Bty 4, C.T. 8.	8'2, eight; 5'9, six; small guns, 38; torpedo tubes, four (submerged).
Scharnhorst												
Fürst Bismarck	400	65	10,700	13,800	19	1,200	540	Kiel	C. & S.	1900	(Kr.) Belt: am. 8; f. 4, a. 4, P.D. 2, Bte 5, cas 4, C.T., 8in.	9'4, four; 5'9, twelve; 3'4 ten; smaller, sixteen; torpedo tubes, 6 (5 subngrd).
Roon	415	65	9,350 *Mine.*	19,000 Nov. 4, '14	21	1,600	500	Kiel Hamburg	Durr ,,	1905 1905	(Kr.) Belt: am. 4, f. 3, a. 3, P.D. 2¾, Bte 6, Bty 4, C.T. 6in.	8'2, four; 6in., ten; 3'4, 12; smaller, 14; torpedo tubes, 4 (3 submerged).
Yorck												
Prinz Adalbert	410	65	*Torpedoed* 9,000 *Mine*	Oct. 23, '15 17,500 Nov. 18, '14	21	1,600	550	Kiel Hamburg	,, ,,	1903 1904	(Kr.) Belt: am. 4, f. 3, a. 3, P.D. 2, Trt. 6, Bty 4, G.T. 9in.	8'2, four; 6in., ten; 3'4, 10; smaller, 14; torpedo tubes, 4 (3 submerged).
F. Karl												
Prinz Heinrich	410	65	9,000	15,000	20	1,500	500	Kiel	,,	1902	(Kr.) Belt: am. 4, f. 2, a. 2, P.D. 2, Trt. 1, Bty 4, C.T. 6in.	9'4, two; 6in., ten; 3'4, ten; smaller, ten; torpedo tubes, four (three submerged).

NOTE TO ARMOUR.—am.=amidships; f.=forward; a.=aft.; P.D.=protective decks; C.T.=conning tower.

* See Turkish Navy.

THE GERMAN NAVY—continued.

CRUISERS

Name.	Length (feet).	Beam (feet).	Tonnage.	Horse Power.	Speed (Knots).	Coal (Max.)	Complement.	Where Built.	Boilers.	Completed	Armament.
*Elbing	426	46	*Gunfire* 4,500	May 31, '17 27,400	27½			Danzig	Schulz	1916	5in., eight; 2½in., four; torpedo tubes, two.
*Pillau											
Bremen								Bremen	Schulz	1904	4"1, ten; smaller, fourteen; torpedo tubes, two (submerged).
Berlin		*Torpedoed Dec. 19,'15*						Danzig	,,	,,	
Danzig	330	40	3,200	10,000	22½	800	300	,,	,,	1907	
Hamburg		*Gun-fire Dec. 8,'14*						Stettin	,,	1904	
Leipzig								Bremen	,,	,,	
Lubeck								Stettin	,,	1905	
Munchen								Bremen	,,	,,	
Arcona		*Gunfire May 31,'16*						Bremen	,,	1903	4"1, ten; smaller, fourteen torpedo tubes, two.
Frauenlob	330	40	2,700	8,000	22	700	250	Kiel	,,	,,	
Undine		*Torpedoed Nov. 7, '15*						,,	,,	1904	
Gefion	...	335	42	3,700	9,000	20	700	300	Danzig	Cylindrical	1894	4"1, 10; smaller, 14; torpedo tubes, 2 (above water).
Amazone								Kiel	Schulz	1901	4"1, ten; smaller, eighteen; torpedo tubes, two (submerged).
Ariadne		*Gun-fire Aug.28,'14*						Bremen	,,	,,	
Gazelle								Kiel	Niclausse	1899	
Medusa	335	40	2,650	8,000	21	600	250	Bremen	Schulz	1901	
Niobe								Kiel	,,	,,	
Nymphe								,,	,,	,,	
Thetis								Danzig	,,	,,	
Hela	328	36	2,040	6,000	20·5	300	175	Bremen	S.T.	1896	15-pr., four; 6-pr.
		Torpedoed Sept.13,'14									

NOTE TO ARMOUR.—am.=amidships; f.=forward; a.=aft; P.D.=protective decks; C.T.=conning tower.

* These were the Russian cruisers "Muraviev Amursky" and "Nevelskoy."

37

PROTECTED CRUISERS

Name.	Lgth (feet)	B'am (feet)	Tonnage.	Horse Power.	Spd (kts.)	Coal (Max.)	Com'mnt.	Where Built.	Boilers.	Completed	Armour.	Armament.
PTD. CRUISERS.												
Wiesbaden	450	44	*Gunfire*	*May 3, '16*	28		370	Stettin	Schulz	1915	Belt, 4in.; ends, 2½in.	4·1in., twelve; torpedo tubes, two.
E. Gelle			5,000	25,500		1,500		Kiel	"	"		
E. ...								"	"	"		
Karlsruhe	450	44	5,000	25,500	28	1,400	370	Kiel	Schulz	1913	Belt, 4in.; ends, 2½in.	4·1in., twelve; torpedo tubes, two.
...			*Sunk*	*Nov. 1914*				Bremen	"	1914		
Regensberg								Bremen	"	"		
Breslau	446	44	*Turkey* 4,478	*Aug. 1914* 24,000	25·5	1,000	370	"	Schulz	1912	Belt, 3½in.; ends, 2in.	4in., twelve; torpedo tubes, two.
Magdeburg			*Wrecked*	*Aug. 27 '14*				Wilh'mshav.	"	"		
Strassburg								Bremen	"	"		
Stralsund												
Augsburg	400	46	4,281	28,000	27·5	900	310		"	1911		4in., twelve; torpedo tubes, two.
Koln			*Gunfire*	*Aug. 28, '14*				Kiel	"	"		
Kolberg			*Gunfire*	*Jan. 24, '15*					"	1910		
Mainz			*Gunfire*	*Aug. 28, '14*				Stettin	"	"		
Dresden	387	43	*Gunfire*	*Mar. 14, '15*	24·5	900	320	Hamburg	"	1908		4in., ten; 3pr., eight torpedo tubes, two.
Emden			*Gunfire*	*Nov. 11, '14*					"	1909		
Koenigsburg	354	43	*Sunk*	*Dec. 14, '14*	23½	850	300	Kiel	"	1907		4·1, 4n; smaller, fourteen; do tubes, two (submerged).
Nurnburg			*Gunfire*	*Dec. 8, '14*					"	1908		
...			3,420	13,200				Kiel	"	"		
...									"	"		
...	380	58	5,800	11,000	19	1,000	450	Stettin	Nicla'se Belle'lle	1898	P.D. 4in.; C.T. 8in.	8·2, two; 6in., eight; 3·4, 4n; smaller, fourteen; do tubes, three (submerged).
...								"	"	1899		
Hertha									"	1898		
Victoria									Durr	1899		

NOTE TO ARMOUR.— am.=amidships; f.=forward; a.=aft.; P.D.=protective decks; C.T.=connin g

* Believed to be ... and "Koln" and " M...

38

The German Navy

NOTE.—The latest type of German destroyers, built since war started, are believed to be vessels of from 1,000 to 1,500 tons displacement, carrying four 4·1in. guns, three funnels, and a speed exceeding 35 knots. Number of torpedo tubes unknown. German losses in torpedo craft is known to have been very severe, but the actual number is not known.

Destroyers.—D 3, D 4 (1887-9), 300 tons, 21 knots ; D 5, D 6 (1880-90), 320 tons, 23 knots ; D 7, D 8 (1892-02), 350 tons, 23 knots ; D 9, D 10 (1893-9), 380 tons, 25 knots ; Taku (1897-9), 280 tons, 30 knots ; S 90-101 (1890-1900), 400 tons, 27 knots ; S 102-7 (1900-2), 400 tons, 27 knots ; G 108-13 (1901-3), 400 tons, 28 knots ; S 114-9 (1902-4), 420 tons, 28 knots ; S 120-5 (1903-5), 420 tons, 28 knots ; S 126-31 (1904-6), 487 tons, 28 knots ; G 132-6 (1905-7), 487 tons, 28½ knots ; G 137 (1905-7), 572 tons, 34 knots ; S 138-49 (1906-7), 525 tons, 30 knots ; V 150-61 (1907-8), 670 tons, 30 knots ; S 162-73 (1908-9), 670 tons, 30 knots. 12 boats 1909-10, 112 boats 1910-11. Germany's programme provided for twelve destroyers a year up to 1917. All these vessels were to be of 670 tons displacement, 30 knots speed, and to carry two 24-pdrs., three machine guns, and three 18in. tubes. She also had 70 torpedo-boats of from 22 to 25 knots.

Submarines.—At the beginning of the war Germany was supposed to have 30 submarines completed, and a number building ; her present position is quite unknown. We do know from captures that she has deliberately faked the index marks on her submarines, but with all her submarine losses it is generally believed that she is at present much stronger in this class of vessel than when war started.

GERMAN NAVY (other losses)

In addition to those ships shown in italics in "The German Navy, Part II," Germany has lost a host of torpedo craft and submarines, especially the latter, also a number of old gunboats of very little fighting value. Some time since the Admiralty decided to publish no further information about the destruction of German submarines, so that the real number lost is only a matter of conjecture ; for that reason we do not attempt to give specific details.

GERMAN NAVAL GUNS

Calibre in Inches.	Weight in Tons.	Length in Calibre.	Projectile in lbs.	Muzzle Velocity (F.S.)	Muzzle Energy (F.T.)
15	90	45	1,650	2,300	90,000
12	52	50	981	2,500	51,000
12	48	45	981	2,500	47,000
11	42	50	760	2,800	42,000
11	40	45	760	2,300	35,000
11	35	40	760	2,200	28,000
9.4	22	40	352	2,800	13,000
8.2	17	50	309	2,800	17,500
8.2	14.8	45	309	2,700	15,000
6.7	8	40	130	3,000	9,000
5.9	6	50	90	3,000	6,000
4.1	2	50	34	3,100	2,300

AUSTRIAN NAVAL GUNS

Calibre in Inches.	Weight in Tons.	Length in Calibre.	Projectile in lbs	Muzzle Velocity (F.S.)	Muzzle Energy (F.T.)
12	52	45	992	2,600	47,400
9.4	21	40	474	2,500	22,000
7.5	11	42	400	2,700	10,000
6	6	40	112	2,600	5,300
4.7	3.5	45	40	3,000	2,800

THE AUSTRO-HUNGARIAN NAVY.

BATTLESHIPS.

Name.	Lgth (feet)	B'am (feet)	Tonnage.	Horse Power.	Spd (kts.)	Coal (Max.)	Com'mnt.	Where Built.	Boilers.	Completed	Armour.	Armament.
Ersatz Monarch Ersatz Wien Ersatz Rudapest Ersatz Hapsburg	570	96	25,300	31,000	21	3,000		Trieste Fiume Trieste Fiume	Yarrow			14in., twelve; 5'9, twelve; 11-pdrs., twenty; torpedo tubes, four.
Prinz Eugen Tegetthoff Viribus Unitis Szent Istvan	469	89	20,000	25,000	22	2,000	1000	Trieste ,, ,, Fiume	Yarrow	1912 1914 1913 1915	Belt: am. 11in.; f. 7in.; a. 6in.; gun positions and C.T. 12in.	12in, twelve; 5'9, twelve; smaller, 22; four torpedo tubes.
Erz. Ferdinand Radetzki Zrinyi	450	80	14,500	20,000	20·5	2,500	950	Trieste	Yarrow	1910 1911 ,,	(Krupp) Belt: am. 9in.; f. 6in.; a. 4in.; gun positions and C.T. 10in.	12in. four; 9'4, eight; 3'9, twenty; 3 torpedo tubes
Erz. Friedrich Erz. Karl Erz. Max	400	72	10,500	14,000	20	1,400	816	Trieste ,, ,,	,, ,, ,,	1906 ,, 1907	(Krupp) Belt: am. 8¼in.; P.D. 2¼in.; B'bette 9½in.; Baty. 6in.; C.T. 8¼in.	9'4, four; 7'6, three; 3in., fourteen, twelve; smaller, 28; torpedo tubes, two.
Arpad Badenberg Hapsburg	360	65	8,300	12,000	19	1,400	875	Trieste Pola Trieste	Belle'le ,, ,,	1903 1904 1903	(Kr.) Belt: am. 8¼in.; f. 2in.; a. 2in.; B'e. 8in.; cas. 6, C.T. 8in.	9'4, three; 6in., twelve; smaller, 28; torpedo tubes, two.
Budapest Monarch Wien	310	56	5,600	8,500	17	700	400	Trieste Pola Trieste	Belle'le Cylindcl	1897 1896 1897	Belt: 10½in.; f. 4½in.; a. 4½in.; P.D. 2½in.; gun positions 10½in.	9'4 four; 6in. six; torpedo tubes, 2.

NOTE TO ARMOUR.—a.m.=amidships; f.=forward; a.=aft; P.D.=protective decks; C.T.=Conning tower.

THE AUSTRO-HUNGARIAN NAVY—*continued.*

ARMOURED CRUISERS AND CRUISERS.

Name.	Lgth (feet)	B'am (feet)	Tonnage.	Horse Power.	Spd. (kts.)	Coal (Max.)	Com' mnt.	Where built.	Boilers.	Completed	Armour.	Armament.
St. Georg	400	62	7,200	12,500	22	1,000	628	Pola	Yarrow	1906	(Krupp) Belt: am. 6½in.; f. 2in.; a. 2in.; PD 3½, B'te8, c. 5in.	9´4, two ; 7´5, five ; 6in., 4 ; smaller, 20 ; torpedo tubes, two (submerged).
Kaiser Karl VI.	367	56	6,200	12,000	20	900	550	San Rocco	Belle'le	1900	(H.)Belt: 8½in.; P.D. 2⅜in.; B'bette 8in.; casemates 3in.	9´4, two ; 6in., eight ; smaller, 22 ; torpedo tubes, four (above water).
Maria Theresia	350	52	5,200	8,000	18½	750	500	San Rocco	Cylindcl	1895	(H.) Belt: 3in.; P.D. 2⅜in.; B'bette 5in.; C.T. 4in.	7´6, two ; 6in., eight ; smaller, twenty ; torpedo tubes, four (above water).
*Ersatz Aspern *Ersatz Szigetvar *Ersatz Zenta			5,000	44,000	30						Belt : am. 2½in.	5´9in., two ; 3´9in., eight.
Helgoland Novara Saida	408	42	3,500 *Torpedoed June*, 1916	25,000	27	850	300	Fiume ,, Trieste	Yarrow ,, ,,	1914 ,, 1913		3´9, nine, 4 smaller.
Admiral Spaun	406	42	3,500	20,000	26	850	300	Pola	Yarrow	1910	Belt: 2in.	3´9in., seven ; 2 smaller.
K. Elizabeth K. Franz Josef	330	49	*Gun-fire* 4,000	Oct. 10, '14 9,000	18	600	400	Pola San Rocco	Yarrow ,,	1892 1891	(Steel) P.D. 2⅜in.; C.T. 4in.	9´4, two ; 6in., six ; smaller fifteen ; torpedo tubes, five (above water).
Aspern Szigetvár Zenta	300	39	2,400 *Gun-fire Aug.*17,'14	7,000	20	500	300	Pola ,, Trieste	Yarrow ,, ,,	1901 ,, 1899	—	4´7, eight : smaller, fourteen ; torpedo tubes, two (above water).

NOTE TO ARMOUR.—am.=amidships ; f.=forward ; a.=aft ; P.D.=protective decks ; C.T.=Conning tower.
Torpedo Gun Boats.—Blitz, Komet, Magnet, Meteor, Planet, Satellit, Trabant. These vessels average 500 tons displacement, and have a speed of 20 knots. Their complement is about the same as our torpedo boat destroyers, 66 men.
33-Knot Destroyers (1912).—800 tons ; 16,000 I.H.P. Six commenced at Fiume, April, 1911. Balaton, Csepel, *Lika (Mined, December 25*, 1915), Orjen, Tatra, *Triglav (Mined, December 25*, 1915).
28-Knot Destroyers (1905-08).—390 tons ; 6,000 I.H.P. Csikos, Dinara, Huzzar, Pandur, Reka, Scharfschutze, Streiter, Ulan, Uskoke, Turul.
Submarines.—U1, U2, *U3 (Sunk, August* 15, 1915), U4, U5, U6, U7, U8, U9, U10, U11, *U12 (Sunk, August* 10, 1915), U13, U14.
*All believed to have been destroyed at Monfalcone, where they were building.

THE TURKISH NAVY.

Name.	Lgth (feet)	B'am (feet)	Tonnage.	Horse Power	Spd. (kts.)	Coal (Max.)	Com' mnt.	Where Built.	Boilers	Completed	Armour.	Armament.
*Rio de Janeiro (now *Erin*)	632	89	27,500	45,000	22	3,000	1000	Elswick	B'bcock	1913	Belt: am. 9in.; P.D., 2½in.; turrets, 9in.	12in., fourteen; 6in., twenty; 3in., twelve; torpedo tubes, three.
*Reshadieh (now *Agincourt*)	525	91	23,000	31,000	21	3,500		Barrow		1914	Belt: 12·6 P.D., 3in.	13·5, ten; 6in. sixteen; torpedo tubes, five.
Sultan Yawuz Selim (late *Goeben*)	610	96	22,640	70,000	28	3,000	900	Hamburg	Schulz	1911	Belt: 8in.; P.D., 2½	11in., ten; 5·9in., twelve; 3·4in., twelve.
†Kheyr-ed-Din Barbarossa	354	65	*Torpedoed Aug. 3, '15* 9,900	9,000	17	1,300	600	Wilhelmsh'n Stettin	,,	1894 1893	Belt: 15¾ in. (C) P.D., 2½in.; T., 11¾ in.	11in., six; 4·1in., eight; 3·4 in., eight.
‡Turgut Reis												
Mesudieh	331	59	9,120 *Sunk*	11,000 *Dec. 13, '14*	17·5	1,000	600	Thames	Nic	1901	Belt: 12in.; P.D., 1in.	9·2in., two; 6in., twelve; 3in., fourteen.
Hamidieh	331	47	7,800	12,000	22	600	300	Elswick Philadelphia	Nic	1904 1904	Belt: 4½in.	6in., two; 4·7in., eight.
Medjidieh			*Mined, April 4, 1915*									

Turkey also has six gunboats of little value, eight destroyers, and eight torpedo-boats, besides the notorious "Goeben" (renamed "Sultan Yawuz Selim") and "Breslau" (renamed "Medilli") for particulars of which see German Navy.

* Purchased by Great Britain. † Ex "Kurfurst Frederich Wilhelm." ‡ Ex "Weissenberg."

Gunboats.—*Burak Reis* (scuttled, Oct. 31, '14), *Pesk-i-Shevket* (torpedoed, April 29, '15), *Peienk-i-Derria* (torpedoed, May 22, '15), *Marmoris* (gunfire, June, 1915), *Buk-i-Satvet* (torpedoed, Aug. 8, '15), and several others. *Timur Hissar* (D.), beached, April 17, '15; *Yar Hissar* (D.), torpedoed, Dec. 2, '15.

THE TURKISH NAVY: OTHER LOSSES.

THE ARGENTINE NAVY.

Name.	Lgth (feet)	B'am (feet)	Tonnage.	Horse Power.	Spd. (kts.)	Coal (Max.)	Com' mnt.	Where Built.	Boilers.	Completed.	Armour.	Armament.
Moreno Rivadavia	557	95	28,000	39,500	22½	4,000	1050	Quincy Camden N.J.	B'bcock	1913 ,,	Belt: am. 12in.; P.D. 3⅜in.; turrets 12in.	12in., twelve; 6in., twelve; 4in., sixteen; torpedo tubes, two.
Belgrano	328	59	7,069	13,000	20	1,000	500	Leghorn	Belle'le	1899	Belt: am. 6in.; P.D. 1⅜in.; turrets 6in.	10in., two; 6in., ten; 4·7in., six; torpedo tubes, four.
Garabaldi	,,	,,	6,732					Pes'ri Po'nte	,,	1896		
Pueyrrdon	,,	,,	6,773					,,	,,	1901		
San Martin	,,	,,	,,					Leghorn	,,	1898		

There are a few smaller cruisers and gunboats, 1 submarine and 15 destroyers, full particulars of which appeared in the 1912 Annual.

Destroyers.—Cordova, La Plata, 1,110 tons, h.p. 19,000, speed 34 knots; 4in., four; torpedo tubes (21in.), four. Catamorca, Sujuy, 995 tons, h.p. 22,000, speed 34 knots; 4in., four; torpedo tubes (21in.), four.

42

UNIFORMS OF THE WORLD'S NAVIES.
GREAT BRITAIN.

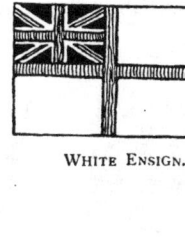

WHITE ENSIGN.

ADMIRAL—FULL DRESS.

Sleeve Distinction.

1. Admiral of the Fleet.
2. Admiral.
3. Vice-Admiral.
4. Rear-Admiral and Commodore, 1st class.

FROCK COAT—SLEEVE
COMMODORE, 2nd cl.

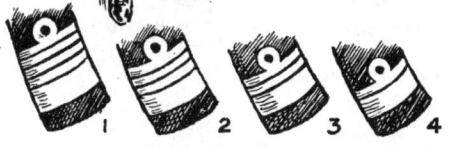

NOTE.

ENGINEERS—The same as below, but a purple line between the lace.

SURGEONS—No curl and a red line between the lace.

PAYMASTERS—No curl and a white line between the lace.

NAVAL INSTRUCTORS — No curl and a light blue line between the lace.

CAPTAIN   COMMANDER   Lt COMr   LIEUTENANT   MIDSHIPMAN AND CADET.

DISTINGUISHING BADGES.—*Continued.*

ROYAL NAVAL RESERVE.

CAPTAIN — SENIOR ENGINEER (PURPLE) — WARRANT ENGINEER (OF 10 YEARS SENIORITY) (PURPLE) — STAFF PAYMASTER & PAYMASTER (WHITE)

ROYAL NAVAL VOLUNTEER RESERVE

CAPTAIN — LIEUTENANT-COMMANDER — STAFF-SURGEON (RED) — ASSIST^T PAYMASTER (UNDER 4 YEARS' SENIORITY) (WHITE)

ROYAL NAVAL AIR SERVICE

WING-CAPTAIN — WING-COMMANDER — SQUADRON-COMMANDER — FLIGHT-COMM & FLIGHT-LIEUT

OFFICERS' BUTTONS

R.N. OFFICERS OF FLAG RANK — R.N. OFFICERS UNDER FLAG RANK — R.N.R OFFICERS — R.N.V.R. OFFICERS — R.N.A.S. OFFICERS

And Naval Year Book

GREAT BRITAIN—*Continued*.

NOTE.

Warrant Officers, Chief Gunners, and Chief Boatswains, 1 row gold lace ½-inch with curl.

Gunners and Boatswains, over 10 years seniority, 1 row gold lace ¼-inch with curl.

Other Warrant Officers buttons only on sleeves.

WARRANT OFFICER.

CHIEF PETTY OFFICER.

Seaman and Stoker ratings below Chief Petty Officer.

WORKING RIG.

46 The Fleet Annual
DISTINGUISHING BADGES.

GUNNERY.

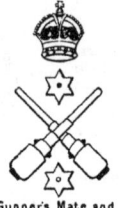

Gunner's Mate and Gunlayer, 1st Class.

Gunner's Mate.

Gunlayer 1st Class.

Gunlayer, 2nd Class.

Gunlayer, 3rd Class.

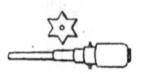

Chief Petty Officer (G). Petty Officer (G). not being Gunlayer or Gunner's Mate — and Seaman Gunner.

TORPEDO

Torpedo Gunner's Mate (Higher Standard).

Torpedo Gunner's Mate.

Torpedo Coxswain.

Leading Torpedo Man.

Chief Petty Officer (T). Petty Officer (T). and Seaman Torpedo Man.

Sketches continued on next sheet.

And Naval Year Book

DISTINGUISHING BADGES—*Continued*.

SIGNALS.

Chief Yeoman of Signals.

Yeoman of Signals.

Leading Signalman.

Signalman.

Ordinary Signalman and Signalboy.

TELEGRAPHISTS

Chief Petty Officer and Petty Officer Telegraphist.

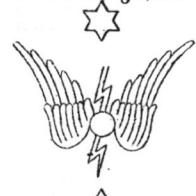

Leading Telegraphist.

Telegraphist.

Ordinary and Boy Telegraphist.

SHOOTING BADGES

1st Class.

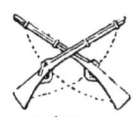

2nd Class.

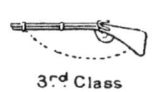

3rd Class.

PHYSICAL TRAINING

Physical Training Instructor 1st Class.

Physical Training Instructor 2nd Class.

The Fleet Annual
DISTINGUISHING BADGES—Continued.

ENGINEER BRANCH

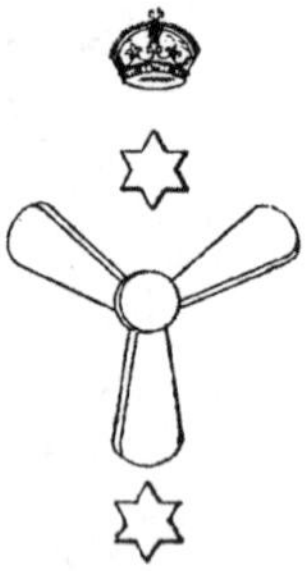

- Mechanician.
- Chief Stoker. 
- Stoker Petty Officer. 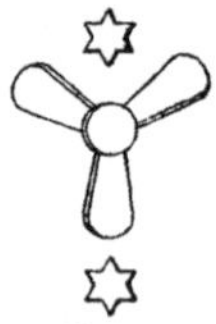
- Leading Stoker passed for Stoker Petty Officer. 
- Stoker. 

ARTISANS

- Chief and other Armourers
- Armourer's Mates and Crews 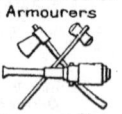 
- Blacksmith, Plumber, Painter 1st Class. All Chief and other Carpenters' Mates, and Skilled Shipwrights of whatever Rating.
- All other Artisans. 

BADGES OF RATING WORN ON THE LEFT ARM

- Petty Officer 1st Class
- Petty Officer 2nd Class
- Leading Seaman and — AFTER 13 YEARS SERVICE.
- AFTER 3 YEARS SERVICE
- Other Leading Hands — AFTER 8 YEARS SERVICE

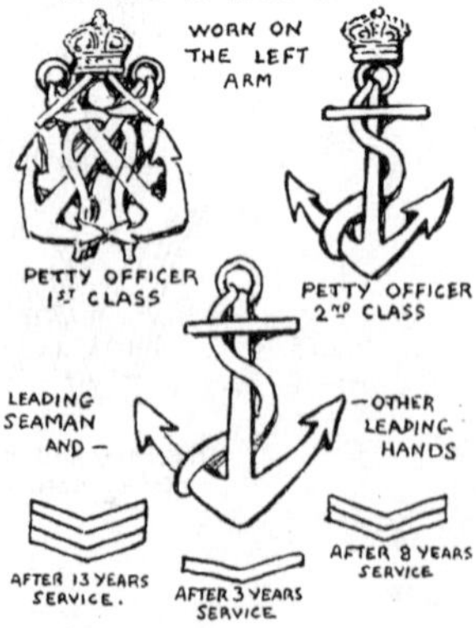

OTHER RATINGS

- Chief Petty Officer Seaman Class not being a Seaman Gunner. 
- N P Naval Police
- Civil Branch 
- Sick Berth Staff 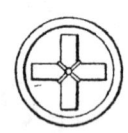
- Buglers

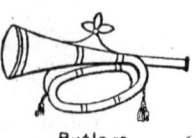

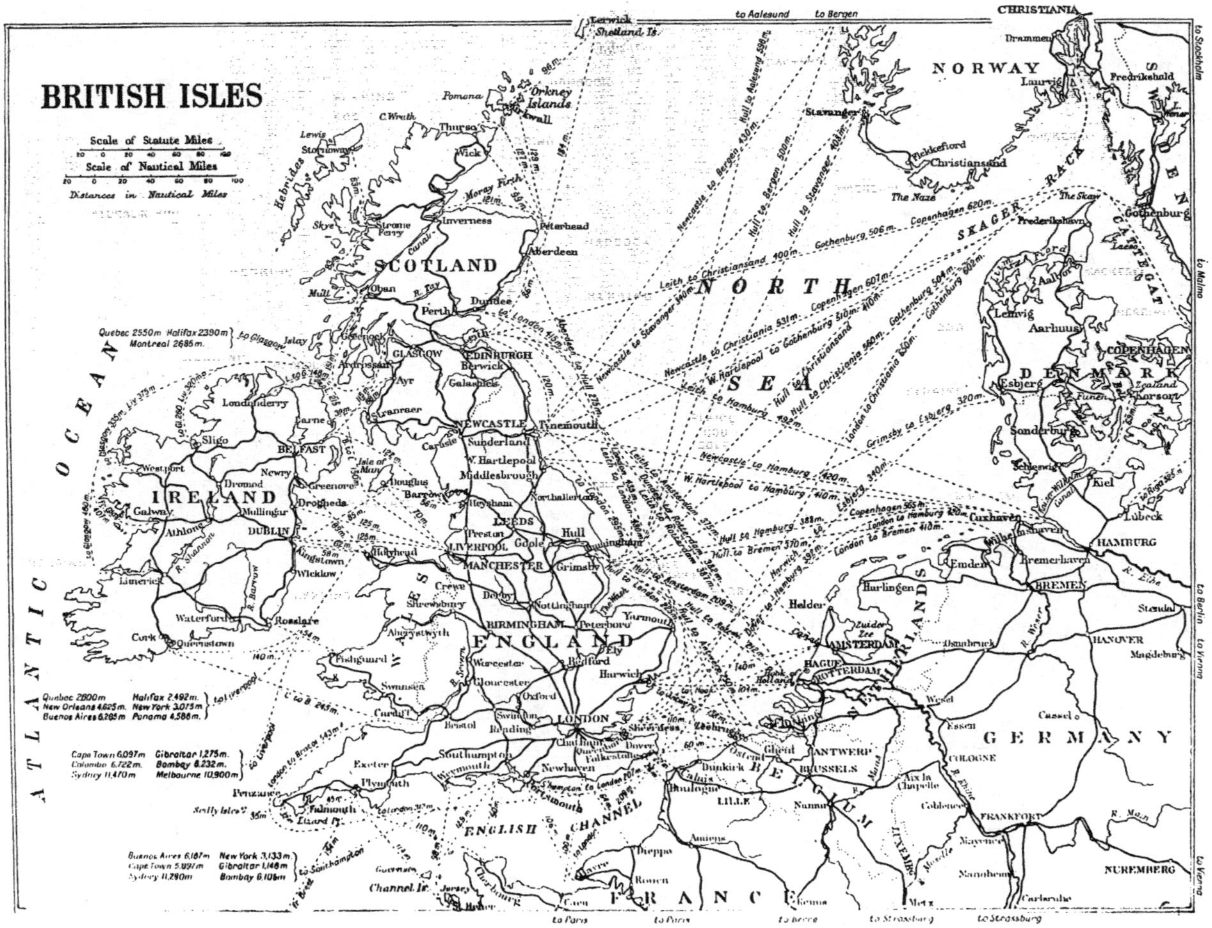

BRITISH ISLES
Scale of Statute Miles
Scale of Nautical Miles
Distances in Nautical Miles
ATLANTIC OCEAN
NORTH SEA
ENGLISH CHANNEL
SKAGER RACK
CATTEGAT
SCOTLAND
ENGLAND
WALES
IRELAND
NORWAY
SWEDEN
DENMARK
GERMANY
NETHERLANDS
BELGIUM
FRANCE
CHRISTIANIA
LONDON
DUBLIN
EDINBURGH
GLASGOW
NEWCASTLE
LIVERPOOL
MANCHESTER
BIRMINGHAM
LEEDS
HAMBURG
BREMEN
AMSTERDAM
ROTTERDAM
ANTWERP
BRUSSELS
COPENHAGEN
to Aalesund
to Bergen
to Stockholm
to Malmo
to Berlin
to Vienna
to Paris
to Strassburg
Quebec 2550m Halifax 2390m
Montreal 2685m.
Quebec 2800m Halifax 2,492m.
New Orleans 4,625m. New York 3,075m
Buenos Aires 6,205m Panama 4,586m.
Cape Town 6,097m Gibraltar 1,275m.
Colombo 6,722m. Bombay 6,232m.
Sydney 11,470m Melbourne 10,900m
Buenos Aires 6,187m New York 3,133m
Cape Town 5,897m Gibraltar 1,148m
Sydney 11,290m Bombay 6,106m

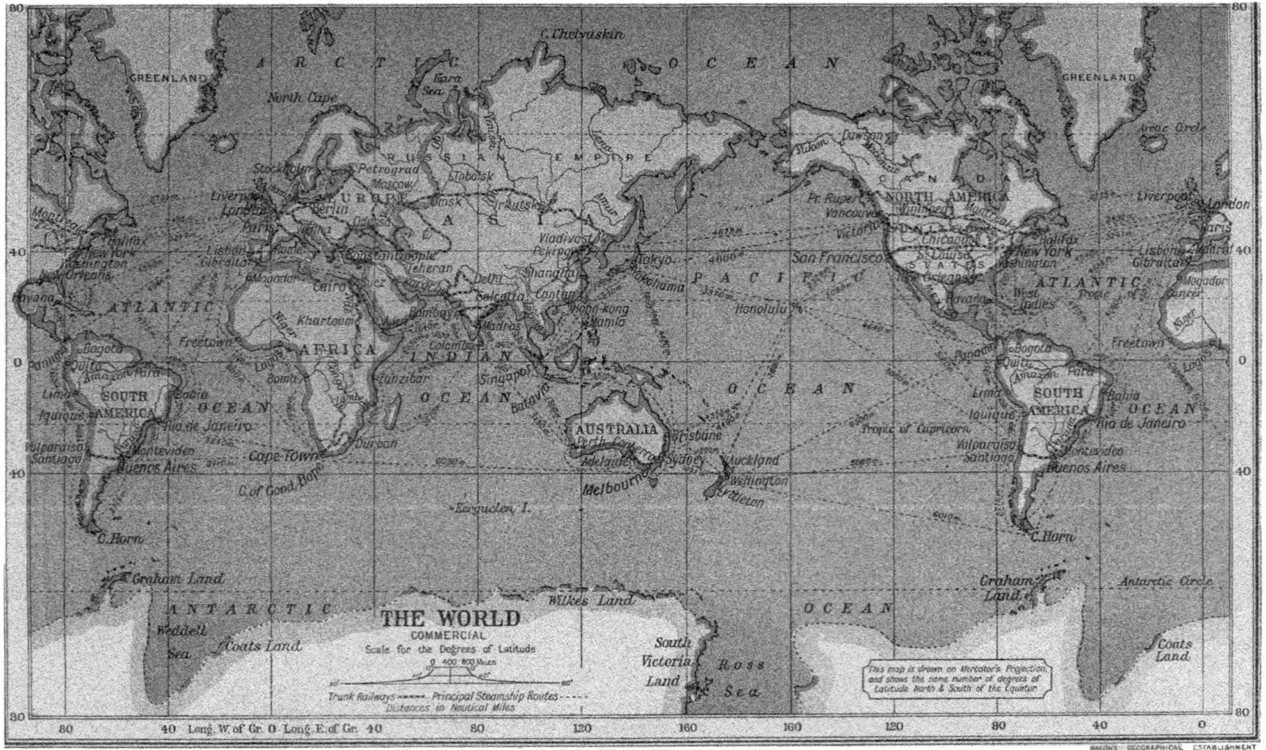

TIME DISTANCES between

LONDON and

	days
ADELAIDE	38
ADEN	16
ALBANY	33
BATAVIA	32
BEIRA (via Cape Town)	28
BRISBANE	43
BOMA (via Antwerp)	20
BOMBAY	21
BRINDISI (Railway)	2
CALCUTTA (via Bombay)	23
CAPE TOWN	17
COLOMBO	22
DURBAN	22
EAST LONDON	21
FREETOWN	11
FREMANTLE	32
GIBRALTAR	4
HOBART (via Cape Town)	37
HONG-KONG	35
KARACHI	22
LAGOS	17
LOURENCO MARQUES	26
MACASSAR	38
MADRAS (via Bombay)	23
MARSEILLES	7
MAURITIUS (via Aden)	30
MELBOURNE	38
MOMBASA (via Aden)	24
MOZAMBIQUE (via Cape Town)	30
PORT ELIZABETH	20
PORT SAID	12
REUNION (via Aden)	29
SHANGHAI	40
SINGAPORE	29
SYDNEY	41
TAMATAVE (via Aden)	26
WELLINGTON (via Melbourne)	44
ZANZIBAR (via Aden)	26

LIVERPOOL and

	days
BELEM (PARA)	16
CALLAO (via Panama)	27
COLON	18
MONTREAL	6
NEW YORK	7
QUEBEC	7
NOME (via Vancouver)	21
VANCOUVER (via Montreal)	13
YOKOHAMA (via Vancouver)	25

SOUTHAMPTON and

	days
AUCKLAND (via San Francisco)	30
BUENOS AIRES	19
HONOLULU (via San Francisco)	18
MONTEVIDEO	18
NEW YORK	7
RIO DE JANEIRO	16
SAN FRANCISCO (via New York)	12
TRINIDAD	13
VALPARAISO (via Buenos Aires	20

NEW YORK and

	days
AUCKLAND (via San Francisco)	23
BARBADOS	6
BUENOS AIRES	20
CALLAO (via Panama)	10
CAPE TOWN (via Southampton)	24
COLON	7
GEORGETOWN	8
GIBRALTAR	8
HONG-KONG (via San Francisco)	29
HONOLULU (via San Francisco)	11
LA GUAYRA	13
LAS PALMAS	13
MONTEVIDEO	19
NAPLES	14
NEW ORLEANS	5
RECIFE (PERNAMBUCO)	12
RIO DE JANEIRO	16
SAN FRANCISCO (Railway)	4½
SYDNEY (via San Francisco)	26
VALPARAISO (via Panama)	23
VANCOUVER (Railway)	6
YOKOHAMA (via San Francisco)	22

MELBOURNE and

	days
ACAPULCO	26
ADELAIDE	2
ADEN	22
AUCKLAND	7
BOMBAY	19
BRISBANE	5
BUENOS AIRES	27
CALCUTTA (via Colombo)	23
CAPE TOWN	22
COLOMBO	16
FIJI Is.	9
FREMANTLE	6
GIBRALTAR	34
HOBART	2
HONG-KONG	26
HONOLULU (via Fiji)	18
LONDON	38
MADRAS (via Colombo)	19
MANILA	23
MONTEVIDEO	26
NEW YORK (via San Francisco)	29
PANAMA (via Wellington)	28
PORT SAID	26
RIO DE JANEIRO	29
SAN FRANCISCO (via Fiji)	24
SHANGHAI	31
SYDNEY	3
TAHITI	14
VALPARAISO (via Buenos Aires)	28
WELLINGTON	6
YOKOHAMA	33

The time distances shown above are calculated from the average time of transit by steamship.

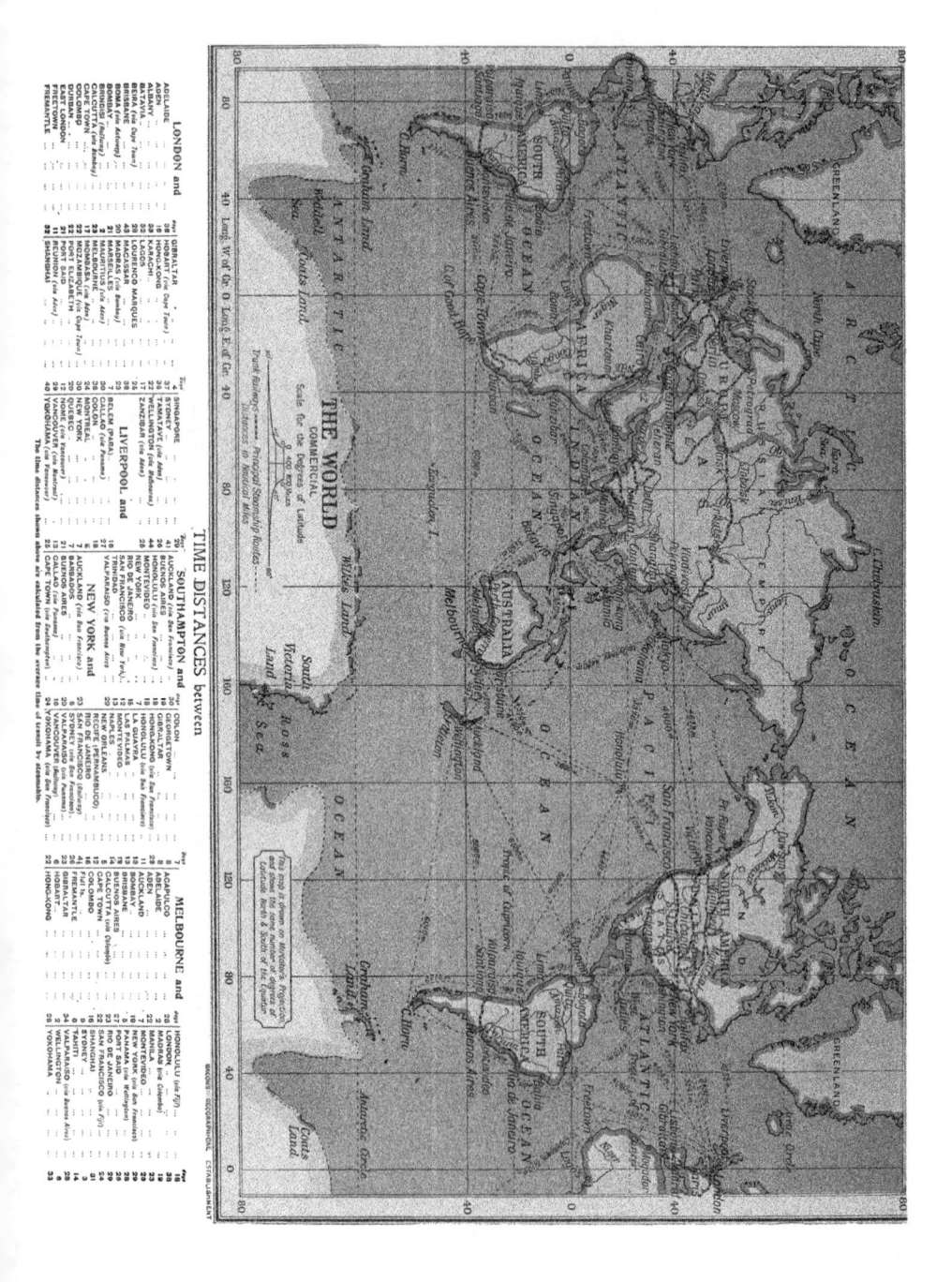

THE FLEET ANNUAL AND NAVAL YEAR BOOK, 1917.   PART III.

The Navy's Immortal Names.

"Glory and peace to her lovely and faithful dead."
W.E.H.

Be it written,
  That all I wrought
Was for Britain,
  In deed and thought:
Be it written,
  That while I die,
'Glory to Britain!'
  Is my last cry.
            MEREDITH.

The Navy's Immortal Names

OFFICERS AND MEN KILLED IN THE WAR.

(Continued from "The Fleet Annual," 1916.)

Note.—Particulars of contractions will be found on the last page of this section.

Captain.
Hugh Edwards, D.S.O.
Pennant A. I. Lloyd (retd.)
Cecil I. Prowse.
Herbert J. Savill.
Hastings F. Shakespear (retd.)
Charles F. Sowerby.
Powell C. Underwood (retd.)
Marcus F. B. Whyte (act.) (retd.)
Charles J. Wintour.

Commander.
Sir Charles R. Blane, Bt.
The Hon. Richard O. B. Bridgeman, D.S.O.
Alfred F. Coplestone-Boughey.
Samuel R. Crabtree (retd.)
Edward H. Currey (retd.)
Manuel Dasent.
Robert G. Fane.
Humphrey Finch-Dawson (retd.)
Francis H. H. Goodhart, D.S.O.
Edwin T. Inman.
Arthur T. Johnstone.
Loftus W. Jones.
Robert H. Llewelyn.
John Marshall (retd.)
Irving B. Miles (retd.)
Harry L. L. Pennell.
Lionel H. Shore.
Arthur E. Silverton.
Richard H. D. Townsend.
John B. Waterlow. D.S.O.
Henry E. D. H. Willoughby.
George F. G. Woodhall (act.) (emergy.)

Commander, R.N.R.
Thomas R. Agassiz.
Cecil De La Mare Goldsmith, R.D.
John Mathias, R.D.
George N. Ramage, R.D.
Charles P. Wilson, R.D. (retd.)
Tempy. Hon. Commander, R.N.V.R.
Lord Abinger.

Wing Commander.
Neville F. Usborne (Com. R.N.)

Lieutenant-Commander.
Geoffrey N. Biggs.
John C. F. Borrett.
Robert F. Chisholm.
Ralph L. Clayton.
Percy B. A. Cooper (retd.)
Thomas S. L. Dorman, D.S.O.
David W. S. Douglas.
Kenneth J. Duff-Dunbar, D.S.O.
The Hon. Hugh C. R. Feilding.
Clarence A. Fulcher.
John E. Grey-Smith.
Alexander H. Gye.
Robert C. Halahan.
William W. Hallwright, D.S.O.
Ralph Ireland.

Leonard H. Lindner.
Charles S. Morris.
Granville Murray-Brown.
Arthur G. Onslow, D.S.O.
Martin Robertson-Glasgow (retd.)
Frank E. M. Roe (retd.)
Douglas R. Saxby-Thomas.
Edward Smyth-Osbourne.
Francis G. Stewart.
George C. Street.
Dudley Stuart.
Julian T. Tenison.
Frank G. Terry.
Aubrey Thomas.
John White.
John S. Wilson.

Squadron Commander.
Ian H. W. S. Dalrymple-Clark.
John J. Petre, D.S.C. (act.)

Lieutenant-Commander, R.N.R.
Thomas R. Heap (retd.)

Lieutenant-Commander, R.N.V.R.
Philip S. Campbell (temp.)
James S. Douglas (temp.)
Frederick S. Kelly, D.S.C. (temp.)
Edward L. Milner-Barry.
William Park, D.S.C. (temp.)

Lieutenant.
Cecil H. Abercrombie.
Harold H. Atkin-Berry.
Alfred Bakewell.
Geoffrey H. V. Bayfield.
Basil A. Beal.
Maurice J. Bethell.
Reginald A. Blyth.
Harold Boase.
Richard G. Bowyer.
Douglas B. Bucham Brown.
James R. Bucknill.
Robert C. Chichester.
James S. Clarke (retd.)
Ronald I. Collier.
Gerald F. T. C. Collins.
Ian C. Cowan.
Ernest T. Donnell.
Stewart B. Dundee-Hooper.
Arthur E. Durham.
John Eadie.
Charles E. F. Egan.
Victor A. Ewart.
Alastair C. N. Farquhar.
John R. B. Farwell.
Robert I. Faulkner.
Edward H. FitzRoy.
Thomas F. S. Flemming.
William J. W. Fletcher.
William N. Gardiner.
Frederick L. Gardner (temp.) (late R.I.M.)
Roderick C. A. Gow.
Eric V. Grey.

Hubert W. D. Griffith.
John M B. Hanly.
Philip Harlock.
Henry W. E. Hearn (act.)
Hugh S. Hornby.
Conrad Jenkin.
George E. Jenkinson.
Richard P. Kellett.
John A. Kemp.
Henry G. S. Laing.
Walter L. Landale
Edward R. M. Lane.
Claude de N. Lucas.
Thomas B. S. McGregor-Robertson.
Alexander P. McMullen.
Eustace N. G. Maton.
Humphrey Matthews.
Edward W. Milsom (act.)
Alexander G. Murray.
Frank P. O'Reilly.
John A. Orr-Ewing.
Reay Parkinson.
Richard E. Paterson.
Eric S. Ray (emergy.)
Edward W. B. Ryan.
Dudley W. Ryder.
William W. Skynner.
Stephen H. Slingsby.
Vincent G. Snow.
Charles A. Sperling.
Percy Strickland.
Andrew N. Swainson.
Herbert J. Webley.
John Welsh (retd.)
Alfred H. Willoughby.

Flight-Commander.
George H. Beard, D.S.C. (act.)

Flight-Lieutenant.
Royce G. A. Baudry.
Harold A. Bower.
Cecil W. Dickinson.
Charles W. Graham, D.S.O.
Leslie H. Hardstaff.
John E. Morgan.
Lewis Morgan (Act. Sub.-Lt. R.N.R.)
Victor Nicholson.
Geoffrey R. H. Talbot.
Taunton E. Viney, D.S.O.
Oswald N. Walmesley.

Temporary Flight Lieutenant.
John T. Bankes-Price.
Richard E. Bush.
George R. S. Fleming.
John D. Hume.
Harold A. Pailthorpe.
Edward L. Pulling, D.S.O.
John C. Railton.
Bertram A. Trechmann.
Harry R. Wambolt.

Lieutenant, R.N.R.
Harold Blow.
George E. R. Browne.
William Clark.
Edwin B. Dalby.

The Navy's Immortal Names

Alfred S. Gilbert.
George R. Hall (act.)
Charles F. Halliday.
Ernest F. Humphrey (act.)
David T. E. James.
Hugh Mc V. Lovett (act.)
William A. McNeill.
Harold O. Master.
Richard Morgan.
Andrew Paterson.
Francis M. Prattent (act.)
George R. Renshaw.
Arthur E. L. Rudd.
Johannes M. Scholtz.
Thomas Steele (act.)
Hugh Twynam (act.)

Temporary Lieutenant, R.N.R.

Ernest R. Aston.
William A. Bell (act.)
Harold M. Bibby.
Fred Boyle.
William A. Carmichael.
Adolph C. Charlton
Henry B. Conby.
Donald Cowan.
Thomas R. Davies.
Thomas S. D. Dickson.
Patrick J. Donovan.
Cyril A. Edmondson.
John A. Evans
Robert E. A. Fox.
Alexander J. Gunn (act.)
John S. Harvey (act.)
Alfred N. Headley.
Andrew Heron.
William Hunter (act.)
Charles T. Klemp (act.)
Frederick H. Lawson (act.)
George Lee (act.)
James R. McClorry.
Alfred F. Maynard.
Harold S. Meats (act.)
Alexander Miller.
Robert C. Milne (act.)
Thomas F. Muir.
Edward F. Newton (act.)
Edwin Nixon.
Edward E. Roberts.
Walter L. Scott, D.S.C.†
Harold Shotton.
Alexander P. Stephen.
Frederick V. Varley.
Leonard C. Warder, D.S.C. (act.)
Evan H. Williams.
George H. W. Williamson (act.)
James A. Williamson (act.)
John N. Wilson.
James H. Young (act.)

Lieutenant, R.N.V.R.

Thomas H. Easton.

Temporary Lieutenant, R.N.V.R.

George R. Airey.
Percy T. Armstrong.
Charles P. Asbury.
George R. Barling.
James Clark.
Oswald H. Crowther.
Reginald A. Davey.
Claude D. F. de la Mothe.
Edward V. Ellis, M.C.

---

†Awarded bar to D.S.C., May, 1917.

Edward W. Ellis.
Charles D. Fisher.
Hon. Vere S. T. Harmsworth.
Ivan Heald.
Samuel G. Hill.
Arthur I. Humphreys.
Charles G. Jackson.
William Ker.
Charles F. Krikorian.
Frederick B. Melland.
Forest H. Mitchell.
James W. Morrison.
Egbert C. Oliver (Asst Paym. R.N. Emerg.)
Cecil A. Schurr.
Cyril A. Smith, D.S.O. (pres. killed)
Gerald H. Tamplin.
William J. Travers.
Cyril A. Truscott.
George K. Turnbull
George W. Wildman
Philip G. Wolfe Murray.
Charles H. P. Wood.

Engineer Captain.

James Barber (retd.)
Albert E. Collings (act.)
George K. Edwards (retd.)

Engineer Commander.

Hubert J. Clegg.
William G. Colquhoun.
Arthur E. Cossey.
George E. A. Crichton.
Reuben Main.
Edward H. T. Meeson, D.S.O.
John M. J. Murphy.
Thomas Shattock.

Engineer Commander, R.N.R.

James H. Watt, R.D.

Tempy. Engineer-Commander, R.N.R.

Charles E. Hurst.

Chief Engineer, R.N.R.

Henry Pollard.

Engineer Lieutenant-Commander.

William V. Benoy.
Reginald G. Hines.
George H. Hirtzel.
William H. F. Hudson.
Patrick J. King.
John M. Murray.
James D. Niven.
Norman Roberts.
Archibald S. de St Legier.
Henry C. N. Simes.
Martin Stuart (retd.)

Tempy. Eng. Lieut.-Commander, R.N.R.

George R. Rutledge.

Engineer Lieutenant.

Francis G. Blake.
Ernest W. Caine.
James Forrest.
Arthur E. Lane.
Francis L. Mogg.
Edwin H. Richards.

Engineer Lieutenant, R.C.N.

Stanley N. de Quetteville.

Tempy. Eng. Lieutenant.

Samuel A. Adams.
John McL. Hine.

Tempy. Eng. Lieutenant, R.N.R.

James Carlisle.
George H. Daymond.
James W. Gibbins.
Thomas Jamieson.
Edward A. R. Larmour.
Henry Maitland.
Robert R. Mitchell.
Francis E. Mortimore.
Archibald B. Perry.
George A. Prescott.
Herbert Sewell.
William W. Sharland.

Colonel (Tempy. Brigadier-General) R.M.

Godfrey E. Matthews, C.B., C.M.G.
(Died while serving in Army).

Major and Bt. Lieut.-Colonel, R.M.

Norman O. Burge (Tempy. Lt.-Col.)
John B. Noble.

Major and Hon.-Col. (tempy. Lt.-Col.), R.M.A.

Warren F. Trotter (Res.).

Major (temp. Lt.-Col.), R.M..

Frederick J. Saunders, D.S.O.
Francis J. W. Cartwright, D.S.O.

Major, R.M.

Robert C. Colquhoun.
Francis J. W. Harvey, V.C.
Gerald C. Rooney.
Ernest F. P. Sketchley, D.S.O.

Captain, R.M.

Alfred W. D. Broughton.
John Goldsmith.
Cyril S. Hazeon.
Valentine H. S. Jones
Vere D. Loxley (temp. Major).
Claude L. E. Muntz.
Arthur S. Tetley (tempy. Lt.-Col.)
Francis H. Thomas.

Tempy. Captain, R.M.

Murdoch C. Browne, D.S.C.
Harry Hoare.
John McIl Pound.
Albert W. Staughton.
Gerald H. Sullivan.

Captain, R.M.A.

Seymour Cruddas.
Ronald W. Hutton.
Guye W. Lushington.
Percy M. C. Wilde.
Montgomery Williams.

Tempy. Capt., R.M.A.

Hubert R. Purser.

Lieutenant, R.M.

Edward Bastin (temp. Capt.)
Alexander D. P. Hamilton (act.)
Francis J. Hanson.
John T. Le Seelleur.
Geoffrey R. Steinthal (act.)
Edmond St. V. St. Vincent-Ryan.
Henry B. Welman (act.)

The Navy's Immortal Names

Tempy. Lieutenant, R.M.
Harold E. Bennie.
Harry G. C. Coulson.
John J. Eaton-Shore.
Frederick W. A. Perry.
William W. Primrose (Attd. R.F.C.)
John W. Richards.
Lawrence W. Robinson.
Herman Shaw.

Chaplain and Naval Instructor.
Rev. Guy A. Browning, M.A.
Rev. William Hall, B.A.
Rev. George S. Kewney, B.A.

Chaplain.
Rev. Philip G. Alexander, B.A.
Rev. Henry D. Dixon-Wright, M.V.O., M.A.
Rev. Wallace M. Le Patourel, M.A.
Rev. Cecil W. Lydall, M.A.
Rev. George W. F. Morgan, B.A.
Rev. William F. Webber, B.A.

Tempy. Chaplain.
Rev. Cyril A. Walton, M.A. (act.)
Rev. Algernon H.- E. Creed, M.A. (act.)

Naval Instructor.
Marshall H. Robinson, B.A.

Tempy. Naval Instructor.
Thomas E. Jones, B.Sc.
John W. A. Steggall
Harry Wallis.

Fleet Surgeon.
Walter J. Bearblock.
Frederick A. Capps.
Herbert L. Geoghegan, M.B.
Francis F. Lobb.
Hugh L. Norris.
Henry G. Williams.

Staff Surgeon, R.N.V.R.
James K. Murphy, F.R.C.S., M.D., M.A.

Fleet Paymaster.
Wingfield W. Alton.
Ernest H. McA. Dyer.
Charles R. Harvey.
Ernest W. L. Mainprice.
John S. Place.

Staff Paymaster.
Percy Cruse.

Surgeon.
Sidney Punch.
John S. Ward.

Surgeon (Emergency).
Frank E. Rock, M.D.

Temporary Surgeon.
Harold G. Chaplin.
Frederick W. T. Clemens.
William H. Edmunds.
Arthur H. Flannery.

Charles H. Gow.
Maurice H. de J. Harper, B.A.
George M. Johnson, M.B., M.A.
Cyril O. H. Jones.
Charles W. Lewis.
John S. D. MacCormac.
Hugh F. McNally, M.B., B.A.
George B. Moon.
Archibald A. Morison.
Charles E. Reckitt.
Archibald M. Russell.
George Shorland.
Godfrey A. Walker.
Thomas M. Wood-Robinson.

Sub-Lieutenant.
Arthur H. C. Barlow.
Russell Bolingbroke.
George L. C. Briggs.
Patrick H. Brooke.
Alan G. Campbell-Cooke.
Thomas H. Cobb (act.)
The Hon. Alan B. de Blaquiere.
Alexander D. Gibson-Carmichael.
Richard Henderson (act.)
William S. Hutchinson (act.)
Henry C. A. Jauncey (act.)
Oswald M. Johnson.
Leopold E. Johnstone (act.)
Henry S. King (act.)
John S. Kirkland.
Geoffrey G. Kitchin (act.)
Cecil R. de V. Law.
Hugh B. Paul (act.)
Raymond S. Portal (act.)
Wilfred B. Price.
Alexander J. S. Richardson (act.)
Clifford H. Rider (act.)
Thomas A. W. Robertson.
Alexander Scrimgeour (act.)
Neville Seymour (act.)
Thomas H. W. Sharples (act.)
Frank A. Single (act.)
William I. Tatham.
Humphrey O'B. Thornhill.
Desmond F. C. L. Tottenham (act.)
Patrick H. G. I. Vance (act.)
Charles P. V. Van der Byl.
Humphrey F. Vernon.

Sub.-Lieutenant, R.A.N.
Joseph Mack (act.)
George W. Paterson.

Mate.
Samuel Anderson.
Thomas H. Clark.
Frederick Cook.
William T. Cory.
Joh H. Manning.
Ernest F. Sheath (act.)
Thomas W. Steggles.

Mate (E).
William F. Brebner.
Henry T. Cleare.
Henry E. Dacey.
Cyril B. Hopkins.
Samuel R. V. Self.

Flight Sub-Lieutenant.
Hon. Arthur C. Corbett.
Leonard W. Hodges.
Arthur J. Whetnall.

Tempy. Flight Sub-Lieutenant.
Samuel L. Bennett.
Raymond W. Berridge.
Rowland Birks.
Charles T. Brimer.
Ian N. Carmichael.
John W. Chuter.
Ronald F. Collins.
George R. G. Daglish.
Arthur C. Dissette.
David A. Duncan.
Oliver B. Ellis.
Neville W. Frames.
Edmund A. Freeman (proby.)
Holbrook L. Gaskell.
Arthur R. Greenwell (proby.)
James D. Haig.
Arthur F. Harvey (proby.)
William H. Hope.
Joshua M. Ingham.
Edward G. O. Jackson.
Patrick S. Kennedy.
Francis A. R. Malet.
John J. Malone, D.S.O.
Alfred T. O. Mann.
Donald H. Masson.
John E. Northrop.
William S. Oliver.
Wallace E. Orchard.
Douglas E. Penney.
Leslie A. Powell.
Lewis Radmore.
James D. Scott.
Thomas R. Shearer.
Herbert R. Simms.
James T. Sims.
Lewis E. Smith.
William S. Stewart.
Alfred L. Thorne.
Stanley V. Trapp.
Ranulph K. J. Vallings.
Kenneth M. van Allen.
Frederic C. Walker.
Hugh D. M. Wallace.
William R. Wallace (proby.)
Louis M. B. Weil.
Robert S. Whigham.
James P. White.
Douglas H. Whittier.
George K. Williams.

Sub-Lieutenant, R.N.R.
Douglas N. Colson, D.S.C.
Eynon L. Jones.
Arthur W. C. Lockwood (act.)

Tempy. Sub-Lieutenant, R.N.R.
Laurence W. Bell.
Alistair G. Cameron.
Edward A. L. Carte.
William Cox.
Benjamin Cuthbert.
Harry T. Doyle.
Arthur R. J. Elven.
Edwin Griffiths.
Fred C. Heath.
Gilbert S. Holbeck.
James F. Kane.
John B. Nevill.
The Hon. Algernon W. Percy.
Robert Thirlwell.

Sub-Lieutenant, R.N.V.R.
Thomas McL. Hutchison.

The Navy's Immortal Names

Tempy. Sub-Lieutenant, R.N.V.R.

William J. L. Aitken.
Douglas R. G. P. Alldridge.
Reginald J. Apthorp.
Eustace M. Aron.
Alwyn L. Ball.
Arthur H. Banning.
Nathan H. Benjamin.
James D. Black.
Leslie G. Black.
John N. Bowden.
Geoffrey C. Bowles.
Charles W. R. Bradley.
James H. Brothers.
John F. Bunce, M.C.
Henry A. J. Burr.
Ernest W. Cashmore.
Arthur E. N. Chance.
Reginald V. Cleves.
James A. Cook.
Arthur S. Cooke.
Major M. Collins.
Thomas K. Cross.
George T. Davidson.
Harold N. B. Daw.
Edgar C. Donovan.
Robert C. G. Edwards.
John H. Emerson.
Christopher G. O. Fletcher
Harold A. Foster.
David Francis
Howard Fry.
William M. Fry.
Leonard S. Gardner.
Harry Gealer.
Roland J. Gee.
Harry Gold.
William R. Haines.
William C. Hakin, M.C.
Alexander C. Hamilton.
Stanley P. Hancock.
Arthur R. Hart.
Edward A. G. Harvie.
Aubrey W. Henton.
Holt C. Hewitt.
Owen J. Hobbs.
Henry V. Howard.
George H. W. Hughes.
Trevor Jacobs.
Gordon Keightley.
Harold Kilner.
Alfred R. Knight.
John A. Langford.
Edmund Langstreth.
Cedric Lee
Walter H. Legge (attd. R.F.C.)
Gerald L. Lesmond.
Ian C. McCormick.
William McCurrach.
John A. McMillan.
John E. Maxwell.
Cyril J. A. Mullens.
Colin F. Neale.
Jack H. M. Newall
Joshua L. Oates.
Edmund J. Palmer.
Arthur E. Payne (pres. drowned).
Sidney G. Poole.
George H. Porter.
George A. Reddick.
Francis L. Rees.
Richard A. W. Robinson.
Alfred J. Rorke.
Arthur Sandell.
Leslie S. Savill.
Claude C. Sennitt.
Herbert A. Siddle.
Richard H. Sikes.
Hubert J. Shea.
Eric W. Squires.
George N. Strang.
Leslie M. Thomas.
Harold W. Troughton.
Frederick A. C. C. Turnbull.
Claude H. Usborne.
Caspar H. G. Wagner.
Alan B. Wallis.
James G. Watson.
George W. A. Wauchope.
Frederick C. Weaver.
William C. J. Williams.
John E. Willis.
Arthur F. Wolfe.

Act. Sub-Lieut. (Act.) R.N.R.

Brian A. Maddison.

Surgeon Probationer, R.N.V.R.

Hugh J. Dingle.

Tempy. Surg. Probationer, R.N.V.R.

William S. Allardyce.
David H. Ferris.
Gerald S. Freeman.
John Hislop.
John E. MacIntyre.
Alexander L. Strachan.
Gordon P. Walker.
Robert Walker.

Tempy. Engineer Sub-Lieutenant.

Eric T. Champness
Arthur L. Daidson.
Charles P. Tanner.
W. Hubert Unsworth.

Tempy. Eng. Sub-Lieutenant, R.N.V.R.

James R. Brown.
Peter Caton.
George L. Elliott.
Bruce Fleming.
John J. Fuller.
Frederick Hall.
James Hogg.
Hugh Lang.
Archibald MacElwee.
Charles J. McKelvey.
John McVicar.
Albert G. G. Maskell.
Ernest E. Midgley.
Stephen J. Moorhouse.
George J. Newlands.
John Rush.
John Shaw.
William Smith.
Frederick W. Stone.

Tempy. Assist Engineer, R.N.R.

Samuel P. Trounson.

Assistant Paymaster.

Harold R. Gore Browne.
Charles H. Doubleday (act.)
Maurice P. Dymocke.
John C. Hart.
Edwin K. Odam.
John P. Rising
Albert D. Stallard (act.)
Lewis R. Tippen.

Assistant Paymaster, R.N.R.

Gilbert M. Ingmire.

Tempy. Assis. Paymaster, R.N.R.

Freund Beaumont.
Thomas B. Brooks.
Harold V. Coombes.
Alexander K. Johnston.
Raymond A. Liversidge.
William G. Macgilp.
Bernard C. C. Newbery.
Thomas H. Noble.
Mark L. O'R. Nugent.
John R. Ormerod.
Harry H. Palmer.
Joseph J. Pearce.
Edgar S. Price.
Raymond A. P. Warlters.

Tempy. Second Lieutenant R.M.

Edward G. Abelson.
Harry C. Brown.
Cecil R. Burton.
Alfred H. Chapman.
Lancelot J. A. Dewar.
William C. A. Elliott.
James Fielding
Charles H. Kearney.
Charles W. Martin.
Alan A. Okell.
Alexander M. Sandison.
Frank Savage.
John W. Somerville.
Louis M. Stokes.
John Swale.
Henry E. R. Upham.

Carpenter Lieutenant.

Benjamin J. Richards.

Chief Gunner.

George F. Collingwood.
Joseph Elliott.
William C. Hunt.
William G. Jones.
Henry W. Lawrence.
Edwin H. Neale.
George Needley.
Frederick S. Scott.
Edmund Sims (retd.)
Albert E. Sturt.

Chief Boatswain.

George Ford.
Frederick Luker.
Frederick H. Mansbridge.
James Mitchell.

Chief Carpenter.

Frederick N. Barber.
William J. Ford (retd.)
William C. Geaton.
Robert Isitt.
Thomas E. J. McCarthy.
James M. Richards.

Chief Artificer Engineer.

John Corner.
Joseph Farrar.
John E. Gifford.
Albert Wilkes.

Gunner.

George Barratt.
Percy Bonneywell (act.)
George Borthwick.
George W. Bradshaw.

The Navy's Immortal Names

Mark W. Cameron.
Alfred Cherry.
Alfred J. Colton (act.)
Arthur Cox (act.)
Frank Ellis.
David Fernie.
William T. Gale.
Herbert H. Gandy (act.)
Herbert Godbehere.
Sidney H. Herlihy.
John P. Hutchings.
William R. Jackett.
John Jackman.
Herbert J. Jennings.
Charles J. Jones.
George A. King.
George R. Kinnear.
Albert G. N. Livermore.
Charles McCarthy (b)
William A. Morrell.
Stephen Munnelly.
Joseph Oates.
Thomas O'Brien.
Michael O'Halloran.
Ernest J. Read.
Henry Riggs.
William R. Roberts.
Donald Simpson.
William G. S. Sledge.
Walter G. Stocker (act.)
Arthur L. Sutton.
William G. Taylor.
Joseph S. M. Uffen.
Albert T. Walker (act.)
William V. Wright.
John J. Young.

R.M. Gunner.

Charles Catley.
George H. Field.
John H. Goss.
Albert E. Nixon.

Boatswain.

Joseph Crabb.
William T. Donovan (act.)
Thomas J. Eustis.
John Gray
William J. Grier.
William T. D. Hancock.
Robert P. Hunnings.
Arthur L. Lilley.
Edward Penny (retd)
Herbert Pratt.
William G. K. Trewin.
Patrick Welton.

Signal Boatswain.

William Baker.
James Crook.
Robert M. Hook.
Michael Kearns.
Percy Meal.
Arthur J. Mortieau.
Arthur W. Phillips.
William F Raper.
Henry H. Rowe.

Skipper R.N.R.

George W. Baldry.
John Barron.
William G. Bowles.
James Butler.
Wilkinson Cappleman.
William Christian.
Ronald R. Digby.

George Gibson.
Montague E. A Gulliver.
William H. Hodgman.
George Mellership, D.S.C.
Gerard Miles.
Albert V. Potter.
Lewis Whyte.
George W. Woodhouse.

Tempy. Skipper, R.N.R.

John Abrams.
Thomas R. Agnew.
George Anderson.
Frederick R. Beckett.
Arthur Bedford.
Henry Belton.
Samuel Blissett.
William Bruce, D.S.C.
Samuel R. Burwood.
Charles A. Campbell.
Alexander Carroll.
Henry Collins.
Albert E. Cook.
Thomas A. Cook.
John Coull.
Thomas Dales.
Thomas Donaldson.
Robert Duthie.
George Findlay.
David Fouquet.
Edward Garrod.
Alexander Geddes.
George Geddes (a)
George Geddes (b)
Robert E. George.
John Grant.
Thomas Grinlaw.
John High.
George E. Hitter.
Charles Holden.
James F. Howlett.
Robert G. Hurren, D.S.C.
Thomas H. Kay.
Horace Kemp.
Alfred G. Kippin.
Frederick W. Limbrick.
George W. Lincoln.
Philip Mason.
James Mitchell.
Alexander Mowat.
William Murray.
George Noel.
Owen L. Owens.
Robert E. Page.
Harry W. Pearce.
Isaac Pearce.
Thomas G. Phipps.
Josiah Pratt.
George H. Preston.
George B. Pulford.
Allan McD. Ramsay.
John A. Rayner.
Archibald M. Radmore.
Charles Slapp.
Alfred Thomas.
Herbert E. Thompson.
Albert True.
Henry E. Walker.
Francis J. Williams.
William J. Winchester.
John Wood.
Herbert J. Woolnough.
Silvanus E. Worth.
James Wright.

Warrant Telegraphist.

Henry Arberry.
Harry Burnell (act.)
Edwin Dymott.
Ernest Kemp.
James Moran.

Temp. Warrant Telegraphist, R.N.R.

Thomas G. Barron.
Richard J. Thompson.
Jack Wade.

Carpenter.

William Johns.
Ernest H. Mortimer.
William J. Pearne.
George T. Stallard.
Thomas A. Walls, D.S.C.
Arthur Wright.

Warrant Officer.

William Reynolds (act.)

Warrant Officer, 2nd Grade, R.N.A.S.

Ernest W. Wescomb.

Artificer Engineer.

John C. R. Blampey.
George K. Brown.
Frederick J. Clark.
Thomas Cole.
Herbert E. Denham.
Frederick W. Edwards (act.)
Benjamin G. Evans.
Cuthbert A. T. Fincken.
James Finlay (act.)
Sydney Fisher.
Frederick C. Fry.
William G. Fuller.
Matthew B. Hobson.
Allan J. Hurst.
Michael J. Lambe (act.)
Albert Middleton (act.)
William G. H. Pike.
Charles E. Rees.
Harold Scott.
Albert Smith.
Harry Southon.
John R. Vickery.
James Woodrow.

Warrant Mechanirian.

Arthur E. Stone.

Warrant Electrician.

Arthur Beales.
Laurence Gatt.
Edwin G. Goad.
Arthur C. Worthington.

Warrant Engineer, R.N.R.

Peter Fisken.
George M. Hunter.

Tempy. Warrant Engineer, R.N.R.

Thomas H. Roberts.

Head Schoolmaster.

George McNamee.

The Navy's Immortal Names

Midshipman.

Charles A. J. Acland-Hood.
Mark Austen.
The Hon. Bernard M. Bailey.
Anthony E. Baldwin.
Edwin R. Bates.
Leonard J. Bidwell.
Douglas A. C. Birch.
Stuart B. N. Bolton.
Kildare H. Burrowes.
Walter S. Burt.
Adair M. G. Campbell.
William F. R. A. Cooper.
Henry P. C. Cotton.
Richard B. Croft.
Archibald W. Dickson.
Richard F. Durlacher.
Humphrey M. L. Durrant.
William N. Eden.
James A. C. Forbes.
Robin G. B. Giffard-Brine.
Denis G. A. Goddard.
William L. Griffith.
Meynell O. Hanwell.
Malcolm A. M. Harris.
Trevor G. L. Hayles.
Cuthbert A. Hill.
Edward T. Hodgson.
George Hopcroft.
Charles R. Longley.
Philip R. Malet de Carteret.
Griffith C. L. Owen.
Ernest C. Peirson-Smith.
Alexander P. Roberton.
Robert Roxburgh.
John M. Shorland.
Herbert A. Snead-Cox.
Edward R. Snow.
Cyril H. G. Summers.
Henry N. A. Taylor.
Denzil C. Tudtall.
Henry J. Tuson.
Percy A. W. Wait.

Tempy. Proby. Flight Officer.

Howard E. Grundy.
Joseph L. Lavigne.
William G. Parry.
Weston W. Pitt.
Randolph H. Seed.
Kenneth Stuart.
Francis H. Y. Titcomb.

Midshipman, R.A.N.

Joseph Mack.

Midshipman, R.N.R.

Bernard W. Davy (proby.)
Edmund E. Fellowes (proby.)
John A. G. Kanaar (proby.)
Thomas Smith.
William R. Sowden (proby.)
Francis R. J. Toughill (proby.)

Tempy. Midshipman, R.N.R.

Robert McD. Auld.
George A. Burkill.
Reginald A. Cotter.
Eric J. Davis.
Harold V. Guest.
William P. Hesketh.
Alfred G. Larking.
Charles A. E. Tucker.
Clement S. B. Mallet.
Archibald C. R. Williams.

Midshipman, R.N.V.R.

Geoffrey T. F. Tothill

Clerk.

Cyril H. Adams.
Ralph T. Butler.
Alan J. Hay.
John W. Powell.

Bandmaster, R.M.

John W. Newton.

JANUARY, 1916.

Anderson, James, Sea. R.N.R. (New.)
Bennett, Samuel, Sapper (R.M.)
Hines, Frank Aubrey, C.P.O.
Jane, Harry, Dckhd. (R.N.R.)
Mason, Septimus. Ld. Tr. (R.N.R.)
Moore, George Henry, A.B.
Nears, Albert, A.B.
Pottinger, Alfred, Ld. Sea.

FEBRUARY, 1916.

Allen, Patrick, A.B.
Angel, Geo. Fredk., Pte. (R.M.L.I.)
Bain, Duncan, Sea. (R.N.R.)
Bates, Henry, A.B. (R.N.V.R.)
Batty, James, Engineman (R.N.R.)
Beckett, James, W/T Op. (R.N.R.)
Belcher, Edwin, C.P.O.
Bennett, Clarence, Sto. 2.
Betts, Ernest John Wm., A.C.
Blakeley, James, Sto. 1.
Blowers, Albert Fredk., P.O. 1.
Byrne, Matthew, Sea. (R.N.R.)
Cain, Charles, Sea. (R.N.R.)
Campbell, Alex., A.B. (R.N.V.R.)
Chammings, Ernest, Ld. Sto.
Colwill, Samuel, Ch. Shipwright.
Congdon, Reginald, A.B.
Cook, George, Sto. P.O.
Cornwell, Albert, A.B.
Crisp, William, Dckhd. (R.N.R.)
Davies, George, Sto. 1.
Dawe, William Hy. Sea. (N.R.N.R.)
Dickinson, George, En. (R.N.R.)
Docherty, John, A.B.
Dundas, Alexander Herman, Ld. S.
Earl, William, Sto. 1.
Flaherty, Joseph, Ld. S. (R.N.R.)
Foad, Sidney John, A.B.
Fraser, Duncan, Sto. 1.
Freeman, Horace James, A.B.
Garvie, Geo. Robert, A.E.R.A. 4.
Gee, Frederick William, A.B.
Gillard, James, Sec Hd. (R.N.R.)
Glue, Alfred, Pte. (R.M.L.I.)
Goodfellow, Rob., E.R.A.I. (R.N.R.)
Green, Arthur Fredk. E. (R.N.R.)
Griffin, James Watson, Ord S.
Hennessey, Garrett, Sto. 1.
Horne, Leonard, Pte. (R.M.L.I.)
Hunt, Maurice, Sea. (R.N.R.)
Iles, Samuel Charles, Sto. P.O.
Jackson, Arthur, Sig.
Keast, William George, Sto. P.O.
*Keefe, James, Sergt. (R.M.L.I.)
King, Wm. David, A.B. (R.N.V.R.)
Laing, Alex., Sea. (R.N.R.)
Lamb, George Wm., Pte. (R.M.L.I.)
Land, Daniel, Ord. Sea.
Leaver, Wm. John, E.R.A.3.
Lee, Fred Gordon, Of. Std. 3.
Leigh, John Edward, Shipwright 1.
Leyland, Albert John Thos., Sto.1.
Lloyd, Albert James, Boy 1.
Loader, Albert, A.B.
McColl, John, Sto. P.O.
McDiarmid, Robert, C.E.R.A.
Macdonald, A. M., E.R.A. (R.N.R.)
Mahoney, Michael, Sea. (R.N.R.)
Meadway, Cecil Harold Ern., Sto.1.
Miller, Edward, P.O.1.
Mills, Geo. Herbt., A.B. (R.N.V.R.)
Moss, William John, Sto.2.
Mugford, Nathan, Sea. (N.R.N.R.)
Murray, Albert Edward, Of. Std. 3.
Murrell, Percy, Sea. (R.N.R.)
Neale, Ted, Sto.1.
Newbiggin, Alex. M., Sig. (R.N.V.R.)
Noble, David, A.B.
Norman, Frederick, Sto.2.
Organ, Evan Thomas, Sto.2.
Pavey, Thomas Edward, Sto.2.
Pearse, Fredk. Richard, Sto.1.
Pearse, John, Sto.1.
Phillips, Robert John, Ord. S.
Pomery, William Henry, Ld. Sto.
Porter, Gordon, Boy 1.
Pridham, William Francis, Sto. P.O.
Prince, William Everard, A B.
Pyne, John, Sto. P.O.
Raeburn, James, Sto.1.
Randall, James Wm., Act. Ld. Sto.
Roach, Ernest Walter, Of. Cook 2.
Roberts, Harold Fernley, Boy 1.
Roberts, Peter, Sto. P.O.
Rowe, Harry Thos., Sh. Std. Assist.
Smith, Charles Sidney, Ld. Sig.
Stevenson, Jack Ern., Pte. (R.M.L.I.)
Stone, Sidney Ernest, A.B.
Style, William Charles, A.B.
Sutherland, Joseph, Sea. (R.N.R.)
Taylor, Fredk. J., Trm. (R.N.R.)
Taylor, Thomas, Sto.1.
Thomas, Joseph Norman, Sto.1.
Tuck, William, Sto.2.
Turley, Bertie, Ord. Sea.
Unwin, James Wm., Pte. (R.M.L.I.)
Waddingham, James, Pte. (R.M.L.I.)
Ward, Geo. E., Deckhd. (R.N.R.)
Warring, James Albert, Sto. P.O.
Specially Entered Mercantile Crew.
Baker, Godfrey Ernest, Fireman.
Bone, Thomas, Greaser.
Broughton, Joseph, C.M. & Jnr.
Brown, Albert, Trimmer.
Dickinson, Thomas. Fireman.
Edmonds, Samuel Herbert, Storekpr.
Eyers, Bertie, Trimmer.
Fielder, Robert, Baker.
Green, W. Clifford, Electrician.
Hallett, Frank, Greaser.
Harper, Albert, Assistant Baker.
Harris, Archibald, Fireman.
Hewitt, James, Trimmer.
Hooper, Albert, Fireman.
Horner, Charles, Fireman.
Hutley, Walter, Fireman.
Kirwan, Thomas, Fireman.
Light, Arthur H., Trimmer.
Longmaid, Richard W., Trimmer.
Lunnon, Thomas, Greaser.
Lynskey, John, Steward.
Miell, George, Fireman.
Pagella, Francis, Steward.
Read, John, Steward.
Riley, Alfred Valentine, Steward.
Routledge, William, Fireman.
Sandford, John, Fireman.

The Navy's Immortal Names 9

Tanner, Frederick, Fireman.
Temple, George F. S., Chief Steward.
Thornhill, Wm. Richard, St. & Pan.
Williams, Robert, Third Cook.
Wilton, Henry, Greaser.
Wyles, Alfred, Trimmer.

MARCH, 1916.

Aldred, Albert, Sto.1.
Allbones, Geo. Wm., En. (R.N.R.)
Angus, Alexander, En. (R.N.R.)
Anthony, John Edwin, Tmr. (R.N.R.)
Arnold, William James, P.O.
Atkinson, Henry Warkman, A.B.
Bailey, Wm. Alf., Sig. (R.N.V.R.)
Bass, Isaac (alias Bastarrechea), E.R.A.2.
Bassett, John Thomas, Ld. S.
Baxter, Forbes S. Dckhd.. (R.N.R.)
Beard, Leonard George, A.B.
Bennett, John, A.B.
Bennett, William, Act. Ld. Sto.
Benson, Geo. Walter, S.H. (R.N.R.)
Bessant, Albert A., Dckhd. (R.N.R.)
Bibbey, Henry Lace, Sto.1.
Biddlecombe, Frank, Air. Mech.1.
Bonner, Wm. Arthur, Act. Ld. Sto.
Boon, George W., Dckhd. (R.N.R.)
Borman, Ch. Richard, Cook (R.N.R.)
Brown, Ernest Samuel, Sto. 1.
Brooks, Charles Wal., Sto. (R.N.R.)
Buchanan, Philip E.R.A. (R.N.R.)
Burnett, Forbes Reid, En. (R.N.R.)
*Burrows, Allan, A.B.
Carpenter, Alec, Ld. Tel.
Chadwick, Alfred Samuel David, A.B.
Chandler, Reg. Alfred, Ord. Tel. (R.N.V.R.)
Charters, Robert, Dckhd. (R.N.R.)
Chinn, Robert Leonard, Sto.1.
Christie, William, Dckhd. (R.N.R.)
Clifton, Thomas, Sec.hd. (R.N.R.)
Clisham, T. A., Dckhd. (R.N.R.)
Connolly, Cornelius, Sto.1.
Cooke, Jesse, Gunner (R.M.A.)
Coultas, Charles, En. (R.N.R.)
Coulter, Wm. J., Tmr. (R.N.R.)
Cowburn, Francis Garrett, Sto. P.O.
Crawford, Alexander, Tmr. (R.N.R.)
Cullen, Murray, Sig. Boy (R.N.R.)
Dale, Alan Denzil, Sto.1.
Davis, Fredk. William, E.R.A.4.
Denney, Alfred, Tmr. (R.N.R.)
Deves, George Edward, Sto.1.
Donne, Augustus, A.B. (R.N.V.R.)
Egan, Frederick, A.B.
Faulkner, Ernest, A.B.
Fitzwater, Samuel D. M., E.R.A.3.
Flack, Arthur James, Ld. Sig.
Ford, Albert Edward, Ld. Sto.
Forrest, John, Deckhd (R.N.R.)
Fowler, John, Sec. Hd. (R.N.R.)
Gange, Edwin Wallace, A.B.
Gilchrist, Bert., Ld. Sig. (R.N.V.R.)
Goff, George, Sto.1.
Greep, Samuel, Sea (R.N.R.)
Hall, Frederick, Cook (R.N.R.)
Harvey, Wm. Saul, En. (R.N.R.)
Hawke, Walter Hubert, Ld. S.
Higgins, Owen, Tmr. (R.N.R.)
Howes, Alfred C., Deckhd. (R.N.R.)
Ireland, James H., En. (R.N.R.)
Jones, William, En. (R.N.R.)
Keat, Henry, Ld. S.
Kelley, William Luxton, Sto.1.
Kerswill, Cuthbert Henry, A.B.
King, Char.. R., Deckhd. (R.N.R.)

Kingcome, Howard William, Sig.
Kirby, Thomas Arthur, A.B.
Lane, Joseph Frederick, Sto.1.
Lefever, James, A.B.
Lewis, James, A.B. (R.N.V.R.)
Lorimer, Thomas, Tmr. (R.N.R.)
Lovell, Victor H. C., C.E.R.A.2.
Lynch, Thomas, A.B.
McDowell, William, Ld. S.
McKinnon, Duncan, Dckhd. (R.N.R.)
McPhail, John, Deckhd. (R.N.R.)
Maeers, Harry, A.B.
Main, Daniel, Dckhd. (R.N.R.)
Martin, Norman, E.R.A.4.
Moody, Edward, Sto.1.
Moore, George Frederick, Sto.1.
Morris, Ernest Richard, C.E.R.A.
Oakley, George, Sto. P.O.
Oates, Charles John, A.B.
Overbury, Thos. W., Dkhd. (R.N.R.)
Owen, Arthur Robert, P.O.
Parker, William, A.B.
Farrell, Charles, C.E.R.A.2.
Pendred, Alfred Joseph, P.O.
Periott, Albert, A.E.R.A.4.
Pilbeam, Arthur Edmund, P.O.2.
Powell, Robert Albert, Act. Ld. Sto.
Proffit, Charles M., Deckhd. (R.N.R.)
Rice, Cecil Frank, E.R.A.4.
Robertson, Peter, Sec. Hd. (R.N.R.)
Rogers, Richard Henry, P.O.
Russell, A. Hy., Deckhd. (R.N.R.)
Scarlett, Edward, E.R.A.1.
Sewell, Walter Henry, A.B.
Shell, Adam, Deckhd. (R.N.R.)
Shepherd, William Edwin, Boy Tel.
Skinner, William Fruin, C.P.O.
Smails, George Oswald, En. (R.N.R.)
Smith, Alfred Ern., Deckhd. (R.N.R.)
Smith, David B., Deckhd. (R.N.R.)
Smith, Ernest, Sto.1.
Smith, Henry M., En. (R.N.R.)
Taylor, Stephen Thomas, Sto.1.
Thirlwell, Arthur Robert, A.B.
Tomlinson, Thos, Deckhd. (R.N.R.)
Trendell, Frederick Arthur. B.
Turner, James, Sec. Hd. (R.N.R.)
Turner, W. Thos., Deckhd. (R.N.R.)
Ulph, Frederick Thomas, Sto.1.
Watson, Charles E., En. (R.N.R.)
Watts, William John. Sto.1.
White, Edward Louis, P.O.
White, John Alfred, Shipwright 2.
Wicks, J. F., Act. Bom. (R.M.A.)
Willcox, Ernest, Sto.1.
Wilson, Robert Hopkins, E.R.A.3.
Witchell, Walter, Sto.1.
Wood, George, Deckhd. (R.N.R.)

Specially Entered Mercantile Crew
Chaplow, William C., Fireman.
Davis, John, A.B.
Piper, R. A., A.B.

APRIL, 1916.

Adams, John Russell, Sto.1.
Ahern, Michael, Deckhd. (R.N.R.)
Bacon, Henry Sabin, Ld. S.
Baldry, Arthur Frederick, A.B.
Ball, Alfred, P.O.1.
Barber, Henry, Deckhd. (R.N.R.)
Barton, Joseph, Pte. (R.M.L.I.)
Batho, Arthur William, Of. Std. 3.
Batter, Fredk. Edgar, Pte. (R.M.L.I.)
Beard, Robert, Tmr. (R.N.R.)
Bewers, Wm. J. Cornelius, Ch. Sto.
Binding, Ernest, A.B. (R.N.V.R.)

Bird, F. A., Deckhd. (R.N.R.)
Blundell, George Henry, Boy 1.
Bonnamy, Ernest Arthur, Ld. S.
Brewer, James William, Sto. 1.
Brodrick, Percy James, Sto.1.
Brooks, Robert J., Sec. Hd. (R.N.R.)
Bull, Charles, A.B.
Burton, John Ed., En. (R.N.R.)
Butchart, J. R., Dckhd. (R.N.R.)
Calder, William Petrie, P.O.
Cameron, Duncan, Tmr. (R.N.R.)
Campbell, Hugh, Tmr. (R.N.R.)
Carey, Geo. C., A.B. (R.N.V.R.)
Carter, Fred, A.E.R.A.4.
Chalk, Alexander, Sea. (N.R.N.R.)
Chapman, P. J., En. (R.N.R.)
Cheston, Herbt. A., P.O. Mec.
Clark, Thomas Alfred, Of. Std. 3.
Coleman, Jabez, Sto. 1.
Conroy, John, Sto. 1.
Cooke, Charles S., Dckhd. (R.N.R.)
*Cotton, Charles S., Dckhd. (R.N.R.)
Cowie, Alexander, Sec. Hd. (R.N.R.)
Culley, Ben. Alf., Tmr. (R.N.R.)
Curtis, Ernest H., Of. Cook 1.
Dadford, Charles Herbert, Sto. 1.
Dumelow, William Henry, Sto. 1.
Durrant, Charles, Cook (R.N.R.)
Dwyer, James, Sto. 1.
Eadie, John, Deckhand (R.N.R.)
Elligott, William, Sea. (R.N.R.)
Elliott, Thos. L., En. (R.N.R.)
Elliott, Wilfred, C.E.R.A. 2.
Ferguson, John, Ld. Tmr. (R.N.R.)
Flynn, Patrick, Sto. 1.
Frederick, S. O., A.B. (R.N.V.R.)
Frost, Charles Albert, P.O.
Gafer, Wm. James, En. (R.N.R.)
Gardner, William Richard, Boy Ser.
Gay, William James, Sea. (R.N.R.)
Gibson, Robert A., Deckhd. (R.N.R.)
Goodwin, Reg. John, Pte. (R.M.L.I.)
Gould, Edward, Tmr. (R.N.R.)
Grimble, William, Sea. (R.N.R.)
Hammond, John A., En. (R.N.R.)
Harlow, Thos. W., Deckhd. (R.N.R.)
Harris, Henry, Deckhand (R.N.R.)
Harvie, Frederick, Sto. 1.
Hayes, Jeremiah, Sea. (R.N.R.)
Hayward, George John, Sto. 1.
Hazleton, Harold, Boy Tel.
Hensley, Fredk. Henry, Sto. 1.
Higman, William John, Sto. P.O.
Hingston, R. Henry B., Sto. 1.
Hollis, Wm. Thos., A.B. (R.N.R.)
Hood, Charles Robert, A.B.
Horn, Percy A., En. (R.N.R.)
Hoskin, John Cleve, Sto. P.O.
Howard, Edward Albert, A.B.
Howe, Sidney, Gun. (R.M.A.)
Hunt, Ernest William, P.O.
Hutt, Alfred Thomas, A.B.
Innes, Alexander, En. (R.N.R.)
Irvine, J. Robt., Deckhd. (R.N.R.)
Jecock, George Webster, A.B.
Jelf, Ernest Samuel, Ld. S.
Johnson, Ernest, Sec. Hd. (R.N.R.)
Jones, J. L., Sec. Hd. (R.N.R.)
Justice, James Ed., Of. Std. 2.
Key, Alf. Thos., Sh. Std. Assist.
Lambert, John. W., En. (R.N.R.)
Langridge, George, C.P.O.
Larcombe, Robert, P.O. Tel.
Larke, James Hy., Tmr. (R.N.R.)
Lawrence, James John, Cooper
Loades, Frank, Deckhd. (R.N.R.)
Lynch, Alfred, Of. Std. 2.
Lyons, George Jack, Sto. P.O.

*MacCutcheon, William, L.C.C.
McKay, William, Deckhd. (R.N.R.)
Mackie, John J., Tmr. (R.N.R.)
McLeod, Donald, Sea. (R.N.R.)
McKury, John, Deckhd. (R.N.R.)
Maher, Joseph, Tmr. (R.N.R.)
Mann, Thomas Edwin Seal, Ord. S.
Manship, J. Wm., Sec. Hd. (R.N.R.)
Mathers, C., Dckhd. (R.N.R.)
Mercer, Thomas, Sto. 1.
Merritt, John Edward Mark. A.B.
Mersey, Ed. J., Deckhd. (R.N.R.)
Micallef, Luigi, Of Ch. Cook.
Miller, Donald, Deckhd. (R.N.R.)
Moore, John Thomas, A.B.
*Moses, James Blackler, Sto. 1.
Nazer, Fredk. J., Deckhd. (R.N.R.)
Neil, Fredk. Robert, Cook's Mate.
Nettleship, Ed. J., Deckhd. (R.N.R.)
Newman, William John, A.B.
Norfor, Geo. A., Deckhd. (R.N.R.)
Norton, Harold Frank, A.B.
Nunn, Arthur, Of. Std. 1.
Oakes, Stanley L., Sea. (R.N.R.)
*Odell, George, A.B.
Organ, Fredk. John, E.R.A. 3.
Packham, Percy Albert, Boy 1.
Payne, Wal. T., Deckhd. (R.N.R.)
Pearce, Thomas George. A.B.
Potter, Fred, Of. Std. 2.
Power, James Aloysius, A.B.
Prin, William, Deckhd. (R.N.R.)
Puckhaber, Herbt. Alb. Victor, P.O.
*Raybrook, Ernest, Sto. 1.
Rayer, Arthur, Ld. Sto.
Regan, Edward Felix Owen, A.B.
Rivett, Albert J., Deckhd. (R.N.R.)
Robson, Thomas, Tmr. (R.N.R.)
Rook, William, Ld. Sto.
Rose, William, A.B.
Rostron, John H., Pte. (R.M.L.I.)
Rowse, Colley Wm., Sto. 1.
Sherrit, D. A. L., Deckhd. (R.N.R.)
Sinclair, James, Deckhd. (R.N.R.)
Skinner, William Hy., Act. Ld. Sto.
Skoyles, Henry Thomas, A.B.
Sluman, Samuel, P.O.
Smith, John, Sto. 1.
Smith, Thos. Ed., Tmr. (R.N.R.)
Smyth, Laurence, Sea. (R.N.R.)
Steer, Harry, Deckhd. (R.N.R.)
Stewardson, R., Deckhd. (R.N.R.)
Stratford, Sidney, P.O.
Symons, Reg. James M., Ld. Sto.
Taylor, Alex. C., Tmr. (R.N.R.)
Thain, Wm. S., Sec Hd. (R.N.R.)
Todd, John Ernest, A.C.
Tooley, Alfred J., Deckhd. (R.N.R.)
Trebble, John, A.B.
Turner, Charles A., Of. Cook 3.
Urquhart, Colin, Deckhd. (R.N.R.)
Vincent, Frank, Ld. S.
Walsh, Richard, Sto. 1.
Waugh, Robert Wm. G., Ld. S.
Wells, Arthur Spencer, Boy 1.
West, J. A, Deckhd. (R.N.R.)
Wilkes, Arthur Thomas, A.B.
*Williams, Albert, Sea. (R.N.R.)
Williams, Alf. John D., Boy 1.
Woodland, Wm. Robert, E.R.A. 2.
Wooler, Harry D., Ld. S. (R.N.R.)
Wright, Ernest, Deckhd. (R.N.R.)

Specially Entered Mercantile Crew.
Ayscough, J., Fireman.
Banks, Alfred, Fireman.
Banks, George, Fireman.

Best, William, Fireman.
Briscoli, A. J., Steward.
Dee, W. V., A.B.
Dick, T. H., Fireman.
Lee, H., A.B.
Lowe, George, Fireman
Major, F. U., A.B.
Penge, A. E., Fireman.
Reed, A., Greaser.
Robinson, F., A.B.
Scarborough, W., A.B.
Smith, Thomas, Assistant Steward.
Stafford, H. H. M., Second Mate.
Stewart, James, A.B.
Toms, George. Fireman.
Wallis, D. G., Fireman.
Warne, William J., A.B.

JUNE, 1916.

Aburrow, John A., Of. Cook, 1.
Adams, Harold, Sto. 1.
Adams, Harry E., En. (R.N.R.)
Adams, Walter Frederick, A.B.
Adams, W. H., Pte. (R.M.L.I.)
Adams, William, Sto. P.O.
Alger, J. Thos., Deckhd. (R.N.R.)
Allen, Ernest Alfred, Act. Ld. Sto.
*Allen, Frank, Cook's Mate.
Allen, Fred Henry, Boy 1.
Allen, George William, Ord. S.
Allen, William Brinkley, Sto. 1.
Allen, Wm. James, Act. Ld. Sto.
Allison, Samuel, A.B.
Allum, George Adin, A.B.
Allwork, Wyndham J., Ord. Sig.
Alner, William Arthur, Sto. 1.
Ames, Ernest B., C.P.O.M.
Amey, Nelson Percival, Sto. 1.
Amey, Wm. John, Pte. (R.M.I..I.)
Amos, Joseph James, Ord. S.
Amy, Wm. M., Shipwright 1.
Andrews, Henry Thomas, A.B.
Anthony, David, Sto. P.O.
Antram, Fredk. Harry, Ld. Sig.
Archibald, Henry, Sto. 2.
*Arda, Edward, Ord. S.
Atkins, Arthur Russell, A.B.
Attwood, Charles Ernest, A.B.
Attwood, George, Cook's Mate.
Austin, Albert, Ld. S.
Austin, Albert Ed., Of. Std. 2.
Austridge, John, A.C.P.O. (Tel.)
*Avery, Sidney James, A.B.
Ayling, George, Sto. 1.
Ayre, John, C P..
Ayton, George, Ord. S.
Ayton, William Charles, Sto. 1.
Axe, Thomas Albert, P.O.
Bagg, Edwin Albert, A.C.P.O.
Baggs, Reginald Geo. R., Ld. S.
Baggs, Walter, Of. Std. 2.
Bagley, John Luke, Sto. (R.N.R.)
Bailey, Charles, P.O.
Bailey, George, Ld. Sig.
Bailey, Henry Richard, A.B.
Bailey, John Charles, Of. Std. 3.
Bailey, Robert James, C.P.O.
Bailey, Sidney Herbert, A.B.
Bainbridge, William, Sto. 1.
Baines, Samuel, Sto. 1.
Baird, Robert Sydney, Of. Std. 2.
Baird, William Alfred Ellison, A.B.
Baker, Albert Edward, Sto. P.O.
Baker, Fredk. Geo., Pte. (R.M.L.I.)
Baker, Percy, A.B.
Baker, Thos. J., En. (R.N.R.)

Ballard, Robert George, Bks.
Banbury, Frederick James, Sto. 1.
Bandcolt, Isaac, A.B.
Banfield, William, Sto. 1.
Banwell, Ernest John, Sto. (R.N.R.)
Barbeary, Harry, A.B.
Barber, John William, A.B.
Bargen, Thomas Edward, Boy 1.
Barlow, Timothy, Yeo. Sig.
Barnard, J. E. T., Painter 1.
Barnes, Edward, Boy 1.
Barnett, John, A.B.
Barrow, Norman, E.R.A. 4
Bartlett, George, A.B. (R.N.V.R.)
Bartlett, George, Mechanician.
Bartlett, Victor Geo. Shipwright 2.
Barton, Edward, A.B.
Barwick, John, Hy., Tmr. (R.N.R.)
Bass, William George, Ld. S.
Bateman, Harvey, Ld. Cook's Mate.
Bateman, John Fredk., Boy 1.
Bates, Arthur, Sailmaker.
Bates, Bernard Emile, P.O.
Bates, George, Act. Ltd. Sto.
Baulk, Arthur Stanley, Ord. S.
Baynes, George Albert, Sto. 1.
Bean, Fredk. Walter, Act. Ld. Sto.
Bear, John Victor, Ld. Tel.
Bearman, Walter John, Ch. Arm.
Beattie, James, A.B. (R.N.V.R.)
Beck, Geo. Edward, Sto. P.O.
Beechy, John Wm. H., Sto. 1.
Beeson, Leonard Joseph. D., A.B.
Beeston, George Stanley, A.B.
Belchamber, Edward, Act. Ld. Sto.
Bell, William Arthur, Sto. 1.
Bellchamber, Sydney Percival, A.B.
Belsham, John Henry, A.B.
*Belson, Alfred E., Gun. (R.M.A.)
Benneton, James, Sapper (R.M.)
Bennett, Albert, Ord. S.
Bennett, Lester S., A.B. (R.N.V.R.)
Bennett, William Henry, Ld. S.
Bentley, Frederick, Sto. 1.
*Berghe, Charles. Wireman 2.
Berry, Thomas, Ord S.
Bettis, James Francis, Sto. 1.
Beversley, Robert, A.B.
Bex, William Luke, Boy 1.
Biles, Edgar Luffman, Sig.
Billingham, Bertie Sto. 1.
Billins, William Ed., Cor. (R.M.L.I.)
*Binstead, Charles Henry, A.B.
Bird, David Samuel, P.O. Tel.
Birkitt, H. D., Act. Ld. Sto.
Birtles, Robert, Boy 1.
Bishop, George Samuel John, A.B.
Bishop, Joseph John, C.E.R.A. 1.
Bishop, Thomas William, Sto. 1.
Black, Robert, Sto. P.O.
Blackburn, Frank, Ord. S.
Blackshaw, George, Boy 1.
Blake, Edward A. J., Sto. 1.
Blake, Walter Harold, A.B.
Blakey, James Henry, Ord. S.
Blandford, Sidney Tom, Act. Ld. Sto
Blewitt, Samuel, Sto. 1.
Bloor, Thomas. Boy 1.
Bobbett, John Joseph, Ld. S.
Boley, Wilfred, Sto. P.O.
Bonass, George Edward, A.B.
*Bond, Arthur William, A.B.
Bond, George H., Ship's Cor. 1.
Bone, Charles Robert, Sto. 1.
Bonnick, Henry Alex. W., A.B.
Boraman, Richard, Pte. (R.M.L.I.)
*Borg, Spiro, Of. Cook, 3.

The Navy's Immortal Names

Borne, James Herbert, Ld. S.
Bostock, John, Sto. 2.
Bosworth, M. J., Of. Std. 3.
Boughen, Walter, A.B.
Boulton, Frank T., Act. Ld. Sto.
Bowen, Geo. William, Sto. 1.
Bowes, John, A.B.
Bowman, Albert Charles, Ch. Sto.
Bowpitt, George Edward, A.B.
Bragg, James Albert, E.R.A. 3.
Brain, William Henry, Boy 1.
Brandon, James Thomas, Ld. Sto.
Bray, Harry, A.B.
Bridger, Ernest Reginald, Ld. S.
Bridges, Wm. F., Pte. (R.M.L.I.)
*Briggs, Henry Charles, S.B.A.
Brindley, Joseph Sto. 1.
Briscoe, John, Sig. Boy.
Broad, William Hugh, Sto. 1.
Brockhurst, J. Wm., Sto. 1.
Brockway, Alf. G. C., Boy Tel.
Brogden, William Richard, A.B.
Brotherton, William B., A.B.
Brown, Aaron, Sto. 1.
Brown, Frederick Wm., Sto. 1.
Brown, John Thomas, A.E.R.A. 4.
Brown, Robert, Sto. 1.
Brown, William, Sto. (R.N.R.)
Browning, Harry, A.B.
Bruce, Sydney Alexander, A.B.
Bruton, Arthur, A.B.
Bryan, G. W., Act. Ld. Cook's Mate.
Buckenham, J. T., Pte. (R.M.L.I.)
Buckingham, Ralph Angus, A.B.
Buckley, John Eustace, Ord. S.
Bucklow, Geo. J. C. A., A.B.
Bunting, Thomas, A.B. (R N.V.R.)
*Burden, Ernest, Sto. 1.
Burnitt, Harry, Ord. Tel.
Burfoot, Charles N. N., A.B.
Burgess, William Herbert, Sto. 1.
Burman, George, A.B.
Burman, William, En. (R.N.R.)
Burren, George Percy, E.R.A. 3.
Burrows, Alfred, Boy 1.
Burton, James R., Act. Ld. Sto.
Burton, Moses, Sto. 1.
Bury, Frederick, Ld. Sig.
Busby, Walter Sydney, A.B.
Butcher, William, Sea. (R.N.R.)
Butler, Frederick Edward, Sto. 1.
Butler, George, Pte. (R.M.L.I.)
Byng, James, Mech.
Byrne, Frederick, A.B.
Cadby, Wm. Geo., Ship's Cor. 1.
Cadman, Charles. Sto. 1.
Cake, William, Sto. P.O.
Cameron, Wm. James, Sto. P.O.
Campbell, Alex., E.R.A. 1. (R.N.R.)
Canham, Archibald Geo., Ord. Tel.
Cannon. James Alfred, Ord. S.
Card, Wilfred Geo. B., Ord. S.
Cardno, John, Tmr. (R.N.R.)
Carmichael, James, Sto. 1.
Carrick, William, Ord. S.
Carson, James Albert, Sto. 1.
Carter, C. C. W. A., Ord. S.
*Carter, Harry, Pte. (R.M.L.I.)
Carter, Thomas Edwin, P.O.
Carvin, Charles, Sea. (R.N.R.)
Cashe, Frank, A.B.
Chadwick, Robert, A.B. (R.N.V.R.)
Chalmers, George Doig. A.E.R.A. 4
Chambers, Arthur H., Shipwright 2.
Chapman, C. F., Pte. (R.M.L.I.)
Chapple, Charles Henry, A.B.
Cheater, Harry James, A.B.

Chesworth, Alexander, P.O.
Child, Albert Ernest, Cooper.
Child, Charles Henry, Sto. P.O.
Chitty, Albert, Sto. P.O.
Chiveralls, Wm. Fredk., Of. Std. 2
Chown, Charles Henry, Sto. P.O.
Clack, Frederick, P.O.
Clark, Alex., Sec. Hd. (R.N.R.)
Clark, Joseph Arthur, Sto. 1.
Clark, William, Master-at-Arms.
Clark, William Edward, P.O.
Clarke, Fredk. John, Sto. 1.
Clarke, William Henry, A.B.
Clay, Francis. Ld. Sto.
Clayton, William, P.O. 1.
Cleary, Frank William, Sto. 1.
*Clements, Albert Edward, A.B.
Clifford, John, Ord. S.
*Clover, Walter, Sapper (R.M.)
Clynes, James, Ord. S.
Cobb, George James, A.B.
Cocks, Thomas, E.R.A. 2.
Cole, Arthur, Ch. Sto.
Cole, Francis Geoffrey, Tel.
Coleman, William Thomas, A.B.
Collar. Alfred V., Dckhd. (R N.R.)
Colleck, Percy, Sig. Boy.
Collecott, Frederick George, Boy 1.
Collett, John William, Ord. S.
Collier, Stanley, A.B.
Collingwood, Robert, Pte. (R.M.L.I.)
Collins, Charles William, Sto. P.O.
Collins, George Samuel, Ld. S.
Collins, Samuel, Ld. S.
*Collins, Wm. A., Pte. (R.M.L.I.)
Collis, William Thomas, A.B.
Coltart, Alfred Stamper, Sto. P.O.
Colwell, Ernest Alfred, Sig. Boy.
Compton, A. W., Pte. (R.M.L.I.)
Connolley, Patrick, Sto. (R.N.R.)
Connor, Patrick, Sto. 1.
Constable, L. A. L., Ord. S.
Coggan, John, Sto. 1.
Cooke, Horatio Nelson, Plumber.
Coombs, Joseph Reginald, P.O.
*Cooper, Alfred, Of. Std. 3.
Cooper, George Henry, Boy 1.
Cooper, Theodore George, Ld. S.
Cooper, William Leonard M., A.B.
Cope, Herbert, A.B.
Copson, George Henry, Sig.
Corney, Sidney George. A B.
*Cornwell, John Travers, Boy 1.
Coulter, William, Sto. 1.
Coulthard, Thomas, A.B. (R.N.V.R.)
Courquin, Edmund, Sto. 1.
Couture, Robert Edward, Sto. 1.
Covey, Jesse Edmund, Ld. Sto.
Cowen, Alexander Webster, Ld. S.
Cowley, George William, Sto. 1.
Cox, Bertie, A B.
Cox, Henry, C.C.
Cox, James, Ch. Sto
Cox, John Christopher, Ld. Sig.
Cox, John William, Sto. 1.
Cox, S., Pte. (R.M.L.I.)
Coyle, John, Sto. 1.
Cracknell, Frederick Charles. A.B.
Cragg, Arthur Harold, Sto. P.O
Craner, Geo. E., Pte. (R.M.L.I.)
Cribben, Alf. Albert, Sap. (R.M)
Crompton, Edward, Pte. (R.M.L.I.)
Cross, Andrew, Pte. (R.M.L.I.)
Crowe, Albert Edward, Sto. P.O.
Cuff, W. N., Act. Cor. (R M.L.I.)
Cullen, Thomas 'Henry, Ord. S.
Cullington, F. T., Sig. (R.N.V.R.)

Cumming. Donald, Ld. Sig.
Cummings, Walter Henry, Sto. 1.
Cuningham, Henry, Boy 1.
Cunningham, James, Sea. (R.N.R.)
Cunnington, Albert Edward, A.B.
Dabbs, Herbert, C.P.O.
Dabinett, C. H., Pte. (R.M.L.I)
Dagwell, Frank, Sto. 1.
Dalby, Joseph, Sto. 1.
Dallas, Wm. A. E., Pte. (R.M.L.I.)
Dalton, Reginald Claude, S.B.A.
Daly, Patrick Joseph, A.B.
Daniells, Edward, Pte. (R.M.L.I.)
Daniells, Harry, Sto. P.O.
Danskill, P. Geo., En. (R.N.R.)
Darby, Wm. George, Bks.
Davey, Ernest, A.B.
Davis, Arthur. Sig. Boy.
Davis, A. Ed., Dckhd. (R.N.R.)
Davies. George, Sto. P.O.
Dawson, A. W. A., Ship's Std.
Dawson, J. B., Pte. (R.M.L.I.)
Dean, Frank P., Sergt. (R.M.L.I.)
Dear, Thomas, Ld. Sto.
Delderfield, James Geo., Sto. 1.
Dempsey, Daniel Hartpole, Ord. S.
Denham, Herbert Smith, E.R.A. 1.
Dennis, Frederick, A.B.
Dennis. Harry, Sto. 1.
Dennison, Norman, Pte. (R.M.L.I.)
*Dent, William, E.R.A. 1.
De St. Croix, Walter Bertram. P.O.
Deveson, Percy William. Ord. S.
Devlin, James, Sto. (R.N.R.)
Diamond, Charles Henry, P.O.
Diaper, Henry, P.O. 1.
*Dinn, George Ernest, Ld. Sig.
Docherty, Robert, Sto. (R.N.R.)
Dodd, Henry W. C., Act. Ld. Sto.
Dodd, Percy Richard Lewis, A.B.
Dodd, William. Sto. 1.
Doherty, Michael, Sto. (R.N.R.)
Dominy, C. J., Pte. (R.M.L.I.)
Donnelly, George Nicholson, A.B.
Donnelly, Joseph, P.O.M.
Dooley, Septimus. Pte. (R.M.L.I.)
*Dore, Herbert F., Pte. (R.M.L.I.)
Doughty, Fredk. J., Act. Ld. Sto.
Dove, George William. Ord. S.
Dowland, Sidney, Pte. (R.M.L.I.)
Downer, R. Ernest, Ld. Cook's M.
Downes, John, 3rd Writer.
Downie, Thomas Arthur, Sto. 2.
Dowson, Joseph, Sto. 1.
Drew, Albert E., Pte. (R.M.L.I.)
Drummond, Frederick Geo., Sto. 1.
Drury, John Wm., Act. Ld. Sto.
Duff, Peter, Sto. (R.N.R.)
Duffin, Andrew Joe, Sto. 1.
Duffield, Percy, Sto. 1.
Duncan, Alex. James C., P.O.
Dunford, Frederick, Sto. P.O.
Dunn, Leslie Geo. Arthur, Tel.
Durrant, Charles, Dckhd. (R.N.R.)
Durrant, George Wynn, P.O. Tel.
Durthie. Robert, En. (R.N.R.)
Dyer, George, P.O.
*Dymond, Edward, Sto. 1.
Eades, James, A.B.
East, Ernest Richard, Sto. 1.
Eccleston, Norman, Sto. (R.N.R.)
Edwards. Cl. H., Ld. Tel.
Edwards, I. S. R. R., Pte. (R.M.L.I.)
Edwards, Richard George, A.B.
Edwards, William Henry. A.B.
Elder, Robert Craig, Act. Sto. P.O.
Ellcome, Isaac; Sto. 1.

*Ellis, Sidney Thomas, A.B.
Ellis, William John, Of. Std. 2.
Ellison, Victor, Sergt. (R.M.L.I.)
Elmer, George Jonathan *alias* Kennett, George, Ch. Sto.
Elson, R. M., Sh. Std. Assist.
Eneas, William J. B., A.B.
English, Francis James, Sig.
English, John, Ld. Sto.
Epps, John Fredk., Sto. P.O.
Evans, George, P.O.
Evans, George Mafeking, Boy 1.
Evans, Joseph, Mech.
Evans, Percy, Pte. (R.M.L.I.)
Evans, Robert, A.B. (R.N.V.R.)
Evans, William Arthur, Boy 1.
Everett, Walter, Ord. S.
Ewing, Walter, A.B.
Eyre, James, Sto. 1.
Falconer, David Alex., Sto. 1.
Fallowfield, Robert, Act. Ld. Sto.
Farindon, Arthur, A.B.
Farlow, Charles A. Alfred, A.B.
Farthing, W. T., Pte. (R.M.L.I.)
Faulkner, Charles Norman. P.O.
Fealey, Harold Colin, Ord. S.
Fear, Edmund C., Pte. (R.M.L.I.)
Fellows, Benjamin, Sto. 1.
Fenton, John, A.B. (R.N.V.R.)
Ferguson, Charles G., Cook (R.N.R.)
Ferrett, S. J. F., Yeo. Sig.
Ferrett, T. C. J., Pte. (R.M.L.I.)
Ferriman, Sydney Clement, A.B.
*Ferry, George Henry, Sto. 1.
Field, George, Sto. 1.
Fielding, Percy, Sig. Boy.
Fielding, William, Sto. 1.
Figgins, Henry Josiah, A.B.
Finch, Albert John, Sto. 1.
*Fisher, Brice, Pte. (R.M.L.I.)
Fitch, John W. N., Ord. Tel.
Findlay, Alexander, A.B.
Fitzgerald, John Henry, Sto. 1.
Flack, Frederick, Sto. 1.
Flanagan, Bernard, Boy 1.
Flavin, Michael, Ld. S.
Flay, William James, Sto. P.O.
Fleming, Martin Thomas, Sig.
Flexman, Ernest F., Ld. Sig.
Foney, Francis John, Ord. S.
Forrest, George Henry, A.B.
Forrest, John, Sto. 1.
Foster, Edward, Boy 1
Foster, Edward, Sto. 1.
Foster, Job, Sto. 1.
Fothergill, Edwin, A.B.
Foulger, Ernest William, A.B.
Fox, Ernest A., Sto. 1.
Fox, Joseph, Sto. 1.
Francis, Charles Robert, A.B.
Fraser, Cecil Samuel, A.E.R.A. 4.
Freeman, William Arthur. A.B.
Freeman, Wm. C., Pte. (R.M.L.I.)
French, Ernest George, Sto. 1.
Friend, John Edward, Sto. 1.
Fromm, Harold Leslie, Ld. S.
Freyr, John Cecil, A.M.
*Fuller, Harry G., Of. Cook, 3.
Fuller, Maurice Harold, E.R.A. 2.
Gaby, George, Tel.
Gale, Herbert Arthur, Sto. P.O.
Gale, Samuel S. C., Boy Tel.
Gale, William, A.B.
Galloway, J. K., E.R.A. 1. (R.N.R.)
Gander, James, Ld. Sto.
Gardner, Walter F., Boy Tel.
Garner, Frederick John, P.O.

Garrett, Samuel, Boy 1.
Garrett, William John, Cook's M.
Garsden, J. W. V., E.A. 2.
Garton, Fredk. J., Sto. P.O.
Gates, George, A.B.
Gausden, William W., Sto. 1.
Gearns, John, Boy 1.
Geary, William R. M., A.B.
Gedge, Edward, A.B.
George, Edward Cecil. A.B.
Geraghty, John, Ste. 1.
Gerrard, Frederick Eustace, Sto. 1.
Gibbs, William, Sto. P.O.
*Gibson, John, Ld. S. (R.N.V.R.)
Gibson, William, A.E.R.A. 4.
Gildersleeve, Henry, Boy 1.
Giles, Harry, E.R.A. 2.
Gisborn, J. F., Pte. (R.M.L.I.)
Glover, Frank, Sto. 1.
Glover, George Albert, P.O.
Goble, A. E., Pte. (R.M.L.I.)
Goddard, Cephas, E.R.A. 2.
Goddard, John, Sto. 1.
Godfrey, Joseph, A.B.
Godward, Cyril Francis, A.B.
Gomm, Charles, A.B.
Goodfellow, Bertie, Cook's Mate.
Gordon, John E. G., Sto. 1.
Gore, Richard, Ch. Sto.
*Gower, John, Pte. (R.M.L.I.)
Gowney, D. E., Act. Bom. (R.M.A.)
*Graham, Walter, Sto. 1.
Grace, William E., Act. Ld. Sto.
Grant, Samuel, Sto. P.O.
Gray, Alf, H. E., Of. Cook, 1.
Green, Alfred Henry. A.B.
Green, George, Sto. 1.
Green, John Joseph, A.B.
Green, Joseph, Sto. 1.
Greenan, John, Sto. (R.N.R.)
Greetham, George Edward, Sto. 1.
Greenwood, Benjamin Thos., Boy 1
Greenwood, Ernest, Sto. 1.
Gregory, Thomas Henry, P.O.
Grehan, Hugh, E.R.A. 3.
Grieg, Wm F., Dckhd. (R.N.R.)
Grier, Archibald James, A.B.
Griffiths, Reginald Maynard, A.B.
Grinham, George Rowley, A.B.
Grinyer, Charles Edmond, Sto. 1.
Groombridge, Victor Albert, P.O.
Groom, David George, A.B.
Groves, Albert John, P.O.
Groves, Thomas Percy, A.B.
Groves, William Ernest, A.B.
Guest, Thomas Edwin, Sto. 1.
Gumbrell, Arthur, A.B.
Hacken, Robert, Pte. (R.M.L.I.)
Haddon, Albert Ernest, A.B.
Haddow, W., Pte. (R.M.L.I.)
Hadlow, Thomas George, A.B.
Hagan, John, Sto. 2.
Hagan, John Sidney Henry, C.C.
Haines, Albert Wm., Shipwright 2.
*Hainsworth, Albert, A.B.
Hainsworth, Henry, A.B.
Hall, Albert George, Sto. 1.
Hall, Edwin Ernest, Sto. 1.
Hall, Frederick, Sto. 1.
*Hali, George, A.B. (R.N.V.R.)
Hall, George Henry, C.E.R.A. 1.
Hamlin, Charles Harold, Ld. Sto.
*Hampson, Abraham, Air Mech. 1.
Handy, Joseph, A.B.
Hansell, Albert, Sto. 1.
Harden, Charles, Sto. 1.
Hardie, John C., Sto. (R.N.R.)

Harding, John, Ld. S.
Hargreaves, Joseph H., Sto. 1.
Harman, David John, Boy 1.
Harper, A. H., A.B. (R.N.V.R.)
*Harper, George, Sea. (R.N.R.)
Harper, Samuel Mungford, A.B.
Harris, George, Act. Sto. P.O.
Harris, Herbert Thomas, Ld. Sto.
Harris, Langton William, Boy 1.
Harris, Samuel John, Ld. S.
*Harris, Thomas James, Sto. 1.
Harrison, Edwin G., Ch. Sh. Cook.
Harrison, Ernest, Dckhd. (R.N.R.)
Harrison, John Wm., Pte. (R.M.I.)
Harrison, Thomas, Ld. S.
Harriss, John Thomas, Sto. P.O.
Hart, Clifford G. C., A.E.R.A. 4.
Hart, George, Sto. 1.
Harvey, Charles Edward, P.O.
Harvey, John Robert, Boy 1.
Harwood, Thomas Joseph, Sto. 1.
Hatch, Walter, Ord. S.
Hawkins, E. A., Act. Ld. Sto.
Hawkins, Edward, Sto. 1.
Hawkins, John Charles, Sto. P.O.
Hawkins, Walter, Pte. (R.M.L.I.)
Hayes, Harold James, Sto. 1.
Hayes, William, C.E.R.A. 1.
Hayler, John, Ld. Sto.
*Haynes, William, Gun. (R.M.A.)
Hazel, Sydney, Ord. S.
Head, Geo. Henry, Pte. (R.M.L.I.)
Hearne, R. J. B., Of. Cook, 2.
Heath, Maurice, Sto. 1.
Heath, Reginald C., Cook's Mate.
Hedges, E. Thos., Wireman, 2.
Heggs, Joseph Herbert, Ord. S.
Heming, Lewis George, P.O.
Heneage, Vincent, Boy 1.
Hennessay, James Edward, Boy 1.
Henry, Thos. E., Pte. (R.M.L.I.)
Henwood, David, Ld. Sto.
Herage, Edwin Frank, A.B.
Heron, Joseph, Sto. 1.
Heseldine, R. W., A.E.R.A. 4.
Heselwood, Robert, Sto. P.O.
Hewitt, Frank, Ord. Sig.
Hick, Harold, Pte. (R.M.L.I.)
Hickman, Albert R. S., A.B.
Hicks, W. H. C., Pte. (R.M.L.I.)
Higgins, Edward, Ld. S.
Higgins, Frank, Sig. (R.N.V.R.)
Higgs, Herbert Thomas, A.B.
Hill, Edward Thomas, Sto. 1.
Hill, Joseph, A.B.
Hill, John James, Sto. 1.
Hill, Joseph, A.B.
Hill, R. J. H., Sergt. (R.M.L.I.)
Hill, Robert, Sto. 2.
Hills, Herbert George, Boy 1.
Hinchliffe, A. J., Ord. Tel. R.N.V.R.
Hiscock, Albert Edward, Tel.
Hiscock, George M., E.R.A. 2.
Hiscock, John T., Pte. (R.M.L.I.)
Hoare, O. C. William, A.B.
Hobbs, Frank Norman, Ord S.
Hobbs, George, Ord. S.
Hockless, Leslie Hector, P.O.
Hodgkinson, John, Boy 1.
Holbrook, William, P.O.
Holden, John, Ord. Sig.
Holder, George W., Sto. 1.
Hollamby, F. H., Cor. (R.M.L.I.)
Holland, Alfred Percy, Act. Ld. Sto.
Holland, Charles Wm., E.R.A. 3.
Holley, James Frederick, A.B.
Hollis, Samuel, Pte. (R.M.L.I.)

Holloway, Frank, Pte. (R.M.L.I.)
*Holloway, William, A.B.
Holtom, Henry E., Of. Std. 2.
Homer, Charles, P.O.
Hook, Fredk. C., Pte. (R.M.L.I.)
Hooker, B. H., Shipwright, 2.
Hookham, Bert, Ld. Sto.
Hope, Charles, Pte. (R.M.L.I.)
Horrocks, Arthur Walker, A.B.
*Horwood, F. J., Cook's Mate.
Houghton, George, A.B.
Howard, Temple, Pte. (R.M.L.I.)
Howard, William, Ld. S.
Howden. Wm. H., Pte. (R.M.L.I.)
Howe, Herbert Wilfred, Sig. Boy.
Hoyland, Arthur, A.B.
*Hubbard, John, Pte. (R.M.L.I.)
Hudson, George Frederick, A.B.
Hudson, John Henry, Ord. Tel.
Hudson, S. A., Pte. (R.M.L.I.)
Huggett, Ernest, Sig.
Hughes, Frank, Sto. 1.
Hughes, Harry J. J., Sto. P.O.
Hughes, Reginald Lawrence, Boy 1.
Humphrey, Alick, Ch. Sto.
Humphrys. Herbert, Boy 1.
Hunt, Charles, Sto. 1.
Hunt, Frank, Pte. (R.M.L.I.)
Hunt, William, Sto. 1.
Hunter, Edward, Sto. 1.
Hunter, Ed. Fry, A.B. (R.N.V.R.)
Hunter, Francis Arthur, A.B.
Hurd, C. Thos. Wm., Ld. Tel.
Hurr, E. Iohn, En. (R.N.R.)
Innoles, Wm. F., Pte. (R.M.L.I.)
Ireland, Henry Amos, Boy 1.
Ireson, William, Boy 1.
Isherwood, Fred, Boy 1.
Ives, John, Pte. (R.M.L.I.)
Jackson, Francis Frederick, A.B.
Jackson, John K., Ord. S.
Jackson, William B., Sto. 1.
*James, George, Of. Cook 3.
James, Gilbert, Boy 1.
Jamieson, William, Sto. 1.
Jarvis, Bertie, Sto. 1.
Jarvis, George, Sto. 1.
Jarvis, John Edward, Sto. 1.
Jeffries, Henry, Boy 1.
Jeffery. Clarence, Ld. Sto.
Jelley, Thos. Wm., Of. Cook, 1.
Jenkins, Stanley Arthur, A.B.
*Jenkins, William Henry, Act. Mech.
Jenkins, William Thomas, A.B.
Jenner, Frank James, Act. Ld. Sto.
Jennings, George Thomas M., A.B.
Jenoure, Arthur S., Ld. Sig.
Jewitt, Lewis, Cook's Mate.
Joels. E. James, Bug. (R.M.L.I.)
Johnson, Alfred George, A.B.
Johnson, Ernest, Tmr. (R.N.R.)
Johnson, William Edward, P.O.
Johnston, James, Sto. 1.
Johnston, John, Sto. (R.N.R.)
Johnstone, Leo Henri, A.B.
Jones, Albert Henry, Sto. P.O.
Jones, Colin, M.A.A.
Jones, Evan. Boy Tel.
Jones, Harry, Pte. (R.M.L.I.)
*Jones, Henry, P.O. 1.
Jones, Hugh Thompson, A.B.
Jones, John, Sto. (R.N.R.)
Jones, John, A.B.
Jones, Thomas, Sto. 1.
Jones, William, Sto. 1.
Jones, William Gratton, Sto. 1.
Jordan. A. H., Pte. (R.M.L.I.)

Kavanagh, A., Pte. (R.M.L.I.)
Kebble, Arthur Alfred, Ld. S.
Keeping, Thomas Leonard, P.O.
Kelly, Herbert Thomas, Ld. Sto.
Kelly, John, Sto. (R.N.R.)
Kelsey, Ernest. Dckhd. (R.N.R.)
Kendall, Arthur, Sto. 1.
Kennedy, John, A.B.
Kenny, Thomas, Sto. (R.N.R.)
Kent, William, Sto. 1.
Kenward, Henry Charles, Sto. 1.
Kidd, James, A.B. (R.N.V.R.)
Kimber, W. J., Sig. (R.N.V.R.)
King, Ezra Carrol, Ld. Tel.
Kirby, Henry, Sto. P.O.
Kirby, James Henry, Sto. 1.
Kirby, William John, Sto. P.O.
*Kirkpatrick, John Nicol, Ord. S.
Kirkup, Frederick, Sto. 1.
Knight, Geo. H., Act. Ld. Sto.
Knight, Harry, Pte. (R.M.L.I.)
Knight, John A. Ed., Sto. 1.
Knight, John George, A.B.
Knowles, Arthur, Ld. Sig.
Knowlson, J. W., Cook's Mate.
Labram, T. C., A.B. (R.N.V.R.)
*Lacey, James Fred, Boy 1.
Lacey, Reginald, Ld. Sto.
Lacy, Arthur, E.R.A. 4.
Laishley, Albert, A.B.
Laity, Joseph Henry, P.O.
Lamb, Joseph Henry, Ord. Tel.
Lammas, Steven John, Sto. 1.
Lampard, Albert Edward, Ld. Sig.
Lampitt. John, A.B.
Lamy, Horace William, A.B.
Landy, Nicholas, Ord. S.
Langdown, Charles F., Sto. 1.
Larkins, Herbert, P.O.
Latter, William Thos, Ld. S.
Lattimore, George Charles, A.B.
*Law, Herbert, Ord. S.
Law, John, Sto. 1.
Lawler, William. Ord. S.
Lawler, William George, Boy 1.
Lawlor, Wm. Benjamin, Ch. Sto.
Lawrence, Leonard, Tel.
*Lay, Wm. H., Gun. (R.M.A.)
Leach, Thomas William. P.O.
Leader, L. J., Pte. (R.M.L.I.)
*LeCornu, Philip Renouf, A.C.
Ledger, Arthur Ernest, A.B.
Ledwood, John William, A.B.
Lee, Joe, Sto. 1.
Lee, William Henry, Sto. P.O.
*Lees, Robert, A.B.
Leonard, Jack, A.B. (R.N.V.R.)
Leslie, Fred Perkins, A.B.
Lever, George, Pte (R.M.L.I.)
Levett, Henry, E.R.A. 2 (R.N.V.R.)
Lewis, James Gregory, Sto. 1.
Lewis, John Henry, Sto. 1.
Lidbitter, Alfred Henry, Ch. P.O.
Liddell, Ernest, Dckhd. (R.N.R.)
*Liley, Ernest, A.C.
Lind, Charles Noel, Sto. 1.
Linden, Albert Edward, A.B.
Lipscombe, Charles Wm., Sto. P.O.
*Little, Joseph. A.B.
Little, R. T., Pte. (R.M.L.I.)
Little, William Bursell, A.B:
Littlewood, Hariph Reginald, A.B.
Livingstone, F., E.R.A. (R.N.R.)
Locke, Frank, Ld. Sto.
Locker, George William, Sto. 1.
Lockham, John Percy, Sto. 1.
Lockton, George, Sto. P.O.

Lockwood, John William, A.B.
Lovegrove, Thos Geo., Cook's Mate.
Lovely, R. H. W., Tmr. (R.N.R.)
*Lovett, George Henry, Sto. 1.
Loving, D. E., Dckhd. (R.N.R.)
Lowe, James, Sto. 1.
Lowe, Tom, Sto. P.O.
Lowe, Wilfred Chambers, Sto. 1.
Lowery, Harry, Sto. 1.
Loy, James Albert, A.B.
Lucas, George, Sto. P.O.
Lyfield, Albert George, Ld. S.
Lynas, Andrew, Ord. S.
Lynn, A. E., Pte. (R.M.L.I.)
*Mabbett, Frank, Pte. (R.M L.I.)
McAdam, William, Sto. 1.
McCall, Daniel, Sto. 1.
McConville, Thomas Farrel, Sto. 1.
McCormick, Thomas, Sto. 1.
McCrea, Harold George, Sig.
McDermott, Archibald. Sto. 1.
MacDonald, Angus, Dckhd. (R.N.R.)
*MacDonald, W. T., Pte. (R.M.L.I.)
McDonnell, Patrick, Sto. (R.N.R.)
McFarlane, Robert McRobbie, A.B.
McGarrigle, Daniel. Sto. 1.
McGarrive, Walter, A.B. (R.N.V.R.)
McGowan, Francis George, Ord. S.
McGowan, Henry, Pte. (R.M.L.I.)
McGrath, Henry, Sto. (R.N.R.)
MacGregor, John D., Ord. S.
McIntyre, Ad., A.B. (R.N.V.R.)
*McKay, David, A.B. (R.N.V.R.)
McKay, Robert, Dckhd. (R.N.R.)
McKenzie, James, Sea. (R.N.R.)
*Mackie, E., Pte. (R.M.L.I.)
*Mackie, R., A.B. (R.N.V.R.)
McLaren, James, Ld. S.
McLaughlin, John, Ld. S.
McLean, James, A.B.
MacLean, J. G., Ch. Writer.
McLoughlin, R. J., Sto. (R.N.R.)
McNeill, Robert, Sto. (R.N.R.)
McPherson, Alex. John, Sto. 1.
Mace, Herbert James, Ld. Sig.
Maddox, Frank Ladbroke, A.B.
Mallam, John, Sto. 1.
Mallard, John Arthur, Ord. S.
Mallett, H. F., Pte. (R.M.L.I.)
Malpass, Hezekiah, Sto. 1.
Manser, Fredk. S. J., Ld. S.
Mapp, William, Ld. Tmr. (R.N.R.)
Marchant, William Cecil A., A.B.
Mariner, Ernest, Pte. (R.M.L.I)
Marlow, Anthony, Sto. 1.
Marner, George, Ld. Sto.
Marshall, Arthur, Sto. 1.
Marshall, Bernard Percy, Sto. 1.
Marshall, Fredk. Geo., Ord. S.
Marshall, Geo. E., Pte. (R.M.L.I.)
Martin, Charles, Sto. 1
Martin, Geo. Fredk., Ship's Cook.
Martin, H. R., Sh. Std. Assist.
*Martin, Leonard J., Pte. (R.M.L.I.)
Martin. Robert Percy, A.B
Maskell, John E., A.C.E.R.A. 2.
Maslin, Arthur Lionel, Sto. 1.
Masters, Benjamin William, A.B.
*Matthews, Albert, Boy 1.
Matthews George Thos., A.S.P.O.
Matthews, Harry, Act. Ld. Sto.
Maxted, Harry, Sto. 1.
Maxted. John, Act. P.O.
May, Joseph Richard, Ld. Sto.
Mayhew. Geo. E., Pte. (R.M.L.I.)
Mead, William Thomas, P.O.
Medhurst, Charles Alfred, Sto. 1.

The Navy's Immortal Names

Melhuish, W. J., Pte. (R.M.L.I.)
Melton, Armine Edward, A.B.
Merritt, C. H., Sh. Std. Assist.
Merwood, Reginald, Act. 1d. Sto.
Metcalfe, George Harold, Ld. S.
Mew, Joseph, Pte. (R.M.L.I.)
Middleton, R. C., Sto. (R.N.R.)
Midgley, Samuel Percy, A.B.
Milford, Sidney, A.B.
Millar, Emil Gernies, Sto. 1.
Mitchell, Robert, En. (R.N.R.)
Mitchell, Sydney Coleman, A.B.
*Mitchinson, F., Pte. (R.M.L.I.)
Mitchner, Harry, A.B.
Mizen, Henry Albert, A.B.
Monier, Charles, A.B.
Monkhouse, Wm., Pte. (R.M.L.I.)
Moore, Fredk. Wm., E.R.A. 1.
Moore, George William, Sto. 1.
Moore, K. Alfred John, Boy Tel.
Moore, Richard, Act. Ld. Sto.
Morel, Louis Sidney Amedee, A.B.
Moreton, William Albert, Boy 1.
Morley, Arthur, Ld. Sto.
Morley, Henry Arnold, Sto. P.O.
Morphew, Geo. Adams, Elec. A. 3.
Morris, Edward Oswald, Sto. 1.
Morris, Frank S., Pte. (R.M.L.I.)
Morris, Fredk. A., Pte. (R.M.L.I.)
Morton, Arthur F., Pte. (R.M.L.I.)
Morton, Cyril Elston Andrew, Sto. 1.
Mottram, Jonathan Bonnar, Sto. 1.
Mould, Albert Charles, A.B.
*Mowatt, John, Sea. (R.N.R.)
Mudie, Douglas Blakely, Ld. S.
*Muir, William, Sto. (R.N.R.)
Mulcock, Arthur, A.B.
Mullen, Daniel, A.B. (R.N.V.R.)
Mullens, Fredk. C., Sto. P.O.
Mulvey, Peter, Sto. (R.N.R.)
Munday, James, A.B. (R.N.V.R.)
Munton, Albert, Sto. 1.
Murphy, Alfred, Dckhd. (R.N.R.)
Murray, John, Ld. S.
Musselwhite, H., Act. Ld. Sto.
Musson, Thos., Pte. (R.M.L.I.)
Nalborough, Arthur, A.B.
Naylor, Albert G. S., S.B.A.
Neeld, Albert William, A.B.
*Nelson, John W., A.B. (R.N.V.R.)
Newbegin, James, Sto. P.O.
Newman, Joseph, Sto. 1.
Newman, Victor Harold, A.B.
Newton, Walter Ernest, P.O.
Nicolson, Murdo, Dckhd. (R.N.R.)
Ninehan, W. E., Act. Ch. P.O.
*Niven, James D., A.B. (R.N.V.R.)
Nobbs, Albert, Sto. 1.
Noel, Harry, Sto. 1.
Nolloth, Joseph, Tmr. (R.N.R.)
Norfield, Thomas Albert, A.B.
Norrington, T. E., Act. Ld. Sto.
Norris, Allan Colquohoun, Sto. 1.
North, Arthur, Ld. Sto.
North, George, A.B.
Northcombe, W. W., E.R.A. 3.
Northover, Ernest, A.B.
Northover, Sidney James, A.C.
Novice, John Arthur Ld. S.
Nowland, Fred, Sto. 1.
Nye, Charles William, Sto. 1.
Nye, Percy James Peter, Sto. 1.
Oakley, James, Ord. S.
O'Connell, Albert Alfred, A.B.
Oliphant, Alexandra, Sto. 1.
Oliver, Fredk. Charles, E.R.A. 3.
Oliver, John, Sto. (R.N.R.)

Orchard, Thomas, Sto. 1.
Ormonde, William Arthur, Sto. P.O.
O'Shea, Michael, Dckhd. (R.N.R.)
Osmond, Albert Victor, Ord. S.
Oubridge, William Bertram, Ld. Sto.
Oulton, William Henry, Boy 1.
Owen, Frederick William, Sto. 1.
Owen, John Thomas, Sto. 1.
Owen, Norman, Pte. (R.M.L.I.)
Owen, W. P., Act. Sergt. (R.M.L.I.)
Page, John Herbert, A.B.
*Page, J. W., Cor. (R.M.L.I.)
Page, Thomas Leonard, A.B.
Palmer, George, C.P.O., Mech.
Pamplin, John Henry, alias Maggs, John Edward, Sto. 1.
Parfett, George James, A.B
Parham, Arthur, Sto. P.O.
Parker, George Henry, Sto. 1.
Parker, James, A.C.
Parkhurst, A. J., Sh. Std. Assist.
Parks, William, Sto. (R.N.R.)
Parsons, Harrie, Of. Std. 3.
Parsons, Stanley Charles, Sig.
Parsons, Wm. R, A B. (R.N.V.R.)
Pashley, Alfred Edward, Of. Std. 3.
Paton, David, Boy 1.
Pattenden, Albert, Act. Ld. Sto.
Payne, Archibald, Ord. S.
Payne, Harry, Ld. S.
Payne, Harry Edward, Sto. 1.
*Payne, R. W, Ld. Cook's Mate.
Payne, Thomas William, Ord. S.
Peake, Alfred, Sto. 1.
Pearce, A. J. J., Shipwright, 1.
Pearce, Charley, A.B.
*Pearce, Edward Thomas, Boy 1.
Pellett, Ernest Alfred, Ord. S.
Pell, George Alfred, Sto. 1.
Pengilly, Percy William, S.B.S.
Percy, J. R., Act. Ld. Sto.
Percy, Harold, Sto. 1.
Perkins, Charles Henry, Ord. S.
Perry, Duke, Act. Ld. Sto.
Perry, John Thomas S., Sto. 1.
Perry, P. E., Pte. (R.M.L.I.)
Pessell, Percy John, Ord. S.
Petch, Fredk., A.B. (R.N.V.R.)
Peters, Wm. R., Act. Ld. Sto.
Petrie, George, Dckhd (R.N.R.)
Pett, Fredk W. R., Ld. Sto.
Pettett, Edward, Sto. (R.N.R.)
Pettett, William James, Sto. (R.N.R.)
Phillips, Arthur, Ld. S
Phillips, Arthur Percy, Ld. Sto.
Phillips, Joseph, Sto. 1.
Piggott, Joseph, A.B. (R.N.V.R.)
Pimbley, John, Sec. Hd. (R.N.R.)
Pipe, Joseph Thomas, Sto. P.O.
Piper, Frank, Pte. (R.M.L.I.)
Plank, Wm., Shipwright, 1.
Plant, John Thomas, Sto. 1.
Pollard, James, Ch Sto.
Ponsford, Claude Henderson, A.B.
Ponting, Ernest Walter, Ld. Sto.
Porteous, Thos., A.B. (R.N.V.R.)
Porter, Allan James, Ld. S.
Potter, Frank, Boy 1.
Powell, John, Sto. (R.N.R.)
Powell, William George, A.B.
Powell, William George, Ord. S.
Pragnell, G. V., Pte. (R.M.L.I.)
Pragnell, Wm., Ship's Cor. 1.
Preece, Ernest James, Sto. 1.
Pritchard, Horace Edward, A.B.
Pue, James, Sto. 1.
Pullin, Alfred, Ch. Sto.

Purkiss, Stanley, Sto. 1.
Purnell, Edgar, Boy 1.
Purvis, George, Sto. 1.
Pyefinch, Edward Charles, Ord. Sig.
*Quick, Richard, Ch. Sto.
Quinton, William Edward, A.B.
Ragless, Percy James, A.B.
Rainey, Arthur, Sto. 1.
Ramsdale, Joseph, A.B.
Ramsey, Percy, A.B.
Randall, Albert Arnaud, A.B.
Randell, Gilbert, Sto. 1.
Rattray, Peter, Sto. 1.
Raven, E. G., Dckhd. (R.N.R.)
Rawlins, William Edward, A.B.
Raymond, Fredk. William, A.B.
*Rayner, Albert Robert, Ld. S.
Redfern, Thomas Henry, Sto. 1.
*Redmond, M., Pte. (R.M.L.I.)
Reed, George Edward. A.B.
Reed, Henry S., E R.A. 1.
Rees, William Hopkin, A.B.
Reeve, Geo. Edward, Yeo. Sig.
Reeves, Harry, Sto P.O.
Reid. William, L.-Cor. (R.M.L.I.)
Reilly, Arthur Edward, A.B.
*Rennie, George Macdonald, Boy 1.
Reynolds, George, Sto. 1.
Reynolds, Palmer, Sto. 1.
Reynolds, Sidney Henry, Boy 1.
Rich, John Llewellyn, Sto. P.O.
Richards, C. A., Sig. Boy (R.N.R.)
Richards, Charles William, Pte. 1.
Richards, Ernest, Pte. (R.M.L.I.)
Richards, John Phillips, Sto. 1.
Rigby, James Edward, Boy 1.
Riley, Ernest, Pte. (R.M.L.I.)
Riordan, Thomas Joseph, Boy 1.
Roberts, Albert Edward, Sto. 1.
Roberts, A. R, Sh. Std. Assist.
Roberts, Hugh, A.B
Roberts, Percy Bentley, C.A.
Robertson, G. H., Tmr. (R.N.R.)
Robertson, James Wallace, Sto. 1.
Robertson, William Harry, A.B.
Robey, William Charles, Ld. S.
Robinson, Arthur Frank, Sto. 1.
Robinson, Eric F. H., Ord. S.
Robson, Henry Albert, Sto. 1.
Rogers, Edward John, Sto. P.O.
Rogers, Herbert H., Elec. A. 3.
Rogers, John Fredk., Sto. 2.
Rogers, William, A.B, (R.N.V.R.)
Rogers, William Edwin, Sto. 1.
*Rolph, Fredk. C., Gun. (R.M.A.)
Rose, Harry D., En. (R.N.R.)
Rose, R. John, Pte. (R.M.L.I.)
Ross, Albert, Ord. S.
Rossiter, Thomas, Sea. (R.N.R.)
Rowell, William George, Sto. 1.
Rowland, George, Sto. 1.
Rowley, Joseph, Ch. Sto.
Royall, Frank, Sto. P.O.
Ruaux, Ernest William, Ld. S.
Rumbold, Edward Charles, Sto. P.O.
Russell, Fredk., Of. Cook, 1.
Ryan, Stephen, Sto. (R.N.R.)
Ryan, William, A.B.
Ryles, Matthew, Sto. 1
Saffery, H. T., Pte (R.M.L.I.)
Salisbury, W. H., E.R.A. 5.
Saloway, William Luke, Sig. Boy.
Sandom, G. C., Pte. (R.M.L.I.)
Sargent, John, Sto. 1.
Saunders, Arthur, Sto. 1.
Saunders, Ernest C., Act Ld. Sto.
Saunders, George Palmer, P.O. 1.

The Navy's Immortal Names

Scott, Frederick Charles, Ord. S.
Scriven, Thomas George, P.O.
Seamer, Edward Thomas, Ld. Sto.
See, C. Wm., Pte. (R.M.L.I.)
Selsby, Henry, Sto. P.O.
Semple, Robert, A.B (R.N.V.R.)
Sexton, R. P. A.. Sig. Boy.
*Seymour, Andrew, Pte. (R.M.L.I.)
Seymour, Herbert Joseph, A.B.
Shaill, Thomas Edwin, Boy 1.
Shanks, John, C.E.R A. 2.
Shanks, John, Sto. 1.
Sharp, W. H., Ch Sh. Cook.
Shaw, J. P.. Cor. (R.M.L.I.)
Shearman, Charles Newman, Sto. 1.
Sheath, Frederick, A.B.
Sheppard, Samuel A., Sto. P.O.
Shepherd, A W., Dckhd. (R.N.R.)
Shepherd, Fredk. Robert, Ord. S.
Shepherd, Samuel, Ld. Cook's Mate.
Shepherd, William, Ord. Tel.
Sherwin, Cyril Ernest, Tel.
Sheurer, Arthur, Sto. 1.
Shields, Walter, A.B.
Shillcock, Joseph R., Ld. S.
Shirran, James. Ld. Sto.
Shore, Austin, Sto. 1.
Short, William Henry, Boy 1.
Shott, Herbert, Sto. P.O.
Sidebotham, W., L.-Cor. (R.M.L.I.)
Silcock, Owen, Sto. 1.
Silk, Ernest Gibbs. Of. Std. 2.
Sills, Ernest Edward, Sto. 1.
*Simmonds, William Thomas, A.B.
Simmons, Charles, Sto. 1.
Simmons, John Fredk. C., Ld. S.
Sirdifield, James Thomas, Sto. 1.
*Sketchley, Thos. A. A.B. (R.N.V.R.)
Skinner, Robert William, A.B.
Skinner, William, Sto. 1.
Slater, Robert, Act. Sec. Hd. (R N R.)
Smalley, Wm., Sergt. (R.M.L.I.)
Smedley, Joseph Henry, Sto. 1.
Smith, Albert, Sto. 1.
Smith. Albert, Sto. 1.
Smith, Albert, Sto. 1.
Smith, Alfred, Pte. (R.M.L.I.)
Smith, Alfred George, Sto. 2.
Smith, Alfred Sidney, Sto. 1.
Smith, Benjamin, Mech.
Smith, Cecil George, Sto. 1.
Smith, Donald Augustus. A.B.
Smith, Ernest, Pte. (R.M.L.I.)
Smith, George Edwin, A.B.
Smith, George Sidney, Ld. Sto.
Smith, Geo. Wm., Of. Std. 3.
Smith, Henry, Sto. 1.
Smith, Henry William, Ord. S.
Smith, James, Sto. P.O.
Smith, Joseph, Ord. S.
*Smith, J. H. R., Ld S. (R.N.V.R.)
Smith, Walter, Sto. P.O.
Smith, William, Boy 1.
Snaith, William, A.B.
Snell, Samuel Solomon, A.B.
Snowden, James Nixon, Sto. 1.
Soanes, C. M.. A.B. (R.N.R.)
Sparkes, S. John, Pte. (R.N.R.)
Sparrow, W. C. J. J. B., Boy 1.
Spedding, Frederick. Cook's Mate.
Spencer, F. G., Elec. A. 3.
Spencer, Wm. E.R.A. 1.
Spiers, Oliver Austen, Sto. 1.
Spooner, J. W., Sec. Hd. (R.N R.)
Spowage, John, E.R.A. 2.
Squire, William Cecil, Sto. 1.
Stables, George, Sto. 1.

Stafford, William Ewart, Boy 1.
Stanley, Samuel, Sto. 1.
Starmore, Ernest Sidney, P O.
Stead, Edmund, Ord. Tel.
Stedman, Jack, Ord. S.
Steele, Cecil Thomas, A.B.
Stephen, George, Tmr. (R.N.R.)
Stephens, Stephen Walter, Boy 1.
Stephenson, C., Tmr. (R.N.R.)
Stephenson, Wm., A.B. (R.N.V.R.)
Stevens, Francis Harry, Sto. 1.
Stevens, Fredk. John, Sig.
Stevens, Richard R., Sto. 1.
*Stevenson, Ernest, Ord. S
Stevenson, William, Ld. Sto.
Stewart, Neil, Pte. (R.M.L.I.)
Stewart, Robert C , Sto 1.
Stokes, Fredk., Dckhd. (R.N R.)
Stott, John, A.B.
Strickland. R. A.. Ord. S.
Stringer, Alex. Douglas, Sto. 1.
Stringer, C. Thos., C.E.A. 2.
Stringer, Harold, Ord. 'S.
Stringer, James Edwin, A.B.
Stirling, E. J., Ld. Cook's Mate.
Stroud, Frederick Charles, A.B.
Stroud, R. E , Dckhd (R.N R.)
Stone, James, Ord. Tel.
Stott, Arthur, A.B.
Studley, Herbert A., Ord. S.
Such, George Henry, Sto. 1.
Suckley, Walter Victor, Sto. 1.
Swannell, Arthur F., Ord. S.
Sweetzer, H. D., Sto. 1.
Tailby, George Alfred, Boy 1.
Talmage, Jeremiah, Sto. P.O.
Tanner, R. Edwin, Ld. Tel.
Tapper, Stanley, Private.
Taylor, Ernest Edward, Mech.
*Taylor, George, A B.
Taylor, Harold de Putorn, P.O.
Taylor, John Albert, Sto. 1.
Taylor, John F., Yeo. Sig.
Taylor, Robert, Sto. P.O.
Terry, Alfred, A.B.
Terry, Percy Wm., Of. Std. 3.
Thackeray, Percy. Sto. 1.
Thomas, David, A.B.
Thomas, Thomas. A.B (R.N.V.R.)
Thompson, John Walace, A.B.
Thompson, R. A., Pte. (R.M.L.I.)
Thompson, William, Sto. 1.
Thornton, W. John, Of. Std. 1.
Thwaites, William Henry, C.P.O.
Tidey, S. W., Sig. (R.N.V.R.)
Tilbury, Wilfred, Pte. (R.M.L.I.)
Tilley, James, Sto. P.O.
Tilling, Henry Charles, Ch. Sto.
Tilling. John Charley, Ord. S.
Tipping, Edward, Sto. 1.
Tisson, Alfred Peter, A.B.
Titley, Alex. Storey, Sto. 1.
Tizard, P. L. E., L.-Sergt. (R.M.L.I)
Toone, Samuel, A.B. (R.N.V.R.)
Treffry, Frederick Charles, A.B.
Trickitt, Frederick, Boy 1.
*Trish, Thomas, A.B.
Trodd, H. V., Cor. (R.M.L.I.)
Trott, John Harry, Boy 1.
Troughton, Percy, Sto. 1.
Townley, Albert Edward, Sto. 1.
Tristram, William Joseph, A.B.
True, Edmund Bishop, Sto. 1.
Tuck, Charles E. A., Ord. S.
Tullock, James, A.B.
Tunnicliffe, James, Sto. (R.N.R.)
Turnbull, John, Sto. 1.

Turner, Arthur Robert, Boy Tel.
Turner, Augustus Wm., Sto. 1.
Turner, Ernest John, Ch. Writer.
Turner, Frank, Cor. (R.M.L.I.)
Turoer, Frederick Henry, Ld. Sto
Turrall, Charles William, P.O.
Twomey, Leo Joseph, S.B.S.
Twoomey, Patrick Joseph, A.B.
Upcraft, Alf. John, En. (R.N.R.)
Usher, P. Day, En. (R.N.R.)
Valenca, Emmanuel, Ord. S.
Varndell, Edward Henry, A.B.
Veale, Michael, Sto. (R.N.R.)
Verlander, George Charles, A.B.
Vince, Stanley John Herbt., A.B.
Vivash, Thomas Arthur, Ord. S.
Vivian, Reginald Claude, L. Tel.
Vyse, John, Sto. 1.
Wagstaff, Alfred Henry, Ld. Sto.
Waight, Fredk. E., Sto. P.O.
*Wainscoat, James Horace, Ld. S.
Waite, Albert. Ord. S.
Wakley, William James, Sto. 1.
Walden, Edwin, A.B.
Walker, Alex., Sto. (R N R.)
Walker, Arthur Edward, A.B.
Walker, William, Sto. 1.
*Walker, W. H , A.B. (R.N.V.R.)
Wallace, William Geo. P., A.B.
Waller, Bertram, Boy Tel.
Waller, Wm. J., Shipwright 1.
Wallis, John, Ld. S.
Walters, Charles C., Elec. A. 3.
Walters, Geo. J. C., Ld. Tel.
Warren, A. A E. W., Pte. (R.M.L.I.)
Warren, J. B., Sec. Hd. (R.N.R.)
Warrington, Robert, Ld. Sto.
Waterman, William F., Ld. Sto.
Waterman, W. G., Sig. (R.N.V.R.)
Waters, Charles, Pte. (R.M.L.I.)
Waters, Henry, A.B.
Watkins, Richard, Tmr. (R.N.R.)
Watthew, Francis Horace, A.B.
Watts, Archibald Grant, Ord. S.
Watts, Charles William, Sto. 1.
*Watts, Fredk. Wm , Cook's Mate.
Waugh, James, Sto. 1.
Wear, Thomas Anthony, Sto. 1.
Webb, William, A.B. (R.N.V.R.)
Webster, John, Ord. S.
Welsby, Walter, Boy 1.
Welsh, Sydney Augustus, A.B.
Wenham, W. F. J., Ld. S.
West, Charles, Sto. P.O.
Westnutt, Alfred, Pte. (R.M.L.I.)
Weston, William Henry, A.B.
Wheeler, Charles William, Boy 1.
Wheeler, Geo. Balford, Ld. Sto.
Wheeler, Wm A., Bug. (R.M.L.I.)
Whelan, Harry Augustus, Ch. Sto.
White, Benjamin, Ld. Sto.
White, Bertie, A.B.
White, Edward Charles, A.B
White, Ernest, A.B. (R.N.V.R.)
White, Frank, Sto. 1.
White, Fred. Sto. 1.
White, Frederick, Ld. S.
White, G. V., Of. Std. 1.
White, James, A.B.
White, John, Sto. 1.
White, William, Sto. 1.
White, William Edward, Sto. 1.
Whitfield, Wm. Geo., 2nd Cook's M.
Whitlock, Harry, Ld. S.
Whitney, Fredk. Wm., Sto. 1.
Whitworth, Jack, Sto. 1.
Wickens, T. J., Act. Ld. Sto.

The Navy's Immortal Names

Wicker, Richard Arthur, S.B.A.
Wiffen, David William, Sto. 1.
Wigfall, Tom, C.E.R.A. 2.
Wigg, William James, Ord. S.
Wilden, Godfrey Paul, A.B.
Wiles, Edward Alfred, A.E.R.A. 4.
Wileman, Harry William, Ld. Sto.
Wilkes, Richard Arthur, Sto. 1.
Wilkinson, Clarence W., E.R.A. 3.
Williams, Alfred, A.B
*Williams, Alfred Tom, S.B.A.
Williams, Charles, C.P.O.
Williams, Charles Alfred John, A.B.
Williams, George. Act. Ch. Sto.
Williams, Joseph George W., P.O. 1
*Williams, Richard, Sto. (R.N.R.)
Williams, William, A.B. (R.N.V.R.)
Williams, William, Sto. 1.
Wills, Wm. S., E.R.A. 2 (R.N.V.R.)
Wilmot, Percy James, Sig.
Wilson, Arthur, Ord. S.
Wilson, Benjamin James, Ld. Sto.
Wilson, Joseph, Boy Tel.
Wilson, Victor, Ld. Sig.
Wilson, William, S.B.S.
Wilson, William James, Sto. 1.
Withington, Clement, Sto. (R.N.R.)
Wood, Charles, Sergt. (R.M.A.)
Wood, Ernest, Sto. 1.
Wood, Frederick, A B.
Wood, George Obed. Ord. S.
Wood, James, Sto. 1.
Wood, William, Sto. 1.
Woodger, John Edward, Sto. 2.
*Wootten, J. E. G., Driver (R.M.A.)
Wright, Samuel R., Dckhd. (R.N.R.)
Wymer, Fredk. L. H., Boy 1.
Yeates, Charles H., Of. Std. 1.
Young, James Geo., Mech.
Ziething, Alex. E., Of. Cook, 2.

CIVILIANS.

Bartlett, Frank Hubert, Can. Man.
*Courtnell, Henry J., Can. Server.
Fleming, J. II., Can. Assist.
Fowler, Alfred, Can. Assist.
*Maydon, Ernest J., Can. Server.
Webb, John H., Can. Assist.

JULY, 1916.

Anderson, Wm., A.B. (R.N.V.R.)
Ayers, Albert Ernest, P.O.
Banks, Wm. Geo., Ld. S.
Bardwell, F. W., Pte. (R.M.L.I.)
Base, Martin, Sto. P.O.
Berry, James, Ld. S.
Blaydon, Charles, Sto. 1.
Brewer, Arthur, A.C.E.R.A. 2.
Bruce, Alfred, Tmr. (R.N.R.)
Burr, William, Ld. S.
Burt, P. L., Pte. (R.M.L.I.)
Caines, George William, A.B.
Chambers, Robert, A.B. (R.N.V.R.)
*Chapman, Hezekiah W., P.O. 1.
Cooke, George Matthew, Ld. S.
Cowie, James, Dckhd. (R.N.R.)
Cowie, William, Sec. Hd. (R.N.R.)
*Cox, Bernard, Sto. 1.
Creber, Charles, Sto. P.O.
Currie, J. Gray, A.B. (R.N.V.R.)
Curtis, Ernest Alfred, Ldr S.
Dalgleish, James B., Tel.
Denwood, Robert, E.R.A. 2.
Devine, Thomas, A.B.
Dixon, C. A., E.R.A. 1 (R.N.R.)

Doman, George, Sto. 1.
Donald, Alex., A.B. (R.N.V.R.)
Doran, J., Sergt. (R.M.L.I.)
*Drynan, Albert, Pte. (R.M.L.I.)
Duncan, R. D., Dckhd. (R.N.R.)
Edwards, E. W. B., Ld. S.
Ferguson, J., Sto. (R.N.R.)
Finch, Harry, Act. Ld. Sto.
Fox, Herbert John, A.B.
Francis, Hugh, En. (R.N.R.)
Frazier, Wm. Fredk., Ld. Sto.
Frearson, F. Warrick, C.C.
Geddes, Joseph, Dckhd. (R.N.R.)
Godfrey, John, Sea. (R.N.R.)
*Gomery, W. F., A.B. (R.N.V.R.)
Green, William Geo., Sto. 1.
Grimshaw, Harry, Sto. 1.
Hall, H. A., Pte. (R.M.L.I.)
Hammond, Georgt Trice, A.B.
Hammonds, G. N., Gun. (R.M.A.)
Harrison, Wm. Ed., Tmr. (R.N.R.)
Hart, Ernest, Sto. 1.
Hendry, John, Sto. 1.
Heslop, John, Sto. 1.
Hesp, J. C., A.B. (R.N.V.R.)
Hobbs, William Henry Geo., A B.
Hodge, Albert Tom, A.B.
Howe, A. William, Sto. 1.
Isaac, Clifford, P.O.
Jameson, Wm. C., Dckhd. (R.N.R.)
Jellard, John, E.R.A. (R.N.R.)
Keay, James, P.O. 1.
Kennedy, John, P.O.
Lay, John Carter, Act. Ld. Sto.
Lee, William, En. (R.N.R.)
Lennon, Peter, Sto. 1.
Ley, E. P., E.R.A. 1.
Logan, R. S., Shipwright 2.
Mabberley, Henry, E.R A. 2.
McCormick, Fredk., Act. Sig.
Mackenzie, A., A.B. (R.N.V.R.)
Mackenzie, J. A., En. (R.N.R.)
Mansfield, Wm. R., Act. Ld. Sto.
Marjoram, E. H., En. (R.N.R.)
Mathews, R. T. P., Sig.
Mayes, Wm., A.B. (R.N.V.R.)
Mernin, Thomas John, A.B.
Mondy, William, Ld S.
Morley, Harry, A.B. (R.N.V.R.)
Morris, George, Sto. P.O.
Newnham, W. G., Ld. S.
Nicholls, Geo. Cyril, Sto. 1.
Oakwell, Alfred A. E., E.R.A. 3.
Page, Arthur William, A.B.
Payne. A. G., Pte. (R.M.L.I.)
Powers, Albert Bennett, P.O.
Procter, T. H., Ld. S. (R.N.V.R.)
*Reaich, George, En (R.N.R.)
*Redford, Peter W., Driver (R.M.A.)
Richer, Albert, Cor. (R.M.L.I.)
Robinson, Thomas Albert, A.B.
Sanford, John, A.B
Sanford, Arthur S. S., P.O.
Sheppard, F. G., Pte. (R.M.L.I.)
Shillabeer, Fredk. Pte. (R.M.L.I.)
Skinner, David, Sea. (R.N.R.)
Smith, F. H, Pte (R.M.L.I.)
Smith, John G., Shipwright 2.
Stanley, John, Temp. Bombardier.
Steen, R., Pte. (R.M.L.I.)
Stevenson, Frank, Sto. P.O.
Stewart, John, Sec. Hd (R.N.R.)
Stubbs, William James, A.B.
Sweeney, James, A.B. (R.N.V.R.)
Thompson. Albert Edward, Sto. 1.
*Thompson, R. S., A.B. (R.N.V.R.)
Thorpe, John F., P.O. (R.N.V.R.)

Toogood, Edwin Albert, A.B.
Towler, George Henry, Sto. 1.
Walker, John T., Of. Cook, 2.
Webb, Sidney H. J., Sto. 1.
Websdale, Samuel A., Sea. (R.N.R.)
*Webster, Albert, Pte. (R.M.L.I.)
*White, Fredk. J., Sto. 1.
White, L. J., Pte. (R.M.L.I.)
*Wild, F. C. J., A.B. (R.N.V.R.)
Wilkes, H. M., P.O (R.N.V.R.)
Williams, Stanley, Dckhd. (R.N.R.)
Williams, Walter Claude, A.B.
*Willis, Harry, Boy Tel.
Wilson, Geo. R., Driver (R.M.A.)
Worner, W. V., A.B. (R.N.V.R.)
Yetman, William Henry, P.O.

AUGUST, 1916.

Addison, David. Sea. (R.N.R.)
Alien, Fredk. (Dckhd. (R.N.R.)
Anfield, John Wm. W., Ld. S.
Ashby, Christopher John, P.O.
Aslett, Edmund Charles, A.B.
Atkinson, J. C., A.B. (R.N.V.R.)
Ayres, N. G., Pte. (R.M.L.I.)
Bacon, Cyril, Sto.
Bacon, James, Sto. 1.
Bagwell, Andrew, A.B.
Baker, Henry, E.R.A 1 (R.N.V.R.)
Baldock, Alfred Henry, Ld. S.
Barber, Richard, A.B. (R.N.V.R.)
Baser, Ernest Rendle, Sto. P.O.
Beall, Albert Victor, A.B.
Beard, Frederick James, Ld. S.
Beck, William Charles, Sto. 1.
Bennett, George Henry, Sto. 1.
Bernard, Patrick, Sto. 2.
Bevan, Edward Wm. R., E.R.A. 3.
Bibbings, Ed. James. Sto. 1.
Boagey, Robert, Act. Ld. Sto.
Bowler, Arthur, A.B.
Brabben, R. N., En. (R.N.R.)
Brace, Wm. J., Sea. (N.R.N.R.)
Broad, Alfred Henry, A.B.
Brophy, Edward, Sto. 1.
Brotherhood, E., Yeo. Sig.
Brown, A. R., Dckhd. (R.N.R.)
Brown, C. V., Dckhd. (R.N.R.)
Brown, Harold, Pte. (R.M.L.I.)
Buckingham, Edred, C.E.R.A. 1.
Budge, K. B. C., A.E.R.A. 4.
Bulbeck, William Henry, A.B.
Bunter, Frederick, C.A.
Butcher, Mark, A.B.
Calvo, George, Sto 1.
Cameron, David A., A.B. (R.N.V.R.)
Campbell, J. M., Dckhd. (R.N.R.)
Carey, Ralph, A.B. (R.N.V.R.)
Carpenter, Henry George, Ld. S.
Carpenter, Thomas, Sto. 1.
Castle, William, P.O.
Chalmers, William, P.O.
Chipchase, A. I., A.E.R.A. 4.
Claridge, Sidney Arthur, Tel.
Claxton, Charles, Ld. S. (R.N.R.)
Coe, Maurice Edward, Sto. 1.
Collier, Andrew Roger, Ch. Sto.
Constable, C. J., A.B. (R.N.V.R.)
Cook, A. J., Sea. (R.N.R.)
Cook, Arthur Owen, A.B.
Cook, Geo. S., Dckhd. (R.N.R.)
Cooley, Frank Edward, A.B.
Couch, Henry, P.O. 1.
Cressy, Geo. J., Sec. Hd (R.N.R.)
Cushing, G. L, Dckhd. (R.N.R.)

The Navy's Immortal Names

Daley, Wm. E. P., Sergt. (R.M.L.I.)
Daniels, Charles Cecil, Sto. 1.
Darkins, Geo., En. (R.N.R.)
Davis, Henry Charles, Sto. 1.
Davis, William, Ch. Sto.
Denison, John. Boy Tel.
Dodsworth, Jos., Sto. (R.N.R.)
Dudley, Charles H., Act. Ld. Sto.
Dyer, Robert Lane, Sto. 1.
Eagle, Herbert, Dckhd. (R.N.R.)
Edkins, Frank, Sto. 1.
Ennis, Robert. Sto. 1.
Evans, Jack, Sto. 1.
Eveleigh, John, Sergt. (R.M.L.I.)
Ewing, Wm. G., Tmr. (R.N.R.)
Fenwick, William Thackray, A.B.
Finch, Bert, Cook's Mate.
Flannery, Wm., Sto. (R.N.R.)
*Flint, G. H. B., A.B. (R.N.V.R.)
Frame, Alex., Ld. Tmr. (R.N.R.)
Frame, James, A.B. (R.N.V.R.)
Frampton, Peter James, A.B.
Frewer, Walter, Ld. Sto.
Fry, Norman Stanley, Sto. P.O.
Gadsby, William W., Sto. P.O.
Garland, John, Ld. Sto
Garry, Arthur Foley, E.R.A. 1.
Gaunt, Frederick Henry, A.B.
Gibbs, Walter, A.B. (R.N.V.R.)
Gibson, John Wm., Act. Ld. Sto.
Gibson, L. V. H., En. (R.N.R.)
Godfrey, Robert Frederick, A B.
Goodman, Ernest, Pte. (R.M.L.I.)
Graham, James Richard, P.O.
Grant, William Alex., Ld. Sig.
Gray, Walter, Act. Cor. (R.M.L.I.)
Gribble, Frederick, Sto. 1.
Grice, Herbert H., Sto. 1.
Griffiths, John, Sto. 1.
Hall, P. Geo., Dckhd. (R.N.R.)
Halls, Wm. C. Ed., Sto. 1.
Harner, William John, Sto. P.O.
*Harrison, C. L., A.B. (R.N.V.R.)
Hatcher, Arthur Ernest, Ld. Sto.
Hayes, Michael, Sto. P.O.
Heaton, Arthur, Ord. S.
Hegarty, Thomas, Sto. 1.
Henzell, Michael, Sto. (R.N.R.)
Hewitt, S. Valentine, Sto. 2.
Hewlett, Harry, Act. Ld. Sto.
Hickery, William Henry, Sto. 1.
Hodgson, Ronald Wm., A.E.R.A. 4.
Horgan, Patrick, Sto. P.O.
Horton, James Ernest, A.C.P.O.
Horwell, Albert Edward, Sto. P.O.
Howells, William, Sto. (R.N.R.)
Hughes, James, Sig.
Hunt, Frank, Dckhd. (R.N.R.)
Hurley, Thomas, Sea. (N.R.N.R.)
James, Archibald N., E.R.A. 4.
James, Henry John, Sto. 2.
Jenner, J. Wm., Tmr. (R.N.R.)
Jolliffe, Francis Henry, Ld. S.
*Jones, J. W., Pte. (R.M.L.I.)
Jones, Thomas Henry, Sto. (R.N.R.)
Kennedy, John, A.B. (R.N.V.R.)
Kinsman, Jabez, A.B. (R.N.V.R.)
Kitching, Charles R., Sto. (R.N.R.)
Lake, Charles. P.O.
Larcombe, Arthur Edwin, A.B.
Lloyd, Percy Norris. Sto 1.
MacAulay, Donald. Sea. (R.N.R.)
McDonald, John, Sea. (R.N.R.)
McIlrath, James, Sto. P.O.
McKenzie, William, Tmr. (R.N.R.)
McMann, John, Sto. 1.
McWalter, J. R., Sto. (R.N.R.)

Mallaby, W. James, Sto. (R.N.R.)
Marks, Maurice John, C.C.
Matthew, William H. H., Sto. 2.
Matthews, Frank Richardson, Ld. S.
Millard, Jocelyn Alfred, E.R.A. 3.
Miller, Wm., Sec. Hd. (R.N.R.)
Monckton, Sidney, A.E.R.A. 4.
Moon, John, A.B. (R.N.V.R.)
Moore, John, Pte. (R.M.L.I.)
Morgan, Geo. E., E.R.A. 4.
Morse, Henry George, Sto. 1.
Nash, J. H., Pte. (R.M.L.I.)
Newson, Robert, En. (R.N.R.)
Nichols, Frederick Noel, A.B.
Nicholson, W., Sea. (R.N.R., Shet.)
Noble, J. D., Act. P.O. (R.N.R.)
O'Neill, John, Sto. 1.
Osborne. L., Boy Cook (R.N.R.)
Page, Edwin Jack, A.B.
Parks, William, Dckhd. (R.N.R.)
Pearse, A. C. J., E.R.A. 1.
Pearson, Albert Thomas, A B.
Peerless, Herbert William, A.B.
Penney, J., A B. (R.N.V.R.)
Perring, William Thomas, Sto. 1.
Perry, Thos. H., Dckhd. (R.N.R.)
Pettman, H. E., Sec. Hd. (R.N.R.)
Pickering, William Geo., Ld. Sto.
Pitt, George, Gun. (R.M.A.)
Pointon, Ed., L.-Cor. (R.M.L.I.)
Pook, Charles, Sto. 1.
Powell, Wm., Pte. (R.M.L.I.)
Preskett, Henry, Ld. S.
Prior, Charles Henry, Ld. Sig.
Prior, John Sampson, Sto. 1.
Pritchard, J. W., Dckhd. (R.N.R.)
Rafferty, John, A.B. (R.N.V.R.)
Rawbone, Albert Charles, Sto. 1.
Reed, William Henry, Ld. Sto.
Reeves, F., Pte. (R.M.L.I.)
Reid, Wm. S., C.E.R.A. (R.N.R.)
Repper, Charles, P.O.
Rice, Owen, Sto. (R.N.R.)
Rising, J. C., Sec. Hd. (R.N.R.)
Roach, George Frederick, A.B.
Roberts, Charles Fredk., A.B.
Salisbury, James Henry, P.O.
Sanderson, George, En. (R.N.R.)
Sanderson, Herbert H., Sto. 1.
Saywell, Herbert N., E.R.A. 3.
*Scorer, William, Ld. S. (R.N.V.R.)
Shanley, Peter, Sto. 1.
Sharp, Fredk. Thos., Ld. Sto.
Sharpe, Percy William, Sto. 1.
*Shaw, James, Pte. (R.M.L.I.)
Shepherd, Alex., Tmr. (R.N.R.)
Shorrocks. R., Pte. (R.M.L.I.)
Silk, Percival G., E.R.A. 3.
Simpson. J. E., Pte (R.M.L.I.)
Slessor, John, A.B. (R.N.V.R.)
*Small, Wm. Carr, A.B. (R.N.V.R.)
Smith, John, Dckhd. (R.N.R.)
Smith, L. Wm., Ld. Tel.
Snow, Sidney, Sto. 1.
Spence, S. G. S., E.R.A. (R.N.R.)
Spoors, Edward, A.B.
Sterling, J., Pte. (R.M.L.I.)
Steward, Alfred George, A.B.
Studd, G. H., Dckhd. (R.N.R.)
*Sullivan, Wm. R., Sap. (R.M.)
Swann, James, Ld. S. (R.N.V.R.)
Symons, Harry, Sto. P.O.
Thom, Geo. Wm., E.R.A. 1.
Thomas, Daniel, Sig. (R.N.V.R.)
Thompson, George Edward, Ord. S.
Thornton, Alfred, Ld. S.
*Throsby, Charles Essam, P.O.

Tovey, Maurice William, Sig.
Tucker, Denis, Sea. (N.R.N.R.)
Wade, A. Ed., A.C.E.R.A 2.
Walker, John D., Sea. (R.N.R.)
Ward, John James, Sto. 1.
Warwick, John C., E.R.A. 3.
Watt, James, En. (R.N.R.)
Webb, Wm., Sto. P O. (Pen.)
*Wedel, A. P., P.O. (R.N.V.R.)
Wells, John, Sto. 1.
West, C., Dckhd. (R.N.R.)
Whent, E. J., Pte. (R.M.L.I.)
Wigg, Wm. James, En. (R.N.R.
Wilbraham, George, E.R.A. 4.
Williams, Ernest Charles, Sto. 1
*Willson, A. J., Pte. (R.M.L.I.)
Wilson, James, E.R.A. (R.N.R.
Wood, R. Wm., Dckhd. (R.N.R.
Wooding, Samuel, Sap. (R.M.)
Woolcock, Ernest Wm., Sto. 2.
Wright, F. S., Dckhd. (R.N.R.)
Wright, William, Sto. 1.
Wright, William Henry, Ord. S.

CIVILIAN.

Underhill, J., Canteen Assistant.

Specially Entered Mercantile Crew.

Armstrong. John, Fireman.
Atherton, George, Fireman.
Beardoe, W., Donkeyman.
Birnie, John, Greaser.
Burnley, Samuel, Assistant Cook.
Carson, Thomas, Greaser.
Castles, Joseph, Greaser.
Cawte, William, A.B.
Cooper, John, Fireman.
Dixon, Frederick, Carpenter.
Glass, Sam, Fireman.
Graham, James, Fireman.
Johnston, Edward C., 3rd Eng.
Lamont, George, Assistant Steward.
Myall, William, A.B.
Phillips, Edward, Fireman.
Porter, Walter David, Fireman.
Rooney, Joseph, Fireman.
Royle, William, A.B.
Smith, Charles, Fireman.
Smith, Edward. Fireman.
Westwood, William, Fireman.

SEPTEMBER, 1916.

Ainslie, Geo Allan, Tmr. (R.N.R.)
Arthur, J. I., Ord. Tel. (R.N.R.)
*Baudet, Louis Fredk., Sto. 1.
*Bickerton, Charles, 3rd Writer.
Blow, Tom. En. (R.N.R.)
Bowles, J. A., Dckhd. (R.N.R.)
Brooks, E. J., Sec. Hd. (R.N.R.)
Cadby, Fredk. N., Sea. (R.N.R.)
Cass, James, Tmr. (R.N.R.)
Collinson, J., Tmr. (R.N.R.)
Cowie, George, Sec. Hd. (R.N.R.)
Cremer, Bertie Leonard, Ld. S.
Denny, Geo., Sec. Hd. (R.N.R.)
Doe. G. H. J., Dckhd. (R.N.R.)
Edwards, H. E., W. Tel. Oper.
(R.N.R.)
Fermoyle, Patrick, Sto. (R.N.R.)
Flynn, John, A.B.
Fraser, T. M., Tel. (R.N.V.R.)
Gardiner, Henry, Dckhd. (R.N.R.)
Gill, Albert, Sto. 1.
Goddard, M. A., Pte. (R.M.L.I.)

Goff, C. Ed., Air Mech. 2.
Green, Thos., A.B. (R.N.V.R.)
Griffin, William, En (R.N.R.)
Harries, Thomas, Dckhd. (R.N.R.)
Hearn, Alfred, Dckhd. (R.N.R.)
Howes, James, Sea. (R.N.R.)
*Hume, Ward, A.B. (R.N.V.R.)
Kiff, Harry W., Ld. S.
Kirkpatrick, C., Dckhd. (R.N.R)
Langford, O. B., Air Craftsman, 2.
Low, Geo. M., En. (R.N.R.)
Macinnes, Norman, Ld. S. (R.N.R)
MacLeod, Wm. A., Dckhd. (R.N.R.)
*McDoal, Dougall, A.B. (R.N.V.R.)
McClure, William Henry, A.B.
McDougall, Arthur, Ord. S.
McGrane, Robert, Gun. (R.M.A.)
McIntosh, W., Ld. Dckhd. (R.N.R.)
Mair, Wm. W., Dckhd. (R.N.R)
Manslow, W. G., Dckhd. (R.N.R.)
Markwell, William Henry, P.O. 1.
Middleton, William, Ord. S.
Miller, Herbert, Tmr. (R.N.R.)
Moore, John Francis, En. (R.N.R.)
Newall, John, Sea. (R.N.R.)
Oxley, Gilbert, E.R.A. 1.
Partridge, Charles L., Sto. P.O.
Pearson, J. T., Tmr Ck. (R.N.R.)
Peel, R. Frank, Tmr. (R.N.R.)
Redding, Albert, A.B. (R.N.V.R.)
Reynolds, Richard James, P.O.
*Rutherford, Henry, A.B. (R.N.V.R.)
Saunders, Fredk., Dckhd. (R.N.R.)
Sclanders, R. E., Sig. Boy (R.N.R.)
Scott, David, Dckhd. (R.N.R.)
Tabone, F. G., Sea. (R.N.R.) (Malt.)
*Tanner, William, A.B. (R.N.V.R.)
Taylor, F. W. G., Pte. (R.M.L.I.), Air Mech. 2.
Thompson, J. W., Dckhd. (R.N.R.)
Turner, C., Ord. Tel. (R.N.V.R.)
Tweedle, Hector, Ld. Sto.
Underwood. Albert Edward, Ld. S.
Warren, Alexander, Ld. Sto.
Widdicombe, R. E., Sec. H. (R.N.R.)
Williams, David, Sig. (R.N.V.R.)
Wills, Wm. S. H., C.E.R.A. 1.
Wood, Alex., Dckhd. (R.N.R.)
Wright, Wm., Gun. (R.M.A.)
Wroe, Richard, Ld. Sto.

Specially Entered Mercantile Crew.
Barber, Alfred O., Assistant Cook.
Frampton, George S., Greaser.
Gandy, Cyril, Chief Steward.
Jinman, Augustus. A.B.
Leach, William W., Fireman.
McPherson, Colin A., 2nd Engineer.
Pearson, William, Assistant Std.
Stubbs, Frank, A.B.

OCTOBER, 1916.

Adams, John, Dckhd. (R.N.R.)
Allen, John Edmund, Ld. Sto.
Allison, G. R, Gun. (R.M.A.)
Anscombe, William Andrew, Sto. 1.
Atherton, George, A.B.
Ayers, S. R., Dckhd. (R.N.R.)
Aylott, Frederick, Boy 1.
Bailey, Alfred, Sto. P.O.
Barnard, J. T., Dckhd. (R.N.R.)
Beamish, F. Wm., Dckhd. (R.N.R.)
Beattie, James, Sto. 1.
Bell, John George, Sto. 1.
Bell, William, Sto. (R.N.R.)

Blackball, Alex, En. (R.N.R.)
Blackball, Geo., Dckhd. (R.N.R.)
Bracken, J. Thos., Ld. Cook's M.
Brady, C. Wm., Dckhd. (R.N.R.)
Bridger, Wm. Alfred, Sto. 1.
Broomfield, Wilson, Sto. 1.
Brown, Fred, A.E.R.A. 4.
Brown, John B., Ord. S.
Bruford, Wm., Dckhd. (R.N.R.)
Buckle, Alfred, 1.d. Sto.
Burdon, Oliver, Sto. (R.N.R)
Burns, J. P., Dckhd. (R.N.R.)
*Bushell, J., A.B. (R.N.V.R.)
Butler, John Stuart, A.B.
Button, Lewis, En. (R.N.R.)
Cadman, Percy, A.B.
Cady, James. Dckhd. (R.N.R.)
Cain, Michael, Sea. (R.N.R.)
Cameron, C. C., Of. Std. 2.
Carroll, James, Sto. P.O.
Carter, Fredk. Samuel, A.B.
Carter, Thos. Wm, Boy 1.
Catchpole, F. C., Tmr. (R.N.R.)
Chambers, T. A., Yeo. Sig.
Channon, J. S., Act. Ld. Sto.
Chapman, A. E, En. (R.N.R.)
Chapman, T. J., Sec. Cook's Mate.
Chappell, T. J., Dckhd. (R.N.R.)
Chase, Henry John, Ld. S.
Chatteris, B. W., En. (R.N.R.)
Christy, O. Wm., Dckhd. (R.N.R.)
Claridge, Leslie Arthur, A.B.
Clark, J. W., Dckhd. (R.N.R.)
Clegg, William Samuel, Sto. 1.
Clewley, Alfred, Sto. 1.
Colebourne, Albert E., Sto. 1.
Connor, Edward T., Ord. S.
Constable, John, Ord. S.
Cotton, C. T., A.B. (R.N.V.R.)
Cox, John R., Sto. 1.
Craig, William, C.E.R.A. (R.N.R)
Crease, William Thos., Sto. 1.
Crespin, A. V. S., P.O.
Crisp, Geo., Dckhd. (R.N.R.)
Croft, William, Sto. 1.
Crooks, John Albert, Sto. 1.
Dargan, George, Sea. (R.N.R.)
Davies, John, Of. Std. 2.
Davies, Percy, Sto. 1.
Daysh, Edward, Sto. 1.
Dean, Wm. H., Tmr. (R.N.R.)
Ditch, J. Wm. H., Sto. 1.
Dolman, Robert, Sto. 1.
Dowsing. T. W, Dckhd. (R.N.R.)
Doy, C. H., Sec. Hd. (R.N.R.)
Doyle, Richard, Sto. (R.N.R.)
Duckworth, Charles, Boy Tel.
Dunk, Wm. Harold, Sto. P.O.
Dyke, A. Wm., Dckhd. (R.N.R.)
Dymock, Malachi, A.B.
Emery, J. Wm.. A.B. (R.N.V.R.)
Fennell, Charles Henry, Sto. 2.
Fisher, H. F., Sec. Hd. (R.N.R.)
Foreman, Wm., Dckhd. (R.N.R.)
Foster, B. Wm., Boy 1.
Fountain, George, Ord. S.
Fowler, Fred, Ord. S.
Fox, James George, Ld. Sto.
Freeman, S. J., Tmr. (R.N.R.)
Funnell, Walter S., Sto. 2.
Gardner, Leslie Fredk., Boy 1.
Geddes, Geo., Tmr. (R.N.R.)
George, Wm. H., Dckhd. (R.N.R.)
Gilbert, Stephen John, P.O.
Glennie, George, Dckhd. (R.N.R.)
Griffiths, Arthur, Sto. 1.
Hague, Joseph Arthur, Sto. 1.

Hall, Albert Edward, A.B.
Hall, J. H. H., Dckhd. (R.N.R.)
Harvey, Geo., Sec. Hd. (R.N.R.)
Haskell, Reginald, A.B. (R.N.V.R)
Hatcher, B. G., Sh. Std. Assist.
Hayson, George Albert, Of. Std. 2.
Heaselgrave, Syd. Geo., Ord. S.
Helyer, A. J., Shipwright 1.
Hendry, James, Sec. Hd. (R.N.R.)
Hodgson, Wm. H., P.O. Mech.
Hoggarth, George, Ord. S.
Holden, Cecil John, Boy 1.
Housley, Leonard, Ord. S.
Howard, William, Sto. P.O.
Hubbard, E. T., Sig. (R.N.V.R.)
Hughes, L., Sea. (R.N.R.)
Hughes, Peter, En. (R.N.R.)
Hughes, William, Sto. 2.
Humphris, Charles Samuel, Ld. S.
Hunt, E., Sec. Hd. (R.N.R.)
Hurren, B. E., Dckhd. (R.N.R.)
Hutchings, A., Ld. S. (R.N.V.R.)
Ironside, Geo, Tmr. (R.N.R.)
Jackson, R. H., Ld. Cook's Mate.
Jenkerson, A. E., Dckhd. (R.N.R.)
Jenkins, Wm. Caleb, C.P.O.
Jinkinson, R. W., En. (R.N.R.)
Johns, W. H. G., Of. Cook, 2.
Johnson, William, P.O.
Johnston, David, Tmr. (R.N.R.)
Jones, D. J., Sig. (R.N.V.R.)
Jones, Wm., A.B. (R.N.V.R.)
Kavangh, John Wm., Sto. 1.
Keeling, William, Sto. 1.
King, J. Fredk, En (R.N.R.)
King, Wm. R., En. (R.N.R.)
Knaggs, Albert Edward, A.B.
Knight, F. Henry James, Sto. 1.
Knights, W. J., Sec. Hd. (R.N.R.)
Lamb, George William, Boy 1.
Lee, Charles Shaw, A.B.
Lee, Edward M., Sto. 2.
Lindo, Fred, Tmr. (R.N.R.)
Livingstone, John, Tmr. (R.N.R.)
Long. Fredk. C., Tmr. (R.N.R.)
Louden, Wm., Tmr. (R.N.R.)
Lovell, Harold W. B., Boy Tel.
Luckhurst, A. E.. Of. Std. 3.
Luff, George D., Sto. P.O.
Lyons, John, Sto. P.O.
McCafferty, Daniel, Ord. S.
McIntosh, Hugh, Sea. (R.N.R.)
McKay, Donald, Sea. (R.N.R.)
McLuckie, Thomas, Sto. 2.
McNab, William, Sto. (R.N.R.)
McQueen, Wm. A., Ld. Tel.
Madden, Robert, Sto. 1.
Malcolm, Fred B., A.E.R.A. 4.
Manning, William Alfred, Boy 1.
Marshall, E. A., Dckhd. (R.N.R.)
Marshall, James Henry, A.B.
Mason, Victor Harry, A.E.R.A. 4.
Mather, Ernest, A.B.
Matheson, Norman, Dckhd. (R.N.R.)
Matthews, Arthur, A.E.R.A. 2.
Maxted, Percy John, Ld. Sto.
Meech, Richard, Sto. S.
Middleton, Thomas E., Ord. S.
Minors, William, Sto. 1.
Mitchell, C. H., Act. Ld. S. (R.N.V.R.)
Moore, Walter Louis, Sto. P.O.
Morrison, William Arthur, A.B.
Murch. L., A.E.R.A. 4.
Murray, Alexander A., Sto. 2.
Murray, F. G., Dckhd. (R.N.R.)
Murray, John, Tmr. (R.N.R.)

The Navy's Immortal Names

Myles, Peter, Sto. 1.
Needham, Christopher, Sto. 1.
Neeve, John S., En. (R.N.R.)
Neslen, Robert, Sec. Hd. (R.N.R.)
Newland, Thos. Samuel, Sto. 1.
Nunn, Alfred Edward, Boy 1.
Nunn, Wm. A., Dckhd. (R.N.R.)
Page. Henry William. Ld. S.
Palmer, Joseph, C.P.O.
Palmer, Joseph William, Boy 1.
Parry. Bertram, Sto. 2.
Parsons, Albert, Sto. 1.
Parsons, G., L.-Cor. (R.M.L.I.)
Patience, William, Sea. (R.N.R.)
Perry, A. Thos., Act. Ld. Sto.
Porteous, Samuel, A.B.
Povey, Austin, Sto. (R.N.R.)
Pratt, H. H., Dckkd. (R.N.R.)
Pringle, Thomas, Sto. (R.N.R.)
Pritchard, James, Sto. 2.
Pronger, Leonard Edward, Sto. 1.
Rapson, James, Sto. P.O.
Reeve, Arthur, Sto. 1.
Richardson, W., Tel. (R.N.V.R.)
Ritchie, Alex., Dckhd. (R.N.R.)
Ritchie, A. G., C.E.R.A. (R.N.R.)
Robertson, John, Sto. 1.
Rogers, Charles-Thomas, Sto. 2.
Rushant, A. S , A.B. (R.N.V.R.)
Sampson, Sydney F., Sto. P.O.
Sapsed, Harold John, Ld. Sig.
Saunders, F. J., Dckhd. (R.N.R.)
Sayers, A. H., En. (R.N.R.)
Sayers, Frank, Sto. 2.
Seager, Harold Arthur, E.R.A. 3.
Sharp, John, Sto. 1.
Shaw, Charles Edwin, Sto. P.O.
Shipp, Harry, Dckhd. (R.N.R.)
Shott, A. H., E.R.A. 4
Sillman, H. T , A.B. (R.N.V.R.)
Simpson, Thos., Sto. P.O.
*Smith, Charles Frederick. Sto. 1.
Smith, Edward, Sto. (R.N.R.)
Smith, F. Wm. Dckhd (R.N.R.)
Smith, Henry, Ld. Sto.
Smith, Joseph Wm., Sto. 2.
Smith, Walter Robert, Sig.
*Smith, William. Sto. P.O.
Soanes, Wm. W., En. (R.N.R.)
Sparrow, James, Sto. 1.
Stainsby, J. R. H., En. (R.N.R.)
Standing, G. T., Dckhd. (R.N.R.)
Steele, Fredk. A. G., A.B.
Stevens, Percy, 2nd Cook's Mate.
Stout, William, Dckhd. (R.N.R.)
Strachan, Wm., En. (R.N.R.)
Stroud, Arthur, A.B.
Sullivan, J. S. J , Act. Ld. Sto.
Swain, A. G., Boy 1.
Tansey, John, Sto. 1.
Taylor, Edward Charles, Ch., Sto.
Taylor, James, Ld. Sto.
Thomas, James, Dckhd. (R.N.R.)
Thornley, Arthur J.. En. (R.N.R.)
Thurston, W. J., Dckhd. (R.N.R.)
Utting, Wm. Ed., En. (R.N.R.)
Walker, John, Tmr. (R.N.R.)
Wallis, J. H., Ld. Cook's Mate.
Wardhaugh, Geo. Estall, Sto. 1.
Warrener, William, Ord. S.
Watson, Alfred, P.O.
Watt, James, Dckhd. (R.N.R.)
Watts, Benjamin, Ld. S.
Wavell, William George, A.B.
West, George Henry, Ch. Sto.
Westoby, E. H., Dckhd. (R.N.R.)
Weston, Arthur, Sto. P.O.

Whaley, J. G., Tel. (R N.V.R.)
Wheatley, George Ernest, Sto. 1.
White, Bertie Alfred. Boy 1.
White, Harry, Ld. S.
White, H. John Wm., Sto. 1.
Whittington, Wm. Geo., Boy Tel.
Williams, D. M., Sea. (R.N.R.)
Wilson, William, Sto. 1.
Wintle, Francis Arthur, A.B.
Wise, Joseph, Ld. S.
Wiseman, William, Cook (R.N.R.)
Wood, John, Ch. Sto.
Woods, George John, Sto. 1.
Woodward, Wilfred, Boy Tel.
Woolnough, E. G., Dckhd. (R.N.R.)
Young, J. W., Air Mech. 1.
Young, Wm., En. (R.N.R.)

NOVEMBER, 1916.

Anderson, A., Dckhd. (R.N.R.)
Annis, John, Tmr. (R.N.R.)
Archer, T. H., Tmr. (R.N.R.)
Aubin, Clifford, Dckhd. (R.N.R.)
Barbour, J. M., Wire. Tel. Opera., (R.N.R.)
Beard, Frank, En. (R.N.R.)
Bentley, Geo., Sergt. (T) (R.M.A.)
Bentley, Harry James, Ld. Sto.
Bessey, John E., Dckhd. (R N.R.)
Bessey, Wm., Tmr. (R.N.R.)
Bills, H., Dckhd. (R.N.R.)
Blyth, H. J., Bov Cook (R.N.R.)
Bonner, F. W., Ord. Tel. (R.N.V.R.)
Boobyer, A. G., Sig. (R.N.V.R.)
Boothman, P., Tel. (R.N.V.R.)
Borman, Jack, Dckhd. (R.N.R.)
Botton, J. F., En. (R.N.R.)
Bowley, Ernest William, A.B.
Braime, W., Dckhd. (R.N.R.)
Brunton, J., Dckhd. (R.N.R.)
Buckle, William Henry, P.O.
Burrows, W. L., Deck Boy (R.N.R.)
Casey, Ed., Sec. Hd. (R.N.R.)
Clark, Alex., Sea. (R.N.R.)
Coleman, M. W., Sec. Hd. (R.N.R.)
Coles, William Albert, P.O.
Cook, B. J., Dckhd. (R.N.R.)
Coombes, James, P.O.
Coulter, W. A., A.B. (R.N.V.R.)
Cowling, Thos. Walter, A.B.
Craven, Joseph, Ld. Sto.
Crichton, John. Sto. 1.
Crocker, Sidney, Sto. 1.
Cumming, J. R., Sea. (R.N.R.)
Davies, Fredk. H , Tmr. (R.N.R.)
Davies, William, Sto. 1.
Doughty, C., Sec. Hd. (R.N.R.)
Emeny, Wm , Col.-Sergt. (R.M.A.)
Englefield, Percy. Cook (R.N R.)
Finlayson, D , Tmr. (R.N.R.)
Fleming, Alfred Robert, P.O.
Fletcher, F. C., Tmr. Cook (R.N.R.)
Fox, Patrick, Ord. S.
Francis, F. R., Dckhd. (R.N.R.)
Galt, John, Sto. 1.
Gardiner, George, Tmr. (R.N.R.)
Garnham, G. L., Dckhd. (R.N.R.)
Garrick, G. A., Dckhd. (R.N.R.)
Goodwin, J. R., Dckhd. (R.N.R.)
Gosling, T. W., Sec. Hd. (R.N.R.)
Gove, Cecil Henry, A.B.
Greenhalf, F. A., Act. Ld. Sto.
Hackford, A., En. (R.N R.)
*Haggon, David, Sto. 1.
Haldenby, John, Dckhd. (R.N.R.)

Hammant, W. E., Tmr. (R.N.R.)
Hand, Alfred Henry, A.B.
Hayward, John Henry, Ld. S.
Hayward, Thomas Alfred, Sto P.O
Hedge, Bertie, Sto. 1.
Henderson, James, E.R.A. 1.
Hewson, Francis William, A.B.
Hicks, C. H., Dckhd (R.N.R.)
Hubbard, Fredk. J., Act. Ld. Sto.
Hughes, Richard. Sto. (R.N.R.)
Hull, Arthur, Air Mech. 1.
Humphries, E.J. Geo., A.B.
Hurlock, Henry, Ld. S.
Jack, Wm., En. (R.N.R.)
Jacobs, Geo. R., En. (R.N.R.)
Jenkinson, Wm., Dckhd. (R.N.R.)
Jermany, R. S., Sec. Hd. (R.N.R.)
Jermy, Arthur J., Tmr. (R.N.R.)
Johnson, Samuel, Dckhd. (R.N.R)
Johnston, John. Sto. 1.
Johnstone, R. D., En. (R.N.R.)
Jones, D. I., Tmr. (R.N.R.)
Jones, John Richard Tel.
Jones, L. G., Ld. Dckhd. (R.N.R.)
Kell, Anthony, E.R.A. (R.N.R.)
Knights, Geo. S., En (R.N.R.)
Knights, W. E. J., Dckhd. (R.N.R.)
Lafferty, Edward, Sea. (R.N.R.)
Langridge, Joseph Golden, A.B.
Lawrence, Oliver H., Boy (R.N.R.)
Lawrie, John G., Sig. (R.N.V.R.)
Lennox, James, Act. Ld. S. (R.N.R.)
Leslie, Stephen, En. (R.N.R.)
Levett, Japheth, A.B
Linder, Charles, Dckhd. (R.N.R.)
McAlpine, Wm., Tmr. (R.N.R.)
McAngus, H.. Sea. (R.N.R.)
McCuish, J.. Dckhd. (R.N.R.)
Macdonald, D., Ld. S. (R.N.R.)
McHardy, Wm. A., Ch. P.O.
McKenzie, Aulay, En. (R.N.R.)
Mackenzie, M., Act. Ld. S. (R.N.R.)
Mackie, Neil, En. (R N.R.)
McLellan, D., Ld. Dckhd. (R.N.R.)
Macleod, M., Dckhd. (R.N.R.)
McLeod, N., Dckhd. (R.N.R.)
McNamara, P. J., A.B. (R.N.V.R.)
McNiven, John, Dckhd. (R.N.R.)
Main, J. F. B., Dckhd. (R.N.R.)
Margerison, C., Dckhd. (R.N.R.)
May, James. C.E.R.A.
Mein, John, Sec. Hd. (R.N.R.)
Mills, J. T., En. (R.N.R.)
Morris, J. William. Sto. 1.
Morrison, John, Dckhd. (R.N.R.)
Mountain, Jesse, A.B.
Neil. A. L., Dckhd. (R.N.R.)
Newell, A. W., Ord. Tel. (R.N.V.R.)
O'Rourke, Michael, A.B.
Owens, Clifford F., A.B. (R.A.N.)
Petherick, D. J., En. (R.N.R.)
Poleson, L., Sea. (R.N.R., Shet.)
Potter, Wm. C. L., Ld. Sig.
Powell, Henry, Sto. 1.
Presswell, John Wm., Ld. S.
Pretten, Albert E., Sea. (R.N.R.)
Prideaux, J. H., Dckhd. (R.N.R.)
Purkiss, A., Tmr. Cook (R.N.R.)
Raffin, W. B., Tel. (R.N.V.R.)
Reeves, Charles Henry. A.S.
Rennison, Thomas F., Sto. 1.
Reid, Alex., En. (R.N.R.)
Ridgers, Arthur, A.B.
Roberts, A. C., A.E.R.A. 4.
Robertson, J., A.B. (R.N.V.R.)
Robinson, Edwin S., E.R.A. 2.
Ross, John H., Ord. S.

Rowe, J. W., Dckhd. (R.N.R.)
Rowland, J., Dckhd. (R.N.R.)
Sadd, George Arthur, P.O.
Sharkey, Geo., En. (R.N.R.)
Sharp, J. H., Dckhd. (R.N.R.)
Simmons, E. S., En. (R.N.R.)
Simmons, Thos., Tmr. (R.N.R.)
Simpson, L. O. S., Sec. Hd. (R.N.R.)
Smith, Albert S., Cook (R.N.R.)
Smith, C., Dckhd. (R.N.R.)
Snowden, Alfred Wm., Sto. 1.
Staniland, Ronald, Tmr. (R.N.R.)
Stebbings, B. E., Tmr. (R.N.R.)
Steed, D., Sea. (N.R.N.R.)
Stevens, Harvey, Sto. 1.
Stone, I. S., Dckhd. (R.N.R.)
Stone, W., Tmr. (R.N.R.)
Stonebanks, W. A., En. (R.N.R.)
Swanson, D., Dckhd. (R.N.R.)
Tait, G. M., Dckhd. (R.N.R.)
*Taylor, James, En. (R.N.R.)
Taylor, J. R., Dckhd. (R.N.R.)
Thomas, Wm., Dckhd. (R.N.R.)
*Thompson, L. C. de C., Air Mech. 1
Thomson, A. W., Act. Ld. S. (R.N.V.R.)
Thomson, John, Tmr. (R.N.R.)
Tozer, James, Tmr. (R.N.R.)
Travers, Wm. R., E.R.A. 3.
Trusler, W., Boy Cook (R N.R.)
Turpin, J., Dckhd. (R.N.R.)
Volze, Fredk. Charles H., A.B.
Walker, J., Dckhd. (R.N.R.)
Walker, S., Dckhd. (R.N.R.)
Walker, Wm., En. (R.N.R.)
Wellfare, Thomas Wm., Ld. Sto.
Wells, Wm. Hy., Tmr. (R.N.R.)
Wetherby, W. J., Sec. Hd. (R.N.R.)
Wiles, A. G., Tmr. (R.N.R.)
Williams, Nathaniel, Sto. (R.N.R.)
Wilson, J. Thos., En. (R.N.R.)
Wood, A. W. M., Tmr. (R.N.R.)
Wright, Wm., Dckhd. (R.N.R.)

Specially Entered Mercantile Crew.

Conroy, W. E. G., Assist. Std.
Lord, Wm. A., Sec. Std.

DECEMBER, 1916.

Adams, John R., Ld. S.
Alexander, J., E.R.A. (R.N.R.)
Allen, B. F., Dckhd. (R.N.R.)
Andrews, George, P.O. 1.
Archer, William Samuel, P.O.
Armour, J., Tmr. (R.N.R.)
Austen, James, A.B.
Bain, J. M., Dckhd. (R.N.R.)
Baines, John Arthur, Sto. 1.
Ball, John, Ord. S.
Barrenger, H. Geo., E.R.A. 4.
Barker, A., Dckhd. (R.N.R.)
Bason, T. H., Pte. (R.M.L.I.)
Battle, Albert Frederick, A.B.
Baumber, W., Dckhd. (R.N.R.)
Bessey, C. G., En. (R.N.R.)
Blake, Herbert L., Sto. 2
Blok, Morris, Sto. 1.
Borrett, William John, Ld. S.
Bowen, Robert, Sto. P.O.
Bradley, W. E., C.P.O. 2.
Bramma, Wilfred, Pte. (R.M.L.I.)
Brandon, C. H. A., Tel. (R.N.V.R.)
Bray, Robert, Tmr. (R.N.R.)
Brooks, G. W., Dckhd. (R.N.R.)
Burgess, A., Dckhd. (R.N.R.)
Burgess, J. W., Tmr. (R.N.R.)

Burt, William, P.O.
Burwood, S. R., Dckhd. (R.N.R.)
*Buurma, John, Sto. P.O.
*Callaby, A., Pte. (R.M.L.I.)
Campagnolo, Ernesto, Sig.
Cartlidge, W., Col.-Sergt. (R.M.L.I.)
Catchpole, Ernest Ord. S.
Chapman, William Henry, Sto. 1.
Charman, Edward George, A.B.
Clark, William Henry, Sto. P.O.
Clem, J. Wm., Of. Sid. 3.
Collis, Edward Charles, Sto. P.O.
Collison, Desper George, A.B.
Colwell, J., En. (R.N.R.)
Cornick, W. H. H., Sto. 2.
Cowlard, Frank Thos., A.B.
Cran, Ernest, A.B.
Creber, Arthur Miles, Sto. 2.
Daly, Peter, Sto. 1.
Davenport, A., Pte. (R.M.L.I.)
Davison, Albert John G., A.B.
Denton, J. A., Ord. Tel. (R.N.V.R.)
Dickens, George John, Sto. 1.
Dorrington, George, Sto. 1.
Downs, J. W., En. (R.N.R.)
Ede, Reuben James, A.B.
Edgcombe, Lambert Henry, Ld. S.
Ekers, Alfred, A.B.
Ellender, Ernest, Sto. 1.
*Ellis, James, Cor. (R.M.L.I.)
Ely, Edward Charles, A.B.
Emery, Harry, A.B.
Evans, Nelson, Sto. 2.
Falloon, A., Pte. (R.M.L.I.)
Farey, H. C., Sig. (R.N.V.R.)
Farmer, Edwin Henry, Sto. 1.
Feather, J. E., Dckhd. (R.N.R.)
Fletcher, J. H., Sec. Hd. (R.N.V.R.)
Flood, James Alfred. Ld. Sto.
Foreman, H. J., Wireman 2.
French, Fredk. John, Ld. S.
Gaines, Thomas Lawson, A.B.
Gallant, Wm., Dckhd. (R.N.R.)
*Galbraith, Robert, Sto. 1.
Gates, G. W., En. (R.N.R.)
Goble, Frederick, Sto. 2.
Goddard, L., Tmr. (R.N.R.)
Grant, Thomas, Tmr. (R.N.R.)
Greaves, Edward, A.B.
Greaves, R., Ord. Tel. (R.N.V.R.)
Griggs, Alma, A.B. (R.N.R.)
Grimes, G. W., Dckhd. (R.N.R.)
Groves, John, Dckhd. (R.N.R.)
Hainsworth, Clarence, A.B.
Hammond, K. Geo. N., Ld. S.
Harle, George, E.R.A. 2.
Harman, R. A. Henry, Tel.
Harmer, William, Ld. Sto.
Harries, William James, Sto. 2.
Hart, Wallace, A.C.P.O.
Hartley, Henry, En. (R.N.R.)
Harvey, R. E., Act. En. (R.N.R.)
Havery, Ralph, C.E.R.A. (R.N.R.)
Haves, V. A. H., Of. Std. 3.
Herbert, Charles H., Sto. P.O.
Herring, James, Sto. 1.
Hoodless, joseph C., Sig.
Horne, C., Dckhd. (R.N.R.)
Hourston, David, A.E.R.A. 4.
Howell, Arthur, Of. Std 2.
Jenkins, H. A., En (R.N.R.)
Jenks, C. Thomas, Ld. S.
Kennard, Geo., A.B. (R.N.R.)
Kerrison, Horace Nelson, Sto. 2.
Kinnaird, William, Ord. S.
Knight, William E. B., A.B.
Larn, Edwin Hubert, A.B.

Learmouth, W., Dckhd. (R.N.R.)
Linklater, A., Tmr. (R.N.R.)
Lyon, Samuel, A.B.
Macdonald, A., Act. Ld. S. (R.N.R.)
Macdonald, John, Sea. (R.N.R.)
McDougall, T. H., Sec. Hd. (R.N.R.)
McUlla, A., Act. Ld. S., (R.N.V.R.)
Manoury, S. J., Tmr. (R.N.R.)
Marriott, E., A.B. (R.N.V.R.)
Martin, Thomas Whatling, A.B.
Matkin, J. A., Act. Ld. Sto.
May, Thomas Henry, Sto. P.O.
Meakin, Geo. E., Sto. P.O.
Mellor, Horace Leonard, A.B.
Miell, Walter John, Sto. 1.
Mockridge, William, Sto. 1.
Moonan, Michael, Ld. S. (R.N.R.)
Munro, R. L., C.E.R.A. 1.
Mutton, Thomas, Ld. S.
Newell, D. C., Act. Ship's Cook.
Newton, R. K., Sto. (R.N.R.)
O'Connor, W. T., Ord. Tel. (R.N.V.R.)
Palmer, Geo. Charles, Ord. S.
Parr, Charles John, Ld. Sto.
Parsons, Henry Charles, Ld. S.
Parton, George, Sec. Hd. (R.N.R.)
Pascoe, J. N., Dckhd. (R.N.R.)
Patterson, A., Dckhd. (R.N.R.)
Pender, Sydney, Dckhd. (R.N.R.)
Powell, A. F., Sig. Boy.
Powell, T. E., Ord. Tel.
Powell, Tom, Sto. 1.
Prout, A. H., Tmr. Cook, (R.N.R.)
*Pugh, Charles, Of. Std 2.
Raper, W. T., Dckhd. (R.N.R.)
Redgrave, A. L., En. (R.N.R.)
Remblance, Wm., Dckhd. (R.N.R.)
*Roberts, Edward, Sto. (R.N.R.)
Robertson, William, Ord. S.
Rogers, Fredk., Tmr. (R.N.R.)
Sadler, Richard, Sto. 1.
Salter, Ernest. Sto. 1.
Sams, J. William, Sto. 1.
Savage, Robert George, Sto. P.O.
Sawkins, John, Ch. Sto.
Scott. Robert, En. (R.N.R.)
*Sharp, Alfred, Ld. S
Shea, Patrick, Sea. (R.N.R.)
Sheader, G. W., Sec. Hd. (R.N.R.)
Smith, Edward, En. (R.N.R.)
Smith, James, P.O.
Smith, Teddy James Arthur, A.B.
Sparkes, S., Sea. (N.R.N.R.)
Stanley, John Henry, A.B.
Stephens, Ernest Alfred, Sig.
Stewart, W. J., E.R.A. 4.
Storey, Arthur, En. (R.N.R.)
Sugden, William A., Ord. S.
Suttle, Garnet, Sto. 2.
Taylor, E. H., Sig. (R.N.V.R.)
Tester, John, L.-Cor. (R.M.L.I.)
Thomas, William, A.B.
Thorpe, Frank, Pte. (R.M.L.I.)
Tyer, Patrick, Boy 1.
Urquhart, William, P.O. (Pen.)
Vincent, John S., Sto. 2.
Walker, J., Sig. Boy (R.N.R.)
Ward, J. R., Dckhd. (R.N.R.)
Watson, William John, A.B.
Welham, H. J., Dckhd. (R.N.R.)
Wells, Herbert E., E.R.A. 2.
Wells, Sidney, En. (R.N.R.)
Wells, William N., P.O. 1.
Whent, Charles Harry, Sig.
White, Arthur, Cook (R.N.R.)
Wilson, George Alfred, Ld. S.
Wilson, Joseph, A.B.

The Navy's Immortal Names

Wooder, Geo. E., Act. Sto. P.O.
Wooldridge, Frederick, P.O. 1.
Wright, G. H., Shipwright, 2.
*Wright, Ronald Rothsay, Boy 1.
Yeardley, J. W., Act. Sto. P.O.
Young, P. P., Tmr. (R.N.R.)

JANUARY, 1917.

Abbott, Fredk. J., Sea. (R.N.R.)
Abbott, J. A., Pte. (R.M.L.I.)
Abbott, M., Dckhd. (R.N.R.)
Alexander, Edwin James, A.B.
Andrews, Albert Henry, P.O. 2.
Anstis, George Henry, P.O. 2.
Astbury, H. T., Cor. (R.M.L.I.)
Atkins, Henry Richard, Ld. Sto.
Atkinson, Alfred, Pte. (R.M.L.I.)
Austin, R. S. M., Ch. A. (Pen.)
Auton, R. Thomas, Ord. Tel.
Ayles, A., Dckhd. (N.R.N.R.)
Baker, William A., Pte. (R.M.L.I.)
Bartlett, Charles, P.O. 1.
Batho, Percy John, Ld. S.
Bennett, Francis Arthur, A.B.
Bennett, G. A., En. (R.N.R.)
Benoit, James J., Sea. (N.R.N.R.)
Bevis, George William, Sto 1.
Birkenhead, T. A., Sea. (R.N.R.)
Black, H. J., Ld. Cook's Mate.
Black, Hugh, A.B. (R.N.V.R.)
Blyth, C., Dckhd. (R.N.R.)
Bonnett, H. E. A., Ord S.
Booth, Albert, Ord. S.
Bower, Alwyn, Pte. (R.M.L.I.)
Boyd, Adam, Sto. 1.
Bradley, Tom. E.R.A. 3.
Brennan, Patrick, Sea. (R.N.R.)
Brenton, Geo., Sea. (N.R.N.R.)
Brinston, L., Sea. (N.R.N.R.)
Browne, C. Charles F., Boy Tel.
Buckley, John, Sea. (R.N.R.)
Buller, S., Wir. Tel. O. (R.N.R.)
Bulley, Thomas, Sea. (R.N.R.)
Burch, R. N., Dckhd. (R.N.R.)
Burke, John, Yeo. Sig.
Burns, James, Sea. (R.N.R.)
Burrans, Geo. Fredk. (alias Burrnas, George Frederick), A.B.
Caine, R. W., Dckhd. (R.N.R.)
Calder, William, Sea. (R.N.R.)
Camp, Victor George, Ord. S.
Carlton, George, A.B.
Carr, Edward, Sto. (R.N.R.)
Carter, N., Pte. (R.M.L.I.)
Catlin, A., F., Pte. (R.M.L.I.)
Cheetham, Arthur B., E.R.A. 2.
Christian, John, Sea. (R.N.R.)
Clark, A. L., A.B. (R.N.V.R.)
Clark, Stephen C., Act. Ld. Sto.
Clarke, A. F., Sec. Hd. (R.N.R.)
Close, Herbert, A.B.
Coafiee, George Edwin, M.A.A.
Cochran, John, Pte. (R.M.L.I.)
Coe, J. A., Act. Ld. S. (R.N.V.R.)
Coles, William, A.B.
Collacott, Thomas James, P.O 1.
Coney, Herbert Henry, Sto. P.O.
Conntely, Patrick, Sea. (R.N.R.)
Cornish, Herbert, Sto. 1.
Cotton, John, Ord. S.
Coughlan, Dennis, Sea. (R.N.R.)
Coulson, John, En. (R.N.R.)
Crellan, Sam, Sea. (R.N.R.)
Crosby, James. En. (R.N.R.)
Crumpler, A. S., Act. Ld. Sto.
Cull, J. W., Pte. (R.M.L.I.)

Cumberland, T., Tmr. (R.N.R.)
Cumby, E., Sea. (N.R.N.R.)
Cunningham, Wm., Pte. (R.M.L.I.)
Cuthbert, Ralph, P.O. 1.
Darker, John, A.B.
Davies, J. V., Ord. Sig. (R.N.V.R.)
Davies, Joseph, Sea. (R.N.R.)
Davis, Roland, A.B.
*Dawes, W. D. S., Air Mech. 1.
Dickinson, John, Sto. 1.
Dickson, David Smart, A.B.
Dinan, Francis Frederick, A.B.
Diston, Amos, Sto 1.
Doddemeade, F. A., Sea. (R.N.R.)
Doe, Frederick, Sto. 1.
Donovan, John, Ld. S.
Dougherty, Alfred, Sea. (R.N.R.)
Doyle, Christopher, Sea. (R.N.R.)
Doyle, John, Sea. (R.N.R.)
Dyer, Harry, Sea. (R.N.R.)
Dymond, Ridgeway, Sto. 1.
Edney, James H., P.O. 1.
Elliott, Frank, A.B.
Elwell, John Wm., Sto. 1.
Evans, Thomas, Sto. 1.
Evans, W. H., Pte. (R.M.L.I.)
Everest, H. W., Aircraftman, 1.
Ewing, Robert Thompson, P.O. 1.
Falzon, F., Sto. (R.N.R., Malt.)
Farley, Joseph, Sea. (R.N.R.)
Farrant, William Thos., Of. Std. 2.
Fenson, Walter A., Ch. Sto.
Fieldwick, George, Sto. P.O.
Fisher, C. A., Pte. (R.M.L.I.)
Fitzgerald, Walter, Sea. (R.N.R.)
Fleming, John, Sea. (R.N.R.)
Forrest, Michael, Ld. Sto.
Fox, Harry, Sto. 1.
Frankish, James S., Sto. 1.
Fraser, Alexander, Ld. Mech.
Freake, E., Sea. (N.R.N.R.)
Futter, Arthur William, Ld. Sea.
Gallant, Alfred William, Ord. S.
Gamble, Albert Edward, Ld. Sea.
Garrett, John E., Sig. (R.N.V.R.)
Gasser, Joseph Henry, P.O. 1.
Gaule, James, Sea. (R.N.R.)
Gentle, John, Pte. (R.M.L.I.)
Gibbons, Martin, Tmr. (R.N.R.)
Gill, George, P.O. 1.
Goddard, Henry Charles, Sto. 1.
Goodall, George, Pte. (R.M.L.I.)
Goodall, W. H., Sig. (R.N.V.R.)
Goodman, Charles Eric, Sig.
Goodrum, C. W., Sig. (R.N.V.R.)
Goss, Edward, Sea. (N.R.N.R.)
Gray, Albert E., Musician (R.M.B.)
Gray, F. B., E.R.A. (R.N.V.R.)
Gray, Wm. M., En. (R.N.R.)
Green, George Lewis, Sig.
Greenwood, John, Sto. 1.
Griffin, John, Dckhd. (R.N.R.)
Griffiths, Denis S., Sig. Boy.
Griffiths, Robert E., Ld. S. (R.N.R.)
Griffiths, Thos., Ld. Tel.
Gurney, Charles Edward, A.B.
Hagan, John, Sea. (R.N.R.)
Hagan, Wm., Sergt. (R.M.L.I.)
Halliham, Timothy, Sto. 1.
Hancock, J., Pte. (R.M.L.I.)
Harding, Alfred Richard, Ld. S.
Hargate, L., Pte. (R.M.L.I.)
Harrington, Charles Henry, A.B.
Harris, Joseph, A.B.
Hart, Wm. H., Air Mech. 1.
Harthill, Harry, Pte. (R.M.L.I.)
Hawkes, Ed. J., Pte. (R.M.L.I.)
Heaney, Daniel, Sea. (R.N.R.)

Heaney, John, Sea. (R.N.R.)
*Heath, William T., C.P.O.
Hedge, J. A., Pte. (R.M.L.I.)
Hickling, Ernest Albert, A.B.
Hill, Robert, Sea. (R.N.R.)
Hill, Wm. J., Sea. (R.N.R.)
Hinchliffe, Percy, A.B.
Hitchin, Frank, Pte. (R.M.L.I.)
Hobbs, W. G., Shipwright, 2.
*Hollidge, W. T., Air Mech. 1.
Honey, S. S., Ord. Sig. (R.N.V.R.)
Hood, Robert, A.B. (R.N V.R.)
Hooper, Richard, Sto. 1.
Hooper, S. M., Sea. (N.R.N.R.)
Howard, Fredk. J., Act. Ld. Sto.
Howe, Arthur, Sto. 1.
Hoyle, Wm. C., Sto. (R.N.R.)
Hughes, Alfred G., Sea. (R.N.R.)
Hyde, Geo. E., Pte. (R.M.L.I.)
Ingham, R. E., Sea. (R.N.R.)
Jago, William H., C.P.O.
James, John, Sea. (R.N.R.)
Jamieson, William J. G., P.O.
Jenkins, Sidney R., E.R.A. 3.
Johnson, Ernest. Ord. S.
Johnson, Wm. A., Of. Std. 3.
Jones, Geo., Act. Ld. S. (R.N.V.R.)
Jordain, Samuel, Sea. (R.N.R.)
Kavanagh, James, Sea. (R.N.R.)
*Keeble, George, A.B.
Keeley, B., Sergt. (R.M.L.I.)
Kennedy, Edward, Act. Bombardier.
Kenny, John, Sea. (R.N.R.)
Kerley, Ethelbert Charles, P.O.
Kewley, Joseph, Sea. (R.N.R.)
Kiddle, Albert Edward, Sto. 1.
Kiely, Bartholomew, A.B.
Knight, Alexander, A.B. (R.N.V.R.)
Knight, Tom Ralph, A.B.
Knott, Charles John Henry, A.B.
Lake, G. A., Dckhd. (R.N.R.)
Lambert, David, Sto. 1.
Laverty, A., Shipwright, 2.
Laverty, William, Ld. S.
Lawrence, Ernest William, A.B.
Ledgard, Arthur, Ord. S.
Lee, Charles Henry, Sto. 1.
Lee, Wm. Geo., Ld. Sig.
Lester, J. R., L.-Cor. (R.M.L.I.)
Lewis, R. V., C.E.R.A. (R.N.R.)
Little, John William, Sto. 1.
Loddey, Sidney W., P.O. 1
Ludby, Alfred George, A.B.
Luscombe, Andrew, P.O.
Lynch, Michael, Sea. (R.N.R.)
McCormack, Alfred, Sto. 1.
McDonald, Angus, Sea. (R.N.R.)
McDonald, Norman, Sea. (R.N.R.)
McEvoy, John, Sea. (R.N.R.)
McGhie, W. W., E.R.A. (R.N.V.R.)
McGirr, John F., Boy 1.
McGregor, Thomas, Sea. (R.N.R.)
McKean, James, Ld. S.
McKibbin, J. E., Sea. (R.N.R.)
McLaren, Arthur M., Sto. 1.
Mcl aughlin, John, Sto. 1.
McLean, James, Sea. (R.N.R.)
McLean, James, A.B. (R.N.V.R.)
McPherson, G., Sec. Hd. (R.N.R.)
McQuade, Alexander, Sto. 1.
Mahoney, Patrick, Sea. (R.N.R.)
Main, Wm., E.R.A. (R.N.R.)
Malony, Martin, Sea. (R.N.R.)
Manning, James Geo , Ld. Sto.
Manzie, Thos., En. (R.N.R.)
Marsh, A. G. T., Pte. (R.M.L.I.)
Marshall, H. P., Sig. (R.N.V.R.)

21

Marston, W., Sto. (R.N.R.)
*Martin, J. H., Dckhd. (R.N.R.)
Martin, Tom, Ld. Sto.
Mason, A. V., Sig. (R.N.V.R.)
Meaghan, William, A.B.
Mickleburgh, S., Pte. (R M.L.I.)
Midwinter, Albert Edward, P.O.
Miller, Andrew, Pte (R.M.L.I.)
Miller, David, Sea. (R.M.L.I.)
Mills, Harry Ernest, A.B.
Milne, Robert, A.B. (R.N.V.R.)
Mitchell, David, A.B.
Mitchell, Thomas, Ld. Sto.
Moore, James, Sig. (R.N.V.R.)
Moyes, William Ernest, Ld. S.
Mugford, J., Sea. (N.R.N.R.)
Mullano, Timothy, Ld. S.
Murphy, Lawrence, Sea. (N.R.N.R.)
Newell, Harry Butler, A.B.
Newman, George Henry, Ld. S.
Newman, Michael, Sea. (R.N.R)
Newman, Robert, Sto. 1.
Nicol, Thomas, Sto. 1.
Nicolson, Duncan, Sea. (R.N.R.)
Niven, Allan, E.R.A. (R.N R.)
Norish, Alfred, C.P.O.
Norris, Richard, Sto. 1.
Notman, Geo. W. William, P.O.
Oatley, Maurice Joseph, Ord. S.
O'Brien, John Sea. (R.N.R.)
O'Brien, M. Ld. Dckhd. (R.N.R.)
O'Connell, Michael, Sea. (R.N.R.)
Odell, William Matthew, A.B.
O'Donnell, Colman, Sea. (R.N.R.)
Olden, Charles R. T., E.R A. 3.
Oliver, John. Sea. (R.N.R.)
O'Reilly, Thomas, Sea. (R.N.R.)
O'Sullivan, Thomas, Sea. (R.N.R.)
Page, Victor Albert, Sto. 1.
Palmer, Horace James, Ld. S.
Parker, G. C., A.B. (R.N.V.R.)
Parker, James, Pte. (R.M.L.I.)
Parsell, John Eric, A.B. (R.N.V.R.)
Penny, Ed. J., Pte. (R.M.L.I.)
Pickering, John, Sto. 1.
Pike, Thomas, C.P.O. (Pen.)
Piper, Walter Ed., Sto. 1.
Porter, Fredk. R., P.O.
Pote, Bertram Cecil, P.O.
Pratt, Sidney Arthur, Sto. 1.
Puddicombe, Wm., Sea. (N.R.N.R.)
Purcell, Charles Thomas, A.B.
Pym, Frank, Sea. (R.N.R.)
Quinlan, Thomas, Sea. (R.N.R.)
Randall, T. C., Sig. (R.N.V.R.)
Randell, Fredk., Sea. (N.R.N.R.)
Randell, Robert, Sea. (R.N.R.)
*Rankin, Edward, Sto. 1.
Reeves, Henry John, Sea. (R.N.R.)
Reid, R A., A.B. (R.N.V.R.)
Revell, Stanley H., Yeo. of Sig.
Reville, Patrick, Sea. (R.N.R.)
Reynolds, Laurence, Sea. (R.N.R.)
Reynolds, M. J., Act. Bom.
Richards, John Charles. A.M.
Richardson, Arthur, Ld. S. (R.N.R.)
Richardson, John Reed, E.R.A. 2.
Rickards, L. Robert, Act. Ld. Sto.
Riddell, J. H., Dckhd. (R.N.R.)
Roberts, James D R., P.O 2.
Roberts, J. A., E.R.A. (R.N R.)
Roberts, William, Sto. 1.
Rogers, Simeon, Sea. (N.R.N.R.)
Rooke, Hubert James, A.B.
Root, Frederick George, A.B.
Rozee, Thos. Geo. Alfred, A.B.
Sandison, R. G., Sea. (R.N.R.)
Sayer, Edward Walter, A.B.

Scarlett, Alfred. Sto. 1.
Scott, Archibald. Ch. Sto.
Scott, Henry Wm., Sto. P.O.
Scott, Robert, Sig. Boy.
Sheody, Fredk. A., A.B. (R.A.N.)
Simpson, Horace, Sto. 1.
Sims, Francis Geo., Ld. Mech.
Sinnott, Thomas. Sea. (R.N.R.)
Smith, Fredk. W. G., C.E.R.A. 2.
Smith, James, En. (R.N.R.)
Smith, John, Sea. (R.N.R.)
Smith, John R., Pte. (R.M L.I.)
Smith, Luke. Sea. (N.R.N.R.)
Snelgrove, F. J., Pte. (R.M.L I.)
Southcott, Henry James, S.B.S.
Southwell, J., Sec. Hd. (R.N.R.)
Sowerbutts, Henry, Dckhd. (R.N.R.)
Spanton, Robert, Sec. Hd. (R.N.R.)
Spink, E. V., Tmr. (R.N.R.)
Stark, Alfred John. P.O. 2.
Starkey, Ernest Roland, A.B.
Stretch, Herbert Charles, P.O.
Stubbings, Geo., Pte. (R.M.L.I)
Sutherland, A. Thos.. Sea. (R.N.R.)
Sutton, Alf., Pte. (R.M.L.I.)
Syers, Charles Henry, Sto. 1.
Tappenden, Alfred Bernard, A.B.
Tardivel, Frank, Sto. P.O. (C.G.)
Taylor, Albert Edward, C.P.O.
Taylor, Charles Albert, C.P.O.
Theakstone, James, A.B.
Thomas, John Wm.. Sea. (R.N R.)
Thompson. E., Dckhd (R.N.R.)
Trickett, Herbert, Ld. Tel.
Troy, Robert, P.O. 1.
Tucker, John C., Sea. (N.R.N.R.)
Turner, Arthur Ernest, A B.
Walls, James, Sea. (R.N R.)
Walters, L E., Dckhd. (R.N.R.)
Walters, S. A., Tmr. (R.N.R.)
Warburton, H. J., Sig. (R.N.V.R.)
Ward, Alfred Edward, A.B.
Webb, L. C., A.B. (R.N.V.R.)
Webster, Edmund, P.O. 1.
Went, F. A M., Pte. (R.M.L.I.)
White, Arthur E., Dckhd. (N.R.N.R.)
White, Leonard, Sto. 1.
Wilcocks, Robert, P.O.
Williams, Robert William, A.B.
Williamson, Geo. J., Act. Sto. P O.
*Wilson. William, En. (R.N.R.)
Windibank, Percy Henry, A.B.
Winterton, Ernest, A.B.
Wisdom, A. J., A.B. (R.N.V.R.)
Withers, M. John. Act. Sto. P.O.
Wooder, James, P.O.
Woodrow, Wm. F., A.B. (R.N.V.R.)
Woods, John Albert, Sea. (R.N.V.R.)
Woolard, Frederick, Sea. (R.N.R.)
Worsfold, William. Bombardier.
Wren, John L., A.B. (R.N.V.R.)
Wrench, Herbert, Ld. S.
Wright, H. B., Sec. Hd. (R.N.R.)
Yallop, E. J., Dckhd. (R.N.R.)
Yarnton, E. J., Pte. (R.M.L.I.)
Young, Wallace, Sea. (N.R.N.R.)
Yule, Victor D., Sig. (R.N.V.R.)

Specially Entered Mercantile Crew.

Allen, William, Fireman.
Archer, G. W., Greaser.
Ashcroft, R., Fireman.
Baldwin, W, F., Steward.
Beesley, T., Steward.
Bell, William, Greaser.
Bowdler, William, Fireman.
Bower, Edward, Bks. Mate.

Bramhall, Thomas, Fireman.
Brooks, A. E., Scullion.
Byers, G., Greaser.
Cain, W. I.., Steward.
Camilleri, L., Fireman.
Campbell. C. D., Trimmer.
Carr, J. J., Greaser.
Chapman, J., Steward.
Chetham, J., Fireman
Clark, N., Assistant Steward.
Coughlin, Henry, Trimmer.
Cove, A. L., Senior Writer.
Coyle, J., Fireman.
Craig, T., Steward.
Craze, Thomas, Fireman.
Crotty, Thomas J., Fireman.
Dodd, R. F., Steward.
Doodson, A. J., Cook.
Dooley, P., Greaser.
Donoghue, John, Fireman.
Dunston, J., Cook's Boy.
Edwards, F., Painter.
Eversfield, Steven, Trimmer.
Fennick, John, Assistant Cook.
Fisher, Richard, Electrician.
Fletcher, J., Fireman.
Forshaw, John, Fireman.
Gardiner, E., Fireman.
Gavin, P., Fireman.
Godfrey, A. E., Cooper
Godfrey, R R., Ch. Cook's Mate.
Green, A. E., Greaser.
Green, N., Greaser.
Groves, Frederick T., Trimmer.
Haines, W. E., Assistant Steward.
Halliday, Rees, Shipwright.
Halsall, T., Trimmer.
Hennessey, J., Fireman.
Hilton, Allen Percy, Greaser.
Hinds, A., Trimmer.
Hodges, A., Fireman.
Holbrook. H., Steward.
Hosier, A., Scullion.
Hughes, W. G., Charge Steward.
Iles, W. H., Chief Cook.
Jackson, L., Trimmer.
James, Henry, Assistant Steward.
Jamieson, Alex, Trimmer.
Jarvis, G. E., Assistant Steward.
Jones, Hugh, Steward.
Jones, James, Fireman.
Jones, J., Steward.
Kelly, Thomas, Fireman.
Kirkham, W., Chief Butcher.
Lacey, Joseph, Assistant Cook.
Langdon, Frank, Ld. Greaser.
Lawrie, J., Fireman.
Lloyd, W. F., Shipwright.
Lucas, H., Trimmer.
McAdam, J., Fireman.
McDonald, R., Trimmer.
McGarry, T., Fireman.
McGregor, L., Trimmer.
Maddocks, L., Greaser.
Magner, J., Shipwright.
Masheder, William. Scullion.
Matthews, Pat, Greaser.
Meek, William, Fireman.
Metcalf, Thomas, Carpenter's Mate
Milton, J. T., Fireman.
Moorhouse, E., Sec. Butcher.
Morgan, Joseph, Ship's Cook.
Morris, A., Steward.
O'Callaghan, A., Scullion.
Oldrey, E. H., Fireman.
Ollosson, C., Steward.
O'Neill, M., Fireman.
Oney, R., Greaser.

The Navy's Immortal Names

Palethorpe, F., Assistant Baker.
Park, E., Steward.
Parsons, C., Steward
Partington, W., Steward.
Pearson, George, Writer.
Perrett, J. J., Assistant Cook.
Piper, William, Trimmer.
Pouncey, G. W., Stoker.
Proctor, R., Trimmer.
Rafter, D., Steward
Rattigan, J., Fireman.
Rich, Charles, Steward.
Riley, T., Fireman.
Roberts, J., Plumber.
Roberts, William, Fireman.
Royle, F., Sailmaker.
Rushbrook, John, Trimmer.
Rushton, C., Steward.
Sherwood, William H. T., Greaser.
Skinner, Hugh, Fireman.
Smart, G. R., Assistant Cook.
Smith, A., Greaser.
Smith, W. J., Trimmer.
Steele, A., Assistant Cook.
Steele, E., Steward.
Stevens, George W., Scullion.
Thompson, John, Trimmer.
Todman, Alfred, Trimmer.
Wallace, C., Steward.
Warren, Charles, Fireman.
Watkins, Fredk. Thomas, Fireman.
Wiggs, A., Shipwright.
Wildman, Arthur, Fireman.
Winker, Thomas, Trimmer.
Woodhall, A. F., Fireman.
Young, H. G., Steward.

FEBRUARY, 1917.

Ashworth, Charles, Dckhd. (R.N.A.)
Ayres, G. H., Dckhd. (R.N.R., T)
Bage, Fred, Tmr. (R.N.R., T.)
Baskcomb, H. O., Sec. Hd. (R.N.R.)
Baxter, Gilbert, Tmr. (R.N.R.)
Bedson, J. W., Dckhd. (R.N.R.)
Bell, Charles Albert, Sto. 1
Bennett, F. C., Act. Ld. S. (R.N.R.)
Bessey, George, Dckhd. (R.N.R.)
Birmingham, Frederic B., E.R.A. 1.
Birnie, Wm. A., Tmr. (R.N.R.)
Black, James, Sto. 1.
Bonner, Daniel, Ld S.
Bowden, Geo., Dckhd. (R.N.R.)
Bright, Donovan Neville, A.B.
Brown, Alfred, Sto. 2.
Brown, Ed. W., A.E.R.A. 4.
Brown, J. L., Boy Cook (R.N.R.)
Bullent, J. E., Dckhd. (R.N.R.)
Bullock, W. E., En. (R.N.R.)
Burnett, E. Wm., Sea. (R.N.R.)
Burnett, James, Tmr. (R.N.R.)
Bush, R., Ord. Tel. (R.N.V.R.)
Butler, J. Wm., Dckhd. (R.N.R.)
Byrne, Patrick, Sto. (R.N.R.)
Cabble, H. O., Sec. Hd. (R.N.R.)
Caldwell, Alexander, Sto. 1.
Campbell, J. A., Air Mech. 2.
Carter, A. E., Tmr. (R.N.R.)
Case, Charles William, A.B.
Christie, Alex., Dckhd. (R.N.R.)
Churchill, Fred, Sto. P.O.
Churchill, Seth, Act. Bombardier.
Clayton, Thos., Dckhd. (R.N.R.)
Clues, William, En. (R.N.R.)
Comben, J. W., Tmr. (R.N.R.)
Constant, John, Sto. 1.
Conway, G. H., En. (R.N.R.)

Cook, James, Dckhd. (R.N.R.)
Cook, Wilfred, Act. Ld. Sto.
Corner, S. Thos., E.R.A. 5.
Cowan, Wm. John, Sea. (R.N.R.)
Cowie, Alex., Tmr. Cook (R.N.R.)
*Cowin, G. L., Air Mech. 1.
Crumpton, A., L.-Cor. (R.M.L.I.)
Cubbins, Wm. George, Sto. 1 (Pen.)
Cutler, William Geo., Sto. P.O.
Davis, Henry James, Sto. 1.
Dawson, F., Tmr. (R.N.R.)
Dean, Percy William, A.B.
Dent, James M., C.E.R.A. 2.
Depper, George, C.P.O. Mch. 3.
Dick, James, Sea. (R.N.R.)
Dickens, T. J., En. (R.N.R.)
Dodds, Matthew Dobson, A.B.
Douds, M. T., Tmr. Cook (R.N.R.)
Doherty, Arthur R., Of. Cook, 2.
Driscoll, James, P.O. 2.
Drodge, Edward John, A.B.
Dromgool, Joseph, Sto 1.
Duchart, George, Sea. (R.N.R.)
Duff, Alexander, Sea. (R.N.R.)
Dumond, George August, Of. Std. 2.
Dyer, H. Wm., Ll. Cook's Mate.
Dyke, J. W., Act. Ld. S. (N.R.N.R.)
Ebling, Bertie, E.R.A. 4
Edgson, E. W., Sig. (R.N.V.R.)
Engwell, George V., Ld. Sto.
Fairless, John, En. (R.N.R.)
Finnigan, John Henry, Sto. P.O.
Flynn, Thos., Tmr. (R.N.R.)
Ford, George Henry R., A.B.
Fortnum, William George, Ld. S.
Fowlow, Z., Act. Ld. S. (N.R.N.R.)
Galbraith, James, Dckhd. (R.N.R.)
Gardiner, Charles James, A.B.
Gerada, G., Fireman (Malt.) (R.N.R.)
Gibbs, Geo. W., En. (R.N.R.)
Gifford, J. L. J., Act. Ld. S. (R.N.R.)
Gill, V. J. A., Air Mech. 1.
Glavin, William, Ld. S. (R.N.R.)
Goble, George Edward, Sto. P.O.
Goble, Thomas, Sto. P.O.
Goldsmith, Alfred Charles, Ld. Sto.
Goodall, Herbert Thomas, Sto. 1.
Goodbrand, A. S., P.O. (R.N.R.)
Greenwood, Richard, Ld. Tel.
Gregson, Henry, Tel. (R.N.V.R.)
Grey, Henry P., En. (R.N.R.)
Grisenthwaite, A. E., Dkhd. (R.N.R.)
Hague, William, Dckhd. (R.N.R.)
Haigh, Frank, En. (R.N.R.)
Harrington, P., Dckhd. (R.N.R.)
Hawker, James Henry F., A.B.
Henderson, James, Dckhd. (R.N.R.)
Hill, Alexander, A.B.
Hodgson, James, Sto. P.O.
Holland, John, Sea. (R.N.R.)
Hollands, Arthur Edward, A.B.
Hook, Benjamin Wm., Sto. 1.
Hopgood, William, Ch. Sto.
Hughes, Owen, A.B.
Hunt, John Wm., Sto. P.O.
Hunter, Wm. L., Sec. Hd. (R.N.R.)
Jackson, Reuben, A.B.
*James, Joseph George, Sto. 1.
Jewell, A. John, Sea. (R.N.R.)
Johnson, John, En. (R.N.R.)
Kendle, William C. Tom, P.O.
Kinrade, Alfred, En. (R.N.R.)
Kirk, G. H., Dckhd. (R.N.R.)
Kirkpatrick, T. W., Cook (R.N.R.)
Lack, Robert John, A.B.
Lamont, D., Dckhd. (R.N.R.)
Landels, William, Sig. Boy. (R.N.R.)
Laurenson, R. D., Sea. (S.R.N.R.)

Lavender, James William, Sto. 2.
Lawrence, A. W., Tmr (R.N.R.)
Lawrence, Wesley M., Sto. 1
Leask. George. Sea. (R.N.R.)
Leask, J. Alex., Sea. (R.N.R.)
Lee, John. Sto. P.O.
Lenman, J. C., Dckhd. (R.N.R.)
Lincoln, Alick, A.B.
Lissett, John Robert, Sto. 1.
Lockyer, Albert, A.B. (R.N.V.R.)
Lodge, Francis, Ord. 1.
London, Peter C., Ord. Tel.
Lowe, Wm. R., Sig. (R.N.V.R.)
Lucas, William George, A.B.
Lupton, S., Dckhd. (R.N.R.)
Macdougall, H., Dckhd. (R.N.R.)
Mackay, Alex., Sea. (R.N.R.)
Mackay, Robert, Dckhd. (R.N.R.)
Maclean, John, Dckhd. (R.N.R.)
Macrae, M., Ld. Dckhd. (R.N.R.)
McAngus, William, Sea. (R.N.R.)
McCallum, J., Tmr. (R.N.R.)
McCarthy, James Sullivan, Arm.
McDowell, Edward Arthur, A.B.
McIntosh, A. C. K., Sig. (R.N.V.R.)
*MacIver, Donald, Ld. S. (R.N.R.)
McKay, J. K. M., Sea. (R.N.R.)
McKay, J. S. D., Tmr. Ck. (R.N.R.)
McKenzie, K., Sea. (R.N.R.)
McLeod, John, Ld. Dckhd. (R.N.R.)
McLeod, Simon, Sea. (R.N.R.)
Mahoney, Edward. Ld. S.
Malcolmson, Wm., Ld. S. (R.N.R.)
Markwell, James, Dckhd. (R.N.R.)
Marnie, G., Ld. Dckhd. (R.N.R., T.)
Martin, J. M., Tmr. (R.N.R.)
Mason, O. C., Dckhd. (R.N.R.)
Matthews, Martin, Sea. (R.N.R.)
Mills, Cecil P. F., Of. Std. 2.
Mills, Charles, En. (R.N.R.)
Mills, John Thomas S., A.B.
Mitchell, Oliver, Sto. P.O.
Mitchinson, R. W., Dckhd. (R.N.R.)
Moore, Reginald, A.B.
Morris, Ernest E., Of. Std. 3.
Morris, Robert. Sec. Hd. (R.N.R.)
Morrison, David, Tmr. (R.N.R.)
Mort, Paul, A.B.
Myers, J. H., Dckhd. (R.N.R.)
Newlove, George Robinson, A.B.
Newman, Ernest James, Ld. S.
Oxenbury, G. E., Dckhd. (R.N.R.)
Pahner, Leslie, Sig. (R.N.V.R.)
Palmer, M., Sec. Hd. (R.N.R.)
Parker, Geo., En. (R.N.R.)
Parker. Lewis. A.B.
Pask, Re. G., Dckhd. (R.N.R.)
Penrose, Alfred, Tmr. (R.N.R.)
Phillips, C. W., Sig. (R.N.V.R.)
Phillips, Frederick, Sto. 1.
Phillips. John, En. (R.N.R.)
Poole, W. F. W., Dckhd. (R.N.R.)
Portsmouth, R. S., Air Mech. 2.
*Pote. Reginald J. R., Sto. 2.
Pullen, A. J., Pte. (R.M.L.I.)
Railton, J. R., Tmr. (R.N.R.)
Randall, William, Sto. 1.
Reddell, Frederick R., Ld. Sig.
Ree, Philip J. R., Ch. Writer.
Repass, John, Ord. S.
Rennie, David. En. (R.N.R.)
Riley, S., Tmr. (R.N.R.)
Robson, H. M., Sec. Hd. (R.N.R.)
Robson. T. A., En. (R.N.R.)
Rollinson, J. R., En. (R.N.R.)
Rook, W. H., Dckhd. (R.N.R.)
Rose. A. E., Sec. Hd. (R.N.R.)
Rose, James, Sea. (N.R.N.R.)

The Navy's Immortal Names

Ruscoe, Joseph. Ld. S.
Ruthen, Samuel, P.O. (R.N.R.)
Sanders, H. H., Tmr. (R.N.R.)
Saunders, William Harris, P.O.
Savory, William, Sto. 1.
*Saver, Ellis Edward, P.O
Scutt, Geo., Tmr. (R.N.R.)
Sherman, Wilfred James, A.B.
Shereman, William, En. (R.N.R.)
Smallman, Francis John, Sto. P.O.
Soutar, James, En. (R.N.R.)
Southwell, Charles, Sto. P.O
Stalker, Robert, En. (R.N.R., T.)
Stockton, William, En. (R.N.R.)
Stone, Alfred, A.B.
Stoyle, A. J., Pte. (R.M.L.I.)
Sutherland, William, Sea. (R.N.R.)
Sweet, William John. A.B.
Symons, W. F, Dckhd. (R.N.R.)
Symons, Gilbert Harold, Sto. 1.
*Taylor, W. D., Dckhd. (R.N.R.)
Tennant, J. W., Tmr. (R.N R.)
Thomas, J. E , Dckhd. (R.N.R.)
Thomson, John, Ld. S. (R.N.R.)
Todd, George, Ord. Tel. (R.N.V.R.)
Todd, H. Lily, A.B. (R.N.V.R.)
Tothill, Rolf Francis Cole. A.B.
*Tucker, Frank E., Sto. 2.
Travers, William, A.B.
*Upstall, Fredk. John, Sto. 1.
Veal, T, C , Dckhd. (R.N.R.)
Waddington, Edgar, Ord. S.
Wagg, Arthur, Act. Ld. Sto.
Walker, Francis, Pte. (R.M.L.I.)
*Ward, Stanley, Ld. Sto.
Watson, C. P., Dckhd. (R.N.R.)
Whalley, Thomas, Tmr. (R.N.R.)
Wharton, Fred, En. (R N.R., T.)
White, Robert, Ord. Sig.
White, William, A.B.
Whitehouse, Rowland, Sto. 1.
Wilks, Alfred Henry, A.B.
Williams, William George, Sto. 1.
*Wills, Herbert William, A.C.
Wilson, Henry, Ld. Sto.
Wintle, Cyril, A.B.
Wood, Frederick Victor, A.B.
Wood, William, Sto. 1,
Wright, Wm. J., Cook (R.N.R.)
Yellow, John G., Sto. (R.N.R.)

Specially Entered Mercantile Crew.

Apsey, Clarence, Sec. Steward.
Bartolo, Guiseppe, Greaser.
Bonett, C., Assistant Steward.
Bragg, R. A., Steward.
Clugston, A., A.B.
Comyn, Frank Chip's Cook.
Cornish, Stephen, A B.
Cruice, George, Fireman.
Duck, Frederick, Assistant Std.
Farrugia, G., Steward
Gibney, Bernard, Assistant Steward.
Greggor, T., Carpenter.
Hamilton, Frank, 3rd Engineer.
Irving, David, Seaman.
Jamie, David, Fireman.
Jones, Robert, 2nd Mate.
Kerruish, John, Trimmer.
Kesson, William, 3rd Engineer.
Lonegar, Matthew, Scullion.
McCarthy, N , Donkeyman.
McLaren, Charles, Fireman.
Marett, Joseph, Fireman.
Noel, Philip. A.B.
O'Keefe, Timothy, A.B.

Pearson, Sidney, Seaman.
Phillips, Edward G., Assistant Cook.
Powell, James,. Fireman.
Salmon, George, Cook.
Shepard, Thomas, Assistant Cook.
Steady, William J., A.B.
Stephen, Alexander, Carpenter.
Stewart, George, 2nd Engineer.
Tardito, C., Fireman.
Thorne, Ernest, Greaser.
Tiley, Henry T., Greaser.

MARCH, 1917.

Allan, Ernest, A.E.R.A 4.
Allison, James, Sig. (R.N.V.R.)
Allwork, Henry William, Ld Sig
Anderson, Henry, Sea. (R.N.R.)
Anderson, H. J., Sea. (R.N.R.)
Anderson, M. J., Sea. (R.N.R.)
Anderson, R. J., Sea. (R.N.R.)
Archer, Ernest, P.O.
Archer, Joseph, Ld. Sto.
Arm, Henry Victor, Boy Tel.
Arnold, James, Sto. 2.
Ashcroft, William Herbert, Tel.
Atcheson, James, P.O. 1.
Bailey, P. R. A., Ord. Tel.
Baker, R. S., Dckhd. (R.N.R.)
*Baker, Tom, Gun. (R.M.A.)
Balls, Harry Arthur, Sig. Boy.
Bashforth, James William, A.B.
Bates, Harry, Sto. 2.
Bell, Tom, Tmr. (R.N.R.)
Belsey, Leonard, P.O.
Bennett, James John, Of. Std. 2.
Bennett, John William, Sig.
Bigsby, Albert E. V., Sto 2.
Birchall, Alfred, A.B. (R.N.V.R.)
Blakey, John William, A.B.
Blewett, John M., Ld Sea. (R.N.R.)
Blows, Frank, Sto. 2.
Bolton, Henry, Ch. P.O.
Boorman, Albert Ed., Ch., P.O.
Bourne, George, A.E.R.A. 4.
Bowen, William, Ch. Sto.
Boxer, William T., E.R.A. 3.
Boyland, C. D., Air Mech. 1.
Bradley, Austin, Ord. S.
Bramwell, Frederick, P.O.
Brandon, J. M., Tel. (R.N.V.R.)
Brashier, Jubilee John, Act. Ld. Sto.
Breeley, Alfred, E.R.A. 4.
Brennan, Alexander, A.B.
Briant, Gordon Walter, Sto. P.O.
Broming, Edmund S., Sto. 1.
Broom, F. H., Dck Boy (R.N.R.)
Brown, A. E., Ld. Cook's Mate.
Brown, Alex. C., Sto. 1.
Bruce, Richard W., E.R.A. (R.N.R.)
Buchan, David, Dckhd. (R.N.R.)
Bull, Joseph Angelus, A.B.
Burgoyne, S. A., En. (R.N.R.)
Burton, J. E., Tmr. (R.N.R.)
Butler, Arthur William, Sto. 1.
Cable, J., Dckhd. (R.N.R.)
Campbell, Robert, Tmr. (R.N.R.)
Cantrill, J. H., Wireman 1.
Carey, Alfred Dckhd. (R.N.R.)
Carr, William, Sto. P.O.
Carrirge, Henry, Sto. 1.
Cartland, Francis, A.B.
Casey, Daniel, A.B. (C.G.)
Cawley, George R., Of. Std. 3.
Chambers, Wilfred, Sto. 2.
Chapple, George. P.O.

Christie, George, En. (R.N.R.)
Clapcott, Frederick, Of. Std. 3.
Clarke, James, Painter 2.
Clay, James Smith, A.B.
Coates, Frederick James, A.B.
Cole, Harold George, Sto. 1.
Collins, Geo., Tmr. (R.N.R.)
Collins, Wm. M., Dckhd. (R.N.R.)
Colton, Terrence, Ord. S.
Connolly, Patrick, Sto. (R.N.R.)
Connor, Timothy, Ld. S (R.N.R.)
Convin, Sidney, Of. Std. 3.
Cook, A. T., Dckhd. (R.N.R.)
Copeland, Alfred, E.R.A. 3.
Cottingham, Victor, A.B.
Coy, Thomas, Ld. Tel.
Crittenden, Howard George, Sto. 2.
Croft, T. C., Sig. (R.N.V.R.)
Crowhurst, Edward John, Ord. S.
Crundall, Frederick W. M , Sto. 1.
Cunnington, R. W , A.B. (R.N.V.R.)
Danes, Albert Victor, Ld. Sto.
Davidson, Douglas, Tmr. (R.N.R.)
Davies, Albert, Tmr. (R.N.R.)
Davies, Alexander, Sto 1.
Davies, David, Sig. (R.N.V.R.)
Davies, N. J., Sig. (R.N.V.R.)
Davies, Richard, Dckhd. (R.N.R.)
*Davies, Thomas Samuel, Ord. S.
Davis, John Hughes, Sto. 1.
Dawson, William, Tmr. (R.N.R.)
Ditchburn, Charles, Tmr. (R.N.R.)
*Doer, William Henry, P.O.
Dolligan, Bernard, Sto. (R.N.R.)
Douglas, O. R., Ord. S.
Dowdall, Patrick Joseph, A.B.
Downer, William Geo., Sto. P.O.
Drew, William, Sec. Hd. (R.N.R.)
Durrand, James, Dckhd. (R.N.R.)
Earle, Edwin, Sto. 1.
Eddolls, F. J., L.-Cor. (R.M.L.I.)
Edworthy, F. W. S., Ord. S.
Elder, George, A.B.
Elkins, George, A.B. (C.G.)
Elsey, Lawrence Jeffery, A.B.
Emerson, Francis, A.B.
Errett, Walter Edwin R., A.B.
Evans, C. F., Dckhd. (R.N.R.)
Evans, Walter, Sig.
Evans, William, Sto. 1.
Evens, Joseph Reginald, Sto. P.O.
Farmer, Joe V. Lloyd, Sto. 1.
Fewtrell, Sydney, A.E.R.A. 3.
Finnerty, Robert, Sto. 1.
Firman, E. J., Sec. Hd. (R.N.R.)
Fisher, Arthur Merton, Ord. S.
Fletcher, Nelson Scott, A.B.
Franklin, S. W. W., Cook's Mate.
Gamblin, Harry, Sto. P O.
Gander. George Arthur, A.B.
Gardiner, John, Sec. Hd. (R.N.R.)
Genower, John Player, A.B.
Gerrie, Arthur, Tmr. Cook (R.N.R.)
Gibbon, T. E., Tmr. (R.N.R.)
Gibbons, Thomas, Ord. S.
Gidley, Ernest, Sto. P.O.
Gillham, Edward, P.O.
Glynn, William, Ord. S.
Goatham, Augustus, Ld. Sto.
Goldsmith, Frederick K., Ld. S.
Goode, A. E., Air Mech. 2.
Gorman, R. E., Air Mech 2.
Gosnell, Charles Albert, Ord. S.
Grantham, James Norman, A.B.
Graves, William, Tmr. (R.N.R.)
Greason, H. Geo., A.E.R. A.. 4.
Greaves, Benjamin Stringer, A.B.

The Navy's Immortal Names

Grebbell, Cyril Wilkinson, L.S.
Grice, J. W. S., En. (R.N R.)
Griffiths, Leonard, Ord. S.
Grimshaw, George Albert, Sto. 1.
Grimston, J. W., En. (R.N.R.)
Groom, Horace E., Ld. Cook's Mate.
Grosse, Frank, A.B.
Gyllenship, Gustavus A., Ld. S.
Halfhead, Herbert Henry, A.B.
Hamblin, Herbert Henry, A.B.
Hamilton, James Hope, A.B.
Hamilton, John, A.B.
Hancox, George William, A.B.
Hands, Henry Lewis, Sto. 1.
Harding, E. J., Dckhd. (R.N.R.)
Harfield, Frederick, A.B.
Hargreaves, William, Sto. 1.
Harris, Alfred, A.C.
Harris, Bert, Ld. Sto.
Harris, George William, Sto. 1.
Hatfield, John Isaiah, Boy Tel.
Hawker, John, Ld. S.
Hawkes, George, Ld. Sig.
Haworth, Samuel Bamford, A.B.
Heeney, Thomas, Sto. P.O.
Heeps, W. H., Tmr. (R.N.R.)
Hodder, John Francis, Sto. 1.
Herbert, James John, Ld. S.
Hersee, Arthur Geo., Of. Std. 2.
Hinchcliff, William Percy, Ord. S.
Hinton, William Thomas, A.B.
Hodson, Fred, Sto. 1.
Holland, Arthur, Ord. Tel.
Holloway, Herbert George, Ld. Sto.
Hollowood, Harry, A.B.
Holmes, Charley, P.O.
Holmes, John, Sto. P.O.
Hopkins, Herbert, A.B.
Hopper, Geoffrey, Act. Ld. Sto.
Horscroft, Alfred, Sto. P.O.
Howard, Charles Thomas, A.B.
Howarth, Tom, A.B.
Howell, Joseph, C.E.R.A. 1.
Hulford. Sidney Arthur, Sto. 1.
Hunt, Henry, Ord. S.
Hyde, William, Tmr. (R.N.R.)
Ilston, John, P.O.
Innes, Clare, En. (R.N.R.)
Irvine, Alex., Ld. S. (R.N.R.)
James, John A., Sea (N.R.N.R.)
James, Thomas Wm , Sig
Johnson, Jack, Sto. 1.
Johnson, William H., Ord. S.
Johnstone, George, Sto 1.
Jones, Ben. George. Ld. S.
Kay, William Livingstone, A.B.
Kayes, Joseph, Ld. S.
Keatley, John, Sto. 1.
Kelly, J. H., Sec. Hd. (R.N.R.)
Kelly, Walter, A.B.
Kemp, Herbert William, Sto. 1.
Kennett, George William, A.B.
Kerr, Alexander, C.E.R.A. 2.
Kerry, Edward, Dckhd. (R.N.R.)
King, Herbert Henry, A.B.
King, P. G., A.B. (R.N.V.R.)
Kipps, H. E., Tel. (R.N.V.R.)
Kitchen, Reed Blackett, Ord. S.
Knight, Cyril Arthur, A.B.
Lacey, Peter, A.B.
Laight. William L., Sto. P.O. (Pen.)
Lamb, Charles, A.B.
Lambert, John Stephen, Sto. 1.
Lampon, Henry James, Sto. 1.
Langmaid, J. P., Ld. Dkhd. (R.N.R.)
Langridge, Albert V., C.P.O.
Langthorp, Thomas, Sto. 1.
Laurence, F., Dckhd. (R.N.R.)

Law, James Henry, Ord. S.
Lillis, Fred, P.O.
Lilly, Cecil B., Act. Ld. Sto.
Lloyd, Alfred, Act. Ld. Sto.
Lockey, Harry, Dckhd. (R.N.R.)
Lockie, Thomas, A.B. (R.N.V.R.)
Lomas, Henry Hugh, Sto. P.O.
Long, Albert Edward, Ld. S.
Loversedge, William, A.B.
McCarthy, Daniel, Sto. P.O.
McCulloch, William, Ch. Sto.
McDonagh, Patrick, Sea. (R.N.R.)
McDonald, Angus, A.B.
MacDonald, N., Dckhd (R.N.R)
McKay, Donald. Sea. (R.N.R.)
Mackenzie, Donald, Sea. (R.N R.)
McKenzie, Matthew, A.B.
McKeown, E. G., A.E.R.A. 4.
McLaughlin, Michael, Ord. S.
McLean, N., Dckhd. (R.N.R.)
McLennan, D. J., Dckhd. (R.N.R.)
Mahoney, Michael, Ch. Writer.
Manning, Richard, Tmr. (R N R)
Marks, Ernest George, Ld. Sto.
Marsh, Edward Arthur, Act. Ld Sto
Marshall, Peter Philip, A.B.
Martin, Henry Thomas, Ord. S.
Maskell, Frederick, Sto. 2.
Mason, Edwin Victor, A.B.
Mason, George, Sto. 1.
Matthews, Robert Sec. Hd. (R.N.R.)
May, Sidney John, A.B.
Maynard, John, Of. Std. 3.
Medway, P. W., Dckhd. (R.N.R.)
Merchant, E., Sig. Boy (R.N.R.)
Merritt, John, Pte. (R.M.L.I.)
Middleton, James Wm., Sto. 1.
Miller, Donald, Sea. (R.N.R.)
Millum, Charles Thos., Sto. 2.
Mitchell, William, Sea. (R.N.R.)
Moat, Geo. H., William. C., Ld. Sto.
Mooney, John, A.B.
Morgan, C. C., Cor. (R.M.L.I.)
Morgan, George Albert, P.O.
Mortimer, Sydney Pace, Sto. 1.
Murchie, T. C., E.R.A. (R.N.R.)
Murphy, William, Sig. (R.N.V.R.)
Neal, E. J. S., A.B. (R.N.V.R.)
Neale, Charles Hilary, Sto. 2.
Needle, Frank, Sto. 1.
Nolan, Wm., Act. Ld. S. (R.N.R.)
Northcott, John Sec. Hd. (R.N.R.)
Norton, Fredk., Tmr. (R.N.R.)
Nunn, H. Wm. Geo., Ld. Sto.
O'Brien, Michael, A.B. (R.N.V.R.)
Pacey, Harry, Sto. 2.
Pack, Walter, Sto. 1.
Padgett, Wm. Frank. Ord. S.
Panther, C. H., Ord. Tel. (R.N.V.R.)
Paterson, Edward, Ld. S. (R.N.V.R.)
Patton, Wm. C., A.B.
Payne, Charles P., Ld. S.
Payne, H. J., Pte. (R.M.L.I.)
Pearson, John, Tmr. (R.N.R.)
Pearson, John Arthur, A.B.
Peek, Samuel, Sto. 1.
Pembroke, James Martin, A.B.
Pearham, George, Sto. 1.
Perrin, G. A., Dckhd. (R.N.R.)
Pirry, William, A.B.
Pledge, B. Sidney, P.O.
Pope, William, Sto. P.O.
Portas, J. H. C., Ord. S.
Porter, William, A.B.
Power, John J., Sea. (N.R.N.R.)
Prout, W. J., Pte. (R.M.L.I.)
Pyle, Thomas, Ord. S.
Randall, Herbert Henry, Ld. S.

Randall, Joseph. A.B.
Rankin, Alex., Dckhd. (R.N.R.)
Rawson, E. A. A., Ld. Mech.
Reed, A. H., Act. Ld. S. (R.N.R.)
Reed, A. J., Pte. (R.M.L.I.) (Pen.)
Reid, John. Tmr. (R.N.R.)
Rich, Sydney, A.B.
Richardson, Fredk. Wm., Sig.
Richardson. H. F., Cook's Mate.
Rickarby, Arthur John, A.B.
Rigby, Charles Armour, Ord. S.
Ritchie, Henry, Dckhd. (R.N.R.)
Roake, Arthur, A B.
Robertson, James, A.B.
Robertson, J. J., Sea. (R.N.R.S.)
Robinson, Bertie Thomas, A.B.
Robus, F. J., Dckhd. (R.N.R.)
Rogers, Cyril Spencer. Sig.
Rogers, Edward, A.B.
Ross, John, Sto. 1.
Runacles, A. Wm., Ord. S.
Russell, Alfred. A.E.R.A. 4.
Rutherford, R., Ld. Dckhd. (R.N.R.)
Ryan, Thomas. A.B.
Salisbury, W. J., Tel. (R.N.V.R.)
Sargent, James, Sto. P.O.
Saunders, Albert E., Sto. 1.
Schofield, John, Ld. S (R.N.R.)
Scott, A. R. N., Tmr. (R.N.R.)
Scott, John Ross, Ld. Sto.
Scriven, Frederick John, A.B.
Searle, Frederick, Sto. 1.
Searle, Percy William, A.B.
Sedwell, John James, Sto. 1.
Shadwell, William C., Ord. S.
*Shapter, Herbert, Ch. Sto.
Sharman, Geo., Dckhd. (R.N.R.)
Sharp, Patrick, Ld. Boat. (C.G.)
Sharp, Stanley R., Act. Sto. P.O.
Sherwell, R. Z. H., E.R.A. 4.
Shipley, Fredk. J., Of. Std. 2.
Shirley, Henry, A.B.
Shotton, Geo., En. (R.N.R.)
Simpson, C. E., Dckhd. (R.N.R.)
Simpson, H. G., E.R.A. 3.
Simpson, Robert. Tmr. (R.N.R.)
Skelton, John, Ld. Sto.
Skewis, Edwin H., Boy Tel.
Skinner, George, Sto. 1.
Slaymaker, W. T., Pte. (R.M.L.I.)
Sleeth, J. F., En. (R.N.R.)
Smith, Arthur John, Ch. Sto.
Smith, Charles, Sto. 1.
Smith, Henry George, A.B.
Smith, John R., Sec. Hd. (R.N.R.)
Smith, Robert, Sto. P.O.
Smith, Wm. H., Of. Std. 3.
Soulsby, Geo., E.R.A. 1. (R.N.R.)
Spells, Charles Edward, Sto. 1.
Stafford, Albert, Ord. S.
Stafford, R. E., En. (R.N.R.)
Stanfield, B. A. J., Dckhd. (R.N.R.)
Stearn, Sydney James, Ld. Sig.
Steell, James, A.E.R.A. 4.
Stevens, John Henry, Ld. S.
Stevens, William Henry, A.B.
Stewart, James B., Ord. Sig.
Stewart, William, A.B.
Sullivan, Jeremiah, Sto. 1.
Sultan, Harry, Ld. S.
Swan, S. T., Dckhd. (R.N.R.)
Taylor, Edward Pearce. A.B.
Taylor, Samuel, Sea. (R.N.R.)
Taylor, Sydney C., Ord. S.
Terry, William J., Sto. P.O.
Tether, Luke. Dckhd. (R.N.R.)
Tew, Charles, Ch. Sto.
Thompson, Robert P., Ld. S.

25

The Navy's Immortal Names

Thorne, John, Sea. (R.N.R.)
Tilley, Robert James, A.B.
Titford, William George, Sto. 1.
Trayhern, Benjamin E., Sto. 1.
Triscott, T. J., Sea. (N.R.N.R.)
Troke, William H., Ord. S.
Truscott, T. H., Tmr. (R.N.R.)
Tucker, Albert Edward, Sto. 1.
Tuffin, Alfred R., P.O. (Pen.)
Tulett, Charles Henry, Sto. P.O.
Turnbull, Hugh Percy M., A.B.
Turner, William. A.B.
Turns, William B., Ld. Tel.
Twyman, Fredk. L., Boy Tel.
*Vaughan, Horace, Sto. 2.
Wakefield, Reginald James, Sto. 1.
Walker, Watson Diston, Sto. 1.
Walshe, William Henry. Ld. Sig.
Ward, Ernest, Pte. (R.M.L.I.)
Warden, C., Dckhd. (R.N.R.)
Watson, Arthur, A.B.
Watson, H. R. H., A.E.R.A. 4.
Watson, James, Dckhd. (R.N.R.)
Watt, W. L., Dckhd. (R.N.R.)
Weaver, Ivor Tom, Ord. S.
*Welham, L. V., Dckhd. (R.N.R.)
Wellings, Thomas Alfred, A.B.
Wheale, Joseph. Sto. (R.N.R.)
White, J. R., Dckhd. (R.N.R.)
White, Wm. Geo., Act. Ld. Sto.
Whitham, Albert, Ord. S.
Wholey, John, A.B.
Wickerson, Charles, Ld. S. (C.G.)
Wight, James. A.B. (R.N.V.R.)
Williams, Walter, Shipwright 1.
Willows, A., alias Taylor, Alfred, Dckhd. (R.N.R.)
Willson, C., Tmr. Cook, (R.N.R.)
Woodland, Walton J., C.E.R.A. 2.
Woodley, E. A , Ord. S. (R.N.C.V.R).
Woodward, William T., Ld. Sto.
Woolcock, H. E., Of. Std. 2.
Wornast, Charles Joseph, A.B.
Wright, Ernest Robert. Of. Std. 3.
Wright, F. J., Dckhd (R.N.R.)
Wright, Richard, Sto 1.
Yearby, F., Act. 'L.-Cor. (R.M.L.I.)

Specially Entered Mercantile Crew.

Brown, W., 2nd Engineer.
Dunn, Cornelius J., Fireman.
Fair, W., Engineer.
Fido, James, Greaser.
Fitzgerald, Edward. Fireman.
Houston, Robert, Steward.
McDonnell, G., Trimmer.
McPherson, Alexander, Assist. Std.
Miller, Russel E., Trimmer.
Ross, Andrew, Greaser,
Smallman, Frederick, Greaser.

APRIL, 1917.

Adam, S. S., Tmr. (R.N.R.)
Allen, Thomas J., Ld. S.
Allen, W. H., Ld Dckhd. (R.N.R.)
Amos, J., Ord. Tel. (R.N.V.R.)
Anderson, Thos., Dckhd. (R.N.R.)
Anderson, Thos., En. (R.N.R.)
Arlington, James, Dckhd. (R.N.R.)
Armstrong, H. E., Sig. (R.N.V.R.)
Ashton, Fredk., Sec. Hd. (R.N.R.)
Babstock, W. J., Qual. S. (N.R.N.R.)
Bagnall, Joe Watson, A.B.
Bailey, Fredk. Robert, Sto. 1.
*Banbrough, Robt., Dckhd. (R.N.R.)

Bannister, Thomas B., Ld. Sto.
Baxter, Albert, Tmr. (R.N.R.)
Baxter, Robert, Dckhd. (R.N.R.)
Bellamy, Epton, Sto. 2.
Benton. Harry, A.B. (R.N.V.R)
Bick, William George. Sto. 1.
Billam, J. F., Tmr. (R.N.R.)
Black, Geo. M., En. (R.N.R.)
Blackley, Wm., Tmr. (R.N.R.)
Blackman. James E., Sto. 1.
Blotham, J. A W., Sto. P.O.
Bolster, J. Millar, Sig. (R.N.V.R.)
Boots, James, Sto. 1.
Bowles, James R., Sec. Hd. (R.N.R.)
Bramley, James, En. (R.N.R.)
Braund, Charles Percy. Ld. Sto.
Brenchley, Alfred E, Sto. 2.
Brian, Daniel, Ld. Sto.
Brooks, Harry E., Sto. P.O.
Brooks, John, E.R.A. 1.
*Broomhead, J., A.B. (R.N.V.R.)
Bruce, M G., Ld. Dckhd. (R.N.R.)
Buchan, John, Sec Hd. (R.N.R.)
Buchan, Wm., Dckhd. (R.N.R.)
Buchan, Wm., Tmr (R.N.R.)
Burgess, J. N., Dckhd. (R.N.R.)
Burton, Ernest, Ld. S.
Burwood, W. J., Dckhd. (R.N.R.)
Byard, W. H, Dckhd (R.N.R)
Canavan, William, Sea. (R.N.R.)
Carbines, Wm. H., Ld. S. (R.N.R.)
Card, Geo. H., D.khd. (R.N.R.)
Carder, Frederick. Sto. 1.
*Carney, R. H., Air Mech. 1.
Carroll, George. En. (R.N.R.)
Carroll, H. J., Shipwright 1.
Castleman, Fredk. George, Ld. S.
Charles, J. H., Sig. (R.N.V.R.)
Chambers, John Alfred, Sto. P.O.
Chivers, Arthur, Ch. P.O. 3.
Clark, Wm. P., E.R A. (R.N.R.)
Clarke, C. T., Tmr. (R.N.R.)
Clarke, Dawson James, A.B.
Clarke, Fredk. J., Ld. S.
Clarke, M. E., Dckhd. (R.N.R.)
Clayfield, E. H., Act. Ld. S. (R.N.V.R.)
Clemett, Phillip George, Sto. 1.
Coghlan, J. L., Air Mech. 1.
Cole, R., Dckhd. (R.N.R.)
Conway, J., Ld. S. (N.R.N.R.)
Cope, George Fredk , Ld. S.
Cottle, Stephen John, A.B.
Coulet, Leonold. Dckhd. (R.N.R.)
Cowls, Fredk. J., A.E.R.A. 4.
Cox, Fredk. John. Sto. 1.
Cox. F. J., R , En. (R.N.R.)
Crawford, J., Dckhd. (R.N.R.)
Crear, E. G., En. (R.N.R.)
Cross, C. B., Dckhd (R.N.R.)
Crothall, George John, Sto. 2.
Croucher, James, Sto. P.O. (Pen.)
Daniels, William, Ld. Sto.
Darby, W., L.-Cor. (R.M.L.I.)
Dart, Charles Ernest. Ld. Sto.
Davies. T. G., En. (R.N.R.)
Dear, Percy, Act. Air Mech. 1.
Denton, Wm. Albert, Ord. S.
Donnelly, Robert, Sto (R.N.R.)
Down, James. Sto. P.O.
Doy, James, Dckhd. (R.N.R.)
Draper, C. J., En. (R.N.R.)
Duthie, C. J., Sec. Hd. (R.N.R.)
Dutton, Fredk., Dckhd. (R.N.R.)
Dykins, J., En. (R.N.R.)
Edwards, George. Dckhd. (R.N.R.)
Edwards, M., Ld. S. (R.N.R.)
Farquhar, David, Ld. Mech.

Farquhar, Geo., En. (R.N.R.)
Farrell, William James, P.O. 1.
Ferrier, J. R., Dckhd. (R.N.R.)
Field, Samuel, Sto. 1.
Finch, Walter Charles, Sto. 1.
Findlay, Wm , Dckhd. (R.N.R.)
Fitzgerald, John J., Sig.
Flatley, William, Sto. 1.
Flood, Thomas, Sto. P.O.
Ford, A. H., Ld. S. (R.N.R.)
Ford, Wm., Pte. (R.M.L.T.)
Foster, S. R., En. (R.N.R.)
Fox, William, Sto. 1.
Foxhall, William, Sto 2.
Fraser, John, Dckhd. (R.N.R.)
Freestone, Francis, Act. Ld. Sto.
Galbraith, J., Ld. Dckhd. (R.N.R.)
Gapper, Charles, A.B. (R.N.V.R.)
Gaunt, John, P.O.
Gay, Arthur Wm., Ld. S.
Gay, Thomas, Dckhd. (R.N.R.)
Gaywood, Harry W., Sto. 2.
Gedge, Harry, Sec. Hd. (R.N.R.)
Gibson, Alfred, Tmr. (R.N.R.)
Gibson, P. M., Dckhd. (R.N.R.)
Gidley, Sydney Herbert, P.O.
Gifford, J., Dckhd. (R.N.R.)
Godwin, Arthur F., Sig.
Gowl, H. C. P., Sec. Hd. (R.N.R.)
Graham, J. J., P.O. Mech.
Gravenor, A. W., Gun. (R.M.A.)
Gray, Herbert, A.C.
Gray, William, Dckhd. (R.N.R.)
Grayson, W. H., Dckhd. (R.N.R.)
Green, Daniel Edward, Sto. 1.
Green. John. A.B.
Grimmer, C. V., Dckhd. (R.N.R.)
Guthrie, G. C., Dckhd. (R.N.R.)
Halcrow, A., Ld. S. (R.N.R.) (Shet.)
Hare, T., Dckhd. (R.N.R.)
Harris, Charles Edward. A.B.
Harris, Ed. Wm., En. (R.N.R.)
Harris, W. T., En. (R.N.R.)
Haycock, A. E., Sig (R.N.V.R.)
Hayes, J., Dckhd. (R.N.R.)
Higginbottom, L., Dckhd. (R.N.R.)
Hilton, E., Wire. Tel. Opera. 1. (R.NR)
*Hoare, Frank, P.O. Mech.
Hodgking, T. H., Act. Bom. (R.M.A)
Hogan. Michael, Sto. 1.
Hope, D. James. Sto. 1.
Horn, W. C., Dckhd. (R.N.R.) (Fishing Section)
Hosier, Harry. Ord. S.
Howie, John Henry, A.B.
Humphrys, Alfred Stanley, A.B.
Hunter, R. E., Tmr. (R.N.R.)
Hutchinson, Wilfred, Ord. Tel.
Ingram, R. T., Tmr. (R.N.R.)
Innes, G. W., En. (R.N.R.)
Ireland. L. G., P.O. Mech.
Ivens, Geofory G., Ld. S.
Ivey, John, Dckhd. (R.N.R.)
Jackson, A. H., Dckhd. (R.N.R.)
James, R. N., En. (R.N.R.)
James, W. G., Sec. Hd. (R.N.R.)
Jeffery, C. G, Dckhd. (R.N R.)
Jellyman, Harry, Sto. 2.
Jewell, Edward, Dckhd. (R.N.R.)
Johnson, Wm., Dckhd. (R.N.R.)
Jones, Albert, Ld. Sto.
Jones, T. O., S. (R.N.R.)
Kavanagh, J. C., En. (R.N.R.)
Keay, A. C., Sec. Hd. (R.N.R.)
Keeble, Alfred, Ld. Dckhd (R.N.R.)
Keech, R., Ord. S. (R.N.C.V.R.)
Kelly, George A. J., Sto. 1.

The Navy's Immortal Names

Kennedy, George A. S., Arm.
Knowles, Robert, A.B. (R.N.V.R.)
Lace, George, Ld. S. (R.N.R.)
Lawrence, Fredk. Gun. (R.M.A.)
Lewis, Wm. J., Tmr. (R.N.R.)
Letley, J. T., Dckhd. (R.N.R.)
Lieper, George, Dckhd (R.N.R.)
Lightly, Jonathan, P.O. 2.
Linton. Andrew, Sto. 1.
Little, John Henry, Sto. 1.
Lockett, W. H., Sig. (R.N.V.R.)
Lockyer, A. G., Act Air Mech. 1.
Lyall, C. B., Dckhd. (R.N.R.)
Lynch, John, Tmr. (R.N.R.)
MacDonald, John, Dckhd. (R.N.R.)
MacFadyen, P., Ld. Dckhd. (R.N.R.)
MacLeod, Donald, Dckhd. (R.N.R.)
*Marjoram, P. J., Dckhd. (R.N.R.)
Marston, John, Tmr. (R.N.R.)
Martin, S. G., Dckhd (R.N.R.)
Marvelly, John, En. (R.N.R.)
Mason, Thomas Henry, A.B.
McAteer, J., Dckhd. (R.N.R.)
McDermott, J., Dckhd. (R.N.R.)
McDonald, N., Act. Ld. S. (R.N.R)
McDougall, P., Dckhd. (R.N.R.)
McGlasson, John, Tmr. (R.N.R.)
McKay, Neil, En. (R.N.R.)
McKenzie, Daniel. Sea. (R.N.R.)
McLean, H., Dckhd. (R.N.R.)
McLeod, George, A.B.
McVeigh, J M., Sto. P.O.
Mills, Joseph, Tmr. (R.N.R.)
Milne, F. J., Tmr. (R.N.R.)
Monk, Alfred George. Ld. Tmr.
Monro, John, Air Mech. 2.
Morrison, D., Sea. (R.N.R.)
Moss, J. O., Sto. P.O.
Muirhead, D., A.I.S. (R.N.V.R.)
Murray, Wm. J. A., Sto. 1.
Mylchreest, D., Ld. Tmr. (R.N.R.)
Nichols, A. George, Ord. S.
Nicolson, Donald, Sea. (R.N.R.)
Nightingale, W. J., Ord. S. (R.N.C.V.R.)
Nixon. R. Gu., En. (R.N.R.)
Norford, R. H., Sto 2.
Orchard, H. Geo., Sto. P.O.
Owens, John, A.B.
Packer, J. E., Dckhd. (R.N.R.)
Paterson, J. L, A.B. (R.N.V.R.)
Paterson. W. W., Dckhd. (R.N.R.)
Peacock, E., C.E.R A. (R.N.R.)
Pengelly, W. G. W., Ld. S. (R.N.R.)
Petrie, A. V. Dckhd (R.N.R., T.)
Phillips. R., Sea. (N.R.N.R.)
Philp, A. B., Sig. (R.N.V.R.)
Pierson, George, A.B.
Pirrie, R. F., Dckhd. (R.N.R.)
Platten, H. W., Tmr. (R.N.R.)
Plumtree, J. H., Dckhd. (R.N.R.)
Prescott, J., Dckhd. (R.N.R.)
*Price, John, A.B.
Prince. A. E, Of. Std. 2.
Puddington, Arthur, A.B.
Rafferty, James Joseph, Sto. 1.
Rampling, A. H., En., (R.N.R.)
Remphry, F. C., Tmr. (R.N.R.)
Reynolds, J. H., Motor Boatman, (R.N.V.R.)
Richards, G. W. P., E.R.A. 4.
Richings, Percy, Sto 1.
Ridgway, Wm., Dckhd. (R.N.R.)
Robinson, H., Tmr. (R.N.R.)
Robinson, H. S., En. (R.N.R.)
Robson, John W., Ld. Sto.
Samways, C. Frank, A B
Saunders, Henry George, P.O.

Scott, Thomas Robert. Sto. 2
Shillito, C., L.-Cor. (R.M.L.I.)
Silk, William Thomas, Ch. Sto.
Sims, Wm., Ld. Cook's Mate.
Smith, Alex., Dckhd. (R.N.R.)
Smith, A. G., Dckhd. (R.N.R.)
Smith, A. J., En. (R.N.R)
Smith, G. H, Tmr. (R.N.R.)
Smith, H. F., Ord. S.
Smith, James, Tmr. (R.N.R.)
Smith, Percy, P.O. Mech.
Snell, Condor, Deck Boy (R.N.R.)
Somerton, H. (Ld. S (N.R.N.R.)
Spink, A. J., Dckhd. (R.N.R.)
Steven, Wm, Ld. S. (R.N.R.) (Shet.)
Stevenson, C. H., Tmr. (R.N.R.)
Stone E. W., Sto. 2.
Strachan, D., En. (R.N.R.)
Stratford. J., Tmr. (R.N.R.)
Stratford, S.. Dckhd. (R.N.R.)
Suatt, C. John, Cook's Mate.
Summers, Albert Edward, P.O.
Swallow, Wm. Henry, Sto. 1.
Sylvester, J., Tmr. (R.N.R.)
Tadd, F., L.-Cor. (R.M.L.I.)
Tavender, A. Vernon, Ord. S.
Tavlor, Charles, Sto. 2.
Taylor, John, En. (R.N.R.)
Thompson, Geo. Wm., Sto. 1.
Thorpe, William. Sto. 1.
Tomkin, Percy, Sto. 2.
Towers, Robert Victor, Ord. S.
Tubb, George, A.B.
Turner, G. V., Air Mech. 1.
Underwood, G. P., Sig. (R.N.V.R.)
Walker, Harold. A.E.R.A. 4.
Wallace, Sidney. Of Std. 2.
Ward, John, A.B.
Watts, Henry. Tmr. (R.N.R.)
Weavers, A.. Air Mech. 1.
Webb, Alfred, Sto. 1.
Welch, M., Dckhd. (R.N.R.)
Wellard, Albert, Ld. Sto.
West. W. R, Dckhd. (R.N.R.)
Whybourn. Geo. E., Ord. S.
Wilcock, F. En. (R.N.R.)
Wilcox, W. E. H., Ord. S.
Wilkes, James T., Ld. Tel.
Wilkinson. Herbert, A.B.
Wilson, A., En. (R.N.R.)
Wilson, George, Sec Hd (R.N.R.)
Wilson, Isaac. Tmr. Cook. (R.N.R.)
Wiltshire, William G.. Ord. S.
Wood, Henry, Ord. S.
Wood, James, Sec. Hd. (R.N.R.)
Wood, John. En. (R N.R.)
Wood, W., Tmr. Cook. (R.N.R.)
Woolnough, G. R., Aircraftman 2.
Worth, Philio Charles. Sea. (R.N.R.)
Young, E. J., Sec. Hd (R.N.R.)

Specially Entered Mercantile Crew.

Allen, S. N., 3rd Engineer.
Bridgewater W., Assist. Steward.
Burnell, I. F., Assist. Motor Eng.
Coombs, H. M., Assist. Motor Eng.
Faircloth F. W., Motor Engineer.
Harvey, G. L., Assist. Motor Eng.
Spillane, David, Assist. Steward.
Taylor, A., Wire. Tel. Operator.
White, H. A. S, Senior Motor Eng.
Wooiton, E. W., Steward.

MAY, 1917.

Adamson. Magnus, Tmr. (R.N.R.)
Alden, John T., Tmr. (R.N.R.)
Andrews, Fredk. John, Sto. 1.

Ashby, Ernest R., Ld. Sto.
Avery, Jack. Sea. (N.R.N.R.)
Bailey. Robert. Sec Hd. (R.N R.)
Baldwin, H. R. P.. En (R.N.R.)
Ball, Douglas Frank, Boy 1.
Ball, Wm. John, Dckhd. (R.N.R.)
Beckett, Fred. Aircraftman, 2.
Peckett, Harold O., Ld. Sig.
Beer, Stanley V. J., A.B.
Bell, George, Sea. (R.N.R.)
Bennett, Ernest, Ld. S.
Bensley, James, Sec. Hd. (R.N.R.)
Berry. Michael, Sto. (R.N.R.)
Biggs, Edwin George. Sto. 1.
Billington, Edward, Sto. 1.
Bird. Robert William, Sto. 1.
Birse, D. John, Ld. Mech.
Bish, Joshua H., Ld. Sig.
Blackburn, Hugh Miller, A.B.
Blake, Reuben, Ch. Sto.
Blowers, H. J., Dckhd. (R.N.R.)
Blowers, J. E., Tmr. (R.N.R.)
Borhon, V. H. A.. A.E.R.A. 4.
Boulton, James. Dckhd. (R.N.R.)
Boyce, A. J., Dckhd. (R.N.R.)
Brady, Sydney, Tmr. (R.N R.
Brearley, Bertram, A.B.
Brookshaw, John James. A.B.
Brown, C., Dckhd. (R.N.R.)
Bryson, Lewis Irvine, A.C.
Buck, Bertie, Dckhd. (R.N.R.)
Burrows, William H., Ord. S.
Butler, Edward, Dckhd. (R.N.R.)
Butler, William, Sto. 1.
Carter, Ernest, Dckhd. (R.N R
Christie, James. Tmr. (R.N.R.)
Clark, Ernest William, A.B.
Clayton, A. E. W., En. (R.N.R.)
Colby, Wm., Dckhd. (R.N.R.)
Cooke, Harold John, Tel.
Cooper, Angelo James. Sto. 1.
Corlett, Wm., Dckhd. (R.N.R.)
Cowie, John, Dckhd (R.N.R.)
Cox, Herbert Edward Ord. S.
Cox, John Egbert, Tel.
Craig, David, E.R.A. 4.
*Crank, John, A.B. (R.N.V.R.)
Crews, C. H., Sec. Hd. (R.N.R.)
Crook, Alfred, Ord. Tel.
Crow, Thomas, Ord. S.
Curl, J. C., Ord. Tel. (R.N.R.)
Dawn. John H., Tmr. (R.N.R.)
Dennehy, J., Dckhd. (R.N.R.)
Dennis, Edgar, A.B. (R.N.V.R.)
Disbrey, Thomas Wm., Sto. 1.
Dodds, G., Ord. S. (R.N.C.V.R.)
Donald, Alfred, Sto. 1.
Draper, William, Pte. (R.M.L.I.)
Edwards, William Henry. A.B.
Ellingworth, C., Air Mech. 2.
Fahy, John, Dckhd. (R.N.R.)
Fawcett, W J., Painter 2.
Filmer, F. H. Chandler, *alias*
    Chandler, F., Of. Cook. 2.
Finch, W. J, Sec. Hd. (R.N.R.)
Flett, A., Sec. Hd. (R.N.R.)
Flintham. Walter. Ld. S.
Forrest, Philip Ernest, A.B.
Fowler, William H., En. (R N.R.)
Garrioch. John, En. (R.N.R.)
Gibson, H. N. J., Aircraftman. 2.
Gidley, Henry Charles. Ord. S.
Gilbey. H. F., Act. Ld Sto.
Gill, Thomas Henry, Sto. 1.
Gill, William George, Ld. S.
Gladwell. G. E.. En. (R.N.R.)
Glazebrook, William. Cook's Mate.
Goodearl, Charles, Sto. 1.

The Navy's Immortal Names

Gordon, A., Sec. Hd. (R.N.R.)
Grant, Alexander, Sea. (R.N.R.)
Grant, A. H, E.R.A. 1.
Gregory, T. J., Tmr. (R.N.R.)
Harding, Charles Leonard, A.B.
Harding, C. J., Sig. (R.N V.R.)
Harkess, Peter. A.B (R.N.V.R.)
Harper, W., Dckhd. (R.N.R.)
Harpham, A., Dckhd. (R.N.R.)
Harris, D. M., A.B. (R.N.V.R.)
Harris, Francis Ward, Sto. 2.
Hay, Alfred, Sec. Hd. (R.N.R.)
Helm, Robert, A.E.R.A. 4.
Hennessey, Archie Leonard, Sto. 1.
Hewitt, J. D., Dckhd (R.N.R.)
Heyworth. Johnny, A B.
Higgins, John. Dckhd. (R.N.R.)
Higgins, W. H., Sea. (R.N.R.)
Highley, Wm., Tmr. (R.N.R.)
Hocking, R. Henry, Ld. Sto.
Hodge, Arthur Henry, Sto. 2.
Hogan, J. H., Tmr. (R.N.R.)
Horridge, Samuel, A.B.
Horsley, G. W., En. (R.N.R.)
Houstoun, George. Ord. S.
Howard, J. W, Tmr. (R.N.R.)
Hulan, E. M., Sea. (N.R.N.R.)
James, S., Shipwright, 2.
Jones, H. E. L., Ord. S. (R N.V.R.)
Jones, John, Dckhd. (R.N.R.)
Jones, T., Pte (R.M.L.I.)
Jones, Thomas, Dckhd (R.N.R.)
Jowett, Arthur, Sto. 1.
Joyes, William Henry, Sto. P.O.
Judge, Stephen William, Sto. 1.
Kay, Ernest, A.B. (R.N.V.R.)
*Keeping, A. John, Ld. S.
Kelly, C., Sea. (R.N.R.)
Kemp, Edward William, A.B.
Kinsella, Christopher, A.B
Lawes, Arthur Henry, A.B.
Lewis, Morgan, Sto. P.O.
Lillie, Felix Maurice. A.B.
Lingard, James Barker, Sto. 1.
Lister, James Frank. A.B.
Lonsdale, H. P., Dckhd. (R.N.R.)
Lovegrove, J. E., Cor. (R.M.L.I.)
Maciver, Roderick, Sea. (R.N.R.)
Mackay, Alex., Ld. S. (R.N.R.)
Mahoney, Patrick, Sea. (R.N.R.)
Martin, James Charles, Sto. 1.
Martin, Thomas, A.B.
McCaskill, Wm. H., Tmr. (R.N.R.)
McCourt, W. F., Dckhd. (R.N.R.)
McDonald, John, Dckhd. (R.N.R.)
MacDonald, M., Sea. (R.N.R.)
McGrievy, Peter, Sen. Res. Attend. (R.N.A.S.B R.)
McKay, P. J., Act. Ld. S. (N.R.N.R.)
McLeod, Angus, Sto. 2.
McLeod, John, Sto. 2.
Melton, C. W., Tmr. (R.N.R.)
Milloy, John Robb, A.B.
Mills, Charles Samuel, Ld. Sto.
Mills, Geo Wm., Sea. (R.N.R.)
Mitchinson, R. W., En. (R.N.R.)
Mitford, Fredk. C., Air Mech. 2.
Money, David, Dckhd (R.N.R.)
Moody, James, En. (R.N.R.)
Morrill, C. C. V., Tmr. (R.N.R.)
Morrison, Angus, Dckhd. (R.N.R.)
Mullins, Martin, Sto. P.O.
*Mummery, L. R., Dckhd. (R.N.R.)
Murphy, Martin, Sig. (R.N.V.R.)
Nash, J. J., (R.N.R.)
Newman, G. Edward, Of. Std. 3.

Northcott, William R, Sto. 1.
Oldman, L., Aircraftman 1.
Ong, William, Sto. P.O.
Osborne, William Thos., Sto. 1.
Osbourne, John S., En. (R.N R.)
Owens, Thos. W., Tel. (R.N.V.R.)
Parker, Lewis Thos, Ld. S.
Pavitt, William. Sig.
Payne, James, Sto. 1.
Pearce, W. T. C., E.R.A. 1.
Perlmal, Samuel, Of. Std. 2.
Peters, T. E., Ord. S. (R.N.C.V.R.)
Pomphrey, R. F., Cook's Mate.
Powell, John Henry, Sto. 1.
Price, C., En. (R.N.R.)
Readding, Wm , Tmr. (R.N.R.)
Ridgley, John Geo., Sto. P.O.
Ridland, L., Sea. (R.N.R.) (Shet.)
Riley, William, A.B.
Ring, Ernest Henry, A.B.
Ritchie, Arch. Geo., A.B.
Ritchie, J. H., Tmr. (R.N.R.)
Roberts, John, Dckhd. (R.N.R.)
Roberts, R., Tmr. (R.N.R.)
Roe, Frank Rivis, Ld. S.
Rogers, Richard Stanley, Sto. 1.
Roll. S. H., Sh. Std. Assistant.
Ross, David, En. (R.N.R.)
Ross, D., Sec. Hd. (R.N.R.)
Russan, W. J., Shipwright 1.
Russell, W. C., Sig. (R.N.V.R.)
Sansom, G. T., Ord. Tel.
Saunders, J. N., En. (R.N.R.)
*Scott, Frank, Ld. S
Shaw, G. W., En. (R.N.R.)
Shaw, Harry, Dckhd. (R.N.R.)
Shenton, E. H., Boy 1.
Shimmin, Wm., Sea. (R.N.R.)
Shimming W. H., Sec. Hd. (R.N.R
Shoebottom, W. A., Tmr. Cook, (R.N.R.)
Simpson, William, Sto. 2.
Sinclair, Alexander, S.B.A.
Skeldon, H., Ord. S. (R.N.O.V R.)
Slater, J., Dckhd. (R.N.R.)
Smith, Albert, A.B. (R.N.V.R.)
Smith, Alfred Henry, Sto. P.O.
Smith, E. H., Sig. (R.N.V.R.)
Smith, Harry Geo., P.O. Mech.
Smith, H. J., Sec. Hd. (R.N.R.)
Smith, James, Tmr. (R.N.R.)
Smith, John. Tmr. Cook (R.N.R.)
Smith, R. W., En. (R.N.R.)
Sparrow, G., Dckhd. (R.N.R.)
Stace, P. M., Tmr. Cook (R.N.R.)
Stanton, George, Tmr. (R.N.R.)
Starkins, W. S. A., Dckhd. (R.N.R.)
*State. George William, Sto. 1.
Stokes, Wm. James, Sto. 1.
Strong, A. H., Ord. Tel.
Styles, R. E. C., Sh. Std. Assist.
Sutton, Percy, Sig.
Sutton, Wm , Dckhd (R.N.R.)
Sweeney, Denis. Ld. S.
Tacey, Henry, Dckhd. (R.N.R.)
Taylor, Fredk. A., Sto. 2.
Thomas, George Victor, Sto. 1.
Tiltman, Wm., Ld. Sto.
Tompkins, G. W., Driver (R.M.A.)
Topham, John, A.B
Trill. Stephen, Sto. P.O
Trott, G. W., Of. Std. 2.
Turner. A. J., Ord. Tel. (R.N.V.R.)
Turner, C. E. W., Ord. Sig. (R N.V.R.)
Turner, Charles R. C., Ld. Sto.

Urquhart, A., Dckhd. (R.N.R.)
Vaughan, J. Charles, Ord. S.
Versey, William, P.O. 1.
Wallace, George Henry, A.B.
Wallace, H., Ld. Tel. (R.N.V.R.)
Wannell, George Robert, C.P.O.
Ward. John W., Dckhd. (R.N.R.)
Wardlaw, Alex. G., Ord. Tel. (R.N.V.R.)
Washbrook, William, Ord. S.
Watson, E., Dckhd (R.N.R.)
Waugh, Harry, Sto. 1.
Webb, James William, Sto. 1.
Welford, Fredk. James, Ld. S.
Wilson, James, En. (R.N.R.)
Wise. Tom, Sto. 1.
Wolfendale, Harry, Sto 2.
Woods, Wilfred Harry, Sto. P.O.
Woollhead, W. H., Ch P.O. Mech. 3
Worden, A. W., A.E.R.A. 4.
Wright, Alfred Edward, Of. Std. 2.
Wright, Cyril Vivian, Ld. Sto
Wright, Edward, A.B.
Wysthoff, W. A., En. (R.N.R.)

Specially Entered Mercantile Crew.

Arnold, Llewellyn. Fireman.
Bell, John James, Trimmer.
Carter, John, Assistant Steward.
Doran, Patrick, Fireman.
Fowler, James, Greaser.
Frame. James, Fireman.
Gallagher, George. Fireman.
George, Emrys, Greaser.
Gilbert, William, Fireman.
Gore, John, Trimmer.
Green, Albert E., Assistant Std.
Hopkins, Griffith, Fireman.
Jones, John, Fireman.
Main, Percy, A.B.
McNulty, Reginald, Trimmer.
Middlewick, William, 2nd Engineer.
Mitchell, Arthur, Greaser.
Muir, Stanley, Fireman.
Robb, Frank, Shipwright.
Saunders, Harry, Greaser.
St. Iedger, John H., A.B.
Taylor, Alfred, Trimmer.
Trimble. William. Assist. Storekpr.
Tyler, Peter, A.B.
Weitzel, Herbert E., Cook.

JUNE, 1917.

Baker, G. W., Tmr. (R.N.R.)
Brown, Alfred, Sec. Hd. (R.N.R.)
Bunn, N. W., En. (R.N.R.)
Callow, H. A., En. (R.N.R.)
Cook, A. R., Dckhd. (R.N.R.)
*Creasey, W., Air Mechanic 2.
Durnin, James, Tmr. (R.N.R.)
Franklin, David. Dckhd. (R.N.R.)
George, W. A., Dckhd. (R.N.R.)
McDonald, John, Sto. (Act. Engineman) (R.N.R.)
*McLean, Murdo, Sea. (R.N.R.)
Rippey, A., Act. Bdr. (R.M.A.)
Shephard, A. L., Aircraftman 2.
Williams, E., Ld. Tmr. (R.N.R.)

Specially Entered Mercantile Crew.

Boyd, J., Ld. Fireman.
Hamilton, Arthur G., Fireman.
McGrath, Maurice. Fireman.

The Navy's Immortal Names

Adams, Frederick William, Able Seaman.
Ashton, Joseph Houghton, Engineman (R.N.R.)
Coxon, James, Engineroom Artificer, 1st Class.
Hudson, Philip, Deckhand (R.N.R.)
Jackson, Albert, Engineroom Artificer, 4th Class.
Jamieson, George Fraser, Leading Seaman (R.N.R.)
Knapp, Christopher John, Boy Telegraphist.
Lambert, Frederick, Greaser (Mercantile rating).
Lewis, Albert Edward, Stoker 1st Class.
Macrae, Daniel, Seaman (R.N.R.)
MacIntosh, John, Trimmer (R.N.R.)
Maher, Leo Joseph, Seaman (Newfoundland) (R.N.R.).

McDonald, Adam Lawson, Trimmer (R.N.R.)
Mitchell, Godfrey, Sergeant (R.M.L.I.)
Mitchell, Charles Henry, Deckhand (R.N.R.)
Moore, Charles, Deckhand (R.N.R.)
Newton, John Thomas, Chief Motor Mechanic.
Peters, James Thomas, Deckhand (R.N.R.)
Simpson, Adam Ray, Engineman (R.N.R.)
Slade, Thomas Charles, Petty Officer.
Tulloch, Magnus, Seaman (R.N.R.)
Wiseman, George Ingram, Air Mechanic, 1st Grade.
Worsley, Albert James Edward, Leading Seaman.

Lieutenant Guy K. Twiss, R.N.
Act. Sub-Lieut. Christopher M. Sylk-Rowlands (R.N.R.)
Mr. Charles H. Young, Gunner, R.N.
Flight Sub-Lieutenant Samuel L. Bennett, R.N.

Surgeon Probationer Raymond F. Pratt, (R.N.V.R.)
Skipper Alexander Geddes (R.N.R.)
Skipper Francis J. Williams (R.N.R.)

Adams, George Alfred, A.B. (R.N.V.R.)
Boddinar, James H., Pte. (R.M.L.I.)
Cowley, Frank, A.B. (R.N.V.R.)
Findlay, Alex., A.B. (R.N.V.R.)
Findlay, Angus M., A.B. (R.N.V.R.)
Hale, William, A.B. (R.N.V.R.)
Hall, David, A.B. (R.N.V.R.)
Hart, Robert, A.B. (R.N.V.R.)
Hepburn, Arthur, A.B. (R.N.V.R.)
Horne, Harry, A.B. (R.N.V.R.)
Hoskin, Harold J., Ld. Seaman (R.N.V.R.)
Jefferson E. J., A.B. (R.N.V.R.)
Knight, Thomas, A.B. (R.N.V.R.)
Lauchlin, David L., A.B. (R.N.V.R.)
Lennox, John T., Pte. (R.M.L.I.)
Marriner, Percy, Pte. (R.M.L.I.)

Middleton, Alex., A.B. (R.N.V.R.)
Norris, Leonard A., A.B. (R.N.V.R.)
Pakeman, Albert V., Pte. (R.M.L.I.)
Riley, Raymond, A.B. (R.N.V.R.)
Roe, Stanley H., Pte. (R.M.L.I.)
Shepherd, Harry, A.B. (R.N.V.R.)
Sherburn, George, Pte. (R.M.L.I.)
Sherwin, Albert, A.B. (R.N.V.R.)
Shields, William, A.B. (R.N.V.R.)
Smith, George H., Cor. (R.M.L.I.)
Spence, J. R., Pte. (R.M.L.I.)
Thomson, Paul, A.B. (R.N.V.R.)
Titchener, Walter J., A.B. (R.N.V.R.)
Webb, Ernest H., Pte. (R.M.L.I.)
White, William, Pte (R.M.L.I.)
Williams, Evan D., A.B. (R.N.V.R.)

Flight Sub-Lieutenant George G. Avery, R.N.
Flight Sub-Lieutenant John R. Bibby, R.N.
Flight Sub-Lieutenant Harry L. Crowe, R.N.
Flight Sub-Lieutenant James E. Potvin, R.N.

Sub-Lieutenant Reginald C. Whiteside, R.N.V.R., attached R.F.C.
Probationary Observer Officer Thomas Rogers, R.N.
Skipper William Allan (R.N.R.)
Skipper Frederick T. Ellison (R.N.R.)

Amos, Hubert William, A.B.
Baker, Alfred George, Leading Cook's Mate.
Bell, David, Ord. Sea. (R.N.C.V.R.)
Bennett, Charles Samuel, Leading Seaman.
Bishop, Walter, P.O.
Bisset, George, Engineman (R.N.R.)
*Boalch, Stanley Richard, A.B. (R.N.V.R.)
Bromilow, Thomas Nelson, Ord. Sea.
Cadwell, William, Seaman (Newfoundland) R.N.R.
Chapman, Charles Edward, A.B.
Clucas, William Henry, Act. Ld. S. (R.N.R.)
Collard, Charles William, Signalman.
Collins, George Albert, A.B.
Colvin, Alexander, Sec. Hand (R.N.R.)
Coombs, Stanley Victor, Ord. Seaman.
Cooper, Sidney Herbert, A.B.
Costello, Patrick, Trimmer (R.N.R.)
Coulthard, John, Act. Ld. S. (R.N.R.)
Curtis, Albert Edward, Act. Ld. Stoker.
Daggett, Harry, A.B.
Daniels, Charles, L.-Cor. (R.M.L.I.)
Davies, Joseph Dominick, Officer's Std. 2nd Class.
Dowdall, Charles Henry, A.B. (R.N.V.R.)
Downing, Frederick Beaton, Leading Signalman.
Dunbavand, Percy, Stoker, 1st Class.
Edmondson, Thomas Lewis, Stoker. 1st Class.
Fish, Henry White, Engineman (R.N.R.)
Fisher, Walter Maurice George, A.B.
Gates, William, Stoker. 1st Class.
Gore, Patrick, Boy Telegraphist.
Graham, Percy Alfred James, Sto. Petty Officer.
Hall, William, Deckhand (R.N.R.)

Harris, John, Sea. (Act. Sec. Hand).
Harvey, George Robert, Trimmer (R.N.R.)
Hawes, Samuel Henry, Chief Armourer.
Hewton, John, Stoker, 1st Class.
Holmes, Douglas, Act. Ld. Sea. (R.N.R.)
Hook, Frank, Act. Ld. Sea.
Horner, William, Deckhand (R.N.R.)
Howden, Arthur, Stoker, 1st Class.
Howsego, William Thomas, A.B.
Hudson, Bertie, Engineman (R.N.R.)
Innes, Alexander James, Deckhand (R.N.R.)
Irvine, Norman, Deckhand (R.N.R.)
Jackson, William, Trimmer (R.N.R.)
Jones, William John, Ord. Sea. (R.N.C.V.R.)
Kennett, George, Deckhand (R.N.R.)
Kilminster, William, Trimmer (R.N.R.)
King, Alfred Hedley, Ld. Deckhand (R.N.R.)
Kingsley, Percy, Trimmer (R.N.R.)
Lamb, Arthur, A.B. (R.N.R.)
Litchfield, Leonard Horace, Signalman (R.N.V.R.)
Littlewood, Thomas Henry, A.B.
Lowry, William, A.B.
McConchie, Reuben, E.R.A. (R.N.R.)
McLeod, Murdo, Seaman (R.N.R.)
McNesby, Victor William, Deckhand (R.N.R.)
MacDonald, Roderick, Seaman (R.N.R.)
Macleod, Finlay, Seaman (R.N.R.)
Maynard, William. A.B.
Middleton, Bertie George, A.B.
Miller, Thomas Yare, A.B. (R.N.V.R.)
Mitchell, William, Seaman (R.N.R.)
Mountford, Joseph, Leading Signalman.

* Accidentally.

The Navy's Immortal Names

Newby, William Wilson, Deckhand (R.N.R.)
Oswald, George, Stoker, 1st Class.
Paul, Alfred, Seaman (R.N.R.)
Payne, Sydney Bernard, Ordinary Seaman.
Pickering, Arthur Lister, Signal Boy (R.N.R.)
Pitcher, Benjamin Walter, Deckhand (R.N.R.)
Potter, Frederick, A.B.
Poultney, Harold Edward, A.B.
Priestly, William, Stoker, 1st Class.
Rae, James, Engineman (R.N.R.)
Riches, John, A.B.
Scott, Joseph Edward, Trimmer (R.N.R.)
Silver, William Frederick, A.B.
Smith, James William, Leading Telegraphist.
Spratt, Percy Harold, Ord. Seaman.
Stedman, William Henry, Leading Stoker.
Summers, Harry, Trimmer (R N.R.)
Sutherland, John Alexander, Seaman (R.N.R.)
Sutton, William Charles, Seaman (R.N.R.)
Tarr, William Henry, Pte. (R.M.L.I.)

Taylor, James, Seaman (R.N.R.)
Thompson, Robert Dick, Ord.-Seaman (R.N.C.V.R.)
Thomson, Laurence, Seaman (R.N.R.)
Tree, Herbert James, Leading Seaman.
Tucker, Chas. Fredk., A.B.
Tyrrell, Stanley George, Ord. Seaman.
Webster, James, Seaman (R.N.R.) (Act. Sec. Hd.)
White, Frank Gordon, Officer's Steward, 2nd Class.
Weedon, James Taylor, Engineman (R.N.R.)
West, Joseph David, Ord. Seaman.
Whippy, James Henry, Pte. (R.M.L.I.)
Wileman, Edgar, Deckhand (R.N.R.)
Williams, Francis Arthur, Ld. Seaman..
Williams, Owen John, Telegraphist (R.N.V.R.)
Williamson, Alfred, Deckhand (R.N.R.)
Withers, Ernest, Ord. Seaman.
Wittup, Harry, Deckhand (R.N.R.)
Wood, Herbert William, Stoker, 1st Class.
Wright, Thomas, Sec. Hand (R.N.R.)
Yates, Frank, Engineman (R.N.R.)

Bailey, Frederick John, Act. Ld. Sea. (R.N.V.R.)
Davidson, Thomas, Act. Ld. Sea. (R.N.V.R.)
Harris, Charles William, Leading Mechanic.

Rippey, Andrew, P. Act. Bombardier (R M.A.)
Simpson, Adam Rae, Engineman (R.N.R.)
Woolley, Samuel, A.B. (R.N.V.R.)

Lieutenant Walter J. Bibby (R.N.R.)
Engineer Lieutenant Joseph Hall (R.N.R.)
Engineer Sub-Lieutenant Wilford S. Sims (R.N.R.)

Flight Sub-Lieutenant John N. McAllister, R.N.
Sub-Lieutenant Malise S. Graham, R.N.
Naval Instructor Marshall H. Robinson, B.A., R.N.

Christie, William, Act. A.B. (R.N.V.R.)
Clark, Alexande., Pte (R.M.L.I.)
Clayton, Laurence, Pte (R.M.L.I.)
Foskett, Walter S., A.B. (R.N.V.R.)
Hill, Elijah, Pte. (R.M.L.I.)

Maskery, Albert E., A.B. (R.N.V.R.)
Roothgen, Philip A., A.B. (R.N.V.R.)
Taylor, Albert, L.-Cor. (R.M.L.I.)
Twibey, Arthur, P.O. (R.N.V.R.)
Young, Henry G. R., Sto. 1 (R.N.)

Lieutenant Samuel Pulford (R.N.R.)
Flight Sub-Lieutenant Augustus C. Jones, R.N.

Skipper John Geddes (R.N.R. S.A. 59).

JULY 9th, 1917.
H.M.S. "Vanguard."

Capt. J. D. Dick.
Com. W. Cadman.
Lt.-Com N. L. R. Bell.
Lt.-Com. A. C. H. Duke.
Lt. O. H. Stoehr.
Lt. S. W. Upcher.
Lt. E. Dunbar-Dunbar-Rivers.
Act. Lt. R. L. Elgood.
Lt. R. E. A. Chessex, R.N.V.R.
Eng. Com. W. N. MacDonald.
Eng.-Lt.-Com. E. G. Smith.
Major H. W. Miles, R.M.L.I.
Act. Chaplain, the Rev. H. A. W. Back, B.A.
Naval Instructor W. F. Hartley, M.A
Flight Surgeon E. Cox, M.B., B.A.
Staff Surgeon W. G. Barras, M.D., C.M., R.N.V.R.
Flight Paymr. P. B Stevens.
Surgeon E. Rayner, M.B., F.R.C.S.
Sub.-Lt. G. Y. Harrison.

Act. Sub.-Lt. C. H. Oldham.
Eng. Sub.-Lt. F. Allender.
Assistant Paymr. E. L. Peirson, R.N.R.
Chief Gunner J. Dennis.
Gunner (T.) W. T. Christmas.
Boatswain D. S. Murphy.
Art. Eng. E. Repetto
Art. Eng. J. W. McAlister.
Mid C. du P. S. M. G. Mauleverer.
Mid. C. A. G. Cooke.
Mid. A. W. A. Wilson.
Mid. R. H. Colbourne.
Mid. M. Marchant.
Mid. R. W. McD. Johnston.
Mid. A. W. De Segundo.
Mid. F. A. V. Wevill.
Mid. J. P. Milton.
Mid. A. S. Ogilvie.

Abbott, H. W., Sto. 1.
Ahrey, D. R., A.B.
Ackrill, R., Ord. S.
Adam, F., Sig. Boy.
Adams, J. W. W., C.C.
Adlam, W. M. A.B.
Agg, G., P.O.
Agnew, T. R., Sto. 1.

Alder, J., Sto. P.O.
Aldridge, F. J., Ord. S.
Allright, J. W. L., Elec. Artfcr. 2.
Ambler, J., Mech.
Amor, G., A.B.
Antcliffe, H., L.-Cor. (R.M.L.I.)
Apps, A. G., Ld. Sto.
Archer, W. L., Sto. 1.

Armitage, H., Ld. Sto.
Armitage, W., Ch. Sto.
Arnold, G. A., Gun. (R.M.A.)
Arnott, A., Sto. (R.N.R.)
Ashford, L. J., Sto. 2.
Aspinall, J. H., Elec. Art. 2 (R.N.V.R.)
Athroll, A. P., A.B.

The Navy's Immortal Names

H.M.S. "Vanguard"—Continued.

Atkins, E. B., Act. Ld. Sto.
Atkinson, L., A.B.
Attwood, W., A.B.
Austin, T. C. B., Boy Tel.
Avis, A. W., Sto. 2.
Ayre, A., Sto. (R.N.R.)
Ayres, J., Sto. 2.
Bacon, D., Ld. Sto
Bailey, J. A., A.B.
Baines, J. H., Pte. (R.M.L.I.)
Baird, A., Ord S.
Baker, A. R., Yeo. of Sig.
Baker, G., A.B.
Baker, W. T., Pte. (R.M.L.I.)
Palaam, E., Ld. Sto.
Ball, A. H., Sto. 2.
Parker, A., A.B.
Barlow, F., Act. Ch. P.O.
Barnard, S. A., Ld. S.
Barnes, B. W., Pte. (R.M.L.I.)
Barnett, F., A.B.
Barrett, E. J., A.G.
Barrett, F., Boy 1.
Barton, C. C., A.B.
Barton, E., Ord. S.
Barty, B., A.B.
Bastian, C. J. C., Shipwright 2.
Bate, A. E. S., Shipwright 2.
Bates, F., A.B.
Bates, W. D., Act. Arm.
Bateson, H., Sto. 1.
Batty, J. C., A.B.
Bean E. G., Pte. (R.M.L.I.)
Beane, A. J., Sto. (R.N.R.)
Beare, F., Sig.
Bearman, S., Of. Cook 3.
Beattie, C., Sto. (R.N.R.)
Beauchamp, C. J., Pte. (R.M.L.I.)
Beeson, J., Cooper.
Beevers-Belvoir, A. C., A.B.
Belcher, W. C. E., Ord. S.
Bellman, H. C., A.B.
Bendall, G. J., Ord. S.
Bennett, G. F. F., Boy 1.
Bennett, W. G., A.B.
Bennett, W. G., E.R.A. 4.
Benson, T., A.B.
Bentley, A. J., A.B.
Benton, C. W., Boy 1.
Bernhard, C., Ord. S.
Berry, B. W., A.B. (R.N.V.R.)
Beswick, H., Cook's Mate.
Betts, P. F., Boy 1.
Bibby, W., A.B.
Biggs, J. P., A.C.
Bird, D., A.B.
Bird, H., Sto. 1.
Birks, G. A., A.B.
Blight, R. J., Sto. P.O.
Bolden, F. F., Gun. (R.M.A.)
Bond, C. I., C.C.
Boulter, A. E., Boy 1.
Bovey, N., Ord. S.
Bowden, F. G., Sto 1.
Bowers, R. A., Ld. S.
Boyes, H. A., Ord. S.
Brackley, W. J., Pte. (R.M.L.I.)
Bradley, A. T., Mech.
Bradshaw, J., Sto. (R.N.R.)
Bradshaw, W. F., Boy 1.
Braidley, W. H., Ord S.
Brazier, W. G., Sto. 1.
Brett, J. J., Sto. 2.
Brideoake, J. T., Pte. (R.M.L.I.)
Bridgman, C. O., Pte. (R.M.L.I.)
Bridgwater, R., Sto. 2.
Brightwell, W., Boy 1.

Britton, A., Sto. 1.
Brockhouse, G. A., A.B.
Brookes, W. H., Ord. S.
Broughton, J. D., Boy 1.
Brown, E. G., E.R.A. 5.
Brown, H., P.O.
Brown, H. A., A.B.
Brown, S., A.B.
Brown, W., Sto. (R.N.R.)
Browne, C., Ld. S.
Browning, P. G., Ch. P.O.
Brownjohn, F., Mech.
Browse, C. H., Ord S.
Bryant, W. J., Ord. S.
Buckley, W. C. Ld. Sto.
Bugg, C., P.O.
Bullen, V. K., Ch. Sto.
Bullock, E., Musician. (R.M.B.)
Bullock, F., Boy 1.
Bunclark, G. S., A.B.
Bundick, B., Sto. P.O.
Bunn, E., Boy 1.
Bunn, W. E., Sto. 1.
Burgess, C. H., Sto. P.O.
Bursill, J. J., Sto. 1.
Bush, A. H., A.B.
Bushell, A. G., Sto. P.O.
Bushell, J. T., Musician (R.M.B.)
Butler, R. E., Sto. 1.
Butterick, G., Ord. Tel.
Butterworth, J. W., E.R.A., 1.
Buttle, A. C., Ord. S.
Callaghan, J., P.O.
Calvert, A. W., A.B.
Cardy, S. H., A.B.
Carney, F., Boy Tel.
Carpenter, A. F., Ld. Sig.
Carrington, T. F. G., Sto. 1.
Carver, E. J., Ord. S.
Cass, W. A. S., Sto. 1.
Carselton, J. W. F., Sto. 1.
Caton, G. T., Yeo. of Sig.
Caughie, R., Ord. S.
Chadwick, W., A.B. (R.N.V.R.)
Chambers, E. W., P.O. 1.
Chapman, F., Sto. 1.
Chapman, G., Bom. (R.M.A.)
Chapman, G. W., A.B.
Chaston, T. G., A.B.
Chilcott, C. O., Ship's Std. Assist.
Chipperfield, H. E., A.C.
Chisman, H. F., A.B.
Chisman, W., Sto. (R.N.R.)
Chittenden, F. W., Shipwright 2
Church, H., Sto. 2.
Clark, A. E., Boy Tel.
Clark, J. B., Sto. 1.
Clarke, R. J., Sto. 1.
Clarke, W., Ch. Sto.
Clarkson, W., Sig. Boy.
Claxton, E., Sto. 1.
Clent, W. J., Ld. Sto.
Clifford, M. J., Cor. (R.M.A.)
Coates, W. J., Sto. 1.
Cochrane, R. A., P.O.
Cockerill, W. H., Ch. P.O.
Coe, J. E., Ch. Sto.
Collett, E. H., Ld. Cook's Mate.
Collins, J., Sto. (R.N.R.)
Collinson, A. W. Sto. 2.
Collis, H. D., Ld. Sig
Collum, H. N., E.R.A. 3.
Colwell, E. C., A.B.
Colwill, F. C., A.B.
Cook, J. T., Wireman, 2.
Cooke, C. F., Ch. P.O.
Cooke, J. H. P., Sto. 1.

Coombs, G. F. T., Sto. 1.
Coombs, G. T., Sto. 2.
Coombs, S. W., Boy 1.
Cooper, C. N., Boy 1.
Cooper, E. J., Sto. 1.
Cooper, E. R., Wireman 2.
Cooper, G. H., Gun. (R.M.A.)
Cooper, H., Sto. 2.
Cooper, H. G., Mech.
Cooper, J. A., Cook's Mate.
Cooper, J., Sto. (R.N.R.)
Corby, F., Pte. (R.M.L.I.)
Core, S. A., Sig. Boy
Cork, J. E., Ord. S.
Cork, W. T., Sto. 1.
Corrigan, P., Sto. 1.
Corser, A., Ch. P.O.
Cory, W. R., P.O.
Coull, R., A.B.
Court, R., Of. Cook 1.
Cox, E. J., A.B.
Cox, H. F., A.B.
Cox, O. C., Ch. Yeo. of Sig.
Cox, W., A.B.
Coy, H., Sto. (R.N.R.)
Cross, L., Boy 1.
Cross, W. A., Ord. S.
Crowhurst, A. J., A.B. (R.N.V.R.)
Crowther, W. A., Sto. 1.
Cullivan, J., P.O.
Currie, N., Ord. S.
Curtis, J., Pte. (R.M.L.I.)
Curtis, J. E., Boy Tel.
Curtis, J. H., A.B. (R.N.V.R.)
Cutmore, S. G. B., Ld. S.
Cutter, L., Sto. (R.N.R.)
Dalton, M., Sto. 1.
Daniels, R. C., Sto. 1.
Davies, A., A.B.
Davis, F. T., Sto. P.O.
Davison, G., Sto. (R.N.R.)
Day, R. E. C., Ship's Std. Assist.
Deadman, A. S., Boy 1.
Deadman, G., Pte. (R.M.L.I.)
Deakin, E. R., Pte. (R.M.L.I.)
Dean, W., Wireman 2.
Denton, A. W., A.B.
Devine, J., Sto. (R.N.R.)
Dexter, H., Ord. S.
Dibbens, C. E., Sig. Boy.
Dickinson, O., Boy 1.
Dicks, W. J., Gun. (R.M.A.)
Diwell, G. C., Sto. 1.
Dixon, M., Sto. 1.
Dobson, C. J., Ord. S.
Dobson, G. C., Boy 1.
Doctrill, A. E., Gun. (R.M.A.)
Dodd, C. R., Ship's Std.
Dolby, A. R., Of. Std. 3.
Donnelly, P., Sto. 2.
Douglas, F. E., Elec. Art. 1
(R.N.V.R.)
Dowley, A. W., Painter, 2.
Down, F., A.B.
Down, T. E., Pte. (R.M.L.I.)
Duckmanton, J., Ord. S.
Dunbar, T., E.R.A. 2.
Dymock, E. H., Ld. S.
Easton, H. T., Musician (R.M.B.)
Eaton, H. G., Sto. 1.
Ede, A. G., Gun. (R.M.A.)
Edgeworth, J., P.O.
Edwards, H., Boy 1.
Edwards, W. A., A.B. (R.N.V.R.)
Eggleton, W. L., A.B.
Egglestone, Shipwright, 2.
Element, C. W., Sto. 2.

H.M.S. "Vanguard"—Continued.

Elkins, W. I., Sig.
Ellis, C. F., Ord. S.
Ellis, H. H., A.B.
Ellis, W. H., Ld. S.
Elvin, J., Sto. (R.N.R.)
Emmett, W. M., Pte. (R.M.L.I.)
Evans, J. H., P.O.
Evans, J. S., Ord. S. (R.N.V.R.)
Evans, R. J., Ord. S. (R.N.V.R.)
Ewing, S. A., Sto. 1.
Fanstone, T. S., Boy 1.
Farrer, J., Sto. 1.
Fenwick, J., Sto. 2.
Ferguson, J. Boy 1.
Ferris, B., C.C.
Field, H. W., A.B
Fisher, H., Sto. 2.
Fitchett. B., Boy Tel.
Flaherty, T., Sto. P.O. (R.N.R.)
Flight, C. S., A.B.
Flindell, H. C., Ld. S.
Foott, A. E., C.C.
Ford, S. E., Sto. 1.
Forrest, A., Ld. Sto.
Foster, J. W., C.E.R.A. 2.
Foster, R., Sig. Boy.
Fox, C., Sto. 1.
Fox, W., Sig. Boy.
Franklin, P. G., Gun. (R.M.A.)
Freeman, F., Sto. (R.N.R.)
French, W. A., Sto. 1.
Frost, D., Ord. S.
Fryatt, A. J., Yeo. of Sig.
Fuller, G. E., Pte. (R.M.L.I.)
Fuller, J. N., Musician (R.M.B.)
Fuller, R. J., A.B.
Gaff, H. J., A.B.
Gaines, F., Sto. 1.
Gait, O., Elec. Art. 4.
Gamble, R. J., A.B.
Gamblen, E. G., P.O. Tel.
Game, B., A.B.
Gammon, W. H., Ord. S.
Gamon, F. O., Of. Std. 3.
Gander, R. J., A.B.
Gandy, J., A.B.
Gapes, J., Pte. (R.M.L.I.)
Gergett, G. W., A.B.
Gaunt, F. T., Bglr. (R.M.L.I.)
Gibbons, H. J., Pte. (R.M.L.I.)
Gilby, W. J., A.B.
Giles, W. G., Gun. (R.M.A.)
Glazier, G. F., Boy 1.
Goodacre, H. W., Ord. S. (R.N.V.R.)
Gooding, M. D., P.O. 1.
Goodwin, R. E., Sto 1.
Goody, L., Sto. 1.
Goodyear, L. C., Gun. (R.M.A.)
Gough, G. R, Ord S. (R.N.V.R.)
Graham, J. W., Boy 1.
Graham, P., Sto. 2.
Granfield, J. T., Ch. Sto.
Grant, F., Pte. (R.M.L.I.)
Grantham, H. R., A.B.
Gray, A., Ld. S.
Gray, F. P., E.R.A. 3.
Gray, F., Boy 1.
Green, E., Cook's Mate.
Green, J. A., Sto. 1.
Green, W. J., Ld. C.C.
Greenaway, alias Foster, W. J. H., Ch. Ship's Cook.
Grinham, O. S., A.B.
Groves, R., Pte. (R.M.L.I.)
Guyton, G. H., Sto 1
Haine, G. H., Sto. 2.
Hall, A. V., A.B.

Hall. G. A., A.B.
Hall, G. W., Pte. (R.M.L.I.)
Hall, J. D., Ld. Sig
Hall, J. J., Boy 1.
Hall, P. H., A.B.
Hall, T. F., Ld. Sto. (R.N.R.)
Halls, J. B., P.O.
Halliday, C. G., Ld. S.
Hamilton, T. P., Ld. Sto.
Hamilton, W. W., A.B.
Hammersley, S. B., A.B.
Hammersley, W. H., Ord. S.
Hammond, A. G., Of. Std. 2.
Hammond, T. F., S.B.A.
Hancock, C. R., 3rd Writer.
Hand, J. A. S., Gun. (R.M.A.)
Harding, S. C, Ord. S.
Harding, W. H., Ld. S.
Hargraves, L., Cook's Mate.
Harod F., Musician (R.M.B.)
Harrold, H. F., Sto. 1.
Harvey, W., Boy 1.
Harvey, W., Ch. Sto.
Hastings, G., P.O.
Hattersley, W., Pte (R.M.L.I.)
Hatton, H., Sto. 1.
Hatton, W., Sto. 1.
Hawkins, H., Sto. 1.
Hawkridge, A. D., P.O.
Hawthorn, W. T., Of. Cook 3.
Hayles, R. J., Boy 1.
Hayward, B., Boy 1.
Heading, W. J., Pte. (R.M.L.I.)
Heale, T., Ord. S.
Healey, J., A.B.
Hebbern, W., Gun. (R.M.A.)
Hert, H. W., Sto. 1.
Hewitt, A. H., Boy, 1.
Hewson, T., A.B.
Hildebrand, T. W., A.B.
Hill, W. H., Ld. S.
Hills, G. H., A.B.
Hillyer, G., Sto. 1.
Hiscutt, F. W., Sto. 1.
Hoadley, E. A., Sto. 1.
Hoare, R., A.B.
Hobbs, W. G., Of. Std. 3.
Hodges, J. H., E.R.A. 1.
Hodson, F., Gun. (R.M.A.)
Holland, A., Of. Std. 1.
Holland, F. F, Sto. 1.
Hollidge, J. J T., Of. Std. 3.
Hollis, A. C. W., Ord. S.
Holloway, S. E. V., 2nd S B.S.
Holmes, A., Sto. 1.
Honor, A. T., Cor. (R.M.L.I.)
Hoper, C. A., Sto. 1.
Hopkins, T. A., Ord. S.
Hopkins, W. J., A.B. (R.N.V.R.)
Horn, F., Sto. 1.
Houghton, R., A.B.
Houston, R. T., Sto. (R.A.N.)
Howard, H. J., Ord. S.
Howden, A. H. E., Sergt. (R.M.A.)
Hoy, E. W., A.B.
Hudson, T., Sto. 1.
Hughes, A. H., Ord. S.
Hull, P., Gun. (R.M.A.)
Humphrey, J., Ord. S.
Hunter, E. F., Sig. Boy.
Hurst, A. W., Ord. S.
Hutchings, F. W., Sto. 1.
Hyland, T., Sto. 2.
Ince, W., Sto. 2.
Inglis, L., Sto. 1.
Inwood, C., Boy 1.
Ireson, L. J., Sto. 1.

Ives, J. O., Sto. 1.
Ives, J. H., Ch. Ship's Cook.
Jacobs, A. J., A.B.
Jakeway, F. A., P.O.
James, G. R., Boy 1.
James, W. E., Sto. 1.
Jameson, A. V., E.R.A. 4.
Jarvis, A. R., P.O. 1.
Jaquest, H., Ld. S.
Jeffreys, J., Sto. (R.N.R.)
Jeffs. W. J., Sto. 1.
Jenner, A. E, Boy 1.
Jessop, B., Sto. (R.N.R.)
Jewell, F. G., Boy 1.
Johnson, C., A.B.
Johnson, G. A. W., Boy 1.
Johnston, G. H., Boy Tel.
Jones, D. J., A.B. (R.N.V.R.)
Jones, G. Gun. (R.M.A.)
Jones, G. C., A.B.
Jones, H., Elec. Art. 4.
Jones, H. A., Ord. S
Jones, J. E., A B.
Jones, R. D., A.B.
Jones, R., A.B.
Jones, R., S.B.A.
Jordan, G., Elec. Art. 3.
Jordan, J. H., P.O.
Jouvenat. C. W., Sto 1.
Judge, O., A.B.
Judson, V. E., Musician (R.M.B.)
Keaveny, W., Sig.
Kelly, J. H., Ld. S.
Kempston, R. P., Ld S
Kinch, G. A., Sto. 1
King, A. W, A.E.R.A. 4.
King, B., Sto. P.O.
King, L. A., Gun. (R.M.A.)
Kingsbury, H., Ord. S. (R.N.V R)
Kirk, J. W., Gun. (R.M.A.)
Knee, D. A., Gun. (R.M.A.)
Knight, A., Sig. Boy.
Knightly, E. W. W., Ord. S.
Lamb, F. V., E.R.A. 3.
Lancaster, R. S., Boy 1.
Lane, A. V., Sto. 1.
Lane, W., Sto. (R.N.R.)
Langham, A., Musician (R.M.B.)
Lanham, H., Ld. S.
Lee, W. G. E., Ship's Std. Assist.
Lewis, A. F., Sto. 1.
Limbrick, H. C., Gun. (R.M.A.)
Lindmeyer. H., Act. Sto. P.O.
Link, A. H., Blacksmith's Mate.
Linnett, M. E., Ld. S.
Lisle, A. S., A.B.
Little, J. R., Ord. S.
Lloyd, E. A. H., A.B.
Long, W., A.B. (R.N.V.R.)
Long, W. E., Sto. P.O.
Lord, W., Boy 1.
Lovegrove, J. W., A.B.
Lowe, W. F., Boy 1.
Luck, A., A.B.
Luckhurst, C. V., Sto. 1.
Luckhurst, W., Sto. 1.
Lumley, E. J., Ord. S.
Lumsden, T., C.C.
Lunny, E. J., Ord. S.
Lynagh, P., Sto. (R.N.R.)
McCargo, S. M, A.B. (R.N.V.R.)
McCarthy, F. T. A., Act. A.M.
McCracken, J., A.B.
McDonald, A., Sto. (R.N.R.)
McDonald, E. J., A.C.
MacDonald, J., Sto. 1.
McDonald, M., Pte. (R M.L.I.)

The Navy's Immortal Names

H.M.S. "Vanguard"—Continued.

McGown, T., A.B.
McGrath, C., C.C.
McIlvenny, S., Sto. 1
McLellan, J., Ord. S.
McPherson, J. H., 2nd Writer.
Mackie, W. F. C., A E.R.A. 4.
Mackrell, P. J., A.B.
Madams, J., Sto. 1.
Maddock, H. J., Tel.
Manderson, F. C., Sto. 1.
Mauger, A. E., Boy 1.
Markwell, C. S. R., Boy Tel.
Marlborough, G., Sto. (R.N.R.)
Marriott, S., Sto. P.O.
Marshall, F. C., Wireman 1.
Martin, A. L., Musician (R.M.B.)
Martin, A, Ld. Sto.
Martin, C. P., Pte. (R.M.L.I.)
Martin, J., Sto. (R.N.R.)
Mason, F., Ord. Tel.
Mason, J. W., Ord S.
Mates, A. E., Musician (R.M.B.)
Maton, A. J., Sto. 1.
Matthews, J., A.B.
May, R., Cor. (R M.L.I.)
Mayhew, T., Of. Cook 1.
Mead. H. A., A.B.
Medhurst, W., Sto. 1.
Metcalf, H., Pte. (R M L.I.)
Mileham, E. G., Boy 1.
Miles, C., Sto. 1.
Milledge, F. W., A.B.
Millen, P. A., A.B.
Miller, C. H., Ld. S
Miller, G. S., Ld. Sto.
Mills, A. R. H., Of Std. 2.
Mills, J. C., A.C.
Milton, H. A., Sto. 1.
Minter, J. E., Gun. (R.M.A.)
Mitchell, H. M. Boy 1.
Mitchell, H, Ord. Sig.
Money, G. W., A.E.R A. 4.
Monk, H. T., Sto. 1.
Monnery, W., P.O. 2.
Moon, A. C., Sto. 1
Moore, H. H., Ord. S.
Morgan, A., Ld. S.
Morgan, R. B., A B.
Morrigan, E., Sto. (R.N.R.)
Morris, A. E., Painter 2
Morrison, R., Sto. 1
Moses, R. C., Sailmaker.
Mould, A., Wireman 2. (R.N.V.R.)
Mountney, W. J., Pte. (R.M.L.I.)
Mulligan, C., Sto. 1.
Mummery, A. R., Ld. Sto.
Munday, H., P.O.
Munder, F. R., Sto. 1.
Murphy, J., Pte. (R.M.L.I.)
Murphy, J. J., Sto. 1.
Murray, H. R., Temp. Naval School master.
Murray, J., Sto. (R.N.R.)
Netley, A. J., Mech.
Neville, J., Joiner.
Newell, A. S., Gun. (R.M.A.)
Newell, W. A., Boy 1.
Newnham, N. R., Bugler (R.M.B.)
Nutt, F., Musician (R.M.B.)
O'Connor, M., Sto. 1.
O'Dea, E, Pte. (R.M.L.I.)
O'Donnell, G., Sto. 1.
Ochiltree, R. R., Ship's St. Assist.
Ogden, A., A.E R A. 4.
Oldham, W. O., Ord. S.
Oliver, A. H., Gun. (R.M.A.)
Omans, A., Sto. 1.

Orr, W. H., Boy 1.
Owen, A., Sto. (R.N R.)
Oxley, A. E., Ldg. S.
Padbury, H. G., Cook's Mate.
Page, A., Ld. S.
Page, W., Ld. Sto. (R.N.R.)
Palmer, A., Boy 1.
Palmer, E. A., Sto. 1.
Parker, E. S, A.B.
Parsons, J. R., Ord. S.
Partington, E., Sto. 1.
Pattle, H., Sto. 2.
Payne, F. J., Sto. 1
Peacock. W., Act. Ld. Sto.
Peak, H. J., Sto. 2.
Pearson, A. H., Boy 1.
Pearson, H., A.B.
Peckham, L. A., Ord. Sig.
Peers, W. M., Boy 1.
Pennington, A., E.R.A., 3.
Pestell, H. S., E.R.A. 3.
Peters, W. B., P.O. 1. (C.G.)
Petre, F. H., Sto. 1.
Phillips, J. T., Sto. 1.
Pickett, D., Boy 1.
Pink, E. A., Boy 1.
Piper, H., A.B.
Plaice, G., Ord. S.
Platt, H. D., C.C
Plumb, W. C. J., A.B.
Pogue, D. G. H., A.B.
Pollard, F. R., Boy 1.
Poole, J. F., Gun. (R.M.A.)
Poor, F. C., Of. Std. 1.
Potter, G. J., William, A.B.
Potter, H. J., A.B.
Powley, J. F., Boy Tel.
Preston, G. W., Ld. S.
Prince, H. A., Sergt. (R.M.A.)
Pryse, J. W O., Sto. 1.
Purchase, E. J. C., Ord. S.
Purchase, H., Boy 1
Radcliffe, P., C.C.
Raspin, C. R., Sig. Boy.
Ratty, A. E., P.O. 1.
Rawlings, W., P.O.
Rawlinson, R., Wireman, 2.
Reeder, G. A., A.B.
Reeves, J. W., Sto. 2.
Reid, W., A.B.
Reid, W. G., Sto. 1.
Renwick, J., Ld. S.
Richards, A. W., Boy 1.
Riddles. R. W., Boy 1.
Ridel, A., Sto. 1.
Rix, J. W., Ord. S.
Roberts, E., Sto. 1.
Roberts, W., Sto. (R.A N)
Robinson, G. H., P.O, 1.
Robertson, P., A.B.
Robson, T., Ord. S.
Rose, E. S., Boy 1.
Ross, G. A., Ord. S.
Rosser, A. W., Gun. (R.M.A.)
Rowden, W. E., Gun. (R.M.A.)
Rudge. W. A., Gun. (R.M.A.)
Rushton, A., A.B.
Russell, A. Sto. 2.
Salisbury, A., Ch. Stg.
Savage, F., Boy 1.
Sayer, J. G., Sto. P.O.
Sayers, E. J., Band Cor. (R.M.B.)
Schembri, F., Of. Std. 1.
Scott, J., Sto. P.O.
Scott, T., Sto. 1.
Scott, W., Sto. 1.
Seal, W. H., Ch. P.O.

Sedwell, A. C., Sto. 1.
Seeley, H., Gun. 2 (R.M.A.)
Shepherd, C. E., Gun. (R.M.A.)
Shepherd, F. R., Ord. Tel.
Sheppard, G. H., Ch. P O.
Shorter. F. R., Sto. 1.
Shutt, J., Sto. 1.
Silcox, E. J., Sto. 1.
Silk, T. A., A.B.
Sillett, G. W., P.O.
Silver, H. G., A.B.
Simmonds, T. A., Gun. (R.M.A.)
Simons, C. J., Sto. 1.
Simpson, N. C., Of. Std. 3.
Simpson, S., A.B.
Sinden, C. H., Sto. 1.
Sinden, J., Sto. 1.
Sines, J. H., Ord. S.
Sivell, W. B., Boy 1.
Skinner, G. W., C.C.
Slow. J., A.B.
Smail, G. W., Blacksmith's Mate.
Smith, E., Ld. S.
Smith, E., S.B.S.
Smith, G. E., Ld. Cook's Mate.
Smith, G. H., A.B
Smith, H. I., Ldg. S.
Smith. H., Sto. 1.
Smith, J. T., Boy 1.
Smith, R. M., Ch. P.O.
Solley, J., A.B.
Soues, A. T., A.B.
Sowden, J. F., P.O. 1.
Sparrow, F. G., Boy 1.
Spence, W., A.E.R.A. 4.
Spencer, F. G., Pte. (R.M.L.I.)
Spiller. W. J., Boy 1.
Stafford, R. B., Ord. S.
Stanley, R, A.B.
Stannard, M. B., A.B.
Stanton, M., Sto. 1.
Stein. A., Pte. (R.M.L.I.)
Stevens, W. E., A.B. (R.N.V.R)
Stewart, H. H. A., Boy 1.
Stimpson, G. W., Ord. S.
Stokes, G., Sto. 2.
Stolton, E. J., Sto. 1.
Stonebridge. H., E.R.A. 3.
Stoneham, H. G., Sto. 1.
Storey. T. W., A.B. (R.N.V.R.)
Storkey, W. G., Act. Ch. P.O.
Strange, G. T., A.B
Stredwick, J. A., A.B.
Styles, H. E., Pte. (R.M.L.I.)
Sully, E., A.B.
Surridge. E. J., Sto. 1.
Swabey, H. J., Boy 1.
Tadman, F. E., A B. (R.N.V.R.)
Talbot, O., Sto. 1.
Tanner, W., Sto. 1.
Tate, E., A.B.
Tatters, T., Sto. (R.N.R.)
Taylor, A. H., Of. Std. 3.
Taylor, C. W., Sto., 1.
Taylor, E., A.B.
Taylor, H., Ship's Std. Assist.
Taylor, H. J., A.B.
Taylor, J., Painter. 1.
Taylor, V. W., E.R.A. 4.
Tebby, H. F., Musician (R.M.B.)
Tebbutt, A. J., Act. Ld. Sto.
Tetlock, R., Sig. (R.N.V.R.)
Teucher, F. C., S.B.A.
Theobald. A. A., Sto. 1.
Thomas, H. T., Sto. 1.
Thomas. R. G., Ch. Shipwright.
Thomas, W. J. E., Boy 1.

H.M.S. "Vanguard"—Continued.

Thompson, C. M., C.C.
Thomson, A., P O.
Thorp, E. B., Sto. 1.
Thorp, W., Musician (R.M.B.)
Thorpe, R., Ch. P.O.
Tickner, F., Boy 1.
Tidmarsh, A. H., Ch. Sto.
Tidnam, W. C., A.B.
Tiller, W. J., A.B.
Tofts, H., Sto. 1.
Tolfree. W., Sto. (R.N.R.)
Trew, W., A.B. (R.N.V.R.)
Tring, E., Musician (R.M.B.)
Trollope, W., Gun. (R.M A.)
Tumber, J. R., Sto. 1.
Turnpenny, T., Sto. 1.
Tutty, F., Gun. (R.M.A.)
Twelftree, E. G., Sto. 1.
Tyrell, E. C. F., Boy 1.
Valentine, R., Ord. S.
Vaugham, E. H., Boy 1.
Vaughan, E. W. H , Ord. S.
Veal, F. T., Ord. S.
Vicary, S., Boy 1.
Vincent, J. E., A.B.
Viton, J. T., Bandmaster 1 (R.M.B.)
Vowell, A. E., A.B.
Wait, R., Sig.
Wakely. D. J., Boy 1.
Wallace, A. J., A.A.M.
Walsh, G. E., Sto. (R.N.R.)

Walsh, R., Sto. P O.
Walton, J. A., Ld. Tel.
Walter, W. R., A.B.
Ward, J. J., Ord. S.
Warne, J. W., P.O.
Warne, W. H., Boy 1.
Wass, J. S., A.B.
Waterhouse, R., A.B.
Waterman, F. E., Boy 1.
Watson, A. S., Sto. 1.
Watson, A. H. J., Ord. Sig.
Watson, B. W., Sto. 1.
Watson, J., Sto. 1.
Watts. W., Sto. (R.N.R.)
Weaire, A. D., A.B.
Weatherly, S. J., 3rd Writer.
Webster, H., Painter, 2.
Weller, E. T., Ld. Sto.
Wellman, H. T., Gun. (R.M.A.
Wells, A. R., Ord. S.
West, H., Sto. 1.
West, L. C. Sto. 1.
Weston, W., A.B
Wharton, F. P., Ord S.
White, G. C. C. J., Boy 1.
Whittaker, F., Sto. 1.
Whittington, G. T., Pte. (R.M.L.I.)
Whitwood, A. C., A.B
Wilcocks, E. E. J., Ld. S
Wilder, J. R., A.B.
Willard, C. J., Sto. P.O.

Williams, H. W., Ord. S.
Williams, O. W., Of. Std. 2.
Wilson, D. P., Shipwright, 1.
Wilson, J. W., A.B.
Wilson, W. H., Pte. (R.M.L.I.)
Winterbone, R. I., Ch. Sto.
Wise, F. S., A.B.
Witheridge, F. J., Act. Ld. Sto.
Wood, A., Arm. Crew.
Wood, J., Boy 1.
Woodhouse, R. H , Plumber's M.
Woodrow, R., Pte. (R.M.L.I.)
Woods, J. W , Pte. (R.M L.I.)
Woodward. A., Ord. S.
Wraight, J., Sto. 1.
Wrench, F. E., Sig. Boy.
Wright, B. A., A.B.
Wright, C. G., Sto 1.
Wright, H., Ord. Ted.
Wright, T. W., A B
Wyatt, W., A.B.
Xuiereb, A., Of. Cook, 3.
Yarnold, H. R., Pte. (R.M.L.I.)
Yates, H. H., Ord. S.

CANTEEN STAFF.

Goddard, E. E., Canteen Assist.
Jackson, F. C., Canteen Manager.
Sawkins, G., Canteen Assist.
Ventham, R., Canteen Assist.

Contractions

A.B.	Able Seaman.
A.C.	Armourer's Crew.
Act. Ld. Sto	Acting Leading Stoker.
A.M.	Armourer's Mate.
Arm.	Armourer.
Bks.	Blacksmith.
C.C.	Carpenter's Crew.
C.E.R.A.	Chief Engine Room Artificer.
Ch. Arm.	Chief Armourer.
Ch. Sto.	Chief Stoker.
C.M.	Carpenter's Mate.
C.P.O.	Chief Petty Officer.
E.R.A.	Engine Room Artificer.
L.C.C.	Leading Carpenter's Crew.
Ld. S.	Leading Seaman.
Ld. Sig.	Leading Signalman.
Ld. Sto.	Leading Stoker.
M.A.A.	Master-at-Arms.
M.W.T.O.1	Marine Wireless Telegraph Operator. 1st Class.
Of. Cook 3	Officer's Cook, 3rd Class.
Of. Std. 2	Officer's Steward, 2nd Class.
Ord. S.	Ordinary Seaman.
P.O.	Petty Officer.
Pte. R.M,L.I.	Private, Royal Marine Light Infantry.
R.M.A.	Royal Marine Artillery.
Sea.	Seaman.
S.B.A.	Sick Berth Attendant.
S.B.S.	Sick Berth Steward.
Sh. Std.	Ship's Steward.
Sto.1	Stoker, 1st Class.
Sto. P.O.	Stoker, Petty Officer.
Tel.	Telegraphist.

The Journal of the British Navy

Edited by Lionel Yexley

MONTHLY **1ᴅ/-** ILLUSTRATED

THE FLEET, which has been run for over twelve years entirely in the interests of the men of the Navy, has been responsible for many of the most far-reaching reforms which have ever been introduced for the benefit of the Lower deck

SEE THE LETTER FROM THE FIRST LORD on Page V

This was the only letter sent to the Press by Sir Eric Geddes on his appointment

ANNUAL SUBSCRIPTION   1/6 post free

General Offices: 11 Henrietta Street, Strand, London

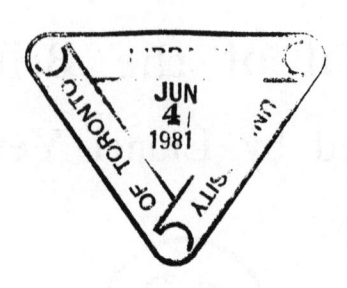

940.45
F62.   41875

LEGISLATIVE
LIBRARY REGULATIONS

1. Books (other than 7-day books) are lent for a period not exceeding two weeks, with the option of renewal for an additional two weeks if no other application is filed. All books are lent at the discretion of the Librarian and are subject to recall at any time.

2. The borrower assumes full responsibility for the value of the book in case of loss or injury.

3. Not more than two books may be borrowed at one time.

142614 21022 OFFICE SPECIALTY

THE FLEET ANNUAL & NAVAL YEAR BOOK, 1917

THE PORTSMOUTH UNITED BREWERIES
LIMITED

Brewers to His Majesty's Forces

UNITED BREWERY, PORTSMOUTH.

55a, GREAT WESTERN DOCKS, PLYMOUTH.

9, STATION ROAD, ALDERSHOT.

THE STONEHENGE INN, LARK HILL, SALISBURY PLAIN.

AGENCIES AT GIBRALTAR, MALTA, and all Naval and Military Ports and Stations.

Printed by The Westminster Press (Gerrards Ltd.), 411a Harrow Road, London, W.

THE PORTSMOUTH UNITED BREWERY LIMITED

Brewers to His Majesty's F[orces]

UNITED BREWERY, PORTSMOUTH.
55a, GREAT WESTERN DOCK, PLYMOUTH.
9, STATION ROAD, ALDERSH[OT]
THE STONEHENGE INN,
LARK HILL, SALISBURY PLAIN.

AGENCIES AT GIBRALT[AR]